Treat this book with care and respect.

*It should become part of your personal
and professional library. It will
serve you well at any number
of points during your
professional career.*

COMPARATIVE ECONOMIC SYSTEMS

Second Edition

Martin C. Schnitzer

Professor of Finance
College of Business
Virginia Polytechnic Institute
and State University

James W. Nordyke

Professor of Economics
College of Business Administration
and Economics
New Mexico State University

Published by

H76   **SOUTH-WESTERN PUBLISHING CO.**

CINCINNATI   WEST CHICAGO, ILL.   DALLAS   PELHAM MANOR, N.Y.
PALO ALTO, CALIF.   BRIGHTON, ENGLAND

ISBN: 0–538–08760–9

Library of Congress Catalog Card Number: 76–9725

2 3 4 5 6 7 8 D 4 3 2 1 0 9 8 7

Printed in the United States of America

PREFACE

The purpose of this book is to present to the student a concise account of existing economic systems so that he or she may secure an intelligent understanding of how they operate. In order to facilitate such an understanding, the book is organized to include separate chapters on the economies of a number of important industrial countries. The economic systems of these countries are treated in a similar organizational manner so that a common frame of reference runs throughout the book.

However, it is necessary to point out that the advanced industrial countries of today do not fall into a rigid ideological system or classification labeled capitalism, communism, or socialism. It is more useful instead to think of a spectrum of systems ranging from those that rely heavily upon market mechanisms to allocate resources to those that rely on central command or planning for resource allocation. The United States lies near the market end of the spectrum. In the realm of economies, great faith has been traditionally placed in the efficacy of individual initiative, private ownership of property, production for profit, competition, and a minimum of interference by government in business. But there has developed a quite substantial element of government control of the economy. Japan and the countries of Western Europe lie near the center of the spectrum. Although resource allocation is achieved primarily through the market mechanism, there is some government ownership of industry and extensive participation by government in the economy. Even in those countries that have command economies, market arrangements are used to some degree to supplement central planning. The degree varies from one country to another.

The book proceeds through the spectrum. Part 1 explains the functioning of a market economy and some of the problems it has raised in the United States and the United Kingdom. Part 2 describes the operation of the economy of the United States, taking into consideration the governmental and other arrangements which have been superimposed upon the market system. Part 3 presents the mixed economic systems of five highly advanced industrialized democracies, France, West Germany, Japan, Sweden, and the United Kingdom.

iii

Part 4 pertains to countries which have economies of modified central command. Three nations—the Soviet Union, China, and Yugoslavia—are examined. Part 5 evaluates the performance of each economic system in terms of fulfillment of the generally accepted goals of full employment, price stability, economic growth, and an equitable distribution of income.

The authors are indebted to Dr. John Hardt of the Library of Congress for his critique of the chapters on the Soviet Union, China, and Yugoslavia, and to Dr. Edwin Jones of the Department of State for his assistance on the chapters on China. The authors are also grateful to Dr. Lloyd Valentine of the University of Cincinnati for his helpful assistance with the organization of the second edition and to Dr. Gertrude Schroeder of the University of Virginia for her suggestions. Many members of the faculties and staffs of Virginia Polytechnic Institute and New Mexico State University who were of assistance are also deserving of thanks.

M.C.S.
J.W.N.

CONTENTS

v

1

Introduction

Most Americans are aware that economic arrangements in their own nation differ from those in others. For example, most productive enterprises in the United States are privately owned businesses, whereas in the Soviet Union most are governmentally owned operations. The programs of welfare payments by governments in western Europe are much more comprehensive than those of the United States. In Japan employees of large businesses are much more likely to be lifelong employees of a single corporation than are American workers, who are more mobile with regard to employment.

Just as economic arrangements differ between countries, so also do economic problems. For example, the Japanese have suffered from a higher rate of inflation than have Americans in recent decades. The problem of unemployment has been more severe, however, in the United States than in either Japan or western European countries. Although the Soviet Union has, in recent decades, apparently had less trouble with either unemployment or inflation than has the United States, the average level of living of the Soviet people is still noticeably below that of Americans.

Not only are economic arrangements and problems different from one country to another, but so also are economic ideals. For example, many Americans firmly believe in the ideal of a "free enterprise system." They seem to desire to keep intrusion by government into economic affairs at a minimum. In contrast, the people of Sweden or Britain appear to be far more tolerant of extensive governmental direction of the economy. And the Soviet people seem to believe rather firmly in the ideal of what they call socialism: the ownership and operation by the government of most of the real property in the nation.

The subject of comparative economic systems attempts to describe how economic arrangements vary betwen nations. It seeks as well to explain how the peculiar arrangements of each nation may alleviate or aggravate that nation's economic problems. And it tries to show how the arrangements and problems have helped to shape the economic ideals and how the ideals in turn have helped to cause the arrangements and problems to be what they are.

This chapter introduces the subject of comparative economic systems. It explains how all national societies are confronted with a common circumstance called economic scarcity. Economic scarcity makes it necessary for every society to have some system of economic arrangements to wrest a living from nature. Medieval society in Europe used manors, guilds, and town governments as economic arrangements and relied heavily upon tradition and direct command to obtain a living for the people. The medieval economy, however, did rather poorly in achieving a high level of living for its people.

Most modern societies, especially those outside the Soviet and Chinese blocs, have partially replaced tradition and command with markets in their economic systems. Part 1 of this book, consisting of Chapters 2 through 6, deals with the market system. Chapter 2 explains how a market system can, ideally, work well in coping with the problems which arise from scarcity. Chapter 3 describes some episodes from American economic history which suggest several weaknesses of market arrangements. Chapter 4 uses the experience of nineteenth-century Europe with the market system to suggest other weaknesses, particularly as seen by that famous critic of market capitalism, Karl Marx. Chapter 5 draws upon the experience of the less-developed countries to suggest still other possible inadequacies of market systems. Chapter 6 draws together these diverse experiences of America, Europe, and the Third World to generalize on the need for deliberate governmental policy to supplement or partially replace market arrangements as a means of coping with scarcity.

Part 2 consists of Chapters 7 and 8. Chapter 7 describes the techniques by which the United States has in recent years attempted to correct some weaknesses of market arrangements, while still retaining the market system. Chapter 8 describes the results of these American techniques.

Part 3, consisting of Chapters 9 through 14, describes the ways in which Japan and several nations in western Europe have supplemented and modified market arrangements. Generally they have gone somewhat further than the United States in relying on governmental and other non-market arrangements.

Part 4, Chapters 15 through 20, explains the Soviet-style economic systems which have gone still further in replacing market arrangements with central commands by government. The Soviet Union, as dealt with in Chapters 16 and 17, is the original active model for this kind of economic system. In recent decades new variations on the model have emerged, notably in China, described in Chapters 18 and 19, and Yugoslavia, described in Chapter 20. The Chinese have sought to go beyond the Soviet model by leaning still more heavily upon command in place of markets. The Yugoslavs have diverged in the other direction, attempting to return to a somewhat more market-like economy than that of the Soviets.

Finally, Part 5, consisting of Chapter 12, draws together for explicit comparison the extent to which each of the major types of economies has achieved the commonly advocated goals of full employment, price stability, equitable income distribution, and appropriate economic growth.

ECONOMIC SCARCITY

Economic scarcity has been a common characteristic of human existence. A thing is regarded as economically *scarce* if there is less available of it than would be needed to satisfy all desire for it, even if the price were zero. The concept of scarcity applies to both products and resources.

Scarcity of Products

Most products are available in quantities insufficient to meet fully the need which people feel they have for the products. For instance, there are millions of new cars produced annually in the United States. However, there are still many people who would like to be able to own more cars than they do. To satisfy their needs and wants, automobile production would have to be many times what it is. The same is true of housing, clothing, medical care, education, and most other goods and services.[1]

One can gain an appreciation of how prevalent scarcity is by trying to think of those few things which are plentiful. Some examples are sand in the Sahara and salt water in the Atlantic. Despite such obvious exceptions, most goods and services have been available generally in quantities smaller than people have desired. The level of living has been less than infinite because of this scarcity of consumable products.

Scarcity of Resources

The scarcity of consumable goods and services is pressing to most people. Underlying this more immediate scarcity is another more basic one—the scarcity of things from which products are made. These things are, as economic writers of a century or two ago called them, land, labor, and capital. Modern terminology labels them *resources*—natural, human, and manufactured.[2]

Some natural resources are soil, sunlight, virgin vegetation, naturally navigable waterways, and mineral and petroleum deposits.

Examples of *human resources* would include people in their capacities as producers of goods and services through their efforts as workers, managers, homemakers, etc.

---

[1] There are some social critics who question whether the United States is still in a state of economic scarcity. It is claimed that preoccupation with trying to reduce the impact of scarcity has blinded the American people to other problems. See John Kenneth Galbraith, *The Affluent Society* (2d ed.; Boston: Houghton Mifflin Company, 1969).

[2] Synonyms for resources are *inputs* or *factors of production.*

Capital resources encompass all manufactured goods used in the production process. They are, according to a classic definition, "the produced means of production," so defined because they are products which are used to make other products. Some obvious examples of capital goods are machinery, factory buildings, and inventories of raw materials. Less obvious examples are highways, fences, courthouses, and artificially fertilized land.

Resources and the Size of Output

The quantity of goods and services which can be produced and the extent to which the degree of scarcity of these goods and services is thus reduced depends importantly upon the available quantity of all kinds of resources. If a full-time farmer has much land, several tractors, and a number of hired hands, a larger crop can be produced than if the farmer is only a part-time farmer with a small acreage, a little garden tractor, and no hired help. So it is with a nation. The nation with large amounts of natural resources, a large labor force, and a great stock of capital goods will ordinarily be able to produce more goods and services than another nation with smaller amounts of the three principal types of resources.

THE ECONOMIC ORGANIZATION OF SOCIETY

The quantity of resources is not the only important determinant of the size of output resulting from production. A given amount of resources can be converted via the process of production into a large amount of consumable goods or services or into a small amount, depending upon the way people are organized to carry on production.

To illustrate this idea, it is useful to consider two situations. In each situation there is a farmer with 600 acres, six hired hands, six tractors, and 6000 pounds of fertilizer. In one situation the farmer assigns one hired worker to each 100 acres with one tractor and a 1000 pounds of fertilizer. Each worker is permitted to work on the assigned acreage independent of the other five. In the other situation the farmer arranges to have the hired hands work together. The probability is that there will be different amounts of crops in the two situations. In spite of similar quantities of resources, different quantities of output result. The different outputs are the result of the different organizational arrangements.

As it is with farmers, so is it with nations. The people of a nation may be organized to carry on production in a variety of ways. For example, each individual or family may undertake production largely independent of other persons or families. Each family is economically self-sufficient, producing by itself those things which it consumes and not relying on outsiders. Another example from the opposite extreme is that in which the people of a nation are organized into communes, similar to those which the Chinese began to use in the late 1950s. In such a commune each person has a very narrow production specialty. Each is exceedingly dependent upon others for needed goods and services. Most economic decisions are determined for most people by others in a rather direct fashion. People are told, for instance, what and how much they may consume and what they are to produce.

It would not be surprising that a society organized in an individualistic way might produce a total amount of goods and services different from that produced by a communally organized society. It would not be surprising even if each society possessed the same natural, human, and capital resources. Both economic organization and the amount of resources are determinants of the size of production.[3]

ECONOMIC PROBLEMS ARISING FROM SCARCITY

The problems which arise from scarcity and the influence of economic organization in overcoming scarcity are complex matters. Initial insight into their nature can be gained by considering the situation of an economically isolated individual like Robinson Crusoe.

The General Nature of Economic Problems

Suppose that Robinson, as the sole survivor of a shipwreck, has just been washed ashore on some uninhabited island. The ship now lies deserted and aground on some rocks several hundred yards offshore. The ship seems likely to sink soon into deep water. Aboard the ship are the supplies and equipment which, if brought ashore, will permit survival. Robinson is faced with the first economic problem of his island existence. In the few trips which can be made to the ship before it sinks, which of the many items aboard the ship should be retrieved? Time before the ship sinks is scarce. Robinson compiles in his mind a list of priorities. He first retrieves what is most essential, then what is next most essential, and so on, until the ship sinks.

This situation faced by Robinson could be called an *economic problem* because it involves the allocation of scarce means among competing uses. What is scarce in this case is the time available before the ship sinks. Robinson must use the time to get some things off the ship while being forced to leave others. It is the contention of many economists that the essence of economics is the wise allocation of scarce means among competing alternative objectives.

Once established on the island, Robinson is faced with other economic problems. The one level site on the island can be used as the location for a hut or a plot for a vegetable garden but not both. His own labor time can be spent building a canoe or hunting coconuts but not both. If seeds salvaged from the ship are eaten, they cannot be planted. If a metal piece is used as a plow, it may wear out before it can be used as a spear.

---

[3] There are still other determinants such as the level of technology of the society. Technology, resources, and organization are interdependent. For example, an effective organization makes it easy to accumulate a large stock of capital and to achieve a high level of technology.

Problems similar to those faced by Robinson confront most societies, although in more complex forms. Economists have studied these problems and made generalizations about them. The problems are typically classified by economists as having to do with the commodity composition of output, the character of production, the distribution of income, and the rate of economic growth.

The Commodity Composition of Output

Because of scarcity, the amount of output of all products is limited. Infinite amounts of all products cannot be produced. Decisions must, therefore, be made about which products are desired and how much is desired of each. In other words, a *commodity composition of output* must be chosen. Usually if more of some good or service is desired, less of others must suffice. To have more of one good, the opportunity of having so much of another good must be given up. A good thus has an *opportunity cost* in the form of an amount of some other good or goods which must be sacrificed in order to have it.

For Robinson Crusoe the opportunity cost of six more coconuts may be 30 pounds of pork. For a modern society the opportunity cost of six military tanks may be 30 automobiles.

It is important that wise choices be made about the commodity composition of output. If Robinson mistakenly devotes his energies to gathering coconuts when he would really rather have pork, he will be worse off than he could have been. If a modern nation mistakenly devotes its resources to the production of a large amount of shoddy clothing when what is really preferred is a smaller amount of better clothing, the people will be less satisfied than they could be. If a nation erroneously devotes its energies to the production of agricultural products which no one wants at a cost of not producing houses which are desired, the people will be less satisfied than they could be.

The Character of Production

Decisions must be made about how resources are to be converted into products. That is, the *character of production* must be determined. Usually there are several ways in which any product can be produced. Robinson can produce pork either by hunting and killing wild hogs or by capturing a hog and a sow, taming them, and raising young pigs. In a modern nation, the variety of possible ways of carrying on production is great and the problem of choice very complex. One method of describing the problem is to break it into three subordinate parts involving techniques of production, assignment of resources, and the kinds of production units.

Techniques of Production. Any particular product can usually be produced in a variety of ways. Some techniques are labor intensive. They involve much labor per unit of output. Other techniques are capital intensive or land intensive. Some techniques depend upon sophisticated technology. Others are technologically primitive. Rice can be grown by the "Chinese" method with little land, almost no equipment, and much labor. Alternatively, it can be grown by the "Louisiana" method with much land, much capital, and little labor. Some techniques which are technologically primitive require more resources of all kinds than do other more advanced techniques.

It is important that wise choices be made regarding techniques. Robinson would be hurting himself economically if he mistakenly chose to hunt wild pigs when a good deal less effort would be needed to domesticate them. The people of a nation lose their maximum opportunity to reduce the impact of scarcity upon themselves if they persist in retaining primitive techniques when more technologically advanced ones using fewer resources are available. Similarly, they are reducing their economic welfare if they persist in using labor-intensive techniques when labor is the scarcest of their resources. When the managers of the government factories in the Soviet Union refuse to install new and more modern equipment because the installation interrupts production and prevents them from fulfilling their current output quotas, inefficient techniques will continue to be used. When labor unions in the United States insist that unneeded extra workers be hired, wasteful techniques are the result.

Assignment of Resources. Even when it has been decided to produce some particular product with some specified technique, there still remains the problem of which units of each resource are to be assigned to production. Each product can be made with a number of different units of a resource, and every unit of each resource has several different potential uses. For Robinson a given plot of land can be used as a construction site for a dwelling or as a garden, and a garden can be set up on any one of several alternate plots. For a nation, each worker has many possible alternative jobs, and any particular job can usually be performed by many different persons.

It is important that good decisions be made regarding assignments. Otherwise, output will be beneath its potential and the impact of scarcity will be more severe. When Nikita Khrushchev ordered wheat to be grown in arid, virgin lands, a poor decision was made, and total output was less in the Soviet Union than it could have been with better decisions regarding assignments. Similarly, racial discrimination in hiring in the United States has sometimes precluded the economically most appropriate persons from assignment to particular jobs.

Types of Production Units. The production of any product can usually be carried on by any one of several kinds of production units or enterprises. A given amount of output can be produced by a few large units or a larger number of smaller ones. The units can be located close together or dispersed. The units may or may not be "vertically integrated" so that several processing steps in converting a raw material to a finished product are conducted by the same enterprise. Even Robinson has a choice of several scattered vegetable plots or one big one. For modern nations, the possibilities are much greater. Steel factories can be big or small. They can be located near the coal mines, the ore deposits, or the users of steel. They can be vertically integrated or not.

Poor decisions regarding the types of production units increase the adverse impact of scarcity. The giant state farms of the Soviet Union are not as productive as smaller farms would be. Resources are wasted. The many filling stations in most urban areas of the United States absorb more land, labor, and capital than would a fewer number of stations which could deliver just as many gallons of gasoline.

The Distribution of Income

For Robinson Crusoe there is no problem of who is to get shares of the output of production. For him there is no problem of the *distribution of income*. However, for nations the problem is a real one and arises directly from scarcity. If anyone is given a larger share of income, that person thereby has a claim on some of the output. Because output is limited, someone else must be content with a smaller share. A continuing, unresolved problem is whether the proceeds of production should be divided among persons in proportion to need, want, worthiness, or the contribution to production.

The Rate of Economic Growth

To some extent even Robinson Crusoe has some control over the time trend of his production and consumption activities. He can choose to work hard and long during his first year or so on the island. He can abstain from using up his supplies of goods and from wearing out his equipment. He can spend part of his energies experimenting and learning better ways of doing things. With hard work, abstention from consumption, equipment maintenance, experimentation, research, and learning, the level of material living achievable by him probably will progressively increase. On the other hand, laziness, consumption of a large amount of supplies, deterioration of equipment without maintenance and repair, and the concentration of his energies on simply producing as much as he can by any method that he already knows will result in less improvement or in the worsening of his economic circumstances as time goes by. Thus, consciously or otherwise, Robinson determines the *rate of growth* of his one-man economy.

Nations also must determine their rate of economic growth. Sometimes deliberate decisions are made. In other cases the rate of growth is simply the result of unplanned circumstances. When Stalin was in power in the Soviet Union, he deliberately forced rapid growth on the people. He required them to work hard and ordered that much of their effort be used to produce capital goods rather than consumer goods. In this way the future productive capacity of the nation was enlarged. On the other hand, economic growth in the United States prior to the 1950s was the result mostly of individuals' decisions and of governmental policies aimed at other objectives. In any case, scarcity makes economic growth important because growth is the chief means of reducing the impact of scarcity.

The Interrelatedness of Economic Problems

Decisions made concerning the commodity composition of output, the character of production, the distribution of income, and the rate of growth are interrelated in complicated ways. This is easily seen in the case of Robinson Crusoe. Suppose he decides to eat more pork and less beans. The fewer beans will now be grown with less square yardage and less labor per plant than before. Increased pig hunting will require ranging farther about the island, perhaps with the assistance of better shoes which were not required before. In order to make the shoes, less time and effort can be spent on providing food immediately. The decision to switch to pork has, therefore, led to abstention from some consumption in the present, a greater accumulation of capital goods in the form of shoes, and perhaps even an increase in technical knowledge in the form of a greater understanding of the whereabouts of pigs. The end result of the original decision to alter the commodity composition of output may entail new techniques of production and a possibly inadvertent acceleration of growth.

THE ADVANTAGES OF ECONOMIC INTERDEPENDENCE

It is possible to imagine a world of Robinson Crusoes. It would be a world in which each person or family is economically self-sufficient. The economic problems faced by each family would resemble those of Robinson with some slight complications created by the need to achieve economic coordination and also to resolve economic conflicts among the members of each family.

The real world is not a world of Robinson Crusoes. It is a world of persons and families who are interdependent economically. It is easy to explain why. First, there are many noneconomic psychological and sociological reasons for contact between persons and families. People, as Aristotle is said to have asserted, are gregarious animals. If contact among people is established for noneconomic reasons, economic contact in the form of exchange of goods, services, and money seems likely to follow. Second, there seem to be strong reasons why economic contact should occur independent of sociological and psychological reasons. There appear to be definite economic advantages to the abandonment of economic isolation and the adoption instead of economic interdependence.

Specialization and Efficiency

The advantages of interdependence seem to center primarily on specialization or division of labor. *Specialization* means mainly the concentration of the efforts of a person or group of persons on some single task. However, machinery and other capital resources and land and other natural resources can also be specialized in this same sense. Specialization usually permits a larger amount of output from a given amount of resources than if self-sufficiency is practiced. Adam Smith long ago in his famous book, *The Wealth of Nations,* suggested some of the reasons why specialization makes possible a greater output of goods and services.[4]

Natural Abilities. Specialization makes it possible to take advantage of the differences in natural talents between persons. There are some people who are very intelligent and others who are physically very dextrous. If those who are intelligent specialize in mental tasks while those who are physically agile specialize in physical tasks, the total amount of output achieved is likely to be greater than if each person tried to do everything for himself. Differences in the natural resources of regions also provide the basis for greater output through specialization. Thus, the people in a rainy region grow rice, and those in a drier one grow wheat. The total output of wheat and rice in the two regions is likely to be considerably greater than if each people attempted to be self-sufficient by growing both rice and wheat.

Acquired Abilities. Specialization also makes for greater output by enabling persons to develop skills through repetition of tasks. Even if there were no personal or regional differences in natural ability, specialization would still be advantageous because it creates the opportunity for acquisition of skill through repetition. Acquired skills of greater degree increase efficiency and, thereby, increase output above that which could be attained in a state of individual or regional self-sufficiency.

Large-Scale Machinery. Specialization makes a larger output of goods and services and, consequently, a higher level of living possible through the use of large-scale machinery. If each family were self-sufficient, it would have a wide variety of relatively small tools and equipment. For technological reasons, small-scale equipment is frequently inefficient. The best 1-horsepower engine frequently uses more than just half as much fuel as a 2-horsepower engine. In addition, if each family were to have all the efficient large-scale equipment for itself, so as to be self-sufficient, the equipment would be idle much of the time. The ratio of the value of output to the investment in capital equipment would be low. This would be especially true if the deterioration of the equipment depended more upon the mere passage of time than upon the intensity of use.

Other Reasons. There are a number of other ways in which specialization may result in a reduction in the impact of scarcity upon the level of living, given a certain amount of natural, human, and handmade resources. Adam Smith pointed out that a jack-of-all trades wastes time and effort in moving

---

[4] Adam Smith, *An Inquiry into the Nature and Causes of the Wealth of Nations,* ed. Edwin Cannan (New York: Random House, Inc., 1937), pp. 7–10. The original edition appeared in 1776.

from one task to another. This waste can be avoided and output increased through personal specialization. Then, too, it might be argued that technological progress is likely to be more rapid when persons, through specialized tasks, gain greater insight into possible improvements in techniques.[5]

Exchange and Satisfaction

Even if it did not permit an increase in output through the efficiencies of specialization, interdependency might still be economically beneficial. Interdependence means that goods, services, and money can be exchanged. Such exchange means that specific types of goods can be traded off by persons who want them less to those who want them more. The ultimate distribution of specific goods among persons or families is improved through exchange. Consequently, the amount of satisfaction derived from consumption of a given amount of output is greater than would be possible under isolated self-sufficiency without trading.

To understand the meaning of this improvement, imagine a prisoner-of-war camp. In the camp each prisoner receives monthly from the Red Cross a bundle of goods identical to those received by the other prisoners: a carton of cigarettes, a pound of cheese, etc. If the prisoners are under no restrictions as to what can be done with the goods they receive, vigorous trading will almost certainly occur. A prisoner who smokes heavily but dislikes cheese will directly or indirectly contact and make a deal with a prisoner of opposite tastes. Many other exchanges will probably occur.

Do the prisoners benefit from trading? The answer is surely yes. The mere fact that they voluntarily undertake the exchanges suggests as much. Such trading and its beneficial results are based upon differences in personal tastes among individuals. If every prisoner had the same tastes or set of preferences, there would be no incentive to trade and no trading would occur. However, granted the realistic assumptions of interpersonal differences in tastes and an initial distribution of goods which fails to match the tastes, trading will almost certainly occur and will mean an economic improvement for all concerned.[6]

In a world of self-sufficient persons or families, each family will try to make the commodity composition of its production match its tastes. Robinson Crusoes who like coconuts will pick coconuts, and those who like pork will hunt pigs. But there will almost always be some condition in the physical environment which prevents perfect or even near-perfect matching of output with tastes. Some families who want coconuts will find themselves on islands where coconuts do not grow.

---

[5] On the other hand, personal specialization may retard technological progress if a discovery made in one field remains unapplied in other fields because of a failure of communication between specialists.

[6] For a more elaborate and true account of such exchange and of other economic activities in a prisoner-of-war camp, see Richard A. Radford, "The Economic Organization of a Prison Camp," *Economica*, Vol. XII (November, 1945), pp. 189–201.

Trade or exchange between persons or families will be beneficial. Even if it did not permit an increase in total output of goods and services, it would still make possible a more satisfactory distribution of them.

THE DISADVANTAGES OF ECONOMIC INTERDEPENDENCE

The advantages of specialization and exchange are so obvious that economic isolation has almost never been followed. Even if most people never made a calculated selection of economic interdependence over isolation, the advantages of the former have directly and indirectly induced people to practice interdependence. The world is one of economic interdependence rather than self-sufficiency.

Yet it would be incorrect to regard the substitution of interdependence for self-sufficiency as without disadvantage. It is, in fact, a mitigated blessing. Specialization and exchange make possible a larger output, faster economic growth, and a better distribution of specific goods and services. Specialization and exchange also create problems. There are costs of achieving the beneficial results. All of the gain is not net gain.

Loss of Control to Others

A basic disadvantage of specialization and exchange is that the individual surrenders to others some control over the situation. The individual becomes subject, in a way unlike before, to the actions of others.

There are numerous examples of individuals subject to this control. A person specializes as a firer on a locomotive and loses the means of living when technological progress, the management of the railroad company, and the public acting through government decree that firers shall no longer be employed. A consumer dependent upon specialists for food is cut off from that food when transportation specialists strike. A renter who purchases housing service from one who specializes in owning rental residential property is subject to eviction. The superior-subordinate relationships within a business organization from assembly-line worker through the board of directors further illustrate control exerted by one person or group upon others. This example can be extended beyond the internal organizational structure to encompass control exerted by shareholders, customers, and government.

Loss of Control to the "System"

Perhaps more serious than the loss of individual control over oneself to others is the loss of control to the "system." When large numbers of people become economically interdependent, their interactions sometimes bring about consequences which no one of them intended and which no one of them finds desirable. This seems to have been the case, for example, with the United States and many other countries during the Great Depression of the 1930s. Almost no one purposely decided to be unemployed. The unemployed were, by and large, eager to work, and it is surely true that they and others could have made good use of the products which could have been produced had they been at work. Yet in 1933 in the United States, 25 percent of the labor force was unemployed, and throughout the rest of the 1930s smaller though still substantial percentages of unemployment existed. It is difficult to imagine anything of the kind happening among self-sufficient individuals and families.

The Costliness of Exchange

Another dismaying aspect of specialization and exchange is that the gains from increased output of products may not be as great as first perceived. Specialization requires exchange, and exchange is a costly process in terms of its absorption of natural, human, and manufactured resources. The vast hordes of people, of inventories of goods, and of equipment employed in retail stores, banks, wholesale operations, and toll and fee collecting activities are among the resources absorbed. The people here are the "middlemen." For the most part they perform useful services. Yet it is perfectly clear that if the distribution process made necessary by specialization could somehow be eliminated while still retaining the advantageous results of specialization, there would be a gain. The middlemen and the real capital associated with them could then be devoted to production proper so that the volume of output and the average level of living would be raised considerably.

Monetary Problems

Another disadvantage of specialization has to do with its connection with money. If specialization occurs, persons and regions must exchange their specialties. Exchange can occur without money by means of a system of direct *barter*, whereby one good or service is directly exchanged between two parties for another. However, barter is an inconvenient, cumbersome kind of exchange. If it were the only kind of exchange possible, not much exchange would take place. The degree of specialization and of productive efficiency achieved would be quite small. The alternative to barter as a means of exchange is money, or more precisely, the general practice of using money as a means of payment.

Money of one form or another has proven to be an indispensable concomitant to any sophisticated system of specialization. It is far more convenient and efficient and far less time-consuming than barter. All modern economic societies from the communist systems of Russia and China to the capitalist systems of the United States and western Europe have found it necessary to use money.

While the social institution of money is indispensable to a sophisticated system of economic specialization, this institution also has disadvantages. If money exists, it must be created. If it is created, there must be some authority which has the power to create it. Whatever authority has the power may abuse it. The abuse usually takes the form of creating too little or too much money. Too little money may cause depression, unemployment, and too low a rate of economic growth. Too much money may cause inflation, which may eventually produce a reaction of deflation and depression, and, in extreme cases, may disorganize production. Because money is a necessary companion to sophisticated specialization, these disadvantages of money may also be regarded as disadvantages of specialization.

INTERDEPENDENCE AND ECONOMIC SYSTEMS

Specialization, exchange, and interdependence make life incomparably more complicated than it would be if the world were made up only of Robinson Crusoes. Interdependent people have to provide solutions to all of the economic problems which arise from scarcity. They have to determine the commodity composition of output, the character of production, the distribution of income, and the rate of economic growth. Moreover, for these problems each individual is likely to have solutions which differ from those of other individuals. Therefore, two additional complicating elements arise in an interdependent situation. One is the need to coordinate the economic activities of the individuals. The other is the need to resolve economic conflicts between them.

It is because of this economic interdependence between persons that economics is properly classified as a *social science*. It is a social science because much of it has to do with a certain class of relationships between individuals who make up each interacting group of people. The group is a society, and the society has economic problems concerning the production, distribution, and consumption of goods and services. The study of these problems and their solutions is *economics*.

Every society has organized one or more ways to provide answers to the basic economic questions which arise from scarcity and interdependence. Such organization consists of various types of economic units within the society and of procedures whereby each unit influences the other units and is influenced by them.

The Case of Medieval Europe

A specific example may make the abstract generalizations of the preceding paragraph clearer. The people who lived in western Europe in the Middle Ages may be regarded as a society. They were, at least to some degree, economically interdependent. Serfs specialized in farming, knights in warfare, and the nobility in government. There were, of course, more specific specialties within each of these broad classes and other specialties such as trading and blacksmithing as well. There had to be some system for answering the basic questions arising from scarcity and interdependence.

Economic Units of Medieval Europe. To answer the basic economic questions, medieval society was organized into various types of economic units.

Individuals made some decisions for themselves, of course, as did families. The manor, a primarily agricultural and largely economically self-sufficient grouping of people, land, and equipment, was the most important type of unit peculiar to the times. As the era progressed, towns, which were both political and economic units, with their municipal governments making economic regulations, became increasingly important. So did guilds, which were groups of people in the same occupation somewhat like a combination of a modern labor union and trade association.

Techniques of Exerting Economic Influence in Medieval Europe. The two principal means by which the individuals and other economic units of medieval society influenced each other were tradition and command. Altruism was a third, perhaps less important, means.

Tradition. Within the manor and throughout medieval society, tradition played a more influential role than in more modern times. What goods and services should be produced? Medieval society would answer, those that have always been produced. How should production occur? Let production be as it always has been. Who should get what share of the output? The division should occur as it always has. So it was that the traditional crops were grown in the traditional way and distributed in the traditional fashion. Lands devoted every year to pasture continued to be so devoted. Sons of plowmen became plowmen, and sons of rulers were eventually rulers.

Command. Command was also used as a means of inter-unit influence in medieval Europe. Where disputes arose because of conflicts in traditions or where uncontrollable changes occurred, resort was made to authority. If a larger percentage of the effort of the manor was to be devoted to war and a smaller percentage to "normal" activities, the change was achieved by command of the lord of the manor. If a new technique of production became known, whether or not it was to be adopted was decided by the relevant guild through its officials and members. If the clergy's share of the produce was regarded as too small, by command of the authorities the taxes supporting the church were raised.

Altruism. No doubt also a sense of obligation and duty influenced economic decisions in this Age of Belief. Serfs remained plowmen because they felt they owed it to their lord. Serfs shared their labor and harvest with the lord because it was their duty. The lord commanded the operations of the manor and organized order for it because that was regarded as the lord's responsibility. Guilds protected their weaker members by price-fixing, and they maintained the quality of their product out of regard for their customers.

Modern National Economic Systems

These then were the types of economic units and principles of inter-unit influence of medieval society. Every society has a system made up of various kinds of units and of techniques for exerting influence. In modern times the most important kinds of societies are national societies. A national society consists of all the people of a nation. Each nation possesses an economic system of various types of economic units and of various types of inter-unit influence. The system of each nation is in part the result of non-deliberate evolution and in part the result of deliberate attempts of the nation to shape its economic system in one way or another. Thus, the people of each nation seek to obtain the advantages of specialization and exchange while avoiding, to the extent they can, the disadvantages.

Each national system is, at least in some respects, peculiarly distinctive and unlike any other. Each has achieved some combination of results, including those both favorable and unfavorable. It is the task of that branch of economics usually called *comparative economic systems* to describe how national economic systems differ and to explain how and why these differences came to be. Such a study seeks to reveal why one national system has produced one set of results and another a different set. It speculates upon how each national system might be altered, perhaps by making the system more like or less like some other, so as to produce a somewhat more favorable combination of results than those already achieved. It also tries to indicate how alterations, if made, may create a less favorable outcome than that presently enjoyed. To describe and to explain these matters are the objectives of the remainder of this book.

SUMMARY

Scarcity of resources and of products is a typical feature of human existence. The adverse impact of scarcity upon the level of living can be reduced, depending upon the way people are organized. Individual self-sufficiency is a poor organizational arrangement because it precludes both production efficiencies arising from specialization and trade by which goods are redistributed in a more satisfying fashion. Economic interdependence is, therefore, the prevailing mode of existence.

Every society must have a system for providing solutions to the problems which arise from scarcity and interdependence. A system is made up of various kinds of economic units and various kinds of techniques for exerting influence among units so that common solutions can be achieved. The problems for which solutions are needed center about the questions of what should be the commodity composition of output, the character of production, the distribution of income, and the rate of economic growth.

It is the task of the branch of study called comparative economic systems and the objective of this book to describe and explain the various kinds of national economic systems which exist.

QUESTIONS

1. Explain the concept of economic scarcity.
2. Are there things which are not scarce?
3. What scarcity underlies the scarcity of consumable goods and services?
4. What are three classic general types of resources, inputs, or factors of production? Why do you think economists bother to classify resources in this way? Are there types of resources other than these three?
5. Apply the concept of scarcity to life in the United States now. Is scarcity still present in the United States? What evidence exists that it is? How does scarcity affect an American's life?
6. What is the meaning of the "economic organization" of people and what has such organization to do with scarcity?
7. What is meant by economic isolation?
8. What is meant by the commodity composition of output, the character of production, the distribution of income, and the rate of economic growth? How is each of these related to economic scarcity?
9. Why are humans economically better off if they do not live in the economic isolation of a Robinson Crusoe? What noneconomic forces have created interdependence for humans?
10. Why specifically does specialization or division of labor enable output to increase?
11. Even if output were not increased by interdependence and specialization, interdependence with trade might still be advantageous. Why is this so?
12. What are the disadvantages of economic specialization, exchange, and interdependence?
13. Extensive specialization requires money. What kinds of problems does the existence and use of money create?
14. To resolve conflicts and coordinate specialists every society is organized into various types of units which influence each other in various ways. What were the peculiar units of the Middle Ages? What forms of influence were used then?

RECOMMENDED READINGS

Grossman, Gregory. *Economic Systems.* Englewood Cliffs, N.J.: Prentice-Hall, Inc., 1967, Chapter 2.

Gruchy, Allan G. *Comparative Economic Systems: Competing Ways to Stability and Growth.* Boston: Houghton Mifflin Company, 1966.

Halm, George N. *Economic Systems: A Comparative Analysis,* 3d ed. New York: Holt, Rinehart & Winston, Inc., 1968, Chapter 2.

Heilbroner, Robert L. *The Making of Economic Society,* 4th ed. Englewood Cliffs, N.J.: Prentice-Hall, Inc., 1972.

Köhler, Heinz. *Welfare and Planning: An Analysis of Capitalism Versus Socialism.* New York: John Wiley & Sons, Inc., 1966, Chapter 1.

Landauer, Carl. *Contemporary Economic Systems: A Comparative Analysis.* Philadelphia: J. B. Lippincott Co., 1964.

Loucks, William N., and William G. Whitney. *Comparative Economic Systems,* 9th ed. New York: Harper & Row, Publishers, 1973.

Oxenfeldt, Alfred R., and Vsevolod Holubnychy. *Economic Systems in Action: The United States, the Soviet Union, and France,* 3d ed. New York: Holt, Rinehart & Winston, Inc., 1965.

Pickersgill, Gary M., and Joyce E. Pickersgill. *Contemporary Economic Systems: A Comparative View.* Englewood Cliffs, N.J.: Prentice-Hall, Inc., 1974.

2

Market Mechanisms

INTRODUCTION

Tradition, command, and altruism are some of the principles by which an economically interdependent society coordinates its members and resolves conflicts among them. It is rather easy to understand how these principles provide answers to the questions which arise from scarcity. *Tradition* suggests that what has been produced continue to be produced as it has been before. *Command* provides direct orders from one person or group to others to resolve these matters. *Altruism* [1] induces people to act in such a .way that answers beneficial to others are provided.

The *market* is another principle of coordination and conflict resolution. It has come to be used increasingly during the last 500 years. Every modern nation uses market mechanisms to some degree as part of its economic system. Some nations, such as the United States, rely heavily on market mechanisms to the near exclusion of command and tradition.[2] Other nations, such as the Soviet Union, find it necessary to supplement their systems of central command with a considerable amount of market arrangements.

Market mechanisms are difficult to understand. Even many Americans, a group who on the average profess faith in the efficacy of market arrangements, do not fully understand them. Failure to understand market arrangements often results in their being incorrectly ignored as useful alternative means of solving economic problems.

---

[1] Altruism is sometimes called *solidarity*. See Carl Landauer, *Contemporary Economic Systems: A Comparative Analysis* (Philadelphia: J. B. Lippincott Co., 1964), pp. 9, 10, 222, and 223.

[2] There are a variety of names used to designate an economy heavily reliant on market arrangements. One is *free-enterprise economy,* a name suggesting economic decisions made by individuals free of direct orders from others, including others in the guise of government. Another is *capitalist economy,* a term indicating the importance of private or nongovernmental ownership and control of property and perhaps indicating the power of persons who own property. Another is an economy of *laissez-faire,* a phrase taken from the French, meaning, roughly, "let them alone," and suggesting that the government should not try to control the economic decisions of individuals. Also used synonymously is *the price system,* a name which emphasizes the role of prices in influencing economic decisions.

For example, in the 1960s unusually large numbers of Americans reached the age of 20, the result of the baby boom of the 1940s, and began to seek jobs. There was an almost automatic assumption in the minds of many observers that some governmental programs of intervention in the economy would be required to cope with the development. It is quite possible, however, that such intervention might not have been required at all. Market forces, if allowed to operate, might induce an almost automatic and relatively painless adjustment. These forces might successfully cope with the development without causing all the undesirable side effects and expense that new governmental intervention often brings.

It is the purpose of this chapter to describe how market mechanisms can effectively produce desirable results. Market mechanisms always operate in practice in conjunction with elements of tradition, command, and altruism. However, these nonmarket elements are largely ignored in this chapter so that attention can be concentrated upon market arrangements.

THE UNITS OF A MARKET ECONOMY

An economy heavily reliant upon market arrangements usually has two chief types of economic units. One is the household, which consists of an individual or a family. The other is the business firm. The household is a consumer and resource owner; the firm, a producer and resource user.

The ownership and control of land, labor, and capital is, directly or indirectly, lodged with households. The ultimate decision about how and whether resources are to be used in production rests with the households. The use of the resources is sold on the market by the households to firms usually in exchange for money payments. These money payments constitute the incomes of the households. The firms, having acquired the resources, use them to produce goods and services. These goods and services are then sold on markets by firms to the households in exchange for money.

The entire process thus consists of a series of two kinds of flows between households and firms. First, there are financial flows of money. Money moves from households via markets for goods and services to firms. Then it flows back again from firms via markets for resources to households. Second, there are real or nonmoney flows. Land, labor, and capital flow from households via resource markets to firms. Real goods and services flow from firms via product markets to households.[3]

The Role of Households

As one of the two types of economic units, households have various kinds of powers and functions in the market mechanisms.

---

[3] Considerable elementary economic analysis is in terms of circular flows of money, goods, and services between households and firms. See, for example, Elbert V. Bowden, *Economics: The Science of Common Sense* (Cincinnati: South-Western Publishing Co., 1977), pp. 78–82; or Campbell R. McConnell, *Economics: Principles, Problems, and Policies* (6th ed.; New York: McGraw-Hill Book Company, 1975), pp 51–54.

Control of Resources. Each household, regardless of size, has the power to decide how and whether the resources it owns are to be used. A husband or wife may decide not to take a formal job. A family head may choose to retire. A teenager may decide to go full time to college. In these cases the household has decided that its labor resources shall not be used. On the other hand, a husband or wife may take a job as a stockbroker rather than remain unemployed. A family head may quit a job in New York to take a similar position in San Francisco. A teenager may decide to take a cooperative work-study program. In these cases the household is deciding how its labor resources shall be used.

A household may decide either to use a plot of land it owns as a site on which to build an automobile service station or to lease the land to a grocery company as a supermarket location. A household may use a building it owns for a storage shed, a mechanic's shop, or a guest house. Alternately, it may tear the edifice down and sell the wood for kindling. A household may deposit its savings with a building and loan association so that funds become available for construction of more residential dwellings. It may instead buy new shares of stock in a telephone corporation so that more telephone equipment can be built. Thus, a household owning land, real property, or money capital determines the use to which the resource is put.

Control of Consumption. Each household in a market economy has some power to determine what and how much it shall consume. From the vast array of goods available, the household chooses those it most desires in the proportions it finds most pleasing. The household divides its income between spending on consumer goods and savings or adding to its stock of real and financial capital.

The decisions which the household makes are interrelated. For example, it may choose to enlarge its consumption of goods. This may be financed by a reduction in saving from current money income. Alternately, the use of more of the household's resources could be offered for sale. Instead it might use up or sell some of its real or financial capital or increase its borrowing.

As a result of all the choices it has made, each household will find itself in a given set of circumstances. It will consume none of some goods and services and certain amounts of others. It will save either none or some of its income. It will add to, subtract from, or allow to remain fixed the amount of each kind of its real and financial capital and its various types of debts.

Maximization of Satisfaction. Each household acting in a market context presumably makes its decisions in such a way that it arrives at the best possible results for itself. The amount of money income it receives is limited. The total amount of money it could spend and save is vastly greater than the income received. Money income is scarce relative to the uses to which it can be put. The household is faced with an economizing problem of allocating the scarce income among competing possible uses.

To increase the amount purchased and consumed of one thing requires either reductions in the amounts of other purchases, more intensive use of the household's resources, more borrowing, or less saving. More of any good or service has its costs in the form of these disadvantageous adjustments which have to be made to obtain it. Presumably each household will make every decision taking into account both the advantages and disadvantages as measured by its own preferences among all the choices and arrive at what is for it the best possible outcome. The household thus maximizes its satisfaction or its net advantage.[4]

The Role of Firms

Each firm, too, has certain powers and functions. Its owners or managers must decide what kinds and how much of the various types of resources the firm shall purchase as inputs, which products and how much output the firm shall produce, which technical processes the firm shall use, and where its operation shall take place. They presumably do so in such a way as to maximize the rate of profit for the firm. That is, actions are taken to maximize the difference between revenues and costs per dollar of ownership capital in the firm.

A decision is never made, for example, to use a production process which absorbs twice as many resources of each type as a second process requires to produce the same amount of output. The second production process is always chosen over the first because it involves only half as much cost and results in the same amount of revenue, thereby providing a greater rate of profit. In the same way there is chosen for the firm a site that keeps costs low relative to the revenues that can be obtained from sale of the product. Those inputs with low prices and considerable contribution to make to the production process are bought and used. Products are selected which can be made at low cost and sold at high prices. Goods and services which are costly to produce because they require large amounts of resources or because they require expensive resources and which can be sold only at a low price because of insufficient consumer demand are not produced.[5]

TECHNIQUES OF INFLUENCE THROUGH MARKETS

The market system leaves economic decisions to be freely made by each household and firm. In this way it enables each unit to do well by itself, given the circumstances in which the unit finds itself. But with each unit making its own decisions independently, are these circumstances not likely to be rather bad? Won't they, in fact, amount to chaos, so that the freedom to make

[4] The theory of consumer behavior in market circumstances is highly developed but still inadequate. See Bernard F. Haley, "Value and Distribution," *A Survey of Contemporary Economics*, American Economic Association, ed. Howard S. Ellis (Homewood, Ill.: Richard D. Irwin, Inc., 1948), Vol. I, pp. 1–10.

[5] For a much more detailed theory of the firm, see any textbook on intermediate microeconomic theory, such as John F. Due and Robert W. Clower, *Intermediate Economic Analysis* (5th ed.; Homewood, Ill.: Richard D. Irwin, Inc., 1966).

decisions is of little advantage? What good, one might ask, does it do me to have freedom to make decisions in my own best interest if all the others exercising their own freedom to make decisions, blithely ignore mine?

The most intriguing aspect of a market system is that, for the most part, giving each unit its own economic freedom to make decisions results neither in chaos nor complacency in regard to the wishes of others. The genius of the system is that each unit, acting in its own self-interest, indirectly will be induced to act in the interest of others. A web of influence, unobtrusive and subtle, conducive but not coercive, connects each household and firm with every other. Let us see how.

The Influence of Households

There are various lines of influence running from households to firms. While the immediate decisions regarding production are made by firms, they are strongly influenced in their choices by the wishes of households. This influence is exercised via the markets for resources and the markets for products. No one household has much influence, but all households in total have considerable influence.

Labor Markets. The influence of households in labor markets is best illustrated by an example. Suppose that most household members who are workers detest hard manual labor and prefer light sedentary tasks. Firms will then find it difficult to hire people for hard physical labor except at very high wage rates. These high wage rates will discourage firms from producing products in ways which require large amounts of physical labor. Firms will seek to reduce their costs and raise their profits by substituting other resources for physical labor in the production process. Perhaps highly mechanized and automated processes will be used.

There probably will be some products for which the substitution of other resources for physical labor is impossible. Inevitably these products require large amounts of physical labor. Because a high wage rate must be paid to induce the reluctant workers into this work, costs of production will be high. High production costs will require high prices for the product, and the high product prices will mean relatively small amounts of these products will be sold. So only small amounts will be produced, and few jobs involving physical labor will exist.

In this way the preferences of the households against physical jobs will cause few such jobs to exist both because firms will substitute other inputs whenever possible for physical labor and because products requiring physical labor will be produced only in small amounts. Preferences concerning such things as the location of work and the working conditions will be similarly effective.

Capital Markets. The preferences of households which own capital will influence the production decisions of firms. If most households are averse to taking risks, they will refuse to make their financial capital available to firms undertaking risky ventures. They will refuse, that is, unless the rate of return on their capital is very high so as to compensate them for the unpleasantness of accepting the risk. The high rate of return which must be paid to obtain capital for risky ventures will deter firms from engaging in risky ventures. Thus, preferences of households will be catered to again.

Household preferences between spending and saving also will be influential so far as the decisions of firms are concerned. Suppose that households generally tend to be conservative. That is, they want to provide for their futures by saving considerable portions of their incomes rather than by spending so much of their incomes for current consumption of goods and services. Two sets of repercussions follow from such preferences. For one thing, the households will be buying less goods and services, and firms will find it necessary to choose to produce fewer consumer products. Firms, consequently, use up fewer resources in consumer goods production. These resources will be released and available for other uses.

What are these other uses? The second set of repercussions reveals the answer. The households place their enlarged savings with financial institutions. Savings accounts are opened. Bonds and stocks are bought. Life insurance policies with savings features are purchased. The financial institutions, acting as intermediaries, seek borrowers for the enlarged savings. In order that all the enlarged savings be loaned out to borrowers, it becomes necessary to lower the interest rates charged. For both savers receiving interest and borrowers paying interest, interest rates tend to be lower. Among the borrowers are firms seeking to obtain funds with which to pay for the expansion of their production facilities, that is, to provide themselves with more real capital. These firms find it increasingly profitable to borrow as interest rates decline. By borrowing, these firms obtain the money capital with which to hire resources to build additional real capital. What resources are these? They are the resources which the first set of repercussions released from use in producing consumer goods.

Once the additional capital goods are built and in place, the economy has a larger productive capacity. A larger output of goods and services is possible. Alternately, as much output as before is possible with less labor effort. So it is that the households' preferences between saving and spending exert, via the market for loanable funds, influence on the choices of firms regarding the capital-intensiveness of production and the rate of growth of total production.

Markets for Consumer Goods. Households as consumers also strongly influence the decisions by firms regarding what to produce. To make a profit, firms engaged in producing consumer goods must choose goods which households want and are willing to buy in preference to other things upon which the same money could be spent. The better a firm is at complying with the wishes of households, the more profitable the firm will be. A business which does not comply will fail entirely, falling into bankruptcy and going out of existence. There will be left only those firms which are willing and able to permit their choice of product to be influenced by household buyers. This power of consumers to influence the commodity composition of gross national product through the market has been called *consumer's sovereignty.*

Influence Between Households. Lines of influence run from one household to another. If some households have strong preferences for certain products, they will buy these products even though the products are priced rather high. In this way other households whose preferences for these products are weaker and who will buy them only at lower prices are precluded from obtaining these products. Essentially the same situation exists in resource markets. If some households have strong preferences for certain uses of their resources, they will accept these uses even at rather low rates of compensation. By so doing, such households preempt these employment opportunities so that they are not available to other households whose preferences for these particular uses of their resources are less strong.

The Influence of Firms

Influence through markets can be exercised from firms to households. One such channel of influence is the market for resources. Suppose firms find that technological conditions and the pattern of demand for products makes necessary the use of large amounts of some type of resources, for example, labor capable of operating lathes. These firms will seek to hire large numbers of lathe operators, and the wage rate will be driven upward for this type of labor. The higher wage rate will encourage more people to seek, through training and other means, to become lathe operators.

So it is also with land and capital. Suppose firms require large amounts of land for the production of a product in great demand by consumers. Then higher rents for land used in this way will induce landowners to make their land available for the production of the product. If firms require buildings as motels to satisfy a growing consumer demand for motel services, owners of money capital will be attracted by the high earnings of the motel industry to make their capital available to motel businesses.

Firms also influence households through the market for products. A product may require a great amount of resources for its production. Alternately, it may require a significant amount of a resource which is priced high either because it is available only in small quantities or because it is much needed for the production of other popular items. In either case firms will charge a high price for the product, and the high price will induce households to buy and consume little of it. Although consumers exercise sovereignty in some respects, in others they have sovereignty exercised upon them.

Not only do lines of influence run in both directions between households and firms, but also they exist between one firm and another. A firm which requires supplies, capital equipment, or services to produce its product creates a demand for these inputs. Some other firm will be induced to fill the demand in order to make a profit. A firm which has a product in the form of supplies, capital equipment, or services can induce other firms to use them by producing them efficiently so that they can be sold at an attractively low price.

MARKET RESPONSES TO CHANGING CIRCUMSTANCES

A market economy has features which allow it to adjust to changes in technology, changes in consumer preferences, and changes in supply. The operation of market mechanisms can be understood best by observing their reactions to change.

Technological Change

Suppose, for example, that a market system has been operating in a given set of circumstances with all adjustments to these circumstances fully made. Now some autonomous technological change occurs. A new synthetic rubber is invented. Its chief ingredient is coal. The new synthetic rubber has, let it be assumed, exactly the same physical properties as natural rubber. If the cost of production of the synthetic is higher than that of the natural rubber, there will be no economic adjustments as a consequence of the invention. It will be purely of scientific interest. If, however, the initial costs of production and, consequently, the selling price of the synthetic are below those of natural rubber, an extensive series of economic reactions is likely to ensue.

Increases in Production. Firms which purchase and use rubber will switch from natural to synthetic because they can lower their costs and increase their profits by doing so. Business users of materials for which rubber is, in one degree or another, a substitute will tend to substitute the newly discovered, lower priced rubber for these other materials. Firms may even substitute rubber for labor by being more wasteful of rubber and reducing the labor used in gathering up scraps of rubber for reuse. In regard to capital, something similar also may occur as old machines are replaced with new ones, less elaborate but more wasteful of rubber.

The price of products made with rubber is likely to fall because of the lower price of this one of their inputs. Both firms and household users of these products containing rubber will respond by attempting to substitute rubber products for other products. A larger quantity of these products made with rubber will be sold as a consequence. Rubber padding in furniture will take the place of feathers and springs. Felt insulation on refrigerators will give way to rubber lining.

Meanwhile, other results will be occurring in the market for coal. The greater purchases of coal by the makers of rubber will tend to drive up its price. The higher price will make it profitable to begin working mines that were previously unprofitable because of inaccessibility or low quality of coal. The higher price will also discourage the use of coal for heating. Users will tend to seek other fuels as substitutes, leaving the coal for purchase by rubber makers. Households who have relied upon coal for heating and who continue to do so will try to make do with less heat, perhaps by using larger amounts of rubber insulation in the walls of their homes and around their doors and windows.

Decreases in Products. Workers on rubber plantations will discover that their wages are falling. Those who least like working there or find it easy to move elsewhere will find other employment, perhaps in the coal mines. Landowners of the plantations, especially those least suitable for the production of rubber, will find their rent returns declining and will seek other uses for their land. Some of the machinery on these plantations will be allowed to wear out without repair or replacement. The funds which might have been used to finance this repair or replacement will be used for other investments such as additional coal-mining equipment or machines to convert coal to rubber.

Indirect Effects. An ever widening circle of ever less violent consequences is likely to spread through the economy from these initial more intensive effects centered on the firms and households most closely connected with the coal and rubber industries. The rise in the price of coal is likely to cause the prices of natural gas and fuel oil to rise also. These effects occur because the higher coal price will drive buyers to gas and oil, the prices of which will rise as the demand increases for them. The higher gas and oil prices will induce resources to be moved into those industries and will cause higher prices for the products made with the use of gas and oil. The higher prices for these products will in turn have further repercussions on the decisions of both firms and households.

In the meantime the prices of materials used in a fashion complementary to rubber will rise in price. Materials such as nylon and rayon will rise because of the greater demand for them to accompany the increased amounts of rubber being used to make tires.

Changes in Consumer Preferences

An example which shows how a market economy adjusts to changes in consumer preferences is the case of tobacco. Imagine that a market system has been in a state of complete adjustment to circumstances. Now an announcement is made that smoking has been found to be a significant threat to health. This information was not known before, but the announcement is believed by consumers, many of whom have been heavy smokers.

What consequences are likely to follow? Consumer preferences are drastically altered against smoking. Tobacco sales and prices decline dramatically. Wage rates for tobacco workers, rent rates for tobacco land, sales prices of tobacco vending machines, values of equipment used in manufacturing tobacco, and profits of tobacco businesses all fall swiftly. Resources are thus encouraged to move out of the tobacco industry. They become available for other uses. They will be channeled into uses in which, under the new circumstances, their owners earn the largest amounts of income and derive the largest amounts of satisfaction. More of other goods most wanted by consumers can now be produced.

Changes in Supply

It is instructive to observe how the market reacts to changes in the supply of some resource or product. An example is provided by the gasoline shortage which occurred in the United States in 1973–1974. One of the immediate causes of the shortage was the so-called Arab oil embargo against the United States. Several of the Arab oil-exporting nations of the Middle East decided not to allow their oil to be shipped to the United States. The result was a decrease in the supply of gasoline in the United States. The immediate reaction of some Americans was to assume that governmental controls would be necessary: gasoline rationing at the retail level, government-directed allocation of gasoline at the refining and wholesale levels, and reduced legal maximum speeds on the highways. There was a tendency to overlook the alternative solution to the situation—the market solution.

How does a market system respond to such a situation? The key variable is probably the price of gasoline. It is likely to rise considerably as the supply of gasoline declines. The higher price causes both households and firms to use less gasoline. Pleasure driving becomes more expensive relative to other entertainment and is therefore reduced. Car pools are formed for commuters. Bicycles and walking are resorted to. Smaller cars which use less gasoline become popular. Thus, the quantity demanded of gasoline is reduced as people are induced by the higher price to accommodate their activities to the situation.

Governmental directives are not necessarily required to cause these accommodations. The higher price of gasoline alone may be sufficient. The households which least value the uses of gasoline will reduce their uses of it the most. Firms will try to keep costs low and profits high by eliminating the use of gasoline. Where production can occur easily without gasoline, it will do so. Where gasoline is essential for production, the price of the product will rise to cover the increased costs of gasoline. The higher price will discourage at least some purchases of the product, and its volume of production will fall. The result will be that the limited quantities of gasoline will be devoted to the most indispensable uses for the benefit of those who appreciate the uses the most.

Meanwhile, on the supply side of the gasoline market, beneficial accommodations will also be occurring. The high price of gasoline will make it profitable for exploration firms to search more vigorously for new oil fields. Some older fields, previously regarded as exhausted, can now profitably be subjected to efforts to retrieve from them additional supplies of oil. The high price of gasoline will also entice more research into techniques for converting coal and shale to gasoline. In these ways the quantity of gasoline supplied will increase because of the new higher price. All of these reactions are the result, not of government commands, but instead, of market forces.[6]

[6] Several good additional examples of the adjustment of market mechanisms to changing circumstances can be found in Harry D. Hutchison, *Economics and Social Goals* (Chicago: Science Research Associates, Inc., 1973), pp. 58–69.

HOW THE MARKET ANSWERS BASIC ECONOMIC QUESTIONS

It is useful to draw together what has been said about market mechanisms thus far. One way to do this is to explain how these mechanisms provide answers to the basic economic questions arising from scarcity. How does a market system determine the commodity composition of output, the character of production, the distribution of income and output, and the rate of economic growth?

The Commodity Composition of Output

The commodity composition of the output of an economy heavily reliant on market arrangements is determined in the first instance by managers of business firms. These managers are directly responsible for converting resources into products, that is, for production. It is they who determine what products will be produced. They are impelled by the profit motive, which causes them to choose products that can be sold at prices which are high relative to costs of production.

Owners of resources and consumers of products exercise their influence on the commodity composition through their influence on costs of production and prices of products. Resource owners who prefer some employments for their resources to others will accept lower compensation for some uses of the resources than for others. In this way they encourage firms to choose to manufacture products which might otherwise go unproduced. Consumers will pay high prices for products which they want very much. In this way they encourage firms to produce these products.

The Character of Production

The character of production is also determined in the first instance by the managers of firms. They select the techniques, the resource proportions, the particular units of each resource, the site, and the scale of operations to be used in production. Again, however, they are motivated by profits; this motivation provides opportunity for resource owners and consumers to determine indirectly the character of production.

The Distribution of Output and Income

There are two aspects of the distribution of output and income which are worthy of discussion at this point. One is the distribution of each specific good or service among the many alternative competing consumers of it. For example, which of the more than 50 million households which may exist in a society are to receive the 8 million new automobiles which may be produced during a year? The other aspect is the aggregate distribution of income. It has to do with the share of each household in the total money income received by the entire society and in the total output of goods and services produced by the firms of the society.

Distribution of Specific Goods. It is relatively easy to explain the market distribution of specific goods. In a market system specific goods are distributed to those who want them the most as evidenced by their going into the market and "outbidding" other households for the goods. The households which get new cars are those that are willing to buy them at higher prices. Households not getting new cars are willing and able to buy them only at lower prices. Cars do not provide much satisfaction to these households, which tend to prefer other goods. Or these households are able to buy cars only at lower prices because their shares in the aggregate national income may be quite small.

Aggregate Distribution of Income. There arises, therefore, the relevance of the other aspect of distribution. In a market society what determines each household's share of the national income? Two immediate determinants are the distribution of the ownership of resources and the prices of the use of resources. Households which own large amounts of land, labor, and capital will receive large shares in the national income. Households which own even moderate amounts of resources which have high prices will also receive large shares.

Behind each of the two immediate determinants there lie many more indirect causes of the distribution. Some of the factors determining the distribution of the ownership of resources are the customs regarding inheritance, the degree to which saving and spending patterns vary from one household to another, the degree to which preferences for education and training vary among households, and the pattern of distribution of natural talent among households. Among the factors which determine the prices of resources are the patterns of preferences of consumers for products, the state of technology, the pattern of preferences of owners of resources as to various uses for their resources, and the distribution of ownership of the resources.

If consumers greatly desire potatoes to eat in large quantities, owners of land which is especially suited to growing potatoes will receive high rents and have large shares in the national income. If technology is advanced by the invention of an internal combustion engine, owners of petroleum deposits will begin to receive higher incomes. If most workers do not like physical labor, then those few who do will receive higher wages than otherwise.

The Rate of Economic Growth

The rate of growth of a market society is greatly determined by the degree of concern which the people have for the future relative to the present. People express this concern in a variety of actions. They save large amounts of their current income. They devote a considerable portion of their current expenditures to education and training. They choose relatively little leisure and much work. They eagerly search through systematic inquiry and experimentation for knowledge of new techniques with which to produce future output. The consequences, as described in greater detail earlier in this chapter, will be a rapid growth in the size of output of the society. The large savings and hard work will enable large additions to be made to the stock of real capital of the society. The education and training will enable the quality of the labor resources to be raised. The experimentation and inquiry will reveal how to get increasingly larger output from ever smaller amounts of inputs through previously unknown production techniques.

On the other hand, if a majority of the people of a market economy are relatively unconcerned about the future, that is, if they are unwilling to make sacrifices in the present for the sake of their future, the rate of growth will be low.

THE ADVANTAGEOUS RESULTS OF MARKET ARRANGEMENTS

It can be claimed that an economy based heavily upon market principles produces good results. The answers provided by market principles to the questions raised by scarcity and interdependence are good ones as judged against reasonable criteria.[7]

The Commodity Composition of Output

A plausible claim is that the best of all possible commodity compositions of total output results from the use of markets. Consumer goods that are most wanted by households are produced. Goods that are not wanted are not produced. Resources are not wastefully drawn away from the production of goods whose consumption would provide great satisfaction to be used for the production of goods whose consumption provides little satisfaction. Goods whose production is very unpleasant to the owners of resources will not be produced. Goods whose production is less unpleasant will be.

For any good which is produced, the quantity will not be so excessive as to absorb resources which if released could produce additional and more satisfying amounts of other goods. Nor will the quantity be so small that resources are released to produce additional but less satisfying quantities of other goods. The preferences of resource owners and consumers operate by way of the market and through the profit motive to assure that the most satisfactory commodity composition is produced. The great bundle of goods and services constituting the national product is of the optimum mixture.

The Character of Production

The character of production, it is claimed, will also be at an optimum under a market system. Firms will never use more resources than are necessary to produce a given amount of output of any product. They will never produce less than the maximum amount of output possible with the use of any given amount of resources. In producing its product, every attempt will be made by each firm to minimize the use of resources which are critically needed for

---

[7] For a more precise elaboration of the criteria in simple mathematical form, see Heinz Köhler, *Welfare and Planning: An Analysis of Capitalism Versus Socialism* (New York: John Wiley & Sons, Inc., 1966), pp. 6–26.

the production elsewhere of other products. Instead every attempt will be made to use resources whose alternative uses are poor or nonexistent. Impelled by the profit motive, firms strain for efficiency.

The beneficial results of households appear most obviously in the form of lower prices for products. More subtly and significantly they take the form of the maximization of the total output of the society, given the quantity of land, labor, and capital with which it has to work. Maximization of the total output is important as a means to maximizing the average level of living of the people of the society and thereby helping to maximize their satisfaction. Hence the claim is made that a society which is based on the market system causes the selection of the best or most efficient techniques of production.

The Distribution of Output and Income

The distribution of specific goods and services among alternative households is also believed to be excellent if a market system is in operation. People who want specific goods more than others obtain them because they are willing to "outbid" the others. Each unit of each good gets to whatever household derives the most satisfaction from it. In this way the total satisfaction of all households and of society is maximized.

The discussion of the preceding paragraph must be qualified by noting that goods go only to those who can pay for them. The distribution of money income, and hence of the means of payment in a market system, is believed by advocates of the free market to be a good one. Households which contribute large amounts of resources or critically important resources to production receive large incomes in return. Persons who think it worthwhile can choose to work hard, save much, train themselves, and concern themselves with making wise choices for themselves. Subsequently, they will receive larger shares in the national income. Those who do not think such extra exertions and sacrifices are worth the compensation choose to have more immediate leisure and to spend more in the present. They should be content with smaller shares in the future. They have in effect freely chosen such shares for themselves.

The Rate of Economic Growth

The rate of growth which results from a market system can also be regarded as optimal. Some advocates of the market system emphasize that there is not necessarily a virtue in a very high rate of growth. Rapid growth has advantages, it is admitted, but it also entails sacrifices, costs, and other disadvantages.[8]

---

[8] In fact, there has been some speculation that in the longer run the world's further economic growth will have such severe disadvantages that either its form will have to change radically or it will have to cease altogether. See the famous study by Donella H. Meadows, Dennis L. Meadows, Jorgen Randers, and William W. Behrens III, *The Limits to Growth: A Report for the Club of Rome's Project on the Predicament of Mankind* (New York: The New American Library, Inc., 1972), and a critical response: H. S. D. Cole, Christopher Freeman, Marie Jahoda, and K. L. R. Pavitt (eds.), *Models of Doom: A Critique of the Limits to Growth* (New York: Universe Books, 1973).

The market system arranges for a rapid or slow rate of growth in accordance with the wishes of individuals. If a large portion of households are acutely concerned with the future and are willing to choose to make present sacrifices for the sake of an opulent future, then under a market system rapid growth will ensure and provide such a future. If most households have little concern for the future and do not believe it worthwhile to make sacrifices in the present for the sake of an affluent future, the mechanism of the market system will provide only a slight rate of economic growth. Then the future will not, for most of the people, be significantly more affluent than the present.

Whatever the rate of economic growth of the whole economy, a market system makes it possible for each household to choose to have its own individual rate of growth by choosing to make few or many sacrifices in the present.

SUMMARY

A market economy is one in which resources are owned and products consumed by households and in which resources are used and goods and services produced by firms. Each household decides for itself how and to what extent its resources shall be used and which products and how much of each product will be consumed by it. Each firm decides for itself which resources it will use and what products it will produce. Both kinds of units presumably make wise decisions for themselves about these matters and thereby achieve results which are beneficial to themselves.

Each unit exerts influence upon and is influenced by the others through a system of markets where products, the use of resources, and money are exchanged. Through these exchanges each unit is led to make decisions which benefit not only itself but also others. Acting to maximize its satisfaction or its own net advantage, each household will tend to supply resources which are most useful and most desirable to others. It will select for its consumption goods and services which are least wanted by others. Acting to maximize its profits, each firm will select for its use resources least needed in other uses. It will maximize its ratio of output to resources used. It will select for production products most wanted by others. Self-interest is thus used to achieve results in the general interest.

The results achieved appear to be very good ones. The commodity composition of output is one that is likely to be most satisfying to the populace. The character of production is such that the level of living is as high as is possible, given the size of the stock of resources, the preferences of resource owners, and the state of technology. The specific products are distributed in a pattern which maximizes the satisfaction of the people. Each family's share in the aggregate distribution of income is proportional to its contribution to the total production of society.

QUESTIONS

1. What are the various types of economic units of an economy heavily reliant on markets? What kinds of economic decisions does each of these types of unit make?
2. In a market economy, by what means does each economic unit influence the economic decisions of other units?

3. What is consumer's sovereignty in a market economy? Is consumer's sovereignty absolutely powerful in such an economy?
4. One test of one's understanding of how market mechanisms work is to try to explain how they would respond to some specific changing circumstance. If, for example, a country relied almost completely upon market mechanisms, how would these mechanisms appropriately respond to an enlargement of the number of twenty-year-olds just finishing school and entering the labor force?
5. How do market mechanisms determine the commodity composition of gross national product? How do they determine the character of production? How do they determine the distribution of income?
6. How do market mechanisms determine the rate of economic growth?
7. Defenders of market mechanisms claim that these mechanisms provide good solutions to the basic economic problems created by scarcity and economic interdependence. What are their arguments?

RECOMMENDED READINGS

Bornstein, Morris (ed.). *Comparative Economic Systems: Models and Cases,* 3d ed. Homewood, Ill.: Richard D. Irwin, Inc., 1974, Selections 1 and 2.

Carson, Richard L., and Gilles Paquet. *Comparative Economic Systems.* New York: Macmillan Publishing Co., Inc., 1973, Chapters 1–5.

Due, John F., and Robert W. Clower. *Intermediate Economic Analysis,* 5th ed. Homewood, Ill.: Richard D. Irwin, Inc., 1966.

Fusfeld, Daniel R. *Economics.* Lexington, Mass.: D. C. Heath and Company, 1972, Chapters 5 and 21–25.

Grossman, Gregory. *Economic Systems.* Englewood Cliffs, N.J.: Prentice-Hall, Inc., 1967, Chapter 4.

Halm, George N. *Economic Systems: A Comparative Analysis,* 3d ed. New York: Holt, Rinehart & Winston, Inc., 1968, Chapters 2 and 3.

Köhler, Heinz. *Welfare and Planning: An Analysis of Capitalism Versus Socialism.* New York: John Wiley & Sons, Inc., 1966, Chapters 2 and 4.

Landauer, Carl. *Contemporary Economic Systems: A Comparative Analysis.* Philadelphia: J. B. Lippincott, 1964, Chapters 4 and 5.

Leftwich, Richard H. *The Price System and Resource Allocation,* 5th ed. New York: Holt, Rinehart & Winston, Inc., 1973.

Loucks, William N., and William G. Whitney. *Comparative Economic Systems,* 9th ed. New York: Harper & Row Publishers, 1973, Chapter 2.

Pickersgill, Gary M., and Joyce E. Pickersgill. *Contemporary Economic Systems: A Comparative View.* Englewood Cliffs, N.J.: Prentice-Hall, Inc., 1974, Chapter 3.

Robinson, Marshall A., Herbert C. Morton, and James D. Calderwood. *An Introduction to Economic Reasoning,* 4th ed. Garden City, N.Y.: Doubleday & Company, Inc., 1967, Chapter 2.

Stigler, George. *The Theory of Price,* 3d ed. New York: The Macmillan Company, 1966.

American Experience and Market Mechanisms

INTRODUCTION

Market mechanisms are used in various degrees in all nations, but no nation relies exclusively on them. They have been found to work best with certain prerequisite conditions. One prerequisite is appropriate governmental policies to provide a framework for them. Their use, therefore, requires a search for such policies. These policies in effect modify and partially replace the market with economic arrangements involving governmental command. Consequently, all present societies combine market and nonmarket elements in their economic systems. All have, in this sense, "mixed" economic systems.

The American economy is no exception. Market mechanisms have worked well for the United States, and a majority of Americans believe that heavy reliance upon markets is desirable. There are, however, episodes in American economic experience which suggest that simple acceptance of market arrangements is an inadequate government policy. This experience indicates that there should be continual reconsideration of certain questions. What constitutes the optimum combination of market arrangements and governmental command? What policies provide the best framework within which markets can operate? What kinds of economic decisions are best left to the market? Which are best decided through government? American experience is one of the most important guides to answers for these questions.

To review all American history in a search for answers would be a cumbersome task. This chapter, therefore, deals with only two elements of this history. These elements are selected because they seem to be peculiarly crucial in the American search for the proper mixture of markets and governmental command. The first of these elements is the Great Depression of the 1930s. The second is monopoly, a problem which arose 100 years ago and still continues.

THE GREAT DEPRESSION

The Great Depression probably did more to reshape the American economic system than any other event of the 20th century. It started in 1929, became more severe until 1933, and stretched on until the beginning of World War II. It involved unemployment, idle production capacity, loss of profits, business bankruptcies, a fall in the level of living, decreases in the value of property, the closing of many banks, and considerable social unrest. At its worst, 25 percent of the labor force was out of work.

This unfortunate period followed the 1920s, a decade in which great faith had been placed in the private market system. The 1920s had been an era of prosperity, full employment, rising levels of living, and stability in the general level of prices. The market system was given credit for this success. But when the success culminated in the disaster of the Great Depression, the blame, too, was placed partly upon the market system.

The Consequences of the Great Depression for the Market System

The Great Depression brought with it a dramatic change in public opinion. Many kinds of governmental intervention in the market economy, previously blocked by majority opposition to change, were now tolerated or encouraged.

New Governmental Economic Intervention. The Federal Deposit Insurance Corporation was created as a government device to prevent economic loss to owners of financial wealth when market pressures forced the closing of banks. The program of government supports for prices of agricultural products was greatly enlarged to prevent losses and bankruptcy for farmers otherwise hurt by market forces in the form of falling or fluctuating prices. Labor unions were encouraged by new legislation so that workers would no longer be forced to bargain individually on the market for labor. For a time through the National Recovery Act, business firms were encouraged to join together to plan to avoid subjecting their products to the fluctuations of the forces of supply and demand.

Legislation was passed requiring compulsory contributions to retirement funds through a government-operated social security system. This had the effect of replacing in part voluntary savings of individuals in response to market forces such as the level of interest rates. Legislation was passed imposing compulsory costs on businesses to finance automatic payments to unemployed workers. In this way reliance upon individual workers' decisions to save part of their income received during prosperous years for use in less prosperous periods was reduced. So was reliance upon an individual business establishment of an unemployment compensation system for its employees as a device for attracting workers.

Realignment of Political Power. The Great Depression provided the political opportunity for reshaping, to some degree, the market system with a system of direct command. It also altered the relative roles of the two major political parties so that after the 1930s it would be more difficult to reintroduce increased reliance upon the market system and easier to introduce into the economy elements of command.

For the 70 years immediately prior to the Great Depression, the Republican party had been the dominant party in the United States. For over 70 percent of these 70 years, the Republicans had held power in Congress. All but three of the 15 presidents during the 70 years had been Republicans. The Republican party had adopted as its traditional position the desirability of relying on market mechanisms for the determination of most economic decisions. It continued to adhere to this position during and after the Great Depression.

The Republicans did not continue, however, to wield power after the Great Depression. They had been in power at the onset of the Depression and were to some degree blamed for it. Moreover, the Republicans continued through the Depression to be the less willing of the two parties to use government command as a means of coping with the Depression. These circumstances lost Republicans many supporters, making the Democrats the majority party, a position which they held into the 1970s.

Between 1932 and the mid-1970s, four of the seven presidents were Democrats, and Congress was controlled during this period of more than 40 years by Democrats for all but four years. The Democrats had adopted as their traditional position a willingness greater than that of the Republicans to resort to government command in economic matters and to rely upon the market to a smaller degree. It is true that, after the 1930s, there was repeated disillusionment with government intervention in the economy and the discovery that such intervention sometimes created more problems than it solved. Nevertheless, the experience of the 1930s continued for decades to influence the economic system and the structure of political power within the American nation.[1]

The Market System as a Cause of the Great Depression

There seems adequate evidence that the Great Depression induced the American people to alter their economic system away from the market mechanisms and toward governmental command. However, the evidence presented thus far does not prove that this alteration was justified; there remains to be considered the vital question of just what caused the Depression. Various possible causal relationships can be entertained. One is that the Great Depression was caused by forces inherent in market arrangements. Another is that the cause may be found in governmental failure to provide the proper framework of public policy within which market arrangements could have worked well. Still another is that the market arrangements did work well, but defective governmental economic policy was the primary cause of the Depression.

---

[1] The socioeconomic consequences of the Great Depression in the United States are dealt with in a number of interesting and readable accounts. Two of the best brief descriptions are these: Frederick Lewis Allen, *The Big Change: America Transforms Itself: 1900–1950* (New York: Harper & Row Publishers, 1952), Chapter 10; and William J. Baumol and Lester V. Chandler, *Economic Processes and Policies* (New York: Harper & Row Publishers, 1954), pp. 137–150. Two more extensive, nontechnical works are these, the latter of which is a book of reprints of newspaper articles and other writings: Caroline Bird, *The Invisible Scar: The Great Depression, and What It Did to American Life, From Then Until Now* (New York: David McKay Co., Inc., 1966); and David A. Shannon (ed.), *The Great Depression* (Englewood Cliffs, N.J.: Prentice-Hall, Inc., 1960).

Excessive and Deficient Spending. There is no complete agreement among economists about the causes of the Great Depression. The most frequently accepted explanation suggests that many private businesses during the 1920s expanded their productive capacity at a rate which was too rapid. It was too rapid to be sustained into and through the 1930s and too rapid relative to the amount of products which could be sold. These businesses expanded productive capacity by ordering and installing new equipment, building additional floor space, and adding to their inventories of materials and products. In the process they spent large sums employing people either directly on their payrolls or indirectly through jobs among supplier firms. These employees spent their earnings buying products of other businesses, which in turn were able to make large profits and were induced to employ large numbers of people.

As long as the spending continued, jobs were plentiful and times were prosperous. The 1920s were, as has already been indicated, prosperous. Beginning in 1929, however, businesses discovered that they had been creating too much productive capacity. Consequently, they decreased their spending. Workers who had had jobs associated with creating additional capacity were discharged or were required to work fewer hours at lower wage rates. Earning less income, these workers, too, spent less on the purchase of products. When other businesses discovered sales of their products declining, they also reduced their labor forces. A cumulative decline in spending on expansion of production capacity, employment, earnings and incomes, and spending on products ensued.

What caused the excessive spending on productive capacity in the 1920s? Partly responsible was World War I. The war had created the need for additional production facilities during the period just before 1920, but it had also prevented the completion of the facilities. Partly responsible was the rapid increase in the desire for certain new products, particularly automobiles. Partly responsible was the inability of business people to judge future rates of growth of demand for their products.

Ideal Market Responses. Was the market system at fault? How would the ideal market system have responded to the situation which developed in the national economy in 1929? How would it have enabled the economy to avoid the undesirable consequences which did in fact occur as part of the Great Depression?

Those consumer and capital products which were found to be available in excessive amounts compared to other goods and services would have fallen in price. The average price level of all goods and services might likewise have fallen. Those types of labor and other resources in especially large supply relative to demand would have fallen in price. Perhaps wage rates and prices of resources in general would have fallen. As the eagerness to borrow funds to use for expansion of productive capacity declined, so would the interest rate on these borrowed funds.

The fall in the prices of products would have induced buyers to purchase larger quantities of them and producers to produce fewer of them. The fall in the prices of certain types of labor would have induced workers to move to other occupations. The fall in the price of all labor would have induced businesses to hire more labor. It would also have induced more workers voluntarily to withdraw themselves, at least partially, from the labor market and to apply more of their hours to leisure. The decline in the interest rate would have encouraged more businesses to borrow to spend on expanding production capacity. It would also have encouraged savers to reduce their saving and to increase their purchases of products. The decline in the prices of products and resources would have increased the purchasing power of holders of money balances and fixed price assets, such as bonds and savings accounts. These holders would have been encouraged in this way to buy more products. With these reactions, the heavy unemployment of the Great Depression could perhaps have been avoided.

Defective Market Responses. Unemployment was not avoided because these reactions did not occur. The American market system of the time was not ideal, and the pattern of responses was defective. There was resistance to price reduction of every kind. Businesses which held monopolistic power over their products chose not to permit their prices to fall. Instead they restricted the volume of physical output of their products to amounts that could be sold at high prices. In this way they created unemployment and idle capacity. Unionized labor chose, through the power which it commanded, to resist wage decreases even though the consequence was unemployment.

Moreover, when prices and wage rates were permitted to fall, reactions were sometimes perverse and inappropriate. A fall in the price of a good created an expectation in the minds of prospective buyers that the price might fall further. The result was that if the purchase was at all postponable, purchases were decreased rather than increased as prices fell. A fall in the wage rate of labor sometimes induced laborers to seek to work even longer hours than before in the hope of maintaining their incomes at the higher level. A fall in the interest rates sometimes made savers try to save even more than before in the hope of achieving a given total amount of interest income even though the interest rates had fallen.

Workers were ignorant of employment opportunities to which they might turn, and they were unable or unwilling to move geographically and occupationally to obtain employment. Likewise, businesses, because of ignorance or inertia, were unable to adjust their choice of product or their technique of production rapidly enough to accommodate swiftly changing circumstances. Consequently, business losses and unemployment were not avoided.[2]

[2] The causes of the Great Depression and of the stock market crash which preceded it are explored in these works: John Kenneth Galbraith, *The Great Crash 1929* (3d ed.: Boston: Houghton Mifflin Company, 1972); Robert Aaron Gordon, *Business Fluctuations* (2d ed.; New York: Harper & Row Publishers, 1961), pp. 428–450; and Paul B. Trescott, *Money, Banking, and Economic Welfare* (2d ed.; New York: McGraw-Hill Book Company, 1965), pp. 459–472.

Nonmarket Causes of the Great Depression

There seems to be considerable evidence that it was the market part of the American economic system which, in large measure, caused the Great Depression. However, there is also evidence to suggest that the great length and the intensity of this catastrophe were caused by nonmarket forces.

Fear of Governmental Policies. The most frequently cited possibility in this regard has to do with the measures of relief, recovery, and reform undertaken by Democratic President Franklin Roosevelt to cope with the Depression after he gained office in 1933. It is contended that these measures were so frightening to conservative business people that they pessimistically delayed a resumption of their employment-creating expenditures on maintenance and expansion of production capacity until the coming of World War II. There is no way of proving this contention, but most moderate scholars of the economics of the Great Depression feel it worthy of mention as a possibility.

Government Policies to Keep Prices High. Another policy of the Roosevelt administration also probably worsened the Great Depression. The administration sought to prevent the fall of prices of labor and products. For example, under the National Recovery Act, in effect in the period 1933–1935, government encouraged business and labor to join together monopolistically to keep prices and wage rates from falling. And under the Agricultural Adjustment Act farm prices were kept high by destroying crops and livestock and by otherwise restricting supply. The preceding section of this chapter suggests that some decline of prices and wage rates was an appropriate market response for ending the Great Depression. If that suggestion is correct, the governmental efforts to keep prices and wage rates high were responsible in part for impeding corrective market forces. Government policy of encouraging high prices may thus have prolonged and deepened the Great Depression.

International Trade Policy. Another probable nonmarket source of the severity of the Great Depression was the passage of the Smoot-Hawley Tariff by the United States Congress in 1930. This piece of legislation against free market forces raised import taxes on a wide variety of foreign goods entering the United States. In retaliation, foreign governments took steps to reduce their peoples' purchases of American exported products. International trade volume was already falling before this new tariff law was passed and would have continued to fall after 1930 because of the Great Depression. Nevertheless, it seems clear that this governmental intervention into the free market mechanism made the Great Depression somewhat more severe than it otherwise would have been.[3]

[3] For brief accounts of the passage and results of the Smoot-Hawley Tariff, see P. T. Ellsworth, *The International Economy: Its Structure and Operation* (New York: The Macmillan Company, 1950), pp. 499–501; and Asher Isaacs, *International Trade: Tariff and Commercial Policies* (Homewood, Ill.: Richard D. Irwin, Inc., 1948), pp. 235 and 236. For longer accounts see U.S. Tariff Commission, *The Tariff and Its History* (Washington: U.S. government Printing Office, 1934); and F. W. Taussig, *The Tariff History of the United States* (8th ed.; New York: G. P. Putnam's Sons, 1964), pp. 489–526.

Monetary Policy and the Federal Reserve System. Still another nonmarket cause of the severity of the Great Depression was the policy pursued by the Federal Reserve System during the 1930s. The Federal Reserve System is a creation of the national government. In fact, it can be regarded as a government agency. While some of its activities are carried on through various markets, it is clearly motivated by nonmarket considerations. Its main activity is control of the quantity of money in the United States.[4] Its aim is to achieve full employment, optimum economic growth, stability in the general level of prices, and a satisfactory balance in international money payments between the United States and the rest of the world.

It is now generally agreed that the appropriate policy for the Federal Reserve during the entire 1930s would have been to make it possible for the commercial banks to increase the money supply and to lower interest rates on borrowed funds. Increases in the money supply and low interest rates would have encouraged borrowing and spending by business for maintenance and expansion of production facilities. Such spending would have provided employment for otherwise unemployed workers directly through the jobs created in the capital goods industry. Indirectly, jobs would have been created in the consumer goods industries whose products would be purchased in enlarged amounts by capital goods workers.

At any rate, the Federal Reserve did not consistently follow such an *easy money* policy. One reason it did not was the legal limitations which Congress had imposed on its actions. Another was misjudgments of the situation by Federal Reserve officials. For example, in 1931 the Federal Reserve took action to raise interest rates and restrict the money supply. It took this action to induce owners of wealth to leave their funds in the United States to earn high interest rates rather than to convert these funds to gold which they then would withdraw to foreign countries. Such withdrawals would leave the United States with what the Federal Reserve and American law judged to be inadequate gold stocks. In this way, maintenance of the gold stock was given higher priority than reduction of unemployment.

Again, in 1936, the Federal Reserve System took action which tightened the supply of money to avoid what it feared was incipient inflation. Yet the effect, if any, was to increase the amount of unemployment which in 1936 was still at a high level of 9 million persons or about 17 percent of the labor force. It is thus the view of some experts that this kind of Federal Reserve policy was one of the main causes of the worsening of unemployment and business conditions which occurred in 1937–1938.[5]

---

[4] Control is partly exercised by the Federal Reserve through its purchases and sales of various types of outstanding United States government securities on the regular market which exists for these securities. Additional control is exerted through direct commands given by the Federal Reserve authorities to commercial banks.

[5] For a generally critical view of the Federal Reserve's actions during the 1930s, see Milton Friedman and Anna Jacobson Schwartz, *The Great Contraction, 1929–1933* (Princeton, N.J.: Princeton University Press, 1965).

General Appraisal

This brief survey of the American experience in the Great Depression suggests that the Depression provided the occasion for a considerable shift of the nation's economy away from the market and toward governmental command. On the one hand, this shift probably was not fully justified. It is possible to make a convincing case that governmental policies, not essentially of a market character but rather of a command nature, helped to make the Depression as great as it was. On the other hand, it seems necessary to concede that the market mechanisms, as they existed in the United States in the 1920s, contained gross deviations from the ideal. Furthermore, any conceivable theoretical market system probably contains inherent problems which would cause it to produce less than ideal results. It is to one of these problems that this study now turns. That is the problem of competition and monopoly.

COMPETITION AND MONOPOLY

The problem of business monopolies and of competition in business became of prominent concern in the United States during the last half of the 19th century. Two groups of forces conspired to make this so. One was the changing character of technology which was occurring at the time. The other was the inherent nature of the market mechanism itself.

Modern Technology as a Cause of Monopoly

Almost everyone is familiar with the technological advances that were rapidly changing the character of production in the 19th century. There were numerous inventions making possible the use of highly specialized and sometimes quite elaborate and large pieces and complexes of machinery. Efficient ways to organize production in big producing units were being discovered, too. At the same time, greater economic contact among larger groups of people spread over wider geographic areas was becoming possible through advances in transportation and communication. The outcome was an increase in the average size of business in many lines of production and a decline in the average number of firms operating in each of many industries. American industry was coming to consist of fewer firms, and these few were of larger size.

Many of these larger firms were beginning to have considerable investment tied up in extremely durable and highly specialized equipment. Interest, maintenance, and depreciation costs were regularly incurred whether the equipment was being used to produce or merely standing idle. These were fixed costs, i.e., costs which are constant in amount regardless of the volume of output. Fixed costs were beginning to be very large and important for some firms. When output volume was below capacity, additional amounts of product could be produced without any increase in fixed costs and, therefore, relatively little total additional costs. The incentive was strong under these circumstances for the managers of these firms to find ways to sell all of the output that could be produced at full capacity.

The emergence of fewer and larger firms in many industries could in itself be regarded as a retreat from the market system. The number of separate economic units exchanging things with each other through market transactions was reduced even though the size of the economy was growing.

The Market System as a Cause of Monopoly

Changing technology was one source of monopoly. What seems to be the inherent nature of the market system was another.

The market system, if working well, produces many generally good results. It succeeds in playing upon self-interest to produce results in the interest of others. It uses lures of profits, income, and satisfaction to induce people to behave in ways which benefit other people. However, the market does not eliminate all the disadvantages of economic interdependence among persons. The market, in fact, is at times a harsh taskmaster, exacting heavy penalties upon those who fail to conform to its demands.

In a market system, the owner of resources which are physically unproductive or only suited to produce goods not greatly wanted by consumers will receive a low income. The consumer whose needs emphasize goods which are difficult to produce and which require the scarcest resources may be able to attain only a low standard of living. The business which finds itself in a high-cost locality, with equipment which is technically obsolete but not physically worn out, or with a product which is little wanted by buyers, may be faced with financial loss or bankruptcy.

Sometimes the market is demanding in the adjustments which it requires its participants to make as conditions change. A worker who is trained in a skill which is in declining demand must seek another skill or suffer the consequences in the form of diminishing income. A consumer who is living in an area of declining economic activity may find the costs of many items purchased rising in price as the local sources of supply of these goods disappear. A business may lose its local market to a distant rival, now able to compete due to a new mode of transportation.

There are not only winners under a market system but losers too. At least to some extent, the more some win, the more others lose. People, disliking to be losers, seek ways to make sure that they, rather than someone else, are the winners. So it is that the market, which emphasizes the pursuit of self-interest, creates situations where conflicts of interest exist.

Devices for Achieving Monopoly Power

The technological developments of the 19th century activated and intensified the already existing tendency for contest among the participants of the market. The enlargements of the technically optimum size of firms meant the inevitable demise of some businesses. The merger of several local markets into a single regional market through advances in transport technology meant the elimination of some of the old local businesses and the survival and enlargement of others. The high proportion of fixed costs associated with the elaborate assemblages of equipment, which the new technology had made possible, increased the efforts of each firm to win over the market sales of other firms. There ensued a variety of economically destructive and ethically repellent business practices exceeding in diversity and intensity anything which had gone before.[6]

Buying and Selling Tactics. A variety of schemes for achieving monopoly through buying, selling, and pricing arrangements were used.

Preemptive Buying. One tactic used to eliminate or prevent competition was *preemptive buying*. Using this tactic, a company would buy up all the supplies or resources suitable for the production of whatever product it was producing. The purchases were not necessarily required for the company's production. They were made because the goods involved could thus be denied to potential competitors.

The first transcontinental railway to reach California was the Southern Pacific. In an attempt to insure for itself a monopoly of rail transport eastward out of the state, it bought up land and constructed rail lines in the few suitable passageways through the Sierras. It did this, not to provide service through these places, but to block the construction of competing rail lines. The Aluminum Company of America (Alcoa) behaved similarly. According to government charges against it, it acted to "acquire bauxite deposits, water power sites and plants in excess of its needs" with the presumable intent of denying use to competitors.[7]

Discrimination. Another tactic used by one company or another was to force a firm supplying an input to agree, as part of a sales contract, not to make sales to any other buyer. Another purchasing tactic was to require a supplying firm to agree to sell an input at unduly favorable terms to a company and at much less favorable terms to other buyers and users. The Standard Oil Company forced railroads to provide it with unusually low freight rates. It went even further and forced railroads to pay to it part of the higher freight price charged rival oil companies. The power to coerce supplying firms in such cases arises in part from the large size of the coercing company relative to its rivals. Supplying firms, under these conditions, are so eager to obtain the business of the large company that they agree to discriminate against its rivals.

Exclusive Sales. Similar tactics were used in selling products. Manufacturing companies agreed to allow distributors and retailers to handle their products only if these distributors and retailers agreed not to handle similar products made by other manufacturers. Manufacturers required all the various products produced by them to be handled by retail dealers so

---

[6] A well-classified description of the tactics can be found in Clair Wilcox, *Public Policies Toward Business* (4th ed.; Homewood, Ill.: Richard D. Irwin, Inc., 1971).

[7] Robert F. Lanzilloti, *The Structure of American Industry: Some Case Studies,* ed. Walter Adams (3d ed.; New York: The Macmillan Company, 1961), Chapter 6.

that no room might be left for the products of other manufacturers. Buyers of one company's products were required to buy all of that company's products so that competitive sellers might be excluded from the market. A company was able to extract these agreements from buyers partly because the company often was the sole source of supply or the cheapest source of supply for some products. Buyers, to get these products at all, could be required to agree to buy other products from the same company.

Predatory Pricing. Companies, in attempts to eliminate competition, also used predatory and discriminatory pricing. Companies with several products or with sales in more than one market area were able to use this tactic. A firm with a chain of grocery stores could lower its prices at one of its outlets which was in close competition with an independent single grocery store. It could sustain the resulting temporary losses at the one outlet by relying on profits at other outlets. In this way it drove the independent out of business. Then it raised its prices in what had become its local monopoly market. Firms with many products were able to use the same tactics in eliminating rival firms with single products.

Vertical Integration and the "Squeeze." A *vertically integrated firm* is a single company performing a whole series of operations from extraction of raw materials through manufacture of an intermediate product to retail sales of a final product to consumers. Such a firm is able to use an interesting combination of the tactics described above to eliminate an unintegrated rival firm engaged in intermediate production only. This tactic was the *squeeze.*

In the squeeze, the selling price of the raw material was raised by the integrated company. In this way the costs of producing were increased for the unintegrated firm buying the raw material. At the same time the purchasing price paid for the intermediate product was lowered by the integrated company. Thus, the revenues of the unintegrated firm from the sale of its product at a competitive price were reduced. The unintegrated firm, with rising costs of production and decreasing product prices, was squeezed out of existence. All stages of operation were left exclusively to the integrated firm, which became a monopoly.

The Erie Case. Occasionally the struggle for protection from competition took the form of devious and complicated financial manipulations and physical violence. A famous example of this was the struggle in the late 1860s over control over the Erie Railroad. On one side of the struggle was Cornelius Vanderbilt, who already controlled the New York Central Railroad. He desired to enlarge and safeguard its near monopoly by acquiring the Erie Railroad, which was, to a degree, in competition with the Central. The Erie was already in the hands of Daniel Drew, James Fisk, and Jay Gould. Vanderbilt began to purchase on the stock market shares of the Erie, hoping in this way to acquire control of it. Drew and his associates at times pretended to cooperate with Vanderbilt. Actually, they printed and sold, probably illegally, more and more Erie shares, the price of which was rising because of Vanderbilt's purchases. They managed to retain control and to profit at Vanderbilt's expense.

Exasperated but still sly, Vanderbilt arranged for a series of court injunctions. The first of these barred the Drew group from issuing more shares and required some of those already issued to be withdrawn. Later court orders provided for the arrest of the Drew group. The Drew group reacted initially by obtaining from another court an order to counteract Vanderbilt's injunctions. When that failed, they fled with money and papers from their Wall Street headquarters across the Hudson River to Jersey City, where the New York courts, which had issued the injunctions, had no jurisdiction. They ensconced themselves in a hotel near the Erie depot. They remained there for much of 1868. On one occasion during the year they withstood, with the help of police and armed guards, an attack of some 40 thugs sent over from New York.

Later Gould went to the New York state capitol at Albany where he successfully lobbied for a law legalizing the issue of the already issued Erie securities. He reportedly spent in the process one million dollars, mainly for bribes to state officials and legislators. Thereafter, a kind of truce was achieved between Vanderbilt and the Drew group, or Erie Ring as it came to be called. As part of the truce, the Ring repurchased from Vanderbilt some of the excessive amounts of Erie stock which he had been duped into buying.

Another episode involving the Erie Ring occurred in 1869. An independently owned railroad, the Albany and Susquehanna, had been constructed between Albany and Binghamton, New York. A major objective of this railroad was to haul coal between the Pennsylvania coal fields near Binghamton and the New England users of coal beyond Albany. The line was adjacent to territory already served by the Erie.

The Erie Ring saw the desirability of their possessing the line. Those already in control of the Albany and Susquehanna line, including J. Pierpont Morgan, resisted. The Erie Ring first tried to buy a majority of the shares of stock in the line but failed, just short of 50 percent. They then attempted through legal maneuvering to gain a clear majority on the board of directors of the line, but did not succeed. They tried by armed assault to gain control of the Albany terminus of the line, but were repulsed. They did, however, install themselves in the line's facilities at the Binghamton end.

Thereupon a group of several hundred men from the Morgan side set out from Albany in a train. They took over and installed themselves in the stations along the route. They ultimately intended to storm the Erie stronghold at the Binghamton terminus. However, upon hearing of the invasion, a group of men of the Erie Ring set out in their own train from Binghamton. The locomotives of the two trains crashed head-on 15 miles from Binghamton, and the Albany locomotive fell from the tracks, severely damaging the other in the process. A battle between the two groups of men ensued. The Erie group lost and retreated, tearing up track and bridges as they went. Ultimately they gave up trying to attain control.[8]

---

[8] For a detailed entertaining account of these and other monopolizing practices, see Matthew Josephson, *The Robber Barons* (New York: Harcourt, Brace & World, Inc., 1962).

Combination and Collusion. It is difficult to estimate the extent either of the physical violence or of the other tactics for attaining monopolistic ends. It seems reasonable to assert that so destructive to the competing businesses and so repugnant to the public were the techniques of rivalry and contest that alternatives were sought in the form of peaceful agreements. These took various forms.

Pools. Among the first of these forms was the *pool*. It came into widespread use in the 1870s among the railroads and some manufacturing industries. Under this arrangement, all or most of the producers of some good or service within a given market reached an agreement. They agreed, usually informally, to share customers, sales, profits, or territories in some fashion. In this way they hoped to avoid price reductions and the more ruthless kinds of cutthroat competition among themselves. Too often, however, the agreement was violated soon after its initiation. One or more of the parties would find it almost irresistible to undercut the others. There were also other reasons for the short duration of pools. One was rapidly changing market conditions. Another was egocentric business managers who believed not only in their own superiority but also in the doctrine of the survival of the fittest in economic affairs. Finally, the pools were legally unenforceable.

Trusts. In the 1880s *trusts* came to replace or exist beside pools as a primary mode of eliminating competition. Under a trust arrangement, the owners of controlling interest in all or most of the firms of an industry would reach an agreement. They would agree to entrust their ownership shares to the control of one or a few people, trustees, and to receive trust certificates in return. The trustees then directed the firms in the trust as though they were one large firm. With monolithic power, they confronted competitive buyers. They maximized profits, not by being best, but by being biggest. Apparently the first and certainly among the most famous trusts was the Standard Oil Trust formed in 1879. The use of the trust device spread to other industries. The trust arrangement was ultimately found to be in conflict with new court decisions and new legislation passed after 1890. Thus, it gave way to other arrangements. Before doing so, it gave its name to the general government campaign against monopolies—the antitrust program.

Thereafter, the use of holding companies, interlocking directorates, and trade associations became prominent as devices to ensure survival for firms and to prevent economic warfare among them.

Holding Companies. A *holding company* is a corporation which has among its assets shares of stock in other corporations. Those who own and/or control a holding company are able through purchases of shares of other corporations to exercise control over a number of otherwise competing companies. In this way, owners and managers of these companies are insulated from at least some of the adverse market effects.

Interlocking Directorates. An *interlocking directorate* is an arrangement wherein one person sits on the board of directors of two or more companies.

Where a complex network of many interlocking directorates exists, the elimination or reduction of competition and warfare becomes possible for the interlocked firms.

Trade Associations. A *trade association* is an organization in which firms of the same industry are members. Trade associations typically conduct research, lobby, advertise, set size and quality standards, and negotiate with labor unions on behalf of all their members jointly. A trade association may also be a means by which the member firms fix prices, share markets, and exact penalties upon disobedient member firms, eliminating economic warfare and market competition among members.

Mergers. Mergers, too, are used to eliminate competition. Mergers may take several forms. One company may purchase the physical assets or the shares of stock of a previously competing company. Two previously competing companies may exchange their stock. A new company may be formed to buy up the assets or shares of two or more older companies, which then disappear. The results are similar to those of effective holding companies and other devices to achieve monopoly. The power to make decisions about such things as production techniques and selling arrangements is transferred. Previously diffused among two or more groups, whose reactions to each other were through the market, the power is transferred to a single group of people, among whom coordination is achieved largely by direct command.

Tradition. In many American industries vigorous competition, unscrupulous tactics, and mergers have reduced the number of firms to a chastened, wary, and experienced few. The managers of these remaining firms have been able, without any agreement at all, to achieve for their firms a pattern of activity and response such that none of the firms is harmed and all benefit. For example, there may be a tradition that one of the firms initiates price changes which are then copied without significant deviation by the rest. The firms may have learned from harsh experience that any behavior other than this *price leadership* may, by encouraging unrestrained competition in price cutting, harm them all. There may be another tradition that each firm has a certain percentage of total sales of the industry. The firms may not try to violate this tradition because attempts to do so in the past have resulted in losses for all the firms. Coordination by the market is replaced by coordination by tradition.

The Undesirable Results of Monopoly

Participating firms may have found these traditionalized arrangements or the alternative of merger or explicit agreement satisfactory for themselves. They are harmful, however, to American society at large. The elimination of market forces within an industry makes the market a poorer mechanism for coordinating that industry with the rest of the economy. Almost all the questions arising from scarcity and interdependence receive inferior answers when market forces operate between but not within industries.

The Commodity Composition of Output. Consider first the question of what the commodity composition of the output of the nation shall be. An intense desire by consuming households for a large amount of a product is supposed to elicit large amounts of it from firms. Yet if the industry producing the product is a monopoly, the response of the industry may be simply to charge a high price and produce small amounts. Consumer sovereignty is thwarted, consumer satisfaction reduced, and economic welfare lessened.

A strong preference of workers for certain jobs producing certain products is supposed to lead to a chain of desirable results. There will be low wage rates, low costs of production, large amounts of output, and many jobs for workers in the industries producing these products. But if the industries are monopolistic, they may restrict output to achieve high profits from high product prices. Then they fail to provide the jobs which satisfy the preferences of workers. Again economic satisfaction is reduced. Economic welfare is lessened.

A natural abundance of some resource in a market economy is supposed to lead to a low price for it and wide use of it. There will be large outputs of products for which the resource is especially appropriate and large use of it by consumers. If the production of the resource is conducted by a monopolistic industry, output will probably be restricted to increase profits. Consumption patterns will be prevented from responding appropriately to the resource endowment of the society. Economic welfare will be less than it could be without the monopoly.

In all of these instances, the monopolistic industry fails to react to external market forces because internal market forces have been stilled. The firms of the industry have arranged to protect themselves from each other's market competition. They, therefore, feel less need to cater to market pressures from outside the industry.

The Character of Production. In a market economy firms are supposed to be under strong inducement to become of such size, locate in such places, select such techniques of production, and choose such land, labor, and capital resources that will maximize output of product relative to the quantity of inputs used. The happy result is that total output of the economy is maximized, given the total resources available. Firms are induced to make these socially optimal choices because they win over competition, survive, and profit if they do and because they are defeated by competition, make losses, and perish if they do not.

However, even those that do not make optimal choices may survive and profit if they are protected from the market and from competitive processes by monopolistic arrangements. They may be too little or too large. They may be located too far south or too far north. They may be using techniques which require too many resources and a combination of resources too heavily weighted with the scarcest resources. They may be selecting individual units of resources which are unsuited to their uses. The consequences of monopoly are poor answers to the question of how production shall be conducted.

Society is penalized by achieving an output and average level of living lower than if the monopolistic elements were absent from the system.

The Distribution of Output and Income. In a market economy working properly, households are supposed to be rewarded with incomes in proportion to their contributions to production. If monopoly is present, they are rewarded partly for their contributions to production and partly for their ability to wield monopoly power. Monopolistic industries raise the prices of their products, reduce the amount of output of their products, and tend to employ fewer resources than they would if they were competitive. Families buying and using the product of a monopoly and owners of most resources of the kind used by a monopoly receive lower real incomes than they would under competitive conditions. Persons who own or manage the monopolies receive higher incomes.

Monopolies may also cause the distribution of specific goods among users to be inferior. Monopolies in transportation, wholesaling, retailing, and storage may, by restricting the amount of these services, reduce the degree to which specific goods get to persons who desire them most.

The Rate of Economic Growth. Monopoly probably alters the rate of growth achieved in a market society. Protected as they are from competition, the firms of a monopolized industry may have less incentive than those in a competitive one to adopt newly discovered techniques or to begin to produce newly discovered products. They are less likely to research vigorously to discover new techniques and products, or to respond to an enlarged flow of savings in the economy by investing in expanded production facilities. If so, the rate of growth of an economy permeated with monopoly may be below the rate of a competitive one.

On the other hand, there are some reasons for believing that the existence of monopolized industries may in some cases cause the rate of growth of an economy to be higher than the competitive one. A monopolistic industry may undertake research into new techniques and new products because the profits of success in these ventures will accrue to the industry and will not have to be shared with outsiders who bore none of the cost. The firm or firms of a monopolistic industry may be large enough to finance sustained and large-scale research and not have to be reluctant to undertake research for fear that one or a few failures will cause bankruptcy. The firms of a monopolized industry, finding that competition in prices or market shares is excluded, may channel their competition into the search for new techniques or new products. It can easily be asserted that monopoly alters the rate of economic growth. It is difficult to determine in which direction the rate is altered.

General Appraisal

The existence of monopoly helps to determine the results which market mechanisms achieve. Monopoly may cause some of these results to be worse than the results of more nearly competitive arrangements. It seems fair to conclude also that the American experience has shown that market arrangements are likely to give rise to monopoly. This does not, of course, mean that there necessarily is any feasible system superior to market arrangements even when those arrangements include some elements of monopoly. The chief alternatives are governmental regulations to prevent the establishment of private monopolies and to break them up if already established, governmental regulation of private monopolies, and governmental monopolies in place of private ones. All these alternatives have disadvantages which limit their attractiveness.

SUMMARY

American experience provides some evidence that a market system, especially without an appropriate framework, can be defective.

The Great Depression, together with earlier similar episodes, suggests that recurrent inability to maintain full employment is a weakness of a market system. The growth of monopoly in America indicates that modern technology and market forces encourage a departure from competition. Lack of appropriate competition makes the economic results of market forces less desirable for society.

These unsatisfactory experiences do not mean that replacement of market mechanisms with governmental command will always produce better results. As later chapters reveal, the economic experience of the United States and of other nations in recent decades can be regarded as a continuing search for the proper combinations of market arrangements and governmental policies.

QUESTIONS

1. Do you, like many Americans, think that market capitalism is a good system? Do you, like them, also think that the American economy is diverging further from market capitalism? Why is this divergence occurring?
2. What causal relevance has the Great Depression for the kind of economic system with which the American nation found itself several decades after the Great Depression?
3. What repercussions did the Great Depression have upon American political life? How are these political repercussions related to changes in the economic system of the nation?
4. What caused the Great Depression? Was the market system primarily responsible? Was governmental policy primarily responsible?
5. How did technology, as it changed during the last 100 years, encourage the growth of monopoly in the United States?
6. How does the market system seem to encourage the growth of monopoly?
7. What does it matter, so far as the general subject of inquiry of this chapter is concerned, whether technology or the market system was the stronger force making for monopolization?
8. What were some of the tactics used to achieve private monopoly power in the United States? Aside from the fact that these tactics may result in monopoly power, do they seem desirable or undesirable to you? Why?
9. How does the extensive existence of private monopoly power cause the market system to produce poorer results than otherwise?

RECOMMENDED READINGS

Adams, Walter (ed.). *The Structure of American Industry,* 4th ed. New York: The Macmillan Company, 1971.

Allen, Frederick Lewis. *The Big Change: America Transforms Itself, 1900–1950.* New York: Harper & Row Publishers, 1969, Chapter 10.

Baumol, William J., and Lester V. Chandler. *Economic Processes and Policies.* New York: Harper & Row Publishers, 1954, pp. 137–150.

Bird, Caroline. *The Invisible Scar: The Great Depression, and What It Did to American Life, From Then Until Now.* New York: David McKay Co., Inc., 1966.

Friedman, Milton, and Anna Jacobson Schwartz. *The Great Contraction, 1929–1933.* Princeton, N.J.: Princeton University Press, 1964.

Galbraith, John Kenneth. *The Great Crash, 1929,* 3d ed. Boston: Houghton Mifflin Company, 1972.

Josephson, Matthew. *The Robber Barons.* New York: Harcourt Brace Jovanovich, Inc., 1962.

Lee, Maurice W. *Macroeconomics: Fluctuations, Growth, and Stability,* 5th ed. Homewood, Ill.: Richard D. Irwin, Inc., 1971, Chapter 7.

Shannon, David A. (ed.). *The Great Depression.* Englewood Cliffs, N.J.: Prentice-Hall, Inc., 1960.

Trescott, Paul B. *Money, Banking, and Economic Welfare,* 2d ed. New York: McGraw-Hill Book Company, 1965, pp. 459–472.

Wilcox, Clair. *Public Policies Toward Business,* 5th ed. Homewood, Ill.: Richard D. Irwin, Inc., 1975.

4

European Experience and Market Mechanisms

INTRODUCTION

In the world outside the United States, the experience which provided the most controversy over the merits and defects of market mechanisms was the *Industrial Revolution*. Britain was the first nation to experience the Industrial Revolution. The British case, perhaps more than any other, provides clues about the process of industrialization and the role which market arrangements may play in that process. The first half of this chapter is devoted to a survey of the British Industrial Revolution and its relation to market mechanisms.

The Industrial Revolution brought to Britain and to the rest of Europe a kind of life unknown previously anywhere in the world. The reactions to this new pattern of life were varied, but there were aspects of it which some observers found repugnant. Consequently, various individuals sought to explain and criticize the existing order and to forecast what might become of it. Of these individuals, none was more prominent than Karl Marx. The last half of this chapter deals with the critique which Marx made of market capitalism at the time of the Industrial Revolution.

THE BRITISH INDUSTRIAL REVOLUTION

What was the British Industrial Revolution?[1] In a sense, it was everything that happened in Britain between the appearance of Adam Smith's *Wealth of Nations* in 1776 and the first publication of Karl Marx's *Das Kapital* in 1867. Out of all that happened, however, it is possible to select various groups of happenings which are of special significance for an understanding of the economics of the era.

Economic Changes

New technology was discovered and introduced into use more rapidly than ever before. Advances in textile production included the spinning jenny, the water frame, and the power loom for spinning thread and weaving cloth.

---

[1] One of the first accounts of the Industrial Revolution as a historical episode is by the older Arnold Toynbee and was first published in 1884. Arnold Toynbee, *The Industrial Revolution* (Boston, Mass.: Beacon Press, 1956).

The steam engine began to be used to pump water from mines, to power trains and ships, and to run manufacturing operations. The railroad, the canal, the steamship, and the telegraph were introduced. The cheap production of iron and precision iron products began. The widespread application of this technology amounted to the mechanization of production and the provision of power from nonhuman sources.

There was, associated with the new technology, a change in the relative importance of different organizational forms for carrying on production. The number of people working in fields and in their own homes on handicrafts or on the fabrication of raw materials supplied by merchant traders declined. The number who found employment in factories grew.

There was a geographical redistribution of the population. People left Ireland, the Scottish highlands, and the south of England. They moved into the Scottish lowlands and the English midlands. A much larger percentage of the population came to live in cities. The number of people in agriculture and in rural areas declined. There was an almost unprecedented growth in the size of the population and the labor force. The total number of persons in the British Isles rose from 10 million in 1750 to 27 million in 1850.

The total amount of real capital with which these people worked and which embodied the new technology greatly increased in the nation. The degree of interdependence and specialization became much larger. The use of money payments grew. There was, as a consequence of all these changes, a considerable growth in the British gross national product.

A change occurred in the types and relative importance of socio-economic classes which shared in the gross national product. The small farmers, tenants, sharecroppers, and hired hands in agriculture tended to disappear. A large urban working class emerged. The upper-income groups came to include the owners and managers of the industrial enterprises as well as the owners of large amounts of land and the most successful merchants.

The Causal Complexity of Change

All of the happenings during the Industrial Revolution were interrelated in a causal and complicated way and such multiplicity of interdependent variables entangles any causal explanation of the British Industrial Revolution.[2]

The technological advances stimulated each other. The invention of the spinning jenny and the water frame provided an abundant supply of thread and furnished a new incentive for finding a more effective way to weave the thread into cloth. Then came the power loom, which provided the way. The textile machinery created the need for and the opportunity to use the steam engine as a source of power for cloth production. To build good steam engines, iron manufacturing had to be improved.

[2] The Industrial Revolution is frequently described briefly in history textbooks. See, for example, R. R. Palmer and Joel Colton, A History of the Modern World (4th ed.; New York: Alfred A. Knopf, Inc., 1971).

The new machinery, power, and technology could be operated best on a large scale. So laborers had to be relocated together for the work. In this way came the rise of factory operations, the process of urbanization, and the regional redistribution of people.

The availability of the new technology encouraged the formation of real capital with which the technology might be put into widespread use. The availability of resources for use in capital formation encouraged the search for new technology which, once discovered, could be embodied in the real capital. Resources for use in capital formation were available because technology had advanced rapidly; the new technology enabled gross national product to be large enough to provide sufficient consumer goods to satisfy the minimum subsistence needs of the populace and still have some resources left over. The population growth also made it possible to use the enlarged amounts of real capital to increase total national output. The increased national output, on the other hand, constituted the goods and services necessary for the living of a larger population.

The discovery and application of technology made possible the emergence of industrialists with large incomes. They were willing and able to spend much of their income and effort on real capital formation and research. The research in turn advanced the state of technology. This class of industrialists was able to secure some political power. As a result, there was a repeal by Parliament of the Corn Laws. These laws had raised the price of wheat and bread through import restrictions. Consequently, both the wage rate for industrial workers and the costs of industrial production had been high. The repeal of the laws reduced costs of production and made possible larger incomes for the industrialists. They could then devote larger amounts of funds and resources to capital formation and technology, with the possible consequence of still greater political power for themselves.

Market Causes of the Revolution

There is, in the above description of the Industrial Revolution, no explicit mention of the market system. Yet markets had a great deal to do with what took place during the Industrial Revolution in Britain.

It has been argued that the demand for British textiles and other products increased in the era just before the Industrial Revolution. It increased because of the establishment and growth of colonies in the New World and in the East, because of the growth of population in Britain and in Europe, and because of the improved international transportation system which was established then. This increased demand provided the opportunity for profits if the supply of the products could somehow be increased.

The technological advances were undertaken by people at least some of whom were discerning enough to recognize the potential profits. They were eager to try to activate the potential for themselves. One invention, such as the spinning jenny, would increase the supply of a product, such as thread. Then complementary inputs, such as cleaned cotton and weavers' services, would rise in price. The rise created the opportunity of profits for anyone who was ingenious enough to find a way to evade the bottlenecks created in these complementary inputs. Profits thus motivated the invention and application of the cotton gin and the power loom.

With the advent of this machinery, the costs of production fell for businesses using the factory method. The factory method was the only feasible way to make use of much of the new technology. Bankruptcy awaited those merchant traders who tried to persist with the old, more costly method of distributing raw materials to the homes of workers, where it was fabricated by hand. These home workers, faced with declining wages or no work, sought a means by which to retain or regain their incomes. They moved to places where there was factory employment.

The most profitable use which the owners of money capital could find for it was in the new production. They invested in the factories, in the machinery, and in urban housing for the workers. The owners and managers who were most successful in the new undertaking reaped the most profits. They used these profits to enlarge their successful businesses.

The success of the British manufacturers with the new production methods enabled them to sell some of their industrial output in international markets, where they took sales away from alternative goods. Part of the earnings from these foreign sales was used indirectly by British firms importing foodstuffs and raw materials into Britain. This importation was in response to the market demand created there by the growing population, the limited natural resources, and the burgeoning industrial production. This demand was made effective by the repeal of the Corn Laws and other legal restrictions on imports.

Nonmarket Causes of the Revolution

The market system with its emphasis upon supply and demand, prices, profits, and incomes played a major part in bringing about the Industrial Revolution in Britain. There were also other causes. There is not now nor perhaps ever can be a complete understanding of these causes. Historians and others have suggested a wide variety of possibilities.

The Historical Background. Some historians emphasize that the basis for an Industrial Revolution somewhere in western Europe was laid in the preceding era. That era is sometimes called the *Commercial Revolution.* It occupied the years from 1500 to 1750. This commercial age, of course, received a heritage of Western civilization from the ancient cultures of the Near East. Additions were made to the heritage by the Greeks and Romans and transmitted by way of the Middle Ages, the Renaissance, and the Reformation. During this commercial era, market forces came to direct economic activity to an extent that they had never before achieved. Scientific and technological advances occurred which provided examples and set the base for the accelerated technological progress after 1750. Wealth, which helped finance the Industrial

Revolution, was accumulated by the merchants and traders. The establishment of colonies and the growth of population during the Commercial Revolution provided the demand for products. This demand played a role in stimulating the increased output during the Industrial Revolution.

The spirit and policy of *mercantilism* helped to prepare the way for the Industrial Revolution. Mercantilism was a body of economic doctrine which dominated Europe during the Commercial Revolution. It advocated the establishment and growth of manufacturing through extensive government encouragement of this activity by subsidies, regulations, and grants of monopolistic privileges.

Natural Geography. Various reasons have been advanced for the occurrence of the Industrial Revolution first in Britain rather than in some other western country. Some of these reasons have to do with the natural geography of the British Isles. The climate is humid so that textiles can be worked up without breaking. The summers and winters are mild with invigorating daily changes in the weather so that people are mentally and physically stimulated. The natural resources are relatively small in amounts but varied in type. Mineral and coal deposits exist, and there are some fairly fertile lands. There is a long coastline with numerous indentations which provide good natural harbors and easy access to the major land masses of the world, especially Europe. The insular situation has provided some protection from invasion, disruption, and destruction by foreign armies. The nearness to the Continent has prevented cultural isolation and provided the opportunity to absorb knowledge and useful social arrangements from the rest of Europe.

British Institutions. Within this context of natural advantages, British society evolved, for the most part gradually and without abrupt discontinuities. By the 18th century the British were more susceptible to stimulation and better prepared for economic advance than any other nation.

The British government of the time was stable and had an efficient and uncorrupt bureaucracy and tax system. Governmental policy encouraged change by elimination of some traditional regulations, such as those enforced by guilds or governmental grants of monopoly. Legislation was introduced, such as poor relief laws, to ease the burden of adjustment which various social classes had to make to economic change. These kinds of governmental policy occurred in part because of a political system less autocratic than those of other European states of the time. This feature made the British government responsive to popular desires and needs.

Social mobility during these centuries was greater among the British people than among Continentals. The British aristocracy had ceased to be purely a hereditary one and came to be one partly of wealth. A high average quality of leadership was probably the result. The more rigid political and social systems on the Continent resulted in the recurrent emigration of skilled laborers and entrepreneurs. Legal and guild restrictions, political upheavals, wars, and religious discrimination in France, the Lowlands, and Germany caused some of the economically most productive individuals and families to migrate from these countries to Britain. In Britain their presence raised the quality of entrepreneurship.

The religious heritage of Protestantism was established in Britain in the 16th century. It emphasized the desirability of hard work, large savings, and productive investment. It probably is accountable in part for the superior British economic progress demonstrated in the Commercial and Industrial Revolutions.

There also developed in Britain, during the era before the Industrial Revolution, the most sophisticated set of financial institutions in the world. These included joint stock companies, central banking in the Bank of England, and organized securities trading. The development of these institutions was stimulated by the superior success of Britain in the Commercial Revolution. Once established in this way, they became important means for advancing the British Industrial Revolution. They made it possible to gather together large amounts of money capital. This capital could then be used to establish businesses that required large amounts of real capital. Large businesses were the primary means by which the technology of the Industrial Revolution was applied.

THE BRITISH AGRICULTURAL REVOLUTION AND MARKET MECHANISMS

The British, succeeding more than any other people in the Commercial Revolution, laid the foundation for their preeminent success in the Industrial Revolution. Market forces played an important role in both successes. However, there was a third series of events, also sometimes called a revolution, which was an important consequence of market forces. This revolution was occurring at the same time as the Commercial Revolution. It was a prerequisite for, and continued into the era of, the Industrial Revolution. It provides the first examples from British experience of defective results of the market system. It was the *Agricultural Revolution*.

Prerevolutionary Agriculture

At the beginning of the Agricultural Revolution, what was the character of British life in the rural areas, where a majority of the population lived? Rural Britain in the 16th and 17th centuries still had many of the aspects of the Middle Ages, including some of the trappings of *manorialism* and *feudalism*. However, it also contained some of the beginnings of modern Western agriculture.

The Village and Its Classes. The basic social unit, other than the household, was the village, which was in many respects like the medieval manor. A number of families, each with a house, lived in the typical village and cooperated in carrying on the village's largely self-sufficient economic activity. Much of this activity involved raising livestock and growing crops in the surrounding fields. There were a number of types of fields, including arable land cultivated for crops, pasture for grazing livestock, woodland for fuel, lumber, and game, and wasteland. Lines of sod rather than walls or permanent fences divided the cropland into small strips or parcels averaging an acre or less each. Each of the parcels was used permanently by one or another of the village families. A single family typically had several scattered parcels to use. The pasture, woodland, and wastelands were used together by the families, who intermingled their livestock and daily activities on this common ground.

There were several classes of families in the village. There might be a noble lord, either resident or absentee. There might be a lord's steward or stewards to supervise the activity of the village on behalf of the lord. There might be freeholders who worked their land parcels without payment of rent or other obligations. There might be lessees who worked land for various payments and obligations and whose possession of the land was granted for a year, for a longer period, or for perpetuity. There were cottagers who lived in homes in the village and who worked for themselves in small garden plots or at handicrafts in their homes. They also tended their livestock in the pastures and hired themselves out to others.

Traditional Cooperation. The diverse village classes were linked together by various rights and obligations which each family had relative to the others. In this way many of the economic decisions and conflicts were resolved by tradition. The lord, if there was one, had a right to receive rents from the lessees. These rents were increasingly taking the form of money payments. The lord, an appointed steward, or a management committee of the village's people customarily made the main economic decisions. They determined the timing of planting and harvesting, the frequency of rotation of fields from crops to fallow, and other matters.

The owner or traditional user of a plot of arable land within a field was required to abide by communal decisions. Otherwise, chaos would have utterly replaced efficiency under this open-field system. The user of a parcel not directly accessible by road had the traditional right to reach it by crossing intervening parcels of others. Traditionally, the user of a parcel too narrow to allow a plow and horse to turn around had the right to make use of a neighbor's land for this purpose. After the harvest, the animals of all had the established privilege of foraging over the harvested fields without regard to individual parcels. All the villagers including the cottagers customarily ran their livestock together on the common pasture. There was thus a good deal of cooperation and communal decision making in the economic activities of the typical English village of the 17th century.

Market Mechanisms as a Means of Change

There was a good deal of inefficiency as adjudged by enterprising lords and stewards. It seemed so, also, to successful merchants who desired to enhance their social standing by acquiring lands which at the same time could be made to earn a good return on investment. The view was also shared by shrewd small farmers and lessees who were eager to use their wits to enlarge their income and raise their status. Individuals of these kinds, motivated by profit and willing to defy tradition, were increasingly in evidence during these centuries. They became more and more impatient with tradition as new technical knowledge of superior farming methods was discovered and disseminated.

Tradition as an Obstacle to Efficiency. The organization of farming in traditional villages impeded the application of the new technology. The maximization of profit by the agricultural entrepreneurs was also prevented. The old parcels of land were too small to be cross-cultivated as the new, more profitable methodology demanded. The village system of deciding upon the same crop for all the parcels of a traditionally bounded field made it impossible to assign crops to the most appropriate areas. The need for getting the consent and cooperation of all the numerous small users for any experimentation with new crops made the introduction of new crops and new rotation systems difficult or impossible. A single farmer found improvements, such as a drainage system, out of the question because of the unlikelihood of obtaining the acquiesence of users of adjacent plots. The herding of all animals together on the common pasture prevented selective breeding and the eradication of disease.

Clearly the old system was inappropriate for the new circumstances. Tradition as the arbiter of agricultural life had to be replaced by profits. How would the replacement occur?

The Enclosure Movement. The process of replacement occurred in part by what has come to be called the *enclosure movement*. This name for the process stems from the fact that the old open fields of arable land and pasture were now fenced or enclosed so that within these confines the new methods might be applied. In fact, a great deal more than this change in outward appearance occurred. The more enterprising and wealthier individuals purchased or otherwise obtained the traditional rights of the others to the use of the land. Some small, outright owners were persuaded to sell their holdings to larger buyers. Some lessees were denied renewals of their leases. Some cottagers were evicted. The rights to use common and waste land were bought out or denied.

In the end, by 1800 or so, the villages with their welter of little strips and their communities of various traditionally privileged and obligated classes had disappeared. In their place were well-managed, economically efficient farms operated by market-conscious individuals.[3]

Were Market Arrangements Harmful?

Some historians and social critics have found grounds in the episode of the British Agricultural Revolution for criticism and even condemnation of the market system.

---

[3] More elaborate accounts of both the European Agricultural Revolution and the Industrial Revolution appear in Witt Bowden, Michael Karpovich, and Abbott Payson Usher, *The Economic History of Europe Since 1750* (New York: AMS Press, Inc., 1970), Chapters 3, 6, 7, 8, 13, and 21.

The Argument of the Critics of the Market. Before the enclosure movements, the rural people of Britain lived a relatively tranquil, traditional life. They possessed known obligations and rights. They felt secure that those rights, confirmed by custom, would be respected so long as the obligations, equally clear, were fulfilled. Most of the families had attachments to pieces of land and homes which gave them the pride and confidence of ownership of property. Most of them were assured thereby of a minimum livelihood from their own efforts. At the same time, their traditional cooperation with the others in their village provided a sense of community and fellowship.

This order was rudely disrupted by avaricious individuals bent on acquisition of more wealth for themselves and motivated by the hope of profit. They were willing to achieve gain without much regard for the welfare of others. They destroyed the social order. They abused, to their advantage, legal processes such as the Enclosure Acts of Parliament. They deprived, often without adequate compensation, a majority of people of their traditional rights, their security, and their homes. They shook these people loose from their country moorings so that they were forced to crowd together in grimy industrial cities. They increased the degree of inequality of income, wealth, and privilege. They left posterity with the impression that ruthlessness is rewarded, at least under the market system.

The Reply of the Defenders of the Market. The elements of accuracy and distortion in the foregoing account are still subject to debate. For example, consider the charge that the market system and the enclosure movement led to the depopulation of the countryside and the forced migration from the country into the dirty cities and the squalid factories. There are several counterarguments to this charge. During the Agricultural Revolution the population of many country districts actually grew. The enclosures sometimes offered additional rural job opportunities. The rising urban population was a result of improved economic conditions and resulting earlier marriages, higher birth rates, and lower death rates among the populace at large.

There is dispute over the charge that the enclosure movement caused a deterioration in the level of living of the lower classes. Living conditions, whether urban or rural, may actually have been better afterwards than before. Indirect evidence of this improvement is the rapid population growth that occurred.

There is disagreement that the plight of the rural working class was caused by the market system operating through enclosures. There were far more important causes of misery among the lower rural economic classes. Among these were wars, such as the Napoleonic Wars, with their high costs. Another was the expansion of the population, which pressed against a countryside devoid of further unused lands. Finally, inappropriate laws, such as the poor relief laws, encouraged workers to remain unemployed or at low paying jobs.

An Appraisal. Two observations on the matter of the market system, the enclosures, and the plight of the rural poor during the Agricultural Revolution are deserving of treatment.

One is whether the market system was actually to blame for the plight of the rural poor or not. Later social critics came to believe that it was and there grew up, in consequence, a tradition among these critics that the market system is defective as revealed by this experience.

The second is that the market system did play an important part in bringing about the Agricultural Revolution, which in turn was a necessary prerequisite for the Industrial Revolution. The increased efficiency in agriculture made possible the foodstuffs for the growing industrial population. Profits and rents of the new agricultural entrepreneurs and owners arose from the increased efficiency. This income provided some of the funds with which the enlarged real capital needed for the industrial expansion was financed.

Both directly and indirectly through its influence on the Agricultural Revolution, the market system was one of the causes of the Industrial Revolution. Both bad and good features of the Industrial Revolution are consequences of the market system. A closer look at these features is warranted.

THE ALLEGED EVILS OF THE INDUSTRIAL REVOLUTION

It is possible to paint a dark picture of the effects of market forces and other influences on the majority of the British urban population of the early 1800s. Many economic historians have done so.

Their description centers on the quality of life of the industrial working classes. The wage rates of these classes were low. Their working conditions were bad. Their children and women worked hard for long hours. They had poor housing and poor public utilities. They felt insecure about their employment. They lacked opportunity for education and entertainment. Consequently, they had an embittered attitude toward their employers and the upper economic classes in general.

The description usually includes the overwhelming role of profits as the motivating force of the upper classes. The drive for profits not only affected their economic decisions, but it also shaped their view of life.

Wages

Average wages were low for a typical industrial worker in the Britain of around 1800. They were certainly low relative to those of modern Western nations in the 20th century. They were low partly because of market forces.

The rapid expansion of population provided large numbers of workers. These workers, sometimes unknowingly, competed with each other for jobs. Each of the large number of workers had less capital and natural resources with which to work than if the working population had been smaller. So the average contribution to production or productivity per worker was low. The market system of the time probably caused a typical employer to make the profitable decision to pay a worker a wage about equal to his productivity.

Many of the technological changes which were occurring so rapidly made skilled labor less necessary. The mechanization of production in many cases reduced the demand for more highly skilled workers. Some of these workers found it necessary to seek employment at less skilled jobs. There, in competition with the unskilled workers, they earned wages lower than before.

The enclosures in agriculture, the consolidation of plots into larger farms, and the conversion of cropland into grazing land reduced the opportunity for employment in agriculture. This reduction in the agricultural demand for labor increased the competition for jobs in industry and reduced the average labor productivity in industry.

Wages were especially low, and their adverse impact on the workers was especially heavy, during financial crises and depressions. These depressions began to recur in Britain during the Industrial Revolution. They, like the Great Depression of the 1930s, were partly caused by the failure of the market system. The market system failed to coordinate properly and smoothly through time the activities of millions of otherwise independent economic units.

Working Conditions

Working conditions in the factories were unpleasant. The equipment was sometimes dangerous and caused workers to have serious accidents which maimed or killed them. The market system was one cause of this trouble. The installation of safety devices or safer machinery cost money and, therefore, seemed to reduce profits. The intense market competition for the jobs prevented workers from declining the jobs even if they were unsafe. The temperature and humidity were sometimes too high or too low for maximum human comfort in the factories. It was costly and hence regarded as unprofitable either to install extra heating or ventilating equipment or to allow the machinery or product to suffer from atmospheric conditions which happened to be pleasant to people. The foremen and other superiors were sometimes arrogant, abusive, and unsympathetic. If they had not been so, especially with the other unpleasant conditions, the workers would have been laggardly. Profits would have fallen off. Interruptions for rests during the working day were discouraged for the same reason. Lengthy working days and the absence of holidays were necessary to keep costs of production low so that the product could be sold for a profit at the competitive market prices.

Children and women were at work in the factories for long hours. It was profitable to employ them rather than men exclusively because there were many children and women available and little else for them to do. The demand for children and women as workers was large because many of the operations in the mechanized factories required unskilled labor and could be done without great strength. The supply of child labor was great for several reasons. For many of the children, schooling was not available or not regarded as necessary or profitable. The low wages received by the parents were inadequate to support the entire family unless the children worked.

Housing

The cities which grew up or expanded to house the workers were unattractive and unpleasant. Many of them consisted of slums with houses of poor quality when constructed and in a state of continual disrepair thereafter.

The houses were crowded together on unpaved and neglected streets. Such buildings were without running water and had open sewage. Residential life was of this quality partly because the market system made it so. The workers received low wages and, therefore, were unable to demand decent housing. The rapid expansion of urban population created a great demand for building materials. In consequence, these materials became high priced. The combination of high costs and low rents made it unprofitable to build better housing.

As for public utilities, there was little profit in them. There was no profit at all in street construction or improvement since no charge by private providers could be made for their use. There was little profit in water and sewage services since the working populace were forced because of low incomes to make do on their own.

Insecurity of Employment

There was little security of jobs. A worker who became ill or who grew old was a less efficient worker, and hence was less profitable, and on that account was discharged. A worker whose skills became obsolete because of mechanization was also less profitable and was released. Workers could be induced to work harder and more profitably, so it went, if there was the possibility of losing jobs for lack of diligence. The threats of unemployment, loss of income, and starvation were potent incentives toward efficiency and profitable conduct.

The Quality of Life

All of this amounted to a wretched life for most of the working classes, at least as judged by Western standards of the 20th century. There was no home life for many of them. The wife and husband had to be away from the home for the long hours of work in the factory. The children were without school to attend and without parental observation. Some of them worked in the factories. Some ran in packs in the neighborhood, not always knowing who their parents were. Some were abandoned by their parents and placed in government orphanages, from which they might be hired out by the authorities to work in the mills.

There was little leisure time except for idleness when unemployment occurred. There was little self-respect, with very small chance of improvement in status either for workers during their lifetime or for their children in their generation. The chance to arrange one's life and to plan and prepare for the future did not exist for most. Illiteracy was widespread. Work was energy-sapping and health-destroying or, at best, routinely boring. Opportunities for vacations and cultural activities were rare. Participation in political life was largely excluded. Few had suffrage.[4]

---

[4] Excerpts from the testimony given during governmental investigations into the working and living conditions in Britain during the early 19th century are reprinted in John Bowditch and Clement Ramsland (eds.) *Voices of the Industrial Revolution: Selected Readings from the Liberal Economists and Their Critics* (Ann Arbor: The University of Michigan Press, 1963), pp. 82–90.

The Upper Classes

Not everyone in Britain in the era around 1800 lived in this degrading fashion. The wealthier classes, the landlords and farm stewards, the merchants and industrialists, and the professionals and intellectuals enjoyed a considerably more attractive life. They were, according to some historians who have looked back on the period, able to rationalize the paradox of widespread misery amid strikingly growing productive power. These groups were impressed by the rapid economic changes which they saw occurring about them. They were awed by the increased productive potential made possible by technology, innovation, and increased capital. They became obsessed with success in the market system. They looked upon the working classes as productive resources to be used to the fullest to maximize production rather than as humans with wants to be satisfied. It was as though their motto had become, "The needs of production must regulate the conditions of life."

IN DEFENSE OF THE INDUSTRIAL REVOLUTION

The market system at work in the British Industrial Revolution produced some unfortunate consequences. It was the fashion during parts of the 19th and 20th centuries to condemn the market system for this reason. In recent decades, however, there has grown up a view that the condemnation is perhaps unjustified. This view rests upon several ideas. First, the general condition of the industrial workers during the Industrial Revolution in Britain may not, in fact, have been so bad. It may have been better, not worse, than the condition of the rural workers of the time and better, in general, than it had been for all workers previously. Second, the Industrial Revolution produced some good consequences for the workers. Third, even if the conditions of the working classes did deteriorate during the decades around 1800, there were causes for it other than the market system. Fourth, it is now believed that many later commentators, looking back on the Industrial Revolution, exaggerated the plight of the working classes of that time.

Improvement Relative to the Rural Past

It is true that the average quality of life for the majority of British urban working people was inferior during the Industrial Revolution to that quality which is typical for people in the United States today. However, there is some evidence that those workers lived better than their rural contemporaries and better than their predecessors, rural or urban. Apparently, rural employers of the time sometimes complained that their laborers were being attracted away from their rural employment by the higher wage rates of the cities. Life in the rural areas in the Middle Ages and on into the Industrial Revolution was harsh rather than idyllic. In the rural areas not only were wages and incomes lowest, but also restrictions on freedom were greatest and hours of work longest. It was in areas and productive operations where older techniques were used and tradition was relied upon that the workers had the hardest time. In the profit-oriented, market-directed activities of the new factories, they fared better.

Political and Economic Gains

Moreover, the market system through the Industrial Revolution actually brought benefits to the workers. It concentrated them geographically. A sense of class consciousness and class willingness to agitate for improvement became possible. Their plight, if such there was, became noticeable to intellectuals and social reformers and, therefore, was subject to amelioration. The political rivalry which developed between the new industrial managers and the older landed proprietors produced changed legislation which aided the workers. The repeal of the Corn Laws tended to reduce the price of food for workers, and passage of the Factory Acts introduced governmental regulation to improve industrial working conditions.

Although not every working class family participated in the improvement, real wages rose and new products became available for use. Finally, the hard work and abstention from consumption that the workers of the time endured made it possible to devote land, labor, and capital to the production of capital goods and to research. As a result, the size of national output could be greater in the future and the standard of living of future generations of workers and others could be higher.

Nonmarket Causes of Troubles

It can also be argued with some cogency that the low quality of life in which many working families found themselves was a result of causes other than the market system and the factory organization which it encouraged.

The British legal system and British governmental policy were partly to blame. The British laws were one-sidedly against the workers. Workers were legally restrained from organizing into unions to confront the employers. The employers were subject to no such restraints. The governmental construction regulations on housing and a tax on windows produced drab dwellings in working-class districts. The inflationary financing used by the government to carry on the Napoleonic Wars raised prices faster than wages and tended to keep the real wages of the workers lower than they would have been otherwise.

The resources that had to be devoted to the conduct of the wars were, of course, unavailable to produce consumer goods for the workers. A period of adjustment which followed the wars was one of moderate depression and created hardship for laborers. Bad harvests at times contributed to the distress of the working class. There would have been crowded housing, inadequate streets, lighting, and water facilities in Britain around 1800, no matter what the economic system, because of the rapid population growth and the accompanying urban migration.

In fact, it can be argued that regardless of the economic system, the process of economic development requires sacrifices. The conversion of a society from agricultural to industrial almost inevitably involves a stage of intense sacrifice. People must then accept unwanted changes, must work hard, must consume little, and, in general, must live poorly.

Historical Controversy Concerning the Facts

Quite a controversy has occurred since the Industrial Revolution regarding the actual conditions of the working classes at that time and the causal forces which produced the conditions. One group, of whose work that of John L. and Barbara Hammond is perhaps the best known, has drawn the picture darkly:

> Thus England asked for profits and received profits. Everything turned to profit. The towns had their profitable dirt, their profitable smoke, their profitable slums, their profitable disorder, their profitable ignorance, their profitable despair. The curse of Midas was on this society: on its corporate life, on its common mind, on the decisive and impatient step it had taken from the peasant to the industrial age. For the new town was not a home where man could find beauty, happiness, leisure, learning, religion, the influences that civilize outlook and habit, but a bare and desolate place, without colour, air or laughter, where man, woman and child worked, ate and slept. This was to be the lot of the mass of mankind: this the sullen rhythm of their lives. The new factories and the new furnaces were like the Pyramids, telling of man's enslavement, rather than of his power, casting their long shadow over the society that took such pride in them.[5]

This group, represented by the Hammonds, which condemns the market system for outrageous excesses has been heavily criticized by other social scientists and philosophers for gross errors in historical research and historiography. Many of the critics are of a conservative, pro-capitalistic bent. The Hammonds' group is accused of seizing upon fragmentary and one-sided evidence in the form of official reports of governmental inquiries into factory and housing conditions. They are blamed for carelessly concluding that urban factory workers were socially abused by the Industrial Revolution and that the cause of the abuse was the market system. The Hammonds' group were not, it is charged, thorough historians. They overlooked much contradictory evidence, which later scholarship has revealed. They were not economists and were not competent to assess the patterns of economic causation at the time. Instead they were social reformers who, moved by injustices they thought they detected, became eager to find a villain and discovered one in the market system.[6]

The Controversy Continues

There is no complete resolution yet of the controversy. Moderate historians today seem to feel that it is easy to exaggerate the real deprivations of the workers of the Industrial Revolution. It is all too difficult to segregate

[5] John L. and Barbara Hammond, *The Rise of Modern Industry* (New York: Harper & Row Publishers, 1969), p. 232. This book originally appeared in 1925. See also Philip A. M. Taylor (ed.), *The Industrial Revolution in Britain: Triumph or Disaster?* (Rev. ed.; Boston: D. C. Heath & Company, 1970). This latter collection of reprinted excerpts compiled by Taylor is often considered the most useful work to consult on the controversy over the Industrial Revolution.

[6] The market capitalism of the Industrial Revolution is defended from the Marxists and the historians by those who strongly advocate a free market society in: F. A. Hayek (ed.), *Capitalism and the Historians* (Chicago: University of Chicago Press, 1963).

from other forces the relative strength of the market system as a cause. No final conclusion is possible regarding the evil which should or should not be attributed to the market system during the British Industrial Revolution. However, it remains true that the experience continues to furnish part of the conventional wisdom of socialists and communists in their attitudes of opposition to market capitalism. In perpetuating this negative view of capitalism and markets, one personality stands out in history. This one is Marx. It is to his ideas that the remainder of this chapter is devoted.

KARL MARX AND HIS VIEWS

Karl Marx was born in Germany in 1818.[7] He was the son of a middle-class family, formerly Jewish but converted to Christianity. His father was a lawyer and a public official. When he reached college age, Marx attended the University of Berlin, where he studied the ideas of the philosopher Hegel. Upon graduation Marx became a newspaper editor, first in the Rhineland, then in Paris, and finally in Brussels. He was forced from one editorship to another and from one country to the next because of his support of radical groups toward whom the existing governments were hostile. In 1853 Marx moved to London, where he spent the last half of his life researching and writing in the British Museum. His chief financial support during these later years came from his closest friend and collaborator, Friedrich Engels. Engels was also a native of Germany, came from wealthy parents, and had arrived in Britain to manage a family branch factory in Manchester. After Marx and Engels met in the 1840s, they worked together first on the brief *Communist Manifesto*,[8] which appeared in 1848, and later on the long and wearisome *Das Kapital*,[9] the second and third volumes of which Engels assembled from Marx's notes after the latter's death in 1883.

The Static Weaknesses of Market Capitalism

Marx was interested in the distribution of income in the market economies of his time. He was especially curious about the great inequality in the

---

[7] A readable, brief biography of Marx can be found in Robert L. Heilbroner, *The Worldly Philosophers: The Lives, Times, and Ideas of the Great Economic Thinkers* (4th ed.; New York: Simon & Schuster, Inc., 1972), Chapter 6. Longer, but still readable accounts of the lives of both Marx and Engels are included in Edmund Wilson, *To the Finland Station: A Study in the Writing and Acting of History* (Garden City, N.Y.: Doubleday & Company, Inc., 1953).

[8] *The Communist Manifesto* has been reprinted in many books including Bowditch and Ramsland, *op. cit.*, pp. 154–180; and in Columbia University Contemporary Civilization Staff (eds.), *Introduction to Contemporary Civilization in the West: A Source Book* (New York: Columbia University Press, 1946), Vol. II, pp. 414–435.

[9] Marx's greatest work is available in an inexpensive edition: Karl Marx, *Capital: A Critique of Political Economy* (New York: Modern Library, Inc., division of Random House, Inc., 1906). Some persons find it difficult reading, and most readers prefer compilations of classified selections from Marx's writings. Two such compilations are these: Karl Marx, *Capital, The Communist Manifesto and Other Writings by Karl Marx*, ed. Max Eastman (New York: Modern Library Inc., division of Random House, Inc., 1932); and Karl Marx, *Marx on Economics*, ed. Robert Freedman (New York: Harcourt Brace Jovanovich, Inc. 1961).

distribution. He recognized that in a market economy one's real income depended upon what one had to sell, upon what one bought, and upon the prices prevailing for what one sold and bought.

So far as what one had to sell was concerned, Marx distinguished two main classes of people. There were those who owned property or capital. These were the capitalists or the *bourgeoisie*. They were able to sell the use of the property or to use it themselves and sell whatever product resulted. Too, there were those who owned only their own labor. These were the *proletariat* or the workers. They were able to sell their labor.

The Labor Theory of Value. So far as prices were concerned, Marx held a *labor theory of value*. He felt that, with some exceptions, the price or value of anything in a market system is determined by the amount of labor which is required to produce it. The relative prices of two products will be in the same proportion as the amounts of labor required to produce them. If two hours of labor are required to make a pair of shoes and five hours of labor are required to build a cart, the price of the shoes on the market will be two fifths of that of the cart.

The price of labor is the wage rate. The wage rate determines the income of the propertyless workers. Marx asserted that the wage rate itself is determined according to the labor theory of value. How much a worker shall receive in income in return for working for an employer depends on how many labor hours are required to produce the necessities of life for a worker. If the necessities can be produced with five hours of labor per day, a worker can "produce" and be available to the employer for work if five hours' wages are paid to the worker each day. Even if the worker actually works 12 hours each day for an employer, the pay will be only for five hours because that is all it takes to sustain the worker. That is all the price can be, under a labor theory of value. In effect Marx thus believed in a *subsistence theory of wages* in a system of market capitalism.

The Theory of Surplus Value. For Marx, labor was a uniquely productive element. To produce enough goods and services to provide a worker with subsistence might require five hours of labor. But if a worker did subsist, more than five hours could be worked. Perhaps the worker could work for as long as 12 hours. In this case, a worker could create seven hours of extra value. Only labor was thus capable, in Marx's view, of creating value. Only labor was capable of creating a surplus above subsistence needs.

With the aid of labor, a piece of land or a machine could transform raw material into finished product, but it could not create additional value. The machine's contribution to the value of the product was equal to the value of that portion of the machine worn out in the process of producing the product. Neither the machine, which was real capital, nor the machine's owner, who was a capitalist, made any net gain possible. Only the worker created surplus value. This was Marx's *theory of surplus value*.

Injustice in the Distribution of Income. What seemed particularly galling to Marx about a capitalist market system was that, although labor created the surplus value, laborers did not receive this value as income. Laborers received only a subsistence income, even though laborers through their work created a volume of products whose total value was considerably in excess of the value of subsistence needs. The total output of production had a value proportional to all the labor exerted, but only a part of the value accrued to labor as wage income.

When a product was sold for its value, what happened to that portion of the sales proceeds not paid out as wages? That portion was retained by the owners of the business, that is, by the capitalists. Consequently, their share in the total income was much larger than their real contribution to production. These income shares of the bourgeoisie took the form of profits, including interest, dividends, and rent.

In summary, Marx's theory of market capitalism involved several ideas. The total value of the gross national product was proportional to and created exclusively by the amount of labor which had directly or indirectly been exerted to produce the gross national product. The total value of the gross national product exceeded the total value of goods and services required to provide a subsistence living for the working population. The working population received from the money proceeds derived from selling the gross national product a total wage income sufficient to buy the goods and services needed for subsistence, but no more. The excess or remainder of the sales proceeds accrued to the capitalists as property income or profits.

In this way Marx saw an element of injustice in a system of market capitalism. This element and other features of capitalism would with time prove to be fatal weaknesses for the market society.

The Dynamic Weaknesses of Market Capitalism

The market distribution of income between workers and property owners was bound, according to Marx, to be a source of increasing difficulty for capitalist economies.

Crises and Depressions. For one thing, it would sometimes be difficult to sell the output being produced. The workers received money income enough to buy only part of the output. This part would necessarily take the form of subsistence or consumer goods. The capitalists received the rest, an amount sufficient to buy the remainder of the output of goods and services. But would they buy it? Of course they would buy some of it to satisfy their own consumption desires. The rest they might purchase in the form of capital goods with which to carry on production and to expand productive capacity. That is, they might purchase capital goods if they found such purchase profitable. Would they find it profitable? Not always, thought Marx. From time to time there would be periods of months or of a year or two when they would not find it profitable. These would be periods of crises and depression. During these times there would be sharply increased financial losses for business, unsold output, business bankruptcies, falling prices, and unemployment.

Marx presented no thoroughly comprehensive and consistent explanation as to why recurrent financial crises occur in market capitalism. They were occurring during Marx's lifetime, and it was natural for him to seize upon them as a manifestation of the fatal flaws of a system which he despised and which he felt was doomed. The cause of the crises might lie, as already suggested, in the maldistribution of income. There was a failure to disseminate purchasing power in a fashion which would insure that all output would be purchased. On the other hand, the cause might lie in the sequential interplay between profit rates and wage rates. Both of these kinds of rates fluctuated in the short run. A rise in the wage rates might reduce profits and so discourage capitalists' purchases of capital goods, the output of which would then be unsold. The unsold output would in turn create a crisis with unemployment. The crisis would cause wages to fall. The fall might somehow result in greater profits. The profits might encourage capitalists' purchases of capital. These purchases might, for the moment, end the crisis and depression. However, they might later cause wages to rise so that the whole cycle of events would be repeated.

Worsening Trends. Marx suggested that these crises and depressions would become increasingly severe. In each successive crisis, the weakest firms would disappear, being absorbed or replaced by a fewer number of larger firms. In the long run the number of firms and the number of capitalists would decline both absolutely and relative to the size of the economy and of the population. The proletariat would be absolutely and relatively enlarged.

The capitalist employers would be impelled by competition among themselves to substitute machinery or capital for labor, even though it was labor which provided surplus value and profits. The capitalists would be impelled to discover and introduce into use new technology. They would do so because such technology would reduce the cost of subsistence needs for labor and thereby enlarge the amount of surplus value and profit. The increasingly severe crises, the substitution of capital for labor, and the introduction of new technology would create a larger and larger volume of unemployment among the workers. There would be an ever increasing *industrial reserve army* of the unemployed.

Marx felt that the rate of profit on capital would fall continually lower. The fall would occur primarily because of the replacement of laborers with machines. The laborers were the source of all surplus and hence of all profits. Machines produced no surplus and, therefore, did not contribute to profits. The capitalists, desperately seeking to sustain profits, would seek ways to increase the surplus value by greater exploitation of the workers. They would resort to longer working hours, more intense work, and the employment of children.

There would be more and more severe crises, fewer and fewer capitalists, larger and larger unemployment, lower and lower profit rates, bigger and bigger amounts of unsold goods, and ever more outrageous exploitation of the workers by the capitalists. These trends would lead, in the Marxist view, ultimately to the end of market capitalism. It would be replaced with a new economic system, or rather, with a whole new society. In Marx's view, economic arrangements were causally determinant of all else in society, and capitalism's inevitable demise would mean a complete change of all else in society.[10]

Economically Determined History

To reiterate, Marx contended that economic conditions were the basic causal forces shaping the nature of society. All other aspects of society—political, religious, and philosophical—were dependent upon the economic system of the society.

Materialism. For example, in a primitive nomad society where horses might be of peculiar importance in enabling the people to gather food and to exist in general, the ownership of horses would also be important to the people. Those persons who owned the horses would be able to control the others. That is, those who possessed the principal means of production would also possess the ability to rule. The religion and philosophy of the nomad society would center about horses and those who owned them. The patterns of marriage and inheritance would be heavily influenced by considerations regarding the use and ownership of horses.

In an agricultural society, land and its possession and use would cause the society to be what it was. The controllers of land would exercise predominant political control. Religion and philosophy might serve primarily as a device for exerting moral compulsion upon individuals to behave cooperatively in the use of the land.

In a society which had amassed considerable real capital and technology, the capital would be the principal means of production. The society would be organized around the existence, ownership, control, and use of the capital. Political power would reside with the owners and controllers of capital, the capitalists. Religion and philosophy would sanctify the ownership and rationalize the social dominance of the owners.

In some advanced societies with great real capital, all ownership and control might be exercised by the government. It would act on behalf of all the people. Political power would rest with all the people. A philosophy of altruism would develop among them.

In the most advanced society, so much capital and such advanced technology would exist that there could be produced goods and services great enough that the desires of everyone could be more than completely satisfied. The ownership of the means of production would cease to matter. Political

---

[10] A clear, entertaining, and brief explanation of Marx's theories appears in: Sir Alexander Gray, *The Development of Economic Doctrine: An Introductory Survey* (New York: John Wiley & Sons, Inc., 1931), Chapter 11. A more technically difficult account, which assumes more knowledge of economic analysis, can be found in: Mark Blaug, *Economic Theory in Retrospect* (Rev. ed.; Homewood, Ill.: Richard D. Irwin, Inc., 1968), Chapter 7.

control over others would cease to have significance. Interpersonal animosity, based on the covetousness of each for the material goods and services of others, would disappear. Government, no longer necessary as the instrument by which some controlled others or by which some were protected from others, would gradually wither away.

Marx felt that the character of a society wholly depended upon its economic system. Hence, his philosophy is labeled one of *materialism.*

The Dialectic. Marx's view of philosophy and history was also *dialectic.* From his teacher Hegel, Marx adopted the notion that what happened in the world could be explained by the clash of opposites. Hegel claimed that a proper understanding of the world could be achieved if all change were viewed as the result of clashing ideas. First, there is an idea, such as scarcity. Then there emerges an opposite idea, such as abundance. Finally the two opposing ideas are combined into a new and superior idea, such as *economy,* which is a means to achieve abundance out of scarcity.

Marx adopted the notion of the clashing of opposites to produce a successor synthesis. However, he rejected the view that this clashing and synthesis took place basically and most significantly in the realm of ideas. Rather, according to Marx, the essentially basic and causal conflict and synthesis took place, as his philosophy of materialism suggests, in the real world of economic events, economic classes, and economic systems.

Dialectical Materialism. Marx welded together his views of the primacy of economic arrangements and of history as progressive conflict into the doctrine of *dialectical materialism.*

A society, such as that of the European Middle Ages, is based on an economic system, such as manorial agriculture. A political structure, such as feudalism, and a philosophical and religious structure, such as medieval Catholicism, grow up in harmony with the economic base. There exist several socio-economic classes: landed nobility, clergy, and serfs. The economic system is successful in filling the material needs of the people. In fact, it is too successful for its own permanence.

The increasing productive ability of manorialism makes it possible for some persons to leave agriculture and become traders or town craftsmen. Others have sufficient time to make discoveries and innovations of an economically useful sort. Gradually the techniques of production and the other economic arrangements change. Local economic self-sufficiency decreases as trading increases. First guilds and then factory workers carry on production in place of the manorial serfs or crafts people. There begins to grow up a new socio-economic class made up of the shopkeeping proprietors, the factory managers and owners, and the merchant traders.

In the meantime, the political power remains, in an increasingly outmoded way, with the hereditary landed aristocracy. The religious rules grow more and more inappropriate for the economic system. For example, the doctrines against usury and in favor of just prices become obsolete. Finally, the economic system and the seat of real powei have changed enough that the new class, the bourgeoisie, is able to wrest political power from the landed nobility. They do so either by forceful revolution, by new laws, or by influence with the sovereign. They also reshape the religious code, perhaps by replacing Catholicism with Protestantism.

Capitalism thereby replaces feudalism. Then, because of its inherent nature, capitalism under the bourgeoisie unintentionally promotes its own replacement. Capitalism brings together the working proletariat and infuses in them a unity born of misery and exploitation. The class conflict between the proletariat and the bourgeoisie sharpens with conditions increasingly favorable to a proletarian victory. The political superstructure of government is in the hands of the bourgeoisie. They have used it as an instrument for the perpetuation of their power. However, it fails to reflect the underlying economic reality of bourgeoisie weakness and proletarian strength. Religion has been used as a device for cowing the workers, for justifying their exploitation, and for drugging them with visions of heaven so that they will accept their earthly misery. However, religion becomes more and more obviously a sham.

Eventually, the workers topple the bourgeoisie government, seize the means of production, abolish private property, and set up a socialist state under the dictatorship of the proletariat. The economic system is thus converted to socialism. Then, because all else follows from economic change, the society becomes ultimately a communist one, with neither government, scarcity, conflict, nor classes.[11]

THE WEAKNESS OF MARXISM

What is wrong with Marx's views? Each of Marx's main ideas can be attacked on a number of grounds.

The Labor Theory of Value

The labor theory of value, as an explanation of what determines relative prices of goods and services, is extremely vulnerable to criticism. Marx anticipated some of the vulnerabilities and tried to deal with them.

Exceptions to the Theory. A piece of fertile, virgin land may exist and command a high price without any human labor at all having been expended on its creation. Such nonreproducible goods, Marx would say, fall in a special category. The prices or values of this category are determined without reference to amounts of labor. Then what of a durable good which was produced some time ago and for whose production a technological improvement has been discovered in the meantime? The value of such a good will fall, Marx would say, in the meantime. It is not the amount of original labor expended but the amount necessary to replace a good that is the determining variable.

---

[11] A readable, but biased account of world history, including the Industrial Revolution, as seen by a modern Marxist is: Leo Huberman, *Man's Worldly Goods: The Story of the Wealth of Nations* (New York: Monthly Review Press, 1952).

What of a unit of a good much like many other units of the same good except that it embodies a much greater amount of labor because it was turned out by a very slow, inept worker? Will it on that account be much more valuable than the other units? No, it will not, because it is not the actual amount of labor used but the amount of *socially necessary* labor that determines values and prices, Marx would answer. What of a good, like a hideous piece of sculpture, on the production of which a great amount of labor has been expended but which cannot be sold for any price because no one wants it? Can it, all in all, be said to be of great value? No, Marx might answer, because labor expended on a useless product is not socially necessary labor. What of a good produced by a monopolist and sold at a high price? Is its price in proportion to the labor in it? Admittedly it is not, for monopoly may distort prices from true values.

The Problem of Diverse Kinds of Labor. What of two goods, one of which embodies four hours of unskilled labor and the other of which embodies four hours of skilled? Will the two goods sell at the same price? Do they have equal value? No, in creating and determining value, one hour of skilled labor counts for more than one hour of unskilled. To compute value, one must convert skilled labor into unskilled labor by multiplying the number of hours of skilled labor by an appropriate conversion number. How can the appropriate number be known? One must observe the number of times higher the wage rate of the skilled worker is above that of the unskilled. What determines this usual number of times? It is determined, in part, by the number of hours of labor socially necessary to produce the goods and services needed to sustain the skilled laborer through the period of his training. It is also determined, in part, by the number of hours required for every laborer, skilled or unskilled, to produce the goods needed to rear that person from infancy and for subsistence during working years.

Too many qualifications and exceptions spoil the attractiveness of a generalization. There is little left of the labor theory of value after all of the obviously necessary modifications are taken into account. Furthermore, the modifications suggested in the preceding paragraphs are incomplete. In the last qualification, for example, the number of labor hours necessary to sustain a worker consists itself of some hours of unskilled labor and some of skilled. To add the two together, a conversion number must be available. Of course, it is not available, for it is precisely what the whole procedure is set up to find.

Alternative Modern Theory. Modern economic theory, developed since Marx, explains values or relative prices in terms of degrees of scarcity. According to this theory, the value of a thing in exchange for something else depends on how scarce it is. Its scarcity in turn depends on the state of its supply and the state of demand for it. Behind supply and demand lie a great many interdependent determinants. The scarcity theory is a complicated one, but it provides a more satisfactory explanation than the labor theory of value. The scarcity theory treats not only labor but also capital and natural resources as productive and value-creating.

Marx's labor theory of value is weak. His use of it as a basis for attacking the capitalistic market society's distribution of income makes that attack weak. One might still condemn market capitalism or market capitalism's distribution of income. However, one would probably do so for some reason other than because one believed that only labor had the power to create value and all value was in proportion to labor used.

The Subsistence Theory of Wages

Another element in Marx's theory of market capitalism was a subsistence theory of wages. There are for this theory two alternative meanings between which Marx vacillated. One is that the wage rate will tend to fall until workers receive only enough income to provide a minimum physical existence for themselves. The other is that the wage rate will tend to fall until workers receive only enough to provide a psychologically or culturally determined minimum level of living for themselves. The latter minimum might change with time as attitudes changed. It might vary from place to place, depending upon what attitudes prevailed in the society of each place. Marx did not give a satisfactory causal explanation of why the wage rate under market capitalism tended toward a subsistence minimum, however defined.

The Malthusian Explanation. Marx rejected the explanation offered by such persons as Thomas Malthus. Malthus had argued that any wage higher than subsistence would reduce the death rate or raise the birth rate. These changes would cause the population and the supply of labor to increase. The increase would depress the market for labor and force the wage rate down. Perhaps Marx rejected the Malthusian explanation because it seemed to place the blame on the workers or to suggest that any economic system, not just market capitalism, would produce the same undesirable result.

Lopsided Bargaining Power. Marx did contend that the bargaining power of each individual worker would be small relative to that of a capitalist employer in the negotiations on wage rates. A worker sometimes has no real alternative, other than unemployment, to accepting a job from one accessible employer. On the other hand, most employers either can offer work to any one of a number of different workers who are competing with each other for jobs or can withhold work entirely by shutting down operations.

Critics of Marx have pointed out that, at least sometimes, workers have considerable bargaining power. Their power arises because of their unusual skills, because they band together in labor unions, because there is competition among employers for their services, or because without their labor real capital is unprofitable. Even with weak bargaining power, there is no proof that the wage rate will fall to the subsistence level.

The Reserve Army of the Unemployed. Marx also contended that there usually would be substantial numbers of unemployed workers. They would always be ready to compete with those who had jobs. They would also furnish an inexhaustible supply of labor at a minimum subsistence wage rate, no matter how strong the demand for labor.

Critics of this argument emphasize that Marx never really convincingly demonstrated that capitalism creates unemployment. Indeed, if Marx was right that only labor creates surplus value and profits, capitalist employers would seek out and employ every available worker because, by so doing, profits could be maximized. Actually, real wage rates in countries heavily dependent upon market capitalism have risen substantially in the long run. A Marxist may choose to dismiss this evidence by claiming that it merely reflects a rising psychological minimum subsistence level. But one can reasonably rejoin that capitalism is performing well, not badly, in this respect. It has raised both aspirations and the means to fulfill them.

The Theory of Surplus Value

The theory of surplus value asserts that workers usually produce more goods and services than are needed for their subsistence. This assertion seems acceptable. It is probably equally acceptable, however, to assert that land is capable of producing more crop than that needed to reseed the land adequately in the next growing season. Likewise, a labor-saving machine may spare more labor hours than were required to make it. As the basis for an attack on market capitalism, the theory of surplus value is no attack at all unless supplemented by a labor theory of value and a subsistence theory of wages. If these latter two ideas are invalid, the theory of surplus value loses its sting for market capitalism.

Actually, land, labor, and capital cooperate in most production activities, regardless of the economic system. The complete removal of any one of these three factors would cause production to cease almost entirely. So long as they do cooperate, the productive output is usually more than enough to replace the worn equipment, maintain the natural resources, and provide for the subsistence needs of the workers. The excess may take the form either of suprasubsistence consumer goods or of capital goods which increase the society's stock of real capital.

The Theory of Crises and Trends

Another element in Marx's attack on market capitalism is the crisis or business cycle. These do occur in many forms of capitalistic economic systems. They had been the object of economists' inquiries and theories before Marx, and they continued to be afterward. Marx's explanation of them was incomplete and faulty. A complete understanding of them has not been achieved. However, most economists believe that, as a result of economic studies undertaken since the Great Depression, mixed economic systems can avoid severe crises and cycles. They can be avoided if rather modest government economic intervention to counteract the cycles is accepted. In any case, crises and cycles have not yet forced the complete collapse of market capitalism and its replacement with Marxian socialism or communism.

Many of the trends which Marx predicted would carry capitalism to its doom have not been corroborated by history subsequent to Marx. Most striking has been the failure of the capitalist owners to become a smaller and smaller percentage of the population and the proletariat, a larger and larger percentage. An increasingly greater portion of the people of western Europe and North America possess property in the form of savings accounts, shares of corporate stock, government bonds, houses, automobiles, and durable consumer goods. The proletarian proportion of the populace has diminished as skilled white-collar and service workers have come to outnumber unskilled, manual workers.

The percentage of the labor force unemployed has not increased in the long run, as Marx predicted it would. The quality of life of the majority of the population has not become increasingly miserable. Working conditions have improved, not deteriorated, on the average at least. In the long run the rate of profit on capital has not fallen as much as Marx predicted. Technological and social changes have provided new, profitable opportunities for the use of machinery and other capital goods. The governments of most capitalist countries have not resolutely blocked every attempt by the majority of the people to obtain legislation to improve their lot. It would be laughable to contend that for most noncommunist, developed countries the government is used as the instrument by which an increasingly small number of capitalists keep subjugated an ever more preponderant working class.

The Theory of Economic Determinism and Dialectical Materialism

Marx's emphasis upon the economic system of a society as determinant of all else about society is also easily criticized.

Economics as Only One of Many Interdependent Forces. The economic system is as much a result as a cause of the general character of society. Religion and philosophy, for example, help to determine economic organization. A people's religion may emphasize the evil of the accumulation of material goods and the virtue of asceticism. In consequence, the economic system is likely to remain a traditional one, and economic growth will not occur. Alternatively, religion may lay stress upon individual responsibility and upon working hard, saving much, and investing productively. As a result, the economic system is likely to become a market one with rapid change. A people's philosophy may accord great prestige to those who are very successful in military, spiritual, or governmental affairs and little prestige to those who are economically successful. Then the economic system of the people is likely to remain organized around the principle of tradition, and what modern Westerners regard as economic progress will probably be absent.

The political system of a society may place and keep in power those who wish to maintain the status quo. Then economic change will probably occur only slowly. The cultural heritage of a people may include a great accumulated stock of technological knowledge. The economic system of that people will probably be very different from that of a people with little such knowledge. The physical environment of a people is likely to shape their economic system. The tropics may offer no challenge to traditional economic organization, which remains primitive. The arctic may offer too great a challenge, which prevents economic organization from being anything but traditional and primitive.

Monocausal Theories of History. It is implausible to view human history simply as a sequence of economic changes which bring about other changes. Such a theory of history probably deserves the same derision as every other monocausal explanation of history. One other such theory is the *hero theory*, which claims that the shape of history is the result of the occurrence from time to time of extremely influential people such as Plato, Christ, Caesar, Charlemagne, Columbus, Luther, Marx, and Lenin. Another is the *idea theory*, which stresses the great historical influence of ideas such as monotheism, asceticism, altruism, capitalism, democracy, and communism. Another is the *war theory*, which claims that conflicts of arms provide the key to the understanding of history. There is also the *political theory*, which claims that history is the sequence of governments.[12]

Marx's selection of struggles between economic classes as the vehicle of historical progress is also not convincing. People generally have not thought of themselves primarily as members of an economic class, but as members of a family, an occupation, a tribe, a race, a district, or a nation, or simply as individuals. A theory of history which explains behavior as arising out of a loyalty which people do not have does not explain much.

THE MERITS OF MARX

Marx was not totally without merit. He did indicate some of the weaknesses of the market capitalism of his time and place. The inequality of income, wealth, and power of 19th century European capitalism was too great. It was too great to be permanently tolerated by the populace and too great by 20th century, Western standards. Marx correctly predicted some of the trends in market capitalism. Recurrent and sometimes severe business fluctuations have taken place. Unemployment has been a persistent problem. Inordinate political and social power has accrued to the economically most successful. Control, if not ownership, has been concentrated in the hands of those who guide the great private corporations.

Marx was perhaps the first to try to explain why history had occurred as it had rather than merely to describe what had occurred. He attempted to integrate economic theory with history. He was undoubtedly one of the few of his time to do so.

[12] A brief elaboration of this kind of criticism of Marx can be found in: William Ebenstein, *Today's Isms: Communism, Fascism, Capitalism, and Socialism* (7th ed.; Englewood Cliffs, N.J.: Prentice-Hall, Inc., 1973), Chapter 1.

Perhaps Marx's greatest achievement was as a propagandist or as an inspiration for revolution and reform. It is ironical that Marx denied the influence of ideas on history and claimed instead the ascendancy of events. His own ideas have inspired and provoked people ever since he propounded them. Perhaps half the earth's population either are led by or desire to be led by those who proclaim their allegiance to Marxism. This is not to say, of course, that the world today is markedly different than it would be had Marx never lived. It is entirely possible that events subsequent to Marx's time, such as the Russian and Chinese Communist revolutions, would have taken place whether or not Marx had ever existed. People like Lenin and Mao, bent on seizing power and on changing society, are likely to pluck from the pages of previous history one name if not another to sanctify their actions and increase the probability of their success. Historical speculation aside, however, it is easy to claim for Marx that no other person did so much as he to besmirch the reputation of market capitalism.

SUMMARY

Market mechanisms helped to produce both the Agricultural Revolution and the Industrial Revolution. These revolutions had many good results, but they also had some bad ones. They destroyed traditional life and created a class of urban poor. Industrial working and living conditions in western Europe in the 19th century were undesirable. The upper economic classes seemed to oppress the lower.

It is still unknown whether these conditions represented a real deterioration from previous circumstances. There is continued debate, too, about the extent to which the market system can be blamed. Nevertheless, opponents of market capitalism have used the experience to attack market arrangements and urge their replacement.

The most prominent of these opponents was Karl Marx. He analyzed the workings of market capitalism to explain what he thought was its unjust distribution of income. He also forecast its inevitable end, brought about by its inherent inconsistencies and by inexorable historical forces.

Marx's analysis is replete with logical contradictions. His theory of economically determined history is grossly simplistic. Still Marx has been influential. As a propagandist against capitalism, he has inspired communist revolutions. His influence may yet spread further in those underdeveloped countries which are dissatisfied with market arrangements as a means for achieving economic development.

QUESTIONS

1. How did market mechanisms help to make possible many of the changes which were part of the Industrial Revolution?
2. If market forces had not been permitted to operate, would the British Industrial Revolution have occurred anyway?
3. What caused the changes in British agriculture between 1500 and 1900?
4. Present as good a case as possible that market mechanisms were a socially beneficial force in British agriculture between 1500 and 1900.

5. What role did market forces have in creating the bad conditions for the working classes of Britain in the 19th century?
6. Defend market mechanisms from the charge that they were socially detrimental during the Industrial Revolution in Britain.
7. What are the facts of Marx's biography? When did he live? Where was he born? What was his father's occupation? What was his religion? Where did he attend college? What occupation did he take up after college? Where did he practice this occupation? Why did he move around so much? Where did he spend the last half of his life? Who was his main collaborator? What were his chief writings?
8. What was Marx's labor theory of value? How can this theory be criticized?
9. What was Marx's theory of wages? How can this theory by criticized?
10. What was Marx's theory of surplus value? Is it a valid theory?
11. What were the causes and consequences, according to Marx, of the distribution of income under market capitalism?
12. What were financial crises and how, according to Marx, were they caused?
13. Marx is said to have had an interpretation of history and explanation of social existence in his "dialectical materialism." What is "dialectical materialism"? Why is it called "materialism"? Why is it called "dialectical"? What alternative explanations of history are there other than the materialistic theory? What forces, other than economic ones, motivate people?
14. How can Marx's theories of conditions under capitalism be combined to indicate the inevitable fall of capitalism?
15. Summarize Marx's theory of economic class struggles from feudalism to communism.
16. To what extent has history since Marx supported or refuted Marx's theory of history and his prediction of the end of capitalism?
17. If Marx was wrong, why has he remained so influential?

RECOMMENDED READINGS

Balinky, Alexander. *Marx's Economics: Origin and Development.* Lexington, Mass.: D. C. Heath and Company, 1970.

Blaug, Mark. *Economic Theory in Retrospect,* Rev. ed. Homewood, Ill.: Richard D. Irwin, Inc., 1968.

Bowden, Witt, Michael Karpovich, and Abbott Payson Usher. *The Economic History of Europe Since 1750.* New York: AMS Press, Inc., 1970.

Bowditch, John, and Clement Ramsland (eds.). *Voices of the Industrial Revolution: Selected Readings from the Liberal Economists and Their Critics.* Ann Arbor: The University of Michigan Press, 1961.

Ebenstein, William. *Today's Isms: Communism, Fascism, Capitalism, and Socialism,* 7th ed. Englewood Cliffs, N.J.: Prentice-Hall, Inc., 1973.

Gray, Alexander. *The Development of Economic Doctrine: An Introductory Survey.* New York: John Wiley & Sons, Inc., 1931.

Hammond, John L., and Barbara Hammond. *The Rise of Modern Industry.* New York: Harper & Row Publishers, 1969.

Hayek, F. A. (ed.). *Capitalism and the Historians.* Chicago: University of Chicago Press, 1954.

Heilbroner, Robert L. *The Worldly Philosophers: The Lives, Times, and Ideas of the Great Economic Thinkers,* 4th ed. New York: Simon & Schuster, Inc., 1972.

Huberman, Leo. *Man's Worldly Goods: The Story of the Wealth of Nations.* New York: Monthly Review Press, 1952.

Marx, Karl. *Capital: A Critique of Political Economy.* New York: Modern Library, Inc., a division of Random House, Inc., 1906.

————. *Capital, The Communist Manifesto, and Other Writings by Karl Marx,* edited by Max Eastman. New York: Modern Library, Inc., a division of Random House, Inc., 1932.

————. *Marx on Economics,* edited by Robert Freedman. New York: Harcourt Brace Jovanovich, Inc., 1961.

Taylor, Philip A. M. (ed.). *The Industrial Revolution in Britain: Triumph or Disaster?,* rev. ed. Boston, Mass.: D. C. Heath & Company, 1970.

Toynbee, Arnold. *The Industrial Revolution.* Boston, Mass.: Beacon Press, 1956.

Wilson, Edmund. *To the Finland Station: A Study in the Writing and Acting of History.* Garden City, N.Y.: Doubleday & Company, Inc., 1953.

5

The Underdeveloped Countries
and Market Mechanisms

INTRODUCTION

A majority of the world's population lives in *underdeveloped* countries.[1] Most of the nations of Latin America, Africa, and Asia are in this category. Until very recently the economies of most of these nations have been organized predominantly on the basis of tradition. However, in the last few decades social, political, and economic changes have come to these countries, and they have begun to acquire new economic systems. They are continuing to struggle in order to convert themselves from underdeveloped poverty to developing wealth. Will heavy reliance upon market mechanisms alone be likely to produce good solutions for the problems which these countries are encountering in their struggles? Many economists and many of the leaders of these countries believe not. In this chapter the apparent suitability of market arrangements for these countries is explored.

The underdeveloped countries are by no means all alike. There is a vast difference between, say, the situation of a typical slum dweller of Mexico City and that of an average Vietnamese peasant. Nevertheless, the underdeveloped countries do seem to have many common features, and a brief summary of some of these is useful at this point.

Typical Economic Conditions

Whether a country should be classed as underdeveloped is sometimes determined by its gross national product per capita. Per capita GNP is a rough measure of the goods and services produced and available on the average to each person. Among the poorest countries in the world are Haiti, Bolivia, Somalia, Yemen, Pakistan, India, China, and Indonesia. For these countries the GNP per capita is less than 5 percent of the annual United States figure, which was about $7,000 in 1975. The poverty which this low percentage figure represents shows up in a tangible way in nutritionally inadequate diets, primitive and crowded housing, ragged clothes, an absence of medical services, and an unavailability of schools. Disease, emaciated bodies, short lives, and illiteracy are other symptoms.

[1] *Underdeveloped* is only one of several adjectives that are used to label less wealthy countries. Some of the others are *developing, emerging,* and *less developed.*

Most of the output of the underdeveloped countries is consumer goods, primarily food. Capital goods are usually a very small part of the GNP. The techniques of production are predominantly primitive. There is very little equipment or other real capital. Labor provides most of the energy. Understanding of the possibility of adoption of more efficient techniques is small.

The vast majority of people are farmers and they live in rural areas. They tend to have rather high death rates but even higher birth rates so that the population size keeps increasing. The age structure of the population is heavily weighted with children. One result is that each person in the economically productive age groups has a greater average number of dependents than is the case for advanced countries.

In some underdeveloped areas the arable land is fragmented into very small, individually owned and managed plots. Elsewhere it is organized into large estates or plantations with most of the labor force as wage laborers or sharecroppers. A typical condition on these lands is supposed by many observers to be *underemployment*. This is a state of affairs in which there are so many laborers per acre that some of them could be removed without a reduction in the size of the output of product. Much of the rural populace gets along by barter or near self-sufficiency. Money transactions are rare.

Typical Social and Political Conditions

Social conditions differ in most underdeveloped countries from those in advanced countries. In many of the poor countries there is an elite class which is wealthy and educated. The families of this class own most of the property and possess most of the political power. This class constitutes a small minority of the total population, the vast majority of whom are, of course, very poor. The middle classes are small or nonexistent.

The rich and powerful elite have, to a considerable extent, adopted European culture as a style of life for themselves. The poor majority remain bound in native tradition. The striking differences between the two major classes have led some people to call the society *dualistic*.

Among the majority there exist such traditions as the *extended family*. This is an arrangement in which all the aunts, uncles, grandparents, grandchildren, nieces, and nephews either by blood or by marriage are regarded as entitled to share in the income earned by their productive relatives. The tradition of *tribalism* survives in many African countries and makes a feeling of national unity difficult.

The governments of most of these countries tend to be autocratic. More than a few are military dictatorships. Some are quite politically unstable with abrupt and sometimes violent changes in leadership occurring rather frequently. Some governments which succeed in staying in power attempt to maintain the status quo in economics. Others press vigorously for some kind of enforced economic change, sometimes including alteration of the economic system.

International Relations

Many of the underdeveloped countries, especially those in Asia and Africa, were colonial possessions of advanced countries until after World War II. Since independence, there has remained a lingering mistrust of foreigners. This mistrust is a result of earlier political domination over native peoples by the Europeans. Some also felt that economic exploitation by Europeans also existed.

The heritage of mistrust continues to manifest itself in various ways. One manifestation is the existence in many poor countries of a vigorous spirit of *nationalism.* Nationalism is a feeling of the importance, merit, superiority, and priority of one's national group and the belief that one's own nation must be made to triumph whenever it is challenged by any other nation. Another manifestation is the resentment felt by the peoples of the underdeveloped nations in their continuing economic relations with the advanced nations. By and large, the underdeveloped nations specialize in the production for export of agricultural and mineral raw materials. They rely upon imports from the advanced nations for manufactured goods, including capital equipment, and for technical services. This is the same trade pattern which existed before independence. Its continuation gives the impression to the underdeveloped peoples that economic independence has not yet been achieved. It is felt that they may continue to be "hewers of wood and drawers of water" for the advanced countries, which exclusively retain the more prestigious and militarily essential manufacturing and service activities.

In matters of international investment and foreign aid, too, resentment arises. Typically, international investment has been undertaken by private businesses with headquarters in advanced countries and with ownership vested with Europeans or Americans. These businesses have established production facilities in underdeveloped countries. Such facilities have consisted mainly of plantations for products like bananas and rubber, mines for the extraction of metallic ores, and petroleum fields. The products of these operations are usually exported to the advanced countries. The ownership and control of these activities have usually remained with the Western foreign investors, and to the underdeveloped peoples the arrangements smack too much of continued colonialism. The grants, loans, and technical assistance which have been extended by the governments of advanced countries to the underdeveloped nations as part of foreign aid programs have been resented in the recipient countries. The resentment arises because of the sometimes justified suspicion that the assistance is given for the purpose of undermining the political and economic independence of the recipients.

Typical Values and Attitudes

The strong resentment felt toward foreigners is only one of the values and attitudes which distinguish the people of the underdeveloped nations from more economically advanced peoples. Typically there is an unquestioning acceptance of the already established modes of production. Change in these matters is seldom considered as an alternative to tradition.

There is also an acceptance by parents of whatever number of children that chance happens to bring or even a positive desire for as many children as possible. There is an expectation that one born of a poor family will remain poor and will give birth to children who will remain poor. Similarly, there is an expectation that the children of the present elite will be the elite of the next generation. There is a presumption that one must share one's material means with one's relatives of the extended family. There is in some nations a strong feeling of loyalty to and dependence upon the tribe.

In some underdeveloped countries there is a cynicism about the government's ability to be anything other than autocratic. There may even exist a failure to imagine that there is any other way for a government to be. There is an apparent inability among many of both the governors and the governed to understand that the government can be used as an instrument for society's improvement rather than as an instrument of personal aggrandizement for those who happen to hold power. There is a failure to comprehend that those who hold power could ever voluntarily relinquish it or that those who are not in power might voluntarily and actively cooperate with those who govern.

In recent decades the people of most underdeveloped countries are supposed to have become aware that there are other peoples whose material existence is significantly more sumptuous than their own. The underdeveloped peoples are believed to have adopted the desire to exist at least as sumptuously. The process by which this adoption has taken place is sometimes called the *revolution in rising expectations*. Among the devices by which the awareness was transmitted and the desire created were colonialism, missionary activities, World War II, and Hollywood movies. In these ways Western individuals, or their likenesses, with habits of high material consumption came among the underdeveloped peoples. Though the desire was thus implanted among them, an understanding of the means by which the desire could be satisfied has not yet fully occurred to them. A gap exists between their economic aspirations and their actual economic achievement. In an attempt to narrow the gap, they have considered and are considering the appropriateness of various economic systems. One of these is, of course, the market system.

MARKET MECHANISMS AS POSITIVE FORCES FOR ECONOMIC DEVELOPMENT

Market mechanisms can play a large role in the conversion of an underdeveloped country into a developed one. The ideas of how they can do so have been formulated from the British experience and from that of other developed nations such as the United States, Japan, and those of western Continental Europe. One of the most famous and controversial theories of economic development based on these experiences was that of Marx. Another and more recent theory, also highly controversial, is that of Walt Whitman Rostow.[2]

2 Walt Whitman Rostow, *The Stages of Economic Growth: A Non-Communist Manifesto* (2d ed.; New York: Cambridge University Press, 1971).

Rostow's Theory of the Stages of Economic Development

According to Rostow, in the process of economic development nations pass through several stages.

The Traditional Society. In the first stage the nation's society is a traditional one. All societies before the Renaissance were traditional societies. These societies have many of the attributes described in the introduction of this chapter. A crucial attribute is the absence of any cumulative, self-reenforcing process of material improvement. Change may occur, but it is not in the form of a systematic trend.

The Prerequisites for Change. In the second stage, as Rostow describes it, there is the establishment of the prerequisites for sustained and systematic change, though such change does not itself begin yet. These prerequisites are of many varieties. Chief among them is an abandonment by at least some of the populace of a philosophy of fatalism and determinism. In its place there arises a belief in rationality, a belief in an ordered universe whose laws are discoverable and advantageous to those who understand them.

Other changes of attitudes and philosophical values also take place. Individuals come to be respected, not because of inherited status, but because of economic efficiency. The maximum number of babies physically possible ceases to be the optimum number as viewed by parents and society. Somehow income above subsistence needs must cease to be distributed to those who use it merely for ceremonial ostentation and instead must begin to be distributed to those who use it for the formation of real capital.

These prerequisites were established in western Europe by the long process the beginning of which can be traced to the ancient civilizations of the Near East. In countries outside western Europe and in today's underdeveloped countries, these prerequisites have been established by contact with Europeans.

The Take-Off. The third stage is described by Rostow as a take-off, which suggests that the pace of social and economic change suddenly accelerates. An important part of this acceleration is the increase in the percentage of the gross national product which is saved and which takes the form of capital goods. Another is the establishment of manufacturing activities. There is also continued alteration in such things as the customs of the people, the governmental forms and practices, and the kinds of economic units in existence. Rostow conceives of the take-off as some stimulating event. The event may be a war, a revolution, or a sudden change in international trading relationships. The event reacts back upon the already established prerequisites in such a way as to set off the accelerated changes named above.

Later Stages. The fourth of Rostow's stages is a period of self-sustaining increases in gross national product both in total and per capita. These increases eventually bring the nation to the fifth stage, one of high mass consumption. There may possibly follow further developments which are worthy of being classed as additional stages but whose character can only be guessed since no nation as yet progressed so far.

Criticisms. Rostow's *theory of the stages of economic growth* has been criticized on a number of counts. Included among these is the charge that it fails to fit with historical fact. There are also assertions that it fails to specify what makes each of the stages peculiarly distinctive relative to each of the others. It is further criticized for its failure to include forces which may be important in causing growth.[3] However, Rostow's terminology has been widely adopted by other writers, and his theory does convey much of the vision which many economic historians have regarding the process of economic development.

The Role of the Market in Economic Growth

What role does the market play in a Rostow-like growth process? In the traditional societies, market mechanisms are only peripherally present since economic coordination is achieved mainly by tradition. In fact, what seems to distinguish the traditional society from societies of the later stages is the small degree to which market mechanisms are relied upon in the former as compared with the latter.

Changes in Religion and Philosophy. In the establishment of the prerequisites for take-off, the market may play a role both as a cause and as an effect. For example, the growth of the practices of specialization in producing, buying, and selling things for money may undermine the traditional religious rules against profit making. When the religious authorities attempt to enforce these religious rules, their prestige and that of their deterministic philosophy may be at stake. If they fail in the enforcement, the philosophy may be discredited, and the way opened for a rational skepticism to replace the determinism. Market mechanisms may thus help to establish what Rostow regards as the crucially important prerequisite to growth.

On the other hand, if determinism has already been replaced with rationalism, the rationality may deliberately lead individuals to engage in specialization in production and concomitant buying and selling. These activities will be undertaken because they prove to be the most rational means by which individuals and groups can achieve their material desires.

Changes in Birth Rates. A further illustration of the role which the market can play in the establishment of the preconditions and the take-off is provided by a study of what sometimes happens to the birth rate during the stages or process of development. In traditional societies the birth rates are high. It is probably appropriate that they be so, for the death rates are also high. These societies would probably dwindle in size and ultimately disappear if birth rates were low.

Typically in most of today's underdeveloped countries, however, the stage involving the establishment of prerequisites to take-off has included the rapid and drastic reduction of death rates. This reduction has occurred as contact

---

[3] A summary of criticism of Rostow's theory and a useful bibliography on the subject appear in Gerald M. Meier, *Leading Issues in Development Economics: Studies in International Poverty* (2d ed.; New York: Oxford University Press, 1970), pp. 59–120.

with Westerners and Western medical technology, public health measures, and transportation techniques have brought about the eradication of epidemic diseases and regional famines. Meanwhile, the birth rates have remained high. The high birth rates in combination with the lowered death rates have created the population explosion. This explosion has had some disadvantageous results for most underdeveloped countries. There are already too many people crowded on the land. There is too little capital equipment for each worker, and the extra mouths to feed leave less output for capital formation.

However, many demographic experts foresee an optimistic outcome, which will be achieved through the operation of market forces. It is this. The changes already occurring in underdeveloped countries are causing a shift in population from rural pursuits to urban ones. In a farm situation large numbers of children in a family are regarded by the parents as assets since they can be put to work at an early age in cooperation with their parents and can thus help to sustain the family income. Hence rural parents choose to have large numbers of children, and the birth rates are high. In an urban situation, however, children are often economic liabilities to their parents. They cannot work until they are almost adults, and they require expensive training and sustenance in the meantime. Moreover, either the mother or the father frequently is prevented from obtaining available work away from the home because of caring for the children.

Circumstances such as these of a market economy suggest to the parents that a rational choice is to have few children. So if urban industrialization is occurring and if most parents act in the way just suggested, the population explosion will be ended. It will be ended not by governmental command or by tradition, but by individual decisions representing rational responses to the economic forces of the market.[4]

The Take-Off. The stimulus of which Rostow conceives as the heart of the take-off stage may also originate in market forces. For example, a business cycle expansion in an advanced country may increase its market demand for the raw material exports of an underdeveloped country. In response, that activity or industry which produces the material in the underdeveloped country may reap unusual profits and may expand. Such expansion may increase the demand for labor and other supplies there so that the whole economy of the underdeveloped country begins to grow faster than before the take-off occurred.

Even a sudden decline in the demand for an underdeveloped country's principal raw material export may act as a stimulus to take-off. For example, suppose a recession occurs in an advanced country so that its import purchases of a raw material from an underdeveloped country dramatically decline. The shock in the underdeveloped country may cause the raw material

[4] Frank W. Notestein, Dudley Kirk, and Sheldon Segal, "The Problem of Population Control," *The Population Dilemma,* edited by Philip M. Hauser (2d ed.; Englewood Cliffs, N.J.: Prentice-Hall, Inc., 1969); and Kingsley Davis, "Population," *Scientific American,* Vol. 209, No. 3 (September, 1963), pp. 62–71.

producers there to begin to process and to try to sell their output to their own nationals. This activity may be the real beginning of manufacturing operations in the underdeveloped country.

Cumulative Growth. The market can provide the mechanism by which growth becomes self-sustaining once something like a take-off occurs. According to Rostow, the growth of one industry is likely to lead to the establishment and growth of others, all through market forces.[5] As one industry grows, it requires and demands increasing amounts of supplies, which are themselves the products of other industries. These other industries can therefore be expected to expand in size, thus creating demand for the products of still other industries, which also then expand. The increased incomes earned by workers in the initially expanding industries provide the demand for products from other consumer goods industries, which then expand. The profits from the initially expanding industries are available and are likely to be used to finance the increase in the productive capacity of these industries. Such expansion probably will create a demand for capital goods so that industries producing capital goods may be established.

In this way it is plausible to argue that market mechanisms can be a vehicle by which economic development can occur.

THE OBSTACLES TO DEVELOPMENT

The fact is, however, that economic development has been occurring very slowly or not at all for the majority of underdeveloped nations. GNP per capita is not only low, it is not increasing very much. It is probably even true that there are periods in which the GNP per capita has been falling in some countries. It turns out that economic development is an extremely elusive objective. The obstacles to its achievement are many.[6] The task of converting backward, poor peoples into progressive, rich ones is not easy. Those who have participated in the "war against poverty" in the United States are all too well aware of the difficulties.

Inadequate Natural Resources

One might claim that the major obstacle to economic development is lack of natural resources. There are certainly some underdeveloped countries that seem to lack climate, soil, minerals, waterpower, and most other features of a rich, natural endowment. Yeman, Chad, Malawi, New Guinea, and India are but a few of these. Then, too, some countries are so small in size as measured in total natural wealth that they seem by themselves economically unviable. Some examples are Guatemala, Mauretania, Oman, Singapore, Trinidad, and Lesotho.

---

[5] Rostow, *op. cit.*

[6] For another summary and critical account of the obstacles to economic development in underdeveloped countries, see Walter Elkan, *An Introduction to Development Economics* (Baltimore: Penguin Books, 1973), Chapter 2.

The fact is, however, that these kinds of obstacles can be overcome. Japan is an example of a nation which, with an extremely poor endowment of natural resources, was able to pursue the development process successfully. Libya is an example of a nation which once seemed hopelessly poor in natural resources, level of living, and prospects. It suddenly discovered in the late 1950s that there was located beneath it one of the world's largest natural petroleum reservoirs, which will probably prove the means to its development. Kuwait, too, is an example of an extremely small desert nation whose path to wealth was through petroleum. One of the most prosperous nations in the world is also the smallest with a population of only about one third of a million people. Luxembourg has been able through specialization and trade with other countries to overcome the diseconomies of small national size.

Finally, there are nations with low, stagnant average levels of living which seem to be rather amply endowed with natural resources. Bolivia, Zaire, and Indonesia are among these. It seems that one could conclude that excellent natural resources and large national size are neither necessary nor sufficient to assure development.

Inadequate Real Capital

Inadequate amounts of real capital and inability to increase the amounts are obstacles to economic development. It is sometimes said that poor countries are, in this regard, caught in a vicious circle. Because the capital stock of each of these countries is small, its real gross national product is small. Because its GNP is small, almost all of the GNP must take the form of consumer subsistence goods such as food, or else the people would starve. But if most of the output must take the form of consumer goods, little can take the form of capital goods. The capital stock remains low as do output or GNP, the level of living, and the rate of economic development. The underdeveloped country is locked in a vicious circle of poverty.

Yet it is well to remind oneself, in assessing this argument, that the advanced countries of today were once in much this same situation. They somehow managed, nonetheless, to develop in the meantime. The British experience discussed in Chapter 4 is a case in point.

Overpopulation

Perhaps the chief obstacle to economic development is people themselves—their numbers, their abilities as producers, their attitudes and values, and the arrangements to which they have become accustomed in their contacts with each other.[7] If one thinks of people as providers of the most important factor of production, labor, one might conclude that the more people, the more labor,

---

[7] A broad and original treatment of the roles of human values and social institutions in economic development occurs in W. Arthur Lewis, *The Theory of Economic Development* (Homewood, Ill.: Richard D. Irwin, Inc., 1955).

the greater the GNP, and the better off the country. For some countries with small populations and access to large natural resources and stocks of real capital, this is appropriate reasoning. Countries such as the United States in the 19th century and Australia or Canada today are in this category.

It is well to remember, however, that for most countries more people mean not only more labor and output but also more consumers among whom to share the output. The more people there are, the less will be the real capital and natural resources per capita. Suppose a country is already large enough to take full advantage of economies of mass production and other advantages of large scale. Suppose that the goal is maximum output per person rather than maximum total output. Then more people are a disadvantage, not an advantage. These suppositions are true for most underdeveloped countries. That is why there is so much concern among so many social scientists and public officials about the population explosion and overpopulation among underdeveloped people.

Unproductive Labor

The majority of people in most underdeveloped countries are workers of only low quality. Whatever may be their virtues as people, as workers they are of little productivity. They are unskilled, uneducated, and untrained. Few of them are capable of acting as business managers with any success. Still fewer of them are able to recognize the opportunities for reorganizing a productive activity in a new way so as to increase output without increasing inputs or to decrease inputs without decreasing output. Few of them are able to put into practice such reorganization even when the opportunity to do so is recognized.

Here again one can explain the predicament in terms of a vicious circle. Without skilled workers, adroit management, and imaginative entrepreneurship, the underdeveloped countries conduct their economic activities in ways which do not require these inputs. Activities are conducted instead with unskilled workers, on a small scale which can dispense with much management, and with a reliance upon tradition rather than upon the imaginative innovations of good entrepreneurship. With activities conducted in this way, there is very little opportunity for workers through practice to develop skills and become trained. Similarly, opportunities are lacking for managers to develop their skills through practice and for a tradition of entrepreneurship to become established. So the underdeveloped countries may be locked in a vicious circle of a low average quality of human resources and backward techniques of production.

Another vicious circle is not unlike that, described several paragraphs ago, between lack of capital and low GNP. This vicious circle has to do with the reenforcing action between untrained labor and low GNP. Because labor is untrained, total output is low. Because output is low, little output can be spared from consumer goods to take the form of training services. Because labor cannot be trained, output remains low.

Values and Attitudes

Behind the large number of peoples and the poor economic quality of human resources lie, partly as causal forces, attitudes and values which are prevalent among the underdeveloped peoples.

Family Size. The attitudes toward births and family size are instructive in this respect. These attitudes were formed during the pre-1900 millennia when death rates were high. Then the chances of a newborn baby's surviving until its first birthday were less than one out of two. The chances of children's surviving into adulthood were almost as low. Under these circumstances, a parental pair would desire many babies, perhaps the biological maximum of which the parents were capable. Many babies would be necessary to have as many as two of them survive to adulthood, when as adults they might be needed to care for aged parents and to perpetuate the family line. Not all parents deliberately and consciously reasoned this argument through, of course; perhaps very few did. Yet the survival not only of the family line but also of the larger society of which the family was a part depended upon achievement of high birth rates. Societies which failed to produce attitudes that encouraged parents to have large numbers of babies probably dwindled out and were replaced.

By the dawn of the industrial and technological age, most societies of the world contained the tradition of high birth rates. The approved mode of behavior among their people was to strive for many babies and large families. This attitude was, at least by this time, predominantly a traditional one rather than a reasoned one. When there became available technological knowledge which permitted death rates to decline, the attitude was outmoded and inappropriate. It persisted, nonetheless, to the economic detriment of the peoples.

Economic Effort. The attitudes and values toward occupational self-improvement of individuals were likewise formed so as to be appropriate to a traditional society. They have persisted into an era which is one of a growing and changing society. They are incompatible with the new society, and they stand as obstacles against it.

In a traditional society one accepted the occupation conventionally reserved for one's family. One's rewards depended upon such acceptance, and the cohesiveness of society depended upon it, too. Individuals were not encouraged by public opinion to seek material gain for themselves through violation of tradition; it was quite the contrary.

Now that the time for change has come, the attitudinal mechanism for the achievement of change is absent. Individuals desire economic improvement for themselves, but there is too little recognition among them of the causal link which can exist between hard work and a higher standard of living. They do not understand that disciplining themselves to an industrial routine is necessary to make available steel mills and cars. They do not see that honesty in observing contracts is prerequisite to greater income and output. They fail to comprehend that saving and training will lead to economic improvement over time.

Success as an entrepreneur is accorded less prestige than success as a military leader, a religious zealot, a civil servant, or a learned scholar. Tolerance of and apathy toward inept, corrupt government prevents the best economic decisions from being made and carried out. Determination by the ruling oligarchy that it shall remain in political and economic power frustrates economic change. Willingness of the popular majority to believe in and follow the demagogic appeals of the latest rabble-rousing politician of expediency provides an atmosphere of insecurity in which good economic decisions are unlikely to be made.

MARKET MECHANISMS AS OBSTACLES TO DEVELOPMENT

In the kind of environment just suggested as typical of underdeveloped countries, it seems unlikely that market mechanisms alone will achieve rapid economic development for these countries. Essentially, market mechanisms consist of permitting individual owners, buyers, and sellers to make economic decisions for themselves and of letting things be as they are or as they will be. In the cases of many underdeveloped countries, this means letting things be as they traditionally have been or letting them be in chaos as they are. This usually will not suffice. The argument against exclusive reliance upon market mechanisms can be given detail as follows.

The Inhibition of Investment

Productive investment induced through market forces is inhibited by several conditions in underdeveloped nations.

Political Insecurity. In many underdeveloped countries the wealthiest portion of the population live considerably above the subsistence minimum and save sizable parts of their incomes. These savings could be spent by them on real capital formation or be loaned to others for the same purpose. In this way the vicious circle of lack of capital and low output might be broken. Unfortunately, the political atmosphere in many of these countries is one of great insecurity. The possibility of revolution or confiscation of capital is quite real. So the savers prefer to buy property outside the country, to purchase land, jewelry, or precious metals within the country, or to invest in quickly saleable merchandise inventories. The corrupt, inept governmental administrators inadvertently encourage the same behavior by the wealthy savers. Consequently, the countries remain without equipment and other real capital and lack economic development.

Lack of Complementary Industries. In order to be profitable to the owners, some types of productive operations, such as factories, require the prior existence of public utilities such as railways, highways, and water, sewage, and electric power facilities. However, these things do not exist, and so investment in factories is not undertaken. The profitable investment in factories may also require the prior existence of a trained labor force, of industries to supply inputs and services, or of a market with buyers who have purchasing power with which to buy the factories' products. Usually one, some, or all of these prerequisites are missing so that there is no investment and no development. Here development by way of market mechanisms is caught up and held back within a vicious circle of lack of complementary industries, each being a prerequisite for the others.[8]

The Inhibition of Enterprise

There may exist among the population of underdeveloped countries individuals with entrepreneurial talents and inclinations. These people may have a sharp sense of what is profitable. Yet the same factors which channel savings and investments into the relatively less productive forms, such as merchandise inventories, land, and foreign property, are likely to direct the entrepreneurial talents into these same lines. Moreover, the entrepreneurs may lack a tradition of honesty in dealings and of a sense of obligation to fulfill contracts. They may aim mainly to devise ways to cheat those with whom they deal. In such cases they are more likely to be an obstacle than an aid to economic development.

The Inhibition of Labor

The reaction of workers on the market for labor may also be a deterrent to economic development. Suppose that as economic development begins, the first increases in real and money wages occur. The reaction of the workers may be to decide that they now need not work as many hours as before the wage increase. They may react in this way because fewer hours of work now provide as much income as before. If they do react in this way, the economic development which made possible the increased wages may grind to a halt for lack of an adequate supply of the right kinds of labor.[9]

This reaction to market forces may be especially likely in countries with a tradition of the extended family. There any extra income earned is likely not to seem worth the extra effort. This is so since the income, but not the effort, must be shared by the worker with so many relatives.

[8] It seems likely that some of the conditions prerequisite for investment in private productive facilities must be provided by governmental action. When prerequisites such as transportation, electric power, and education are lacking, it is usually a government which must create them. Government expenditures to create them are said to constitute either public investment in *social overhead capital* or public provision of an *infrastructure*. Specific discussion of the infrastructure and of social overhead capital appears in Everett E. Hagen, *The Economics of Development* (Rev. ed.; Homewood, Illinois: Richard D. Irwin, Inc., 1975), pp. 170–176. The infrastructure of agriculture is discussed in Clifton R. Wharton, "The Infrastructure for Agricultural Growth," Chapter 4 of Herman M. Southworth and Bruce F. Johnston (eds.), *Agricultural Development and Economic Growth* (Ithaca, New York: Cornell University Press, 1967), pp. 107–146. Additional general discussion of the accumulation and use of real capital can be found in Meier, *op. cit.*, pp. 165–250.

[9] The economic phenomenon in which the amount of labor supplied may decrease when the wage rate rises is called by economists *the backward bending supply curve of labor*. One brief criticism of it occurs in Elkan, *op. cit.*, pp. 37–39. The supply curve of labor is probably more likely to be backward bending when there are few additional attractive goods available to be purchased by workers than when many such goods are available.

In other cases the market may encourage partially inappropriate decisions with regard to the purchase by a worker of training or exertion of effort to improve skills. The market may fail to induce the worker to take into account all the benefits which occur from such training and effort. The market inducement to the worker, of course, occurs mainly in the form of higher income which can be earned through increased training or improved productive ability. The worker makes the decision by weighing the improvement's cost against the higher income to be earned. In some instances the worker rationally decides against undertaking the training when, from society's viewpoint, the decision should be in favor of the training. The worker's decision is socially inappropriate because there are benefits which accrue to society from the training in addition to and apart from the direct benefits of greater output and higher income which occurs to the worker.

The additional social benefits include the better citizen the worker is likely to be because of the training. They also include the knowledge that associates absorb, gratis, from the worker because of that trained status. There is, in addition, the increased probability that through additional training the worker will discover production improvements for which there is no personal compensation but which, nevertheless, raise the productive capacity of the society of which the worker is a part.

Reliance exclusively upon market forces to determine the amounts of training, education, and other improvements in labor quality produces too little of these. This may be a crucially important defect of the market system for underdeveloped countries.

SUCCESSES IN DEVELOPMENT

The latter portions of this chapter have dwelt upon possible weaknesses of market mechanisms as devices for achieving economic development. One should keep in mind, however, that market mechanisms can, in combination with the right government policies, sometimes be positive forces in promoting economic development. Indeed, there are numerous instances in which market mechanisms have obviously contributed to economic development in underdeveloped countries. Some of the empirical evidence of these instances is summarized in this section.

Mexico

Mexico has achieved considerable economic progress in recent decades. Real gross national product, both per capita and in total, has risen at high rates. This achievement has occurred while the Mexican economic system has consisted of a unique and interesting combination of market and governmental arrangements.

Over ninety percent of all production in Mexico is conducted by privately owned and operated enterprises. Much of the new investment is financed from privately generated savings channeled through private financial institutions. Private foreign investment has been important in promoting growth. Much of the agricultural sector is organized as private commercial farms. The transactions conducted by all of these economic units are basically motivated by the desire for maximizing profits and income, in response to market forces. Rewards in income and wealth have gone in great measure to those who act efficiently in response to market opportunities. For the most part, comprehensive detailed central planning of the economy by the government has been absent.

On the other hand, the Mexican government has exercised pervasive influence in the economy. It has not hesitated to take over the ownership and control of a few entire industries such as petroleum production. It has established government enterprises in competition with private ones in the same industry, such as in the case of steel production. It has exercised considerable control over access to financial credit through government financial institutions and through regulation of private financial firms. It has constructed social overhead facilities, such as ports and roads, with a clear intention of influencing the geographical location and other characteristics of new private real investment. It has controlled access to imported goods and to foreign sources of capital.

It is impossible to indicate exactly the extent to which Mexico owes its economic development to private market forces as opposed to governmental direction. What does seem clear is that Mexico's combination of the two has at least not impeded fairly successful economic development. The particular combination of the two probably is an effective one and has been an important force in Mexico's economic success.[10]

Underdeveloped Countries as a Group

All underdeveloped countries are like Mexico in the sense that they combine market arrangements with governmental policy. Economic growth results from both. A crucial question is to what extent the market arrangements rather than the governmental policies are the cause of growth. No very accurate answer to the question can be given. However, one respected scholar of economic development has made relevant estimates.

Angus Maddison studied the growth rates in 22 underdeveloped countries for the period 1950–1965. He concluded that on the average "autonomous growth influences" accounted for almost two-thirds of the growth while governmental policy accounted for the remaining one-third. Autonomous growth influences refer mostly to market forces but also include some economic aid from foreign governments.

[10] A basic long-run description and assessment of the Mexican economic system can be found in Raymond Vernon, *The Dilemma of Mexico's Development* (Cambridge, Mass.: Harvard University Press, 1963). A more recent brief summary of Mexico's economic status is Calvin P. Blair, "Mexico in the World Economy," *Current History*, Vol. 66, No. 393 (May, 1974), pp. 217 ff.

Maddison's study cannot be regarded as decisive, but it does suggest that market mechanisms have played an important role in achieving development in underdeveloped countries in recent decades. Some of the countries where market forces seem to have been the cause of much growth in real gross national product in the period 1950–1965 are Israel, Venezuela, Taiwan, Greece, and South Korea. Some of the countries where market forces were probably very important as causes of growth, *relative to* government policies as causes of growth, are Venezuela, Israel, Argentina, and Chile.

On the other hand, Maddison's study indicated that countries where government policy seemed to have been a cause of much growth are Yugoslavia, Spain, Taiwan, and Thailand. Countries where government policies were unusually important as causes of growth, *relative to* market forces as causes of growth, are Yugoslavia, Peru, Sri Lanka, and Thailand.[11]

SUMMARY

A majority of the world's people live in underdeveloped countries where per capita output and income are very low. The people in these countries aspire to be affluent. Perhaps they will become so by following a process of development similar to that already experienced by Western nations. In the West, market forces played a significant role in development. These forces may be equally useful for the underdeveloped countries. The profit motive may encourage investment and innovation, for example, and the desire for economic self-improvement among individuals may induce them to work hard and to make decisions which cause themselves and their countries to advance economically.

However, there are many obstacles to development for today's poorer countries. Inadequate natural resources, too little capital, overpopulation, backward attitudes, and inefficient governments all interact to constitute a self-perpetuating set of mutually reenforcing impediments to economic growth. In such a set of circumstances, market arrangements may work poorly as a mechanism for development. Investment may be inhibited or induced to take perverse forms because of political insecurity. Entrepreneurial effort may not be forthcoming because little social prestige is attached to economic success. Social institutions such as the extended family may stifle market incentives to work.

Market mechanisms have been considerably less than a perfect means for achieving economic development for poor countries. This evidence of the inadequacy of market mechanisms alone to achieve economic goals can be added to similar evidence drawn from the experience of the United States, Britain, and the other advanced nations. The basis can thus be provided for a generalized exposition of the need for market mechanisms to be supplemented and partially replaced by other arrangements. Such an exposition is the subject of the next chapter.

[11] Angus Maddison, *Economic Progress and Policy in Developing Countries* (New York: W. W. Norton & Co., Inc., 1971).

QUESTIONS

1. Upon what basis is a country classified as underdeveloped?
2. What are the typical economic features of underdevelopment?
3. What is the typical class structure of most underdeveloped countries?
4. What kinds of feelings exist among many underdeveloped peoples toward Westerners? Why do these feelings exist?
5. What is the "revolution in rising expectations"?
6. What is Rostow's theory of the stages of economic growth?
7. In Rostow's theory, what role do market forces play in each stage?
8. In traditional societies, what is the typical attitude toward family size? Why does this attitude exist? How can market forces induce a beneficial change in this attitude as economic development occurs?
9. What do you regard as the paramount and overwhelming obstacle to economic development in underdeveloped countries? Why?
10. What is the vicious circle of small real capital and low income in underdeveloped countries?
11. When and how are more people a detriment rather than a benefit in achieving economic development?
12. What is the vicious circle of low labor quality and low income?
13. What are some examples of social customs which block economic development? What are some examples of values or attitudes which block economic development?
14. How can market mechanisms, in combination with other circumstances, impede investment, enterprise, and labor effort in underdeveloped countries?

RECOMMENDED READINGS

Bhagwati, Jagdish. *The Economics of Underdeveloped Countries.* New York: McGraw-Hill Book Company, 1966.

Dalton, George (ed.). *Economic Development and Social Change: The Modernization of Village Communities.* Garden City, N.Y.: The Natural History Press, 1971.

————. *Economic Systems and Society: Capitalism, Communism, and the Third World.* Baltimore: Penguin Books Inc., 1974, Chapter 7.

De Gregori, Thomas R., and Oriol Pi-Sunyer. *Economic Development: The Cultural Context.* New York: John Wiley & Sons, Inc., 1969.

Elkan, Walter. *An Introduction to Development Economics.* Baltimore: Penguin Books Inc., 1973.

Hauser, Philip M. (ed.). *The Population Dilemma,* 2d ed. Englewood Cliffs, N.J.: Prentice-Hall, Inc., 1970.

Heilbroner, Robert L. *The Great Ascent: The Struggle for Economic Development in Our Time.* New York: Harper & Row Publishers, 1963.

Higgins, Benjamin. *Economic Development: Principles, Problems, and Policies,* rev. ed. New York: W. W. Norton & Company, Inc., 1968.

Kindleberger, Charles P. *Economic Development,* 2d ed. New York: McGraw-Hill Book Company, Inc., 1965.

Lewis, W. Arthur. *The Theory of Economic Development.* Homewood, Ill.: Richard D. Irwin, Inc., 1955.

Maddison, Angus. *Economic Progress and Policy in Developing Countries.* New
    York: W. W. Norton & Company, Inc., 1971.
Meier, Gerald M. *The International Economics of Development: Theory and Policy.*
    New York: Harper & Row Publishers, 1968.
————. *Leading Issues in Economic Development: Studies in International Poverty,*
    2d ed. New York: Oxford University Press, Inc., 1970.
Morgan, Theodore, and George W. Betz (eds.). *Economic Development: Readings in
    Theory and Practice.* Belmont, Calif.: Wadsworth Publishing Co., Inc., 1970.
Myint, Hla. *The Economics of the Developing Countries.* Atlantic Highlands, N.J.:
    Humanities Press, Inc., 1973.
Myrdal, Gunnar. *The Challenge of World Poverty: A World Anti-Poverty Program in
    Outline.* New York: Random House, Inc., 1971.
Novack, David E., and Robert Lekachman (eds.). *Development and Society: The
    Dynamics of Economic Change.* New York: St. Martin's Press, Inc., 1964.
Ranis, Gustav (ed.). *The United States and the Developing Economies,* rev. ed. New
    York: W. W. Norton & Company, Inc., 1973.
Rostow, Walt Whitman. *The Stages of Economic Growth: A Non-Communist Mani-
    festo,* 2d ed. New York: Cambridge University Press, 1971.
Schiavo-Campo, Salvatore, and Hans W. Singer. *Perspectives of Economic De-
    velopment.* Boston: Houghton Mifflin Company, 1970.

6

Market Mechanisms, Economic Problems, and the Need for Governmental Policy

INTRODUCTION

The United States, Britain, and other countries, primarily those of European culture, have had several centuries of experience with market arrangements. More recently the underdeveloped nations have had such experience, too. All this experience provides the empirical basis for generalizations about the kinds of problems which seem likely to arise in an economy heavily reliant upon market mechanisms. Such generalizations are the essence of this chapter.

It is useful to divide these generalizations into two groups. The first group involves the prerequisite conditions within which market mechanisms operate most effectively. The absence of these conditions usually necessitates governmental action to create them. The second group involves the problems which seem to arise as results of the effective operation of market forces and which usually require governmental actions as correctives for those results.

This chapter deals with the prerequisites and the problems. Most of the remaining chapters deal with the kinds of corrective governmental actions which have been tried in various countries. The successes and failures of these actions and the new problems which these actions have in turn created are also treated in later chapters. In the real world it is not always possible to know whether a given problem arises from the operation of market forces or from governmental actions. However, in this chapter the emphasis is placed upon market forces as possible sources of trouble. In later chapters governmental policies are subjected to similar analysis.

PREREQUISITES OF A MARKET SYSTEM

In order to work well, a market system requires that the people of the society in which it is to operate have certain personal qualities, including entrepreneurship. A minimum degree of political stability must exist, and it is necessary for the government to provide a framework of law and order within which the market can operate. There should be at least some degree of competition and of price flexibility. In general, a market system works well if the cultural heritage is appropriate for market forces.

Personal Qualities

Market mechanisms widely diffuse among individuals the power to make economic decisions. It is therefore important that the individuals be able to make good decisions. To do so, they must be informed, prudent, honest, and willing to adjust to changing conditions.

Knowledgeableness. Lack of information has been a basic source of the economic troubles in societies relying heavily on market mechanisms. The Great Depression occurred in the United States in the 1930s partly because the managers of individual American firms had been poorly informed of prospective demand for their products and of each other's expansion activities. Once the depression began, these business people had no accurate information about how long it might last or how deep it might become. This uncertainty probably caused the depression to be deeper and longer than it otherwise would have been.

Lack of information contributes to the monopoly problem, too. Both consumers and purchasers of inputs for businesses are open to exploitation by monopolistic sellers because of lack of knowledge. The buyers may lack knowledge of other sellers who may exist, of the existence of other products which may serve as close substitutes, or of techniques which would make the use of such substitutes possible. Resource owners, such as 20th century American farmers or 19th century British factory workers, experience difficulties partly because they are poorly informed of alternative uses for their land, labor, or capital. Millions of underdeveloped people are caught in their poverty partly because they are not informed of new productive techniques which they might employ, new skills which they might acquire, and new products which they might produce.

Just as individuals need to be informed if they are to function efficiently within a market system, they must also be able to use the information prudently on their own behalf. They must be able to select from all the information available that which is relevant for their situation. They need to understand the causal relationships between their actions and the consequences. Business people may expand their production facilities when they already are informed of a prospective decline in the demand for their product. Workers may move into a region which they already know is one of surplus labor supply. Consumers may choose to purchase a durable appliance even though they realize it is technically obsolete. All these people create problems for themselves and others.

Honesty. To a minimum degree at least, commercial honesty seems also to be a requisite for a populace relying upon market mechanisms. Suppose that an overriding propensity existed among a people to strive to cheat each other in exchanges. This propensity would probably divert so much effort away from making good decisions that poor results would follow. The employer would spend so much time and effort checking on the suspicious activities of thieving employees that there would exist little opportunity to work out new, more efficient, productive arrangements. The consumer would become so wary of deceitful sellers that exchange and specialization would tend to decline. Considerable resources of the society might have to be devoted to police activities. Market mechanisms, which depend upon the exercise of economic decision-making power by many individuals, become ineffective when that power is used primarily and consciously to deceive.

Adaptability. Individual willingness to adjust to changing conditions is necessary for the effective working of a market system. A great many of the historical difficulties of market-oriented societies seem to have occurred partly because of the people's unwillingness to adjust. Some American farmers have been unwilling to adapt to the relative decline of agriculture. They have helped to create the problem of rural poverty by their reluctance to move off the farms. The British rural population at the time of the Enclosures acted in the same way. Business firms, too, have disliked having to adjust to changing forces of the competitive market and have striven for monopolistic arrangements by which to insulate themselves. Workers have refused to accept lower wages when declining demand for or increasing supply of their type of labor called for such a decline. Unemployment for some of them has resulted.

Entrepreneurship

To work at their best, market mechanisms require that some of the market participants possess at least a minimum degree of entrepreneurial inclination and ability. An *entrepreneur* is one who is willing and able to supervise production, to organize workers, materials, and machinery to produce a product, and to strive to achieve efficiency in production. An entrepreneur is eager to experiment with new techniques to increase efficiency and to risk loss for the sake of such experimentation.

Entrepreneurs must be persons of some imagination in order to envision the possibility of improvement in the production of goods and services. They must be leaders so that they can obtain the cooperation of workers and property owners. They must believe that it is important to achieve excellent performance in production. They must be venturesome so that they take the initiative in introducing new techniques of production. Lest it be thought that in order to be an entrepreneur a person must possess all the admirable human qualities and none of the despicable ones, it should be noted that a person might be ruthless, tyrannical, intolerant, egotistical, and miserly and still be a good entrepreneur.

Entrepreneurs are essential to a market system. Achievement of productive efficiency and economic growth to provide a high and rising average level of living for the population of a market system depends upon their presence. It is they who make consumer sovereignty work by discovering what consumers want and by producing it. It is they who provide the opportunities for the efficient employment of each unit of land, labor, and capital. It is they who diligently seek ways to increase the output size without increasing the volume of resources used. It is they who provide the opportunities for the efficient employment of each unit of land, labor, and capital. It is they who break constraining traditions with the result that there emerge new products, new ways of producing old products, new sources of natural resources, and new ways of conveying products to users.

Political Conditions

A market system frequently is regarded as the antithesis of a governmentally directed economy. Although in a market system the government does not assume total directive activity, it is impossible to conceive of a market system's working well in the complete absence of an effective government. Without government there is anarchy, and a market system could not function within anarchy.

Therefore, it is concluded that a stable government is necessary to supply a framework of law and order within which a market system works. Government, with its nonmarket power to punish offenders, provides a means of protecting property from destruction or seizure. As a result, owners have an incentive to accumulate and productively use their property, as their preferences and market forces direct. Government enforces agreements or contracts between private transactors in markets and thereby encourages market transactions to take place. Government provides a population with the means of preventing hostile incursions by foreign peoples. Thus it permits market transactions to continue uninterrupted.

When governments become so weak that they cease to perform these requisite functions, market systems become less effective. In early Medieval Europe, because there was no effective central government, a market system could not have existed as an important coordinator of intermanorial economic affairs. Today in some underdeveloped countries with weak and unstable governments, market systems have failed to develop or have disintegrated and produced perverse results.

Competition and Price Flexibility

There are a number of more technical prerequisites necessary for a market system to work well. One of these is effective competition, which was discussed in Chapter 3. Another is price flexibility.

For a market system to work well and to provide for adjustments to changing conditions, it is necessary that the prices of specific goods, services, and resources be able to rise and fall. Changes in these prices are the means by which independent consumers, producers, and resource owners are induced to make adjustments beneficial to others.

Product Price Changes. Thus, if consumer preferences change in favor of some good, its price rises as a result, and the higher price induces producers to supply more of the good. Sometimes a price is not permitted to rise because there are legal *price ceilings*. In other cases political pressure is brought to bear upon the suppliers not to raise a price. There may also be social and moral pressure against price increases. In these instances the inducement to the producers to increase the quantity supplied is reduced or eliminated, and consumer sovereignty is frustrated.

For example, in a large city, increased population or increased incomes may lead people to desire more apartments. However, apartment rent rates may be prevented from rising by city or state law. Then market mechanisms will be prevented from responding to the changing consumer needs. The number of apartments being built will not rise because the return to capitalists on their property as apartments is not allowed to increase.

Consider another example. Suppose there is an increased demand for copper. Suppose presidential pressure is used to prevent the copper companies from charging a higher price. Then these companies are discouraged from increasing copper production to match increased demand.

Assume that there is a bad harvest of wheat but prevailing morality prescribes no more than a just price for wheat, as it did during the Middle Ages in Europe. Then a price higher than that which normally or customarily prevails may not be charged. Storers of wheat will not be as strongly induced to dishoard their wheat supplies to satisfy the shortage as they would be if the price were permitted to rise.

Resource Price Changes. Changes, including decreases, in the prices of resources are often necessary if a market system is to work well. If a technological innovation reduces the demand for a given type of labor, a fall in the relevant wage rate is called for. Such a fall would encourage employers to reemploy some of the labor. They would substitute it for other factors, and they would use it to produce more of the product. More of the product could now be sold because the labor costs of production would be lower. Lower production costs would permit lower prices for the product, increasing the quantity demanded of the product.

A decrease in the wage rate would also encourage some of the workers to cease to offer the skill for sale and to offer themselves, instead, in other occupations. However, the power of labor unions, the humanitarianism of employers, or minimum wage legislation may prevent the wage rate from falling. Then those thrown out of work by the technological innovation are likely to remain jobless and constitute an unemployment problem.

Flexible wages and prices are necessary prerequisites for markets to work well.

The Cultural Heritage

There have been many societies in which the prerequisites discussed above were absent. Therefore, it must be conceded that heavy reliance upon market mechanisms cannot be a universal prescription for all societies, at all times, in all places. The recent difficulties of the underdeveloped countries suggest as much. There exists no ubiquitous human nature such that, if just allowed to do so, all persons will always pursue profits, income, and satisfaction, and will always benefit each other in the process. The pursuit of profits, income, and satisfaction is learned behavior, and it is not innately present in humans. It is acquired by some from their environments when those environments are appropriate. It is not acquired by others at all. It is socially beneficial only when the environment is appropriate, and the environment is not always appropriate.

Values and Behavior Patterns. *The environment* in this context refers primarily to the social traditions which make up the cultural heritage of the people of a society. There are social traditions in the nature of mental attitudes, philosophical values, or moral principles which are possessed by the people of a society. These they pass on from one generation to the next, and, according to these values, they make decisions or choices which result in their behavior in one way or another. Other social traditions are in the nature of behavior patterns themselves, patterns common to most or all of the people of a society. The values help to determine the behavior patterns, and behavior patterns help to shape the values. An individual who is born into a society learns to accept most of its values and soon learns to repeat its behavior patterns.

Uncertainty About Basic Causes. What causes the cultural heritage of one society to contain most of the prerequisites of a successful market system and that of another to contain few of these prerequisites? Economists generally do not know and are not particularly equipped to discover the answer. Such matters would seem most appropriately to lie within the provinces of sociologists, historians, cultural anthropologists, and social psychologists. These specialists have not thus far been able to provide adequate explanations.[1] It is really not known, for example, why one nation has political revolutions frequently while another has none. Consequently, there remains ignorance about the deeper determinants of the suitability of a market system for a society. There is, however, more knowledge about the immediate requisite social conditions for the proper working of a market system. In other words, it is not possible deliberately to shape a society so that a market system will work well for it. Nevertheless, it is possible to predict with some accuracy whether, for any given society, a market system has a good immediate chance of working well for it.

COMMON PROBLEMS UNDER MARKET SYSTEMS

The cultural heritage of some societies seems to contain all or most of the necessary requisites for the effective operation of a market system. Even for

---

[1] One famous example of an attempt by a psychologist to discern the origins of entrepreneurial spirit is David C. McClelland, *The Achieving Society* (New York: The Free Press, 1967). See also, as a kind of sequel, David C. McClelland and David G. Winter, *Motivating Economic Achievement* (New York: The Free Press, 1971).

these societies, excessive reliance upon the market, to the exclusion of tradition, command, and altruism, seems to produce some undesirable results.[2] Each of these troublesome results will be taken up in turn in the following sections.

Unequal Distribution of Income and Wealth

A market system tends to distribute income among the participating households in proportion to their contribution to production. Large shares in the national income go to those persons who work hard, who own resources in great demand or in small supply, who are discerning enough to make wise choices for themselves, and who are willing to be mobile in the use of their resources. Small shares go to those who have opposite traits. It is almost a certainty that the distribution of these attributes among the population will be such as to cause income to be distributed unequally to households.

The Argument That Inequality in Incomes Is Unjust. If it is conceded that a market system is likely to distribute incomes unequally, there are some people who would judge the inequality to be unjustified. Their arguments can be summarized as follows.

First, they argue that at least some of those people who work hard enjoy work. Consequently, they should not be rewarded with large incomes just for working hard.

They also assert that, in many cases, those who happen to own the scarcest and highest paying resources may have come into the ownership through no effort or choice of their own. For example, they may have inherited the resources they own. Therefore, they do not deserve large rewards for such ownership since the income which the market system accords them is a matter of chance.

Some who adjudge income inequality to be unjust contend that persons who own large quantities of property do not necessarily merit large incomes simply for allowing that property to be used in production. They may passively allow compound interest and, in the case of land, increased population to provide them with ever enlarging wealth and income.

Critics of the way in which the market system distributes income also argue that persons who make wise choices for themselves regarding such matters as what jobs to take or what use to make of their property are not necessarily meritorious. Some of them simply were lucky to be born in a society that contained a cultural heritage of wisdom. Their parents transmitted great intelligence to them genetically and provided a home environment in which a process of wise decision making was constantly carried on. The process became deeply etched into the impressionable minds of the children as a behavior pattern to follow.

[2] General surveys of the strengths and weaknesses of a market system appear in these: Gregory Grossman, *Economic Systems* (Englewood Cliffs, N.J.: Prentice-Hall, Inc., 1967), pp. 49–55; Heinz Köhler, *Welfare and Planning: An Analysis of Capitalism Versus Socialism* (New York: John Wiley & Sons, Inc., 1966), Chapter 5; William N. Loucks and William G. Whitney, *Comparative Economic Systems* (9th ed.; New York: Harper & Row, Publishers, 1973); and Gary M. Pickersgill and Joyce E. Pickersgill, *Contemporary Economic Systems: A Comparative View* (Englewood Cliffs, N.J.: Prentice-Hall, Inc., 1974).

Finally, those who contend that unequal income distribution is unjust say that persons who are willing to shift their resources from one use to another derive adequate satisfaction from the spirit of adventure which is associated with such change. Additional reward for such mobility in the form of large incomes is unwarranted.

Most people living in market system countries do not feel that unequal distribution of income is necessarily unjust. Many feel that absolute equality of income is undesirable since this could only be attained by the suppression of individual freedoms which would result in the destruction of existing social and legal institutions.

The Interaction of Wealth and Income. Inequality of income interacts with and mutually reinforces inequality of wealth. Those with large incomes have a greater ability to save part of their income and accumulate it in the form of wealth or property than do those with small incomes. A family with a low income will probably expend its entire income in essential consumption goods. A family with a high income has extra income after expenditures on essentials; this extra income may be saved.

A family which possesses property or wealth derives more income than just its labor income in wages and salaries. It receives in addition rent, dividends, interest, and profits. It tends, therefore, to be a family with a high income.

A family with a large income and with considerable wealth can afford to take risky ventures in choosing its occupations and in the use of its wealth. If these ventures are successful, they will augment the wealth and income further. A poor family is usually without a cushion of wealth or *discretionary* income on which to rely in case a risky venture fails. That family cannot undertake the risky venture for fear of jeopardizing income which is essential to them.

So it is that in a market system inequality of wealth and income may be cumulatively self-reinforcing.[3]

Unemployment

The spectre of large numbers of people who are capable and desirous of working but who are unable to find a job has haunted market economies for two centuries. The severity of the problem has varied with time. During the Great Depression of the 1930s, it was the foremost problem in the United States, but it disappeared during World War II. There is no complete agreement about why unemployment occurs in a market system, but modern economic analysis emphasizes two important types of unemployment, classified by cause. These are unemployment caused by too little total spending in the economy and structural unemployment.

[3] Discussions of economic inequality in a market economy are included in: George N. Halm, *Economic Systems: A Comparative Analysis* (3d ed.; New York: Holt, Rinehart & Winston, Inc., 1968), Chapter 5; and Carl Landauer, *Contemporary Economic Systems: A Comparative Analysis* (Philadelphia: J. B. Lippincott Co., 1964), Chapter 7.

Unemployment Caused by Too Little Total Spending. The theory of unemployment caused by too little total spending was developed primarily by the foremost economist of the 20th century thus far, John Maynard Keynes. This Englishman, writing in his *General Theory of Employment, Interest, and Money* [4] in the 1930s, sought to explain the Great Depression.

Keynesian Determinants of Employment. According to Keynes the volume of employment in the economy is determined by the volume of production of goods and services by business. This volume of production in turn depends upon the volume of sales of goods and services by business, in other words, upon how much businesses are able to sell. Sales depend upon how much spending is being done to buy the products. If spending is large, employment will be large, but if spending is small, there will be much unemployment.

Total spending to buy final products is called *gross national product spending.* GNP spending has three main components. (1) There is *consumer spending.* This is spending by households to buy newly produced consumer goods and services. (2) There is *business investment spending.* This is spending by businesses to buy newly produced capital goods in the forms of plant, equipment, and additional inventories. (3) There is *government spending* for newly produced goods and services. When these three types of spending are too small in total, unemployment will occur.

Keynesian Determinants of Spending. What determines these three types of spending? Consumer spending is determined mainly by two variables. One is the size of consumer income. This is directly and closely related to the size of total spending or the GNP. The other is the willingness of consumers to spend their income. Business investment spending is determined by business expectations regarding the profitability in the future of additional plant, equipment, and inventories created now. Such expectations are influenced by the interest rates prevailing on funds borrowed to undertake this investment spending, by the extent of idle plant and equipment, and by the current size of GNP and sales of products. Government spending is determined by the need for publicly provided goods and services and by the felt need to minimize government deficits and debt.

There are a number of reasons why GNP spending may be too low and why unemployment caused by too little total spending may thus exist. Consumers may be too unwilling to spend out of their incomes. Business expectations regarding the future profitability of additional plant, equipment, and inventory may be too low. The interest rate may be too high. The amount

---

[4] John Maynard Keynes, *The General Theory of Employment, Interest, and Money* (New York: Harcourt, Brace & World, Inc., 1936). This is a classic but very difficult work, and one might best use one of the standard guides to it: Dudley Dillard, *The Economics of John Maynard Keynes: The Theory of a Monetary Economy* (Englewood Cliffs, N.J.: Prentice-Hall, Inc., 1948); Alvin H. Hansen, *A Guide to Keynes* (New York: McGraw-Hill Book Company, 1953). Keynes and his ideas are presented in a more elementary and entertaining style in Robert L. Heilbroner, *The Worldly Philosophers: The Lives, Times, and Ideas of the Great Economic Thinkers* (4th ed.; New York: Simon & Schuster, Inc., 1972), Chapter 9.

of idle equipment may be too great. Product sales may be too low. The willingness of governments to engage in *deficit spending* may be too small. That is, governments may be too unwilling to have their own spending exceed tax receipts.

This is Keynes' explanation for unemployment. It is still largely accepted today among economists as an explanation for one of the two important types of unemployment in a market system.

Structural Unemployment. The second kind of unemployment is structural unemployment. It came to be the center of economists' attention in the United States in the late 1950s and early 1960s.[5] *Structural unemployment* is unemployment caused by changes in the structure of the labor market. These are changes in the demands and supplies of various specific types of labor. Adjustment to these changes is slow and imperfect.

Changes in Demand. Structural changes may originate on the demand side of the labor market. For example, there may be a shift in consumers' preferences from coal as a residential heating fuel to natural gas. There will then be a decrease in the demand for the labor of coal miners. A delayed and incomplete transfer of enough workers from mining to other occupations may then cause unemployment for some of the miners. As another example, geographical shifts of economic activity may decrease the demand for labor in the locality which the activity is leaving. This was the case during much of the last century as the American textile industry shifted from New England to the South. New England textile workers were, for a time, structurally unemployed. If a technological advance such as automation occurs, the new methods may decrease the demand for certain types of workers, who may then become unemployed. If it becomes the practice for employers to provide large pensions to their employees, the demand for older workers may decrease since they involve large pension costs relative to the length of time worked. Older workers may then experience unemployment.

Changes in Supply. Structural changes may also originate on the supply side of the labor market. One cause might be a large increase in the birth rate, such as occurred in the United States in the 1940s. Fifteen or twenty years later there will be an increase in the supply of teenage labor, some of which may go unemployed. Another cause might be an increase in the average length of life so that the supply of labor from older people increases. Then some of these people may go unemployed because the quantity of labor demanded of them fails to increase rapidly enough to employ all of them.

The Possibility of Unemployment in a Market System. Is a market system likely to feature unemployment? The answer appears to be yes, at least sometimes. There appears to be no automatic mechanism to assure that total spending will always be sufficient to avoid unemployment caused by too little total

---

[5] One good discussion of structural unemployment occurs in this governmental publication: *Economic Report of the President: January, 1964* (Washington: U.S. Government Printing Office, 1964), pp. 166–183.

spending. Suppose that consumers wish to save more and spend less. Apparently there is no market force which will assure that business investment spending will increase enough to offset the decreased consumer spending and thereby avoid unemployment.

It was once thought that decreases in the interest rate and in the general level of money wages would, in such a case, keep total spending adequate to avoid unemployment. However, now most economists agree that changes in interest rates have rather little influence on the volume of investment spending. Changes in interest rates are too weak to increase investment spending sufficiently to offset decreases in consumer spending. Furthermore, it is now recognized that decreases in wage rates are likely to have as many effects which reduce employment as they have which increase it. Finally, there is a strong resistance to decreases in money wages, in any case.

History also suggests that structural unemployment may be rather common in a market system. Ignorance of employment opportunities, unwillingness to make adjustments in occupations or location, and failure to realize or admit that any alternatives to previous jobs exist seem sometimes to characterize workers thrown out of work by change. Sometimes, too, employers appear to be unable to discover ways of attracting, retraining, and utilizing unemployed workers.

Inflation and Deflation

Inflation is an increase in the average prices of goods and services, a rise in the general level of prices.[6] *Deflation* is a fall in the general level of prices. Both are regarded as serious socio-economic problems because both have undesirable consequences.

Redistribution of Income and Wealth Through Inflation. Inflation tends to hurt those people who receive fixed money incomes. Examples are pensioners, social security recipients, earners of interest income, and civil servants. These people are hurt because during inflation the prices of the goods and services they buy tend to rise faster than their money incomes. Thus the real purchasing power of their incomes decreases; i.e., their real incomes decline.

Inflation also tends to hurt those who are owners of fixed price assets, such as bonds, savings accounts, and demand deposits at banks. The prices of these assets remain the same while the prices of other goods and services rise. In this way the real purchasing power and the real wealth of the owners of these assets decline.

Inflation is, of course, advantageous to some groups of people. During inflation the real burden of debt declines so that debtors have an easier task of repaying their debts. Owners of some businesses may find the prices of their products rising faster than their costs of doing business so that their profits grow.

---

[6] Two useful volumes on inflation are George Leland Bach, *The New Inflation: Causes, Effects, Cures* (Englewood Cliffs, N.J.: Prentice-Hall, Inc., 1973); and Robert Lekachman, *Inflation: The Permanent Problem of Boom and Bust* (New York: Random House, 1973).

Since inflation harms some people and helps others, one might assert that the net effect is not undesirable because the harm is offset by the help. However, this is probably an unwarranted conclusion for two reasons. First, the redistribution of income, wealth, and advantage from those who are hurt to those who are helped is not judged as just by many. Those who are hurt do not particularly deserve to be hurt nor do those who are helped deserve the help. Second, inflation may have other effects which are harmful to all of society.

Other Disadvantages of Inflation. What are these other harmful effects of inflation? First, inflation diverts the attention of entrepreneurs from the attainment of efficiency in production to the attainment of speculative gains from price increases. Society depends upon productive efficiency for a high level of living. Society therefore suffers as business managers and others become absorbed in the speculative purchase and sale of real estate, shares of corporate stock, and inventories of goods from which extraordinary gains can be made in a time of inflation.

Second, prices of various goods and services rise at different rates during inflation, and prices cease to be as good guides to production and consumption decisions as they should be. Consumers make fewer wise decisions for themselves when confronted by a crazy quilt of rising prices. Business people become confused as to what the truly lowest cost production choices are.

Third, inflation may cause social unrest. People look upon their wage and salary increases as long delayed, highly justified, richly deserved, and finally received recognition of their true merit. At the same time, they resent increases in the prices of things they must buy as unjustified exploitation. Of course, both the wage and salary increases and the price increases are really parts of a single inflationary process, but people do not realize this. Consequently, they become dissatisfied.

Finally, inflation of moderate amounts might be acceptable because it involves only moderate disadvantages. However, it can be argued that moderate inflation tends to give way to and to produce inflation of quite immoderate intensity with great disadvantages. If prices rise slowly for a time, people may begin to expect them to continue to rise. These people will then accelerate their purchases before prices rise further. This very acceleration will constitute increased demand, which will drive prices up further and faster.

Deflation. Deflation has analogous disadvantages. An unjustified redistribution of income, wealth, and advantage may occur with deflation. Consumption and production decisions are likely to be disturbed in the confusion of differentially falling sets of prices. Social unrest is likely. Particularly, deflation is likely to be accompanied by unemployment since purchases of products are likely to be delayed in anticipation of lower prices to come, and lowered purchases and sales induce lower employment.

Market and Nonmarket Causes of Inflation. Inflation and deflation, particularly inflation, have occurred frequently in societies which have relied heavily on a market system. There is, however, substantial evidence that much of these changes in the general price levels have been the result, not of the market system, but of governmental activities of a non-market sort. This is so since the size of the money supply, which is the most important determinant of the general level of prices, has usually been under the control of the government rather than having been left to market forces. This governmental control of the money supply has existed even in those societies otherwise heavily reliant upon markets.

There are, nevertheless, strong logical reasons and some historical evidence that a market system without government control of the money supply would produce undesirable results including inflation and deflation. In a system where any enterprising private person can print up currency, mint coins, or create money in the highly abstract form of book credits, there is strong inducement to do so almost without limit. Such money creation is a very profitable method for paying for real goods purchased by the money creator or for earning interest on loans made with created money.

Such money creation may be limited by several circumstances. Tradition and the attitude of the populace may require that money be based on some real commodity such as gold. If the real commodity is itself limited in amount, so also will be the money. If a political authority decrees a legal limit, then the money will be limited. Fear that the money will decline in purchasing power may limit acceptance of the money. Then its creation may be limited as a result. If none of these conditions is present in sufficient degree, excessive quantities of money are likely to be created. Inflation will be the consequence.

Indeed, it seems likely that several issuers of money will exist in a market system. Each is likely to issue a different kind of money, and the price of each kind is likely to fluctuate in terms of each of the others. A probable consequence is a chaos of prices and price changes. There will be a price of each money in terms of every other, and a price of each good and service in terms of each money. In such circumstances a revulsion against money may occur, and there will be a resort to barter with all its economic disadvantages.

Changes in the Velocity of Money. Even if the quantity of money is fixed in some way, market forces may cause inflation and deflation through changes in the velocity with which money is spent. Suppose that, for some reason, people's expectations change in the direction of higher prices or greater shortages of goods in the future. Then people will begin to spend money faster, and inflation probably will occur. If lower prices or increased supplies of goods are expected, people will spend the existing money more slowly, prices will fall, and deflation will occur.

Recurrent Instability: Business Fluctuations

Experience with market systems suggests that, without nonmarket controls, these systems tend to produce recurrent periods of prosperity alternating with periods of depression. A period of prosperity and the period of depression following it are together called a *business cycle*, or a *business fluctuation*.

"Business fluctuation" is now the preferred term. The word "cycle" connotes a sequence of events quite regularly repeated, whereas each actual historical sequence of prosperity and depression has been unique. The duration, intensity, amplitude, and other characteristics of each fluctuation are peculiar to it.

There are several phases to a typical fluctuation. First there is a period of prosperity or *expansion,* which may last from a few months to several years and which is characterized by increasing employment, incomes, prices, and gross national product. The expansion inevitably ends at a point of time called a *peak, crisis* or *upper turning point.* There follows a period of depression, recession, or *contraction,* which may last from a few months to several years and which is characterized by declining employment, incomes, prices, and GNP. There is something about a contraction which causes it, at a point of time called a *trough* or *lower turning point,* to end and to become reversed, initiating the next expansion phase.

Causes of Business Fluctuations. Business fluctuations are supposed to be self-generating in a market system. One of the most intriguing problems of economics is to explain why this should be so. Why does an expansion continue and intensify for a time? Why must it end? Why should it not continue indefinitely? Why, if it does end, must a contraction, rather than a plateau, follow? What is it about the expansion which necessitates an ensuing contraction? [7]

The modern, generally accepted explanation for business fluctuations in a market system is an eclectic one. It draws upon and weaves together older, monocausal theories into a rather untidy and still incompletely resolved synthesis. It is admitted that forces quite outside the economic system may initiate or end a contraction or an expansion or may modify one already underway. Such forces include a season of good or bad weather and good or bad harvests, a war or war's end, an international diplomatic crisis, a revolution, an election outcome, and an invention or discovery.

Psychological Factors. Psychological factors may play an important and real role in business fluctuations. For example, once an expansion has begun, the higher incomes, employment, profits, and sales may cause both consumers and business people to become optimistic about the economic future. Their optimism causes them to increase both consumer spending and business investment spending. The increased spending stimulates the expansion, causing further optimism, and so on, with behavior and outlook interacting in a mutually reenforcing manner. Similarly, waves of decreased spending and pessimism may cause a contraction to become cumulatively more severe.

---

[7] If one wishes to pursue the subject of business fluctuations in a market economy, one might look at some of the standard texts in that field: Carl A. Dauten and Lloyd M. Valentine, *Business Cycles and Forecasting* (4th ed.; Cincinnati: South-Western Publishing Co., 1974), especially Chapters 2–5 and 10–13; and Maurice M. Lee, *Macroeconomics: Fluctuations, Growth, and Stability* (5th ed.; Homewood, Ill.: Richard D. Irwin, Inc., 1971). A readable survey of business cycle theory appears in Gottfried Haberler, *Prosperity and Depression: A Theoretical Analysis of Cyclical Movements* (4th ed.; Cambridge, Mass.: Harvard University Press, 1964).

The Psychology of Turning Points. It is more difficult to explain on psychological grounds why the turning points occur, but it can be done. For example, suppose that most consumers and business people have in the backs of their minds some notion of normal or average levels of prices, incomes, profits, and employment. Suppose they possess a conviction that large and sustained departures of these economic variables from normal or average levels are unlikely. Imagine that an expansion is progressing with higher and higher prices, incomes, profits, and employment. First a few and then more consumers and business people begin to believe that the expansion will not continue. As a result, they begin to reduce their spending in anticipation of less prosperous times ahead. When the expansion has gone far enough to induce a sufficiently large number of the market participants to believe its end is imminent, total spending will decline, and it will end. An upper turning point will have occurred, and a contraction will have begun. Analogous explanations of the lower turning point can be given.

The Competitive Illusion. Another partially psychological theory of the turning points in a market system has to do with what has been called *the competitive illusion.* Suppose that an expansion is underway so that the demand for the products of most industries is increasing. Suppose that in each of these industries each of the many competing firms begins to enlarge its capacity to produce. Each firm does so through investment spending. Suppose each fails to take into account that its rivals are also undertaking enlargements. To some degree, each firm is expanding to be able to fill the same demand on which each of its rivals is counting. The enlargement process takes time. In the meantime, the investment spending stimulates the expansion. Then, at last, each of the firms completes its enlargement project and begins to produce and put on the market enlarged quantities of the product just at the same time that all of the other unsuspecting firms do. The market for the product is glutted. Losses are incurred. Investment spending is drastically reduced by many firms, all at once. The expansion has ended and the contraction begun.

Analogous errors of excessive change in production capacity will be made by most firms in most industries in the contraction. These errors will be made because of the failure to know of and take into account the similar activities of rival firms.

Differential Rates of Reaction. Differential rates of adjustment to change among various economic magnitudes in a market system may be partially responsible for business fluctuations. For example, suppose that an expansion is just underway. An increased demand for products occurs as a part of the expansion. In combination with market conditions such as flexible prices, the increased demand causes a rise in the prices of products. There is also at the same time likely to be an increase in the demand for labor and other resources, but the prices of these may be prevented from rising for a time by contractual arrangements. Therefore, salary increases must await the expiration of employment contracts. Rental increases must await the expiration of leases. Interest rate increases must await the expiration of loans. In the meantime, the prices of the products businesses sell increase, and the prices of the inputs businesses buy remain the same. Profits, which are the difference between businesses' gross incomes and total costs, increase. The increased profits provide both the inducement and the means for businesses to increase real investment spending. The result is that the expansion is further stimulated.

As the expansion reaches its later stages, however, the prices of labor and other resources do at last begin to rise because the contractual arrangements expire and are renewed on new terms. Business costs rise, and profits are squeezed. The decrease in profits prompts businesses to decrease their investment spending, and this causes total spending to decrease. The decline in total spending constitutes the upper turning point and the beginning of the contraction. During the early stages of the contraction, product prices fall rapidly, but resource prices remain high. Profits decline further or give way to losses. Investment spending is depressed further, and the contraction becomes more severe. Later, however, resource prices fall, allowing an end to the contraction.

General Appraisal. There is worthy of note one aspect which is present in most of the various explanations of business fluctuations in a market economy. The fluctuations occur because the power to make economic decisions is diffused among many independent businesses which are imperfectly informed and coordinated by the market mechanism. The individual businesses have inadequate understanding of what their competitors are doing. They do not fully understand what the aggregate effect of their own decisions, together with those of their competitors, will be. Furthermore, there is no means by which an individual business can commit itself to certain courses of future action on condition that many other firms simultaneously commit themselves. The consequence is that heavy reliance upon a market system is likely to result in fluctuations which are troublesome to virtually all of the market participants.

Economic Insecurity

A market system features instability in the aggregate levels of employment and prices. There are also constant changes in prices, quantities produced and sold, techniques of production, and particular resources used in the production of specific goods and services. These changes produce a feeling of insecurity for the people of the society using the system. *Economic insecurity* is the fear that there will occur in the future changes which are not entirely foreseeable and which will require painful and undesired adjustments.

Causes of Insecurity. These adjustments may be made necessary by a wide variety of events. Most business cycle contractions occur rather unexpectedly. Workers never know when they may suddenly be without work. Similarly, owners never know when their income from profits may suddenly shrink. The timing, duration, and intensity of the expansions of business fluctuations with their accompanying inflation cannot be accurately forecast. Consequently, owners of fixed price assets and recipients of fixed money incomes stand in almost perpetual fear that the real value of their income and wealth may be greatly reduced.

There is always a possibility of the introduction of new technology. A constant threat is thus posed that workers may lose their old jobs, may have to undergo expensive and psychologically distressing retraining and relocation, and then may find that their new jobs and locations are less rewarding both monetarily and psychically than their old ones. Consumer preferences may erratically shift away from some product, whose producers then experience a drastic reduction in the value of machinery which produces the product and into which they as owners have already invested their wealth. An industrial firm may suddenly discover that it would reduce its costs if it relocated elsewhere. It may then actually relocate. The relocation may cause the value of homes in the old location to fall. Those homes may be the only property that some families have.

A new marketing technique, such as a discount house, may be introduced. It may destroy the wealth of a family who owned a traditional department store, which is no longer able to exist. A smoky factory may be established someplace, reducing the value of the residential properties nearby. A worker may suddenly discover that a supervisor, with whom a congenial working relationship has been established, has been replaced by an irascible person under whom little pleasure on the job is possible.

Market Mitigation of Insecurity. It should be pointed out that not all changes create pain and disadvantages. Furthermore, not everyone is troubled by insecurity. There are those venturesome individuals who enjoy the excitement of not knowing what the future has in store for them and who welcome the challenge of adjustment.

It should also be noted that a market system provides some opportunities of self-protection for individuals who dislike having to make unexpected adjustments and who tend to suffer from insecurity. An individual who fears unemployment can, when selecting a job or an occupation, choose those which experience shows are the steadiest and most likely to endure. Someone who is afraid of the loss of income which occurs when unemployment comes can build up savings while employed. A person who fears the possibility that residential property may fall in value may rent a house rather than buy one. One who fears that inflation may wipe out the value of fixed price assets may place personal wealth instead in real estate or common stocks. Someone who is afraid that the ability to earn income may be unexpectedly eliminated through death or illness may buy insurance. A person who dreads a pauperous old age can buy an annuity or take a job with a company which has a program of large pensions. One who fears that all personal wealth will be destroyed in some single catastrophe can make diversified investments. That person can have some real property and some financial, some fixed price assets and some variable, and some in one industry and some in another.

Nevertheless, it must be admitted that some insecurity will remain in a market system. There are some risks that remain uninsurable, and the elimination of one kind of risk often means the introduction of another.

In later chapters various nonmarket governmental techniques are described for coping with insecurity. There it will become clear that reduction of insecurity through government may have disadvantages. Under a governmental program like the American social security system, for example, individual economic freedom is sacrificed and political insecurity may be increased. Perhaps insecurity of one type or another is an inherent part of the human condition.

Inadequate Economic Growth

Economic growth refers to increases through time in either the per capita or the total GNP. Among the chief immediate causes of growth are enlargement of the stock of real capital through the processes of saving and investment, improvement in the quality of the people as workers and entrepreneurs through education and training, and advances in technology. There may be a tendency for a market system to produce a growth rate which is too low.

It is useful to recall the process by which growth is brought about in a market economy. The basic decisions regarding growth are made by individual households and firms. Each of these separate units decides such things as how much to save, how much to invest, how much education to purchase, and how much research and exploration to undertake on the basis of a comparison of the benefits and costs to itself of the activities. If the benefits to itself exceed the costs to itself, the activity is undertaken. If the benefits to itself are less than the costs, the activity is not undertaken.

Saving. For example, consider a family trying to decide whether to save some of its income. What is the principal cost of this saving to the family? It is the sacrifice now of the goods and services which the family could buy and enjoy if it did not save. The principal benefit to the family from saving is the goods and services which the family will be able to buy and enjoy some time in the future, when the savings are finally spent. If the family decides that goods in the present are less satisfying than goods in the future, combined with interest income earned in the meantime, it will save.

In an *ideal* market economy this decision to save should lead to increased economic growth. The money savings are transmitted through financial institutions and loaned to businesses. The businesses use the borrowed funds to purchase the use of resources which have been released by the saving from the production of consumer goods. The businesses now use these resources to create capital goods. The capital goods so created make possible thereafter a larger real GNP.

However, in a *real* market economy the process might work differently. The attempt to save, which constitutes a decrease in spending for consumer goods, may discourage businesses. There may be no increase or perhaps even a decrease in borrowing and the creation of capital goods by businesses. With decreased consumer spending and no increase in business investment spending to create capital goods, unemployment is likely to result.

The unemployment can be a cost of the attempted saving. It is a cost, not to the family making the decision to save, but to society. The family does not take this cost into account in making its decision. There is no reason for it to do so since the unemployment resulting from its own decision is extremely unlikely to affect its own members. However, if many families, acting in this way, decide to save, the consequent unemployment is likely to be quite large. Furthermore, the unemployment and the failure of the capital formation will probably result in a rate of growth lower than appropriate.

Education. Something similar happens when a family determines whether to buy education for its members. In a market economy a family buys the education if the education's cost to the family is less than the education's benefits to the family. The main real cost to the family is the other goods and services whose purchase and use is foregone by the family because it buys the education. The main benefits to the family are the increased income which the education, once received, enables the family to earn and the increased enjoyment of life which the education makes possible for the family. Comparing the costs and benefits, the family makes a decision. In many cases, a family will decide not to buy the education because the cost to it exceeds the benefits to it.

However, in many of these cases, the education should have occurred. There are additional benefits to people other than the family itself when the family is educated. These additional benefits cause the total benefits to exceed the cost of the education. What are these additional benefits which accrue to people other than the family? An educated person is more likely to respect the property of others than an uneducated one. All property owners are benefited when education occurs. An educated person is more likely to make a technological discovery, which increases the real GNP and causes economic growth. An educated person is more likely to vote intelligently and adopt wise views on political issues, all to the benefit of other people.

Education is a major source of economic growth. Inadequate amounts of education could be chosen by people acting in a strictly market framework. Hence, a market system may produce a rate of economic growth which is too small.

Research and Development. A major means of achieving technological progress is research. In a market system each business firm decides for itself the amount of research it will undertake. It does so on the basis of the cost and benefits to itself of the research. The main cost is the expense of undertaking the research. The main benefit is the greater profit from reduced costs, which, through an advantage over competitors, enable the firm's profits to be larger.

However, often when an individual firm's research is successful, it is difficult or impossible to prevent the resulting knowledge from being diffused among rival firms. These rival firms benefit from the expensive research undertaken by the researching firm, whose competitive advantage is then lost. Because of this prospective loss of advantage, many firms do not undertake the research in the first place. The private profits to one firm do not justify the research, even though the benefits to society in the form of economic growth and a higher level of living clearly do justify the research.

A Nonoptimal Commodity Composition of Gross National Product

A market economy, unless modified by at least a little government intervention, may produce relatively too few of some goods and services and relatively too many of others.

External Benefits. The preceding section on economic growth indicated that a market system may produce too few capital goods, too little educational services, and too little research. It may do so because the individual decision makers take into account only the benefits to themselves and ignore benefits to others. When there are *external benefits,* too little of some goods and services may be produced and used.[8]

External Costs in Production. When there are *external costs,* too much of some goods and services may be produced and used. An example is steel. One of the costs external to the steel firms but quite real to society is the pollution of the air and water. This pollution is inherent in the production of steel in a market society with the techniques known in the 20th century.

Suppose a steel firm is deciding whether to establish and operate a steel mill. The firm adds up the expected revenues from selling the product and subtracts therefrom the costs of production, including the cost of labor, raw materials, and machinery and buildings. To the steel producer there is no cost in sending smoke into the air to blacken the drying clothes in neighborhood yards. To it there is no cost in raising the temperature and the noxious chemical content of the local river, even though fish are killed and the potability of water downstream is decreased. These are costs to society, but they are costs which are external to the steel producer. In a market economy without enforceable and established property rights in the air and water, these costs are not taken into account.

If these external costs were taken into account, there would be at least some instances in which the total costs, internal and external, would exceed the benefits. As a result, some of the steel mills would not be established and less steel would be produced. The GNP would then consist of less steel and more of other things. In that sense, a market system may produce relatively too much of some goods, such as steel. The commodity composition of the GNP may then be other than optimal.

---

[8] One of the classics on the effect which the existence of external costs and benefits has in creating imperfections in the results of a market system is William J. Baumol, *Welfare Economics and the Theory of the State* (2d ed.; Cambridge, Mass.: Harvard University Press, 1965). See also Richard L. Carson, *Comparative Economic Systems* (New York: Macmillan Publishing Co., Inc., 1973), Chapter 15.

External Costs in Consumption. For some products the external cost exists in connection with their consumption rather than their production. Liquor is an example. A purchaser and consumer of bourbon decides how much of it to buy and thus helps to determine how much of it will be produced. This consumer makes a decision on the basis of the costs and benefits of the liquor. The costs which are external to the consumer, but very real to others, are ignored. These external costs occur when the consumer shouts loudly at a party so that neighbors cannot sleep or drives drunkenly into a pedestrian. Consequently, more bourbon, relative to some other product, may be produced in a market system than is best.

The case of bourbon is but one example. The reader is invited to consider in this connection the cases of such other products or activities as pornographic literature, violence on television, opium, billboards, redwood lumbering, prostitution, strip mining, and gambling.

Other Causes. There are several reasons other than the existence of external costs and benefits for believing that a strictly market system produces a nonoptimal GNP. Some goods and services seem to be incapable of division so as to be sold to individual buyers on the market. National defense is usually cited as the prime example of such an indivisible good, much needed but not supplied by a market system. Other goods and services require excessively costly arrangements for the market collection of the fees for their use. Even though their benefits are large relative to their costs exclusive of collection fees, little of them would be produced in a market economy. Examples of these goods are highways, sidewalks, and parks.

Unattractive Personal Qualities

Some critics of market systems argue that such systems tend to encourage the development of unattractive personalities and characters for those people who participate in the markets. Their argument, shorn of modifications and expressed in vivid terms, could be stated that to work well, a market system requires people to be adaptable, competitive, and enterprising. It accords wealth and power to those who are most so. However, people who are adaptable can also be said to be rootless, unprincipled, and unsteady. Those who are competitive may be aggressive, hostile, and unscrupulous. Those who are enterprising may be domineering, materialistic, and callous. In a market system it may be, indeed, that the race is to the swiftest. The devil takes the hindmost, and good guys finish last. In a market system, children may arrive at adolescence with certain impressions, never to be altered. They may believe that a person's worth is to be measured by the number of subordinates commanded on the job, the number of bathrooms in a house, or the number and intensity of a person's ulcers. They may believe that if anything is worth striving for, it is money, because almost all else worthwhile and subject to one's control follows from it.

There is no way of proving that a market system produces these qualities among its people to a greater degree than does any feasible alternative system.

Furthermore, there is no scientific way of demonstrating that these qualities are really bad ones. However, the suspicion remains among critics of the market system that both may be the case.[9]

SUMMARY

When the appropriate prerequisites are present, a market system functions at its best. Even then, however, some of the results may be imperfect and necessitate governmental actions as correctives.

In a market system the distribution of income and wealth can become quite unequal and, in the judgment of some persons, inequitable. Unemployment may persist or recur. The general level of prices may rise or fall with harmful results to groups in society and to society as a whole. Business fluctuations may take place. In consequence of this instability and for other reasons, the people may feel economically insecure. Economic growth may be lower than the people really desire. The commodity composition of GNP may be other than optimal. A market system may cause people to acquire unattractive characteristics.

The above description should not be allowed to suggest that a market system produces nothing but undesirable results. Market mechanisms can be extremely effective means for achieving economic coordination and for producing good results.[10] In addition, it would be incorrect to infer from the contents of this chapter that nonmarket arrangements do not also produce many defective results. The inference would be incorrect whether the arrangements took the form of governmental intervention in an otherwise predominantly market economy like that of the United States or the form of a governmentally directed, centrally commanded economy like that of the Soviet Union.

All in all, however, there is ample cause for a people of a society not to seek to retain an economic system based strictly and exclusively on markets. There is sufficient reason for them to modify their economy in one way or another, so as to try to alter at least some of the results of market mechanisms. The American experiment in modification, primarily through governmental action, is the subject of the next chapter.

QUESTIONS

1. Have you yourself, living within a predominantly market economy, ever made poor decisions for yourself as to what consumption goods you should buy, what job you should take, or what investment you should make? Why did you make them? It could be argued that such poorly made decisions have adverse effects, not only on the person making them and upon that person's family, but on others as well. How is this so?
2. Suppose that everyone in the United States suddenly began to behave dishonestly in their buying and selling relations with others. What might happen as a result to the average degree of economic well-being in the United States? Why?

[9] For an attack on the personal qualities that a market system seems to encourage, See R. H. Tawney, *The Acquisitive Society* (New York: Harcourt, Brace & World, Inc., 1920).
[10] These good results have been described in detail in Chapter 2.

3. Imagine two countries, both with predominantly market-oriented economic systems. In country A the level of entrepreneurship is high; in B, low. In which country would the average level of living be likely to be the higher? Why? In which would the economic growth rate be higher? Why? Now consider carefully the following question: In which country would the people be likely to be happier?

4. "A truly market economy implies little government intervention in the economy, that is, a weak government." Comment on the validity of this statement.

5. Can you think of some realistic examples in the United States—other than those described in the text of this chapter—in which price rigidity has prevented the market from working well? Carefully describe the causal relationship between the price rigidity and the poor results in your examples.

6. The cultural heritage of a nation is supposed to have something to do with how well a system of markets might work in a nation. Consider a foreign nation whose cultural heritage you know differs from that of the United States. In the light of the differences in the cultural heritages of the two nations, would markets be expected to work better in the United States or in the other nation?

7. Suppose a market economy was in operation without taxation or spending by government. Why would you expect inequality in the distribution of income? Now suppose someone proposed to impose taxes upon the people with high incomes and to give the tax proceeds to those with low incomes? Would you agree or disagree with the proposal? Why? What do you suppose would be the most convincing arguments of those who took the side opposite your own?

8. What is the difference between unemployment caused by too little total spending in the economy and structural unemployment? Are both likely to occur in a market economy? Why? What use do you think there is in distinguishing between the two kinds of unemployment?

9. "Since inflation harms some people and helps others, the net effect of inflation is not undesirable because the harm is offset by the help." Comment.

10. "Market forces, not governmental actions, are primarily responsible for most of the inflation that has occurred in nations with market systems." Comment.

11. Present an eclectic or synthesized theory of business fluctuations in a market economy.

12. What is meant by economic insecurity? Do you personally welcome uncertainty about your economic future or do you find it worrisome? Do you think most people share your view? Try to suggest some of the things which government intervention in the economy can do to reduce the economic insecurity.

13. What does it mean to say that "external" benefits unrecognized in a market economy may cause inadequate economic growth?

14. What does it mean to say that "external" costs unrecognized in a market economy may cause a nonoptimal commodity composition of gross national product?

RECOMMENDED READINGS

Bach, George Leland. *The New Inflation: Causes, Effects, Cures.* Englewood Cliffs, N.J.: Prentice-Hall, Inc., 1973.

Baumol, William J. *Welfare Economics and the Theory of the State,* 2d ed. Cambridge, Mass.: Harvard University Press, 1965.

Carson, Richard L. *Comparative Economic Systems.* New York: Macmillan Publishing Co., Inc., 1973, Chapters 14–17.

Dauten, Carl A., and Lloyd M. Valentine. *Business Cycles and Forecasting,* 4th ed. Cincinnati: South-Western Publishing Co., 1974.

Dillard, Dudley. *The Economics of John Maynard Keynes: The Theory of a Monetary Economy.* Englewood Cliffs, N.J.: Prentice-Hall, Inc., 1948.

Grossman, Gregory. *Economic Systems.* Englewood Cliffs, N.J.: Prentice-Hall, Inc., 1967.

Haberler, Gottfried. *Prosperity and Depression: A Theoretical Analysis of Cyclical Movements,* 4th ed. Cambridge, Mass.: Harvard University Press, 1964.

Halm, George N. *Economic Systems: A Comparative Anaylsis,* 3d ed. New York: Holt, Rinehart & Winston, Inc., 1968.

Heilbroner, Robert L., *The Worldly Philosophers: The Lives, Times and Ideas of the Great Economic Thinkers,* 4th ed. New York: Simon and Schuster, Inc., 1972.

Keynes, John Maynard. *The General Theory of Employment, Interest, and Money.* New York: Harcourt, Brace & World, 1936.

Köhler, Heinz. *Welfare and Planning: An Analysis of Capitalism Versus Socialism.* New York: John Wiley & Sons, Inc., 1966.

Landauer, Carl. *Contemporary Economic Systems: A Comparative Analysis.* Philadelphia: J. B. Lippincott Co., 1964.

Lee, Maurice W. *Macroeconomics: Fluctuations, Growth, and Stability,* 5th ed. Homewood, Ill.: Richard D. Irwin, Inc., 1971.

Lekachman, Robert. *Inflation: The Permanent Problem of Boom and Bust.* New York: Random House, 1973.

Loucks, William N., and William G. Whitney. *Comparative Economic Systems,* 9th ed. New York: Harper & Row, Publishers, 1973.

McClelland, David C. *The Achieving Society.* New York: The Free Press, 1967.

———, and David G. Winter. *Motivating Economic Achievement.* New York: The Free Press, 1971.

Mermelstein, David (ed.). *Economics: Mainstream Readings and Radical Critiques,* 2d ed. New York: Random House, 1973.

Tawney, R. H. *The Acquisitive Society.* New York: Harcourt, Brace & World, 1955.

Weaver, James H. (ed.). *Modern Political Economy: Radical and Orthodox Views.* Boston: Allyn and Bacon, Inc., 1973.

7

The American Economic System

INTRODUCTION

The United States has retained heavy reliance upon competitive market mechanisms in its economic system. In addition, nonmarket and noncompetitive economic arrangements have developed. These arrangements have arisen partly through unguided and spontaneous evolution and partly as a result of deliberate choice. They supplement and modify the effects of the market mechanisms so that the consequences are other than they would be with a market system alone.

One of these arrangements is the very large firm, usually organized as a corporation. As indicated in Chapter 3, the impetus for the emergence of these large corporations was partly technological. The economies of large scale become available with bigness. The impetus was also partly monopolistic. Bigness can provide power over market conditions and over rivals. These large corporations modified the market system. Some of their results were socially desirable, and some were not.

The large businesses have been one of the reasons for the development of two additional arrangements—labor unions and government intervention in the economy. Both of these have become major features of the economic system in the United States and in other nations still relying heavily on the market system. Both have been major means for counteracting some of the undesirable results of large businesses and for mitigating some of the other defects of a market system. Of the two, government intervention is by far the more important. After brief surveys of the internal workings in large corporations and of the modifying role of labor unions, this chapter turns to its major subject—government intervention in the United States economy.

LARGE CORPORATIONS

The typical, large American corporation is insulated from pure market pressures, at least to some degree. Competition impinges on it to a smaller extent than on a small firm in a pure market economy.[1]

Reduced Market Pressures

A large firm may achieve its insulation from competition in the market for its products in a variety of ways. In some cases, there are no other firms whose products are similar. In others, there may be an understanding with other firms not to engage in price competition. Sometimes the firm controls or is controlled by other firms. Occasionally it may succeed in persuading its buyers that its product is so different from those of other firms that substitution of products does not seem possible to the buyers of the goods.

The large firm may have less market pressure from a changing pattern of demands for specific products than does a firm in a purely market economy. The large firm may make many products, some quite unrelated productively to others. A loss sustained in the production of some of its products can be tolerated because offsets are provided from the profits of others.

The large firm might experience less market pressure from the inputs which it requires for production than would a firm in a fully competitive position. There are several reasons for this reduced pressure. The firm may produce or own these inputs. It may be a *monopsonistic* or sole purchaser of them. It may have an agreement with other purchasers concerning the maximum price any of them will pay for the input.

The typical, large corporation may be under little market pressure as to the acquisition of funds for expansion. Its major source of such funds may be its own undistributed profits.

Separation of Ownership from Control

The large corporation is usually somewhat insulated from the pressure of those who technically are the legal owners of it. It is, to a degree, relieved of having to maximize profits. This is so because ownership is usually vested in a group of shareholders, who are great in number, scattered geographically,

---

[1] For some purposes a large firm should be thought of as one which is *large relative* to the size of the market in which it buys inputs or sells a product. In measuring monopoly power, this definition of a large firm is a useful one. Thus even an absolutely small firm may possess strong monopoly power if it is the only firm selling products in its market. A small grocery store may have considerable power if it is the only grocery store in an isolated community.

For other purposes a large firm should be thought of as one which is *absolutely large*, in the sense that it has a great many employees or produces many millions of dollars of product or possesses great amounts of capital, regardless of how big it is relative to the markets in which it operates. In assessing the influence of market forces versus the influence of command, this definition is often the more useful one and is the one primarily used in this section of this chapter.

and changing in composition. Each of the shareholders may own only a small percentage of the total shares of the corporation. These owners may find it difficult to meet together to make decisions for the corporation. The consequence is that this power falls to a board of directors, to the executives, and to the chief technical experts of the corporation. These officials often have the real control. The members of this controlling group sometimes are able to perpetuate themselves in their positions regardless of the wishes of the owners. It is difficult for the owners, dispersed and diffused as they are, to mount a coordinated attack on the entrenched management. Such is the meaning of the much discussed *separation of ownership from control.*[2]

Decisions Not Motivated by the Market

Under these circumstances of partial insulation from market forces, what causes the corporation to make the decisions it does? On what principles are such matters as the product prices, the product mix, the acquisition of subsidiaries, the rate of expansion, and the selection and promotion of personnel determined? The answers to these questions are of considerable significance since the economic achievement of the American people depends to a considerable extent upon them. However, surprisingly little is really known about such matters.

It would seem inadequate to assume that profit maximization alone motivates the decision makers, especially since the profits usually accrue not to them but to the separate absentee owners. Prestige, power, security, and a clear conscience may motivate them. They may decide, unprofitably, to expand the firm in order to be in charge of something bigger. On the other hand, they may choose, unprofitably, not to expand it, in order to keep it small enough that control of it does not have to be shared with other persons. They may dissipate its profits by giving its funds away to charity or by retaining unneeded employees for whom they have compassion. They may buy inputs at high, unprofitable prices from supplying firms in which they have an ownership interest. They may display their patriotism by having the corporation buy high priced domestic inputs rather than low priced foreign ones.

On the other hand, will the attainment of at least satisfactorily large, if not maximum, profits not still be an important goal for these managers? After all, it is out of profits that they find the means to expansion. Furthermore, most of them may simply want to do a good job and may believe that the size of profits is the main indicator of a job well done. Finally, it is the size of profits that determines their prestige and their ability to mollify dissident stockholders who may be inclined to try to organize a rebellion.

[2] This theme was probably first emphasized in the classic work by Adolph A. Berle and Gardiner C. Means, *The Modern Corporation and Private Property* (New York: The Macmillan Company, 1933). As suggested in subsequent paragraphs, those in control, the managers, are seldom completely independent of the owners. Dissatisfied owners may band together to oust incumbent managers. Or the owners may sell their shares of stock, driving down the price of the stock and thus creating difficulties for the managers.

It may be true that the large corporation is not under as great a pressure from market forces as the small firm typical of a strictly market economy. Many of its decisions may be approximately the same, nonetheless.[3]

LABOR UNIONS

An economic institution which has developed in the American economy, as well as other market economies, is the labor union. Its development has been partly in response to defects in a strictly market system. Perhaps this development has made the societies of market nations better societies than they would otherwise have been. Perhaps unions have helped market systems to continue to exist in modified form rather than being replaced because of irremediable and intolerable defects.

Redressing an Imbalance of Market Power

Without labor unions, the markets for many types of labor would be one-sided, with the employers possessing great bargaining advantage over the workers. This one-sidedness appeared in blatant form in the British Industrial Revolution. Then, as in other instances, there were usually but a few employers in each labor market. Most of these employers could easily dispense with the labor of any one worker and could even continue to exist for a time without any of the laborers. On the other side of the market was a large number of poorly informed, almost propertyless, unorganized employees. They were directly and immediately dependent upon their employment. Frequently, alternative jobs were not available to them; and without their jobs, their livelihoods were threatened.

Viewed against this background, unions may be regarded as a means of modifying the market system so as to improve the results. By banding together into unions, the workers increased their bargaining power vis-à-vis the employers. Competition among the workers for jobs was substantially reduced by unionization. By means of strikes, the unions could realistically confront the employers with alternatives. Either higher pay, more lenient treatment, shorter hours, and more pleasant working conditions would be granted, or all the workers' services would be lost.

Benefits of Unions to Members

It is fairly clear that the development of unions has been of net advantage to the majority of union members. For them unions have made possible increased income from higher wages and steadier income from a decrease in temporary involuntary furloughs from work. Paid vacations have been enlarged. Compensation has been paid for injuries received while at work and for temporary unemployment. Other benefits include pensions, increased

---

[3] John F. Due and Robert W. Clower, *Intermediate Economic Analysis: Resource Allocation, Factor Pricing, and Welfare* (5th ed.; Homewood, Ill.: Richard D. Irwin, Inc., 1966), Chapter 3.

security through such arrangements as seniority, and shorter and better scheduled hours of work. Unions have secured greater political power for workers. Consequently, the workers have had greater ability to secure legislation which they may regard as favorable. An example is a law which prohibits wages below legally specified minimums. Unions have enabled workers to gain greater concern from employers. They have given workers the camaraderie of participation in a group of peers and also a means of reviewing mistreatment by employers.

Benefits of Unions to Society

There is also reason to believe that unions have had some favorable effects on society as a whole. It can be argued that the distribution of income has been made somewhat less unequal by unions. Perhaps the inequality of opportunity to become wealthy and to use political power has been reduced.

It is quite possible that unions have, in a number of ways, made possible for society greater economic efficiency and faster economic growth. For example, the existence of a union in a factory may provide a much needed avenue of communication. Through a union, information about inefficiencies in production and opportunities for improvement may be conveyed from the lower levels of a factory to the upper hierarchy of managers. The managers may be surrounded by obsequious assistants and may never otherwise obtain this information. Unions have also given their political support to governmental programs of education, training, and welfare, which have accelerated economic growth. Unions have increased the morale of the workers and thus probably have increased worker efficiency.

The Argument over the Effects of Unions

Most of the arguments about the socially desirable effects of unions, of course, are disputed. Consider as an example the dispute concerning the effect of unions on efficiency.

On the one hand, there are those who believe that people, including workers, are selfish, rational, and individualistic and that these forces shape the motivations of people. Specifically, they believe that most workers dislike their work and must be driven to do it. They must be driven by the fear of unemployment or even starvation and by the reward of higher money income. Since unions tend to reduce this fear, unions reduce efficiency. Unions, therefore, are harmful to society because a reduced GNP and a lower average level of living result.

A different point of view is held by those who believe that work is not naturally detested. Rather, work is for many people their chief social activity, their principal outlet for creativity, and the chief determinant of their social status. Those holding this view believe that the motivations and attitudes of an individual worker are shaped by his group of fellow workers. They contend that, without unions, the formal organization of a factory usually fails to take positive advantage of this power of the work group to shape motivation.

Unions can be used to create favorable attitudes among workers. A sense of responsible participation among them is likely to result in harmony and efficiency. Finally, even if unions did not increase efficiency, they might still be desirable. Unions may increase the satisfaction which workers derive from working. After all, the economic welfare of society cannot be measured by real GNP per capita alone. The utility, not only from consumption, but also directly from production must be taken into account.[4]

Disadvantages of Unions

It is, of course, true that unions have social disadvantages, as well as advantages. It is debatable whether the net social effect of unions is good or bad.

Unions contribute to inflation by insisting on higher and higher wage rates, which push up the prices of products. They, in combination with monopolistic businesses, are the chief causes of *cost-push inflation.*

Unions may also cause unemployment. They do this partly by restricting entry into occupations which they control. They also may raise wage rates. Then, because of higher prices for the product, less of the product can be sold. As a result, fewer workers can be employed. Furthermore, with high wage rates, capital is substituted for labor by producers, and the labor may go unemployed.

Unions may alter the distribution of income in what is judged by some people to be an undesirable way. The poorest workers are migrant laborers, unskilled laborers, and domestic servants. They tend to remain ununionized. Thus the poorest remain poor in spite of the existence of unions in the economy. The poorest are further hurt since the prices of the goods they buy are pushed up by unionization in other industries. By exercising their control of unionized occupations, unions may get large incomes for those workers already receiving the highest wages.

Unions restrict freedom. They reduce the freedom of workers to enter occupations and the freedom to refrain from joining a union in a *union-shop* industry. They restrict the freedom of property owners to do with their property as they choose. The freedom of managers to control production is reduced.

Unions create economic insecurity by their strikes, which cut off supplies or services that may be essential to the work or the welfare of consumers and others. By their boycotts, unions may endanger property values and people's livings.

Unions may decrease economic efficiency, economic growth, and the average level of living. They may do so by featherbedding and by obstructing the introduction of new techniques of production. By their harassment of management, they may direct attention from the achievement of efficiency.

Unions may have undesirable political repercussions. Labor leaders, by controlling union funds for campaign contributions, may exert excessive influence on politicians. Unions may occasionally provide an avenue of infiltration into society for communists or other extremists.

---

[4] For an elaboration of the latter view, see J. A. C. Brown, *The Social Psychology of Industry: Human Relations in the Factory* (Baltimore: Penguin Books, Inc., 1954).

GOVERNMENTAL POLICIES

Governments in the United States and in most modified market economies intervene in a variety of ways in economic affairs. They intervene by taxing, partly to transfer purchasing power from private spenders to the government and partly to discourage various consumption and production activities. They spend, partly to purchase goods and services including resources, partly to transfer purchasing power to consumers, and partly to encourage various consumption and production activities. They regulate some activities directly, in order to change the amounts or other aspects of these activities. They undertake production of some goods and services. The justification for this intervention is the need to provide the prerequisites and remedy the defects of the market system, which continues to be relied upon heavily.

Public Education

Government in the United States is a means by which the personal qualities of the population are influenced. This influence is achieved primarily through the system of public education. The overwhelming portion of elementary and secondary education is conducted by local governments. Probably over three-fourths of the higher education occurs in state colleges and universities.

Market and Nonmarket Elements in Education. Education is financed mainly by taxes rather than fees paid by buyers of education. The institutions are government enterprises conducted without regard for profit in the market sense. The capital goods connected with them are government property. The students at the lower levels are compelled by force of law to attend. Those at the upper levels are induced to do so by what amounts to heavy subsidization. The character of the education is not allowed to be principally determined by permitting several schools to compete with each other for students. Each school is not usually given freedom to design a curriculum with which to attract students as customers. Instead, most schools possess local monopolistic franchises.

However, the market system is allowed to intrude in the purchasing of inputs—hiring teachers, buying supplies, constructing buildings, and borrowing funds. Further, market considerations sometimes influence the quantity and quality of education. For example, the market may indicate, by high interest rates on borrowed funds, a great relative scarcity of capital in the society. Then the decision to forego a new school building may be made. Nevertheless, market forces are, for the most part, kept on the periphery.

Federal Government Intervention in Education. In recent years the American national government has intervened in the educational process in a variety of nonmarket ways. It has granted scholarships to students and provided funds for their part-time employment to enable them to finance their education. It has caused military veterans' benefits to take the form of payments for education and has subsidized school lunch programs. It has awarded funds for the construction of educational buildings and granted research funds to universities to indirectly sustain their teaching. It has set up or financially sponsored vocational training programs, adult education programs, and preschool kindergarten programs.

The federal government has intervened in these ways partly because it is better able to transcend market forces than are state and local governments, the relations among which may be governed by market considerations. For example, the public universities in two states may bid against each other for the same professor. This professor could be hired instead by the federal government and then directed to go to one or the other of the universities. Another example occurs when a state is loathe to spend great amounts on higher education because many of the students, once educated, leave the state. They are attracted by market forces, such as higher incomes, to other states. These other states become the main beneficiaries of the external advantages of the education. A third example is provided when one state is fearful of raising its property or income taxes to finance more education lest it thereby induce businesses to locate in a different state.

Other Governmental Programs. Local, state, and federal governments have sought through a predominantly nonmarket process of public education to create a populace able to be informed, prudent, honest, and mobile. Other smaller government activities have had the same end. For example, the post office, a government enterprise, charges mail fees below cost for newspapers, books, and advertising matter. This practice may be regarded as subsidization for the sake of disseminating information. Personal income taxes are reduced for those who move geographically so that they will be more mobile. Advancement in some civil service programs is contingent upon acquisition of additional education. Truth in advertising, packaging, and lending is required by law. Programs such as the federal Volunteers in Service to America (VISTA) attempt to instill entrepreneurial ingenuity among groups who lack it. Supposedly exemplary people who possess this attribute are sent in to live and work among these groups.

There are many governmental programs to influence personal qualities. However, the main means by which these qualities of the American people are shaped continue to be the family and the upbringing it provides for children, largely based on the cultural traditions of the society.

Government and Business

The government in the United States has intervened in the economy to deal with competition and monopoly in several important ways. It has tried to prevent the formation of monopolies and to break up monopolies by means of an antitrust program. It has accepted the existence of some monopolies and attempted to regulate their activities to prevent undesirable social results. It has assumed the ownership and operation of some production undertakings.

It has attempted to shape the form which competition has taken and has acted in such a way that competition has sometimes been reduced.[5]

Antitrust Legislation. English common law and American common law, which followed, had provided the legal basis for private persons injured by monopolies to sue and obtain some relief from monopolies. However, it was only in 1890 that the first federal law was passed in the United States explicitly making monopoly a crime against the state. This was the Sherman Antitrust Act. It was enacted as a reaction against the monopolistic activities which had then become common. In brief, broad, and rather vague language, it made illegal and punishable both monopolies of trade and agreements between two or more parties "in restraint of trade."

After more than two decades of rather lax enforcement and interpretation, the Sherman Act was supplemented in 1914 by the Clayton Act and the Federal Trade Commission Act. The Clayton Act explicitly listed certain monopolistic practices as illegal. Among these was *discriminatory pricing*. That is, variation in the price charged for a product by a seller from one buyer to another was outlawed when such variation was unjustified by variations in cost of production. Also prohibited were sales of a product on condition that the buyer not buy the same or other products from other sellers. In addition, purchases by a corporation of shares in a competing corporation were banned. So was the holding by a person of directorships in two or more competing corporations. The Federal Trade Commission Act created that independent federal agency. The agency was directed to police against "unfair methods of competition," which were declared illegal. Presumably, the object was to prevent competition deliberately and mainly designed to lead to monopoly.

The Robinson-Patman Act of 1936 attempted to improve the competitive position of small, independent retail businesses against larger retailers, including chains. It did so by making more specific and stringent the rules against discriminatory pricing. The Cellar-Kefauver Antimerger Act of 1950 made the Clayton Act more restrictive. Under this act it became illegal for a corporation to acquire assets, not just the stock, of a competing corporation.

Enforcement of Antitrust Laws. Mere passage of laws does not assure their observance, of course. Enforcement agencies are required. In the case of the American federal antimonopoly laws, there are two such agencies. These are the Antitrust Division of the Department of Justice and the Federal Trade Commission.

The Antitrust Division of the Department of Justice. The Antitrust Division receives complaints from customers or competitors of alleged monopolizers. It can accept or reject these complaints. Upon acceptance of a complaint, the Division calls upon another federal agency, the Federal Bureau of Investigation, to gather evidence. The Division possesses no investigative

---

[5] For a more thorough treatment of the issues in this section, see Clair Wilcox, *Public Policies Toward Business* (4th ed.; Homewood, Ill.: Richard D. Irwin, Inc., 1971).

staff of its own. If sufficient evidence can be gathered, it may be presented by the lawyers of the Division to a grand jury. An attempt is made to convince the jury that a trial is warranted. If the grand jury agrees that it is warranted, the Division and its lawyers act as prosecutors in a regular federal court against the alleged monopolists. Conviction of the accused is usually difficult to achieve. In any case, appeal to higher courts is possible. When found guilty, the offending corporation and its officers are subject to fines or imprisonment or both. The cost of the litigation and the adverse publicity for the defendant can also be regarded as punishment.

The Antitrust Division may also seek through a lawsuit to persuade a court to take other action. The court may order by injunction that a business cease a certain monopolizing practice. The court may also decree that a business break itself up or sell off some of its parts. Sometimes before a court decision is reached, the Division and the defendant agree to a settlement. The court will enforce such a settlement by what is called a *consent decree*. Any decision by a court requires subsequent enforcement partly through surveillance by the Division. The Division may or may not be diligent in this activity.

The Federal Trade Commission. The Federal Trade Commission has, in addition to execution of antimonopoly policy, a number of other duties. It tries to prevent deception and fraud by sellers against customers. These other duties sometimes have preoccupied the Commission almost to the exclusion of antimonopoly action. However, the Commission has investigated, compiled reports on, and publicized general monopolistic practices of businesses. It has attempted to persuade businesses to refrain voluntarily from monopolistic practices. It has received complaints from parties aggrieved by the monopolistic practices of others. It has heard the evidence on such complaints and has issued orders to businesses to end monopolistic practices. It has appeared before regular federal courts to obtain enforcement of such orders.

The Commission and the Antitrust Division thus overlap with respect to their duties and responsibilities. In addition, private persons or businesses who believe themselves economically harmed by the monopolistic practices of others may sue the alleged monopolists. They may thus attempt to force an end to the practice or obtain compensation for the harm. They may take this action with or without the aid and cooperation of the Commission or the Division.

Regulation. For some industries it has long been recognized that enforcement of competition and prevention of monopoly are inappropriate approaches. For these industries the technical efficiency achieved by allowing but a single, monopolistic firm to exist is great. Therefore, the monopoly is tolerated. Included among these industries are the public utilities. Some of these are also called *natural monopolies*. In general for these activities, the larger the firm and the fewer the number of competing firms, the less is the average cost of production and the smaller the social disadvantages. It is easy to see, for example, that five telephone companies in a city would be costly. There would have to be duplication of lines. In addition, a user might need to have five telephones to be assured of direct communication with any other city resident.

In these cases monopoly is tolerated. However, to prevent monopolistic exploitation, governmental agencies are set up to regulate the monopoly. In the United States federal and state and local commissions are used as regulatory agencies. Among the federal agencies are the Interstate Commerce Commission, the Federal Power Commission, and the Federal Communications Commission.

The primary aim has been to control prices charged for products. This control is exercised both to prevent monopolistically high prices and to prevent unjustified variations in the price from one buyer to another. The regulation of price so as to prevent monopolistic profit requires as a concomitant the regulation of the quality of the product. Monopolistic profits can be made and monopolistic exploitation achieved through either price or quality. Furthermore, accurate determination of profit depends upon an accurate calculation of the value of the real capital goods in which the business has invested and an accurate record of the expenses of the business. Therefore, regulation of accounting procedures becomes necessary. Moreover, another corporation may be related to the monopoly as a subsidiary or as a parent. This other corporation may try to circumvent the restrictive regulation on monopoly profit by charging excessively high prices for supplies, for capital goods, or for borrowed funds. So both the intercorporate relations of and the flotation of securities by the monopolist seem to require regulation. Adequate regulation can thus be both extensive and complicated.

Government Ownership. Governments in the United States have taken over the ownership and control of a few productive operations. Widely held ideology in the nation has opposed government operation of production activities. What little there is has been undertaken partly to control monopolies. It has also been undertaken because public regulation of privately owned monopolies has not always been successful. Other reasons for government ownership seem to be scattered and incidental; they appear to be almost matters of historical chance.

The federal government has a monopoly over mail through the postal system. This activity was specifically designated as a governmental function in the original Constitution of 1789. The federal government also produces and distributes electricity, researches and produces atomic energy, prints and distributes publications, produces a little metal, and has built and operated shipping fleets and a few railroads. It buys, sells, and stores agricultural products and minerals, makes a variety of loans, sells several kinds of insurance, and manages the use of land in the national forests and parks. It operates vocational training and welfare counseling services and, of course, produces national defense. The federal government became engaged in many of these activities as a result of war or as a part of its intervention for other purposes, such as redistribution of income and of opportunity.

State governments, in a pattern which varies somewhat from state to state, produce a few products. Included are higher education, liquor retailing services, unemployment and worker disability insurance, park services, electricity, rental housing, and highway and other transportation. The total amount of production by all governments in the United States is still quite a small percentage of total production in the nation. The governments buy much of what they use from privately owned and operated enterprises rather than producing it themselves.

Reduction of Competition. It has to be recognized that some forms of government intervention in the United States economy have had the effect of reducing competition and promoting monopoly, though that effect has been unintended in some cases. For example, the patent laws have provided legal monopolies to patent holders. Labor unions have been encouraged and protected so as to acquire a monopoly over specific labor skills. Unions have been exempted by the Clayton Act of 1914 from the antimonopoly rules. Import taxes and other restrictions on products brought into the United States have been imposed to protect American producers and workers from foreign competition. Competition among producers of raw petroleum has been prevented by legal limitations on the amount of oil each can produce.

State governmental policies have reduced competition in the sale of supplies to state and local government and in the construction of buildings for government. These policies have excluded purchases from firms whose headquarters are outside the state. Personal and corporate income tax laws in the United States have features which hamper the easy establishment and growth of new firms which would compete with older ones. Licenses are required to enter some occupations or to establish certain kinds of businesses. Since the number of licenses granted is limited in various ways, the opportunity for competition is reduced. In the Great Depression, the National Industrial Recovery Act was in operation from 1933 to 1935. It deliberately encouraged the firms in each industry to plan together to control output and prices in what amounted to a monopolistic manner.[6]

Redistribution of Income, Wealth, Opportunity, and Power

Governments in the United States have intervened in economic affairs in a variety of ways in order to alter the distribution of income, wealth, opportunity, and power. One means has been the tax system. Another has been cash grants and the provision of goods and services without charge to all or part of the population. Finally, there are a variety of miscellaneous regulatory policies which have probably had the effect, sometimes incidental to other objectives, of reducing inequality.

Taxes. Taxes which take a larger percentage of the income of a person with a high income than of a person with a low income are called *progressive taxes*.

[6] Government encouragement of monopoly is attacked in Milton Friedman, *Capitalism and Freedom* (Chicago: University of Chicago Press, 1962), Chapter 8.

Such taxes decrease the degree of inequality of income among a population. Then the percentage share of upper-income groups in the national income is smaller after taxes are paid than before. In the United States, the personal and corporate income taxes and the gift and inheritance taxes appear at first glance to be steeply progressive. They are probably moderately so in fact.

Progression in the Federal Personal Income Tax. In the early 1970s, the federal personal income tax had a marginal tax rate on taxable income rising from 14 percent for the first $500 of annual income to 70 percent on income above $100,000.[7] The word *marginal* is used here to indicate that percentage rate applied to an extra or marginal dollar of income, not to all income. For example, if one had a taxable income of $101,000, the tax payable was not 70 percent of $101,000, which would be $70,700. Instead, it was some amount considerably less because only the last, or marginal, $1,000, that above $100,000, was taxed at 70 percent. At the same time, the first $100,000 was taxed at lower rates, 14 percent of the first $500 plus 15 percent of the second $500, and so on.

The phrase *taxable income* is used to indicate that not all income earned is taxed. From the gross income earned are subtracted certain sums as deductions. Examples of deductions are some medical expenses and state and local taxes paid. Also subtracted are exemptions of $750 for the taxpayer and each legal dependent. The residual amount after these subtractions is taxable income.

Thus the effective degree of progression is somewhat different than first appears. In the early 1970s the average, not marginal, tax rates ranged from 0 percent on very small incomes to 53 percent and higher on incomes of $100,000 and higher.

There are, however, numerous legal avenues by which taxpayers can avoid having to pay income taxes. These are so-called loopholes. One loophole is to let what is really personal income take the form of a business expense account. Another is to let corporate profits be retained by corporations rather than be paid out as dividends to shareholders. Too, one can invest in state and local government bonds, the interest income from which is not taxable. If one owns the house in which one lives, there is no money income received from the wealth represented by the house. Consequently, there is no income tax. These loopholes are utilized primarily by upper-income groups. It is these groups who are most able to hire lawyers and to seek ways to take advantage of the loopholes. It is they for whom it is most worthwhile to take advantage of loopholes, since absolut tax savings are so large for them. Hence, the loopholes reduce the degree of progression of the tax to something less than first appears.

Other Progressive Taxes. The federal corporate income tax is a tax on corporate net profits. In the early 1970s its rate was 22 percent on the first

---

[7] These rates apply to incomes of unmarried individuals and of married persons who report their incomes separately for tax purposes. Somewhat different rates apply to incomes of married persons who report their incomes together.

$25,000 of annual profits and 48 percent on all profits above that amount. The owners of corporations are, for the most part, persons in the high income groups. Therefore, this tax would seem to be progressive. However, it is less so to the extent that corporations shift the real burden of the tax away from the owners to other groups, such as the employees and customers. This shifting can occur through lower wages for corporate employees or higher product prices for customers.

Death and gift taxes in the United States are probably quite progressive, but this effect is somewhat diluted by loopholes, which are extensive.

Regressive Sales and Property Taxes. The questions of to what degree and in what direction the burden of a tax is shifted and where the final burden falls are difficult to answer. Unfortunately, they are of considerable significance for the sales tax and property tax. These are probably *regressive taxes*. A regressive tax is one for which the percentage burden decreases as the size of the income increases.

The typical state sales tax is a flat-rate tax on most sales. The final burden of this tax seems to fall mainly on consumers. As a consumer, one can escape the burden by saving rather than spending one's income. It is the upper-income groups who are most able to save and do in fact save. Amounts of savings as a percentage of income rise as income rises. Hence, a typical upper-income person pays a smaller percentage of his income in sales tax, though not a smaller absolute amount, than a lower-income person.

In the same way, property taxes are probably regressive. Those levied upon business property are, like a sales tax, passed on to consumers in the form of higher product prices. Those on residential property tend to be borne by the residents. Lower-income groups spend a larger percentage of their income for residences than do upper-income groups. Such spending takes the form of rent, interest, mortgage, and maintenance costs.

The Redistribution Effect of the American Tax System. Several important studies of the distribution of the burden of all taxes taken together for the United States were made for the years in the 1960s. They stressed the difficulty of making accurate estimates, but reached several conclusions. State and local taxation was somewhat regressive. Federal taxation was progressive for most income ranges. Overall, the combined effect was perhaps one of slight and irregular progression.[8]

Nontax Policies of Redistribution. Governments in the United States have also altered the distribution of income by free gifts of money, goods, and services to some or all people. Similar effects are achieved by governmental sales of goods and services at prices lower than those which would have prevailed otherwise. In the case of money grants, the share of the lower-income

---

[8] W. Irwin Gillespie, "Effect of Public Expenditures on the Distribution of Income," *Essays in Fiscal Federalism*, ed. Richard A. Musgrave (Washington: The Brookings Institution, 1965), pp. 122–186; *Tax Burdens and Benefits of Government Expenditures by Income Class, 1961 and 1965* (New York: Tax Foundation, Inc., 1967).

groups in the national money, and hence the real, income is increased. Examples are unemployment compensation, relief payments, and old age pensions. In the case of gifts of or low cost sales of goods, the share of the lower-income groups in the national real income is directly increased. Examples are the food-stamp plan, subsidized public housing, free or low cost medical and hospital services, and free vocational training services. Some goods and services are given to all people. Examples are police protection, national defense, and the use of sidewalks and streets. It could be argued that although these go to the upper-income groups as well as the lower, their approximately equal availability to and use by all reduces the inequality of real income.

New Programs of the 1960s. In the 1960s, at the instigation of the federal government and in cooperation with state and local governments, there were established a variety of new programs. These were authorized by the Manpower Training and Development Act of 1962, the Appalachia Act of 1965, and the Economic Opportunity Act of 1964. These programs provided various services to the poor. The aim was to improve the ability of these people to help themselves to greater incomes and opportunities and thus to reduce the causes of inequality.

Among these programs was the Job Corps. It provided free training and living expenses for young people at special centers. Another, the Neighborhood Youth Corps, provided subsidized local work-training for low income groups. There were also programs of loans and subsidized services for low income farmers, adult education programs, prekindergarten and kindergarten training for children from poor families, and low cost loans to small businesses to create employment in communities where the poor were concentrated. VISTA provided the services of social workers to the poor.[9]

Other Policies. By a variety of other policies, the governments in the United States have caused, sometimes unintentionally, the degree of economic inequality to be reduced. Minimum wage legislation requires that wage rates in certain businesses be no less than specified amounts. Such legislation probably has increased the incomes of some poor workers. However, it may have reduced that of others who have become unemployed or who have been forced to shift to work where the legislation does not apply. Encouragement of labor unions through governmental policy may have reduced inequality. The reduction of monopoly through government antitrust policy has probably made for more nearly equal distribution of income. Laws against racial and other discrimination in employment have perhaps enabled some of the poorest persons to earn higher incomes. Finally, government intervention to reduce depressions has reduced poverty by keeping the poor employed during such periods.

[9] For a summary account of these programs, see Thomas J. Hailstones and Frank V. Mastrianna, *Contemporary Economic Problems and Issues* (4th ed.; Cincinnati: South-Western Publishing Co., 1976).

Public Finance

The theory of Keynes implicitly provided a partial solution to several problems of a market economy. Keynesian theory suggested how unemployment and deflation caused by too little total spending could be combated. Inflation caused by too much spending was also correctable. So, too, were business fluctuations, insofar as they were caused by too little or too much spending. Keynes' theory was distilled to its purest form and labeled *functional finance* by one of Keynes' foremost American followers, Abba P. Lerner.[10] Functional finance indicates how public finance may be used to solve problems caused by too little or too much aggregate spending. These problems are to be dealt with through variations in the rate of government spending and taxation.

Fiscal Policy. The rules of functional finance replace or supplement the older rules of governmental finance. The latter had traditionally served as guides to government spending and taxation in predominantly market economies.

According to the old rules, the main purpose of government spending is to provide goods and services which are needed but which the private market system fails to provide. The main purpose of taxation is to provide the funds which the government requires to finance its spending. The relationship between the amount of government spending and the amount of taxation should be one of equality. In this way a governmental budgetary deficit does not occur, and a governmental debt, with all its disadvantages, does not accumulate.

The new Keynesian functional finance provides different rules. A main purpose of governmental spending is to add to the total spending in the economy. The aim is to raise total spending until it is large enough to eliminate unemployment. An additional purpose of governmental spending is the provision of public goods and services. The main purpose of taxation is to reduce consumer and business investment spending. In this way, inflation of the kind caused by too much total spending will not occur.

Private spending may be inadequate to support full employment. Then either governmental spending should be increased or taxation reduced or both. The purpose of tax reduction in such a situation would be to provide private spenders with more after-tax income to spend. Likely consequences of these government actions are a budgetary deficit for the government and perhaps continual increases in the public debt. However, according to the Keynesian view, the greatest alleged disadvantage of public debt is an unreal one. Moreover, the real disadvantages are small. Therefore, it is better to enlarge the debt and avoid unemployment than to avoid debt and cause unemployment of people who are willing and otherwise able to work.

At times private spending may be so excessive as to lead not only to full employment, but also inflation. Then, according to the Keynesian rules, either

---

[10] Abba P. Lerner, "Functional Finance and the Federal Debt," *Social Research,* Vol. X, No. 1 (February, 1943), pp. 38–51; or Abba P. Lerner, *The Economics of Control: Principles of Welfare Economics* (New York: The Macmillan Company, 1944), Chapter 24.

government spending should be reduced or taxation increased or both. There will be a consequent reduction in the government deficit or an emergence or enlargement of a government surplus. The money from the surplus can be used to reduce the public debt, be held idle, or be eliminated.

Official federal government philosophy in the United States has gradually abandoned at least some of the older rules and come round to a somewhat modified form of the Keynesian view. The rules of this modified Keynesianism are usually called *fiscal policy*.[11] Thus the Tax Reduction Act of 1964 was passed at a time when the federal government already had a deficit and was increasing its spending. A main aim of the reduction was to increase employment, and in this it was successful.

Automatic or Built-in Stabilizers. It is also recognized that governmental economic intervention in the United States has features which may be called automatic or built-in stabilizers. These features tend, without any new policy decisions, to moderate increases or decreases in aggregate spending.

What are built-in stabilizers? One of them is the progressive income tax. When spending begins to decline and to cause unemployment and recession, personal incomes decline. With lower incomes, people find themselves subject to lower tax rates, which become applicable under a progressive tax system. With lower tax rates and lower incomes, the total taxes which have to be paid are considerably less. Consequently, people do not cut back their spending by so much as they would have with a nonprogressive income tax. Likewise, when total spending becomes so large as to cause inflation, the spending and the higher prices cause higher incomes. Under a progressive income tax, people then become subject to higher tax rates so that more taxes are taken. After-tax incomes, spending, and the inflation are less than they would be with a nonprogressive tax.

Other built-in stabilizers are the unemployment compensation program and the system of relief payments to the needy. When unemployment and a recession occur, the newly unemployed people automatically apply for unemployment compensation or relief payments. The government's expenditures for these purposes increase, and the decline in total spending is not as great as it would be otherwise. Even the old age pension program, a part of social security, operates in this way. When unemployment and a recession come, people, who otherwise would not have done so, formally retire and apply for pension payments from the government. With these payments, their spending is greater than it would be without them. Hence both the decline in total spending and the severity of the unemployment and recession are moderated.

The program of farm price supports acts in much the same way. In a recession, farm prices may fall to the support levels. Under the program, the government automatically increases its spending to buy farm products. In this way, it prevents total spending from falling as far as it would otherwise.

---

[11] For a brief survey of how Keynesian theory eventually became accepted by United States governmental officials and others, see John Kenneth Galbraith, "Came the Revolution," *The New York Times Book Review* (May 16, 1965), p. 1 ff.

The automatic stabilizers do not, of course, eliminate unemployment and inflation since they are not set in motion until some unemployment or inflation occurs. They only moderate unemployment and inflation caused by too little or too much total spending. They must be supplemented by deliberate decisions by government to change government spending or taxation. These deliberate decisions are sometimes called *discretionary fiscal policy*.

The Banking System

Automatic stabilizers and discretionary fiscal policy are supplemented by another form of government economic intervention called *monetary policy*. Monetary policy has to do with the total quantity of money in existence in the nation, with limitations on the ability to create money, and with the terms on which credit or borrowed funds are made available.

The Federal Reserve System and Commercial Banks. In the United States, the power to exert monetary policy is centered in the Board of Governors of the Federal Reserve System. The Federal Reserve is technically a privately owned corporation but is actually an independent government agency subject to loose control by the federal legislature and the President. It may be regarded as the central bank of the United States, comparable, for example, to the Bank of England in the United Kingdom or the Deutsche Bundesbank in Germany.

The money supply in the United States consists of currency, including coins, in circulation and checking accounts or demand deposits at about 14,000 commercial banks. These banks are privately owned businesses. The Federal Reserve prints and issues most of the currency in circulation. The amount of currency, in this sense, is subject to the control of the Federal Reserve.

The demand deposits are actually nothing more than paper credits on the books of commercial banks. They denote the obligation of the banks to honor both checks drawn by the depositors on the deposits and requests by the depositors for conversion to currency. They are created by the commercial banks when they make loans or purchase securities. They are destroyed by the commercial banks when the banks receive repayment of loans and when securities are sold by the banks. Therefore, the Federal Reserve does not have power to control directly that portion of the United States money supply in the form of demand deposits.

Powers of the Federal Reserve. The Federal Reserve does have fairly effective *indirect* control over the quantity of demand deposits in existence. Commercial banks are legally required to have for each dollar of demand deposits on their books no less than a specified number of cents of *reserve*. This reserve may take the form either of currency in the vaults of the banks or of book credit at the Federal Reserve. The specified number is the *percentage reserve requirement*. The Federal Reserve ordinarily has control over the quantity of currency in existence. It also controls the amount of book credit noted on its books and owned by the commercial banks. It also specifies the percentage reserve requirement. In these ways, the quantity of money in the United States is indirectly but fairly effectively under the control of what is really a federal government agency.

Monetary Policy. How does the government use its control over the money supply to combat unemployment, deflation, inflation, and business fluctuations? Suppose there is a period when unemployment, perhaps with deflation, is the problem. The Federal Reserve may either reduce the percentage reserve requirement or increase the paper credit on its books on behalf of the commercial banks. It can achieve the latter by making loans to the commercial banks and allowing the loans to take the form of this credit. Alternatively, it can purchase securities from the commercial banks or from the customers of these banks. It then pays for the securities by creating this credit for the sellers. In any case, the commercial banks find themselves with the ability to make additional loans to their customers. They may do so by creating demand deposits for these customers. This increased availability of loanable funds usually will cause interest rates to decline. Businesses and consumers will be encouraged to obtain bank loans and to spend the resulting newly created demand deposits. The increased spending may reduce the deflation and unemployment.

In this way governmental monetary policy administered through the Federal Reserve is expected to work in a time of unemployment. The money supply is increased. Interest rates are reduced. Other conditions of lending are liberalized. Total spending is increased. So ends the unemployment.

In a time of inflation, a "tight" monetary policy is used. This policy is usually accomplished by sales of securities by the Federal Reserve. Sometimes the means used is a reduction in loans by the Federal Reserve to the commercial banks. Only rarely are percentage reserve requirements raised. All of these actions tend to reduce the quantity of money, raise interest rates, restrict other terms of lending, reduce total spending, and moderate or eliminate the inflation.

Economic Growth

Government in the United States had traditionally intervened in the economy in ways which had the effect of accelerating economic growth. Then in the 1950s, Soviet Russian growth seemed to offer a new challenge. Consequently, new programs to promote American growth were begun in the late 1950s and the 1960s.

Traditional American Policies. The size of the labor force was increased in the 19th century by a liberal immigration policy. This policy, essentially, let the market system operate in this regard without impediment. During that century, too, a liberal and subsidized policy of frontier land settlement encouraged the market to cause the country's economy to grow.

In both the 19th and 20th centuries, the quality of the labor force has been raised through subsidized and compulsory education. The government has sponsored some research, such as that undertaken by the agricultural experiment stations and the land grant colleges. It has encouraged the dissemination of knowledge through agricultural extension agents. The patent system has been a governmental device for stimulating private research. The government's sponsorship of research into the technology of war has resulted in discoveries useful to nonmilitary production. An example is the knowledge of atomic energy derived from the development of the atomic bomb.

The Soviet Challenge. In the late 1950s Americans became alarmed by the rather low rate of economic growth which had been achieved during the past two or three decades. The immediate stimulus for the alarm was the almost spectacular economic and technological achievements of the Soviet Union. The Soviet growth rate was revealed at that time to have been considerably more than most Americans had thought at all possible. The Soviet orbiting of the first scientific satellite in 1957 was an accomplishment which America could not until later duplicate.

New Growth Policies. A number of federal governmental policies were introduced thereafter in the United States in an attempt to accelerate the rate of economic growth.

Two new tax policies were used. These were an investment tax credit and accelerated depreciation. These policies reduced businesses' income tax payments if they bought or built additional plant and equipment. In this way, the nation's stock of real capital and its ability to produce would increase more quickly.

Increased governmental assistance to research was provided outside the traditionally aided areas of defense and agriculture. Included was research in such fields as space, medicine, psychology, and education. As a result, there might be greater knowledge of how to increase the output from a given amount of resources.

Increased varieties and amounts of federal aid were given to education so that, in part, people could be better producers. Additional training and retraining programs were sponsored by a variety of federal agencies to raise the quality of the labor force and reduce unemployment of the structural sort.

Laws were passed against racial and other discrimination in employment. These laws were designed primarily to achieve a noneconomic, ethical goal. Nevertheless, they accelerated growth by increasing the degree to which human resources could efficiently match the uses to which they were put.

Measures of fiscal policy designed to achieve full employment and avoid a recession also had the beneficial effect of promoting growth. Growth is measured primarily by actual production rather than mere ability to produce. Fiscal policy assured that the gap between actual production and ability to produce was narrowed.

A Clean Environment

Beginning in the late 1960s, a new view regarding growth arose among Americans. Some of the adverse side effects of past growth began to receive greater attention. Chief among these effects were air pollution and water pollution.

Air and water pollution occur partly because so much production of goods and services is being carried on. In earlier decades the real gross national product was smaller than now. The noxious fumes and harmful chemicals which were given off were able to be absorbed and converted by the earth's natural capacity to cleanse itself. There were, in effect, little or no external costs or disadvantages to most production. As growth occurred, the volume of production increased. So also did the volume of potential pollutants. Production became large relative to the earth's natural capacity to cleanse itself. Air and water pollution came to be significant external costs which private producers frequently did not take into account. Economic growth and the market system combined to produce pollution.

Pollution also occurs partly because the techniques of production in use are those which pollute rather than those which do not. Frequently the private or internal production costs of the polluting techniques are less than those of nonpolluting ones. A competitive firm which chose the nonpolluting but more expansive techniques would be undersold and outcompeted in its product market by rival firms which chose the polluting but less expensive techniques. Hence, the polluting techniques are used by all the firms. Smelter companies do not freely choose to filter their air discharges. Chemical companies do not freely choose to treat their liquid sewage. For *local* government, too, pollution is often an external effect, and costly measures to avoid the pollution will not voluntarily be undertaken by these governments. Why should a city go to the expense of treating its municipal sewage if the main adverse effect of nontreatment is on other (downstream) communities?

Federal Governmental Policy Against Water Pollution. In recent decades the American national government has acted in several ways to reduce water pollution. It has stood ready to pay over half the costs of constructing sewage treatment plants for municipalities. This subsidy is available only to municipalities in states which have set up a plan for achieving acceptably pure water. A federal governmental unit, the Environmental Protection Agency, determines the acceptability of such plans. Subsidies of this kind are supposed to encourage municipalities to construct and operate adequate sewage treatment plants, which they would otherwise not undertake because of the expense.

Since 1969 the national government has permitted private enterprises to reduce their income taxes if the enterprises have set up waste treatment facilities. For tax purposes the enterprises are permitted to count almost all the cost of such facilities as depreciation expense in the first few years of the life of the facilities. This arrangement is sometimes called accelerated depreciation of investment in waste treatment plants. The arrangement is supposed to encourage the construction and operation of these facilities.

The national government has sought to encourage private and local pollution control by holding conferences attended by governmental officials and polluters. The aim presumably is to encourage an awareness of the need for pollution control.

Each state has been required by the national government to establish water quality standards and to develop a plan for achieving the standards. The states are to issue licenses for pollution and to limit the number and circumscribe the conditions of the licenses so that the standards can be achieved. The Federal Environmental Protection Agency is to assist the states in enforcing the standards, if necessary, through prosecution in the courts.

Federal Governmental Policy Against Air Pollution. The American national government has acted in a number of ways to reduce pollution of the air. It sponsors research into the causes, extent, effects, and possible remedies of air pollution. It makes grants to state and local governments to develop their air control programs. It holds conferences among government and private officials to encourage an awareness of the problem and of the need for solutions. Beginning in 1965 national restrictions on auto exhaust pollution were planned. The federal Department of Health, Education, and Welfare began to designate regions called "air sheds," to establish air quality standards for such sheds, and to require state governments to plan to achieve these standards. In 1970 a federal "Clean Air Bill" required states to plan more thoroughly against air pollution. This bill also set nationally uniform limits on air pollution by each type of new industrial plant and by automobiles after 1975 or 1976.

The degree of failure and success of these policies against pollution and some of the reasons for failure and success are discussed in Chapter 8.

Economic Security

Governments in economies primarily directed by market forces have intervened in a variety of ways which reduce economic insecurity. Sometimes the reduction in insecurity occurs as an incidental result of policies principally designed to cope with other problems.

Policies Which Incidentally Reduce Insecurity. Unemployment is both a problem itself and a cause of insecurity. Governmental activities successfully undertaken to reduce unemployment also reduce insecurity. Fiscal policy is such an activity. There are programs designed to reduce structural unemployment by increasing the geographical and occupational mobility of labor. Examples are retraining programs and tax reduction for moving expenses. These programs also reduce the insecurity of those workers who are concerned with their abilities to maintain their incomes.

Inflation is a major source of insecurity for those people receiving fixed money incomes or owning fixed price assets. Therefore, government undertakings designed to reduce inflation may also reduce insecurity. An example is tight monetary policy.

Some governmental programs are mainly intended to redistribute income or to raise the incomes of the poorest people in the population by assuring them of no less than a certain minimum income. These programs have the effect of reducing the insecurity felt by these people regarding the continued receipt of at least some income. Into this class of programs fall encouragement of the growth of unions, the imposition of tariffs upon imported goods, and agricultural price supports.

Through special tax laws, governments encourage private savings and the purchase of private insurance and annuities. Such encouragement also reduces insecurity.

All of these policies have been used by government in the United States.

Social Security. The American governmental program which most directly and explicitly has been directed against economic insecurity is what is commonly called *social security*. The social security program has three main components. One is the unemployment compensation system. Another is the old age, survivors, and disability insurance system. The third is the public assistance system. The present forms of all three took shape initially in the 1930s.

Unemployment Compensation. The unemployment compensation system places a payroll tax upon most employers. The tax receipts are placed in a fund or reserve. From the reserve, payments are made to workers when they become unemployed. Under such a system workers may feel secure in the knowledge that, whether or not they continue to hold jobs, they will continue to receive an income.

Old Age, Survivors, and Disability Insurance. The old age, survivors, and disability insurance program places a payroll tax upon both employers and employees. The tax receipts are placed in a reserve fund. From this fund, payments are made to workers who have retired or who are disabled and to the spouses and young children of workers who have been killed. In this way, workers and their families may feel secure that at least part of their income will continue when they retire or should the worker die or become disabled. An expansion of the program occurred in the mid-1960s. Free hospital care began to be provided for older persons, and voluntary governmental insurance for doctors' fees became available to them. For these persons the insecurity which was caused by the possibility of large, imperative, and unexpected drains upon their incomes was reduced.

Both unemployment compensation and old age, survivors, and disability insurance are, as they work in the United States, compulsory insurance systems operated by government. Employees or employers or both pay premiums in the form of taxes. Employees then receive benefits paid out of the tax funds. The size of the benefit to be received depends in part on the size of the tax payment. The employees receive the benefit as a matter of right, regardless of need. Not all people, not even all employees, are included in the systems. The law compels only some employers and employees to pay taxes. Even some of those who pay are ineligible to receive benefits. Moreover, the unemployment compensation can be paid to any worker for no more than a maximum number of consecutive weeks and a maximum number of weeks in a year.

Public Assistance. The third component of the social security program, public assistance, is designed to supplement the other two components. It provides payments to needy persons not included in the other components. It is not an insurance system. The funds are provided from general taxes or government borrowing, and a person must prove need to receive payment. Payments are made to dependent children, the blind, the aged, and the permanently and totally disabled Public assistance resembles the relief payments that have been made to the poor in most Western countries at least since Elizabethan times.

Justification for Social Security. Public assistance payments are probably defensible on two grounds. They provide security for everyone regarding a minimum level of real income. In addition, they result in a less unequal distribution of income. However, what is the justification for the two compulsory insurance systems run by government? Could not private insurance, voluntarily purchased, be relied upon for unemployment, old age, survivors, and disability protection?

Historically the coming of compulsory programs seems easy to explain. In the 1930s the Great Depression revealed the need for some protection against the uncertain cessation of income. Yet neither then nor before had privately produced, voluntarily purchased insurance been provided or sold on an adequate scale. The only alternative seemed to be compulsory governmental insurance.

The logical justification for compulsory governmental insurance is more difficult to discover.[12] If people need the insurance, why don't they buy it? If such insurance is needed, why don't private businesses arrange it and sell it in appropriate amounts?

One answer is that the need for compensation for unemployment, for example, unlike the need for compensation for fire damage and for death, is not reasonably predictable. This risk does not occur in truly random fashion subject to the "law of large numbers." Instead, unemployment is dependent upon such things as business fluctuations whose occurrence is largely unforeseeable. Since forecasts of frequency of occurrence are not possible, private companies are unable to set fees at appropriate levels for the insurance. Also, they are necessarily without the supplemental power of taxation.

Moreover, the employers and employees with the least risk would not buy voluntary insurance. They would feel that they did not need it. Therefore, for those others who would buy it because they had considerable need, the fees would have to be discouragingly high.

Furthermore, many individuals are ignorant or poorly informed of risks. They underestimate the uncertainty or danger which confronts them and so do not buy insurance. The insurance as an asset is highly intangible and, therefore, is not sufficiently prized.

---

[12] Milton Friedman, in fact, believes there is no such justification. See Friedman, *op. cit.,* pp. 182–189.

Also, the administrative costs and difficulty of collection of insurance fees are high in cases in which buyers have small or irregular incomes.

All in all, compulsory governmental insurance may be a useful device. It redistributes income; lower-income people typically receive insurance benefits greater than in proportion to their insurance tax payments. It also paternalistically forces individuals to buy something which they need but the need for which they may not recognize. It is provided by the government since provision by private businesses would be difficult for technical reasons.

SUMMARY

Three important types of economic organizations have developed in the United States. These three are the large corporation, the labor union, and government in an economic role. The three have arisen partly in response to the needs and deficiencies of market mechanisms.

The large corporation uses a nonmarket system of coordination by command within itself. It is partially insulated from external market forces. Nevertheless, it may make decisions similar to those which would be made to maximize profits in a market situation.

Labor unions in part offset the power of corporations and reduce the power of market forces in labor markets. Unions probably improve the positions of their members. However, the unions have had both good and bad effects on society and are still an object of controversy.

Undoubtedly, the most important American modification of the market system has been achieved through governmental measures in the economy. Public education has been provided. Business monopolies have been curbed. Progressive taxation, transfer payments, and vocational training have been used to reduce economic inequality. Fiscal and monetary policies have been aimed at the achievement of full employment and price stability. A variety of governmental regulations, including tax arrangements, have been adopted to shape economic growth and to curb pollution. The social security program has reduced economic insecurity.

All in all, government in the United States has come to occupy a large and growing role in the economy. Still, government only supplements rather than predominantly displaces the market system. The economic importance of government relative to the market is not precisely measurable, but statistics are suggestive. For example, government purchases of output rose from 10 percent of the GNP in 1930 to 22 percent in 1970. It is clear that governmental intervention in the economy has become large enough to justify the classification of America as a *mixed* rather than a strictly market system. How successful this mixture has been remains to be discussed.

QUESTIONS

1. In what ways can the development of large corporate businesses be regarded as a departure from a market system?
2. Are the decision makers in large corporations motivated by the desire to maximize profits? What else could possibly motivate them?
3. In what ways can the development of labor unions be regarded as a departure from a market system?

4. Suppose that Congress was considering legislation to reduce the power of labor unions. Would you support or oppose such legislation? Why?
5. Supposing that labor unions reduced efficiency in production, one, nevertheless, might justify the existence of labor unions. How?
6. Some Americans who have received their entire education from kindergarten through college in public schools are incredulous when told that one of the nation's largest industries, education, is governmentally owned and operated and is mostly socialistic. Is it correct to say that, primarily, the education industry is not part of the market system in the United States?
7. Why do you think the American government has not been successful in preventing or abolishing private monopoly power in the United States?
8. If it is unwise or impossible to break up private monopolies, what can be done other than simply to accept their existence?
9. How has governmental policy in the United States actually encouraged private monopolies which might not have existed in the absence of governmental intervention?
10. Which American taxes are progressive? Which are regressive?
11. How can the distribution of income be altered by governmental policy other than taxation?
12. Compare and contrast the old rules of public finance with the new rules of functional finance or fiscal policy. Which set of rules do you prefer? Why?
13. The next chapter contains a critique of the new rules of fiscal policy. You might, however, try to do some independent thinking by attempting now to answer the question of what might be wrong with the new rules in practice in the United States.
14. What are automatic or built-in stabilizers? Do you know of any automatic stabilizers built into governmental economic policy other than those described in the text? Do you know of any automatic stabilizers in the way private participants behave in a market system?
15. What, in general, is monetary policy? Who has control over monetary policy? Is this power lodged in private or governmental hands? Is the power exerted through market channels or simply by command?
16. A critique of American monetary policy appears in the next chapter, but a good exercise in creative thinking is to review the description of monetary policy in this chapter and then to answer this question: How and why might monetary policy fail to work as it is supposed to, particularly in a time of business cycle recession?
17. What new governmental policies were used in the United States in the 1960s to accelerate the rate of American economic growth? What information would you need to have to know if these efforts were successful?
18. Is there any justification for the government's compelling people to buy life insurance or old age annuities in the United States?

RECOMMENDED READINGS

American Economic Association. *Readings in Industrial Organization and Public Policy.* Homewood, Ill.: Richard D. Irwin, Inc., 1958.
——. *Readings in the Social Control of Industry.* Philadelphia: The Blakiston Company, 1949.

Bowen, William G. and Orley Ashenfelter (eds.). *Labor and the National Economy,* rev. ed. New York: W. W. Norton & Company, Inc., 1972.

Brown, J. A. C. *The Social Psychology of Industry: Human Relations in the Factory.* Baltimore: Penguin Books, Inc., 1954.

Freeman, A. Myrick III, Robert H. Haveman, and Allen V. Kneese. *The Economics of Environmental Policy.* New York: John Wiley & Sons, Inc., 1973.

Friedman, Milton. *Capitalism and Freedom.* Chicago: University of Chicago Press, 1962.

Galbraith, John Kenneth. *American Capitalism: The Concept of Countervailing Power,* rev. ed. Boston: Houghton Mifflin Company, 1956.

Hailstones, Thomas J., Bernard L. Martin, and George A. Wing. *Contemporary Economic Problems and Issues,* 3d ed. Cincinnati: South-Western Publishing Co., 1973.

Hayek, Friedrich A. *The Road to Serfdom.* Chicago: University of Chicago Press, 1944.

Heller, Walter W. *Economic Growth and Environmental Quality: Collision or Co-Existence?* Morristown, N.J.: General Learning Press, 1973.

Okun, Arthur M. (ed.). *The Battle Against Unemployment,* rev. ed. New York: W. W. Norton & Company, Inc., 1972.

Slesinger, Reuben E. *National Economic Policy: The Presidential Reports.* Princeton, N.J.: D. Van Nostrand Co., Inc., 1968.

Wilcox, Clair. *Public Policies Toward Business,* 5th ed. Homewood, Ill.: Richard D. Irwin, Inc., 1975.

―――. *Toward Social Welfare: An Analysis of Programs and Proposals Attacking Poverty, Insecurity, and Inequality of Opportunity.* Homewood, Ill.: Richard D. Irwin, Inc., 1969.

8

An Appraisal of the American Economy

INTRODUCTION

Is the American economy a success? Has basic reliance on a market system, but with extensive superimposition of governmental controls, produced a highly desirable set of results?

Suppose everyone who wanted a job had one. The average level of prices was not increasing at all. The average level of living was high and rising very rapidly. There was what almost everyone regarded as a fair distribution of income, wealth, and power. People confronted the future without fear of economic difficulties. Everybody felt free to buy what they wished, to work at what they wanted, and to do with their property as they chose. There was equality of opportunity to become wealthy. Then the American economy could be regarded as a complete success.

Of course, these conditions have not all been fully achieved. There is some unemployment. Some inflation occurs. The character of economic growth is not optimum. There are inequities in the distribution of economic power. Some economic insecurity is felt. Economic freedom is incomplete. The imposition of governmental controls has cured only some of the defects of a market system. In the process, governmental intervention has created some undesired results.

The goals of this chapter are several. An attempt is made to indicate the extent to which the American economy is a success. Suggestions are offered as to how it is most successful and least successful. The reasons for its successes and failures are explored.

THE LEVEL OF LIVING

The outstanding success of the United States economically is the high average level of living that has been achieved for its people.

Difficulties of Measurement

Of course, there is great difficulty in indicating with any precision just how high the average level of living is for any people. Accurate measurement of levels of living is subject to many conceptual and empirical obstacles. The most obvious objective measure might seem to be consumption per capita. This measure is calculated by adding together the total value of all goods and services purchased by consumers during a period of time and dividing the sum by the number of people in the population.

Ambiguities in Per Capita Consumption. Per capita consumption as a measure of the average level of living, however, fails to account for some important economic and social costs. Should one include those services, such as defense and police services, which are not purchased directly by consumers? Services such as commuter transportation may not add anything directly to consumer satisfaction. Should not the amount of leisure be taken into account? Is not the quality of the environment relevant? Does not the degree of air pollution, the attractiveness of the streets and countryside, and the extent of physical violence make a difference? Should not the introduction of new products or the improvements in old ones be taken into account, regardless of whether there is an increase in the total money value of consumption purchases? [1]

Problems in Making Comparisons. Such problems as these become particularly troublesome when an attempt is made to compare the levels of living of two or more nations or of the people of a nation at different times.

For example, the money value of per capita consumption might be greater in Iceland than in Samoa. However, the actual level of living might be higher in Samoa. The physical environment, mainly the climate, of Samoa may require a much smaller expenditure to achieve a given level of living than may that of Iceland.

Americans in 1960 received more doctors' services per capita to cope with lung cancer than did their ancestors in 1860. Does this suggest that the American level of living in 1960 was higher than it was in 1860 or does it suggest that there is simply more lung cancer in 1960 than there was in 1860?

Suppose average per capita consumption in the Soviet Union is 100 rubles per month while that in the United States is $200 per month. How do the levels of living compare in the two countries? In order to make the comparison, one must at least know how many dollars a ruble is worth. However, what does one use to determine this worth? Should one really use the official exchange rate of the Soviet government, a rate which is obviously set arbitrarily? On the other hand, should one use the quite different black-market rate at which an American tourist might surreptitiously exchange his dollars for rubles on some street in Moscow? [2]

---

[1] Many of these difficulties arise because of ambiguity in the concept of "income." See, for example, Myron H. Ross, *Income: Analysis and Policy* (2d ed.; New York: McGraw-Hill Book Company, 1968).

[2] For a brief summary of the problem of measuring differences in levels of living, especially for underdeveloped countries, see Stephen Enke, *Economics for Development* (Englewood Cliffs, N.J.: Prentice-Hall, Inc., 1963), pp. 41–46.

Aggregate Measures

Even though many difficulties of measuring and comparing levels of living exist, statistics still serve well as rough indicators of the level of living. Personal consumption expenditures per capita in dollars of 1958 purchasing power were $2,631 in the United States in 1973, more than double the $1,145 figure for 1929.[3] The implication is that the American average level of living more than doubled in this period of 44 years. Moreover, the amount increased in every year from 1958 through 1973. All of this is evidence that the United States economy, since it took on substantially its present form in the 1930s, has enabled the American people to raise their level of living by significant amounts.

Another measure of the level of living, closely related to per capita consumption, is per capita gross national product. Per capita GNP includes the value of consumption goods and services and, in addition, the value of capital goods and governmental purchases of goods and services. It has been estimated that the per capita GNP of the United States in 1971 was $5,076 in then-current dollars.[4] This was an amount considerably larger than that of any other major country. The amount in United States dollars for that year for second-ranking Sweden was $4,348. For third-ranking Canada it was $4,227. For fourth-ranking Switzerland it was $3,816. Several other countries which are large and are considered economically advanced had still smaller amounts: $3,697 for West Germany, $2,892 for France, and $2,381 for the United Kingdom.[5]

Specific Measures

Aggregate measures, like personal consumption spending per capita and GNP per capita, have deficiencies as measures of the level of living. Such aggregates also fail to convey vividly enough contrasts between one level of living and another. Therefore, additional kinds of comparisons in terms of specific commodities and services are sometimes made between nations. These, too, generally support the contention that the United States enjoys a higher level of living than any other major nation.

For example, it has been calculated that to secure enough income to buy one kilogram of butter required 43 minutes of the typical factory worker's time in the United States in 1960, but 52 minutes in Canada, 67 minutes in the United Kingdom, 146 minutes in Argentina, 148 minutes in West Germany, 250 minutes in France, and 390 minutes in Japan.[6] Again, it was estimated that

[3] United States Department of Commerce, *Survey of Current Business*, Vol. 54, No. 6 (June, 1974), pp. S–1 and S–13; and *Economic Report of the President* (Washington: U.S. Government Printing Office, January, 1973), p. 213.

[4] *Ibid.*, pp. 193 and 219.

[5] United Nations, Statistical Office, *Monthly Bulletin of Statistics*, Vol. 26, No. 10 (October, 1972), pp. 1–5 and 186–190; and International Monetary Fund, *International Financial Statistics*, Vol. 24, No. 9 (September, 1971), p. 27.

[6] Gertrude Deutsch (ed.), *The Economic Almanac, 1962* (New York: National Industrial Conference Board, 1962), p. 493.

in 1970 there were more telephones per person in the United States than in any other country. The United States had 59 telephones per 100 people; second-ranking Sweden had 53; the United Kingdom, 27; Japan, 25; West Germany, 23; France, 17; the Soviet Union, 5; and Yugoslavia, 4.[7] In the same year the United States also had more television sets per person than any other country. There were 41 sets for each 100 persons in the United States, and 31 in Sweden, 28 in West Germany, 27 in the United Kingdom, 26 in East Germany, 22 in Japan, 20 in France, 14 in the Soviet Union, and 9 in Yugoslavia.[8] Such fragmentary bits of evidence are not conclusive proof of relative levels of living, but when they all point in the same direction, they cannot be ignored.

The Problem of Causation

Suppose one accepts as correct the proposition that the American level of living is the highest of any major nation in the world. There is still no necessary implication that the major cause of this achievement is the American economic system. It might be argued, for example, that the high American level of living is the result of forces other than the economic system. It might even be contended that the achievement has occurred in spite of, rather than because of, that system.

All kinds of speculation are possible. For example, one who was an ardent advocate of laissez-faire could argue that free enterprise had created a strong American economy by 1929. It was so strong, it might be asserted, that the extensive government intervention which occurred in the decades afterward was unable to prevent considerable continued forward momentum. On the other hand, there are some who believe that modern technology requires considerable government regulation. They might admit that free enterprise was good for America in the 19th century. However, they might insist that progress would have slowed and ceased in the mid-20th century, had not the United States significantly altered its economic system by increasing the amount of government direction which was practiced.

A fairly good case can be made for the contention that the type of economic system applied in America has been at most a necessary, but not at all a sufficient, condition for American economic progress. The United States had advantages for its economic development which had little to do with its economic system. A continent full of rich, unexploited natural resources is one of these advantages. A cultural tradition of hard work and enterprise inherited from Europe is another.[9] The opportunity to borrow technology and capital as well as culture and people from Europe is still another. Having achieved a good start with these advantages, America became wealthy. Being

[7] United States Bureau of the Census, *Statistical Abstract of the United States* (93d ed.; Washington: U.S. Government Printing Office, 1972), pp. 829–830.

[8] *Ibid.*

[9] Alfred R. Oxenfeldt and Vsevolod Holubnychy, *Economic Systems in Action: The United States, the Soviet Union, and France* (3d ed.; New York: Holt, Rinehart & Winston, Inc., 1965), p. 62.

wealthy in 1929, America found it easy to become even wealthier in the decades thereafter. More wealth came easy to America for many of the same
reasons that an underdeveloped country's being poor makes it very difficult
for it to do anything other than remain poor.

All in all, it seems necessary to reach a favorable conclusion regarding
the modified market system which the United States fashioned for itself after
1929. At the very least, it was not an obstacle to continued progress in raising
the level of living. In fact, it probably was a substantial contributor to that
progress.

ECONOMIC GROWTH

A high level of living in the present is made possible by the economic
growth of the past. A rising level of living is made possible by continued
economic growth in the present. The high level of living of the American
people in the mid-20th century implied great economic growth previously. A
central concern of Americans in the mid-20th century was their rate of economic growth at that time. This concern arose partly from a desire to continue to enjoy a rising level of living. It also arose because economic growth
is an avenue to achieve national prestige and international power.

The chief measure of economic growth is the rate of change of real
gross national product, either total or per capita, over time. The total real
GNP of the United States measured in dollars of 1958 purchasing power rose
from about $204 billion in 1929 to $837 billion in 1973, as indicated in Table
8–1. The real per capita GNP rose from about $1,673 in 1929 to about $3,978
in 1973. The period from 1950 until 1973 excludes the unusual years of the
Great Depression and of World War II. From 1950 to 1973 the average annual

TABLE 8–1

REAL GROSS NATIONAL PRODUCT, UNITED STATES, 1929–1973

Year	Total Real GNP Billions of Dollars of 1958 Purchasing Power	Percentage Change from Preceding Year	Per Capita GNP Dollars of 1958 Purchasing Power	Percentage Change from Preceding Year
1929	204	—	1,673	—
1930	184	− 9.8	1,493	−10.8
1931	169	− 8.2	1,361	− 8.8
1932	144	−14.8	1,152	−15.4
1933	142	− 1.4	1,129	− 2.0
1934	154	8.5	1,217	7.8
1935	170	10.4	1,334	9.6
1936	193	13.5	1,505	12.8
1937	203	5.2	1,574	4.6
1938	193	− 4.9	1,485	− 5.7
1939	209	8.3	1,595	7.4

TABLE 8–1, Continued

Year	Total Real GNP		Per Capita GNP	
	Billions of Dollars of 1958 Purchasing Power	Percentage Change from Preceding Year	Dollars of 1958 Purchasing Power	Percentage Change From Preceding Year
1940	227	8.6	1,718	7.7
1941	264	16.3	1,979	15.2
1942	298	12.9	2,210	11.7
1943	337	13.1	2,465	11.5
1944	361	7.1	2,608	5.8
1945	355	− 1.7	2,537	− 2.7
1946	313	−11.8	2,214	−12.7
1947	310	− 1.0	2,151	− 2.8
1948	324	4.5	2,210	2.7
1949	324	0.1	2,172	− 1.7
1950	355	9.6	2,331	7.3
1951	383	8.5	2,473	6.1
1952	395	3.1	2,507	1.4
1953	413	4.6	2,578	2.8
1954	407	− 1.5	2,497	− 3.1
1955	438	7.6	2,640	5.7
1956	446	1.8	2,641	0.0
1957	453	1.6	2,634	− 0.3
1958	447	− 1.3	2,556	− 3.0
1959	476	6.5	2,677	4.7
1960	488	2.5	2,701	0.9
1961	497	1.8	2,705	0.1
1962	530	6.6	2,839	5.0
1963	551	4.0	2,909	2.5
1964	581	5.4	3,024	4.0
1965	618	6.4	3,176	5.0
1966	657	6.3	3,336	5.0
1967	673	2.4	3,380	1.3
1968	707	5.1	3,515	4.0
1969	726	2.7	3,580	1.8
1970	722	− 0.6	3,525	− 1.5
1971	742	2.8	3,582	1.6
1972	790	6.5	3,781	5.6
1973	837	5.9	3,978	5.2

Source: Derived from *Economic Report of the President* (February, 1968), pp. 210 and 227; *Economic Report of the President* (January, 1973), pp. 194 and 219; and *Survey of Current Business*, Vol. 54, No. 6 (June, 1974), pp. S–1 and S–13.

rate of increase in total real GNP was about 4 percent. The average annual rate of increase in per capita real GNP was about 2½ percent. These are moderately high rates and suggest the American economy was fairly successful in achieving growth. However, closer examination of growth figures for the United States in Table 8–1 and for other countries in Tables 8–2 and 8–3 suggest a slightly less satisfying conclusion.

TABLE 8–2
PERCENTAGE CHANGES IN REAL GROSS NATIONAL PRODUCT, EIGHT ADVANCED COUNTRIES, 1950–1965

| | Percentage Change, 1950–1965 | |
Country	Total Real GNP	Per Capita Real GNP
Canada	92.2	34.8
France	96.9	67.4
West Germany	169.0	127.7
Italy	127.7	108.0
Japan	136.5	154.3
Sweden	78.1	62.4
United Kingdom	54.2	43.0
United States	71.6	34.2

Source: Agency for International Development and The National Industrial Conference Board, *The Economic Almanac, 1967–1968*, pp. 502 and 503.

TABLE 8–3
ANNUAL PERCENTAGE CHANGES IN REAL GROSS NATIONAL PRODUCT, EIGHT ADVANCED COUNTRIES, 1965–1970

| | | Annual Percentage Change | |
Country	Years	Total Real GNP	Per Capita Real GNP
Canada	1965–70	4.4	2.6
France	1965–70	5.7	4.9
West Germany	1965–70	4.7	4.0
Italy	1965–69	6.0	5.2
Japan	1965–70	12.1	10.9
Sweden	1965–70	3.9	3.2
United Kingdom	1965–69	2.4	1.9
United States	1965–70	3.3	2.3

Sources: United States Bureau of the Census, *Statistical Abstract of the United States, 1972*, p. 814; and United Nations Statistical Office, *Monthly Bulletin of Statistics* (July, 1972), pp. 2 and 212.

Erratic Growth During Depression and War

For one thing, the rate of growth was not entirely steady. During the Great Depression decade of the 1930s, there were year-to-year decreases in total and per capita real GNP in half the years because of unemployment and idle production capacity. However, perhaps that experience is of historical rather than current interest. As has been indicated in earlier chapters, the American economic system was considerably altered thereafter, and economic understanding of how to avoid the recurrence of such a disaster was greatly increased. Thus those depression years should not be used to judge the ability of the American economy to perform well in the latter half of the 20th century.

Growth occurred very rapidly during the war years from 1940 until 1944. This rapidity was probably evidence of how well the American economic system, as it then existed, could respond under forced draft in a situation of crisis. It also showed how effective government stimulation can sometimes be in eliminating depression and unemployment.

The declining real GNP at the end of the war in the years 1945 through 1947 probably should be regarded as a result of removal of the forced draft of war. For example, women left the defense plants and returned to their homes. The labor of homemakers does not count as part of the GNP. However, this decline in real GNP can be regarded also as a result of the inability of the economy to adjust perfectly to rapidly changing conditions. Nonetheless, positive credit is due the economic system for negotiating the immediate postwar readjustment without a major relapse into depression.

Unsteady Growth Since 1947

The period since 1947 provides perhaps the best evidence of the ability or inability of the American economy, as it was constituted in the mid-20th century, to achieve steady growth. Several aspects of the statistics in Table 8–1 deserve emphasis.

First, growth was slowed or even reversed during the contraction phases of the five recognized business cycles in the period from 1947 to 1973. These contractions occurred in 1948–49, 1953–54, 1957–58, 1960–61, and 1969–70. At least until the 1970s and probably even thereafter, the American economic system was not structured to avoid business cycles completely. On the other hand, the five cyclic recessions that did occur were of rather modest proportions, especially when compared with the Great Depression.

Second, in the late 1950s and early 1960s, the rate of growth noticeably slowed. In the years 1956 through 1961, the average annual increase in the total real GNP was only about 2.2 percent. The average annual change in per capita real GNP was about .4 percent. These low figures are partly the result of the fact that these years included two recessions. Nevertheless, it is probably significant that the length of the interval between recessions was growing briefer as the 1950s wore on. Furthermore, the rates of increase in real GNP during the nonrecession years of the period were alarmingly small.

Third, beginning about 1962, an unusually long period of substantial increases in GNP began. The average annual increase in total real GNP in the years 1962 through 1968 was about 5.2 percent. That of per capita real GNP was a striking 3.8 percent.

What conclusions seem to emerge from this review of statistics for the United States? By the 1970s, the American system was probably able to avoid major interruptions in growth and to increase growth if that was desired. The system seemed to be enlarging its ability to determine the rate of growth within increasingly narrow limits. On the other hand, precise determination and control were still not attained. One has only to note the recession of 1969–70 to understand that perfectly steady growth was not yet achieved.

National Growth Comparisons

American economic growth was somewhat unsteady in the period after World War II. It was also less, on the average, than that of a number of other countries. This was unsettling to some Americans. Table 8–2 reveals the percentage changes in total and per capita real GNP from 1950 to 1965 for eight noncommunist advanced countries. Of these eight, the United States had the lowest growth rates. Table 8–3 indicates the average annual growth rates for the same eight countries for the more recent period from 1965 to 1970. In this period the American growth rates were still lower than those of six of the other countries. The United Kingdom had the lowest rates of all.

Problems in Achieving Growth

One should not necessarily conclude from the data in Tables 8–2 and 8–3 that the American performance was poor.

First, many of the other countries listed in the tables were just recovering in the early 1950s from the destructive effects of World War II. Their percentage growth rates were abnormally high in the period from 1950 to 1965 because during these years they were returning from the temporarily low levels of production of the immediate postwar years to more nearly normal levels. The United States, on the other hand, suffered relatively little damage during the war and was already operating at normal production levels in 1950. Partly for this reason the percentage increases for the United States from 1950 to 1970 is less than those of some of the other countries.

Second, the United States was in 1950 already at a higher stage of economic development than most of the other countries. One can perhaps accept the idea that better developed countries can be expected to grow at lower rates than those not quite so developed. In that case the relatively slower American growth is simply a consequence of its advanced state and not necessarily a result of its economic system.

It is probable, however, that there are additional reasons for the relatively slow American growth. One, already mentioned above, was the inability of the American economic system to avoid recessions. Each recession meant that fewer goods, including capital goods, were produced than could have been produced. Hence, the real capital stock of the nation grew less than it could have otherwise. Consequently, the nation inherited a smaller capacity to produce than it would have if there had been no recessions.

Another reason was the volume of unemployment, which remained high relative to other countries in the late 1950s and early 1960s even during non-recession years. Much of the persistent unemployment was of the structural sort, which came to be recognized and emphasized beginning about 1960. Structural unemployment represents human resources which perhaps could be, but actually are not, contributing to the production of GNP. If structural unemployment exists, then the GNP will be less than it could be. If structural unemployment increases, the rate of increase of GNP will be less than it could otherwise be.

Still another reason for the slow growth is related to those just given. The American government was sometimes unable or unwilling to use vigorously policies which could promote growth. For example, Keynesian fiscal policy to fight recessions was not wholeheartedly accepted and used by American presidents until after 1961, when John Kennedy was in office. National programs to reduce structural unemployment require government spending, government intervention in the economy, and subsidies to the poor. All three of these government activities were contrary to ideology popular among many Americans. An easy monetary policy can be used to lower interest rates and to encourage business investment spending on capital formation. Restrictionist fiscal policy can be used to reduce consumption spending and hence to keep total spending at low, noninflationary levels. These two policies used together may accelerate growth, but they have a real cost of reduced consumption. They also have a political disadvantage of alienation of voters. The voters resent the higher taxes and the reduced spending which are the essence of restrictionist fiscal policy.

Coping with the Environmental Side Effects of Growth

One aspect of economic growth that received increased attention in the United States beginning in the late 1960s was the effect of growth on the natural environment. Some of the first steps undertaken by the American federal government to prevent pollution of the environment were described in Chapter 7. Policies against pollution of the air and water included governmental subsidization of sewage treatment plants, public relations campaigns against pollution, licensing of the right to pollute, and requiring controls on vehicular and factory exhausts.

It is hard to measure the extent to which the environment has been preserved from pollution. There was general agreement by the mid-1970s that the United States was still considerably short of restoring a sufficiently clean environment or perhaps even of significantly retarding environmental deterioration. There seemed to be a number of reasons for the lack of greater success in the fight against pollution. For one thing, there began to be recognition that there are disadvantages as well as benefits in curbing pollution. For example, to subsidize the construction of sewage treatment plants requires higher taxes. To fail to issue a local license to a company which is looking for a site for a new factory may cause the local unemployment to persist. To require exhaust controls on cars raises the prices of cars and reduces the number of miles per gallon of gasoline consumed. To refuse to allow a coal-burning electric generating plant to be built creates a shortage of electricity. All in all, insistence that the environment be cared for probably means that economic growth must be slower than otherwise.

Another reason for the failure to reduce pollution more was the inadequate techniques used. Anti-pollution laws were not always enforced. Exceptions to the laws were too often made. Subsidization of sewage treatment was perhaps not as good a technique as charging the polluters a fee for the right to pollute. The rights of the general populace to a clean environment were not as well established in law as were the rights of individual businesses to carry on their production as they chose. Too often, too, the fight against pollution was conducted on an excessively fragmented basis. Environmental planning for an entire river basin was required. Instead, a sewage treatment plant here or there was subsidized whether or not it was crucial to the overall quality of the basin's environment.

A final reason why the fight against pollution was not more successful was the political process. Congress and state legislatures wanted to please the environmentalists, but they did not want to anger the businesses, workers, and cities that were polluting. In an attempt to please both sides, the legislators passed laws which were vague and which left considerable discretion to the governmental agency officials who implemented the laws. The tendency of the officials was to intrude to no more than a minimal degree in the activities of the polluters. This tendency was encouraged by the fact that the officials were not accountable, except very indirectly, to the populace. In addition, their decisions were not very visible to the public, and their accessibility to the public was often small. The result was one of considerable inertia in the agency activities and of a continuation of pollution.[10]

EMPLOYMENT AND UNEMPLOYMENT

As suggested in a preceding section, the American modified market system succeeded in reducing unemployment, but not in eliminating it.

The unemployment rate is usually expressed as a percentage of the civilian labor force. In the depths of the Great Depression, the unemployment rate for the United States was as high as 25 percent. The rate did not again reach that high figure in subsequent decades, as can be seen from Table 8–4. During World War II the rate fell to 1.2 percent. The maximum annual rate in the period between 1946 and 1973 was 6.8 percent in 1958, closely followed by 6.7 percent in 1961. The average rate in the period from 1946 until 1973 was about 4.7 percent.

---

[10] For a readable account of the American experience with anti-pollution policy, see A. Myrick Freeman III, Robert H. Haveman, and Allen V. Kneese, *The Economics of Environmental Policy* (New York: John Wiley & Sons, Inc., 1973).

TABLE 8–4

UNEMPLOYMENT RATES, UNITED STATES, 1929–1973

Year	Percentage of Civilian Labor Force	Year	Percentage of Civilian Labor Force
1929	3.2		
1930	8.7	1952	3.0
1931	15.9	1953	2.9
1932	23.6	1954	5.5
1933	24.9	1955	4.4
1934	21.7	1956	4.1
1935	20.1	1957	4.3
1936	16.9	1958	6.8
1937	14.3	1959	5.5
1938	19.0	1960	5.5
1939	17.2	1961	6.7
1940	14.6	1962	5.5
1941	9.9	1963	5.7
1942	4.7	1964	5.2
1943	1.9	1965	4.5
1944	1.2	1966	3.8
1945	1.9	1967	3.8
1946	3.9	1968	3.6
1947	3.9	1969	3.5
1948	3.8	1970	4.9
1949	5.9	1971	5.9
1950	5.3	1972	5.6
1951	3.3	1973	4.9

Sources: National Industrial Conference Board, *The Economic Alamanac, 1962,* pp. 36 and 37; *Economic Report of the President* (January, 1973), p. 223; and *Survey of Current Business,* Vol. 54, No. 6 (June, 1974), p. S–13.

One can then conclude that the American system was successful in preventing a recurrence of the large-scale unemployment of the Great Depression. However, some unemployment persisted. Moreover, the problem was apparently becoming moderately worse in the period from 1956 until 1963 and again after 1970. Concern arose over this persistent and moderately increasing unemployment. Such concern can be better understood when it is known that the average rate of unemployment in most of the other economically advanced nations of the world in the period from 1961 until 1971 was considerably lower. Relevant statistics are given in Table 8–5. It is also useful to know that the unemployment in the United States was more heavily concentrated among certain portions of the labor force, such as teenagers and nonwhites.[11]

[11] *Economic Report of the President* (Washington: U.S. Government Printing Office, January, 1973), p. 223.

TABLE 8–5

UNEMPLOYMENT RATES, EIGHT ADVANCED COUNTRIES, 1961–1971

Unemployment Rate
as a Percentage of the Civilian Labor Force

Country	1961	1962	1963	1964	1965	1966	1967	1968	1969	1970	1971
Canada	7.1	5.9	5.5	4.7	3.9	3.6	4.1	4.8	4.7	5.9	6.4
France	2.0	2.0	2.4	1.9	1.8	2.3	3.0	2.7	2.1	2.2	2.7
West Germany	0.4	0.4	0.4	0.4	0.3	0.4	1.0	1.2	0.8	0.5	0.7
Italy	3.7	3.2	2.7	3.0	4.0	4.3	3.8	3.8	3.7	3.4	3.4
Japan	1.3	1.1	1.1	1.0	1.2	1.1	1.4	1.2	1.1	1.2	1.3
Sweden	1.5	1.5	1.7	1.6	1.2	1.6	2.2	2.2	1.9	1.5	2.5
United Kingdom	2.3	2.8	3.3	2.4	2.3	2.3	3.1	3.7	3.7	4.0	5.3
United States	6.7	5.5	5.7	5.2	4.5	3.8	3.8	3.6	3.5	4.9	5.9

Sources: National Industrial Conference Board, *The Economic Almanac, 1967–1968*, p. 508; United States Bureau of the Census, *Statistical Abstract of the United States, 1970*, p. 811; and United States Bureau of the Census, *Statistical Abstract of the United States, 1972*, p. 812.

INFLATION AND PRICE STABILITY

Moderate amounts of inflation characterized the United States after the mid-1930s. The record is summarized in Table 8–6. The general level of prices of all goods and services produced as a part of the gross national product had risen by 1958 to twice its level of 1929. Further, from 1958 to 1973 an additional 54 percent increase occurred in this level. In the late 1950s and early 1960s, the average annual increase in the level was about 1.5 percent. In the mid-1960s it was about 3 percent. In the late 1960s and early 1970s, it was almost 5 percent. By 1974 the highest rate of inflation since 1950 was occurring. There was thus a moderate increasing and worrisome tendency toward inflation.

The amount of inflation which occurred in the United States between 1963 and 1972 was almost as little as that which occurred in the least inflationary of the other major noncommunist advanced nations. In the period from 1963 until 1972, the prices of consumer goods and services rose about 37 percent in the United States. West Germany, Canada, and Italy had about the same amount of inflation, with comparable figures of 33, 35, and 40 percent, respectively. But France had 46 percent, the United Kingdom 57 percent, Japan 60 percent, and the Netherlands 63 percent.[12]

PROBLEMS WITH KEYNESIAN FISCAL POLICY

A small part of the cause of inadequate economic growth and a major cause of unemployment and inflation in the United States in the middle decades of the 20th century was the failure of Keynesian fiscal policy to work perfectly in practice.

[12] *Ibid.*, p. 301.

TABLE 8—6

GROSS NATIONAL PRODUCT DEFLATOR, UNITED STATES, SELECTED YEARS, 1929—1973

Year	Index (1958 = 100)	Year	Index (1958 = 100)
1929	50.6	1965	110.9
1930	49.3	1966	113.9
1933	39.3	1967	117.6
1939	43.2	1968	122.3
1940	43.9		
		1969	128.2
1945	59.7	1970	135.2
1950	80.2	1971	141.6
1955	90.9	1972	146.1
1958	100.0	1973	153.9
1960	103.3		

Sources: *Economic Report of the President* (February, 1968), p. 212; *Economic Report of the President* (January, 1973), p. 196; and *Survey of Current Business*, Vol. 54, No. 6 (June, 1974), p. 16.

Keynesian fiscal policy, as explained in preceding chapters, calls for unemployment to be reduced by increases in governmental spending or decreases in taxation or both. These actions tend to increase total spending in the economy and thus to reduce unemployment. They also cause the governmental budget to move from surplus to deficit. Keynesian fiscal policy calls for inflation to be reduced by decreases in governmental spending or increases in taxation or both. These actions tend to reduce spending in the economy and thus to reduce inflation. They also cause the governmental budget to move from deficit to surplus. Fiscal policy can be used to moderate business cycles. To do so, the government must move its budget in the surplus direction as a business cycle expansion becomes excessive. The budget must be moved in the deficit direction as a business cycle recession gets underway.

Simultaneous Unemployment and Inflation

One trouble with Keynesian fiscal policy in practice occurred because inflation and unemployment took place simultaneously at times in the United States. Keynesian policy provides one set of actions for inflation and the opposite set for unemployment. It offers no guide as to how to cope with simultaneous inflation and unemployment. According to a simplified version of Keynesian theory, inflation and unemployment do not occur simultaneously: inflation is caused by too much total spending in the economy; unemployment, by too little. Therefore, there is some precisely right amount of spending which will produce full employment without inflation. Keynesian policy is designed to achieve that right amount.

Nevertheless, in the United States in the mid-20th century, inflation and unemployment did occur simultaneously. They did so because there were kinds of inflation other than demand-pull inflation, which is caused by too much total spending. Further, there were kinds of unemployment other than general or cyclical unemployment, which is caused by too little total spending. There were also cost-push or seller's inflation and structural unemployment. Even when total spending was inadequate to cause full employment, cost-push inflation could and sometimes did exist. Even when total spending was so excessive as to cause inflation, unemployment of the structural sort could and usually did exist.

Another deficiency in Keynesian fiscal policy is that it provides a remedy neither for structural unemployment nor for cost-push inflation. For a considerable time in the 1940s and early 1950s, preoccupation with Keynesian economics prevented adequate recognition in the United States of cost-push inflation and of structural unemployment. When, beginning in the 1950s, these problems began to receive greater recognition, Keynesian policy provided no real solution for them.

Timing

An equally important defect in Keynesian policy in practice in the United States was the matter of timing. To cope with business fluctuations, the proper timing of governmental policy was very important. For example, increases in taxes and decreases in spending should have occurred at the time in each cyclic expansion at which total spending would have otherwise become excessive. However, such timing was extremely difficult to achieve for three primary reasons.

First, economists and government officials were unable to predict when a crucial stage in the business cycle would be reached. Indeed, at any given time, they were not sure what stage had already been reached, since it took several months to gather and interpret the statistics and other data. It was thus impossible to alert governmental officials as to what precise policy was required before or even at the time such policy was to be put into effect.

Second, even if this predictive and analytical lag had not existed, a decision lag would have made proper timing impossible. That is, even with an understanding among economists of what the situation was, there was still need for agreement among political officials as to what should be done about it. Such agreement was achieved only after a time of discussion and debate. Sometimes the debate was quite prolonged. It was 20 months after President John Kennedy requested Congress to lower taxes that the Tax Reduction Act of 1964 was finally passed by Congress. It was 17 months after President Lyndon Johnson first suggested a tax increase that Congress passed the tax raises of 1968.

Third, even after political agreement on a change of policy, there elapsed a time before the new policy was implemented. Tax changes and governmental expenditure changes, once agreed upon and passed into law, required months to be put into effect.

Thus it took a long time for the economists to determine that a business cycle boom had become excessively inflationary, for Congress to agree that a tax increase was desirable, and for the bureaucracy to notify taxpayers to begin paying higher taxes. By the time all this had been done, the business cycle could have reached a new phase. So it might happen that people began paying higher taxes and reducing their own spending just at a time when a recession had begun and when spending increases, not decreases, were the appropriate measures.

Deficits and Debt

Keynesian fiscal policy may be further regarded as defective because it may involve considerable increases in the federal governmental debt. The change in the size of this national debt is indicated in Table 8–7.

TABLE 8–7
FEDERAL GOVERNMENTAL DEBT AND GROSS NATIONAL PRODUCT, UNITED STATES, SELECTED YEARS, 1929–1973

Year	Debt (in Billions of Current Dollars)	GNP (in Billions of Current Dollars)	Debt as a Percentage of GNP
1929	16.3	103.1	15.8
1930	16.0	90.4	17.8
1933	24.0	55.6	43.2
1935	35.1	72.2	48.6
1940	50.9	99.7	51.1
1945	278.7	211.9	131.5
1950	256.7	248.8	103.2
1955	280.8	398.0	70.6
1960	290.4	503.7	57.7
1961	296.5	520.1	57.0
1962	304.0	560.3	54.3
1963	310.1	590.5	52.5
1964	318.7	632.4	50.4
1965	321.4	684.9	46.9
1966	329.8	749.9	44.0
1967	345.2	793.9	43.5
1968	358.0	864.2	41.4
1969	368.2	930.3	39.6
1970	389.2	976.4	39.9
1971	424.1	1,055.5	40.2
1972	449.3	1,155.2	38.9
1973	480.7	1,289.1	37.3

Sources: *Economic Report of the President* (February, 1968), pp. 209 and 285; *Economic Report of the President* (January, 1973), pp. 193 and 272; and *Survey of Current Business*, Vol. 54, No. 6 (June, 1974), p. S–1 and S–19.

Fallacious Fears of a National Debt. There is a popularly held fear of a large and growing governmental debt. This is a fear that such a debt bankrupts a nation, must be paid off, and constitutes an almost intolerable burden on future generations. This fear is probably naive.

A growing governmental debt will not bankrupt an economically growing nation any more than a growing debt owed by a vigorous business corporation which borrows to expand will bankrupt the corporation. It is true that individual securities which represent parts of the debt must be paid off as their maturity dates arrive. However, such payments may be financed by the government through the issuance and sale of new securities. This refinancing means that the debt in the aggregate can be successfully perpetuated.

Suppose that in the future it were for some reason decided to pay off the debt. The people who were taxpayers among the generation alive at that time would indeed be burdened with extraordinarily, but temporarily, heavy taxes. However, those among that generation who were owners of governmental securities would receive the tax proceeds. The quantity of real resources available for use and the amount of real national income and product would not necessarily be diminished. There would need to occur no reduction in the real level of living of that generation comparable to the reduction in the level of living of the generation alive during World War II, when much of the debt was originally incurred and when the American people worked hard and consumed relatively little.

Real Disadvantages of a National Debt. There may be, however, some real difficulties created by a large and growing public debt.

Interest Payments. One of these difficulties involves the interest payments which must be made on the debt. In 1974 these interest payments amounted to $28 billion for the United States federal government. In a time of full employment and inflationary pressure, the funds to make these interest payments should come from taxes. Taxes are troublesome in that they reduce taxpayers' incentives to work hard, to save, to invest productively, and to be efficient. Workers and entrepreneurs may reduce their efforts because too much of the reward for extra effort is taken away by the government in taxes. If effort and efficiency decline as a result, the real GNP and the rate of economic growth decline. The level of living of most people in the nation may be less than otherwise. Hence a large national debt can be harmful.

This harmful effect of a large debt upon incentives will be so small as to be insignificant if the ratio of the size of the debt to the size of the national income or GNP is small. The trend of this ratio for the United States for the period 1929–73 is shown in Table 8–6. It should be noted that the ratio has declined since 1945.[13]

---

[13] The significance of a large, growing national governmental debt is still a matter of dispute, even among experts. See Milton H. Spencer, *Contemporary Economics* (2d ed., New York: Worth Publishers, Inc., 1974), pp. 202–206. For debate by professional economists on aspects of the burden of national public debt, see William Gordon Bowen, R. G. Davis, and D. W. Kopf, "The Public Debt: A Burden on Future Generations?" *American Economic*

Debt Owed to Foreigners. There is another significant sense in which a public debt that arises from Keynesian fiscal policy may be a real burden on the people of a nation. This burden may occur in those cases in which the debt is owed to foreigners. For example, in the mid-1970s the Arab oil-exporting nations were acquiring more of the securities representing the United States national debt. To pay the interest on such debt or to repay the debt itself, foreign funds may have to be earned. The chief means of earning them is to export goods and services which have been produced in the nation. These goods are then lost as far as the consumption and the level of living of the nation are concerned. In this way, repaying a debt owed to foreigners can be a real burden upon the generation which obtains the means to repay it. In 1974 about 12 percent of the American federal government debt of $500 billion was owed to foreigners.

Discouragement of Growth. The creation and existence of public debt, even if it is not owed to foreigners, may distort economic decisions and economic activities from what they would otherwise be. This distortion may be undesirable in itself and may also be disadvantageous to future generations.

In the competition for borrowed funds, governmental borrowing may drive up interest rates. High interest rates may discourage private borrowers who wish to spend on real capital formation. The results will be a slower growth of productive capacity for the economy, consequent less ability to produce goods in the future, and a lower level of living for future generations. This is significantly true, however, only if governmental spending financed by the deficit is for purposes which increase current consumption rather than increase productive capacity.

Governmental deficit spending and the creation of public debt may cause fear among private real investors. They may then decide to reduce private capital formation. Again, the same disadvantageous results for economic growth will follow.

Politically Inspired Waste

There is still another way in which Keynesian fiscal policy may be disadvantageous. In pre-Keynesian times it was thought by most government officials and economists that deficit spending by government and the incurrence of governmental debt were things to be avoided. There was a kind of moral rule that it was wrong for the government to go into debt. Not everyone understood why, on grounds of cause and effect, such behavior by government was wrong. Nevertheless, the rule did serve a useful purpose. It served to remind government spenders that there was a cost to government spending. It said, in effect, if it is desirable that the government spend, then to get the funds to spend, there must be taxes. Taxes are immensely obvious financial

Review, Vol. 50, No. 4 (September, 1960), pp. 701–706. Arguments and counterarguments resulting from this article appeared in the *American Economic Review,* Vol. 51, No. 1 (March, 1961), pp. 132–143, and in the *Review of Economics and Statistics,* Vol. 44, No. 1 (February, 1962), pp. 98 and 99.

costs to taxpayers. Consequently, both the government and the people were, under the rule, constantly reminded of the cost of governmental spending.

The financial cost in the form of taxes represented a real cost in terms of sacrifices of alternative opportunities foregone when governmental spending occurred. Suppose, for example, the government wished to build a dam. Then the man-hours, natural resources, and machinery use required to build the dam would be lost forever so far as alternative uses, such as building houses, were concerned. To construct the dam, the rule required tax financing. The prospect of more taxes forced people to decide whether they really wanted the dam more than the houses.

Keynesian thinking overturned the old rule against deficit spending. In its place was the idea that governmental deficit spending was something appropriate and could serve the useful purpose of preventing unemployment. Freed of the old rule and carelessly interpreting the new Keynesian rules, politicians could justify to themselves governmental deficit spending in almost any circumstance. Under old rule or new, there is a persistent temptation for people and politicians to wish for increased governmental spending. The temptation exists because someone obviously benefits from the spending. There is also a persistent aversion to taxes, since they obviously hurt someone. Now Keynesian economists say government spending can, and sometimes should, occur without taxation. It must seem to the people and the politicians that they can have the best of two worlds: more dams and more houses.

Under conditions of already substantially full employment, however, this is simply not possible. If resources are used to build dams, they are not available to build houses. Under the Keynesian rules, the real costs of governmental spending become obscured. It becomes possible to avoid the financial costs, taxes, which represent the real costs. The Keynesian rules, by removing the moral stigma against deficit spending under some circumstances, seem to enlarge greatly the opportunity for governmental deficit spending under conditions in which such spending is unjustified.[14]

PROBLEMS WITH MONETARY POLICY

Monetary policy, too, had deficiencies as it existed in practice in the United States in the period from 1929 through the following decades. These deficiencies explain in part the failure of the United States to attain a better record during those years as steady growth, full employment, and price stability are concerned.

Like fiscal policy, monetary policy is partially dependent upon forecasts of forthcoming conditions and takes time to make its effects felt. Forecasts may be inaccurate. There are lapses of time between forecasts and policy

---

[14] One who wished to pursue briefly the criticisms against Keynes might read William Harold Hutt, "Keynes: Obsolete But Influential," *The Wall Street Journal*, Vol. 166, No. 49 (September 9, 1965), p. 12. For lengthier criticisms, see William Harold Hutt, *Keynesianism —Retrospect and Prospect: A Critical Restatement of Basic Economic Principles* (Chicago: Henry Regnery Co., 1963); and Henry Hazlett, *The Failure of the "New Economics": An Analysis of the Keynesian Fallacies* (Princeton, N.J.: D. Van Nostrand Co., Inc., 1959).

decisions and between policy decisions and effects. These lapses mean that the effects may occur at inappropriate times.

Moreover, there are substantial segments of the financial sector which are, at most, subject to only indirect control by the Federal Reserve authorities. Among these are nonbank financial intermediaries, such as personal finance companies, savings and loan associations, and life insurance companies. These institutions may, contrary to Federal Reserve policy, continue to make loans or cease to make loans. For example, suppose the Federal Reserve is attempting to fight inflation by reducing the quantity of money. At the same time, the financial firms and the general public may be increasing the average speed with which money circulates. In such a case, the volume of spending may be increasing when the money supply is decreasing.

Finally, it is alleged that tight monetary policy is discriminatory. It cuts off the flow of loanable funds to small firms and to the industry which constructs houses. Both of these are heavily dependent upon borrowed money. At the same time this policy may permit large, established firms and other industries to continue to expand and to spend. They do so from their own undistributed profits or from funds received because of preferential treatment by banks. In a period of credit stringency, the banks are likely to ration loans to borrowers, with understandable priority given to their largest customers.

PRIVATE CONCENTRATION OF ECONOMIC POWER

Behind several of the unsolved economic problems in the American economy lies the existence of large business firms and large labor unions with considerable monopoly-like power. These concentrations of power may be partially to blame for a surprisingly large share of the American economic difficulties.

Wage-Price Guideposts

The American economic system has developed no really effective arrangement for coping with these large concentrations of economic power. In this regard one policy which has been tried in one form or another several times in recent decades is direct control over prices and wages. In the 1960s this control took the form of *wage-price guideposts* or *guidelines*.

These were first made explicit by the President's Council of Economic Advisers in 1962. The guideposts indicated that the average level of prices in the economy should remain stable. They also suggested that the average level of wage rates should rise at a rate equal to the average rate of increase of labor productivity. This rate was about 3.2 percent per year. The guides were primarily for the monopolistic and unionized sectors of the economy. They were intended to stop inflation and to keep approximately constant the labor and nonlabor shares of the national income. They were qualified by several exceptions.

The guides can perhaps be regarded as having been moderately success-ful from 1962 until 1966. In any case, the rate of inflation and wage increases were very moderate during that period. Beginning in 1966, the rate of inflation rose, and negotiated wage increases in several important industries were considerably in excess of the guides. A major defect in the guides seems to be that they involved no reliable and effective means of enforcement. Plead-ings and denunciations by public officials and the pressure of hopefully aroused public opinion were the primary techniques of implementation. Such techniques are unlikely to be successful in the long run.[15]

Wage-Price Freezes and Phases

When President Nixon succeeded to the Presidency in 1969, he at first rejected the idea of price and wage controls and abandoned the policy of guideposts. However, by 1971 inflation was growing worse. The use of Keynes-ian fiscal policy and monetary policy in a restrictive direction to fight the in-flation would probably have caused unemployment. Therefore, in August, 1971, President Nixon suddenly announced a *wage-price freeze*. For several months most product prices and wage rates were legally prohibited from rising. This period of several months came to be called Phase I. Phases II, III, and IV followed during the next two years. During these later Phases the rigidity of the controls was decreased and exceptions to them were increased. By 1974 the program had been ended. In 1974 Nixon's successor, President Ford, established a small federal agency to monitor prices and wages and to publicize and try to exert pressure against excessive increases in prices and wage rates. The agency was without any real power to prevent price and wage increases.

The mandatory controls by the government over prices and wage rates in the early 1970s were generally regarded afterward as failures. The rate of inflation was higher at the time the controls expired than it had been at the time they were started. While they were in operation they were enforced in a sporadic and halfhearted fashion. It was found necessary to riddle them with exceptions. They were blamed for various economic ills, such as beef and gasoline shortages.

New Proposals

In place of direct controls as techniques for fighting inflation, economists suggested various governmental policies. Among these was more vigorous en-forcement of the antimonopoly laws, elimination of tariffs and restrictive quotas on goods entering the country, new labor laws to reduce the power of unions to restrict entry into various occupations, and alteration of the tax laws so as to encourage enlargement of the productive capacity of businesses.

---

[15] One review of the policy of guideposts may be found in Reuben E. Slesinger, *National Economic Policy: The Presidential Reports* (Princeton, N.J.: D. Van Nostrand Co., Inc., 1968), pp. 100–127.

Many of these new techniques were unlikely to be adopted because of political opposition. Others of them probably would not effectively decrease the
private power to raise prices and wages.[16]

It must be concluded that by the mid-1970s, the United States had still
to find a satisfactory means of coping with private concentration of economic
power and with inflation.

TABLE 8—8
PERSONAL DISTRIBUTION OF INCOME IN THE UNITED STATES, SELECTED
YEARS, 1947–1970

Income Rank	Percentage Share of Aggregate Income Received by Families and Unrelated Individuals in Each Fifth-of-Income Rank and by Top 5 Percent					
	1947	1950	1955	1960	1965	1970
Families						
Total	100	100	100	100	100	100
Lowest Fifth	5	4	5	5	5	5
Second Fifth	12	12	12	12	12	12
Middle Fifth	17	17	18	18	18	17
Fourth Fifth	23	24	24	23	24	24
Highest Fifth	43	43	41	42	41	42
Top 5 Percent	18	17	17	17	16	14
Unrelated Individuals						
Total	100	100	100	100	100	100
Lowest Fifth	3	2	3	3	3	3
Second Fifth	5	7	7	7	8	8
Middle Fifth	12	14	13	13	13	14
Fourth Fifth	21	27	25	26	25	25
Highest Fifth	59	50	52	51	51	50
Top 5 Percent	33	19	22	20	20	21

Sources: National Industrial Conference Board, The Economic Almanac, 1967–1968,
p. 391; and United States Bureau of the Census, Statistical Abstract of
the United States, 1972, p. 324.

[16] For an elaboration of these techniques, see Hendrik S. Houthakker, "A Positive Way
to Fight Inflation," The Wall Street Journal, July 30, 1974, p. 6; and Walter W. Heller,
"An Open Letter to President Ford," The Wall Street Journal, August 12, 1974, p. 6.

TABLE 8–9
EXTENT OF POVERTY IN THE UNITED STATES, SELECTED YEARS, 1959–1970

Year	Number of People in Poverty (In Millions)	Percentage of the Total Population
1959	39.5	22.4
1965	33.2	17.3
1968	25.4	12.8
1969	24.3	12.2
1970	25.5	12.6

Source: United States Bureau of the Census, *Statistical Abstract of the United States, 1972*, p. 329.

ECONOMIC INEQUALITY AND POVERTY

Tables 8–8 and 8–9 are useful in judging the progress which the United States has made in dealing with economic inequality and poverty. Table 8–8 suggests that the degree of inequality in the distribution of income remained about the same during the two decades after 1950. This could be regarded as a failure of the nation to make progress toward widely held egalitarian goals. The clamor in the 1960s and 1970s over the inequality of opportunity for ethnic and racial minorities, women, and the aged probably was a reflection of this failure.

Table 8–9 has better news. It indicates that the extent of absolute poverty declined substantially in the United States between 1959 and 1970. The number of people living in poverty decreased from approximately 40 million to about 25 million during the period. Of the total population, the percentage living in poverty declined from about 22 percent to about 13 percent during these same years. Considerable credit for this reduction in poverty probably belongs to the economic growth achieved by the nation. Somewhat less credit perhaps belongs to the specific anti-poverty programs begun in the 1960s. Some of these latter programs had come to be regarded as failures, and many of them were abandoned by 1974.

SUMMARY

Perhaps the most successful aspect of the American modified market system of the mid-20th century was the high average level of living. Economic growth, too, was considerable. Inflation was moderate. Unemployment was, on the average, fairly low.

For none of these criteria of success was the American record perfect, of course. The search went on for the causes of these imperfections and for techniques of improvement. Mild business fluctuations continued to occur. Structural unemployment was recognized as a problem beginning in the 1950s.

Fiscal and monetary policies helped to achieve the good record but were also found to possess at least minor flaws in practice. Fiscal policy tended to overlook structural unemployment and cost-push inflation. Fiscal policy was also difficult to operate in timely fashion; it could involve increases in public debt; and it possibly encouraged wasteful government spending. Monetary policy was rather ineffective against recessions and was hampered by political opposition during inflation.

Conflicts arose in part from the semimonopolistic character of some sectors of the American economy. The power of large businesses and labor unions over prices and wage rates made it difficult to achieve full employment and price stability simultaneously. No fully satisfactory American technique had been devised by the 1970s to deal with this power.

The degree of economic inequality remained rather high in the United States during the first 30 years after World War II. However, considerable reduction in the number of people in poverty was achieved by the nation in the 1960s. The improvement was probably the result of general economic growth more than of specific anti-poverty programs.

QUESTIONS

1. Why is it hard to measure the level of living of a people? Why is it difficult to compare accurately the levels of living of two nations? What purpose is served if such comparisons are made?
2. What sort of objective evidence is there that Americans live better economically than any other people?
3. Do you believe that the American modified market system is primarily responsible for the achievement of a high level of living for the American people? Why or why not? Would you then recommend the American system for use in other nations?
4. The American economy has grown greatly since the 1930s. Can one conclude that the American economic system is well designed to achieve economic growth?
5. What is the causal relationship between unemployment and economic growth?
6. Should the rate of inflation which the United States has experienced during the last decade be regarded as evidence of the superiority of the American economic system? Why or why not?
7. Present a good case against Keynesian economic policy.
8. What did the "guideposts" of the 1960s have to do with private concentrations of economic power?

RECOMMENDED READINGS

Batchelder, Alan B. *The Economics of Poverty*, 2d ed. New York: John Wiley & Sons, Inc., 1971.

Budd, Edward C. (ed.). *Inequality and Poverty.* New York: W. W. Norton & Company, Inc., 1967.

Denison, Edward F., and Jean-Pierre Poullier. *Why Growth Rates Differ: Postwar Experience in Nine Western Countries.* Washington: The Brookings Institution, 1967.

Edel, Matthew. *Economies and the Environment.* Englewood Cliffs, N.J.: Prentice-Hall, Inc., 1972.

Freeman, A. Myrick, III, Robert H. Haveman, and Allen V. Kneese. *The Economics of Environmental Policy.* New York: John Wiley & Sons, Inc., 1973.

Friedman, Milton, and Anna Jacobson Schwartz. *The Great Contraction, 1929– 1933.* Princeton, N.J.: Princeton University Press, 1965.

Galbraith, John Kenneth. *The Affluent Society,* 2d ed. Boston: Houghton Mifflin Company, 1969.

———. *Economics and the Public Purpose.* Boston: Houghton Mifflin Company, 1973.

———. *The New Industrial State,* 2d ed. Boston: Houghton Mifflin Company, 1972.

Hamilton, David. *A Primer on the Economics of Poverty.* New York: Random House, Inc., 1968.

Harrington, Michael. *The Other America: Poverty in the United States.* Baltimore, Md.: Penguin Books, Inc., 1963.

Heilbroner, Robert L. *An Inquiry Into the Human Prospect.* New York: W. W. Norton & Company, Inc., 1974.

Moskoff, William (ed.). *Comparative National Economic Policies: A Reader for Introductory Economics.* Lexington, Mass.: D. C. Heath and Company, 1973.

Pechman, Joseph A., and Benjamin A. Okner. *Who Bears the Tax Burden?* Washington: The Brookings Institution, 1974.

Silk, Leonard. *Capitalism: The Moving Target.* New York: Praeger Publishers, 1974.

Snider, Delbert A. *Introduction to International Economics,* 6th ed. Homewood, Ill.: Richard D. Irwin, 1975.

Theobald, Robert (ed.). *The Guaranteed Income: Next Step in Socioeconomic Evolution?* Garden City, N.Y.: Doubleday & Company, Inc., 1967.

Will, Robert E., and Harold G. Vatter (eds.). *Poverty in Affluence: The Social, Political, and Economic Dimensions of Poverty in the United States,* 2d ed. New York: Harcourt Brace Jovanovich, Inc., 1970.

9

Mixed Economic Systems

INTRODUCTION

Many comparative economic systems texts tend to stratify countries on the basis of *isms—capitalism, socialism, communism,* and *fascism.* A set of institutions are defined for each system and various countries are then classified as belonging to one or another system. At one time there was certainly a clear-cut line of demarcation between the various systems, but developments in recent years have tended to obfuscate differences that existed.

Today, most of the advanced industrial countries cannot be dumped into a box which is neatly labeled capitalism or socialism, for elements of each are prevalent. In general, then, it is best not to label countries by *isms.* It is better to apply the term *mixed,* which indicates that the economic systems of many countries combine some of the institutions of both capitalism and socialism.

A fundamental dilemma of any economic system is a scarcity of resources relative to wants. Decisions are necessary to determine how a given volume of resources is to be allocated in production and how the income derived from production is to be distributed to the various agents—capital, labor, and land—that are responsible for it. The market forces which allocate resources in production and determine the rewards in distribution are supply and demand. The relationship of supply and demand determines the relative values of individual resources and commodities. Explained in terms of money, these values are prices, and the pricing system is the unconscious planning mechanism which guides private individuals, in pursuit of maximum individual rewards, to allocate fully the resources of the economic system. Productive agents then are allocated or distributed on the basis of prices in a capitalistic system.

Capitalism

In a capitalistic system, ownership of the agents of production is held by individuals. This, however, does not preclude government ownership and operation of certain public services—post office and communication facilities—or natural monopolies. These agents of production have multiple uses. Price relationships determine their use. The use of land is determined by the prices individuals and firms are willing to pay. Capital will normally go into the fields where there are the greatest returns. Rewards go to the owners of the agents of production in the form of wages, rent, interest, and profits.

Under capitalism, consumer sovereignty is an important institution for the reason that consumer preferences in the market place determine what and how much will be produced. These preferences will be expressed through the price mechanism which operates on supply and demand in the markets for goods and services. If consumer demand for color television is great relative to the supply, prices will be bid higher than cost of production, and, in response to demand, expansion will occur on the part of existing firms and new firms that may choose to enter the market. Eventually the output of color television will be equal to the demand. However, if consumer demand is less than the supply of color television, prices will fall below costs, firms will stop producing sets, and eventually supply will adjust to demand.

Consumers are unequal in their ability to bid for various goods and services because incomes are not distributed equally. The question of for whom goods are produced is resolved by the price system operating in the market place. Some consumers have more money than others and can bid higher for certain goods. If this seems unfair, it is necessary to point out that in a free market system, supply and demand largely determine the distribution of income to individuals. Labor, as an agent of production, is rewarded according to its productivity. If it is scarce relative to the demand for it, then its productivity is high and it can command a large income; if it is abundant relative to demand, then its productivity and income will be low.

Capitalism has a set of institutions that serve as a frame of reference, or a point of comparison, to other systems. One institution is that of *private property ownership,* which involves a set of rights granted by society. These rights are enforced by laws and regulations. Owners can use their property as they desire as long as they do not infringe upon the rights of others. They can transfer it by sale or they can pass it on to their dependents. These property rights are supposed to provide incentives in a capitalistic system.

Freedom of enterprise is also an important institution. This refers to the right of an individual to select an occupation, to found and operate a business in any field, or to invest capital in whatever enterprise he or she chooses. As a consumer, one is also free to buy the products of one's choice. There is a libertarian element in this institution which is easy to reconcile with the development of political democracy in the United States. The element of self-interest is probably a stronger rationale for freedom of enterprise because it is probably the strongest motivating force in individual decisions.[1] Tied to freedom of enterprise is economic motivation, which involves the profit motive for the entrepreneur and the maximization of income for workers and their families.

Socialism

Socialism as an economic system represents a significant departure from the institutions of capitalism. The socialists contend that there are several major flaws in a capitalistic system—unemployment, income inequality, and social waste. The socialists would amend these flaws by changing the capitalistic institutions that presumably are responsible for them. There would be public ownership of the agents of production. Most industries would be nationalized and the profit motive would be eliminated. Income distribution would also be a public function, and income disparities based on the receipt of rental income, interest, or inheritance would be eliminated. Great emphasis would be placed on social welfare measures—medical care, family allowances, retirement benefits, and unemployment compensation. The institution of private property is an anathema to the socialists and would be completely discarded. However, the right of the individual to select any occupation would be preserved. A socialist system, then, would involve the elimination, or at least a major modification, of private profit making, public ownership of the agents of production, economic and social planning for the common good, and a distribution of income which would be much more even than under capitalism.[2]

Under socialism, decisions concerning the kinds and quantities of goods to be produced, the allocation of available productive factors to various industries and enterprises, and the distribution of resources between consumption and capital formation would be made by the government planners. The planners could not rely in the capitalistic guides of prices and costs in making these decisions, for prices and costs are determined by the planners under socialism. The socialists would not rely on price relationships in making economic decisions to the degree that a capitalist market economy would, but would handle through economic planning most of the decisions which are made under capitalism by the reactions of individuals and firms to these relationships. These decisions would be arbitrary since socialist planners would have no market-determined price system to guide them in making decisions as to what kinds and quantities of goods to produce and as to the distribution of the agents of production among various industries.

---

[1] The idea is prevalent in a capitalistic system that acting in one's self-interest benefits other members of society. Adam Smith, for example, expressed the view that the wealth of nations would increase most rapidly if everyone were allowed to follow whatever occupation seemed best in each person's eyes and to invest capital in whatever enterprise thought to prove most profitable.

[2] Although modern socialism was born in the stress and strain of Europe's rapid 19th century economic development, it is indebted to the French Revolution for its egalitarianism, as well as for state interference in economic matters. Emphasis was placed on environmental factors and the perfectibility of human nature.

Mixed Economic Systems

A mixed economic system combines some of the basic features of capitalism and socialism. In this examination five countries—France, the United Kingdom, Japan, Sweden, and West Germany—are used as prototypes of mixed economies. In mixed economic systems, certain characteristics are apparent.

1. There is a commitment to full employment as a fundamental economic objective. This has meant that postwar monetary and fiscal policies have been subverted to this end.[3] Price stability, as an economic goal, has been secondary in importance. Massive unemployment was experienced in each country during the period between the two world wars. In the United Kingdom, for example, the unemployment rate rarely got below 10 percent for the entire interwar period.

2. There has been the creation of elaborate social welfare programs, which has caused the name *welfare state* to be utilized in describing the systems of these countries, particularly the United Kingdom. These programs, which are largely a postwar development, provide a wide variety of social welfare measures and constitute a sizable proportion of government expenditures.

3. There is considerable reliance on economic planning of the indicative type. Economic planning, as it is utilized in these countries, is a system for centrally guiding the whole economy in the direction the planners would like for it to go. Supporters of economic planning, particularly the French type, contend that it is free from the elements of political authoritarianism and economic regimentation which are associated with planning of the Soviet type and from the defects of the unplanned, free market economies that existed in the United States and western Europe prior to World War II.

4. There is recognition that the objectives of full employment, social welfare, and economic planning can be accomplished without recourse to the nationalization of industry. Most nationalization that occurred took place during the period immediately after World War II, for reasons that had little to do with socialism.[4] Nationalization, for the most part, is a thing of the past—a *shibboleth* worshipped by die-hard socialists.

5. There is a basic reliance on free enterprise and the market system in all five countries. Most industry is privately owned. Facilities for production and

---

[3] However, preoccupation with monetary and fiscal measures to maintain full employment has caused an overheating of the economies of these countries. Dependence on foreign trade means that the inflationary bias that exists has caused balance of payments problems. The United Kingdom is pursuing a deflationary economic policy which is aimed at strengthening its domestic economy.

[4] The nationalization of the United Kingdom's coal industry is a case in point. It is considered probable that had the Conservative party remained in power after the end of World War II, the coal industry would have been nationalized anyway. The cause was the desire of the coal owners themselves that their industry be nationalized. The coal-mining industry had been subject to considerable state interference during the interwar period. In 1919 the Liberal party recommended nationalization. In 1930 the government imposed by statute a cartel system, giving producers fixed quotas to produce and sell and the power to fix prices. Coal was made an artificial monopoly. In 1938 coal itself, as distinct from its operation, was nationalized. Coal, then, had a history of unemployment, state interference, and cartelization before it was nationalized in 1948.

distribution remain primarily in the hands of private enterprise. Nevertheless, the governments play an important role in the economies of these countries through the use of monetary and fiscal policies. Control over the budget and credit gives the governments enormous leverage over the economic decisions of business firms. Income redistribution in these countries has been accomplished, not so much through progressive taxation, but through transfer payments in the form of a variety of social welfare measures.

Before examining the economic systems of the United Kingdom, France, Japan, Sweden, and West Germany, it is desirable to explore some of the above characteristics in some detail to provide a frame of reference to be followed. Perhaps the key point that should be remembered in connection with these countries is that the free market is recognized as the normal mechanism of economic adjustment.

ECONOMIC PLANNING

The purpose of a national economic plan is to harmonize the economic activities of different sections of society in the interest of optimal economic growth and structural balance. A good plan provides information on two matters. First, it provides a forecast of how an economy should perform in the future. Secondly, it provides a set of targets which can be attained through the implementation of necessary measures.

Virtually all countries have government planning policies of one sort or another to accomplish economic growth through proper resource allocation. In developing a plan, two questions are involved—the choice of the objectives and targets and the extent to which the government is committed to the implementation of the plan.

Economic planning can be classified as *imperative* or *indicative*.[5] The former would apply to a centralized *macroeconomic* plan in an economy dominated by its public sector. The government would assume direction by control and regulation of output, prices, and wages. Indicative planning would apply in an economy in which the government indicates a series of goals and indirectly stimulates certain economic activities through the budget, taxation, and interest rates to accomplish planning by inducements. The free market, however, is recognized as the normal mechanism of economic adjustment.

Economic Planning in Russia

The Russian economic plan is an example of imperative planning. The planners, as would be true in any country, start with limited resources and must allocate these resources to each economic sector to maintain some kind

---

[5] Actually these two concepts can be too circumscribed. There are several degrees of planning, ranging from the authoritarian, *command,* type of plan as used in Russia and China, to the very broad, and not defined as such, monetary and fiscal plans of the American Council of Economic Advisers. Most plans are somewhere in between these two extremes, including the French and Japanese economic plans.

of balance for the normal production of goods and services needed for the country. Russian planning consists of selected physical targets for output, employment, and consumption by sectors and regions. A plan is built around output goals and the expansion in capacity needed for leading industries and their supportive branches and for other sectors of secondary importance. A system of input-output balances is used to derive the various output and employment targets. Plans are drawn up on the basis of directives from the leadership of the Communist Party, which also controls the government. Consumer sovereignty is pretty much disregarded in the Soviet Union, and failure to fulfill the goals which have been defined by the planners redounds to the serious disadvantage of those who were responsible.[6]

Economic Planning in France

French economic planning is an example of indicative planning.[7] It is much less extreme or coercive than Russian planning, and it is essentially viewed as a set of directives or guidelines which help to guide the planning of private industry as well as the public sector of the economy. Nevertheless, there is a certain amount of government intervention in the implementation of planning, which has taken the form of indirect control over credit and taxation to encourage desirable objectives. There exists in France a whole range of measures which enable industries that conform to the plan to be rewarded. There is access to credit. There are tax concessions and, within the policy for regional development, subsidies for factories and equipment. There are favorable interest rates to encourage investment in certain areas.

The five countries studied in the section on mixed economies use planning. However, the degree of planning varies considerably among countries. French planning has consisted of a series of plans which have remained in effect for a period of usually four years.[8] The primary *raison d'etre* of French planning is the stimulation of economic growth. The Fourth and Fifth French Plans contained attempts to formulate a growth path for the French economy which postulated not only a certain rate of growth but a certain pattern of growth. In the Fourth Plan, the growth of private consumption was held back to allow a greater effort in the field of social investment. French plans are end-point plans, which construct an image of the economy in the horizon year of the plan but not for the intervening years.

It is an ineluctable fact that the public sector of the French economy determines the trend the economy is to follow. The national budget plays a

[6] It has been said that a Russian plan is reducible to an input-output table, plus a firing squad, plus a monopoly of propaganda.

[7] The term "indicative" may be a misnomer. Although French planning is not imperative or mandatory, it does attempt to guide the economy in a certain direction, and it does have the machinery to make its preferences effective. Although it does not fix an exact, detailed, and rigid program for each industry, the French plan does attempt to fit economic activity into a general framework which it has outlined.

[8] The need for planning in France grew out of the exigencies of the immediate postwar period and the memories of economic stagnation and unemployment of the interwar years.

very important role in determining the role that public investment is to play during the gestation period of the plan. About 25 percent of total fixed investment is financed out of public funds. More than half of the investment financed by specialized lending institutions and by medium-term credit is under direct state control.[9] The public sector on the average has accounted for around 40 percent of the gross savings of the capital market.

Economic Planning in Sweden, the United Kingdom, and Japan

Economic planning in Sweden is not nearly so comprehensive as French planning. There is no formal plan which is supposed to be operative over a specific time period. Swedish planning takes the form of a forecast usually spanning a five-year period. The purpose of the forecast is to provide business firms with information about the prospects for the economy to help them with their planning decisions. The government also has a guide for the planning of long-term capital expenditures. The aim of Swedish planning is to outline a flexible strategy for resolving the long-term difficulties with which economic policy is faced, in order to ensure full employment, rapid production increases, and financial stability.

The United Kingdom's planning is indicative in that a target is set up for the growth of national output over a period of time, accomplished by a detailed series of figures showing what might happen to particular industries and sectors—of which the public sector is one—if the target is achieved. There is also a statement of government policies which are supposed to help in achieving the target. The government is in a position, through its decisions on fiscal and monetary policies and other credit instruments, to directly influence the action of private firms. It is through the use of these instruments that the economy is directed to faster growth. The National Plan and the associated incomes and prices policy provide the framework in which public policy is to operate.

Japanese economic planning is also indicative in that objectives and targets are established as guides for the economy to follow. There have been a number of plans, but economic circumstances, particularly conditions external to the Japanese economy, have been responsible for their quick obsolescence. Current economic planning in Japan, as expressed in the Five-Year Plan which runs from 1972 to 1976, places emphasis on economic growth. A blueprint for this growth is developed, and certain sectors of the economy are assigned public investment priorities. The rate of capital accumulation, a major factor in economic growth, can be influenced by various fiscal and monetary measures. The international balance of payments problem is less amenable to influence by these measures.

[9] The French government exercises, both directly and indirectly, considerable influence over investment. Decisions to invest are left to private enterprise, and no effort is made to compel conformance to national policy objectives. Obviously, however, these decisions can be influenced by control over credit.

Objectives of Economic Planning

It can be said that the objectives of planning are certain general aims of economic policy expressed in qualitative terms: achieving a high rate of economic growth, with full employment, and in conditions of price stability and balance of payments equilibrium; improving the relative income distribution of the poorer classes; industrializing underdeveloped regions; and so on. Planning is geared to public expenditures and to investments made by some, but not all, individual firms, and through these to the growth rate. The latter is influenced through the instruments of monetary and fiscal policy.

However, planning is powerless to control certain determinants of the rate of economic growth, such as technological progress or international developments. Often specific increases in the growth rate are proposed in the plans, but no clear indication as to how this is to be accomplished is given.

FISCAL AND MONETARY POLICIES

Fiscal and monetary policies play an important role in the operation of the mixed economies of western Europe and Japan. Fiscal measures—government expenditures and taxes—change aggregate demand directly by altering private income and expenditure streams, while monetary measures affect aggregate demand indirectly by altering prices and the absolute and relative supplies of different kinds of financial assets.

The primary purpose of fiscal and monetary policies is economic stabilization. By this we mean controlling tendencies toward inflation or large-scale unemployment. A third objective, which is interrelated, is a desirable rate of economic growth.

A basic objective of any economic system should be full employment. It is reasonable to demand of an orderly economy that people should not be exposed to the vagaries of involuntary and prolonged unemployment. The prevention of mass unemployment is a fundamental desideratum for the social stability of any economic system.

The western European countries and Japan have maintained unemployment rates below 2 percent of the labor force throughout most of the postwar period. Full employment has been the supreme economic goal. The unemployment rate generally associated with full employment in the United States would topple governments throughout western Europe and Japan.

Price stability is a second fiscal and monetary objective. Inflation can wreak havoc on the development of an economy. To a major degree, price stability and full employment are mutually exclusive phenomena.[10] In attempting to accomplish full employment goals, many countries have sacrificed price stability with the concomitant of unfavorable trade balances and loss of export

---

[10] There has to be an allowance for frictional and seasonal unemployment.

markets. However, as a matter of political necessity, full employment as a goal takes precedence over price stability.[11]

Economic growth is also a most important economic policy objective. This refers to real per capita increases in goods and services over a time period. A high rate of economic growth is reflected in higher living standards. Full employment without economic growth is in itself meaningless. In comparing the efficiency and effectiveness of various economic systems, economic growth is certainly a valid criterion. In the process of maintaining price level stability and full employment, fiscal and monetary policies can also influence the rate of economic growth.

Fiscal Policy

Fiscal policy involves deliberate changes in government expenditures and taxes as a means of controlling economic activity. The budget of the national government is the key instrument through which fiscal policy is effected. Government expenditures for goods and services directly affect the level of economic activity because they are a component part of the demand function. Transfer payments and taxes, on the other hand, affect disposable income and also the two major components of aggregate demand—consumption and investment. Fiscal policy controls the provision of public goods and services through expenditures and income redistribution through taxes and transfer payments.

On the whole, fiscal policy carries the major responsibility for providing the conditions requisite to economic growth in the western European countries and Japan. To a considerable extent, this follows from the relatively substantial government participation in economic activity which is regarded in the United States as properly the sphere for private action. The term *public investment* would embrace a substantially wider range of economic activities in such countries as France and Sweden than it would in the United States. Because of relatively large government ownership in public utilities, transportation and communication facilities, and many basic industries, expenditure polcies in these countries are much more directly involved in the expansion of total productive capacity than is true in the United States. Public investment in the expansion of the capacities of these industries has been pursued vigorously to stimulate employment and economic growth.

Tax policies in the United Kingdom, France, Japan, Sweden, and West Germany reflect governmental concern with the promotion of economic growth, social welfare, and economic stability. Extensive use is made of liberal depreciation allowances and special tax incentives to stimulate private investment. Government transfer payments are utilized to accomplish an

---

[11] Economists favoring some unemployment as the cost of price stability seldom specify the percentage of the work force to be unemployed. This, however, can be done through the medium of the *Phillips curve* which makes it possible to estimate the proportion that would be involved. In the United Kingdom, the Phillips curve shows that inflation becomes a problem when unemployment drops to 2.5 percent.

extensive redistribution of income, while tax rates have been manipulated to encourage compliance with specific national policy objectives. In Sweden, for example, specific fiscal measures, such as an investment tax, have been used to encourage or discourage activities in various sectors of the economy.

Monetary Policy

Monetary policy refers to central bank actions to lessen fluctuations in investment and consumer spending through the regulation and use of the supply of money. It indirectly produces its effects upon the performance of an economy by influencing the aggregate amount and composition of effective demand for goods and services and the interest rate charged in the financial markets. Its influence on aggregate demand and the interest rate is indirect, being primarily upon the stock of money held by households, business firms, and nonbank financial institutions.

The basic instruments of monetary policy are rediscounting, changes in reserve requirements, and open market operations. In the United States, the Federal Reserve is responsible for the implementation of monetary policy; in the European countries—France, the United Kingdom, Sweden, and West Germany—and Japan, the central banks are responsible. The central banks, however, are government operated and controlled, whereas the Federal Reserve banks are owned by member banks of the Federal Reserve System.[12]

Commercial banks are privately owned in the United Kingdom, Japan, Germany, and Sweden. In France, most are publicly owned. Also in France, the government owns all, or a controlling part, of institutions operating in the field of medium- and long-term credit. It has used this ownership to direct their borrowing and lending policies toward the attainment of economic and social objectives.

Monetary System of France. In France principal responsibility for stabilizing rates of employment and the price level rests with monetary and credit instruments. The National Credit Council, consisting of representatives of the government and of various economic and financial interests, sets the broad lines of monetary and credit policy. Within this framework, the Bank of France, nationalized since 1946, has considerable autonomy and makes the important decisions concerning the day-to-day operations of the central bank.

The French government remains a large accumulator and investor of funds, and it exercises a great deal of control over both external and internal capital transactions. Thus the impact of market forces on the allocation of funds remains limited. The capital market has been to some extent segmented by the preferential treatment given to certain sectors of the economy.[13] The

---

[12] Government ownership does not necessarily mean government control. There are a number of instances where the central bank, once created and given its terms of reference, is left to go its own way. This is also true of other government financial institutions. In France, for example, the public authorities exercise a tighter control over the private credit banks than over the state-owned institutions engaged in medium- and long-term credit.

[13] This statement also holds true for the United Kingdom, Japan, and Sweden. It illustrates the fact that government control over credit can be effective in achieving certain objectives.

government has consistently encouraged investment in housing and has channeled capital into this area. The Bank of France itself has become an important source of medium-term financing in agriculture and construction.

Monetary System of Sweden. In Sweden the central bank (*Sveriges Riksbank*) is also state owned. Its functions have been, until recent years, subverted to the economic policies of the Swedish government. Full employment and social welfare took precedence over price stability, and an easy money policy was pursued. However, mounting inflationary pressures have resulted in increases in the rediscount rate and a general tight money policy, with the approval of the government.

The commercial banks are privately owned. Their major function is to grant long-term loans to industry; in addition, they act as underwriters for bond issues and hold large portfolios of bonds and housing mortgages. The Bank of Sweden exercises control over the commercial banks through the setting of liquidity ratios as well as legal reserve requirements.

The government controls all but certain specified, new capital issues in an attempt to maintain low long-term interest rates for priority borrowers. This is particularly true in housing. The provision of low-cost funds for residential construction is a major determinant of central bank monetary policy, and access to long-term funds is determined by control over capital issues rather than by free movements of interest rates in the market.

Monetary System of the United Kingdom. The Bank of England was nationalized in 1946. Although it enjoys autonomy in determining and guiding monetary policy, its policies are closely coordinated with those of the government. It has great influence over the commercial banks of the country, both through moral suasion and through the use of the customary central banking devices and techniques. The Bank has statutory powers to obtain information from and make recommendations to commercial banks, if this appears necessary or desirable in the public interest.[14]

Commercial banks operate under private ownership and management. Eleven banks which are members of the London Clearing House are responsible for about nine tenths of the resources of all commercial banks in the United Kingdom. For the most part, the credit of the commercial banks consists of securities, primarily government paper and particularly the Treasury bills. The heaviest suppliers of investment capital are the insurance companies and not the commercial banks.

Monetary System of Japan. The modern financial system of Japan was created during the Meiji Restoration and was patterned after the British banking system, with the Bank of Japan placed at the apex and supplemented by commercial and savings banks. In recent years it has been extremely difficult to

---

[14] However, this power over the commercial banks has never been employed, and the relationship between the Bank of England and the commercial banks has long been based on informal discussions. Nevertheless, the Bank of England undoubtedly derives wide power from this provision. It illustrates the point that the government does have the ultimate power over the British banking system.

satisfy the enormous fund requirements needed by the Japanese economy to continue its rapid rate of economic growth. As a result the government itself has had to assume a role in providing funds through the creation of special banks, which are designed to provide capital for economic activities.

The rapid rate of economic growth has created several characteristics which make the Japanese financial system different from other countries. First, the biggest borrowers in the money markets are business corporations, while the biggest lenders are private individuals. Although this feature is not unique, it is more pronounced in Japan for the reason that the prime mover of economic expansion has been the investment activities of private corporations. Second, the bulk of funds from the personal sector flows to the corporate sector through a channel of financial intermediaries. Savings are primarily held in the form of time deposits with commercial banks and other financial institutions, rather than in corporate securities. Third, there is constant reliance on the part of the commercial banks on the Bank of Japan for credit for the reason that there is consistent overborrowing by business corporations.

Monetary System of West Germany. In West Germany the law of 1957 which created the *Deutsche Bundesbank* provides that the central bank should keep in line with government economic policy, although the law adds that it should do this so far as it is consistent with its proper duty, which is to safeguard the currency. The law also provides the Deutsche Bundesbank with considerable independence—and independence which it has in fact used. However, the law also requires consultation between the Bundesbank and the government; there is no provision for government directives to the Bank.

There are a number of various financial institutions in West Germany, some of which are privately owned and others of which are publicly owned. The German commercial banks are privately owned. Savings banks, however, are owned by the German municipalities and are used to provide a source of capital for local needs. Specific purpose banks are important in West Germany; they have served to channel funds from the social security system and budgetary surpluses into economic areas in need of development.

Monetary systems vary from country to country. Control may be divided in different ways between the national government and the central bank. Although the central bank is state owned in all five of the countries, autonomy in matters of monetary policy varies considerably. The commercial banking system in the five countries, with the exception of France, is for the most part privately owned. Outside of the commercial banks, among the very large number of institutions concerned with medium- and long-term credit, the main distinction is between those countries where a good part of these institutions are state created bodies, such as in France, and the countries, such as the United Kingdom, where nearly all of them are private institutions. It is also necessary to remember with respect to the provision of credit the role of social security funds. In Sweden, for example, the National Pension Fund is a major source of medium- and long-term credit, particularly to provincial and municipal governments.

NATIONALIZATION

Nationalization of industry is a distinct manifestation of socialism. The reasons for nationalization are perhaps obvious. It is alleged by the socialists that production for profit under a capitalistic system leads to social waste and unemployment. The socialists contend that the price system, as it is utilized under capitalism contains three flaws—the difficulty of expressing wants through prices, inattention of the price system to social costs, and the influence of income inequality on prices.

Certain wants, such as public health and education, are difficult to express through the medium of prices in the market place and, as a result, are often not adequately fulfilled under capitalism. Since profit is the basic entrepreneurial motive in a free enterprise system, social costs—polluted streams, polluted air, and wasted national resources—are not taken into consideration. Since money means votes in the market place, income inequality means that those persons with the most money have the greatest number of votes in determining what will be produced and who will get the results of production. This means that many inconsequential and trivial things are produced for those who have large incomes, while many basic wants are left unsatisfied.

Unemployment has been the *bête noire* of capitalism. The socialists contend that production for profit is the reason. When profits decline, production is reduced and unemployment is the result. The reduction in aggregate demand which results from less production and employment has a pervasive effect throughout the economy. Mass unemployment and social unrest are the results. The solution, according to the socialists, is to nationalize industry. When this is done, production can be based on social need instead of profits. Also, certain industries affect the public interest more than others and should by necessity be nationalized. Examples would be transportation and communications.

However, nationalization of industry, as an economic fact of life, has simply not taken place to any significant degree in France, West Germany, the United Kingdom, Sweden, or Japan. The nationalization that has occurred in these countries either took place in the period immediately following World War II, for reasons that can be attributed only in part to socialism, or in periods far in the past, when socialism was no issue. In several countries, certain industries have always been operated by the government. In France, for example, a mixed system of public and private ownership and control existed before the Franco-Prussian war. The government of the United Kingdom, wishing to coordinate telegraph services with the post office, had the Postmaster General take over all telegraph companies in 1869. In 1896 the post office bought all the long-distance telephone lines from private telephone companies, and in 1911 it bought all privately owned telephone properties. In Japan government control and operation of certain industries dates back to the Meiji Restoration. In Sweden no nationalization has occurred in the last thirty years.

A wave of nationalization took place in the United Kingdom and France in the period immediately following World War II. However, it is necessary to point out that socialism was only one of several factors which were responsible for this development. Economic stagnation and internal problems in several industries during the interwar period made it quite likely that nationalization would have occurred in these countries, regardless of the political party in power. In the United Kingdom, for example, the Conservative party in 1939 had brought under government ownership and operation both domestic and overseas air transportation systems.

The Experience of the United Kingdom with Nationalization

When the Labour party came into office in the United Kingdom in 1946, a limited number of industries were nationalized. Coal was one industry that was nationalized. For reasons that have already been pointed out, it is probable that the Conservatives, had they remained in office, would have nationalized the coal industry also. The railroads, nationalized by the Transportation Act of 1947, were subject to public control pretty much from the outset.[15] During the interwar period, the railways went into the doldrums because of the growth of road competition. At the outbreak of World War II, the British government took over railway operation under the Emergency Defense Powers Act. War operations and war damages placed a heavy burden on the railway system in facing the problems of postwar readjustment. It was necessary (so the Labour party thought) to coordinate transportation policies with the postwar redevelopment of the British economy; the railroads, canals, all London Metropolitan bus, subway, and streetcar facilities, all long-distance truck lines, and all dock and harbor facilities were nationalized.

The nationalization of the steel industry by the Labour party, however, was a much more specific socialistic measure, and it aroused considerably more controversy than the other acts of nationalization. There were two reasons for the nationalization of steel:

1. There was the paramount idea that it was desirable for the government to assume control over an industry upon which the economy was dependent.
2. There was also the belief that there was too much concentration of economic power by a few companies in the industry. Through trade associations, these companies had adopted price fixing and other cartel practices.

In retrospect, the main reason for nationalization in the United Kingdom during the immediate postwar period was to use public investment as a compensatory device for offsetting the vagaries of the private sector and maintaining employment at a higher level than during the prewar period. In the case of some industries, nationalization was neither so revolutionary nor

[15] Railways have been considered an appropriate industry for nationalization in other countries not given over to socialism. Bismarck realized the enormous importance of the control of the railroads if Germany was to be unified and militarily strong. A state owned railroad system was one of his domestic policy objectives. In 1879 he obtained approval from the Prussian Parliament of a plan for state ownership of railroads in Prussia. By 1914 almost all German railroads were operated by the state. Rates were fixed with the objectives of promoting foreign trade and helping agriculture.

so controversial as might have been supposed. The Bank of England was already in effect a public institution. Its changed status was hardly more than a change of title. The railroads and coal mines had been losing money for years, and the Conservatives themselves were perfectly ready to accept the nationalization. Moreover, the road toward consolidation and control of industry had been opened by the Conservatives in earlier years when they had sponsored state-chartered monopolies for shipping and air transportation.

The Experience of France with Nationalization

In France a similar pattern of nationalization occurred. Certain parts of the railroad system were nationalized long before World War I. The telephone was made a government monopoly in 1889. In 1936, under the reforms of the Popular Front, the Bank of France was nationalized.

Most nationalization took place in the period immediately following World War II. There were two reasons, which are as follows:

1. France emerged from the German occupation a stripped and debilitated country, desperately short of raw materials, consumer goods, and food supplies. Transportation was paralyzed; industrial production had fallen to 40 percent of the 1938 level; a generalized black market had replaced the usual channels of trade; and an inflated currency threatened to bring the whole economy down in chaos.
2. Economic stagnation occurred during the interwar period. The unemployment rate was high. The depression struck France late, but when it came, it was worse and more intractable than in many other countries. By 1935 French exports stood at less than a third of the 1928 figure. There was imbalance at the top of the economic and social structure in that much of French national wealth was concentrated in the hands of several hundred families.

After the war, the view was adopted that, in order to achieve economic recovery, the French government had to play an important role. The immediate postwar years were consequently characterized by a policy of economic *dirigisme* as opposed to a quick return to a liberal, or market economy, which was the way that West Germany chose. This policy had three principal characteristics:

1. It brought with it some important nationalizations, affecting the gas and electric power industries, almost the whole of coal mining, the Renault motor works, the Bank of France, the four largest deposit banks, and the larger insurance companies.
2. It retained for some years most of the wartime system of price, rationing, and licensing controls.
3. It gave the government, through the *Monnet Plan*, a dominant influence over the direction of investment.

To a certain extent, postwar nationalization was a continuation of economic policies that were started by the Popular Front government in 1936.

It represented an amalgam of economic necessity and socialist influence. However, no significant nationalization has taken place since 1946.

The Experience of Sweden with Nationalization

In Sweden government ownership of industry did not follow the clear-cut pattern that developed in the United Kingdom and France. After World War I the government became co-owner of the iron mines in Lapland by acquiring a participation in a subsidiary of the Graensburg Corporation. Mixed enterprises with government and private control have become a characteristic of Sweden's industrial structure. In the field of electricity production, the Swedish government is responsible for about 40 percent of total production, local governments, 5 percent, and private utilities, the remainder. Nearly all of the railway mileage is operated by the Swedish government, which took over the development of the major routes in the mid-19th century.

Nationalization of industry has not been a part of the program of the Social Democratic party, which has been in power since the 1930s. Nevertheless, government control is substantial as a result of fiscal, monetary, and regulatory measures of the kinds familiar in other highly developed industrial countries, and the government has large interests in certain areas of the economy.

The Experience of Japan and Germany with Nationalization

Government ownership of industry in Japan has followed a similar pattern to that in Sweden. Control of certain industries by the Japanese government dates back to the early period of the Meiji Restoration and had nothing to do with socialist doctrine. The two paramount reasons for government ownership of industry were the need to develop a strong and viable economy which could compete with success against the established powers of the West and to prepare for military aggrandizements against neighboring countries.

In Germany government ownership of industry predates Bismarck. In Prussia state ownership of mines existed until 1865 when a mining law did away with state operations. Also in Prussia, ownership of the railroads was taken over in 1876, and the other German states soon followed suit. With the formation of the German Empire, Bismarck realized the need for a coordinated railroad system under state control if Germany was to become militarily strong. Accordingly, he took steps to nationalize the railroad system, particularly in Prussia. By 1914 most of the railroad system was under state control. By 1919 the entire system had been nationalized.

State control and regulation of industry has always been important in Germany. Under the Nazis all the economic activities in Germany, with the exception of transportation and agriculture, were centralized under the control of an Economics Minister, and many restrictions were placed on German enterprise.

In the five countries—France, the United Kingdom, Sweden, Japan, and Germany—a limited number of industries have been nationalized. This leaves each with what can be called a mixed economy. Private enterprise is dominant in that it employs by far the greatest percentage of workers and contributes the greatest part of the gross national product. The profit motive is still the cornerstone of enterprise in the economies of these countries, and market forces influence the decisions of what and for whom to produce. Nevertheless, fiscal and monetary policies and government control over public investment and credit can exercise considerable leverage in these decisions.

SOCIAL WELFARE

The public sector of an economy is engaged in two major types of activities, both of which can be measured by the expenditures incurred in carrying them out. One activity involves a government in the provision to its citizens of a broad array of goods and services including expenditures on roads, education, and police protection. These expenditures represent a transfer of resources from the private sector of an economy to the public sector, and they also represent the contribution of the government sector to total gross national product. A measurement that will be used to indicate the extent to which the governments of France, West Germany, Japan, Sweden, and the United Kingdom contribute to the national output of goods and services is the ratio of government expenditures on goods and services to gross national product.

The other activity involves the use of transfer payments as an instrument for the redistribution of income, generally with the dual objectives of greater income equality and the provision of some minimum standard of living for everyone. *Transfer payments,* as distinguished from government expenditures on goods and services, involve only the transfer of income from one group to another through taxation and provide no equivalent value in terms of goods and services in exchange. There is no return flow to the government of goods and services. Transfer payments include family allowances, old age pensions, and unemployment compensation. Some services, such as free medical care, are normally considered to be direct governmental expenditures for services which absorb resources the same way as do other government expenditures for services.[16]

The extent to which governments redistribute income can be measured by comparing transfer payments to national income, which is the factor cost of producing gross national product, or, more specifically, the aggregate earnings of labor and property which arise from the production of goods and services by a nation's economy. It is a concept of fundamental importance, for it represents to an economy as a whole the major source of money income or spending power for the purchase of the bulk of the national output.

Resource allocation to the public sector is accomplished by the process of taxation. This means that the cost of public activity is borne by the taxpayers of a nation. Taxation will have an income redistribution effect if various income groups have a different proportion of money income after payment

---

[16] Government expenditures can be classified as exhaustive and nonexhaustive. *Exhaustive expenditures* use up resources to provide goods and services. *Nonexhaustive expenditures,* such as transfer payments, do not use up resources.

of taxes than they do before. This will occur, particularly if the tax system is progressive. However, there are limits to the extent to which progressive taxation can be used, and in France and West Germany the bulk of welfare expenditures are financed by indirect taxation. It can also be said, with respect to all the countries considered in this section on mixed economies, that the growth of welfare expenditures brings with it an increase in the dependence of the government on indirect taxation.

The economic influence of governments is of paramount importance in the analysis of mixed economic systems. This influence has intensified in all major industrial countries, including the United States, and will be measured in the following chapters by using several criteria:

1. The relationship of government expenditures to gross national product to indicate the extent to which resources have been diverted from private to public use.
2. The relationship of transfer payments to national income to indicate the extent to which the percentage of earned income has been redistributed by government action.
3. The relationship of taxes to gross national product to indicate the extent to which governments have control over economic resources.

Table 9–1 presents these relationships for the five countries under review.

TABLE 9–1
THE RELATIONSHIP OF THE PUBLIC SECTOR TO GROSS NATIONAL PRODUCT AND NATIONAL INCOME FOR FRANCE, UNITED KINGDOM, JAPAN, SWEDEN, WEST GERMANY AND THE UNITED STATES FOR 1972

Country	Relationship of Government Expenditures to Gross National Product in Percentages *	Relationship of Transfer Payments to National Income in Percentages	Relationship of Taxes to Gross National Product in Percentages
France	15	21	40
United Kingdom	18	10	33
Japan	10	6	20
Sweden	28	14	44
West Germany	19	19	36
United States	21	6	29

* Government expenditures do not include capital expenditures.

Source: *National Accounts Statistics, 1960–1972* (Paris: Organization for Economic Cooperation and Development, 1973).

It is necessary to point out that they are absolute relationships and do not show a trend in expenditures and taxes relative to other major expenditure components of the private sector over a period of time.

Income redistribution in favor of the lower-income groups is a cardinal objective of socialism. While few socialists would favor complete income equality, most would favor the elimination of wide income disparities between rich and poor. The socialists object to the concentration of wealth in the hands of a few, which leads to considerable income inequality. The rentier class, or "coupon clippers," is looked upon with disfavor. The socialists would attempt to correct this unequal distribution of income through the use of progressive income taxes, gift and inheritance taxes, and a variety of transfer payments which are designed to raise the incomes of the poor.

The term *welfare state* is certainly applicable to the mixed economic systems that exist in most countries of the world. The main principles of a welfare state are a commitment to a minimum standard of living for all of its citizens and to full employment as the most important social goal to be supported by public policy. This, in itself, is not socialism as it is properly defined.[17] An objective of socialism is, however, to distribute income and social opportunity more equitably than they are presumed to be under capitalism.

The comprehensive social welfare programs that exist in West Germany, the United Kingdom, France, Japan, and Sweden are, for the most part, recent phenomena. Most of these programs, such as the British national health insurance scheme, were developed after World War II. The main reason for their adoption was the high rate of unemployment that existed in the interwar period in these countries. This unemployment and the concomitant economic and social miseries brought about considerable political discontent. There was the realization on the part of the government that a reversion to the interwar period must be avoided by all practical means. Postwar blueprints for economic recovery and development included the adoption of comprehensive social welfare measures. Currently, contributions for these programs are much larger than in the United States, and expenditures are also larger because these countries, such as France, have programs of health insurance, and the benefit levels of pension and unemployment programs represent larger fractions of wage income.[18] France also has an extensive program of family allowances.

Social Welfare in the United Kingdom

In the United Kingdom the current social welfare program had its genesis in the Beveridge Report of 1942, which was the first comprehensive survey of the British system of social insurance ever made and a carefully reasoned scheme for the abolition of wants as they had been known before the war.[19]

[17] Webster's dictionary defines socialism as an economic and political theory of organization based on collective or government ownership and democratic management of the essential means for the production and distribution of goods.

[18] Social welfare expenditures, as a percentage of gross national product, came to 14.4 percent in France, 10.8 percent in United Kingdom, and 9.2 percent in Sweden, as compared to 4.8 percent in the United States in 1967.

[19] "Social Insurance and Allied Services," Report by Sir William Beveridge, Command Paper No. 6404 (November, 1942).

The Beveridge Plan was essentially an insurance scheme giving in return for contributions benefits up to a subsistence level as a matter of right and not as the result of a means test. In return for contributions which all would pay, a minimum income sufficient to meet basic needs would be guaranteed for all periods of interrupted earnings, whether through sickness, disability, unemployment or old age. In addition, there would be grants for the normal incidences of life that called for unusual expenditures—for birth, maternity grants; for families, family allowances; and for death, funeral grants. The Plan involved three fundamental principles: (1) coverage of all persons regardless of income; (2) flat rate subsistence benefits and contributions from everyone; and (3) unification of all social insurance and assistance programs under a Ministry of Social Security with local Security Offices in reach of all insured persons.[20]

When the Labour party came into power after the war, it adopted the basic principles of the Beveridge Plan. A national health service was established, which provided free and comprehensive medical service including medical, dental, specialist, and hospital services. Maternity allowances, maternity grants, death grants, widows' pensions, and family allowances were also provided. The family allowance provided a weekly cash grant to parents for each child after the first. Unemployment benefits were made more comprehensive. Sickness and retirement benefits were improved and made more uniform. In addition, a host of broad social welfare measures were incorporated into the social welfare system. These included general welfare activities for children, youth organizations and recreational facilities, activities which catered to the special welfare needs of older people, special aids to the handicapped, the provision of housing, and activities in connection with town and country planning. Food subsidies were also provided to those in the lower-income groups. Thus, the so-called welfare state was established in the United Kingdom, and remains today as an important facet of the British economy.[21] Approximately 50 percent of the expenditures of the national government are on social welfare services.

Social Welfare in France

The burden of French taxation, one of the heaviest in the world, may to a considerable degree be explained by an extensive social welfare system. In few countries do transfer payments from the social security system account for a greater proportion of national income than in France. The bulk of French social welfare expenditures is financed by special taxes. These taxes are paid

[20] Sir Winston Churchill, in a note to his Cabinet soon after the Beveridge Report appeared, commented, "It is because I do not want to deceive the people by false hopes and airy visions of Utopia and El Dorado, that I must refrain from making promises about the future."

[21] Actually the precursor to the "welfare state" was the social welfare program of the liberal government in 1908, which included social insurance for health and unemployment, old age pensions, and assistance to low-income workers through the statutory fixing of minimum wages by various trade boards.

to special social security funds from which the benefits are paid, and expenditures are reflected in a special social budget but not in the national budget. The importance of the social welfare system is reflected in the fact that transfer payments amount to 20 percent of total personal income. On the reverse side of the coin, however, the taxes to finance the social welfare benefits on the average amount to 51 percent of the employers' payroll cost.

Although certain elements of the social welfare system extend back to the 19th century, most current welfare measures date from the Popular Front reforms of 1936. These measures were consolidated by the French government in 1945 into one general system which is in existence today. This system provides disability and old age pensions, medical benefits, unemployment compensation, rental allowances for low-income groups, and family allowances. The family allowance, which is financed by a levy on employers only, provides tax-free monthly payments for the second, third, and subsequent children in a family. The allowance often is the equivalent of a French family's regular salary.

Social Welfare in Sweden and Japan

Sweden also has an extensive system of welfare benefits, and a considerable part of the national income is redistributed through transfer payments which take the form of unemployment compensation, maternity benefits, family allowances, and old age pensions. Attempts at income leveling have been made through tax financed social security and other welfare expenditures, as well as through the income tax structure which is the most comprehensive in the world. Certain welfare benefits, such as the family allowance, are financed entirely out of general tax revenues. Other benefits, such as old age pensions, are financed out of taxes which are levied on both the employer and employee.

Sweden is supposed to be a country in which poverty does not exist. To a major extent, this statement is correct because transfer payments do increase the incomes of families and individuals that have small incomes. However, this does not mean that no low income families exist in Sweden; it simply means that welfare measures place a minimum income floor which assures every Swedish family a basic living standard.

Japan's social welfare programs are less ambitious than the other countries. There is no family allowance, and benefits are lower in general for other programs. This can be explained in part by the traditional thrift and general conservative outlook of the Japanese people, respect and the assumption of responsibility for elders on the part of their children, the paternalism of the Japanese employers toward their employees, and the fact that many, if not most, of the Japanese do not change jobs during their lifetimes.

Social Welfare in West Germany

Social welfare programs in Germany date back to 1883 when Bismarck's opposition to socialism and his jealousy of the trade union movement led him to sponsor the health insurance law of 1883. This law was the first national insurance law in the world, and it covered most industrial workers. Workers contributed two thirds and employers one third of the cost. The coverage of the law was constantly widened. By 1911 when the Insurance Consolidation Act brought all German insurance systems under one statute, the majority of workers were insured against sickness and invalidity. Benefits included medicine, hospitalization, maternity benefits, and payment of 50 percent of the wages lost by illness.

Bismarck also sponsored the workmen's compensation act of 1884 and the old age insurance law of 1889. The workmen's compensation law (Accident Insurance Law) was also the first of its kind in the world and provided benefits regardless of the circumstances of the injury. The cost was placed entirely on the employer. The Old Age and Invalidity Law of 1889 provided an old age pension payable to persons who had been regularly employed and who had reached the age of seventy. It was financed by a tax on both the employer and employee, with each paying half; the government granted additional subsidies.

German social welfare represented a combination of paternalism on the part of the state as well as an acceptance of state responsibility for those in need. This overall concept prevails in the German social welfare system of today. A considerable part of the German national income is transferred from one segment of the population to another through the medium of transfer payments which take the form of family allowances, medical benefits, old age pensions, and other benefits.

SUMMARY

The five countries discussed in this section—the United Kingdom, France, Japan, Sweden, and West Germany—have mixed economic systems. The governments of these countries pursue policies of participation and intervention in the economies to a degree that would not be acceptable in the United States. Nevertheless, private enterprise is dominant and a market system prevails in all five countries. Government participation in economic activity, however, cannot be minimized as an influence and covers several specific areas, which are as follows:

1. Economic planning is employed which, although indicative, has involved a certain amount of state intervention. A plan involves more than government forecasts and exhortations, because private decisions concerning investment and pricing policies can be influenced through government control and regulation of the supply and through tax policies.
2. General fiscal and monetary measures are used, which has permitted a state of excess demand to exist during most of the postwar period.
3. Use is made of selective protection and promotion policies which include favorable credit terms for specific industries, special depreciation allowances for certain industries, favored treatment under various taxes, preference on government orders, and favored access to imports of equipment that ordinarily would be restricted.

4. Nationalization of key industries which can influence the volume of public expenditures has occurred. These industries are indeed very large businesses and are often the largest employers in the country.
5. Transfer payments, through the medium of social welfare expenditures, have an important effect on income redistribution. Broad and comprehensive welfare schemes cover the masses of wage earners in all the countries.

The governments of these countries, then, stimulate certain economic activities through the budget, taxation, interest rates, and planning through inducements. However, the market system is preserved, and production and distribution are determined by a cost-price relationship. Economic adjustments are brought about by normal supply and demand relationships in the market. Profits, rent, and interest, as distributive shares to the agents of production, are far from being eliminated. Freedom of enterprise and private property ownership are largely unchallenged as economic institutions. Consumer sovereignty exists in all five countries, and individual and mass preferences determine what is going to be produced, at what quality, and in what quantities. Modern marketing and advertising techniques used in these countries are quite similar to those which are used in the United States.

It is assumed that a mixed economic system, through government direction and participation, can ameliorate or eliminate the major flaw of a capitalistic system, namely unemployment, as well as accomplish a high rate of economic growth. Whether this is actually the case is highly problematical.

QUESTIONS

1. How are supplies of productive agents allocated or distributed among industries in mixed economic systems?
2. Discuss the effects of great income inequality on the distribution of goods and services in a capitalistic system.
3. Discuss some of the reasons for the nationalization of industry in the United Kingdom and France.
4. All important economic decisions would be made without reference to price relationships under socialism. Do you agree?
5. The term "mixed economy" is probably more applicable to the economic systems of the western European countries, than the terms "capitalism" and "socialism." Do you agree?
6. In a mixed economy, such as the United Kingdom's, the government can control the field of investment credit. Do you agree?
7. Discuss the role of government with reference to monetary and fiscal policies in a mixed economy.
8. Discuss the importance of economic planning in a mixed economic system.
9. The major flaws of a capitalistic system—unemployment, income inequality, and social waste—have been eliminated in such countries as France and the United Kingdom. Do you agree?
10. Discuss the importance of social welfare expenditures in a mixed economic system.

RECOMMENDED READINGS

Beveridge, William. *Full Employment in a Free Society,* 2d ed. Atlantic Highlands, N.J.: Humanities Press, Inc., 1960.

Blodgett, Ralph H. *Comparative Economic Systems.* New York: The Macmillan Company, 1949.

Dobb, Maurice H. *On Economic Theory and Socialism.* London: Routledge & Kegan Paul, Ltd., 1965.

Ebenstein, William. *Today's Isms,* 7th ed. Englewood Cliffs, N.J.: Prentice-Hall, Inc., 1973.

Friedman, Milton. *Capitalism and Freedom.* Chicago: University of Chicago Press, 1962.

Myrdal, Gunnar. *Beyond the Welfare State.* New Haven: Yale University Press, 1960.

National Bureau of Economic Research. *Foreign Tax Policies and Economic Growth.* New York: Columbia University Press, 1966.

————. *National Economic Planning.* New York: Columbia University Press, 1967.

Sweezy, Paul W. *Socialism.* New York: McGraw-Hill Book Company, 1949.

Tinbergen, Jan. *Economic Planning.* New Haven: Yale University Press, 1966.

Wright, David M. *Capitalism.* Chicago: Henry Regnery Co., 1962.

10
France

INTRODUCTION

France is both a leading industrial country and the largest agricultural producer in western Europe. The economy is highly developed and diversified. Although the French government is dedicated to a policy of planned economic and social development, private enterprise is the backbone of the French economic system. The economy of France is a *managed market economy* in which the government attempts to modify, but not directly control, production and distribution. Direct government ownership of industry is, by European standards, average.

French economic planning is regarded by many persons as being a middle-ground approach between free, unregulated market capitalism and directive, controlled communism. French economic growth was remarkably high and comparatively regular during the 1950s, and many observers are convinced that French planning must have had something to do with this.[1]

French economic planning is indicative in that it indicates directions in which the economy ought to go, but does not provide specific targets or quotas for individual firms and industries. It relies on policies of selective promotion and protection to encourage economic growth. These policies include public credit to favor areas of the economy that need development, special depreciation allowances for certain industries such as steel, favorable treatment of exports under the value-added tax, and preference in government orders. The French government has the power and the desire to influence business decisions involving investment, prices, and plant location.

THE FRENCH ECONOMIC SYSTEM

The French economic system can be classified as a free enterprise or neo-capitalistic system in which the government plays a direct and important role. Most production activities are in private hands, and the government indicates

[1] The average growth rate for France in the period 1950–61 was 4.6 percent. This rate was higher than the growth rates of the United States and the United Kingdom but lower than those for West Germany and Italy.

rather than determines the direction that these activities should take. Distribution is also basically in private hands, with the government modifying rather than determining the flow of income to the agents of production.

The government participates directly or indirectly in business and industry to a far greater degree than is the case in the United States or West Germany. It controls all of the railroads and coal mines, virtually all of the electrical power production, and has controlling interest in the airlines. The Bank of France and the four largest deposit banks are controlled by the government. A segment of the insurance industry is nationalized. The government also has a large interest in the petroleum and natural gas industries, and is involved in the production of motor vehicles and planes. Direct regulation and selective intervention in other industries is also common. Investment plans of major companies are often discussed with government agencies able to help provide financing; and the government tries to promote mergers and other changes in the organization of private firms.

Government ownership of industry resulted from a series of nationalizations that occurred immediately after World War II. The Bank of France, the four largest deposit banks, 34 insurance companies, the electric and gas industries, the coal mines, Air France, and one automobile and one aircraft company were nationalized.[2] There were several reasons for nationalization.

One reason for nationalization was a desire to continue the Popular Front program of 1936, which was an assault on economic institutions that had for decades preserved a hopelessly outmoded capitalism. Manufacturing and agriculture were both protected by high tariffs and import quotas and, in many cases, by subsidies and by producers' agreements allocating production and markets. This had led to a static economy with restrictive competition and little incentive to improve production methods or to experiment with new products.

A second reason for nationalization was the need to develop a blueprint for France's future after the war, which called for formal and systematic economic planning that would rehabilitate the war-torn economy and stimulate economic growth. Discussions in France, concerning the way in which economic recovery could most quickly be accomplished, led to the view that an active role would have to be played by the French government. A policy of economic *dirigisme* was selected. This policy, it was felt, could be carried out best by the nationalization of a number of basic industries.

There have been no significant nationalizations in recent years, and nationalization is not a part of the program of the Fifth French Republic. The operation of public enterprises has been kept consistent with the basic objective of the French government—the maintenance of a high rate of economic growth.

Table 10–1 shows the composition of the French gross national product for 1972. The influence of the government sector is understated considerably as

---

[2] The automobile and aircraft companies were nationalized as punishment for collaboration with the Germans.

TABLE 10–1

FRENCH GROSS NATIONAL PRODUCT FOR 1972 *

Components		Billions of Dollars
Consumer expenditures		104.19
Government expenditures		24.45
Defense	6.12	
Civil	18.33	
Gross domestic investment		47.86
National and local governments	7.15	
Private enterprises	33.60	
Public enterprises	7.11	
Changes in inventories		3.89
Exports of goods and services	35.19	
Less: imports of goods and services	34.94	
Net exports of goods and services		0.25
Gross national product		180.64

* The French franc has fluctuated in value relative to the U.S. dollar. As applied to the 1972 table, the franc exchanged at 5.1 to $1.

Source: Commissariat du Plan, *Rapports sur les Comptes de la Nation,* Paris, 1973, p. 2.

transfer payments are not reflected in total expenditures. Transfer payments in 1972 amounted to $33.31 billion compared to direct government expenditures on goods and services of $24.58 billion. Gross domestic investment is divided into three categories: direct investment by the national and local governments, investment by private enterprises, and investment by public enterprises.

Public Finance

France has two budgets—the national budget and the social budget. The national budget is general in nature in that it contains the receipts from basic revenue sources, such as the value-added tax and the personal income tax, and it contains the national expenditures, including expenditures on goods and services, gross capital formation, interest on the public debt, and capital transfers. The social budget covers both social security expenditures—old age and disability insurance, medical care, family allowances, and workmen's compensation—and outlays for veterans' pensions and miscellaneous welfare payments. The social budget is used because the bulk of French social welfare expenditures is financed, not out of general national revenues, but by special taxes on employers and, to a minor extent, on employees. These taxes are not paid to the national treasury, but to special social security funds from which the benefits are paid. The social budget measures the importance of transfer payments to the French economy and reflects the use of government power as an instrument for the redistribution of income.

French public finance is highly centralized. The national government accounts for about 87 percent of the total tax receipts and local governments for the remaining 13 percent. Local taxes, however, are levied under authority granted by the National Assembly and, for the most part, are administered and collected by the National Tax Administration. Local taxes are also "local" only in the sense that the revenue raised, which is reduced by a small charge for collection by the national government, goes to the local governments.

An important characteristic of both the national and local tax systems is the reliance upon indirect taxes as revenue sources. Approximately 75 percent of all national and local government tax receipts come from indirect taxes; and the remaining 25 percent, from direct taxes.[3] The most important national tax, the value-added tax, and the most important local tax, the retail sales tax, are indirect taxes. The two major direct taxes, the personal income tax and the corporate income tax, are both national taxes and have no counterpart at the local level. The property tax, which is the major source of tax revenue to local governments in the United States, is not an important source of revenue at the local level in France.

Taxation is used as a direct instrument of economic policy to promote economic stabilization or social welfare objectives. French exports have been an important factor in the country's economic growth, and the national government has made use of its taxing power so as to facilitate the ability of business firms to adjust to foreign competition. Tax policy is also used to stimulate industrial decentralization and regional development. A more equitable distribution of the national income has also been a goal of taxation and transfer policies in France. France has one of the most comprehensive social welfare systems in the world. In 1972 social welfare expenditures amounted to 16.7 percent of the French gross national product and 18.5 percent of household income.[4]

The French Tax System. The tax system of France has several characteristics which are different from the tax systems of most advanced industrial countries. These characteristics are as follows: [5]

1. Greater reliance is placed on sales taxation in France than in other advanced industrial countries. The value-added tax is the keystone of the French tax system and accounts for one third of the revenues of the national government. There is also less reliance on income taxation as a revenue source than in most industrial countries.

2. In few countries are tax incentives as numerous or as varied as in France. Tax incentives are used for a variety of purposes—to stimulate scientific research and development, to encourage the modernization of plants and

---

[3] Social security contributions are excluded from the calculations for the reason that they are not a part of national government revenues, but go directly to a special fund. When they are included as tax receipts, the ratio is 55 percent indirect and 45 percent direct.

[4] *Le Budget Social de la Nation de 1972*, p. 44.

[5] Harvard Law School, *Taxation in France*, World Tax Series (Chicago: Commerce Clearing House, Inc., 1966), p. 67.

equipment, to facilitate regional development and the decentralization of the Paris region, to encourage housing construction, and to develop export markets. French tax incentives are available not only under the income tax, but also under the value-added tax.

3. Another major characteristic of the French tax system is the role of tax innovation. In the value-added tax, France possesses the most refined and economically neutral type of indirect tax in the West.[6] This tax is used to stimulate economic growth. France was also the first country to rely on the income tax as a source of revenue.

4. The yield of the French tax system is also an important characteristic. French tax collections equal 41 percent of gross national product—the second highest percentage in the world for any industrial country.[7]

The major French taxes and their importance as revenue producers are shown in Table 10–2.

TABLE 10–2
MAJOR REVENUE SOURCES FOR THE FRENCH NATIONAL BUDGET, 1972

Tax	Amount (Millions of Dollars)
Value-added tax	17,294
Personal income tax	7,510
Gasoline tax	2,490
Corporate income tax	3,804
Tobacco and alcohol excises	1,765
Registration and stamp taxes	1,510
Other receipts	2,941
Total budget receipts	37,314

Source: Ministere de L'Economie et des Finances, *Le Budget de 1972*, p. 9.

The Value-Added Tax. The most important tax in France is the value-added tax, which accounts for approximately 33 percent of the tax receipts of the national government. The French value-added tax is levied only on the value added by a given enterprise. Value-added is the difference between the selling price of the product and the cost of the various inputs used by the enterprise in the course of the manufacturing and distribution process. Because the tax is levied only on the value added by the enterprise, it is not a cumulative levy like the general turnover tax, which is used by several other European countries, and thus does not pyramid. The French value-added tax is calculated by applying the tax rate to gross sales and then crediting all taxes on purchases against the tax due; thus each taxpayer pays a tax only on the difference—the value added. The rates of the value-added tax range from 7 percent to 33 percent. However, the normal rate is 20 percent. Lower rates

[6] Carl Shoup, "Some Distinguishing Characteristics of the British, French and United States Public Finance Systems," *American Economic Review*, Vol. 47, No. 2 (1957).

[7] This percentage reflects the inclusion of social security contributions.

are applied to goods regarded as necessities; higher rates are applied to goods regarded as luxuries.

The value-added tax is used as a conscious instrument of French economic policy in several ways:

1. French exports are exempt from the value-added tax. Exemption occurs if delivery is made outside of France or to a point within France for eventual export. Invisible exports, such as tourist expenditures, are also exempt.
2. Capital goods are generally accorded favorable treatment under the value-added tax. This treatment, combined with the exemption of exports, results in a general tax on consumption expenditures. The tax has a restrictive effect on consumer spending and encourages capital formation and exports.
3. The value-added tax is used as a tax incentive to encourage expansion and modernization in the petroleum industry.[8] A rate of 17 percent is applied to petroleum as it leaves the refinery or storage depot. As a tax offset, petroleum companies may claim credits for taxes incurred on purchases of goods, equipment, and services for exploration, and for the construction and operation of refineries and pipelines.
4. The value-added tax is also used as an incentive to housing construction. Favorable rates are applied to land purchased for housing and to the construction of houses. The value-added tax is applicable to all phases of housing construction—land acquisition, construction, and sale of the house.

The Income Tax. The French income tax is progressive. Rates range from 10 percent on taxable incomes from 3,300 to 5,750 francs ($647 to $1127) to 60 percent on taxable incomes in excess of 86,500 francs ($16,961). However, the *family quotient system* reduces the progressivity of the income tax as the size of the family increases. The family quotient system allows the income to be divided into a certain number of shares based on the number of dependents in a family. Each adult is entitled to one share each and each dependent child is entitled to half a share. The income tax is then levied on each share. Thus, a couple with four children would have four shares. The income tax is paid on each of the four shares at a rate which is calculated for portions of each share contained in various tax brackets. For example, the couple with four children would pay the same tax on an income of 40,000 francs ($7,843) as four single persons with an income of 10,000 francs ($1,961) each or two childless couples with incomes of 20,000 francs ($3,922) each.

The income tax is levied on income from wages and salaries, dividends and interest, capital gains, and profits from industrial-commercial activities and agriculture, net after deduction for social security contributions. From net income, two basic deductions are permitted—a 10 percent deduction for personal expenses (up to 30 percent is permitted for certain professions) and an additional deduction of 20 percent on the balance. Wage and salary earners are also entitled to a tax credit of 5 percent on net taxable salary or wage.

[8] The value-added tax is normally applied to transactions at every stage in the production and wholesale cycle, with each taxpayer enjoying a tax credit to ensure that each person is taxed only on the value each adds to the taxable product. However, for petroleum products, the value-added tax is applied only at one stage—when the product is shipped for consumption.

The rates of the personal income tax are shown in Table 10–3.

TABLE 10–3
RATES OF THE FRENCH PERSONAL INCOME TAX AS OF JULY 1973

Income in Dollars *	Percentage Rate
0 to 814	0
815 to 1,417	10
1,418 to 2,342	15
2,343 to 3,464	20
3,465 to 5,424	30
5,425 to 10,724	40
10,725 to 21,326	50
21,327 and over	60

* 1 Franc equaled $.24655 in 1973.

Source: Les Impots en France (Paris: Bureau d'Etudes Fiscales et Juridiques, 1973), p. 32.

Other French Taxes. There are three other major French taxes—the employers' payroll tax, the corporation income tax, and the gasoline and petroleum tax. The employers' payroll tax is based on the total amount of wages and salaries paid to employees. The tax is levied at progressive rates. The standard rate is 4.25 percent, and the rate increases to 8.5 percent on the portion of salaries between $5,882 and $11,765 and to 13.6 percent on amounts in excess of $11,765. The corporation income tax is levied at the rate of 50 percent of net taxable income. In general, no reduction is granted on the part of the profits that is distributed. However, dividends paid in new shares issued for purposes approved by the government are deductible. Petroleum products are subject to a tax known as the "internal consumption duty" which is levied at the same time the product is shipped for consumption.

Taxation and Economic Development. Taxation, as mentioned previously, plays a very important role in French economic policy. A basic desideratum of French economic policy is the development of exports. This is done through the use of several tax incentives—exemption of French exports from the value-added tax, deduction from the corporate income tax of the cost of setting up overseas sales offices, exemption from the tax on services, and refunds from the portion of the employers' payroll tax and of social security charges borne by employers deemed to be attributable to production for export.[9]

Government Expenditures. As mentioned previously, the French government utilizes two budgets—the national budget and the social budget. In 1972 total government expenditures in the national budget amounted to approximately $36.71 billion. These expenditures are shown in Table 10–4, page 208.

[9] When France joined the European Coal and Steel Community, reimbursement ended regarding exports of coal and steel products to member countries. Reimbursement also was ended on all exports to members of the European Economic Community.

TABLE 10—4

EXPENDITURES OF THE FRENCH NATIONAL BUDGET FOR 1972

Expenditures	Amount (Millions of Dollars) *
Administrative expenses	$ 3,845
National defense	6,185
Foreign aid	932
Education	6,463
Social welfare	6,285
Economic development	7,831
Housing	1,546
Other expenditures	3,925
Total	$37,012

* 1 Franc equaled $.196078 in 1972.

Source: Ministere de L'Economie et des Finances, Le Budget de 1972, p. 22.

France has one of the most comprehensive social welfare systems in the world. There are three significant characteristics of the system:

1. It is expensive—in 1972 transfer payments amounted to $35.3 billion out of a gross national product of $180.6 billion.
2. It is financed primarily by levies on French employers.
3. It is administered by a large number of different social security and family allowance funds.

There are two separate social welfare systems—a family allowance system and a general social security system. The family allowance system, which is financed by a tax on employers only, provides tax-free monthly payments for the second, third, and subsequent children in a family, a special allowance for families with only one wage earner, prenatal and maternity allowances, and, in certain circumstances, a housing allowance. The general social security system provides insurance, maternity benefits, pension benefits, and old age and survivor's benefits. The system is financed by a tax levied on the employer, which amounts to 17 percent of the employee's wage up to a ceiling of $3,240 a year, and a levy on the employee of 6.5 percent up to the same ceiling, plus a rate of 2 percent on earnings above the wage ceiling on the employer and a rate of 1 percent on the employee.

Family Allowances. France's comprehensive system of family allowances has been called the most original and important part of the French social security system.[10] It was introduced into the French revenue and tax systems in 1932. The primary reason for doing so was to stimulate an increase in the birthrate to compensate for the tremendous war losses sustained by the French in World War I.

[10] Wallace Peterson, *The Welfare State in France*, No. 21 (Lincoln: University of Nebraska Studies, 1960), p. 2.

The family allowance is financed by a tax on the employer which is levied at the rate of 12 percent on wages paid to each worker on incomes up to the social security ceiling of $274.57 a month. The employee contributes nothing. Families with more than one child are eligible for an allowance which is computed on the basis of a base salary of $77.65 a month. This base salary represents the average gross weekly earnings for an unskilled worker in the Paris area. The rate of the allowance is 22 percent of the base salary for the second child or 22 percent times $64.31, which is equal to $17.08 a month. For successive children through the sixth child, the rate increases by 33 percent of the base salary per child. For all children over the sixth child, the rate is a flat 33 percent of the base salary. The family allowance is not subject to the French income tax.

Social Security. The social security system in France is complex and fragmented. Special systems exist for farmworkers, coal miners, railroad workers, public utility employees, seamen, and public employees, in addition to the general social security system which covers about 50 percent of the population. There is some intermingling of the general and special systems, with workers receiving benefits from both systems. The social security system is decentralized, with a number of funds (*caisses*) operating at a primary, or local, level. These funds are managed by boards chosen by the employee and employer contributors. The boards are responsible for the collection and disbursement of revenues. There does not exist a single system for the administration of all social security benefits.

The basic or general social security system provides disability and old age pensions for ordinary workers, as well as widow's and survivor's benefits. Supplementary schemes provide additional benefits for higher paid employees and benefits for the self-employed. A medical program provides sick pay and reimbursement for a major portion of medical expenses. In addition, there is workmen's compensation for industrial accidents, unemployment compensation, pensions to war veterans, local relief for the poor and infirm, and miscellaneous welfare outlays.

The following benefits are provided under social security proper: old age pensions, death and survivors benefits, and sickness and maternity benefits.

The old age pension is paid to persons 60 years of age and over who have had 30 years of insurance coverage. Benefits are reduced if the coverage is less. The pension is 20 percent of average earnings in the last ten years of work (40 percent if the worker has engaged in arduous work). An increment of 4 percent of average earnings is added per year for postponed retirement. Forty percent of earnings is payable at age 65, and 60 percent of earnings is payable at age 70. There is a reduced pension for workers who have had less than 30 years of coverage. There is also a dependent's supplement of 50 percent of the pension for the spouse and 10 percent of the pension if three or more children are cared for. There is also a special supplement of $196.08 a year which is paid to low income pensioners and a special allowance of $343.14 a year for low income workers who are not eligible for old age pensions. The old age pension is adjusted to changes in the cost of living and to annual changes in the national average wage.

In the event of the death of a worker who is covered by the social security system, survivors receive a lump-sum payment, or "death grant," which is equal to three month's salary of the deceased. Fifty percent of the old age pension paid or payable to the insured is paid to the surviving spouse. There is also a children's supplement payable to widows or widowers with three or more children.

Sickness and maternity benefits cover the costs of sickness and birth. Sickness benefits compensate for loss of earnings, as well as the medical cost of being sick. There is compensation for loss of earnings which amounts to one half of a worker's earnings payable for a period of up to 12 months for ordinary illnesses and up to three years for a prolonged illness. Two thirds of earnings are available to families with three or more children after a lapse of 30 days. Medical benefits provide cash refunds of part of expenses and include general and medical care, dental care, hospitalization, maternity care, and laboratory services. A patient is free to choose any doctor, and the doctor is free to prescribe whatever treatment is deemed appropriate. Fees are fixed between the doctor and the patient and are paid by the patient who is then reimbursed by the government for a portion of the outlay, normally for 80 percent of the amount set by a standard scale. Patients are reimbursed also for a major portion of outlays for drugs and hospital expenses. For low income patients, the entire outlay is reimbursed by the government.

Income Redistribution. In few countries do transfer payments from the social welfare system—social security and family allowances—account for a greater proportion of national income than in France. In 1972 total financial aid from all sources as expressed in the social budget amounted to $36.9 billion, the equivalent of 20.6 percent of the gross national product.

The social budget is an excellent measure of how the state distributes income. It reflects all financial measures of a social nature which are conducted by the state. This financial aid takes into account not only social security benefits and family allowances, which constitute two thirds of state expenditures, but also expenditures resulting from the provision of sanitation, housing, education, assistance to Algerian repatriates, and other activities.

The French social budget for 1972 is shown in Table 10–5.

Probably the fundamental point concerning the income redistribution effects of transfer payments in the French economy concerns their financing. Since the social security and family allowance taxes are levied almost exclusively on the employer, there is a strong presumption that their incidence is on the French consumer. The taxes can be considered as part of business costs, and employers will presumably attempt to shift them to the consumer in the form of higher prices. The extent to which they can be shifted depends on a complex of variables, including the elasticity of demand for the employer's product, the degree of monopoly possessed in the market for the product, and the effect of the tax on consumer demand. Since aggregate

TABLE 10–5
THE FRENCH SOCIAL BUDGET FOR 1972

Items	Millions of Dollars
Expenditures	
Sickness benefits	$ 7,431
Old age pensions	9,725
Family allowances	6,725
Accidents at work	1,413
Other expenditures	11,608
Total	$36,902
Receipts	
Contributions from beneficiaries	$ 5,020
Contributions from employers in the private sector	17,274
Contributions from public employers other than the state	4,372
Contributions from the state as an employer	3,548
Contributions from the state as a public authority	6,315
Miscellaneous receipts	373
Total	$36,902

Source: *Le Budget Social de la Nation Pour 1972*, p. 49.

demand has tended to exceed aggregate supply in France, as well as in other European countries, during the postwar period, it can be said that conditions favorable for the shifting of these taxes to the consumer exist.

There is little taking from the "classes" and giving to the "masses" taxation in France. The value-added tax, rather than the personal income tax, is the single most important source of revenue. The progressivity of the personal income tax is reduced through the use of income-splitting and through special professional allowances to certain types of workers. This means that the burden of transfer expenditures is placed on an array of indirect taxes which fall on the employer and the consumer with consequent price and income effects. The external effect could mean that French products would be priced out of competition in the world markets; however, exemptions of exports from the value-added tax and other factors exercise a counterbalancing effect.

Transfer payments represent a significant part of household income in France. In 1972 household gross income in France amounted to $159.4 billion. Of this amount, earnings from employment (wages and salaries) amounted to $75.88 billion, social security and family allowances amounted to $35.3 billion, gross entrepreneurial income amounted to $39.6 billion, property income amounted to $5.3 billion, and income from other sources amounted to $9.61 billion.[11] In the same year social security and family allowance payments equaled 27 percent of the sum spent on private consumption.

[11] "France," *Economic Surveys* (Paris: Organization for Economic Cooperation and Development, May, 1973).

Although the personal income tax is progressive, its income redistribution effect is rather limited for two reasons:

1. Transfer payments, such as social security benefits and family allowances, are not financed out of general tax revenues, but out of special taxes levied on the employer and employee. In France 97.7 percent of the cost of all social welfare programs—social security and family allowances—is financed by taxes on employers and employees and less than 1 percent out of general government revenues.[12]
2. The family quotient system reduces the progressiveness of the income tax. Tax preference is given to families through the use of this system. This has meant that income is redistributed more within income classes than between income classes.

Fiscal Policy. Since approximately 20 percent of French industry is government owned, public expenditure policies are, to a substantial degree, directly concerned with the expansion of productive capacity. In 1972 public investment expenditures as carried in the national budget amounted to $8.43 billion.[13] These expenditures provided for 31.2 percent of total investment in agriculture, 50.4 percent of total investment in power facilities, and 27.2 percent of total investment in construction.[14]

The importance of the government to the French economy is immediately apparent when the national budget is compared to gross national product. In 1972 French gross national product was an estimated $180.59 billion and total expenditures in the national budget amounted to around $36.67 billion.[15] The size of the budget indicates the extent to which the nation's resources are channeled through the public sector and also provides, to a considerable degree, a measure of the extent and character of state intervention. When the social budget is also considered, over 40 percent of the gross national product passes through the central government. The outstanding features of the French budgetary system are the heavy volume of transfer payments and the large capital investment program financed by the government. When revenues from various tax sources are also taken into consideration, the aggregate role of the government, as reflected in its budgetary accounts, is considerable. Changes in expenditures and revenues in the budget have a powerful fiscal impact on the French economy.[16]

French fiscal policy during the postwar period, for the most part, has been expansionary. After a period of reconstruction which ended around 1949, France experienced a sustained rate of economic growth, which was helped in part by budget deficits that were attributable to public investment. In 1953 and 1954, tax relief was provided to stimulate private investment.

---

[12] Harvard Law School, *Taxation in France,* World Tax Series (Chicago: Commerce Clearing House, Inc., 1966), p. 67.

[13] Ministere de L'Economie et des Finances, *Le Budget de 1972,* p. 51.

[14] *Ibid.,* p. 55.

[15] *Le Budget de 1972,* p. 22.

[16] Transfer payments alone in 1972 amounted to more than $35.3 billion and taxes amounted to $72.94 billion compared to a gross national product of $180.59 billion.

This relief took the form of a reduction of excise taxes on the purchase of investment goods and the provision of more favorable depreciation allowances. The primary target of the French government during the 1950s was the maintenance of a rapid rate of economic expansion. However, inflation and an unfavorable balance of payments brought about fiscal and monetary changes. The Fifth Republic, under De Gaulle, adopted an anti-inflationary fiscal program in 1959 that helped to bring financial stability to France.[17] Taxes were raised and government subsidies were cut in an attempt to reduce distortions in the price structure. Fiscal measures were also used to increase the volume of savings. These measures provided exemptions from the personal income tax, including interest on Treasury bills and other government securities, interest on deposits in the national savings bank system, and interest on bonds issued by the national agricultural bank.

Fiscal policy, for the most part, was moderately expansionary during the 1960s. The fiscal measures used were primarily selective rather than general. Tax relief was provided for lower-income groups and specific measures were taken to encourage private investment.[18]

The Banking System

France has a comprehensive banking system which is headed by the Bank of France. The system includes three types of banks—commercial banks, investment banks, and medium- and long-term credit banks. Unlike the banking systems in the United Kingdom and Sweden, French banks are, for the most part, publicly owned. The control of business financing through government ownership of the major credit institutions has been of importance to the postwar development of the French economy. Ownership has provided the state with direct leverage for the implementation of credit policies which are consonant with the objectives of the French economic plans.

The Central Bank. The Bank of France was organized by Napoleon Bonaparte in 1800 as a privately owned company. In 1803 it was given a monopoly for note issuance in the Paris area, and in 1848 that monopoly was extended to all of France. With the victory of the *Popular Front* government of Leon Blum in 1936, legislation was passed which gave the French government the dominant position in the management of the bank. In 1946 the Bank of France was nationalized, the shareholders receiving negotiable government securities in exchange for their stock.

With the nationalization of the Bank of France, the French government was able to assume ultimate control over monetary policy. A National Credit

---

[17] The franc was also devalued.

[18] Many types of tax-free depreciation reserve allowances are available to reduce the effective tax rate on business firms. These allowances can be changed from year to year as economic conditions change. The French tax system, with its heavy reliance on indirect taxes, does not readily lend itself to general fiscal policy measures, such as an income tax increase. The personal income tax does not affect the majority of taxpayers. French fiscal policy must be selective rather than general.

Council was created and given power to regulate the operations of all classes of banks, this power being exercised through the Bank of France.[19]

The Bank of France can discount commercial paper and government securities for private individuals and enterprises, and all classes of banks and public institutions, provided that the maturities do not exceed three months. The Bank also rediscounts short-term paper for commercial banks and rediscounts medium-term (two to five years) paper for public and semipublic credit institutions. The Bank has become an important source of medium-term financing for industry, agriculture, and construction.

The Commercial Banks. The four largest commercial banks—Banque Nationale pour le Commerce et L'Industrie, Crédit Lyonnais, Comptoire National d'Escompte, and Société Genéralé—were also nationalized in 1945. These banks maintain branch banks in most cities throughout France. Monetary policy is easily implemented through the nationalized sector of the banking system.

Two major commercial banks—the Crédit Industriel et Commerce, and the Crédit Commerce de France—are not nationalized. The French banking system also includes a number of regional banks, the largest of which is the Credit du Nord, and also local banks which operate in single towns only.

Apparently the nationalized commercial banks have not changed the structure of the banking system to any significant degree. They actively compete against themselves and against the private banks for the deposits of the French public. The nationalized banks also do not play an important role in expediting the objectives of the French economic plans.[20] Of more importance in this respect are the specialized credit institutions.

Specialized Credit Institutions. There are in France a number of semipublic and public credit institutions. It is through these institutions that the French government exercises its considerable financial powers to determine the allocation of savings into particular investment channels. The specialized credit institutions existed before World War II; however, they have been adapted specifically during the postwar period to deal with the need to furnish financing for investment. They are diverse in that some are banks while others are not. But, as a common feature, they tend to specialize in one or a few lines of activity. Their funds are made available by grants from savings deposits, bond issues, and the French Treasury.[21] In 1962 grants and deposits

---

[19] The National Credit Council has 43 members, including a president, who is a minister designated by the government, and a vice-president, who is also the Governor of the Bank of France. Seventeen members of the Council represent government departments concerned with economic problems, and the remaining 24 members represent various economic and financial interests.

[20] John Hackett and Anne-Marie Hackett, *Economic Planning in France* (Cambridge: Harvard University Press, 1963), pp. 81–84.

[21] The French Treasury plays a central and dominant role in the French capital market, and it accounts for approximately 50 percent of savings in France. The Treasury controls the capital market to the extent that no important borrower can have access to funds without its consent. Moreover, control over the financial circuits of the country means that the Treasury has a priority claim on resources. This state of affairs has developed over an extended time as a result of unstable financial history rather than political and economic ideologies. Control over the capital market gives the government an effective instrument to encourage compliance with investment objectives of its economic plans.

from the Treasury accounted for $9 billion, savings deposits accounted for $7.41 billion, and bond issues accounted for $2.76 billion out of total resources of $22.45 billion.[22] These specialized credit institutions are discussed in the following paragraphs.

The Crédit Foncier. The purpose of the Crédit Foncier is to provide medium-term credit for homebuilding. It is a semipublic institution in that, although it is privately owned, the French government has the right to appoint the governor and two deputy directors. It provides medium-term loans which are supported by first mortgages. The funds of the Crédit Foncier come from special credits in the national budget, deposits, and bond issues.

The Crédit Agricole. This institution provides financing for the local and regional agricultural credit societies. It is a public institution which is controlled by the Minister of Agriculture. It receives funds from the Treasury, private depositors, and through the issue of bonds in the capital market.

The Caisse des Dépots et Consignations. This publicly owned institution manages the funds of the social security and postal savings systems. It is one of the most important financial institutions, and its total deposits are equal to those of the sight deposits of all the deposit banks combined. In 1962 it accounted for approximately 45 percent of all financial resources made available through the specialized lending institutions.[23] Its funds are used primarily to finance low rental housing. It also lends to local authorities to finance various types of public works. It invests in a wide variety of financial instruments including Treasury bills and medium- and long-term government bonds.

The Crédit National. The main function of this government owned institution is the provision to private industry of a part of the funds from the national budget for investment purposes. It receives its funds from the Economic and Social Development Fund, which is an important instrument of French economic planning and which is a special item in the French budget.

Monetary Policy. Principal responsibility for stabilizing rates of employment and the price level rests with monetary and credit policies which are set by the National Credit Council. Within the policy framework set by the Council, the Bank of France has the responsibility for implementing monetary policy. It utilizes all sorts of measures of credit control—changes in the discount rate, the imposition of rediscount ceilings, the control of minimum reserves to be held by the banks in the form of Treasury paper, open market operations, and certain measures of qualitative control. However, the power of the Bank of France to implement monetary policy is circumscribed, to a certain extent, by the existence of the specialized credit institutions, which have considerable influence on both the volume of money-market demand and the character of the investment program for which financing is sought.

[22] *A Description and Analysis of Certain European Capital Markets* (Washington: Joint Economic Committee, 88th Congress, 2d Session, 1964), p. 103.
[23] *Ibid.*, p. 102.

During most of the postwar period, monetary policy has been used to accommodate financial demands arising from investment activity. Emphasis was placed on the stimulation and maintenance of a rapid rate of economic expansion, and monetary policy was subverted toward this end. However, inflation and monetary instability, which occurred during the middle of the 1950s, ushered in the Fifth Republic under Charles de Gaulle, and monetary policy was used to restore financial stability to France. It made the franc one of the most stable currency units in the world and contributed to increasing the gold reserves of the country. A rise in private consumption in 1963 coincided with a worsening of the trade balance, and monetary measures which were designed to moderate the rate of expansion of private demand were adopted. Since then, monetary policy generally has been expansionary.

Labor-Management Relations

There are a number of national federations of unions in France. These federations are not as highly organized nor as powerful politically as their counterparts in the United States. Although no reliable information is available on the number of French workers in trade unions, estimates place union membership as one fourth of the total labor force.[24]

The French trade union movement is dominated by several large labor confederations which, although ideologically different, are united in a general unwillingness to accept the basic institutions of capitalism. These confederations were also united in their opposition to Charles de Gaulle.

The largest trade union confederation is the CGT (Confederation Generale de Travail). It is Communist-led and has a membership of about 1.4 million. It is militant in philosophy and activity and is affiliated with the Communist World Federation of Trade Unions. The CGT is divided into departmental unions and industrial federations. To be affiliated with CGT, each union must first join a departmental union which brings together all unions of the region, whatever their trade.

A second major union is the CGT-FO (Force Ouvriere), a dissident group which broke away from the CGT. It has some 600,000 members and supports the Socialist party. It is traditionally strong in the government services.

A third union confederation is the CFTC (Confederation Federale des Travilleurs Chretiens), which was also organized as a result of a split within the CGT. Its membership, amounting to 500,000, is found primarily in the staunchly Catholic and conservative areas of Brittany and western France.[25] The organization of the CFTC is centralized. It is the least revolutionary of the three major French unions and the most inclined to work for labor-management cooperation.

Two other important French unions are the General Confederation of Supervisory Employees (Confederation Generale des Cadres), which has a

---

[24] *Labor Digests on Countries in Europe,* Bulletin No. 1737 (Washington: U.S. Department of Labor, 1972), p. 3.

[25] To broaden its appeal, the CFTC in 1964 dropped its religious reference (Chretiens) and renamed itself the Democratic Confederation of Labor.

membership of 200,000, and the Federation of Public Education Personnel, which has a membership of 400,000 and attracts teachers of varied political persuasion.

Employers are also organized into associations. The overall employers' organization is the National Council of French Employers (Conseil National du Patronat Francais). It comprises some 150 trade associations and three major federations. The trade associations represent their members in the negotiation of collective agreements.

A split occurred within the CNPF in 1965 between old and young employers over economic policies of the French government. The split resulted in the formation of the Center des Jeunes Patrons. The Center supports government economic planning, maintenance of full employment, and participative labor-management relations.

Collective bargaining contracts are reached either by direct negotiations between labor and management or with government assistance. In 1950, the French government enacted legislation which set the conditions under which collective bargaining agreements could be made. This legislation provides for permanent employee commissions through which agreements can be worked out at any time. Before an agreement can be effective, it must be filed with the government.

There are three types of labor-management agreements in France: extended agreements, which are negotiated by commissions established by the Minister of Labor and which apply to more than one employer and to all employees—manual, white collar, technical, and supervisory; ordinary agreements, which are also multi-employer in scope, but which are negotiated without the direct intervention of the Minister of Labor; and plant agreements, which concern company level contracts involving wages.

In recent years the productivity of French workers has been exceeded by wage increases, despite the efforts of the French government to slow down the increase in wages and prices. This can be explained in part by a shortage of labor which existed throughout the 1960s, even with the repatriation of the French colons from Algeria.

In the nationalized sector of the economy, the French government has attempted to hold wage increases to 4 percent a year. This has caused wage increases in the public sector to lag behind increases in the private sector, with the result of acrimony between the government and the labor unions and extensive strikes occurring among public employees.

Government and Business

The involvement of the French government in the business sector of the economy is considerable. This involvement dates back to the time of Jean Baptiste Colbert, Minister of Finance under Louis XIV. Colbert, a practitioner of mercantilism, was concerned with France's development as an international power. To achieve this objective, he subsidized certain industries and attempted to regulate the methods and the quality of industrial output, using for this purpose the French guilds.

Government Control Devices. The French government exercises control over business activities in several ways: through public investment both in the nationalized sector of the economy and through the guidance of investment into officially approved channels; through taxes, subsidies, preferential treatment in government operated transportation, and selective import licensing; through compulsory profit sharing; and through price controls. In France, little natural prejudice exists against the active state manipulation of these devices to produce desired economic results. The power of the government in the economy is considerable, and it has at its disposal a vast number of controls and financial devices which it can use to alter business decisions. Thus politics is very much a part of business.[26]

The Nationalized Industries. Nationalization of important sectors of the economy has given the government control over the prices and products of key industries. It has also given the government considerable control over the allocation of credit through the public lending institutions which channel savings into favored sectors of the economy. A shortage of capital after World War II gave the government considerable leverage in the manipulation of credit to influence business decisions. For example, from 1947 through 1949 approximately two thirds of all investment financing was provided either from public funds or state owned credit agencies.[27] As business profits and private credit sources developed during the 1950s, internal financing became more important than financing provided by public funds, and government control over business policies has been reduced.

The nationalized industries function for the most part under the nominal control of public boards on which representatives of labor, management, and the customers of the enterprise in question are represented. In practice, however, the government has retained a strong hand through its authority to appoint the general managers, whose powers have increased at the expense of the public boards. More and more basic policy is determined by the ministries under whose jurisdiction the nationalized industries fall, and in some cases by interministerial committees. Basic decisions with respect to prices, costs, and investment have become the responsibility of various government agencies.

The nationalized industries have been operated within the framework of a number of objectives, the principal of which have been the raising of production to meet certain economic goals, the implementing of a large-scale modernization program to expand capacity and raise productivity, the lowering of industrial costs, the subsidizing of various economic and social groups, the improving of working conditions and labor relations, and the achieving of financial balance in the accounts of the nationalized enterprises.[28]

---

[26] For a comprehensive treatment of the relationship of government and business in France, see John Sheehan, *Promotion and Control of Industry in Postwar France* (Cambridge: Harvard University Press, 1963).

[27] *Ibid.,* pp. 32–34.

[28] Warren C. Baum, *The French Economy and the State* (Princeton: Princeton University Press, 1958), p. 189.

Compulsory Profit Sharing. Aside from the nationalized industries, the interference of the French government in business is considerable. For example, in January 1968, the government established an obligatory profit sharing plan affecting the employees of all private enterprises in France employing more than a hundred persons. The workers' share of profits is to be calculated on the percentage contributed by labor to the total value added by the enterprise. Prior to calculating the amount of profits which are to be distributed to the workers, however, enterprises are permitted to deduct from taxable profits the corporate income tax as well as a 5 percent return on invested capital, including legal reserves. Employers and employees are supposed to form company works committees to select the method by which profits are distributed.

Monetary and Fiscal Devices. The French government has been very active in the use of monetary and fiscal devices which are designed to foster investment and influence regional development. Regional development is a fundamental goal of French economic policy, and many tax incentives are provided to industry to encourage industrial decentralization. Special grants are provided to firms that locate in regions that have below average incomes. Exemptions from local business taxes and special depreciation provisions are also provided. The government has also used tax incentives to encourage corporate mergers.

Price Controls. Direct price controls have been used extensively since the end of the war. Three separate systems of controls were established in 1945 and form the basis of current controls: *liberte totale,* in which industries are subject to no price controls or in which the price of a product is free of control through several stages of production; *liberte surveillee,* in which industries are subject to direct price controls fixed by the government; and *liberte controlee,* in which producers or distributors may set or change prices but are required to explain to the government the reasons for their decisions. The price control authorities may accept or reject their reasons, and in either case firms must delay price changes for a 15-day examination period.

Recourse to price controls has varied considerably in the postwar period. The trend, however, has been toward the relaxation of controls. Nevertheless, the government is not reluctant to use price controls to achieve desired economic objectives and continues to maintain controls on certain key products, such as wheat, gasoline, and milk.[29]

Economic Planning

French economic planning has received considerable attention in Western countries in recent years. It is regarded as a middle ground approach between

---

[29] In April, 1963, as an anti-inflationary measure, the government placed price controls on some 80 products. Rent control has also been used, and in certain cities, including Paris, rent controls are still used for certain types of buildings. Controls have also been used in the Paris area to regulate hotel charges.

an unplanned, free market capitalistic system and an imperative, or directive, planned economic system. The worst evils of each system are presumably eliminated by French planning. There is also the belief that planning has been responsible for the above average, postwar economic growth rate in France.

Development of French Planning. The formation of the Popular Front government under Socialist Premier Leon Blum marked the first phase of the development of economic planning in France in that it extended the responsibility of the government more deeply than ever before into the economy. The Popular Front nationalized the armament industry, introduced a graduated income tax, and institutionalized a government protected system of collective bargaining.

In 1944 the National Council of the Resistance produced a plan for France's future which called for the nationalization of primary resources and energy, state control of banks and insurance, and the participation of labor in industrial management. Most of the nationalization measures were formalized following World War II.

Formal economic planning occurred with the creation of the Commissariat General au Plan in 1946. The Monnet Plan, or "First French Plan," was developed with the objective of reconstructing six basic areas of the French economy—coal, electricity, steel, cement, transportation, and agricultural equipment. Its primary objectives were set out in terms of the growth in capacity and output needed in these sectors. The corresponding investments were, in large part, financed out of funds provided by the Treasury. Controls were placed over new capital issues and over the distribution of medium- and long-term credit. Priority allocations of raw materials, building permits, and permits to install new equipment were also used in order to channel production and investment in the desired direction.

Altogether, five plans have been completed. The First Plan was designed to develop basic sectors of the economy which would exert a motive force on all economic sectors. The State, through the First Plan, achieved a dominant influence over the direction of investment. The First Plan covered the period from 1947 to 1953.

Less authoritarian, or directive, methods were used by the French government in succeeding plans. The First Plan was of necessity an imposed reconstruction of the French economy. By the early 1950s, however, the worst scarcities had been eliminated and direct controls—allocations of goods and wage and price controls—moderated considerably.

The Second French Plan (1954–57) differed from the First Plan in that it applied to the entire economy rather than to a few basic sectors. The objectives of the Second Plan were improving productivity in the agricultural sector of the economy, modernizing processing industries, constructing housing, upgrading the less developed areas of the country to the level of more prosperous areas, and developing export markets.

The Third Plan (1958–61) had as a general goal a high rate of economic expansion—a 20 percent growth rate in four years—with monetary stability and balanced foreign payments. Its objectives were also similar to those for the Second Plan. In 1958 the franc was devalued in an attempt to achieve a more favorable balance of foreign payments—a move which proved successful.

The Fourth Plan (1962–65) included social, as well as economic, objectives. Social action was taken in support of the less favored sections of the population—farmers, the aged, low-income workers, and students. This was accomplished by increasing subsidies and allowances to students, implementing a guaranteed minimum wage to aid low income workers, improving welfare benefits to the aged, and increasing loans and price supports to farmers.

Other objectives included attaining a 24 percent increase in gross domestic output, full employment of the labor force, increasing exports and a favorable balance of payments, and increasing the level of fixed gross investment to 22 percent of disposable income.

The Fifth Plan (1966–1970) ran for five years instead of four as in the three preceding plans. There were two innovations in the Fifth Plan. For the first time in the development of French planning, an incomes policy was adopted. The objective of the incomes policy was to develop goals for distribution of increases in national income among income groups. Under the incomes policy, average annual increases in incomes, in real terms, were planned over the five-year period of the Plan. The second innovation was the adoption of a warning system to identify inflationary or deflationary trends in time to take remedial action. The Plan also contained social and economic goals which were to be attained during the planning period.

The Sixth Plan, 1971–1975. Like the five plans which preceded it since 1945, the Sixth Plan set the main guidelines of economic and social development in France over a five-year period. As in the other five plans, the Sixth Plan provided a series of economic and social objectives which govern public policy and the activities of the nation as a whole. These objectives are not hardfast; to the contrary, procedures have been provided for adjustment or revision to allow for unforseeable development and to enable the Plan to remain as close as possible to reality. The basic objectives of the Plan as it was originally implemented by law in July, 1971, are as follows:

1. Given a projected reduction in the average working time of one and one-half hours, the Sixth Plan set the growth rate per year of the gross national product at 5.8 percent. This growth rate presupposed an average growth in industrial production of 7.5 percent a year.
2. Four types of public facilities were given top priority for development: telecommunications, roads with 870 miles of expressways to be opened, ports with the improvement of Dunkirk and Marseilles, and transportation and traffic infrastructures in large cities. The annual growth rate in volume of the public facilities in terms of the gross formation of fixed capital was set at 9 percent a year.
3. For social investments, the main one was that which concerned job training; in effect, it was held essential to reduce the discrepancies between job opportunities and job requests. An objective was to double post-school job training between 1970 and 1975.

4. All social welfare benefits, including health insurance, retirement benefits, and family allowances, were to be increased during the Sixth Plan. By 1975 benefits were scheduled to total 200 billion francs (approximately $40 billion) compared to a projected gross domestic product of 1,050 billion francs (approximately $210 billion).

5. An increase in productive investments and the completion of construction programs required the nation's rate of saving to amount to around 30 percent of gross domestic product during the planning period. To this end, the government was to stimulate household savings to the point that they would increase to 16 percent of personal income as compared to 15 percent during the Fifth plan.

6. Regional planning has been an important goal of French planning, especially as concerns the creation of jobs. In the less favored economic regions which are mostly rural, jobs in industry and in the service industries were to be increased by 75 percent during the Sixth Plan. In the Alsace-Lorraine region, 30 percent of all new jobs created in the mechanical engineering industry, automobile construction and chemical industries were to be set up.

7. As far as prices were concerned, the goal of the Sixth Plan was to set an annual growth rate of 2.5 percent for the general level of prices and 1.7 percent for the prices of industrial products.

The type of economic growth chosen for the Sixth Plan was quite different from past plans in that the chief stimulus for growth was not to come from domestic demand but from foreign trade. The basic strategy of the Plan was to rely upon a rapid expansion of exports of industrial products—a consequence and a condition of diversification and fast development of the industrial sector. This meant faster growth of value added.

The Mechanics of French Planning. French planning is essentially a forecast of the direction the economy should take over a period of time. The government, in concert with representatives of agriculture, business, and labor, draws up a plan for the future development of the economy. Reliance is placed on input-output tables and national income sector accounts in the development of the plan.

The Planning Commissariat (Commissariat au Plan) is the administrative agency responsible for the development of the plan. The Commissariat has no power of its own, but prepares the plan, submits it for approval to the government authorities, and sees to its implementation once it is approved. It is responsible to the Prime Minister for its actions. It is headed by a director (Commissaire General) and has a staff of about 40 planning specialists and 50 executive personnel. A large contribution toward the work of preparing the plan comes from other public or semipublic offices.[30]

At the regional level, there are Regional Economic Development Committees, which are consultative bodies set up in 1965. These Committees

---

[30] For the most comprehensive discussion of the administration and preparation of French plans, see Pierre Bauchet, *Economic Planning: The French Experience* (New York: Praeger, 1964) and Stephen Cohen, *Modern Capitalist Planning: The French Model* (Cambridge: Harvard University Press, 1969).

represent local regions and organizations and are responsible for an analysis of the economic and social impact of the plan in the region they represent.

Three interministerial agencies were created in 1966—the Administrative, the Public Enterprise, and the Private Enterprise Committees. These committees were created to supervise the implementation of the plan and to offer solutions for any problem that arose in the administrative, public, or private sector of the economy.

Instruments of French Planning. French economic planning relies on priority allocation of investment funds and on tax incentives to accomplish its implementation, rather than on authoritarian directives or exhortations. Physical restraints are few and are primarily limited to the granting of permits which are required for opening new petroleum refineries or expanding old ones. Special installation permits are required for new plants and plant extensions of more than a certain size in the Paris area.

Credit Allocation. Allocation of credit is an important instrument of French planning. The Treasury, operating out of several types of budgetary funds, is a major source of funds which finance investment in the public and private sectors of the economy. The major part of these funds is channeled through a special Treasury account called the Fund for Economic and Social Development. The Fund makes three types of loans, which are as follows:

1. Loans to the nationalized enterprises, which are made directly through the Treasury.
2. Loans to basic industries in the private sector, which are made by the Fund but with the Crédit National acting as intermediary; and
3. Loans to other industries, which are made by the Crédit National out of funds provided by the Treasury.

Since interest rates are below what the borrower has to pay in the market, the Fund can see that there is conformity with the objectives of the Plan, both in the nature of investments and the priority of investments.

There are other ways in which investment can be influenced to favor the objectives of the Plan. One is selective control by the Ministry of Finance over all capital issues; another is control by the Planning Commissariat over long-term borrowing from the major semipublic credit institutions—Crédit National, Crédit Foncier, and Crédit Agricole.[31] These public institutions can make long-term loans out of advances from the Fund for Economic and Social Development, from their own resources, and from funds raised in the capital market.

Selectivity in the granting of short-term credit was utilized for the first time in 1963. Although the basic reason for the use of selectivity was in connection with a stabilization plan to reduce the inflationary pressures prevalent in the economy, favoritism was shown by the commercial banks to borrowers who

---

[31] The Crédit National deals mostly with industrial credit, the Crédit Foncier with real estate credit, and the Crédit Agricole with farm credit.

intended to follow the objectives of the Fourth Plan, particularly with respect to investment in labor surplus areas. This favoritism represented an attempt by the government to influence investment decisions through the short- and medium-term lending policies of the commercial banks.[32] Favorable consideration was also to be shown to borrowers who intended to finance investments that would reduce costs and prices.

Tax Incentives. A second instrument of French economic planning is the use of tax incentives. These incentives are selective as between one activity which conforms to the aim of the Plan and another which does not.[33] There are several examples of selective tax measures.

1. As mentioned previously, incentives are provided under the value-added tax. Special credits under the value-added tax are also provided for the construction of housing. [34]
2. Although dividends are not generally deductible from taxable income in computing the corporate income tax, corporations can make this deduction provided that the proceeds paid for the stock have been used in connection with regional development or plant and equipment modernization plans. Application for deduction must be filed with the Planning Commissariat, and approval or disapproval is given by the Ministry of Finance.
3. A reduction is also given on the transfer tax on land and buildings when the transfer is connected with the program for regional development and industrial decentralization.
4. There is partial relief or total exemption from the business license tax for firms that help promote the Plan's regional development program.

The use of tax incentive devices to hasten the modernization and decentralization of French industry is an essential feature of the French tax system. Tax incentives are used by many European countries to accomplish the same objectives, plan or no plan. It happens to be that modernization and decentralization of industry are objectives of the French Plans. Since this is the case, tax incentives can be considered a legitimate instrument of French planning.

Public Investment. Public investment is also an important instrument of French economic planning. A large part of French gross fixed investment is financed out of public funds. In 1972 total gross fixed investment financed

---

[32] The commercial banks were asked, not ordered, by the government to pursue a selective lending policy.

[33] The use of tax incentives is not a new phenomenon in France. Its use dates back to the time of Colbert and French mercantilism. It reflects a view that taxation should not be neutral but should be used to achieve certain economic objectives. However, the neutrality aspects of the French tax system considerably outweigh the incentive aspects. Tax incentives are basically confined to regional development, housing construction, exports, and scientific research, and to a considerable degree are automatic in that no government approval is needed.

[34] A shortage of housing is an acute problem in France. Tax incentives are considerable. In 1963 as an incentive to housing construction, the value-added tax was extended to housing construction. Since tax credits are available under the value-added tax, this extension meant a reduction in the tax burden on housing construction.

by the Treasury amounted to $8.5 billion. Some $3.16 billion were spent on investments made by the government and on grants made to local governments for investment expenditures in social fixed capital. Another $1.8 billion were used to finance the expenditures of the nationalized enterprises. The remaining $3.53 billion were divided between investments in housing, tourism, and agriculture.[35]

If investment expenditures of the nationalized industries are added to the investments made directly by the French government, the percentage of gross fixed investment directly or indirectly financed by the government amounted to 38 percent in 1972.[36] This, of course, means that a large percentage of investment can be influenced by the government, and the objectives of the Plans are more easily expedited through this influence.

Although there are rewards given for conformance to the objectives of the Plan, there are no penalties for nonconformance. Industries and firms are under no obligation to reach quotas or targets as set forth in the directives of the Plan.

Results of the Plans. It is difficult to evaluate the effectiveness of French economic planning for two reasons:

1. It is hard to compare the unplanned French economy before World War II with the postwar planned economy. For one thing, the economic base, which could have been used for comparison, was completely altered by the war. The French economy had to be rebuilt after the war. Also, institutional arrangements were altered by the war and by the postwar nationalization of industry.
2. Numerous factors in addition to economic planning have also had an effect on the postwar development of France. It is difficult to isolate planning from these factors. For example, it is possible that inflation may have had more influence on the course of French development than planning.

A comparison of growth rates also presents difficulties for several reasons:

1. The growth rate depends on the existence of resources, such as labor, over which a country has no control in the short run. The shortage of French labor is not the fault of economic planning but of the birthrate.
2. Maximization of the growth rate, as a desirable economic goal, varies among countries as to the degree of intensity.
3. The economic base, or point of comparison, differs among countries.

On balance, the performance of the French economy has been good relative to other major industrial countries, particularly with respect to the real growth rate. However, despite targets set in successive plans, the relative development of prices have been far less satisfactory. There have been conflicts between an emphasis on the attainment of specific growth rates and the goal of price stability. This conflict has usually been resolved in favor of price stability, and growth objectives frequently have been modified. Aside from

[35] Ministere de L'Economie et des Finances, *Le Budget de 1972*, Paris, 1972, p. 11.
[36] *Ibid.*, p. 13.

growth and price stability goals, planning has had beneficial effects on the French economy in that there has been a reorganization and improvement in the quality of the labor force. In addition, there has been a regrouping of business firms into larger and more efficient units through persuasion exercised by the consultative machinery of planning.

The performance of the French economy over the last two decades and extending into the 1970s has been rather outstanding. Although shifts in the positions of countries occur from time to time, as of early 1974 it can be said that France possesses the most dynamic economy in Europe. France has the fastest increase in the rate of productivity in Europe. From 1961 to 1970 worker productivity increased by 58 percent, and industrial productivity increased at an average annual rate of 5.2 percent.[37] These rates of increase have been maintained in the 1970s.

The rate of economic growth in France has been the highest in West Europe for the period 1960 to 1973. During the period 1960 to 1965, the French average annual growth rate in real terms was 5.8 percent compared to a West European average of 4.8 percent.[38] The rate of 5.8 percent was the highest for all countries. For the period 1965 to 1970, the French economy grew at a rate of 5.6 percent, a rate well above the average of 4.4 percent for West Europe, but exceeded by a rate of 6 percent for Italy. From 1969 to 1972, the French real gross national product increased by 26.1 percent—an average annual growth rate in excess of 6 percent. In 1973 the French growth rate increased by 6.5 percent. It can be said that the only major country with a higher growth rate than France since 1960 is Japan.

However, the performance of the French economy with respect to price stability has been rather erratic. In the 1950s, the aspect of French economic performance which drew the greatest attention was not the high average rate of growth of the gross national product, but the successive waves of inflation. This inflation led to balance of payments difficulties and culminated in the crisis of mid-1958 when the nation's gold and foreign exchange reserves had for the second time within six months virtually disappeared despite repeated recourse to foreign credits. This situation led to the devaluation of the franc in 1958, the sixth devaluation since 1944. For some time after the devaluation the rate of French inflation was below that of other countries. In 1967 the rate of inflation began to increase, and for the five-year period 1968–1972, the consumer price index increased by an annual average of 5.8 percent.[39] Since 1972 the inflation has become more severe.

Employment in France has held at a high level, with few yearly exceptions, since the end of World War II. In 1973, for example, the rate of unemployment was 2.5 percent, compared to 2.2 percent in 1972.[40] To some extent the low

[37] Organization for Economic Cooperation and Development, *Employment Policy in France* (Paris: 1971).

[38] Deutsches Institut für Wirtschaftsforschung, "Stabilitatspolitik in der E G," *Wochenbericht* (Berlin: November 8, 1973).

[39] International Monetary Fund, *International Financial Statistics* (November, 1973).

[40] Agence Nationale pour L'Emploi, *Annual Report for 1973* (Paris: 1973), p. 7.

rate of unemployment is misleading given the fact that France has a surplus of farm labor that is underemployed in agriculture. There has also been some problem with regional unemployment as certain areas of France have experienced economic problems associated with the closing of obsolete industries. Nevertheless, the performance of the French economy in maintaining full employment has been good.

The proportion of the French national income that is redistributed via the tax-transfer machinery is considerable, and a welfare state of the first order exists. The proportion of the national income that is redistributed via the machinery of the French government is about twice as large as it is in the United Kingdom and almost four times greater than the United States. To the extent that the welfare state means protection for the worker against the hazards and uncertainties of contemporary economic life, France has been as successful as any other nation in establishing the necessary machinery for this purpose. However, reliance on indirect taxes to finance the bulk of welfare expenditures tends to have a moderating effect on income redistribution, particularly between income classes. The implication of indirect taxes is clear, as it means that a considerable portion of the real costs of the welfare expenditures are borne, in the final analysis, by the beneficiaries of these expenditures.

SUMMARY

The French economy may be best described as partially planned. Although most of it remains under private ownership, an effort is made by the government to secure the compliance of private, as well as public, enterprises with the established economic and social objectives set forth in the Plans.

The French government participates in the economy in several ways, which include:

1. The ownership or partial control of a number of important industries. However, nationalization took place during the period immediately after World War II, and it has not been a basic economic desideratum of subsequent French governments. The nationalized industries behave, to a considerable degree, like private industries, and there is no particular evidence to indicate that their operation plays an important role in influencing the activities of the private sector of the French economy.

2. Economic planning, which has taken the form of a series of plans, the latest of which is the Sixth Plan. The objective of planning is to develop a series of blueprints for the French economy to follow over a specific period of time. The planning is indicative rather than imperative. The government exerts an influence in that it can divert the allocation of capital into areas that are in conformance with the objectives of the Plan and also can use selective tax measures to achieve the same conformance. Public investment by the government also plays an important role in accomplishing the objectives of planning.

3. Income redistribution, accomplished through a comprehensive social welfare program, including a system of family allowances. Most of the welfare programs are financed by taxes on employers with the result that an inordinate tax burden is placed on the employer. Transfer payments comprise a sizable fraction of French national income.

Although production and distribution in France are primarily controlled by private enterprise operating within the framework of the market system, the government, with its power to deny a firm access to credit or to tax exemptions which could prove important to the firm, is in a rather powerful and persuasive position to influence the decisions of what to produce, where to locate, and whether to undertake certain investments. This is exactly what has been done to achieve the objectives of the Plan, and it can have a distorting effect in that investment funds can be withheld from more profitable uses in favor of less profitable ones through the use of credit controls and selective tax incentives.

QUESTIONS

1. French economic planning can be called indicative rather than imperative. Explain.
2. Discuss the mechanics of the value-added tax and the ways in which it can be used to achieve national economic objectives.
3. Discuss the reasons for the postwar nationalization of certain of the French industries.
4. The French government plays an important role in the banking system. Do you agree?
5. What were the objectives of the Sixth French Plan?
6. The French government can influence the decisions of business firms to invest in several ways. What are these ways?
7. French economic planning has been called *soft planning*. What is meant by this term?
8. Discuss the policy instruments which are used to implement the French Plans.
9. An important social welfare measure in France is the system of family allowances. What is the system and what are its effects on income redistribution?

RECOMMENDED READINGS

Ardagh, John. *The New French Revolution.* New York: Harper and Row, 1969.

Bauchet, Pierre. *Economic Planning, The French Experience.* New York: Frederick A. Praeger, Inc., 1964.

Cohen, Stephen. *Modern Capitalist Planning: The French Model.* Berkeley: University of California Press, 1975.

Denton, Geoffrey and Malcolm MacLennan. *Economic Planning and Policies in Britain, France, and Germany.* New York: Frederick A. Praeger, Inc., 1969.

Lutz, Vera. *Central Planning for the Market Economy: An Analysis of the French Theory and Experience.* New Jersey: Humanities Press, Inc.

Milward, Alan. *The New Order and the French Economy.* Oxford: The Clarendon Press, 1970.

Servan-Schreiber, Jean-Jacques. *The Radical Alternative.* New York: Dell Publishing Co. Inc., 1972.

Sheahan, John. *An Introduction to the French Economy.* Columbus: Charles Merrill, 1969.

Thompson, Ian. *Modern France: A Social and Economic Geography.* Totowa, N.J.: Rowman & Littlefield, Inc., 1971.

11

The United Kingdom

INTRODUCTION

The year 1945 is often represented as a line of demarcation in British history. The welfare state, as the phrase has come to be used, stems from the victory of the Labour party in the general election of that year. The phrase is really tied to the publication of the Beveridge Report of 1942 and is roughly descriptive of government activities which are redistributive in character. The welfare state developed in the United Kingdom partly as a result of the deprivations sustained during World War II and partly as a remembrance of prewar British capitalism, in particular the high rate of unemployment and excessive and widespread inequalities in the distribution of wealth and income. In 1924, for example, two thirds of the total wealth in the United Kingdom was owned by 1.6 percent of all wealth owners.[1] Also, the United Kingdom, being one of the older capitalistic countries, had had more time for the institution of inheritance to do its work.

Distinct economic policy changes have occurred since 1945. There is no longer the extreme emphasis on income equality and other egalitarian measures. Nationalization of industry and socialization of medicine are past history, and the current concern in the United Kingdom is over the rate of economic growth and a persistently unfavorable balance of payments. Indirect taxes have increased in importance relative to direct taxes, and measures to stimulate economic growth have become more important than measures to achieve income equality.

THE ECONOMIC SYSTEM

The British economic system is mixed. Although private enterprise is dominant, the government plays an important role in economic activity in three ways; through the nationalized sector of the economy, through social welfare measures aimed at achieving income redistribution and economic and

---

[1] James Wedgwood, *The Economics of Inheritance* (London: George Routledge and Sons, Ltd., 1929), p. 42.

social well-being, and through fiscal and monetary policies which have been used to pursue a policy of full employment.

The process of nationalization took place in the period immediately following World War II. Affected by the nationalization program of the Labour government were the Bank of England, the railways, the coal mines, the steel industry, trucking, and the public utilities—especially the electrical and gas industries. The owners were compensated at approximately the market price of their holdings. In the case of some of the industries, nationalization was neither as revolutionary nor as controversial as might be supposed. The Bank of England was already, in effect, a public institution; its changed status was hardly more than a change in title. The railroads and coal mines had been losing money for years, and the owners were perfectly willing to accept nationalization.[2]

Nationalization has not figured prominently as a part of British economic policy in recent years with the exception of the steel industry. When the Conservative party came into power in 1951, the steel industry was de-nationalized and remained so until 1966 when the Labour party nationalized it for the second time.[3]

Apart from the nationalized industries, economic activity is organized pretty much in the capitalistic fashion. Business firms are free to organize in any of the traditional forms, and may make their decisions on the usual capitalistic bases of price and cost. Through the use of monetary and fiscal policies, however, the government can exert indirect control on the activities of private enterprises. For example, the government has wide powers to encourage the development of industries in areas which are depressed because of the dependence on a single industry, usually coal mining or shipbuilding. The government can also influence and control industrial, residential, and public construction.

The economic record of the United Kingdom since the end of World War II shows a favorable rate of employment accompanied by a low rate of economic growth, instability in the price level, and a balance-of-payments problem. Relatively heavy emphasis has been given until recent years to the maintenance of a high rate of employment. However, balance-of-payments problems and price instability necessitated the use of Draconian measures in the late 1960s and early 1970s. In 1967 the British pound was devalued for the purpose of balancing accounts with the rest of the world by stimulating exports and restraining imports. Subsequent fiscal and monetary measures were also designed to limit the rise in costs in order to maintain as much as possible a competitive advantage conferred by devaluation. In the early 1970s the Heath Government stressed an increase in the rate of economic growth,

---

[2] The road to nationalization had been opened by the Conservative party in earlier years when it sponsored state-chartered monopolies for shipping, air transportation, radio broadcasting, and other industries.

[3] The renationalization of the steel industry was done primarily to please the more doctrinaire and left-wing members of the Labour party, who felt that Prime Minister Wilson was too moderate, rather than as a matter of economic policy.

with an annual average rate of 3.5 percent set as a target. However, the British economy was confronted at the end of 1973 by its greatest crisis since World War II, with one result a $3 billion cut in government spending.

In 1973 the British gross national product amounted to $128.36 billion. The major components are shown in Table 11-1.

TABLE 11–1
BRITISH GROSS NATIONAL PRODUCT FOR 1973

Expenditures	Millions of Dollars
Consumer expenditures	94,231
Government expenditures on goods and services	28,085
Gross domestic fixed capital formation	26,914
Inventory adjustments	− 1,056
Total domestic expenditures	148,174
Exports and property income from abroad	31,994
Imports and property income paid abroad	−32,256
Less: Taxes on expenditures	−22,270
Subsidies	2,719
Gross national product at factor cost	128,361

Source: Central Statistical Office, *Monthly Digest of Statistics*, Table 1 (London: Her Majesty's Stationery Office, October, 1974).

Government savings and investment make a significant contribution to the British economy. In 1973 public saving which emanated from public corporations, the national government, and local governments amounted to more than one third of total savings, a rate which is considerably higher than that for the United States for the reason that the nationalized sector also contributes to public savings. Government investment in 1973 contributed 45 percent of total investment. Out of gross domestic fixed capital formation of $26.91 billion, public corporation contributed $4.3 billion, the national government $1.7 billion, and local governments $5 billion.[4]

Public Finance

The British budget is a powerful weapon for influencing the general level of activity in the economy. Its purpose is not only to raise revenue to meet government expenditures, but also to regulate the national economy. It is part of the budget's job to help bring about a balance between the total goods and services that are likely to be available to the nation and the total claims that will be made upon them.

The budget does not include all public sector expenditures. It includes all national government expenditures other than payments out of the National

[4] Central Statistical Office, *Monthly Digest of Statistics*, Table 2 (London: Her Majesty's Stationery Office, October, 1973).

Insurance Funds. However, it does not include either local governmental expenditures or nationalized industry investment, although it does cover grants to local authorities and loans and deficit grants to the nationalized industries, as well as the British government's contributions to the National Insurance Funds. The expenditure figures in the budget are one measure of the national government's contribution to the demand for goods and services.

The nationalized industries, local authorities, and other public bodies need to borrow from year to year mainly to finance expenditures on capital projects. Most of this borrowing is done from the National Loans Fund, which is responsible for the bulk of domestic lending by the government. The National Loans Fund and the Consolidated Fund, which balances current revenue against current expenditures, are the two basic components of the budget.

The British Tax System. Taxation in the United Kingdom is fairly evenly balanced between direct and indirect taxes. The most important direct tax is the personal income tax. No other European country, except Sweden, imposes personal income taxes to a greater degree than does the United Kingdom, nor do personal taxes account for nearly so high a percentage of gross national product in France, Germany, or the United States as they do in the United Kingdom and Sweden. There is also a heavy reliance on indirect taxes on tobacco, alcohol, and gasoline. The tax yield on these three commodities amounts to nearly 7 percent of the British gross national product, over half as much again as Sweden, twice as much as Germany and France, and three times the American proportion.

The Personal Income Tax. The most important tax in the United Kingdom is the personal income tax. It was first introduced during the Napoleonic Wars when the Income Tax Act of 1799 was passed. The tax was levied at a flat rate per pound without regard to a taxpayer's income. However, a measure of graduation was achieved through the operation of exemptions for small incomes.

For many years the British income tax structure included an income tax and a surtax. However, in 1973 this system was replaced by a single graduated income tax. Much revision was entailed in the changeover to a straight progressive tax. There is some differentiation between earned and investment income, with investment income of up to $4,800 being subject to the same rates as earned income and income in excess of $4,800 subject to a 15 percent surcharge. The income tax is graduated by means of personal allowances and progressive tax rates. These rates, as of April 1973, ranged from 30 percent on incomes of $12,000 or less to 75 percent on incomes in excess of $48,000. Incomes of husband and wife may be aggregated and treated as one income or treated as separate incomes. However, a higher personal allowance is given to couples who file jointly.

A series of allowances reduce the base of the personal income tax. For example, there is a flat allowance of $1,428 for a single person, and $1,860 for a married couple. There are also allowances for children which vary with their ages. In addition, there are other types of allowances and deductions.

In some cases allowances are permitted for dependent relatives. An earned income allowance is given to families where the wife is working. Life insurance premiums may be deducted for tax purposes, and so may interest up to a given amount. All in all, the allowances and deductions reduce the progressiveness of the personal income tax. Nevertheless, despite allowances and deductions, the effective rate of income taxation, i.e., what the taxpayers actually pay in taxes relative to the amount of their income, is higher in the United Kingdom than in most other countries.

The Corporate Income Tax. Corporate incomes are taxed at a rate of 40 percent. However, in considering the general level of corporate taxation, allowances have to be made for various forms of investment incentives. The British have been liberal with measures which are designed to stimulate investment. Investment grants are made available for capital expenditures on new machinery or equipment installed for use by manufacturing, construction, and extractive industries. The rate of the grant is 25 percent of expenditures. The purpose of the grant is to stimulate the development of the capital intensive industries in order to increase the rate of economic growth.

Excise Taxes. Excise taxes are levied on consumer goods, especially tobacco, alcohol, and gasoline. In the fiscal year 1972–1973, taxes on these three commodities accounted for 25 percent of the national government's total tax revenues. The tobacco tax rate varies, with tobacco of Commonwealth origin being admitted at a preferential rate. The tax rate on alcohol varies according to the type of liquor involved, with beer and light wines carrying the lowest rates. The rates of the gasoline tax also vary depending on its use. One feature of the taxes on tobacco, alcohol, and gasoline is the large proportion they represent of the sales price. For example, the tax on cigarettes is 80 percent of the purchase price.

Value-Added Tax. The value-added tax replaced the purchase and selective employment taxes in April 1973. The value-added tax is a general turnover tax on consumption; it has a broader base than the purchase tax and applies to a wide range of goods and services. It is calculated as a percentage of the value of a given good or service, with a single flat rate of 10 percent applicable to most times. However, there are certain exemptions to the value-added tax. First of all, exports of goods and services are exempt. Secondly, basic necessities of life, such as food, drugs, and medicines, are exempt from the tax. Finally, children's clothing, books, coal, gas, electricity, and gasoline are also exempt. The value-added tax adds an element of regressivity to the British tax system in that it is passed on to the final consumer.

Government Expenditures. Total central government expenditures for the fiscal year 1972–1973 amounted to $42.2 billion.[5] These expenditures can be divided into two categories—current and capital. Current expenditures can be divided into four categories—expenditures on goods and services, subsidies, current

---

[5] Chancellor of the Exchequer, *Financial Statement and Budget Report, 1973–1974* (London: Her Majesty's Stationery Office, 1974), p. 14.

The sources of British tax revenues are shown in Table 11–.

TABLE 11–2
BRITISH TAX RECEIPTS BY SOURCES FOR FISCAL YEAR 1973–1974

Taxes	Millions of Dollars
Personal income tax	17,359
Surtax	864
Corporate tax	4,908
Wealth tax	955
Tobacco tax	2,472
Alcohol tax	2,050
Petroleum tax	3,960
Value-added tax	2,760
Miscellaneous	6,554
Total	41,882

Source: Chancellor of the Exchequer, *Financial Statement and Budget Report, 1973–1974*, Table 9 (London: Her Majesty's Stationery Office, 1974), p. 17.

grants to the personal and public sectors, and interest on the public debt. Capital expenditures include gross domestic fixed capital formation, capital grants, and loans. When local government expenditures are added to central government expenditures, total public expenditures of all types are around 40 percent of the gross national product. One reason for this is that the public sector contribution to investment is very much higher in the United Kingdom than in the United States because of the importance of public enterprises. These enterprises own about 40 percent of the nation's capital assets and are responsible for nearly 45 percent of the annual fixed investments of the nation.

The United Kingdom has a comprehensive social welfare system. It can be divided into two categories: the medical care and social security program which includes family allowances, and the national insurance program which provides unemployment and sickness benefits, old age pensions, maternity benefits, and death grants. In contrast with the income-based contributions common in other European countries, the British welfare system, like that in the United States, is based mainly on flat-rate contributions. These contributions introduce an element of regressivity into the fiscal system.

Medical Care. The best known social welfare program is medical care, which is provided in the United Kingdom under the National Health Service as a free public service and is not a part of the regular social insurance program. All residents are eligible for health services. General practitioner care, specialist services, hospitalization, maternity care, and treatment in the event of industrial injuries are provided by the National Health Service.

The British government pays for about 80 percent of the cost of the National Health Service from general revenue. The employee and employer pay weekly contributions that meet about four fifths and one fifth, respectively, of the remaining 20 percent of the cost.

National Health Service hospitals account for the great majority of hospitals in the country and are vested in the government. Medical staffs are paid on nationally agreed scales. For general practice, nearly all doctors participate in the National Health Service. Unlike hospital doctors, who are paid by salary, their remuneration is based on a system of fees and allowances which are designed to relate pay to the work load, expenses, and experiences of each individual doctor.[6] Patients are free to select any doctor within their home area.

Prescribed medicines are free.[7] Dental services and false teeth, eyeglasses, hearing aids, and other devices are supplied through the National Health Service but with some cost sharing on the part of the patient. There is no charge for dental services to children or to expectant or recent mothers.

Family Allowances. Family allowances are cash payments for the benefit of the family as a whole. They are of recent origin in the United Kingdom, dating back to 1946, and are financed out of general revenues rather than from taxes on employers and employees. They are paid to all families with two or more children under certain age limits. No allowance is paid to a family with only one child under the age limit. The allowance is 18 shillings a week for the second child and 1 pound a week for subsequent children.[8] For example, a family with three children would receive 38 shillings a week and a family with five children would receive 78 shillings a week. There is no income limit or means test, but allowances must be declared as income for tax purposes. In 1972 the family allowance represented as a transfer payment 5.8 percent of average family income in the United Kingdom.

National Insurance. Separate and apart from the National Health Service, there exists a comprehensive program of social security which comes under the category of national insurance. This program provides flat-rate sickness benefits at a rate of 5 pounds a week for men, single women, and widows up to a period of a year. In addition, national insurance beneficiaries can also receive benefits for dependent children. Married women and divorced women who receive some alimony get lower benefits. Earnings-related supplements to the flat-rate benefits are payable to persons who, because of their higher earnings, have paid additional graduated contributions. The supplement is payable for up to six months in any uninterrupted period of sickness and the

---

[6] There is an acknowledged shortage of doctors in Britain. A factor in the situation is the emigration of British doctors to North America and elsewhere, though its effects have been mitigated by the immigration of doctors from overseas. The factors underlying emigration are not fully established, but the principal ones seem to be a desire for better facilities, higher pay, and greater professional freedom.

[7] However, on June 10, 1968, changes were made and some prescriptions are no longer free.

[8] There are 20 shillings to a British pound. For many years the pound was valued at $2.40. It has been devalued and now has a floating exchange rate.

rate is one third of a person's average weekly earnings between 9 and 30 pounds during the previous year, but the supplements cannot raise the total benefit, including allowances for dependents, above 85 percent of earnings.

Old age pensions and unemployment benefits are similar in makeup to sickness benefits. Flat-rate unemployment benefits are the same as sickness benefits; this has the advantage that there is nothing to be gained from claiming one benefit rather than the other. Old age pensions are payable to persons who have reached minimum pension age, 65 for men and 60 for women, and have retired from regular work. The standard weekly flat-rate pension is 5 pounds for a man or woman who qualified on his or her own insurance record. A married woman who has made no contribution is entitled to a lower pension of 3 pounds, 2 shillings a week. As a corollary to regular old age pensions, there is a graduated pension scheme which provides higher rates to higher paid contributors. There is no set maximum amount that any contributor can receive.

There are other benefits payable under the national insurance program. A maternity allowance of 5 pounds a week is paid to women who give up paid employment to have a baby. The benefit is usually paid for 18 weeks, beginning with the 11th week before the expected week of confinement. In addition to the allowance, there is a lump-sum maternity grant of 25 pounds which is paid to most mothers, either on their insurance or on their husband's insurance. There is also a death grant of 25 pounds which is payable on the death of an insured person or the wife, husband, or child of an insured person. There is a widow's allowance, which is separate from a widow's pension and is payable at a standard rate of 7 pounds a week for 26 weeks after the husband's death. There is also a widowed mother's allowance which is payable when the widow's allowance ends, provided there are dependent children.

Total government expenditures on national health, family allowances, and national insurance amounted to $12.2 billion in 1972, or approximately 10 percent of gross national product.[9]

All public sector expenditures in the United Kingdom are covered in the current and capital transactions of the central government, including the National Insurance Fund and all other central government funds and accounts, and the transactions of local governments, together with the transactions of the nationalized industries and other public corporations on appropriation and capital accounts. Public expenditures exert much influence on the British economy, particularly on capital formation. In 1972 public sector expenditures on fixed capital formation accounted for 9.2 percent of the gross national product compared to 10.1 percent for the private sector.[10] Public expenditures on goods and services accounted for 18.8 percent of the gross national product —a percentage which is about average by European standards. In the same year, transfer payments to individuals amounted to 10.1 percent of personal income and 10.3 percent of national income.[11] Transfer payments can be

[9] Central Statistical Office, *National Income and Expenditures,* Table 41 (London: Her Majesty's Stationery Office, 1973).

[10] *Ibid.,* page 32.

[11] *Ibid.,* p. 3.

compared to personal income to show the proportion of income which has been redistributed by government action.

Table 11–3 presents central government expenditures for the fiscal year 1973–1974.

TABLE 11–3

CENTRAL GOVERNMENT EXPENDITURES FOR FISCAL YEAR 1973–1974

Items	Millions of Dollars
Current expenditures	
Current expenditures on goods and services	32,707
Subsidies	2,659
Debt interest	6,566
Current grants to:	
Local authorities	1,121
Private sector	14,798
Abroad	732
Total	58,583
Capital Expenditures	
Gross domestic capital formation	13,932
Capital grants to:	
Local authorities	—
Public corporations	—
Private sector	2,237
Net domestic lending	802
Loans to overseas government	142
Miscellaneous	1,440
Total	18,553
Total Expenditures	77,136

Source: Chancellor of the Exchequer, *Financial Statement and Budget Report, 1973–1974*, Table 5 (London: Her Majesty's Stationery Office, 1974), p. 13.

Income Redistribution. The British government has become an instrument for effecting changes in the distribution of income. Taxes and transfer payments are the major means for accomplishing this objective, with taxes reducing the incomes of some persons and transfer payments adding to the incomes of others. However, with respect to transfers, it should be noted that some of the services provided by the government are, in effect, nonmonetary transfers. This would be true for such expenditures as free medical care, since the recipients of this service benefit through obtaining it at a cost price below its real cost as measured by the government expenditures for the resources necessary to provide the service.

Taxation. Income redistribution is accomplished through the progressiveness of the personal income tax. There is a redistribution of income in the direction of greater equality because of the proportionate share of upper-income groups in total income is reduced and the proportionate share of the lower-income groups is raised. A progressive tax structure must bring about this result because the effective rate of taxation—the ratio of total taxes paid to income received—increases with the size of income.

The distribution of incomes before and after taxes for 1968 is shown in Table 11–4.

TABLE 11–4
DISTRIBUTION OF INCOMES IN THE UNITED KINGDOM BEFORE AND AFTER TAXES FOR 1968

Income Range (Dollars)	Number of Incomes (Thousands)	Income Before Taxes (Millions)	Tax (Millions)	Income After Taxes (Millions)
$ 120 and under $ 600	5,611	1,183	—	1,183
600 and under 1,200	11,894	5,419	96	5,323
1,200 and under 2,400	15,125	16,142	1,255	14,887
2,400 and under 3,600	16,178	19,802	2,270	17,532
3,600 and under 4,800	6,646	11,330	1,622	9,708
4,800 and under 7,200	3,115	7,346	1,176	6,170
7,200 and under 12,000	888	3,286	905	2,381
12,000 and under 24,000	360	2,400	866	1,534
24,000 and under 48,000	84	1,121	588	533
48,000 and over	17	559	422	137
Total	59,918	68,588	9,200	59,388

Source: Central Statistical Office, National Income and Expenditures, 1968 (London: Her Majesty's Stationery Office), p. 33. This publication is also known as the Blue Book. For a definition of income, see pp. 32–33.

Government Assistance. Income redistribution is also accomplished through the provision of government assistance to individuals and families. For the family with children, family allowances and general social welfare measures are provided, irrespective of need; and for the aged, an old age pension is provided plus supplementary benefits to individuals and families whose incomes are below a defined scale. For the infirm, there are sickness benefits; and for all persons, there are general medical and health benefits. However, transfer payments when expressed as a percentage of national income and personal income are lower in the United Kingdom than in Sweden, France, and West Germany.[12] This can be attributed in part to the slowing down of the growth of the gross national product and to the deflationary policies which were pursued by the Wilson government during the latter part of the 1960s.[13]

[12] For example, the proportion of the French national income that is redistributed through the machinery of the central government is almost twice as large as it is in the United Kingdom.
[13] Some welfare benefits have been placed on a "need" basis rather than on a "right" basis. Charges and fees are also being levied on certain goods and services that were previously provided free.

Greater Income Equality. A great deal has been written in recent years concerning the strong influence of egalitarian considerations upon economic policy pursued by the British government since the end of World War II. Studies indicate that the concentration of personal income, both before and after the income tax, in the hands of the top 5 percent of income recipients was reduced after the war compared with 1938, and this tendency toward greater equality continued during the postwar years.[14]

However, more current studies tend to dispute the idea that there is a trend toward greater income equality.[15] After 1957 the trend toward greater income equality tended to stabilize, with shifts occurring in the rate of income taxation. But there were other factors at work to slow down the trend toward greater income equality. Rent, interest, and dividends, which had increased from $2.9 billion in 1949 to $3.8 billion in 1957, more than doubled during the 1958 to 1967 period. Income from self-employment remained fairly constant from 1949 to 1957, but increased by 50 percent from 1958 to 1967.[16] Wages and salaries increased from $17.5 billion in 1949 to $31.2 billion in 1957, and from $32.4 billion in 1958 to $58.1 billion in 1967.

Table 11–5 shows the distribution of before- and after-tax incomes for the

TABLE 11–5
DISTRIBUTION OF INCOME AND TAX PAYMENTS FOR THE UPPER 1 PERCENT AND 5 PERCENT OF BRITISH INCOME UNITS FOR SELECTED YEARS

	Before Taxes		After Taxes		Percentage of Tax Payments	
	Top 1 Percent	Top 5 Percent	Top 1 Percent	Top 5 Percent	Top 1 Percent	Top 5 Percent
1949	11.2	23.8	6.4	17.7	46.0	69.6
1953	9.8	21.9	5.8	15.9	41.1	62.3
1957	8.2	19.1	5.0	14.9	35.3	54.2
1958	8.2	19.5	5.1	15.8	34.8	54.3
1959	8.3	19.9	5.2	16.8	34.5	54.6
1960	8.5	19.9	5.1	15.6	34.4	54.1
1961	8.1	19.2	5.5	16.0	30.0	49.9
1962	8.1	19.2	5.5	16.2	28.4	46.9
1963	7.9	19.1	5.2	15.7	28.0	47.3
1967	7.9	19.2	5.0	15.5	22.8	38.1

Source: Central Statistical Office, *National Income & Expenditures, 1960 and 1968* (London: Her Majesty's Stationery Office, 1960 and 1968), p. 32 (1960) and p. 28 (1968).

[14] F. W. Paish, "The Real Incidence of Personal Taxation," *Lloyds Bank Review* (January, 1957), and H. F. Lydall, "The Long-Term Trend in the Size Distribution of Income," *Journal of the Royal Statistical Society*, Series A, 122, Part 1 (1959).

[15] Richard M. Titmuss, *Income Distribution & Social Change* (London: Simson Shand Ltd., 1962), and R. J. Nicholson, "The Distribution of Personal Income," *Lloyds Bank Review* (January, 1967).

[16] Central Statistical Office, *National Income & Expenditures, 1972* (London: Her Majesty's Stationery Office, 1972), pp. 4–5.

upper 1 percent and 5 percent of income units for selected years. In 1949, for example, the upper 1 percent of all income units received 11.2 percent of before-tax income and 6.4 percent of after-tax income, while the top 5 percent received 23.8 percent of before-tax income and 17.7 percent of after-tax income. As can be seen in the table, there has been little change in income distribution from 1957 to 1967.[17] Also shown in the table is the percentage of total income taxes paid by the top 1 percent and 5 percent of income units for the same years. The percentage of taxes raised from these groups has shown a decline over time.

Inequality of Wealth. Inequality in the distribution of wealth is perhaps more closely identified with the United Kingdom than with any other major industrial country because, after all, the Industrial Revolution really developed in this country. A concomitant of the Industrial Revolution was the concentration of property in the hands of a few persons. Vast fortunes were made, particularly during the development of the British Empire with its markets and resources. These fortunes, for the most part, were not touched by taxation, but were allowed to accumulate and be passed down from generation to generation.

Studies of the distribution of wealth are not often made. One of the first studies of the distribution of wealth in the United Kingdom covered the years 1912 and 1924.[18] In 1912, 43 percent of all wealth was owned by 0.2 percent of all wealth owners, while well over half of the wealth of the country was owned by only 0.8 percent of wealth owners.[19] During the intervening 12-year period World War I occurred, causing some dislocations in the British economy. The tax structure was also revised considerably in 1914, and in subsequent years during the war, by the imposition of a surtax on incomes exceeding a particular level—$7,200 in 1914 and $4,800 in 1918. Minor shifts occurred in the distribution of wealth. In 1924 two thirds of the wealth was owned by 1.6 percent of all wealth owners, compared to 0.9 percent in 1912.[20] Some 93 to 94 percent of all of the wealth was owned by 13.3 percent of the owners in 1912 and by 23.0 percent of the owners in 1924.

Considerable shifting has occurred in the distribution of wealth since 1924. Current data indicate that the top 1 percent of all wealth owners in the United Kingdom own around 21 percent of all wealth, while the top 5 percent own 41 percent of the wealth.[21] On the basis of individual net wealth, 0.3 percent of all wealth owners with assets covered by estate duties had property valued in excess of $240,000.[22] However, this 0.3 percent of wealth owners owned around 10 percent of wealth and had average property valued at around

[17] Central Statistical Office, *National Income & Expenditures, 1968–1969* (London: Her Majesty's Stationery Office, 1968–1969), pp. 27–28 & 34–35.

[18] Wedgwood, *op. cit.*, p. 47.

[19] *Ibid.*, p. 47.

[20] *Ibid.*, p. 48.

[21] Central Statistical Office, *Social Trends*, Table 35 (London: Her Majesty's Stationery Office, 1972), p. 86.

[22] *Ibid.*

$960,000. Based on estate duty returns, evidence indicates a greater concentration of individual wealth. The top 1 percent owned about one third of total wealth in 1971, while the top 5 percent owned more than 50 percent.[23]

Fiscal Policy. The primary objectives of fiscal policy in the United Kingdom as in other countries, include a high level of employment, a satisfactory rate of economic growth, and a reasonably stable price level. To these is added, with special importance for a highly open economy such as that in the United Kingdom, a viable balance-of-payments position. Finally, the objectives are to be achieved with a satisfactory distribution of income. Successive governments—Conservative and Labour—have followed these objectives, with the Conservatives placing more emphasis upon economic growth and the Labour party placing more emphasis upon a high level of employment. The instruments of fiscal policy are the standard tax and transfer payment devices that are used by the United States and other countries. In particular, however, the British have tended to place reliance upon changes in the tax system to manage the economy. For example, to stimulate investment demand and hence the rate of economic growth, income taxes have been cut. To counteract inflation and excess demand, income taxes have been raised.

Stop-Go Stabilization. The term *stop-go* has been applied to British stabilization policy. It refers to deliberate government action to alternately restrain and stimulate economic activity. It has been followed rather continuously through the use of fiscal and monetary measures. Examples of the fiscal measures can be catalogued chronologically, as follows:

1. During the Korean War period, as an anti-inflationary measure, imports were restricted through the imposition of higher import duties, and a deflationary budget which involved reduced government spending was utilized.
2. During the period from 1953 to 1955, antirecessionary measures were adopted. The boom which followed World War II had slowed down, and there was concern over potential unemployment. As mentioned above, there was a reduction in taxes, and the budget was made expansionary.
3. In 1957 and 1958 a leveling off of economic activity occurred, and an increase in unemployment evoked an easing of fiscal restraints. Purchase tax rates were reduced, and initial allowances on new depreciable facilities were liberalized. At the same time, public investment outlays through the budget were expanded, and efforts were made to spur public housing. The budget was expansionary.
4. In 1961 balance-of-payments problems, brought about by speculation which followed the revaluation of the West German and Dutch currency units, resulted in the imposition of fiscal restraints. Indirect taxes were raised.
5. In 1965 rising prices and a deteriorating balance-of-payments position brought about tax increases and budget cuts.
6. In 1971 fiscal policy was switched to go. To encourage consumer demand reductions were made in indirect taxes and the budget was expansionary.

[23] A. B. Atkinson, *The Distribution of Wealth in Great Britain* (Unpublished Monograph, University of Essex).

The Banking System

The British banking system consists of the Bank of England which is the central bank of the nation, and a few large commercial banks which have assumed an oligopolistic structure as a result of mergers and integration. Besides the commercial banks, whose primary function is the financing of the economy in general, there are other institutions whose activities are more specialized but whose aggregate importance is very great. These are the merchant bankers and the acceptance houses, whose primary concern is with the financing of foreign trade. The insurance companies and building societies are the most important suppliers of investment capital in the United Kingdom.

The Bank of England. The Bank of England was chartered by an act of Parliament in 1694. In 1844 it was given the sole right of note issue. By the second half of the 19th century, the public service aspects of the Bank's activities began to eclipse its private banking business. It became the lender of last resort to the money market and the regulator of the great international gold and capital markets in London.

In 1946 the Bank was nationalized by an act of Parliament. The government acquired the entire capital stock of the Bank and was empowered to appoint the Governor, Deputy Director, and Directors of the Bank for fixed terms. The Treasury has the power to give directions to the Bank, after consultation with the Governor.

The Bank has the overall responsibility for the management and control of the monetary and financial system. It exercises monetary control through a combination of open-market operations and discount policy. This is done on the basis of institutional arrangements peculiar to the British monetary system. Unlike the Federal Reserve System of the United States, the Bank does not lend to commercial banks, but only to discount houses, whose main business is to underwrite the weekly Treasury bill issue with call loans secured mostly from London clearing houses.

Credit is restricted by selling Treasury bills or government bonds through discount houses and securities dealers, thus absorbing cash from the banking system. The discount market chiefly consists of twelve major houses which are members of the London Discount Market Association, the organization which is responsible for bidding on Treasury bills each week. To restore their cash and liquidity positions, banks can withdraw their call loans from the discount houses; the discount houses, in turn, may be forced to borrow money from the Bank of England at a penalty rate, which is set higher than the average yield from the discount houses' earning assets.

The Commercial Banks. The commercial banking system operates under private ownership and management. There are five major commercial banks—Barclays, Lloyds, Midland, National Provincial, and Westminster. Two other large banks are the District Bank and Martins. These banks undertake all normal types of banking business, such as deposits, advances, bill discounting, and foreign exchange. They do not participate directly in industry; their financing of industry is limited to short-term advances and overdrafts which are formally repayable on demand. British banks have a traditional preference for financing working rather than fixed capital expenditures.

Discount Houses. *Discount houses* play a very important role in the British financial system. Their most important function concerns the financing of Treasury bills. The discount houses purchase the Treasury bills on a weekly basis with loans which they obtain from the commercial banks or with their own funds. This purchase provides the government with day-to-day finance. The discount houses are also the intermediary through which the Bank of England acts as a lender of last resort to the banking system. As mentioned above, the discount houses obtain a substantial amount of their funds to purchase Treasury bills from the commercial banks on a *call loan* basis. If loan repayment is demanded by the banks, the discount houses can borrow from the Bank of England through rediscounting bills or by advances against collateral. The minimum rate at which the Bank of England will make funds available to the discount houses is called the *bank rate,* and it is the key rate in the whole structure of interest rates in Great Britain.

Other Financial Institutions. Capital funds are also provided through other sources, such as insurance companies, building societies, investment trusts, and pension funds. The insurance companies, pension funds, and building societies are the dominant sources of long-term finance. Insurance companies are privately owned and provide a supply of capital to the long-term market. In 1962 investments by insurance companies represented more than 10 percent of the total amount required to finance gross fixed capital formation, public and private, and more than 20 percent of net fixed capital formation.[24]

Building societies, also privately owned, are second only to the insurance companies as a source of long-term loanable funds. The building societies rely on the savings of the public, and they provide financing for about two thirds of private home building. The societies offer both shares and deposits to the public. Shares are nonmarketable and pay a higher rate of interest.

Investment trusts are also an important source of long-term capital funds. In the past, trusts played an important part in the development of the Commonwealth countries. During the period from 1870 to 1914, they also contributed much to the economic development of the United States.

In investment banking, there is no doubt about the power of the government to exercise control. Under the Banking Control and Guarantee Act of 1947, the government has the power to regulate new access to the capital market and establish priorities which are deemed essential to the national interest. The Act also empowered the Treasury to guarantee long-term loans made to facilitate industrial development.

Monetary Policy. Monetary policy in the United Kingdom is used as a stabilization device and consists of several arrangements.

[24] *A Description and Analysis of Certain European Capital Markets* (Washington: Joint Economic Committee, 88th Congress, 2d Session, 1964), p. 235.

Hire purchase controls are used to regulate the volume of consumer expenditures. This type of control is a selective control in that it involves the amount of down payment required to consummate the purchase of consumer goods and also involves the maximum period of repayment. It has proven to be an important monetary policy instrument and has an advantage over other monetary and fiscal policy instruments in that it can be imposed immediately. During the period from 1951 to 1960, hire purchase controls were imposed eleven times.

The use of the *bank rate* is also an important monetary policy device. The bank rate is the price which the Bank of England will pay when rediscounting bills. It is a penalty rate which is usually set above the market rate of discount and has its impact on the discount houses. As mentioned previously, the discount houses occupy a special position in the market for Treasury bills, and from the standpoint of monetary policy, the Treasury bill is a major instrument in the money market. The discount houses link the commercial banks to the Bank of England. They purchase Treasury bills with money borrowed at call from the commercial banks; if they have to borrow from the Bank of England, the bank rate, or "penalty rate," can be employed. Changes in the bank rate force changes in other interest rates.

Open market operations is another monetary policy instrument. It refers to the buying and selling of Treasury bills and other short-term obligations in the money market by the Bank of England. These transactions affect the liquidity of the commercial banks by expanding or contracting their balances with the Bank of England.

A direct control, which takes the form of special deposits, can be imposed on commercial banks by the Bank of England. The purpose of this device is to alter the liquidity ratio of commercial banks. The *liquidity ratio,* which is the ratio of liquid bank assets to total assets, is set at 30 percent of total bank assets. Special deposits have the effect of reducing the liquidity ratio.

Monetary, as well as fiscal, policy has been an integral part of the policy of "stop-go" which British anticyclical policy has been called. Aggressive use of monetary policy as a stabilization device has been made by both Conservative and Labour governments during the postwar period in an attempt to maintain full employment as well as to preserve a semblance of price stability.

Labor-Management Relations

A minority of British workers belong to trade unions. Of the approximately 23 million workers, 8.8 million, or almost 40 percent, are members of trade unions. Of these, 8.3 million belong to the British Trades Union Congress (TUC). The TUC is a permanent association which is constituted by the affiliation of different trade unions.

The unions affiliated with the TUC vary in size and character and in the views they hold regarding organization. There are craft unions, industrial unions, general workers' unions, and nonmanual and professional organizations. Although the unions operate individually, they come together, industry by industry, through federations which are set up for the purpose of collective bargaining. A single union may have members in several industries and may, therefore, be affiliated with several federations. The principal federations are the Confederation of Shipbuilding and Engineering Unions, the National Federation of Building Trades Operatives, and the Printing and Kindred Trades Confederation. There are also federations in cotton and woolen textiles.

The executive body of the TUC is the General Council. The members of the General Council are elected at the annual meeting of the TUC.[25] Affiliated unions are entitled to send to the annual meeting one delegate for every 5,000 members. There are 34 members on the council. For purposes of representation, affiliated unions have been divided into 18 trade groups, and seats on the council are allocated according to the size of the group. For example, one group—mining and quarrying—has three members, while another group—shipbuilding—has one.

Current industrial relations in the United Kingdom are governed by the Industrial Relations Act of 1971. The Act sets a framework of rules for industrial action. First of all, unions have to register if they wish to continue to receive certain rights and privileges such as recognition by an employer or a limit to the amount they can be fined. Secondly, a collective bargaining agreement is presumed to be legally binding, and strikes become unfair industrial practices and can be declared illegal because they involve breach of contract. Third, certain industrial practices such as the secondary boycott are illegal. Thus workers in one firm cannot encourage others to withhold supplies from that firm. A National Industrial Relations Court is supposed to maintain jurisdiction over industrial disputes. The court has the power to order a cooling-off period during a dispute.

Unions occupy a powerful position in the United Kingdom. During the postwar period full employment contributed to the development of union power, and wages increased faster than productivity. This fact, however, cannot be attributed to the strength of unions. In general, labor-management relations have been rather acrimonious, with some of the worst labor disputes occurring in the public sector. The coal miners' strike of early 1974 was with a public enterprise. Many British labor unions are afflicted with a class struggle mentality, and there is no question that union intransigence on issues involving productivity has been a factor contributing to the general decline of the British economy during the postwar period.

Government and Business

The government has control over several industries, such as coal, inland transportation, telecommunications, central banking, civil aviation, and steel. This control came about through various nationalization acts in the period immediately following World War II after the Labour party came into office. With the exception of the steel industry, which was denationalized by the

---

[25] The annual Congress invariably meets on the first Monday of September and remains in session for four days.

Conservative party when it came to power in 1951 and which was nationalized again by the Labour government in 1966, no significant nationalization has taken place for 20 years.

Several basic reasons for government takeover of the above industries were as follows:

1. They were of key importance to the economy, not only as to production, but as to volume of aggregate employment as well.
2. They had not been efficient in the past and needed reorganization along radically different lines.
3. They needed large capital expenditures, which were forthcoming only from the government or through guarantees.

The Coal Industry. The coal industry is a case in point. The number of workers employed in coal mining fell between 1924 and 1930 from 1,259,000 to 1,069,000. Despite this shrinkage in the labor force, unemployment rose from 6.9 percent in 1924 to 28.3 percent by 1930; some kind of government intervention was inevitable.[26] In 1930 the coal-mining industry, by an act of Parliament (the Coal Mines Act), had obtained authority for production quotas. A central council set the tonnage of coal to be mined each year and gave quotas to coal districts, which in turn, under the control of district boards, allotted tonnages to individual collieries.[27] The district board also fixed minimum prices.

The first step toward state ownership occurred with the passage of the Coal Act of 1938 when the Conservative government made provision for the nationalization of royalties. In the matter of compensation, the Act set a precedent for the future. The owners of the coal mines were given $172.8 million. This was equivalent to 15 years of the estimated income from the mines.

The coal industry was nationalized under the provisions of the Coal Industry Nationalization Act of 1946. The National Coal Board was created and given responsibility for running the coal mines. It was not set up as a department of the government. The Nationalization Act which created the Board laid down the rule that the coal industry should break even, after paying interest charges on the capital advanced by the government to finance the industry. Within this particular statutory obligation, the industry is left free to conduct the day-to-day management as it sees fit. The coal industry operates in a highly competitive field and is run on a commercial basis.

When the National Coal Board took over control of the coal-mining industry in 1947, there were nearly 1,000 pits in operation employing 750,000 men. The industry had suffered for many years from the lack of capital investment, the depression, and high unemployment rates.

[26] Charles Loch Mowat, *Britain Between the Wars* (Chicago: University of Chicago Press, 1955), p. 273.
[27] This effort to salvage the coal-mining industry proved a partial success but did not solve long-run problems of capital modernization and earnings. Unemployment was reduced from 40.6 percent in 1932 to 18.9 percent in 1937. Output fell from 244 million tons in 1930 to 207 million tons in 1933 but recovered to 241 million tons in 1937.

From 1947 to 1957 employment in the coal mines was stabilized at around 700,000 men. However, toward the end of 1957 the employment picture began to change for the following reasons:

1. An increase in the use of other sources of energy, especially oil.
2. A generally lower level of industrial activity.
3. Much greater efficiency in the use of coal.

Employment in the collieries declined from 700,000 at the end of 1957 to 210,000 by the end of 1972. Also by March 1965, 270 collieries employing 212,000 people were losing money. Consequently, the National Coal Board has concentrated on phasing out the operations of the unprofitable mines and transferring unemployed coal miners to profitable areas.

The Steel Industry. The steel industry was nationalized by the Labour government for the second time in 1966. The government acquired nine major, privately held steel companies for which it issued new securities worth $3.1 billion in exchange for the shares of the steel companies. Later the government will acquire four more companies that are currently parts of larger organizations; this will require an additional security issue. Together, the nationalized companies account for 91.6 percent of the nation's steel output and 95 percent of its iron output.

Politics played an important part in the renationalization of the steel industry in 1966. Prime Minister Wilson felt that it was necessary to placate the left-wing elements within the Labour party who were critical of his foreign and domestic policies. These elements, many of whom were old-line socialists, regarded nationalization of steel as a basic desideratum of domestic policy. The steel industry was more of a symbol than anything else. Nationalization of steel had been a part of the socialists' platform for many decades.

The Labour government also felt that the nationalization of the steel industry was necessary for domestic economic growth. Efficiency in steel production was necessary to enable the British to compete with steel producers in other countries. The government alone has sufficient finances to stimulate modernization of plants and equipment.[28]

Function and Purpose of Nationalization. With respect to the nationalized industries, the function of the government is to ensure that they are organized and administered efficiently and economically to carry out their responsibilities. Although the industries have obligations of a national and noncommercial nature, they are not regarded as social services absolved from economic and

---

[28] This reason tends to obfuscate the real reason for nationalization, namely, the need for Wilson to pacify members of his own party to gain support for his foreign policy.

Steel production has shown continued expansion since the end of World War II. In 1966 production was more than double that of 1946.

Britain's iron and steel industry, the greater part of which was nationalized under the Iron and Steel Act of 1949, was denationalized by the Iron and Steel Act of 1953. The 1953 act, however, provided for the creation of the Iron and Steel Board to continue public supervision of the industry in cooperation with representatives of the industry.

commercial justification. They are expected to pay their way, and most of the nationalization statutes contain a requirement to this effect. Their statutory obligations prescribe that their revenues should, on an average of good years and bad years, be not less than sufficient to meet all items chargeable to revenue, including interest, depreciation, the redemption of capital, and the provision of reserves. Thus the statutes prescribe a minimum performance and not a maximum.

In 1967 explicit price and investment rules were established for the nationalized industries. On pricing, marginal cost pricing was laid down, though accounting costs were to be covered by revenue.[29] Unit prices proportional to marginal cost were recommended for the apportionment of fixed costs among consumers where necessary to cover total costs. Social cost-benefit analysis was proposed for investment appraisal, and it was stated that the returns on investment should be presented in terms of discounted net present value. A test discount rate of 8 percent was laid down for project appraisal. The government explicitly recognized the noncommercial operations undertaken by nationalized industries, and stressed the need to distinguish social obligations from commercial operations. When social obligations were involved, subsidies from the government could be provided to cover costs. For example, the 1968 Transport Act provides for grants for unremunerative rail services as required for social or economic reasons.

Some comparison can be drawn between the return on capital in private enterprises and the rate of return in the nationalized industries. The rate of return has been considerably higher in private industry. In 1959 net income after depreciation expressed as a proportion of net assets after depreciation amounted to 14.9 percent in manufacturing (private) and 13.3 percent in iron and steel (private), compared to 1.6 percent for the National Coal Board (public), 3.3 percent for the Gas Council and Board (public), and −1.3 percent for the British Transport Commission.[30] However, this does not necessarily mean that nationalized industries are more inefficient than private enterprise. In fact, a nationalized industry may be efficient and yet incur a deficit, for the reason that the operation of the nationalized industries is subject to government intervention on economic and social grounds.

Government Influence on Private Enterprise. Most of the British economy, however, remains in the hands of private enterprise. The automobile, chemical, engineering, textile, food processing, metal products, paper products, aircraft, and rubber products industries are all privately owned.

The government influences the development of British industry through the use of monetary and fiscal policies and through laws governing mergers, restrictive trade practices, and resale price maintenance. It also has control over credit and investment policies and can establish priorities that it deems to be

[29] *Nationalized Industries: A Review of Economic & Financial Objectives,* Command Paper 3437 (London: Her Majesty's Stationery Office, November, 1967).
[30] *The Financial & Economic Obligations of the Nationalized Industries,* Command Paper 1337 (London: Her Majesty's Stationery Office, April 1961).

in the national interest. A case in point involves the use of the tax powers of the government to achieve various economic and social objectives. In particular, successive governments, Conservative and Labour, have attempted to stimulate investment by various kinds of tax incentives and investment grants. A major feature of these incentives is the extent to which they are discriminatory. They make investments in certain areas more profitable than in others and some types of investment more profitable than other types. This, of course, is by design, and is intended to stimulate investment in the places and in the forms the government desires. The bases for this intervention hinges on the conviction that the market, if left to itself, will lead to misallocation of investment and to regional imbalance in the level of employment.

Aside from tax incentives and grants, the British government budget itself has an impact on private enterprise. For example, in 1969 out of the $2.6 billion spent on research and development in the United Kingdom, approximately half was financed from government sources. It can be said that a large part of the cost of promoting industrial efficiency is supported by public funds. Moreover, the size and structure of important private industries, such as agriculture and aircraft production, are in effect determined by government budget decisions; and the purchases of the public sector also provide a large and in some cases dominant part of the demand for the products of other industries, notably construction, electronics, and pharmaceuticals.

In the United Kingdom, as in the United States, legislation seeking to improve the performance of the private business sector has proceeded both to regulate the structure of markets and to govern the conduct of firms in the market place. The aim of British legislation with respect to mergers and monopolies has been expressed in a number of acts. The Monopolies and Restrictive Practices Act was passed in 1948 and defined a monopoly situation as one in which one third of the supply of goods is controlled by a single firm or a group of linked firms. A Monopolies Commission was created but was largely ineffective. In 1965 the Monopolies and Mergers Act was passed to give the Monopolies Commission control over mergers and unfair pricing practices. The Monopolies Commission has the right to investigate industries with market structures of near monopoly. Restrictive trade practices were dealt with in the Restrictive Practices Acts of 1956 and 1968. Defined as restrictive practices were price fixing agreements, control over supply, and other anticompetitive practices by firms.

Economic Planning

The British economy has suffered from a number of long-standing problems. Some problems can be attributed to the structure of the economy and to the fact that Great Britain is an old, industrial country. Other problems arise from her changed position in the world. In the last two decades, Great Britain's status as a world power has changed drastically. Former colonies in the British Empire are now independent nations. This change has had considerable repercussions on British trade and overseas investment.

These problems are reflected in a growth rate which has been below average for major countries and in an unfavorable balance of payments. To some extent the latter is responsible for the former, because the periodic imposition of restrictive domestic policies which slow growth have been necessary in order to correct payment deficits.

It is evident that the rate of growth of the British economy has not been satisfactory. During the 1960s, the rate of growth of total output per person employed was the lowest in Europe. There was a considerable difference in growth rates, with the United Kingdom ranking at the bottom among major industrial countries. This fact is illustrated in Table 11–6.

TABLE 11–6
GROWTH RATES IN MAJOR INDUSTRIAL COUNTRIES, 1955–1968

Countries	Growth in Domestic Product	Industrial Production
Japan	9.7%	14.6% *
West Germany	5.0	6.9
Italy	5.3	7.5
France	5.5	7.7
Sweden	4.5	4.8
United States	3.9	4.1
United Kingdom	2.8	3.0

* Average annual rate of growth.
Source: *The Growth of Output* (Paris: OECD, 1970), p. 220.

The low growth rate and the balance of payments problems were responsible for the institution of a number of economic policy measures by the Labour government under a general blueprint for economic development called the National Plan.

The National Plan. The National Plan was presented to Parliament in September 1965. Its objective was to provide a basis for greater economic growth. An essential part of the Plan was to provide a solution to the United Kingdom's balance of payments problem.[31]

The philosophy of the Plan and the Labour government was articulated quite succinctly.[32] Although manufacturing industry is, and will continue to be, largely governed by market forces, this does not necessarily bring about the results which the nation needs to solve the problem of economic growth. These forces of competition operate too slowly. Inadequacy of investment has caused home demand to be met by a greater flow of imports than the economy can afford.

In certain cases, such as regional development, important social costs arise which are not expressed in market prices, and positive government action is

---

[31] Secretary of State for Economic Affairs, *The National Plan,* Command Paper 2764 (London: Her Majesty's Stationery Office, September, 1965).
[32] *Ibid.,* pp. 1–3.

necessary to supplement market forces. However, care must be exercised so as not to destroy the complex mechanism upon which the market economy is based. Cooperative planning and the market economy must be blended together to produce an internationally competitive industry.

This, then, was the rationale of the Plan. Ambivalence existed to some degree, and some supporters of the Labour party, who had visualized a continued march onward toward socialism, were disappointed.

The Plan was designed to achieve a 25 percent increase in national output between 1964 and 1970. Interrelated problems, which had to be overcome before this goal could be achieved, were the restoration of the international balance of payments to a sound position, an increase in industrial efficiency, and improvement in the utilization of labor. In determining the pattern of government expenditures, emphasis was to be given to those forms which directly assist economic growth.

A program of action to achieve a higher rate of economic growth was also set forth in the Plan. The first point in the Plan was to improve the balance-of-payments deficit by a reduction in overseas spending. The phasing out of defense operations in West Germany and the Far East were examples of this action. Also, private investment abroad and aid to developing countries were to be reduced. Exports were to be promoted through the use of an export rebate scheme, whereby certain indirect taxes bearing on exports were refunded. Government financial assistance was to be made available to support trade missions and marketing relevant to the expansion of exports.

The second point in the Plan was to increase investment in manufacturing through the use of tax incentives. The Plan recommended that investment in manufacturing should increase at an average rate of 7 percent a year for the period 1964–70. Priority in incentives was to be given to those sectors that could make the greatest contribution to improving the balance of payments. The set of investment incentives, as mentioned previously, took the form of cash grants. The cash grant, the Labour government believed, was the most direct and easily understood form of investment incentive.[33]

Regional economic policy, the third point in the Plan, also played an important role. The objective was to achieve a fuller use of manpower and investment in the less prosperous areas of the country. Measures to attract industry into underdeveloped areas of the United Kingdom took the form of grants per job created and grants to cover the cost of construction. The cost of training workers was also defrayed by the government.

Manpower policy, the fourth point under the Plan, involved more emphasis on improving labor mobility through the use of relocation allowances and an upgrading of job skills. Government training centers were to be expanded; the aim was to create 8,000 such centers. Grants were given to employers to

[33] The investment grant can be used to manipulate investment in the desired direction for the reason that it amounts to a direct rebate of part of the cost of acquiring a capital asset. This rebate can vary in amount, ranging from 40 percent for investment that contributes to the objectives of the Plan to nothing for investment in areas that do not contribute to economic growth or the solving of the balance of payments problem.

cover the cost of training or retraining personnel. The grants included the training of all types of personnel. The 25 percent growth in output visualized by the Plan had to take place against a backdrop of a working population which was expanding slowly. The problem with respect to labor involved more effective utilization. This was one of the Plan's objectives.

A fifth essential feature of the Plan was a policy for prices and incomes. To achieve economic growth, the competitive position of the British economy, vis-à-vis other countries, had to be improved. Over a period of ten years, the United Kingdom's share of world exports of manufactured goods declined from 20 percent to 14 percent. This decline was reflected in a weakening of the balance of payments. In 1964 the international payments deficit on current and long-term capital accounts amounted to 756 million pounds. An attack on the problem of costs was one of the essential measures for strengthening the balance of payments position.[34]

Prices and Incomes Policies. The major purpose of prices and incomes policies involves the problem of how to avoid inflation at full employment. Generally, prices and income policies have attempted to introduce into wage, nonwage, and price decisions criteria which, if followed, would produce greater price stability without sacrificing employment objectives. Policies may take the form of a short-term curb on the rise of money incomes and prices, or it may seek to secure a longer-run change in economic behavior. It may focus primarily on wages or, as in the forms more popular in the United Kingdom, on the broader set of incomes, prices, and productivity.

In 1965 a prices and incomes policy was adopted by the Labour government. Its basic objectives were to keep the general level of prices stable; to raise productivity and efficiency so that real national output could increase; and to keep wages, salaries, and other forms of income in line with this increase.[35] An average rate of annual increase of money wages was set at 3 to 3½ percent. A list of four criteria was established that could be used to justify exceptional pay increases. These criteria were related to worker productivity, manpower shortages, and inequitable pay differentials for similar work.[36] Price criteria were also established. For example, companies could raise prices only if costs could not be offset by increased output per employee or if inavoidable increases in nonlabor costs could not be offset by reductions in labor and capital cost per unit of output.

In June 1966 an emergency income and price freeze was announced. The government called for a six-month standstill on wages and income.[37] A similar standstill of 12 months was imposed on prices. Criteria for price increases were made more stringent, and the standstill was applied to all goods and services. It was also applied to dividend payments and other forms of income.

---

[34] The National Plan was discontinued in 1968.

[35] Department of Economic Affairs, *Prices and Incomes Policy,* Command Paper 2639 (London: Her Majesty's Stationery Office, 1965).

[36] *Ibid.,* p. 8.

[37] Department of Economic Affairs, *Prices and Incomes Standstill,* Command Paper 3073 (London: Her Majesty's Stationery Office, 1967).

However, cooperation on the part of labor and management was voluntary. Also, in 1968 statutory powers were invoked to enforce compliance with prices and income policy, and a short-term freeze was imposed on both incomes and prices. This freeze was eventually relaxed, and ceilings were placed on both income and price increases. Increases in income above the ceiling limit were allowed only if they could be justified by a list of criteria which emphasized direct contributions to increased productivity.

AN APPRAISAL OF THE BRITISH ECONOMY

Full employment, economic growth, price stability, and an equitable distribution of income are basic objectives of any economic system. Added to these objectives, particularly in the case of the United Kingdom, is the need to also maintain a viable balance of payments. More than most other countries, the United Kingdom has felt the threat of rising prices to its balance-of-payments position. Therefore, recurrent experiments with an incomes policy has become a fact of life to the British economy.

Since the trauma of high interwar unemployment, the United Kingdom has placed heavy emphasis on full employment as a central objective of national economic policy. With respect to this objective, the overall performance of the British economy has been good. Since 1950, the average annual rate of unemployment rose above 2 percent, a record substantially superior to that of the United States, but about average in comparison to other European countries. However, the weight that has been attached to a low rate of unemployment in the formulation of British economic policy came into conflict with price stability and balance of payments problems. There has been a trade-off between unemployment and the balance of payments. On several occasions, the British government has reduced domestic demand substantially to improve the balance of payments, and on each of these occasions unemployment rose above 2 percent.

In addition to maintaining full employment, the British government has also attempted to maintain an adequate rate of economic growth. This effort reflects two concerns: observations of higher rates of growth in all other industrial countries, and continuing frustration in meeting from Britain's limited output the numerous claims by housing, social services, defense, and exports. However, the goal of economic growth must be given a low rating. The British growth rate has been the lowest in Western Europe. During the period 1950–1960 the British growth rate expressed as an average annual real rate was 2.7 percent compared to a 4.7 percent average rate for 13 countries in Western Europe.[38] For the time period 1960–1965 the comparable rates were 3.4 percent and 4.8 percent respectively, and for the period 1965–1970, the rates were 2.3 percent and 4.4 percent.[39] Regardless of the time period used, the British growth rate was lower than all of the Western European countries and all of

[38] Deutsches Institut fuer Wirtschaftsforschung, "Wochenbericht" (April 26, 1973), pp. 222–227.
[39] Ibid., p. 223.

the OECD countries. In comparison to such major countries as France, Japan, and West Germany, the United Kingdom ran a very bad last.

The third goal of price stability has also not fared particularly well over time. During the period 1950–1970 the average annual price increase was 3.5 percent, and during the period 1965–1972 the average annual increase was 5.8 percent.[40] In 1973 the increase was 6.7 percent. In comparison to other countries, the performance of the United Kingdom in achieving price stability has been average. During the period 1960–1970 consumer prices in France and Italy increased by 49 and 51 percent respectively compared to an increase of 45 percent for the United Kingdom.[41] On the other hand, this increase exceeded those of West Germany and the United States for the same time period. However, during the period 1970–1973 increases in consumer prices in the United Kingdom exceeded those in all of the above-mentioned countries including Japan.[42]

Probably the greatest problem confronting the British economy has been an imbalance in its balance of payments position. Imports have exceeded exports for most years since 1950 with repeated crises in terms of substantial deficits occurring. The balance of payments is, in principle, a record of all transactions, during a period of time, between residents of the United Kingdom and residents of the rest of the world. The balance of payments problem may be attributable in part to British decline in the share of world exports. Neither the price nor the quality of British exports and import-competing goods has been favorable enough to protect its export market position and to combat increasing penetration of the home markets by many types of imports. Wartime destruction of merchant shipping, together with the forced liquidation of profitable overseas investments, has also had an adverse effect on Britain's balance of payments.

The distribution of income and wealth involves social valuations about equity, opportunity, and power. In general it can be said that distributional objectives in the United Kingdom have fared better than growth and balance of payments objectives. They have played a major part in public policy, especially through the provision of public welfare services. Income differentials have been narrowed to some extent over time through the use of progressive income taxation, and a reduction in wealth inequality has also occurred. This is not to say, however, that there is overall satisfaction with the distribution of income and wealth, particularly given the class stratification of British society. Economic interest groups cannot be expected to agree over the proper relationship among wages, salaries, profits, and rent. The strike of the British coal miners in late 1973 and early 1974 illustrates a disagreement in British society over income distribution issues which may well be very difficult to resolve.

    [40] *The British Economy: Key Statistics 1900–1970* (Cambridge: Cambridge Economic Service, 1972), pp. 2–8.
    [41] International Monetary Fund, "International Financial Statistics" (November, 1972).
    [42] *Ibid.*, p. 5.

TABLE 11–7

UNEMPLOYMENT RATES, PRICE LEVEL CHANGES, AND ECONOMIC GROWTH IN THE UNITED KINGDOM, 1963–1973

Year	Unemployment Rates [1]	Price Level Changes [2]	Growth Rate [3]
1963	2.5%	2.0	4.0
1964	1.6	3.1	5.5
1965	1.4	5.3	2.5
1966	1.5	4.8	2.1
1967	2.4	4.9	2.4
1968	2.4	5.1	3.7
1969	2.4	5.0	2.5
1970	2.6	5.2	2.6
1971	3.6	5.8	1.5
1972	2.9	6.7	2.1
1973	3.8	8.5	3.1

[1] Unemployment statistics of the United Kingdom are based on a count of unemployed registrants at employment exchanges and youth offices.
[2] All final goods and services sold on the home market.
[3] Changes in real gross domestic product.
Source: *The British Economy, Key Statistics 1900–1973* (London: Times Newspapers, Ltd.), pp. 1–12.

Table 11–7 summarizes the British economy for the period 1963–1973. The table presents unemployment rates, price level changes, and the real rate of economic growth. The performance of the economy over this period of time was at best erratic, with unemployment rates and price level changes holding at a stable level for only two years over the period.

A number of explanations have been offered for the generally poor performance of the United Kingdom during most of the postwar period. A few reasons can be summarized as follows:

1. In general, both labor and management practices have been wedded to the past rather than the present. Unions have become more interested in rights and security than in productivity, and management has failed to adopt new techniques of organization.

2. To some extent, conditions beyond the control of the United Kingdom were responsible for economic problems. Most Western countries started at a lower economic point than the United Kingdom and have caught up by taking advantage of technical advances. In other words, the United Kingdom has had to pay the price for being a pioneer in industry.

3. In terms of such growth determinants as the education of the labor force, hours of work, and capital inputs, the United Kingdom has lagged behind the other major industrial countries.

4. Restrictive fiscal and monetary policies, which have been taken by the government largely because of an unfavorable balance of payments, have tended to stultify economic growth. These measures, although reducing the pressure of domestic demand in the economy, increased unemployment and created excess capacity.

5. Large and persistent differences in the level of employment have exacerbated labor shortages which have caused productivity to drop.

SUMMARY

The economic record of the United Kingdom since the end of World War II shows a fairly high level of employment, a low rate of economic growth, and inflation. There has been a persistently sensitive balance of payments problem caused by several factors: the need to import roughly 50 percent of the nation's food supply and virtually all of its industrial raw materials; the burden of debt payments resulting from the war; overseas payments required in consequence of postwar policy commitments; and the loss of many of its markets, which was brought about by the dissolution of the British Empire.

The United Kingdom, like its European neighbors, has a nationalized sector of industry as well as an important public investment sector. Decisions in both areas have been conditioned by overall economic policy considerations. Economic policy directed to the private sectors of the economy has relied on general monetary and fiscal measures coupled with such specific fiscal measures as a purchase tax, which has been used to curb inflation, and investment allowances, which have been used to stimulate regional economic development.

Another important area of government intervention in the economy is the comprehensive social welfare system. Budgetary expenditures here have been a significant component of total consumption. An important key to the high level of employment which has characterized the British economy since the end of the war lies in the fact that total demand has been well sustained from the public sector.

The economic health of the United Kingdom is poor and there is serious doubt that the problems which confront the country can be remedied. During 1970 and 1971 the country drifted into its deepest recession since the end of World War II. Although some improvement in employment and growth was made in 1972 and 1973, the British economy was affected severely by the energy crisis which occurred in late 1973, and by a concomitant series of strikes. The British economy was placed on a three-day work week and sharp cuts were made on government spending. The strikes, in particular the one launched by the British coal miners, have an ominous portent for the future for the reason that they reveal the deep and apparently irreconcilable class divisions within the country. Perhaps the British penchant for muddling through all emergencies may save the economy from collapse.

QUESTIONS

1. The rate of economic growth in the United Kingdom has lagged behind growth rates of other major countries. What are some of the reasons for this lag?
2. What trends have occurred over time in the distribution of income and wealth in the United Kingdom?
3. Discuss the relationship of taxes and transfer payments to gross national product and national income in the United Kingdom.
4. Discuss the role of fiscal and monetary policy as economic stabilization devices in the United Kingdom.

5. Discuss the relationship of the Bank of England to the British banking system.
6. List some of the factors contributing to the low British growth rate.
7. Discuss the reasons for the postwar nationalization of a segment of British industry, such as coal or inland transportation.
8. What are the problems confronting the British economy and what measures should be used to solve them?
9. What were the basic objectives of the National Plan?
10. What is the purpose of the prices and incomes policy?

RECOMMENDED READINGS

Atkinson, A. B. *Unequal Shares.* London: The Penguin Press, 1972.

Bland, D. E., & K. W. Watkins. *Can England Survive?* London: M. Joseph, 1971.

Caves, Richard E., and Associates. *Britain's Economic Prospects.* Washington: The Brookings Institution, 1968.

Brittan, Samuel. *Government & the Market Economy.* Levittown: Transatlantic Arts, Inc., 1972.

Cockcroft, John. *Why England Sleeps.* London: Arlington Books, 1971.

Cohen, Charles. *British Economic Policy, 1960–1969.* London: Butterworths, 1971.

Glyn, Andrew, and Robert Sutcliffe. *Capitalism in Crisis.* New York: Pantheon Books, 1972.

Meyer, Frederick. *Problems of a Mature Economy.* London: Macmillan, 1970.

Prest, A. R., and Coppock, D. J. *The U.K. Economy: Manual of Applied Economics.* London: Weidenfeld & Nicholson, 1972.

Smith, David M. *Industrial Britain.* New York: A. M. Kelley, 1969.

12
Japan

INTRODUCTION

Japan has emerged as a world power for the second time in this century. This fact can be attributed almost exclusively to the amazing performance of its economy. With the highest sustained growth rate in the world (an average of almost 10 percent a year), Japan has achieved a gross national product which now places it third among the world's industrial nations.

The phenomenal growth rate is even more remarkable when one considers the economic base from which the Japanese have to operate. The land area of Japan is small, the natural resources are limited, and the population is large. Dependence on exports and imports is a way of life for the Japanese economy. There has been considerable pressure on foreign reserves to cover a balance of payments deficit incurred to pay for the imports necessary to sustain industrial development.

The Japanese economy is mixed in that although private enterprise is dominant, the government also plays an important role through direct control and operation of certain industries and through indirect control of the supply of credit. Japanese tax policy has as a basic economic objective the stimulation of growth through the encouragement and support of all export-oriented industries.

The history of modern Japan began with the Meiji Restoration of 1868. Before this time Japan had remained in complete isolation from the Western world. However, British and American commercial encroachments into China, which resulted in the Treaty of Nanking, made it only a matter of time before attention would be diverted to Japan.

During the Meiji Restoration, Japan became a world power. The one event which brought this about was the Russo-Japanese War, which resulted in a decisive victory for the Japanese. Rapid advances in commerce and industry had occurred before the war, and Japanese economic hegemony had been established in Korea, the Liao-tung Peninsula, and southern Manchuria. The Bank of Japan was established in 1882 and was modeled along the lines of European central banks. The Constitution of 1889 fostered the development of political parties and the hope for the eventual realization of a democratic parliamentary system of government.

Japanese capitalism was characterized by the concentration of economic power in the hands of such *zaibatsu* combines as Mitsui, Mitsubishi, Sumitomo, and Yasuda.[1] These combines were larger than any American corporation. Mitsui, for example, employed 1,800,000 workers and Mitsubishi employed 1,000,000 workers.

With the defeat and subsequent occupation of Japan in 1945 came the problems of reform and reorganization of the economy. A new constitution, which incorporated Western principles of democratic parliamentary government, was promulgated in November 1946. The dissolution of the zaibatsu into a number of independent enterprises was carried out. This policy, in effect, retarded postwar economic recovery, for it diluted the base upon which the prewar economy had been built However, the zaibatsu combines have regrouped and exist in Japan today.

THE ECONOMIC SYSTEM

Japan has an economic philosophy which embraces the basic concepts of a modern capitalistic society. Economic phenomena are permitted free play to the extent that their actions are not inimical to national objectives. Implicit in this philosophy, however, is an element of control by the government over economic activity at whatever point it is considered necessary. Historically, however, there has been a close relationship between government and business in Japan.

The Meiji Restoration of 1868 marks the beginning of the development of Japan as a modern industrial nation.[2] In the first years after the Restoration, the most important development in Japan was the creation of an atmosphere conducive to economic growth. Fear of conquest by the leading maritime powers of Europe, as well as the United States, caused a deep sense of national emergency among the new leaders of the nation. In order to survive the encroachments of the Western powers, it was felt that Japan, by national policy, had to master the secret of industry. To gain the knowledge necessary to develop industry, Japanese students were sent to study the technology of Western nations, and engineers and technicians from Western nations were temporarily employed in Japan. To this day, the Japanese are known for their ability to use the technology of other nations.

The government became a major operator of key industries. The modernization of Japan during the latter part of the last century included the nationalization of certain sectors of the economy—the postal service, telephone and telegraph communications, and railways. The government also built and operated iron foundries, shipyards, machine shops, and factories. Tobacco, salt, and camphor became government monopolies. The government also provided

---

[1] Zaibatsu combines are vast industrial empires which are under control and management of a few family dynasties.

[2] The Meiji Restoration of 1868 was called a "restoration" because the powers of government which the *Tokugawa Shogunate* had usurped were restored to the Emperor of Japan who came to be known posthumously as the Emperor Meiji.

technical and financial assistance to private interests in key industries. A financial and monetary base for the economy was provided in 1882 when the Bank of Japan was formed. Although the government was involved in providing the conditions requisite to economic growth and industrial development, private enterprise also developed and flourished during the Restoration.

The Japanese government has relied extensively upon fiscal and monetary policies to stimulate economic growth. Special tax incentives are utilized to encourage a high rate of investment and exports. Tax policy is also used to achieve specific policy objectives. For example, there are special tax incentives to promote the introduction of new products and technology. Monetary policy has been relied upon to check inflationary pressures inherent in the postwar development of the economy. New financial institutions, such as the Japan Development Bank, have been created to encourage Japanese business enterprises to invest in special areas of the economy that are in need of development, such as the construction of new buildings and equipment.

Although economic planning exists in Japan, it is indicative rather than imperative. The economic plans, as developed by the government, serve as guidance for public and private decisions. These decisions are influenced by the fact that governmental economic regulation and control is more pervasive than it is in the United States and by the fact that fiscal and monetary incentives are used by the government to encourage compliance with the basic objectives of the economic plans.

Japan is characterized as having a *dual economy*. Highly developed industries exist side by side with small unmechanized workshops. Approximately 50 percent of business firms in Japan employ 50 workers or less, as compared to 15 percent in the United States; and rates of pay in such firms average less than 50 percent of rates in large firms employing more than 1,000 workers. However, small firms are important to the Japanese economy for the reason that there is a widespread practice of subcontracting on the part of large firms.

Certain sectors of the Japanese economy have shown a remarkable rate of economic growth. The iron and steel industry has been the backbone of the postwar economic boom. Production in 1970 exceeded 90 million tons, an amount surpassed only by the United States and the Soviet Union. Iron and steel products account for about 15 percent of all Japanese exports.

Japan is the world's largest shipbuilder. Revolutionary techniques have been developed for the construction of enormous tankers, involving the building and launching of sections which are subsequently joined together while the vessel is afloat. Japan ranks third in the world in the production of automobiles and third in the world in the production of chemicals. Rapid development has also occurred in the production of electrical machinery, electronics equipment and commercial aircraft.

A shift to heavy and sophisticated industries and the development of the domestic economy have contributed to the postwar growth of the economy. Rising living standards have created a broad and affluent domestic market to backstop the advantages of mass production. Although the domestic market now absorbs the great bulk of industrial output, exports have become more critical due to Japan's need to import raw materials and food.

The Japanese gross national product for 1972 is shown in Table 12–1. The increase in the gross national product both in real and monetary terms has been remarkable during the postwar period.

TABLE 12–1
THE JAPANESE GROSS NATIONAL PRODUCT FOR 1972 *

Expenditures at Current Prices	Billions of Dollars
Consumer expenditures	155.44
Government expenditures	26.84
Gross fixed asset formation	109.26
Changes in inventories	5.12
National expenditures	296.66
Exports of goods and services	34.28
Less: Imports of goods and services	27.18
Gross national product at market prices	303.76
Less: Indirect taxes	23.18
Statistical discrepancy	−2.88
Gross national product at factor cost	277.70

* In 1972 a yen was equal to $0.0033.

Source: Japanese Economic Planning Agency, *Annual Report on National Income Statistics* (Tokyo, 1973).

Public Finance

The leaders of the Meiji Restoration did not ignore the tax field in their ardor for borrowing new ideas from the forefront of advanced Western thought. Thus in 1887 Japan became one of the first countries in the world to have a national income tax.[3] However, the rate of progression went only from 1 percent to 3 percent, with the result that only meager amounts of revenue were raised. A corporate income tax was also introduced in 1899 when Japan found itself saddled with ever increasing expenditures to meet new demands, such as the expansion of armaments.

Government expenditures and transfers are handled in the national budget which consists of general accounts, special accounts, and government agency accounts. General accounts are incorporated into a general accounts budget and include expenditures for education, science and technology, social security, land conservation and development, allocations to local governments, and national defense. Main revenue sources are taxes, monopoly profits, and bond revenues. Special accounts are used for purposes where the government either

---

[3] The United Kingdom introduced an income tax in 1799, and Prussia introduced one in 1851. The United States used the income tax during the Civil War but dropped it when the war was over.

undertakes specific projects or finances a specific expenditure with a specific revenue. Principal among the special accounts are those for national hospitals, harbor improvement, and export insurance. The government agency accounts are for those public corporations which are financed by the government and whose budgets are subject to the approval of the Diet.[4] These agencies are: the three public corporations—The Japan Telegraph and Telephone Company, the Japan National Railways, and The Japan Monopolies Corporation; two banks—The Japan Development Bank and The Japan Export-Import Bank; and several other credit institutions, including the Small Business Finance Corporation and the Housing Loan Corporation.

An adjunct to the national budget is the Financial Loan and Investment Program, which is designed to provide government corporations with funds. Although the program is submitted to the Diet, the law does not require its approval by this legislative body. Funds, which are loaned to public corporations, are provided by collecting part of national savings through postal savings and postal insurance, pension funds, and the sale of government guaranteed bonds.

The Japanese Tax System. The two most important taxes in the Japanese tax system are the personal and corporate income taxes. In 1973 these taxes accounted for 63.2 percent of national revenue obtained from tax purposes.

The Personal Income Tax. The personal income tax ranges from 10 percent of taxable income under 400,000 yen (approximately $1,333) to 75 percent on incomes in excess of 80 million yen (about $266,667).[5] The taxpayer is allowed an exemption of 200,000 yen ($667) and another 200,000 yen for a spouse provided that the spouse's income is less than 150,000 yen ($500), an exemption of 140,000 yen ($467) for each dependent, and deductions for social insurance and life insurance premiums. Income from dividends, interest, and royalties is segregated from ordinary income and taxed at a rate of 15 percent.[6] The actual income tax is computed by applying the tax rate to each category of taxable income. The tax cumulates for each income bracket.

The Corporate Income Tax. The corporate income tax is the most important source of tax revenue to the national government. In 1973 it accounted for 35 percent of all national tax revenues. The corporate income tax rate on ordinary income which is not distributed as dividends is 28 percent on incomes up to 3 million yen ($10,000) and 36.5 percent on incomes of over 3 million yen. Rates are reduced on ordinary income which has been redistributed in the form of dividends to 22 percent on incomes of under 3 million yen and 26 percent on incomes over 3 million yen. The income base for tax purposes is reduced considerably by favorable tax provisions in the Japanese

---

[4] The Diet is Japan's legislative body to which representatives of the political parties are elected.

[5] The Japanese-United States exchange rate is approximately 300 yen to $1.

[6] The tax rates and exemptions were in effect in 1973. However, the rates and exemptions are revised annually.

tax system which have been instituted by the government to facilitate economic policy objectives. An example would be deduction of expenses involved in developing overseas markets.[7]

The Liquor Tax. The liquor tax is the third most important source of revenue to the government. In 1972 it accounted for 9.3 percent of national tax revenues. The tax rates on liquor are substantially higher than those of other commodities subject to consumption taxes, and the tax base is the quantity of liquor shipped from the manufacturer. The tax is a flat-rate levy which is based on the kind, class, and percentage of alcohol.

Special Provisions of the Tax System. A peculiar characteristic of the Japanese tax system is an enormous number of special tax provisions under which taxes are reduced selectively to accomplish specific national policy objectives. These provisions fall into several categories, which are as follows:

1. Provisions to stimulate personal savings. The supply of savings is necessary to maintain a high rate of capital formation and economic growth. To stimulate savings, provisions of the personal income tax provide for tax exemption of interest income from small deposits, separate low taxation of interest income, favorable tax treatment of dividend income, exemption of capital gains on securities, and deduction of life insurance premiums.
2. Provisions to promote the introduction of new products and technology. These include exemptions from personal or corporate income taxation of income from the sales of new products approved by the Ministry of Finance, duty-free importation of certain types of machinery and equipment by industries approved by the Ministry of Finance, and favorable treatment of royalties on patents and technology approved by the Ministry of Finance.
3. Provisions to stimulate investment. Considerable use has been made of accelerated depreciation provisions to encourage investment.[8] They are selective in their application and apply only to industries designated by the Ministry of Finance as contributing to exports or to the modernization of the economy.
4. Provisions to stimulate exports. A certain part of income from exports is exempt from the personal and corporate income taxes.[9] Accelerated depreciation privileges are also granted to export industries, provided that income from exports in one year shows a gain over the preceding year.

The major Japanese taxes are presented in Table 12–2 on page 264.

---

[7] For a comprehensive discussion of the Japanese tax system, see *An Outline of Japanese Taxes,* which is published by the Ministry of Finance.

[8] *Accelerated depreciation* is essentially the same as a loan at zero interest. It encourages investment for three reasons: (1) It reduces the effective tax rate by postponing some of the tax payment until a later tax period; (2) it decreases the investor's uncertainty about having sufficient income in the future from which to deduct his depreciation allowance; and (3) by increasing after-tax receipts in early periods at the expense of later receipts, it increases a firm's funds for financing investment.

[9] The use of devices to foster exports and restrict imports is discouraged under the provisions of the General Agreement on Tariffs and Trade (GATT). This means that since Japan is a member, she must abandon quantitative restrictions on imports.

TABLE 12–2
JAPANESE NATIONAL TAXES BY TYPES FOR 1973

Taxes	Amount in Billions of Dollars
Personal income tax	13,735
Corporate income tax	14,690
Liquor tax	3,743
Gasoline tax	3,582
Commodity tax	1,522
Customs duties	1,397
Monopoly profits tax	774
Stamp revenues	729
Miscellaneous	818
Total	40,990

Source: An Outline of Japanese Taxes (Tokyo: Ministry of Finance, 1973), p. 281.

TABLE 12–3
THE JAPANESE GENERAL ACCOUNTS BUDGET FOR 1973

Items	Billions of Dollars *
Revenue	
Taxes and stamp revenue	40.99
Monopoly profits	1.35
Receipts from government enterprises	0.04
Miscellaneous revenues	1.00
Surplus from preceding years	0.82
Public bonds	8.66
Total revenues	52.86
Expenditures	
Social Security	7.83
Promotion of education and science	5.81
Pensions	1.75
Tax transfers to local authorities	10.29
National defense	3.46
Public works	10.51
Miscellaneous	13.21
Total expenditures	52.86

* In 1973 1 yen equaled $0.0033.

Source: "Japan," Economic Surveys (Paris: Organization for Economic Cooperation and Development, 1973), p. 47.

Local Governmental Revenues. The Japanese have sought in the post-war period for a viable system of local public finance. Local government units in Japan rely on a system of grants from the national government, as well as a number of taxes, to support their expenditures. Half of the revenues of local governmental entities are provided by grants and subsidies from the national treasury. However, Japan has had a long tradition of local autonomy, and the importance of local finance in relation to national finance is greater in Japan than it is in the United Kingdom, France, and West Germany. In 1969 local tax revenues amounted to $7.84 billion. The most important local tax is a business enterprise tax which is levied on earned income. The municipal property tax is also an important revenue source to local governments.

Government Expenditures. In 1972 national and local government expenditures on goods and services accounted for approximately 19 percent of the Japanese gross national product. Fixed capital expenditures by the government amounted to 10 percent of gross national product and one third of domestic investment expenditures.[10] Total government expenditures in Japan are lower relative to gross national product than they are in the other countries with mixed economic systems.

The General Accounts Budget. National government expenditures on goods and services and transfer payments are a part of the general accounts budget which also contains the sources of revenue to finance these expenditures. The general accounts budget is presented in Table 12–3.

The Financial Loan and Investment Program. Separate from the general accounts budget is the Financial Loan and Investment Program, which is similar to a capital budget in that it contains expenditures for capital investments which are to be used over an extended period of time. Items included in the Financial Loan and Investment Program are expenditures for: housing, water, and sewage facilities; agriculture and small industries; roads, transportation, and regional development; and key industries and export promotion. In 1972 total expenditures in the Financial Loan and Investment Program amounted to $22.86 billion.[11] Total combined government expenditures, which included the general accounts budget, amounted to $31.26 billion in 1972— approximately 19 percent of the gross national product.

Welfare Expenditures. Social welfare benefits amount to 15 percent of the general accounts budget and are of four types: old age pensions, sickness and maternity benefits, work injury compensation, and unemployment benefits. The family allowance, which is one of the most important social welfare measures used by other industrial countries, is not used in Japan. Old age pensions account for the largest percentage of social security expenditures and are financed out of a tax on insured persons of 3.25 percent on incomes of up to $198 a month and a tax of 3.25 percent of payrolls on the employer. There is also a dual system for special classes of workers—those at sea, teachers, and public servants. The old age pension is paid monthly and is based

---

[10] "Japan," *Economic Surveys* (Paris: Organization for Economic Cooperation and Development, 1973), pp. 32 and 48.
  [11] *Ibid.*, p. 48.

on the years of coverage multiplied by a sum of approximately $0.91 plus 1 percent of lifetime average monthly earnings. There are also supplements for dependents of about $1.98 for the spouse and for each child under 18.[12]

Sickness and maternity benefits are financed out of a tax of 3.25 percent on insured persons on incomes of up to $198 a month and a 3.25 percent payroll tax on employers. Sickness benefits amount to 60 percent of earnings, according to wage class, payable for up to 26 weeks. Maternity benefits amount to 60 percent of earnings for 12 weeks before and after confinement, plus a lump-sum maternity grant of half of one month's wages. Patients pay for a part of their medical care.

Work injury is financed out of a tax on the employer which ranges from 2 to 8 percent of the payroll costs, based on a 3-year accident rate. Permanent disability benefits are based on the degree of disability.

Unemployment compensation is financed out of a tax of 1 percent of earnings of insured persons and a tax of 1 percent of payrolls on the employer. Benefits amount to 60 percent of earnings, with a maximum benefit of $3 a day for a period which ranges from 180 to 270 days, depending on the number of years of coverage.

Income Redistribution. Transfer payments and taxes are lower in Japan when compared to such factors as household incomes and gross national product than they are in the four other countries which are included in the section on mixed economic systems. In 1972 transfer payments amounted to about 6 percent of personal income in Japan compared to 19 percent in France, and 16 percent in West Germany. In the same year, receipts from taxation and social security contributions amounted to 20 percent of gross national product in Japan compared to 40 percent in France, 44 percent in Sweden, and 33 percent in the United Kingdom.[13] Social security contributions amounted to 5 percent of national income in Japan compared to 19 percent in France.

A major explanation for the fact that government social welfare payments are lower in Japan than in other industrial countries lies in the role of the industrial enterprise as a social force in modern Japan. It is considered to be a social unit from which the nation expects more than mere production of goods and services. It provides employees with the security of a lifetime commitment to employment, and it provides family allowances, housing and travel allowances, substantial retirement allowances, medical benefits, and many non-cash benefits as well. The industrial enterprise can be regarded as an industrial family. The employees, rather than being hired, are adopted as members of the family, and their participation in it is based on grounds larger than actual contribution in terms of skill. The wage system is not simply compensation for work but is rather a kind of "life income" determined by the employees' ages

---

[12] These rates and benefits are from the publication "Social Security Programs Throughout the World," which was published by the Office of Research and Statistics, U.S. Social Security Administration, 1972.

[13] *National Accounts Statistics, 1965–1974* (Paris: Organization for Economic Cooperation and Development, 1975), pp. 44, 60, 68, 144.

and family changes. The basic wage often comprises only 50 percent of annual income; the remainder is paid in various allowances and benefits.[14]

Government expenditures and tax policies have placed more emphasis on the attainment of a high growth rate than on income redistribution. Priority within the budget is given to expenditures that increase capital formation and, thus, the capacity of the nation to increase its output of goods. A lower priority has been assigned to social welfare expenditures. Also, even though the personal income tax is progressive, the government has pursued a policy of continued tax cutting to stimulate aggregate demand. As Table 12–4 indicates, the mass of Japanese income earners are concentrated in the lower-income brackets, while the few with high incomes simply do not have enough income to redistribute.

TABLE 12–4
DISTRIBUTION OF JAPANESE TAXPAYERS BY INCOME BRACKETS FOR 1969

Income Brackets	Percentage of Taxpayers	Percentage of Income
$ 0 and under $ 1,667	22.4	9.1
1,667 and under 2,333	19.7	11.8
2,333 and under 3,333	24.8	20.9
3,333 and under 6,667	27.2	35.7
6,667 and under 10,000	3.5	8.4
10,000 and under 16,667	1.7	6.2
16,667 and under 33,333	0.6	3.9
33,333 and under 66,667	0.1	1.9
66,667 and over	0.0	2.4
	100.0	100.0

Source: Tax Bureau of the Ministry of Finance, *Annual Report 1971* (Tokyo: 1971), p. 258.

Fiscal Policy. Fiscal policy has played an important role in the postwar economic development of the Japanese economy. Changes in the level of taxation, in expenditures in the government general accounts budget, and in the government financial loan and investment program are the three devices which have been used to affect the level of aggregate demand. Maintenance of a high rate of economic growth, as opposed to income redistribution and the provision of socially desirable goods and services, has been the dominant objective of fiscal policy.[15] However, this emphasis on economic growth can also be recognized as an acceptance of responsibility on the government's part

---

[14] James J. Ballon, *Labor Relations in Postwar Japan,* Industrial Relations Seminar Bulletin, No. 9 (Tokyo: Sophia University, 1966), p. 3.

[15] Hugh T. Patrick, "Cyclical Instability and Fiscal-Monetary Policy in Postwar Japan," *The State and Economic Enterprise in Japan,* edited by William W. Lockwood (Princeton, N.J.: Princeton University Press, 1965), p. 598.

to provide a sustained rate of economic growth, which redounds to the advantage of the Japanese people in the form of a continued increase in the per capita output of real goods and services. Government fiscal policy, which has supported a continuous increase in private and public investment, has been conducive to a high rate of growth in Japan.

Taxation. Annual changes in the tax laws constitute an important part of government fiscal policy. A policy of cutting taxes has been followed each year as the rate of economic growth has increased. This tax cutting has taken two forms with respect to the personal income tax—increases in basic exemptions and decreases in tax rates. During the period between 1950 and 1972, the basic exemption for a taxpayer was raised from $82.50 to $660 and the exemption for a spouse was raised from $39.60 to $660. Tax rates, particularly at higher levels, have also been reduced. For example, the marginal tax rate at $990, which was 55 percent in 1950, was 10 percent in 1972. The decline in progressivity of the personal income tax may be considered as a factor which has contributed to the postwar rise in the rate of savings in Japan. A high ratio of personal savings to disposable income has existed in Japan and can be attributed in part to the inherent thriftiness of the people. This savings, as will be pointed out later in the chapter, is channeled into investment outlets through the existence of a number of specialized financial institutions which serve as repositories for savings. Savings, far from being a leakage from the income stream, have been directed into an abundant supply of investment outlets. The policy of tax reductions has succeeded because prosperity has prevailed during the postwar period and there has been no existence of idle or unused capacity to dampen investment. It is the type of policy to follow if it is desirable to raise the growth rate under conditions of prosperity.

Expenditures. Throughout most of the postwar period, the Japanese adhered to a conservative policy of financing the general accounts budget and limiting its size relative to national income. The public debt was kept low and little recourse was made to public borrowing. However, this policy was broken in 1966 when a bond flotation of $2 billion was utilized to cover a deficit which had been incurred to stimulate the economy. In the same year one of the largest tax cuts of the postwar period was introduced, amounting to more than $1 billion, or 1 percent of the gross national product. In subsequent years the general accounts budget and the financial loan and investment program continued to be used to either stimulate the economy or dampen down inflation.

Changes in fiscal policy measures have been occasioned primarily by balance-of-payments considerations. In 1967, for example, tightened fiscal measures were adopted when a deterioration in the external balance of payments occurred. Government expenditures on goods and services were held at a fairly constant level for the fiscal year 1967–1968, while the ratio of government current receipts to gross national product increased. In 1969 expansionary fiscal policy measures were utilized in order to maintain a rapid rate of economic growth. These measures included tax cuts and an increase in deficit spending. In 1971 and 1972 budget expenditures were increased at an average rate of 15 percent.[16] For the fiscal 1972–1973 period, total government expenditures, as reflected in the national income accounts, were projected to increase by 24 percent over the previous fiscal year.[17] In addition, the financial loan and investment program, which is kept separate from the general accounts budget, was increased by 50 percent over the 1971–1972 fiscal year.[18]

The Banking System

The financial system of Japan can be divided into a number of institutions with the Bank of Japan forming the nexus of the system. Japanese banks may be classified under the headings of ordinary banks, long-term credit banks, and foreign exchange banks. There are also financial institutions which specialize in financing medium- and small-sized enterprises and agriculture, forestry, and fisheries. In addition, there are government owned financial institutions which operate to supplement the functions of the private financial institutions. Included among the government financial institutions are the Japan Development Bank, the Export-Import Bank of Japan, the Housing Loan Corporation, and the Small Business Finance Corporation. Most of these financial institutions were created after the end of World War II and currently play an important role in the financial operations of the nation.

The largest borrowers of funds in Japan are the corporate business concerns which dominate investment activities in the country. The biggest source of savings is private individuals. In Japan, most of the savings flow from individuals to corporate enterprises through the channel of the financial institutions mentioned above. The use of direct financing through the securities market is small. However, the development of securities investment trusts has broadened the sphere of the securities market.

The Central Bank. The Bank of Japan was established in 1882. Since its establishment, the Bank has always served as the fiscal agent for the government. It provides the government with lending facilities and has also assumed over the years a wide range of activities including the handling of public receipts and payments, government debt, Treasury accounts, and the buying and selling of foreign exchange.

The Bank of Japan also carries out a wide variety of activities with commercial banks and other institutions. These include receiving deposits, making loans, discounting bills and notes, and buying and selling Treasury bills. The lack of financial capital has caused commercial banks to turn to the Bank of Japan as a source of funds. Since the commercial banks are dependent upon the central bank for credit, discount policy has played an important and effective role in maintaining general economic stability. A restriction of central bank credit has an immediate and significant impact on commercial bank lending and investment activities.

---

[16] Bank of Japan, *Monthly Economic Statistics* (April, 1973), p. 7.
[17] *Mitsubishi Bank Review*, Vol. 4, No. 5 (May, 1973), p. 162.
[18] *Ibid.,* p. 163.

Commercial Banks. The commercial banks are privately owned and are divided into two types—city banks and local banks. City banks are located in large cities and operate on a nationwide scale with a network of branch offices widely distributed throughout the country. Since the Meiji period, these banks have played a principal role in supplying the funds necessary for the rapid expansion of the economy. City bank loans, for the most part, are granted to large-scale enterprises; however, in recent years they have become more oriented toward the consumer mass market and have gone into the area of consumer credit. The city banks account for one third of the total fund resources of all financial institutions, public and private, in Japan, and account for 62 percent of the deposits of all banks.[19] There are 13 city banks in Japan.

Local banks are commercial banks conducting business principally in local economic areas. There are 63 local banks, and each is based in a prefecture and extends its operations to neighboring prefectures.[20] Loans to medium- and small-sized enterprises make up the greatest part of local bank loans, and time deposits of individuals make up the greatest part of total deposits. Local banks also lend to local public entities and are an important supplier of call loan funds. Local banks account for 33 percent of the deposits of all banks and 28 percent of all bank loans.[21]

In addition to the commercial banks, there are also long-term credit banks and trust banks. To raise funds for loans, they are allowed to issue debentures up to 20 times their combined total of capital and reserves. Trust banks provide long-term funds for investment in equipment. Both the long-term credit banks and the trust banks are privately owned.

Government Financial Institutions. The government itself is engaged in substantial financial activities through the ownership of a number of specialized credit institutions. Funds to support these institutions are obtained from a special counterpart fund in the budget and from individual savings in the form of postal savings, postal annuities, and postal life insurance. These savings and the surplus funds from special budgetary accounts are deposited in a Trust Fund Bureau, which can use these funds for loans to public enterprises and the financial institutions. Loans are also made to the private sector of the economy, particularly to industries that are export related. However, as a rule, this type of financing is undertaken in cooperation with private lending institutions.

The Export-Import Bank. Through its specialized credit institutions, the government provides capital for long-term industrial development, export financing, and for agriculture, as a part of its policy for stimulating economic growth in an economy where capital is scarce. The Japan Export-Import Bank provides long-term loans at subsidized interest rates to exporters of Japanese products. For example, loans have been provided for the construction of

---

[19] The Bank of Tokyo, *The Financial System of Japan* (1967), p. 27.
[20] A *prefecture* is an administrative unit which corresponds to a metropolitan area or a province.
[21] *The Financial System of Japan, op. cit.,* pp. 28 and 37.

tankers, textile machinery, and rolling stock. Loans have also been provided for the financing of projects, such as the development of iron ore mines in India and the construction of textile mills in South America. The Bank also provides import financing and debt guarantees to attract foreign capital into Japan. To stimulate economic development in Southeast Asia, the government set up a special account with the Bank and called it the Southeast Asia Development Cooperation Fund. Funds were provided out of the national budget. The Fund was eventually transformed into an independent corporation and currently finances long-term investment in Southeast Asia.[22]

Japan Development Bank. Another important government owned financial institution is the Japan Development Bank. This bank was created in 1951 for the purpose of aiding in the reconstruction of the economy. Most of its loans were originally concentrated in the electric power, shipbuilding, and coal industries. However, in recent years its loans have been channeled into the petrochemical and rubber industries and also into the promotion of regional development, city transportation, and international tourism. The Bank provides long-term loans at low interest rates to basic domestic industries. Through its control over investment resources that are in the hands of official financial agencies like the Japan Development Bank, the government is able to exercise some control over national investment and thereby exert some influence with respect to its economic plans.

Other financial institutions directly owned and operated by the government include the Small Business Finance Corporation, which exists for the purpose of supplying long-term loans to small businesses when financing by ordinary financial institutions proves difficult, and the Agriculture, Forestry, and Fisheries Finance Corporation, which provides long-term, low interest loans for agricultural equipment investment on the part of agricultural co-operatives and individual farming enterprises. Funds for both corporations are obtained from the general accounts (national) budget and from investments in securities and the provision of call loans.[23]

Monetary Policy. The Bank of Japan has three instruments which are used to control the volume of credit and money—bank rate policy, open market operations, and reserve deposit requirements. Bank rate policy involves the lowering or raising of discount rates and interest rates. The alteration of these rates is the most important monetary policy instrument in Japan because city banks rely heavily on loans from the Bank of Japan, and industries, in turn, rely heavily on bank loans.[24] Costs in general and the availability of bank funds are highly responsive to changes in the discount and interest rates on

---

[22] The Fuji Bank, *Banking in Modern Japan* (Tokyo, 1967), pp. 222, 223 and 278, 279.

[23] *Ibid.*, pp. 266–268.

[24] Overborrowing on the part of business corporations is a characteristic of the Japanese financial system. The most important borrowers in the money markets are the business corporations. In the postwar years, investment funds have come primarily from the banks and not from internal financing or through the sale of securities.

commercial and export trade bills, overdrafts, and general secured loans. In addition, the Bank also can place a lending ceiling for each bank, above which it can impose a penalty rate or refuse to make loans. Open market operations are inhibited by the lack of a well developed capital market and are not important as an instrument of monetary policy. Legal reserve requirements are far below the standard of reserve requirements in other major countries, and manipulation of these requirements by the Bank of Japan is a supplementary instrument of monetary control.[25]

In Japan the function of monetary policy is more circumscribed than that of fiscal policy. In general, monetary policy has been expansionary in order to facilitate the high rate of economic growth. Successive cuts in the official discount rate brought it down to the all-time low level of 4.25 percent in June of 1972. Lower rates of interest resulted in the stimulation of new housing and residential construction. In 1972 the government adopted a series of measures aimed at reducing an overall balance-of-payments surplus and at stimulating economic activity. In addition to lowering the rediscount rate, the Bank of Japan also lowered the rate of interest paid on time deposits as well as the required legal reserves for both time and demand deposits. In 1973 the revaluation of the yen exerted a deflationary impact on the Japanese economy and monetary measures were linked to the maintenance of a favorable balance of payments.

Labor-Management Relations

An outstanding feature of Japanese trade unions is that they are usually company unions, organized enterprise by enterprise. The typical Japanese labor union is made up of the employees of a single company or of a single operational unit within a company, regardless of their occupation. Approximately 85 percent of all basic union units, embracing almost 80 percent of total union membership, are organized along enterprise lines; that is, their members are confined to a single shop, establishment, or enterprise.[26] The remainder are divided about equally between *industrial unions* and *craft unions* in which the local units are not based simply on enterprise membership. The *enterprise union* typically includes all branches and plants of a firm whether engaged in the production of single or multiple lines.

National Labor and Employer Confederations. At the present time there are four national labor confederations and two major currents of the labor movement—industrial democracy and socialism. The national confederations are loosely knit from the standpoint of organization and control, and they play a policy-making role. They enjoy little authority over the enterprise unions,

---

[25] Japanese commercial banks are characterized by extended lending, low liquidity, and large indebtedness to the Bank of Japan. In recent years the ratio of loans to deposits has often stood near 100 percent. Nearly two thirds of commercial bank deposits are in time and savings accounts, compared to 35 to 45 percent in the United States.

[26] Solomon Levine, *Industrial Relations in Postwar Japan* (Urbana: University of Illinois Press, 1958), p. 91.

which are free to carry on bargaining with employers. Negotiations between labor and management are mostly conducted within each enterprise, but some industrial unions, notably those of private railways, coal mining, textiles, and shipping, hold collective bargaining with a number of companies. Political, as well as economic, issues are brought to bear during labor-management negotiations. Typical examples of political issues involve campaigns which express opposition to the war in Vietnam or opposition to the Japan-Republic of Korea normalization talks.

Japanese employers are also organized into several major confederations, the largest of which is the Federation of Economic Organizations (*Keidenran*). It is made up of 102 financial, industrial, and trading associations, and almost 800 leading business firms.[27] Membership in the federation is institutional, and its work is carried out through nineteen standing committees. It is interested in national economic planning and the development of the economy. Keidenran wields considerable influence in government economic affairs because many business and political leaders are bound together by a common educational background and family and matrimonial ties. Also, both business and the nation depend upon export-import exchange for survival.

Two other business confederations which are of importance are the Japanese Federation of Employers Association (*Nikkeiren*) and the Chamber of Commerce and Industry (*Nisho*). Nikkeiren is made up of around 100 regional and industrial employers associations, and its function is also to influence the economic policies of the government. Nisho represents 400 chambers of commerce and industry.

Government and Union Relations. The relationship of the government to unions has followed a series of convolutions since the development of unions in Japan. They were originally suppressed by the government, but after World War I, the government adopted a more liberal attitude toward them and declared that it would not oppose their development. However, the government's policy of toleration ceased in 1936 when some unions were declared illegal. In 1940 the government outlawed all unions except the labor front, which it had established two years before. At the end of World War II, no unions existed in Japan. Prewar unionism had died completely.

During the early American military occupation following World War II, the Japanese government played a permissive role in the area of union-government relations. It had no choice in the matter, for the Allied Powers endorsed a series of labor reforms which had as their objective the development of a strong trade union movement in Japan. There were several reasons for this policy—the desire to democratize industrial society, the intent to develop unions as a countervailing force against the potential rebirth of the zaibatsu, and the need to raise incomes of the industrial masses.[28] Unions were

[27] Koji Taira, "Participation by Workers' and Employers' Organizations in Economic Planning in Japan," *International Labor Review*, Vol. 94, No. 6 (December, 1966), pp. 511–534.

[28] Levine, *op. cit.*, p. 66.

given the right to organize and bargain collectively, and labor courts were set up to adjudicate labor disputes. Union membership, which had been zero during the war, increased to around 7 million by 1949.[29] However, during the Korean War the United States reversed some of its occupational policies and encouraged the Japanese government to purge many unions of Communist members.

Government and Business

The combination of free enterprise and government control in Japan dates back to the Meiji Restoration.[30] The government was active during the Meiji era in introducing Western industrial methods into Japan and also took the lead in promoting the development of industries of strategic importance. Throughout a period, dating from the Russo-Japanese War of 1904 to World War II, responsibility for development and innovation was shared between the government and the large zaibatsu combines. Fundamental shifts took place in government policy during the economic and political crises of the 1930s. To counteract the effects of the world depression, the government compelled closer cooperation between producers to mitigate the excesses of competition. Later in the decade, when the militarists gained the ascendancy in Japan and war appeared inevitable, government intervention in the economy increased. The electric power industry was nationalized in 1938, and strategic industries were brought under direct government supervision.

With respect to government control of business, the occupation authorities attempted to democratize the economy by destroying the concentration of economic power which was held by the zaibatsu combines during the period before World War II. Antimonopoly and antitrust decrees, which prohibited mergers, interlocking directorates, and undue restrictions of production, price, or technology through combinations and agreements, were utilized in the attempt. An economic purge was applied to a number of key officials in some 250 major companies, and members of listed zaibatsu families were prohibited from holding positions of responsibility in any restricted company.[31] The whole approach to the dissolution of zaibatsu economic power ran counter to the need for extensive economic planning in order to accomplish the rehabilitation of the economy, and eventually Japanese government policies, particularly with respect to the promotion of exports, have favored mergers which result in large-scale business operations.[32]

---

[29] Ministry of Labor, *Yearbook of Labor Statistics, 1956* (Tokyo: Division of Labor Statistics and Research, 1956).

[30] However, the Tokugawa Shogunate encouraged the development of Western-style factories to produce iron, armaments, and other products considered militarily essential. A state policy of encouragement of agricultural production was also adopted.

[31] Jerome B. Cohen, *Japan's Economy in War and Reconstruction* (Minneapolis: University of Minnesota Press, 1949), pp. 429–435.

[32] The curret Economic and Social Development Plan mentions the need for business firms to merge and consolidate in order to strengthen their international competitive conditions. Antimonopoly laws are to be less punitive against business mergers.

Government Promotion of Businesses. As has been mentioned, there has long been a tradition in Japan for the government to promote business interests by the means of special financial privileges, subsidies, and low interest rates. Selective or discriminatory treatment of various industries has been an integral part of postwar Japanese economic policy. The government has tried to favor certain industries, certain types of economic activity, or certain groups of firms, through such measures as an import licensing system, control and allocation of investment funds, and special tax policies to promote investment and corporate savings. Examples of tax policies include: accelerated depreciation provisions to stimulate the modernization of industrial facilities and the advancement of new technology; and tax-free reserves, which are deductible from the Japanese corporate income tax and which are used to increase the total supply of national savings.[33]

In general, government economic policies have favored the following types of industries.[34]

1. Export- and import-competing industries which help improve the balance of payments.
2. Heavy and chemical industries where the possibility of technological progress and expansion of export demand is considered to be greater than in other industries.
3. Industries which supply important basic materials, energy, or basic productive services—iron and steel, electric power, coal, marine transportation, and chemical fertilizers.

Government Savings and Investment. A conspicuous feature of postwar Japanese public finance has been a high level of government savings and investment, which has made a significant contribution to capital formation. During the postwar period, the government and its agencies have been accounting for as much as one fourth of all investment spending in Japan— a high percentage for an economy based so largely on private enterprise. Investment and lending activities have been financed to a considerable degree from surpluses in the budget and other forms of public savings. Funds from the national budget have been channeled through various lending institutions to help provide industries with the finance necessary for expansion. Government investment and savings have been accomplished in large part because Japanese expenditures on national defense and social welfare have been lower than those of other countries. This has meant that in the absence of wasteful investment in armaments, investment can be directed into uses that yield quick returns.

The government has also made use of monetary instruments in shaping the direction of industry toward desired economic goals. The official government banks can direct capital resources into preferred fields. By controlling

[33] National Bureau of Economic Research, *Foreign Tax Policies and Economic Growth* (New York: Columbia University Press, 1966), pp. 39–75.
[34] *Ibid.,* pp. 65–67.

the flow of funds from the Bank of Japan and thence to industry, the government can also influence the development of industries that are considered essential to the attainment of economic growth.

Nationalization of Industries. Japan is in itself a major operator of a number of industries. Part of the program of modernization during the late 19th century, in fact, included nationalization of wide sectors of Japanese business —the postal service, telephone and telegraph communications, and railways. In addition, tobacco, salt, and camphor were made government monopolies. These activities have been organized into public corporations which are under the ultimate control of the Japanese Diet. There are three public corporations: The Japan National Railways, The Japan Telegraph and Telephone Company, and The Japan Monopolies Corportion. In addition, there are the credit institutions which are owned and operated by the government: The Japan Export-Import Bank, The Japan Development Bank, and others.

However, there is relatively little public ownership of industry when Japan is compared to other countries such as France and the United Kingdom. During the occupation, the Japanese government was forced to divest itself of certain monopolies, such as steel, which it had before and during the war. The electric power industry, which was nationalized before the war, is now privately owned.

Economic Planning

Japanese economic planning is indicative rather than imperative and is similar to French planning in that a rather formal and highly structured plan is developed which is to cover a specific period of time. National policy objectives are specified in the plan. However, there is no element of coercion or centralized government control, but rather an arrangement which is based on induced cooperation on the part of business enterprises through the use of monetary and fiscal controls, and through planned expenditures on the part of the government. Planning provides a framework which gives Japanese business enterprises an idea of the direction in which the economy is going.

Since the end of World War II, there have been several sets of economic plans. The first set of plans was aimed at the reconstruction of the postwar economy.[35] When this was accomplished, a second set of plans was adopted for the purpose of developing a viable economy in the absence of economic assistance from the United States. A third set, including the National Income Doubling Plan and the Economic and Social Development Plan, placed emphasis on economic growth. These sets of plans coincided with the actual stages of postwar economic development.

National Income Doubling Plan. The objective of the Income Doubling Plan was to accomplish a doubling of the Japanese national income over a 10-year

---

[35] The first plan was the Draft Plan for Economic Reconstruction, which was completed in 1948, and the second plan was the Economic Reconstruction Plan, which was completed in 1949.

period, 1961–1970, for an average growth rate of 7.2 percent compounded annually. The plan involved a blueprint of national expectations accompanied by a budget of government investment programs. The plan was centered on the government sector of the economy. The allocation of funds for several types of public investments over the decade was determined and fitted within the framework of the national budget. Desired economic targets were to be achieved by such indirect measures as fiscal and monetary policies and various inducements designed to encourage private enterprise to expand in a desirable direction.[36]

The plan aimed at increasing the ratio of public investment to private investment from one to three to one to two by 1970. Investments were to be made for improving the backward economic structure of agriculture and forestry, upgrading the transportation system, strengthening the facilities for land conservation, and redeveloping major cities. Priority was to be given to public investments which would strengthen the industrial infrastructure of the country. Regional imbalance in economic development was also to be eliminated.

The task of fiscal and monetary policy under the Income Doubling Plan was to insure a proper supply of funds for economic growth, while maintaining price stability and minimizing business fluctuations. Funds for private investment were to be obtained by measures to stimulate both corporate and personal savings and by the development of more outlets for enterprises to procure needed capital funds directly. Taxes were also to be reduced to stimulate domestic consumption and investment. In the area of monetary policy, the inflow of foreign capital and Japanese investments overseas were to be encouraged through the liberalization of foreign exchange transactions.

The Income Doubling Plan presented a forecast for the private sector of the economy. Private enterprises were supposed to make their own long-range plans based on the projections of trends during the life of the plan. Government participation vis-à-vis private enterprise was to take the form of expenditures on social capital.

The Economic and Social Development Plan. In February 1973 the Japanese government announced a new five-year economic plan covering the fiscal years 1973 to 1977. This plan superceded the Economic and Social Development Plan which was designed to run from the fiscal years 1970 to 1975. The new plan is designed to cope with new problems in the Japanese economy, such as the wide gap between the rate of national economic growth and expenditures on social welfare, the enormous trade surplus, and the growing public concern over environmental problems. The objectives of the Plan are as follows:

1. To stabilize prices at a more orderly rate in order to accomplish a more uniform rate of economic growth. The Plan seeks to hold the average annual rise of consumer prices to 4 percent. Wholesale prices are also to be stabilized at a rate of increase of 5 percent a year. Real economic growth is to be held to an annual average increase of 9 percent a year.

[36] Economic Planning Agency, *National Income Doubling Plan* (Tokyo: Japan Times, Ltd., 1961).

2. Major priority is to be given to the preservation of the environment. In the major metropolitan areas of Tokyo and Osaka, the quantity of pollutants discharged in the air will be reduced by half by 1977 over the 1970 level. The diffusion rate of sewerage is to be raised from 19 percent in 1972 to 42 percent in 1977. All other environmental standards are to be improved over a 1972 base. During the plan period the Japanese government proposes to invest $1.8 billion to protect the environment, and another $1.8 to combat pollution expected from industry.

3. Significant changes are to be made in the area of social welfare. The ratio of transfer payments is to be raised from 6 percent in 1972 to 8.8 percent in 1977. Old age pensions are to be doubled during the plan period and the retirement age is to be reduced to 60 years. There is to be increased government investment in social capital in order to raise living standards. For example, four million houses are to be constructed during the plan period.

Table 12–5 shows the projected increase of the various components of the Japanese economy during the course of the Plan.

TABLE 12–5
PROJECTED RATES OF INCREASE IN THE ECONOMIC AND SOCIAL DEVELOPMENT PLAN—1973–1977

Components of the Economy	Average Annual Rate of Increase (Percentage)
Gross national product	9.0
Personal consumption	14.0
Government consumption	10.0
Government investment	18.0
Private equipment investment	11.0
Private residential investment	20.0
Exports	14.0
Imports	16.0

Source: Economic Planning Agency, *Economic and Social Development Plan* (Tokyo, February, 1973).

Fiscal and monetary policies are to be utilized to maintain a stable rate of economic growth. The government plans to raise the ratio of taxes to national income from 20 percent in 1972 to 27 percent in 1977. The rate of increase in government expenditures is to be greater than the increase in real gross national product, and reliance is to be placed on the use of countercyclical fiscal policy—increases or decreases in public spending and the rate of business depreciation—to adjust economic activity.

The Mechanics of Japanese Planning. Economic planning is optional on the part of the government and the initiative for it rests with the Prime Minister. Unlike the French economic plans, which have been usually for four-year periods, Japanese plans do not adhere to a particular time schedule. The plans usually set a goal of long-range economic growth per annum over a base period and provide guiding principles for the accomplishment of various economic and social objectives.

The National Resources Development Law, which was passed in 1950, provided the current framework for economic planning. The formulation of a plan involves the creation of a set of objectives and the collection and analysis of data which lead to the preparation of a formal framework within which the plan is to operate. The Economic Council, which consists of not more than 30 members appointed by the Prime Minister, is responsible for the development of a plan, and the Economic Planning Agency, which is attached directly to the office of the Prime Minister, is responsible for the technical work associated with economic planning.

The Economic Council is comprised of key members of the financial community, industry, and government, who are appointed to a two-year term by the Prime Minister. In addition, a number of experts on technical matters are utilized in the formulation of the plan. There is a General Policy Committee and a number of specialized committees, each of which is concerned with certain areas of the economy, such as agriculture and forestry. Their reports are appended to the draft of the plan, which is sent by the Council to the Prime Minister.

The Economic Planning Agency is responsible for the technical work associated with economic planning. It also has the responsibility for coordinating the principal policies and plans of other executive agencies of the Japanese government, analyzing and measuring national economic resources, and preparing policies and plans concerning the development of electricity resources. It has as its advisory agent the Economic Council.

To carry out its functions which are not limited exclusively to long-term economic planning, the Agency must work through various executive departments and such agencies as the Bank of Japan, whose support is crucial because it is the center of Japanese financial policy formulation. It is also necessary to work with the Ministry of Finance, because of its control over expenditures and the budget, which affect the successful operation of any plan. Planning policies involving foreign trade, agriculture, transportation, and labor are effectuated through cooperation with the various ministries that are responsible for these activities. However, the Economic Planning Agency does not possess the power of a ministry and can exercise little independent initiative or coordination.

As in the past, the government and business have been closely associated in working out national economic policy. From this association, the plans which concern the future of the Japanese economy develop. These plans are more than just estimates of the future, for the government is able through various fiscal devices and through control over various financial institutions, such as the Japan Development Bank, to encourage or compel growth along the desired lines.

AN APPRAISAL OF THE JAPANESE ECONOMY

The growth rate of the Japanese economy has been the highest for any major industrial country. The average annual rate of growth in terms of real gross national product for the period 1950–1964 was 9.6 percent in Japan compared to 6.7 percent for West Germany and 3.1 percent for the United States, and the average annual rate of growth in terms of industrial production was 14.4 percent for Japan compared to 8.1 percent for West Germany and 3.6 percent for the United States.[37] During the 1960s Japan's annual rate of economic growth was 16 percent in monetary terms and 11 percent in real terms. In 1970 the gross national product increased 10.3 percent in real terms, in 1971 the increase was 6.2 percent, and in 1972 the increase was 9.2 percent.[38]

A certain mystique surrounds the phenomenal growth rate of the Japanese economy. How can a country with the size and resource base of Japan mount such a sustained effort over a prolonged period of time? Several aspects are familiar—a low level from which postwar recovery started, an abundant and productive labor supply, and a traditionally high rate of personal savings—but these factors do not fully explain the extraordinary viability of the Japanese economy.

Actually the Japanese growth rate is an integral extension of a century of development, the roots of which can be traced to the emergence of a mercantile class during the latter period of the Tokugawa Shogunate. A continuity of growth continued during the Meiji period up to the present, and the basic reasons for it have survived—a pervasive spirit of enterprise which combines the profit motive with economic nationalism, a regulatory but sponsoring relationship of government to business, the managerial competence of the business and financial class, and the frugality and industry of the masses of workers.[39]

A number of new elements have been injected into the postwar growth process. The occupation-inspired program of land reform eliminated the system of feudal tenancy and made possible an increase in agricultural productivity, while at the same time it released labor for the expanding industrial sector. Japan's large, modern, manufacturing establishments were able to recruit manpower both from agriculture and from the country's many small and backward concerns. The productivity of the workers thus transferred was substantially increased. Her ability to draw upon this reservoir of manpower undoubtedly contributed to Japan's rapid growth during the postwar period. Italy and France also benefited by similar movements into occupations where productivity was higher.

Another new element in the growth process is the absence of major military expenditures in the national budget. With the United States assuming the

---

[37] Thomas Wilson, "Stability and the Rate of Growth," *Lloyds Bank Review*, No. 81 (London: July, 1966), pp. 16–32.

[38] Bureau of Statistics, *Japan Statistical Yearbook 1973* (Tokyo: Office of the Prime Minister, 1973), p. 10.

[39] G. C. Allen, *A Short Economic History of Japan* (London: Unwin University Books, 1961), pp. 13–47.

major responsibility for Japan's defense, the Japanese are able to divert their resources into more productive channels. Defense-related expenditures account for about 7 percent of total budgetary expenditures and less than 1 percent of gross national product.

Personal savings have averaged around 17 percent of disposable income—a high rate even by comparison with the United States. This can be attributed to several factors—the frugality of the Japanese, a substantial increase in disposable income during the postwar period, and tax policies, such as the tax exemption of interest income from small deposits, which are used by the government to encourage personal savings. These savings have aided the high rate of capital formation which has taken place in Japan.[40] The nation's banks are the major recipients of private savings and the medium for channeling these investment funds to industry.

Although private sources have furnished most of the capital, and wealth ownership remains largely in private hands, the government has played an important and crucial financial role in the economic development of Japan. The government, through its investment and lending activities, has controlled at least one third of the nation's investment spending during the last decade and has also provided savings to finance these activities through surpluses in the general accounts budget.

Japan has achieved a rising rate of productivity in industry as well as in agriculture. Productivity increases have been in excess of wage increases, and the margin has made possible a high rate of capital accumulation by companies and thus a high rate of capital investment. Labor has been released from inefficient areas, such as agriculture, and has been more efficiently used in combination with modern equipment. The introduction of new technology and processes, organizational improvements in management, improvements in cost and production control, and efficient quality control standards have also helped to increase productivity.

Nevertheless, Japanese economic growth has not been an unmixed blessing. The Japanese have come to the realization that they have paid heavily for their obsession with rapid growth. Tokyo, Osaka, and other metropolitan areas have become megalopolitan nightmares, hopelessly congested and permeated with choking fumes. The atmosphere is killing the famous cherry trees in Tokyo, and in nearby Kawasaki it has killed people as well. In a nation that ranks third among the top economic powers of the world, only 15 percent of the homes are connected to sewers. The Japanese are having to undertake a vast restructuring of the nation and its economy.[41] To check pollution and urban congestion, factories are to be dispersed to the countryside and dozens of new towns are to be created and linked by networks of highways and

---

[40] Domestic capital formation has been an important factor in economic growth, accounting for about 90 percent of corporate investment funds, much of which went into new plant construction and acquisition of modern equipment. Since 1963 investments have represented around 33 percent of GNP, compared to 16 percent in the United States.

[41] Mitsubishi Economic Research Institute, "Survey of Economic Conditions in Japan" (May, 1973), pp. 2–5.

express railways. It is estimated that a trillion dollars will be spent to clean up pollution and redeploy industry.

The rapid increase in economic development has created a number of socioeconomic changes with which Japan must reckon. For one thing, it has become necessary to revamp attitudes toward work and leisure. The Japanese have become torn between their devotion to work and an increased desire for more leisure. Moreover, by stressing exports Japan has, in effect, given away products to the world at low prices—and at the expense of its own people who produced the goods. Revised national goals will drastically alter the strategies of Japanese corporations in ways that will undoubtedly affect world trade for years to come. There has also been a shift away from reliance on heavy industry toward new sources of economic growth.

One important problem confronting the Japanese is the wide disparity between national wealth and social welfare. It is openly acknowledged that Japan is a backward society by many measures of economic and social well-being. A recent government survey revealed that the country lags a decade behind Western Europe in housing, sanitation, and other essentials. Social security benefits are also very low in comparison to other major industrial nations. Japan devotes only 6 percent of its national income to social security compared with 15 to 20 percent for the Western European countries. Though most workers retire at 55, they must wait until 60 to qualify for retirement pensions, which typically are totally inadequate in terms of providing a decent standard of living.

SUMMARY

The Japanese economic system is essentially capitalistic. With the exception of certain public services and monopolies which are operated by the Japanese government, private enterprise is dominant in the economy. The government leaves the initiative for production and distribution in private hands, and it has for many decades devoted itself to creating an environment which is favorable to investment by private enterprise. Business firms have flourished under the protection of the government, and leaders in both fields are often connected by common educational and marital ties.

Nevertheless, the government intervenes constantly to turn industry into directions thought to be desirable for the economy as a whole. By controlling the flow of funds from the Bank of Japan to commercial banks and from thence to industry, the government has exerted pressure on industry. Through tax benefits, special depreciation allowances, and favorable interest rates, the government has stimulated savings and investment. Pervasive pressures are exercised one way or another on the investment decisions of business firms. The government also has controlled a considerable proportion of the nation's investment during the boom of the last decade. A policy of tax reductions has served to stimulate aggregate demand which in turn has caused yearly surpluses in the budget. From this source came 25 percent of the nation's savings over the last decade.

The rate of economic growth has been the most rapid of all major industrial countries. Although the increase can be predicated in part on the fact that the economy had no where to go but up after the devastation brought about by World War II, other factors are much more important in explaining the growth rate. A stimulus to growth has come both from rising consumption demands at home and market opportunities abroad. Other stimuli include a reverse gap between productivity and wages, an abundant labor supply, a high rate of personal savings, and an undervalued currency.

Economic planning is indicative rather than imperative. A series of plans have been used since the end of World War II to accomplish set economic objectives. Japanese planning points out a series of desirable goals which the economy should try to achieve. Industry has a frame of reference within which to operate. No direct coercion, which would be used in imperative planning, is used to make industry operate within the framework of the plan. The government, however, has indirect and more subtle ways to assure compliance with the objectives of planning. Control over the supply of credit gives the government leverage in enforcing compliance. Selective fiscal measures which are designed to favor exports, certain types of industries, investment, or personal savings can also be used to encourage conformance with the plan. The national budget can also be used to allocate expenditures into desirable areas. Even where no fiscal and monetary controls exist, it is customary for the government to provide personal guidance to industry or, conversely, for industry to consult the government before making major business decisions.

The Japanese economy is not free from problems. An adverse balance of payments has existed throughout most of the last decade. Rising standards of living at home are a mixed blessing in that although consumer demand has increased, expectations of still higher living standards may redound to the disadvantage of the rate of growth. Political instability, although currently nascent, also poses a problem for the future.

QUESTIONS

1. What factors have been responsible for the high rate of Japanese economic growth?
2. Discuss the objectives of Japanese economic planning.
3. Discuss the relationship between government and business in Japan.
4. Fiscal policy has played an important role in stimulating savings and investment in Japan. Do you agree?
5. Compare Japanese and French economic planning.
6. Explain some of the factors which have been responsible for a high rate of personal savings in Japan.
7. What are the objectives of the Economic and Social Development Plan?
8. Discuss the role of fiscal and monetary policies in the implementation of Japanese economic planning.

RECOMMENDED READINGS

Brzezinski, Zbigniew. *The Fragile Blossom: Crisis and Change in Japan.* New York: Harper and Row, 1972.

Guillain, Robert. *The Japanese Challenge.* Philadelphia: L. B. Lippincoth, 1970.

Hunsberger, Warren S. *Japan: New Industrial Giant.* New York: American-Asian Educational Exchange, 1972.

Kahn, Herman. *The Emerging Japanese Superstate.* Englewood Cliffs, New Jersey: Prentice-Hall, 1970.

Lockwood, William W. *The State and Economic Enterprise in Japan.* Princeton: Princeton University Press, 1965.

Reischauer, Edwin O. *Japan: The Story of a Nation,* rev. ed. New York: Knopf, 1974.

Patrick, H. T. *Monetary Policy and Central Banking in Contemporary Japan.* Bombay: East India Press, 1962.

Yanaga, Chitoshi. *Big Business in Japanese Politics.* New Haven: Yale University Press, 1968.

13
Sweden

INTRODUCTION

Sweden is a prime example of what is called *welfare capitalism*. The social welfare program has perhaps created in some American minds the picture of the welfare state par excellence. The name "Sweden" automatically conjures up visions of socialism in its most advanced form with government enterprise abounding everywhere.

However, as will be pointed out, the Swedish economic system is a mixed system. Private enterprise dominates almost all forms of economic activity. Swedish industry, with some exceptions, is privately owned and must attempt to earn a profit the same as its American counterparts. The ownership of private property, although not so prevalent as in the United States, is certainly a prominent characteristic of the Swedish economic system. Freedom of choice of one's occupation is also as prevalent in Sweden as in the United States.

Probably the basic difference between Sweden and the United States lies in the very comprehensive and all-inclusive social welfare program which covers every Swede from the "cradle to the grave." The rationale for this program lies both in a set of Swedish institutional factors different from those in the United States and in the depression of the 1930s, which probably caused a greater dislocation in the economy of Sweden than in that of the United States.[1]

Sweden is a country well worth examining. It has one of the highest standards of living in the world. From the standpoint of labor-management relations, Sweden has the most stable relations of any industrial country. It is also a country which has eliminated poverty—and even signs of poverty are hard to find. Worker productivity is higher than in any other European country. Programs to create employment are probably as varied as in any country in the world. Indeed, Sweden can be considered a showcase country.

THE ECONOMIC SYSTEM

Sweden has the highest standard of living in Western Europe and is second only to the United States and Canada in the world. In 1972 the average family

[1] The average unemployment rate in Sweden was around 15 percent during the 1930s.

income amounted to approximately 44,000 kronor ($9,240), and the median income amounted to approximately 41,000 kronor ($8,610).[2] In 1972 the per capita income of Sweden was $5,300 compared to $4,400 for Canada, $5,600 for the United States, and $2,600 for Great Britain. In such outward manifestations of living standards as number of automobiles, radios, television sets, and telephones, Sweden is second only to the United States.[3]

In viewing the structure of the Swedish economy, at first glance it does not appear to be strikingly different from other contemporary mixed capitalistic industrialized economies. It is clear that Sweden has what can be called a nonsocialized economy. Some 90 percent of all enterprises in industry are privately owned. Private enterprise accounts for 86 percent of steel production, 93 percent of chemical production, 89 percent of forest production, and 84 percent of food production.[4] The automobile industry is privately owned. Eighty-nine percent of Sweden's retail business is in private hands, and the same holds true of 91 percent of the banking business. Agriculture is entirely in the domain of private enterprise, and agricultural land is privately owned. Private enterprise accounts for the employment of 84 percent of the labor force.

Government ownership is largely limited to railroads, telephone and telegraph systems, and other utilities. There is one government-owned steel mill, situated in northern Sweden, which was built to stimulate local employment. Today, as is the case generally in Western Europe, the Swedish government is the dominant supplier of electric power in the country. The Swedish, Danish, and Norwegian governments together own 50 percent of the Scandinavian Airlines System (SAS). The other 50 percent is in the hands of private nationals of the three countries. In addition, the Swedish government has some ownership of banks.

Nevertheless, the role of the public sector of the economy, that is, the national and local government sector, is very significant. The share of the public sector in the total economy is large and has increased in importance during the postwar period. This share can be measured by using two criteria, as follows:

1. The relationship of public consumption and public investment relative to gross national product.
2. The relationship of taxes and social welfare contributions to gross national product.

The relationship of public consumption and public investment to gross national product is shown in Table 13–1.

---

[2] The Krona is worth $.21. The income is before taxes and transfer payments and is based on Swedish tax data provided by the Ministry of Finance.

[3] See the *Quarterly Review* (Skandinaviska Banken, First Quarter, 1971). Erik Lundberg has developed a series of economic indicators to measure standards of living in various countries. According to Lundberg, Sweden's standard of living is exceeded only by the United States.

[4] Ministry of Finance, *The Swedish Budget, 1973–1974* (Stockholm, 1973), pp. 73–77.

TABLE 13—1

GROSS NATIONAL PRODUCT OF THE SWEDISH ECONOMY FOR 1972

Source	Millions of Dollars *
Private consumption	20,646
Central government consumption	3,336
Local government consumption	5,690
Private gross domestic investment	4,193
Central government domestic investment	1,596
Local government domestic investment	2,371
Changes in inventories	255
Exports	9,446
Less: Imports	9,061
Gross national product	38,472

* In 1972, 1 krona equaled $.21.

Source: *Statistisk Arsbok för Sverige, 1972* (Stockholm: Statistiska Centralbyran, 1972), p. 340.

Approximately 31 percent of the gross national product was utilized by the national and local governments within the public sector. The goods and services that are produced by public or private enterprises go either to public consumption or public investment or private consumption or private investment. In 1946 the share of public consumption and investment was 17 percent of gross national product; in 1972 the share had increased to 33 percent.[5]

When taxes and social security contributions are compared to the gross national product, the importance of the public sector to the Swedish economy becomes obvious. Taxes, of course, provide the state with control over economic resources. They are the means by which resources are transferred from the private sector to the public sector. In 1972 direct and indirect taxes and social security contributions amounted to 44 percent of the Swedish gross national product.[6]

The public sector of the Swedish economy has also grown in importance relative to the private sector. In 1950 private consumption expenditures amounted to 62 percent of the gross national product. In 1972 private consumption expenditures amounted to 53 percent of the gross national product. Private investment expenditures have remained relatively stable. In 1950 they amounted to 17.4 percent of gross national product, and in 1972 they amounted to 14.1 percent of gross national product. Central and local government investment expenditures increased from 9.7 percent of gross national product in 1950 to 10.5 percent in 1972.[7]

[5] *Statistisk Arsbok för Sverige, 1972* (Stockholm: Statistiska Centralbyran, 1972), p. 342.

[6] Ministry of Finance, *The Swedish Budget 1973–1974* (Stockholm, 1973), p. 60.

[7] *Statistical Reports, 1973* (Stockholm: National Bureau of Statistics, 1973), pp. 3 and 4.

Public Finance

A feature of Swedish public finance is the division of the budget into a current operating budget and a capital budget. The former deals with the government as a going concern while the latter deals with the government's capital investments. There is also a national budget, which is an annual report on the prospects of the Swedish economy, both public and private.

The current operating budget shows on the revenue side tax receipts and profits of the government's capital funds and enterprises—receipts from the tobacco, alcohol, and telephone monopolies, the post office, and the like. On the expenditure side of the current budget are shown the customary government expenditures for such programs as education, social welfare, and roads, and expenditures for the state capital funds. The latter is dominated by interest payments on the national debt.

The capital budget separates those items which, although built in the present, are intended to give up their services for some years in the future. Since these items will cease to give service at some future period, they are charged off under the assumption that they are used up to some degree each year. The capital budget regards the government as any other business providing service to the public. The government forms capital assets as do private businesses, and they are treated similarly. The result of capital budgeting has been to permit an expansion in the rate of government fixed capital formation, as compared to other types of expenditures, without appearing to increase taxes to do so.

The Swedish governmental budget is regarded as an instrument for influencing short- and long-term economic development. A policy of attempting to balance the budget every year proved undesirable from the standpoint of overall economic stability and was replaced during the 1930s by a policy under which the budget is used explicitly to create deficits during recessions and surpluses during boom periods. Unfortunately, commitment to a policy of full employment at all cost has resulted in deficits in the Swedish budget even during years which obviously called for a surplus.

The Swedish Tax System. The tax system of Sweden is relatively uncomplicated when compared to the systems of other countries. The income tax is the most important national and local tax. Another tax, which is of increasing importance as a source of national revenue, is the value-added tax. This tax is of recent origin and is patterned after the French value-added tax. General sumptuary taxes are also important. In recent years, indirect taxes have increased in importance relative to direct taxes as a source of government revenue.

Table 13–2 presents tax revenues for the national and local governments for the fiscal year 1973–1974. Excluded from the table are revenues from the public enterprise funds and other sources of nontax revenues, such as receipts from annual depreciation allowances and the liquidation of assets.

TABLE 13—2
NATIONAL AND LOCAL TAX REVENUES IN SWEDEN
FOR THE FISCAL YEAR 1973—1974

Taxes	Millions of Dollars *
National	
Income and capital taxes, including old age pension fees	4,899
Death duty and gift tax	92
Value-added tax	3,220
Liquor tax	736
Tobacco tax	414
Gasoline tax	1,058
Customs duties	276
Miscellaneous	1,518
Total	12,213
Local	
Local income tax	6,210
Total	18,423

* 1 krona = $.23.
Source: Skattebetalarnas Forening, "Fakta för Skattebetalare" (Stockholm, 1973).

Personal Income Taxes. Sweden has a national and local income tax. The national income tax is progressive, but all local income taxes are proportional. The local rates, however, vary from commune to commune. The average rate of all local income taxes in 1973 was 23.94 percent of taxable income. Local income taxes are levied at the same rate for individuals, partnerships, corporations, and trusts. The national and local income taxes are collected by one administrative organization, usually by means of withholding from wages and salaries. The county governor's office pays to each commune local income taxes collected on its behalf.

The national income tax rates vary from 7 percent on incomes of $3,000 or less to 54 percent on incomes of $31,500 or more. There are various standard deductions of $900 for every taxpayer and a maximum deduction of $420 from earned income in families with children under 16. There are no deductions for children.

The communal system of local government in Sweden underlies the structure of the local income tax rate. While only one local income tax is levied, the rate is made up of several separate components. For example, the local income tax rate for the county of Kalmar was 24.60 percent in 1972, but is divided into a communal portion of 14.90 percent, a portion for the support of the state church of 1.10 percent, and the remaining portion of 8.60 percent for the county council. These amounts are set by the commune and county councils. The rate for the state church is determined when the local church council submits its budget to the commune council, which then includes in the rate of the local tax an amount sufficient to meet any deficit. The combined average rate of all local taxes for the whole of Sweden for 1973 was 23.94 percent of taxable income, that is, assessable income after deductions and exemption. Of this amount, 14.78 percent went to the communes, 0.85 percent went to the support of the state church, and the remainder went to the counties.

The national and local income taxes are computed together and are generally withheld by the employer. However, every person earning an annual income of at least $630 or owning capital assets valued at $21,000 or more is required to fill out and submit an annual tax return in February of each year which states the amount of income during the previous year and the amount of any capital assets at the end of that year.

The Corporate Income Tax. The corporate income tax is also an important source of revenue to the Swedish government. Corporations are subject to both national and local taxes on income. The national income tax is levied at a flat rate of 40 percent. At the local level, corporations are taxed at the same rates as individuals. The amount of the local income tax assessed during the year against a corporation is a deduction which is subtracted from net income to give the assessable income for national income tax purposes. The effective rate, national and local, is approximately 49 percent.

The Value-Added Tax. The value-added tax was introduced in Sweden in January 1969, replacing a general retail sales tax which had been in existence for a number of years. It is an ad valorem tax payable on the price that the consumer pays and can be considered a broad form of consumption tax. The rate of the tax is 15 percent of the taxable value, which is the price paid by the consumer with the amount of the tax included. The rate corresponds to 16.5 percent of the price before the tax. For certain transactions, the tax rate is based on reduced taxable values according to special reduction rules. For example, there is a reduction rule of 60 percent which is applicable to the purchase of machinery. The effective rate of the tax is reduced to 9 percent of the total price including the tax, or 9.65 percent when it is excluded.

Sumptuary Taxes. These taxes are designed to penalize the consumption of certain products which are generally considered to be harmful. The taxation of liquor and tobacco represents specific examples. In Sweden taxation of these two products is an important source of national revenue. Sales of liquor are limited to the two government owned monopolies, one the importer and wholesaler and the other the retailer. A sales tax is added to the price when sales are made from the wholesaler to the retailer. This tax amounts to a flat rate plus an ad valorem surcharge, both of which vary according to the type of liquor sold. The value-added tax is then imposed on the sale of liquor to the consumer.

The government also has a monopoly on the manufacture, importation, and sale, other than at retail, of tobacco. The tax on tobacco is composed of two elements—a flat rate calculated per piece or per package, in the case of cigars and cigarettes, and the value-added tax which is imposed on the sales price to the consumer. The combined rates are high. For example, on a package of cigarettes, the total tax amounts to 93 percent of the sales price.

The Impact of Taxation in Sweden. When direct and indirect taxes and social security contributions are compared to gross national product, it is evident that a considerable percentage of the gross national product is diverted from the private to the public sector of the Swedish economy. A recent article by Erik Lundberg revealed that taxes and social security contributions represent 48.1 percent of the Swedish gross national product.[8] The comparable statistic which he developed for the United States is 30 percent. He also estimated that a 100 million kronor ($21 million) increase in gross national product would be accompanied by a total rise in taxes of close to 50 million kronor ($10.5 million).

Table 13-3 presents the average burden of direct and indirect taxes for various income earners in Sweden. Included as direct taxes are the national and local income taxes, the old age pension, and the national health insurance premium—all of which are withheld by employers from the wages and salaries of employees. Indirect taxes would include sales and excise taxes. Transfer payments, which would redound to the advantage of those persons who are in the lower income groups, are not included in the table.

TABLE 13-3

BURDEN OF SWEDISH TAXATION FOR VARIOUS INCOME CLASSES *

Income Classes (Dollars)	Direct Taxes (Dollars)	Indirect ** Taxes (Dollars)	Total Taxes (Dollars)	Percentage of Income
1,680	—	420	420	25
3,150	448	675	1,124	36
4,200	831	842	1,673	40
8,400	3,044	1,339	4,383	52
10,500	4,354	1,536	5,891	56
15,750	7,692	2,014	9,706	62
21,000	11,420	2,395	13,815	66
42,000	27,263	3,684	30,948	73

* Taxes are for a family with one wage earner.

** Indirect taxes are estimates.

Source: Skattebetarnas Forening, "Fakta för Skattebetalare" (Stockholm, 1973), p. 7.

Government Expenditures. Total national government expenditures as set forth in the 1973–1974 budget amounted to $15.23 billion. The two most important categories of expenditures are for national defense and social

[8] Erik Lundberg, "Sweden's Economy in an International Perspective," *Quarterly Review* (Skandinaviska Banken, First Quarter, 1971), p. 7.

welfare. The latter includes expenditures on education and research, health and social services, general social security measures, and family allowances. Sweden has a highly developed social security and welfare system. The major components of the system are summarized below.

The Family Allowance. A family allowance of $260 per child per year is paid to families with children. It is paid in quarterly installments to the mother and is not subject to the Swedish income tax. It is the second largest transfer payment item in the Swedish budget after old age pensions. It is financed out of general government revenues. There are no contributions from employers and employees. In 1972 family allowance expenditures amounted to 1.4 percent of the Swedish gross national product, 4 percent of national budget expenditures, and 8 percent of total transfer payments.[9] In addition to the family allowance, there are free holiday grants to children under 14 who come from families with taxable incomes of less than $1,450 a year.

Housing. The provision of adequate housing for all persons is a paramount socioeconomic objective in Sweden. Much emphasis has been placed on housing construction and, to some extent, Swedish credit policies have been subverted to this end. Government housing credits are designed to have priority on credit available in the open market and are used as a means for controlling the volume of housing construction in the country. In addition, housing allowances, which are designed to cover at least a part of rents, are paid to about one third of all Swedish families. A system of rent control also is in effect, with rent increases subject to government approval.[10]

Old Age and Invalidity Pensions. Family and housing allowances are designed to improve the economic status of the family; pensions, to improve the economic position of the aged and disabled. There is a basic old age pension for everyone who reaches age 67, as well as a supplementary old age pension. The basic old age pension amounts to $110 a month for a single person and $180 a month for a married couple. At their discretion, however, Swedish citizens can apply for their old age pensions at the age of 63 or defer it until 70 by accepting a reduction or premium in the amount of the pension. The pension is financed by a tax on the employee of 5 percent of income, with a maximum payment of $315 a year. The employer contributes nothing, and the central government finances 70 percent of the cost of the basic pension out of general revenues.

The supplementary old age pension is also payable at age 67. The benefits under this pension program depend upon one's earned income during the period of active employment. The pension amounts to 3 percent of average annual earnings between $1,323 and $11,498 times the years of coverage with the maximum set at 60 percent of earnings. The pension is tied to the cost of living. It is financed by a tax on the employer of 10 percent of each employee's wages between $1,323 and $11,498.

---

[9] *The Swedish Budget, 1973–1974,* p. 61.
[10] *Ibid.,* p. 63.

The general level of total old age pensions—basic national pensions plus supplementary pensions—amounts to approximately two thirds of the average annual earnings of the pensioners during their 15 best years of income.

There are also basic and supplementary invalidity pensions which provide the same amounts as the regular old age pensions and are financed out of the same taxes. Both types of pensions provide for children's and housing supplements, as well as for a widow's pension which amounts to 90 percent of the basic pension and 40 percent of the supplementary pension.

The Compulsory Health Program. A compulsory health program is financed by contributions from the insured which are based on income. A person who makes less than $378 a year pays nothing. On incomes above this amount, the insured pays an amount for both case and medical benefits which is based on income and the region in which the insured lives. The employer contributes to the health program through payment of a 3 percent tax on payrolls up to $11,498 a year. The national government contributes to the cost out of general revenues.

There is a guarantee of income for loss of work caused by illness. A standard sickness benefit of $1.26 a day is payable to all insured persons. Also there is a supplement, which ranges from $1.26 to $10.92 a day and which varies directly with income, payable to all persons earning more than $546 a year. In addition, there are children's supplements which range from $.21 a day for one to two children to $.63 a day for five or more children. Workers with two children, hospitalized for two weeks, would receive two thirds of their income in sickness benefits.

Maternity allowances, which also range from $.21 to $10.92 a day depending on income, are payable for a period of 180 days. There is also a lump-sum maternity grant of $226.80. Besides these, there is the free service of a trained midwife before, during, and after childbirth and free maternity care in a hospital.

The compulsory health program covers all of the population. It pays three fourths of medical fees and travel expenses, part of the cost of medicines (vitally important medicines, such as insulin, are free), and the total cost of hospital treatment.

Unemployment Insurance. Unemployment insurance, which is voluntary, covers the majority of persons who are exposed to the risk of unemployment. There are 49 unemployment insurance societies, each representing a particular union, but administered separately from the union to which the worker belongs. Benefits, which range between certain maximums and minimums, are paid on a daily basis and can amount to a maximum of $12 a day, payable up to 200 days. There is also a dependent's supplement of $.42 a day for the spouse and all children under 16. The compensation is financed by a levy on all insured persons, which ranges from $1.05 to $5.04 a month according to the society, and government subsidies to the various funds, which range from $.42 to $1.05 per day of unemployment, the actual amount varying with each society's incidence of unemployment.

Approximately one third of the cost of unemployment compensation is met by worker contributions and two thirds by national government contributions. The employer contributes nothing.

A summary of central government expenditures in the 1973–1974 draft budget is presented in Table 13–4.

TABLE 13–4
SWEDISH GOVERNMENT EXPENDITURES FOR 1973–1974

Expenditures	Millions of Dollars *
Defense	1,822
Education	2,415
Social Security **	2,263
Health and related services	699
Communication	1,341
Support to families with children	945
Housing	752
Labor market policies	865
Miscellaneous	2,109
Total	13,211

* In 1973, 1 krona equaled $.23.
** The basic old age pension scheme is the only part of the social security system that is listed in the national budget.
Source: Ministry of Finance, *The Swedish Budget* (Stockholm, 1973), p. 39.

Income Redistribution. Income redistribution in Sweden is accomplished through progressive income taxation and transfer payments from the public to the private sector. As mentioned previously, there are two income taxes in Sweden—a national income tax levied on behalf of the national government and a local income tax levied on behalf of the local government units.

Distribution Through Taxation. Regardless of the criteria used, the level of taxation in Sweden is the highest of any industrial country. A comparative study made by Erik Lundberg indicates that taxes and social security contributions amount to 48.1 percent of Swedish gross national product in comparison to 20.6 percent for Japan, 30.0 percent for the United States, 37.1 percent for West Germany, and 37.4 percent for the United Kingdom. When direct taxes, i.e., income taxes, are isolated from total taxes, Sweden has the highest level relative to personal income of all industrial countries. For example, direct taxes amounted to 30.0 percent of personal income compared to 10.1 percent for Japan, 19.8 percent for the United States, and 18.9 percent for the United Kingdom. The average marginal income tax rate is 46 percent in Sweden compared to 20 percent in the United States and 13 percent in Japan.[11]

[11] Lundberg, *op. cit.*, p. 7.

Swedish personal income taxes have an important impact upon the distribution of income in that they divert a part of the flow of personal income away from savings and private consumption, and thus alter the distribution of money income that results from the play of market forces. In Sweden, as a result of the extensive use of income taxes, the upper income groups have to pay more for government services and transfers than do the lower income groups. The end result is that there is a substantial equalization of both money and real income. But Swedish income taxes, given their nature, inevitably reduce the volume of investment, partly by reducing the volume of savings that would normally come from the upper income groups, and partly by reducing the level of consumption and thus the profitability of additional investment.

TABLE 13–5

INCOME DISTRIBUTION IN SWEDEN BEFORE AND AFTER TAXES, 1970 *
(In Millions of Dollars)

Income Classes	Taxpayers	Income Before Taxes	Taxpayers	Income After Taxes
$ 0 to $ 760	39,489	18.8	135,215	63.6
761 to 1,899	576,457	792.5	824,745	1,156.9
1,900 to 2,849	522,364	1,213.2	860,812	2,021.0
2,850 to 3,799	437,945	1,430.8	693,538	2,293.9
3,800 to 4,749	455,811	1,925.1	479,209	2,044.5
4,750 to 5,699	426,011	2,206.4	337,599	1,762.7
5,700 to 7,599	587,634	3,898.2	306,342	2,034.8
7,600 to 9,499	345,665	2,951.9	82,894	707.6
9,500 to 11,399	178,500	1,863.3	29,783	310.7
11,400 to 18,999	172,931	2,461.2	25,082	356.8
19,000 and over	38,554	1,031.2	5,142	146.2
	3,781,361	19,792.6	3,780,361	12,898.7

* In 1970, 1 krona equaled $0.19.

Sources: Statistika Centralbyran, "Inkomst och Formogenhetsfordelningen Ar 1970," *Statistiska Meddelanden, 1971* (Stockholm, 1971), pp. 16 and 18; and Statistika Centralbyran, *Statistiska Arsbok för Sverege 1972* (Stockholm, 1973), pp. 333–334.

The extent to which income taxes affect Swedish income distribution is apparent in Table 13–5. The reduction in the number of upper income taxpayers is particularly significant. Approximately 10 percent of all taxpaying units had net incomes of $10,000 or more before taxes in 1970, but less than 2 percent had after-tax incomes of that amount. The upper 1 percent of all taxpayers was reduced to 0.15 percent after taxes. The impact of income taxation as well as the cost of the Swedish welfare state is reflected in the table. Total taxes amounted to $7.6 billion out of total taxable income of $21.9 billion. The magnitude of direct taxes in Sweden is reflected in the fact that almost half of a given increase in household incomes is consumed by taxes.

No other country is anywhere near Sweden in this respect. Conversely, the rate of saving is much lower in Sweden than in most countries. For example, savings average around 5 percent of Swedish personal income compared to a ratio of 20 percent for Japan.

Distribution Through Transfer Payments. Large sums of money are redistributed through the medium of transfer payments in Sweden. As mentioned previously, there are transfers designed to benefit certain sectors of society, such as family allowances and old age pensions. There are also grants to certain sectors of the economy, such as agricultural subsidies, which result in lower prices for goods and services. Finally, there are some services provided by the government that are, in effect, nonmonetary transfers, such as free education. This analysis, however, is limited to direct monetary transfers to households, which amounted to $5.88 billion in 1972, or around 18 percent of personal income. The extent to which incomes are redistributed through income transfers is going to depend on a taxpayer's position on the income ladder.

Swedish studies on income redistribution tend to confirm that major gains in redistribution through transfer payments and other forms of government expenditures are confined primarily to the lowest income groups.[12] A break-even point, where taxes counterbalance gains from expenditures, is reached rather rapidly. For example, in 1967 this break-even point was around $2,200 on a per capita basis. What this means is that taxes more than counterbalance gains for the majority of taxpayers who received more than 80 percent of total income. It is not only the upper income groups, but the average income groups as well who defray the cost of income redistribution.

Distribution of transfer payments between income groups favors the non-active segment of the Swedish population over the active segment. For example, the average annual income of all persons who were fully employed was $5,208 in 1967.[13] Average taxes amounted to $1,659, while average income from various transfers amounted to $252—a net loss, so to speak, of $1,407. On the other hand, those who were partially employed, or who were receiving old age pensions, showed a net gain in terms of income. For low income earners, typically those receiving $1,050 or less in 1967, transfer payments accounted for around 60 percent of total income. But again, it is not necessary to reinforce the point that on balance the loss in terms of redistribution hits the active segment of society. In 1967 the average annual income in agriculture was $1,470. Direct taxes amounted to $693, while income from government transfers amounted to $630—a net loss of $63.

Fiscal Policy. The general economic policy of the Swedish government has been to achieve a high level of employment. This objective stems from circumstances which prevailed in Sweden between the two world wars. The average unemployment rate in the period 1923–1930 was 11 percent; in the period

---

[12] The studies used were as follows: Lars Soderstrom, *Laginkomstproblemet* (Stockholm: Statens Offentliga Utredningar, 1972); and Lars Soderstrom, *Den Svenska Kopkraftsfordelningen 1967* (Stockholm: Statens Offentliga Utredningar, 1971).

[13] *Den Svenska Kopkraftsfordelningen, ibid.,* p. 52.

1930–1933, the unemployment rate was 19 percent; and in the period 1933–1937, the average rate was 16 percent.[14] In the period 1929–1939 the average unemployment rate was 16 percent.[15] However, Sweden has had a very high level of employment in general since World War II. Unemployment has averaged less than 2 percent since the war, and the supply of labor has been so short in some areas that many workers have been brought in from other countries.

Investment Reserve as an Instrument of Fiscal Policy. One of the main sources of economic growth is investment. It is required, not only to increase the total stock of equipment and buildings, but also to allow labor to be employed on increasingly productive jobs as old plant and machinery is replaced by new. However, investment is the most unstable component of aggregate demand, and economists have long been interested in measures that would stabilize investment practices.

The Swedish government has attempted to influence the timing of private investment projects through special tax concessions to firms that are willing to postpone their particular investment projects so as to fit them into a more stable general pattern.[16] The device used is the *investment reserve*. Its purpose is to encourage private corporate savings in periods of high profits and private capital expenditures in periods of unemployment. Companies are encouraged to set aside part of their pretax profits in a reserve which is deposited in the Bank of Sweden (*Sveriges Riksbank*), and if these funds are used for investments in buildings, machinery, and inventories during a period when investment is desirable for employment purposes, substantial tax privileges are obtainable.

The investment reserve operates as follows: Swedish companies are permitted to set aside, at their own discretion, up to 40 percent of pretax profits in a reserve for economic stabilization. This amount is deductible for purposes of both the national and local income taxes. Forty-six percent of the amount must be deposited in a non-interest-bearing account in the Bank of Sweden, and the remaining 54 percent remains a part of a company's working capital. No government permission is needed to set aside this reserve.

The investment reserve has been released to stimulate the Swedish economy on four occasions—in 1958, 1962, 1967, and 1971. The funds were released for specific investment purposes, spelled out either by geographical area,

---

[14] Erik Lundberg, *Business Cycles and Economic Policy* (Cambridge, Mass.: Harvard University Press, 1957) p. 52.

[15] Post World War II economic policy in Sweden stems from the economic conditions that prevailed in the country between World Wars I and II. An emphasis on maintaining a high level of employment regardless of the consequences has characterized Swedish economic policy.

[16] The World Tax Series volume, *Taxation in Sweden,* makes this statement on p. 69: "No country has sought more vigorously to use taxation, together with other fiscal, monetary, and regulatory measures, as a tool to affect the business cycle. Sweden has employed pioneering tax devices to make the economy more resistant to depressions and to influence the propensity to invest on the part of business firms; in this way it has sought to enlist private capital in leveling the business cycle."

economic sector, or both. For example, the reserve was released in 1967 to stimulate employment in the construction industry. In 1962 the investment reserve was released to stimulate employment in the paper and pulp, building construction, and machine tool industries.[17]

If Swedish companies use their investment reserve funds when they are authorized to do so by the national government, they are entitled to certain tax benefits. When the reserve is used, it is not restorable to taxable income. In addition, companies are entitled to an extra investment deduction of 10 percent of the reserve used, which is permitted in the tax assessment in their next income tax return.[18]

Budgets as Instruments of Fiscal Policy. In the postwar period there has been much interest in the fact that the Scandinavian countries, including Sweden, have made a thorough trial of the use of national economic budgets as a means of providing the general framework for the coordination of economic policies, both public and private. The purpose of the national economic budget is the projection of national economic goals or objectives within which fiscal, monetary, wage and price policies could be worked out and coordinated in the national interest. It is an aid to economic policy.[19] The national budget is prepared by the Ministry of Finance, and it contains a survey of the general economic development anticipated for the fiscal year based on the preliminary national economic accounts for the previous calendar year. The budget also provides an estimated balance of resources, that is, a table showing the expected total supply of goods and services within the country, and the use of these for different purposes.

The regular budget for the fiscal year 1973–1974 provides a good example of anti-recession fiscal policy. Because of various factors, such as a decline in consumer expenditures and exports, the Swedish economy experienced some unemployment in 1972 and 1973. For the 1973–1974 fiscal period, a deficit was planned for the Swedish budget. Changes were made in income tax payments that were designed to put more money into the hands of consumers. Government outlays, particularly of the transfer payment type, were to be increased by 12 percent during the fiscal year. More funds were to be allocated to public

[17] The Swedish investment reserve is a well known fiscal policy device which has received international attention. For a comprehensive treatment of the investment reserve, see Martin Schnitzer, *The Swedish Investment Reserve, A Device for Economic Stabilization* (Washington: American Enterprise Institute for Public Policy Research, 1967). Also see Gunnar Eliasson, *Investment Reserve Funds in Operation* (Stockholm: National Institute of Economic Research, 1967), and Sven-Erik Johansson, "An Appraisal of the Swedish System of Investment Reserve," *The International Journal of Accounting,* Vol. 1, No. 1 (Fall, 1965) pp. 85–92.

[18] In other words, a company which used its investment reserve in 1967 would be permitted to deduct 10 percent of the amount from taxable income in its income tax return for 1968.

[19] The national budget is not the same thing as the regular budget. The *regular budget* consists of the current and capital budgets and contains the proposals on government incomes and expenditures during the coming fiscal year. The *national budget* is really an economic survey or forecast. It is submitted together with the regular, or *state budget,* in January of each year to the Swedish Parliament for approval. The Swedish fiscal year begins on July 1.

works projects in order to provide employment for the unemployed, and special measures designed to encourage business investments were continued.[20]

Taxes and expenditures through the use of the regular budget are the instruments of Swedish fiscal policy. On the expenditure side, it is mainly public investment outlays that can be varied for economic stabilization purposes. Since investments involving practically all road building, electric power stations, railroad transportation, and telecommunications are covered by the budget, there is wide leverage for stabilization policies. Even more important is the fact that the volume of housing construction is directly influenced by the government. About 90 percent of all houses are built with government loans at subsidized interest rates. By changing the amounts allocated in the budget for housing loans, the government is able to influence the volume of housing construction.[21]

The Banking System

The Swedish credit market is characterized by a multiplicity of types of credit institutions, public and private, among which the division of functions is not clearly defined. Some institutions are limited by statute to one particular type of lending operation as in the case of mortgage banks; other institutions, like the commercial banks, conduct highly diversified operations and compete very actively with almost every type of specialized credit institution. Swedish credit institutions can be classified under the following four headings: the central bank, commercial banks, savings banks, and various specialized credit institutions.

The Bank of Sweden. The Bank of Sweden is the oldest central bank in the world. It was organized in 1668 as a state owned bank responsible to the Swedish Parliament, after the failure in that year of a predecessor institution, the Bank of Stockholm, chartered in 1656 and considered to be the first bank in the world to issue ordinary bank notes.

The Bank of Sweden is state owned and legally responsible to the Swedish Parliament, which elects six of its seven directors. The chairman is appointed by the King in Council. Current administration of the Bank is handled by a Board of Management consisting of the Governor of the Bank, a Deputy Governor, two directors, and several managers. The chief executive officers, the Governor and Deputy Governor, are elected by the Board of Directors from among its seven members.

The functions of the Bank are as follows:

1. It regulates the supply of money and the level of interest rates on the credit market, for which purposes it exercises the regular powers of monetary policy.
2. It also holds the country's main gold and foreign exchange reserves and is responsible for the fixing of official exchange rates.

---

[20] The Swedish draft budget for 1973–1974.

[21] Martin Schnitzer, *Unemployment Programs in Sweden* (Washington: Joint Economic Committee, 88th Congress of the United States, 1964), p. 48.

3. It conducts lending operations on a limited scale—such lending being concerned primarily with loans to state owned corporations and certain small loans which are made out of special funds appropriated for social purposes.

The Commercial Banks. There are 16 commercial banks in Sweden, of which 15 are privately owned, and one, Sveriges Kreditbank, is government owned. The four largest privately owned commercial banks, the Svenska Handelsbanken, the Skandinaviska Banken, the Stockholm Enskilda Bank, and the Goteborgs Bank, account for about 70 percent of all commercial banking in Sweden. These banks operate throughout Sweden as well as internationally. The largest bank, the Svenska Handelsbanken, accounts for approximately one third of all of commercial banking. The Sveriges Kreditbank, which was created as a result of a bank reorganization in 1951, accounts for about 6 percent of the commercial banking business.

The functions of the Swedish commercial banks are as follows:

1. They engage in the long-term financing of industry.
2. They act as underwriters for bond issues and hold large portfolios of bonds and housing mortgages.
3. They maintain stock exchange departments, which act as brokers on the Stockholm Stock Exchange.[22]
4. They receive savings and time deposits.[23]
5. They are responsible for foreign trade transactions—a very important responsibility since foreign trade is a vital factor in Sweden's economy, and fluctuations in it are quickly reflected in the country's general level of prosperity.

The Savings Banks. Private savings banks also play a significant role in Swedish banking. In 1972 there were 403 of them. They are small in size and differ from the commercial banks in that they are nonprofit institutions with no shareholders. Although the savings banks are private in ownership, they are subject to governmental control since at least half of their governing bodies must be appointed by local government authorities.

Savings banks collect small- or medium-sized savings. These funds are invested in mortgage loans, loans to small business firms, loans to local governments, personal consumer loans, and government bonds. Swedish savings banks are of particular importance in the urban real estate market. In addition to the regular savings banks, the Post Office Savings Bank (Postsparbanken) also provides an outlet for savings. These savings are used to finance housing construction.

Specialized Credit Institutions. Sweden also has a great many specialized credit institutions, which are mainly concerned with mortgage lending. Some are privately owned; others are publicly owned. There are special mortgage banks for agriculture, home building, and shipbuilding. An example of a

---

[22] Around 90 percent of all transactions on the Stockholm Stock Exchange are handled by the stock exchange departments of the commercial banks.

[23] A preponderance of time and savings deposits characterizes the structure of Swedish commercial banks. Time and savings deposits account for approximately 85 percent of total deposits.

mortgage bank is the Ship Mortgage Bank. Its purpose is to grant long-term loans on the security of ship mortgages. It is a semi-official institution in that its chairman is appointed by the Swedish government. Its loan funds are obtained from open market bond sales.

In 1967 a special lending institution, Sveriges Investeringsbank (Investment Bank of Sweden) was created by the Swedish government for the purpose of providing for the long-term financing of industrial investment. The objective is to guarantee the long-term prospects for full employment in Sweden through the provision of funds that would be used to promote structural concentration in the older branches of Swedish industry, such as pulp and steel, and to accelerate the growth rate of new industries. The source of capital to the Bank is the sale of government bonds to the National Pension Fund.

The National Pension Fund is also an important credit institution. In fact, since its creation in 1960, it has become the largest credit institution in Sweden. It obtains its funds from taxes which finance old age pensions. The government, however, does not have direct control over the Fund's operation; it is run by a tripartite board consisting of union, employer, and government representatives. The Fund is limited in that it cannot lend directly to industry; it is entitled to buy only national, municipal, and industrial bonds.

Monetary Policy. Monetary policy is exercised by the Bank of Sweden in several ways, including the following:

1. Through open market operations;
2. Through rediscount rate adjustments; and
3. Through the use of liquidity ratios which are established for commercial banks and other lending institutions.[24]

In general, monetary policy has been subverted during the postwar period to the general economic policy of the Swedish government, which has been the attainment of a high level of employment. Until the latter part of the 1950s, monetary policy was passive. The Bank of Sweden had to pursue a cheap money policy in accordance with the full employment and social welfare policies of the government. Until 1955 the Bank pegged the government bond market in order to permit the flotation of the large number of bond issues necessary to finance the budget deficits and the housing program. The Bank also exercised control over capital issues, under which applications to float long-term securities were screened to assure that loans for priority sectors, that is, the national government and the housing market, received preferential treatment.

---

[24] Commercial banks' holdings of *liquid assets*, that is, mainly cash and short-term government securities, are fixed at a certain percentage of total deposits, excluding savings accounts. These liquidity ratios are differentiated according to the size of the banks. For example, for the largest banks they are 30 percent of deposits, and for the smallest banks, 25 percent. These ratios, of course, are varied from time to time in accordance with monetary policy objectives. A decrease in a bank's liquidity ratio reduces its capacity to lend.

However, monetary policy in recent years has been given freer reign by the Swedish government. Sweden is an export-oriented country, and rising domestic prices have affected the international competitiveness of Swedish industry. Imports have exceeded exports in each year from 1963 to 1972, while the consumer price index has increased 53 percent during the same period of time.

Labor-Management Relations

Management and labor in Sweden are strongly organized. Both have formed central organizations—the Swedish Employers' Confederation for the employers and the Confederation of Swedish Trade Unions and the Central Organization of Salaried Employees for the workers. In addition to these groups, there is the Swedish Confederation of Professional Associations which includes professional workers—doctors, lawyers, engineers, and teachers—and an organization representing civil service personnel called the Central Organization of State Employees.

The Confederation of Swedish Trade Unions (LO). The Confederation of Swedish Trade Unions represents about 95 percent of all production workers in the country and has about 1,500,000 members. Thirty-nine unions with 6,202 branches are included in this organization. There is a congress which consists of 300 delegates elected by the members of the unions. It meets every fifth year. The congress elects the executive board. This consists of 13 people. There is a general council of 140 members which meets twice a year. Its members are also elected by the unions.

The local organizations which constitute the fundamental units of LO are of three different kinds. In each place where a productive enterprise is in operation, the workers join a local union which, in turn, is associated with an industry-wide union. If there are several enterprises in the same industrial branch in one place, independently working organizations, called *factory sections*, are organized at each plant and are parts of the local union. In places where there are several branches of production represented and there is more than one local union involved, these unions are combined into *local trade councils*. These have no duties with regard to wage policies.

The Swedish union movement has been marked by centralism. There have been worked out within LO so-called model statutes which the affiliated unions must accept. According to these rules, the locals do not have the right to take any sort of coercive action without receiving the national union's permission. In connection with negotiations for wage agreements, the members involved elect delegates to a wage conference which discusses and decides on the cancellation of existing agreements. The wage conference appoints a delegation whose purpose is to negotiate for a new agreement. When the negotiations are over, the result is laid before the wage conference and the national union's board for examination and approval or disapproval.

If a union has exhausted the possibilities of negotiation without being able to reach an acceptable result and decides in favor of open conflict, it must, according to law, announce the work stoppage seven days before the strike is called. Union rules in such cases require a union to obtain LO board approval of the strike announcement if as much as 3 percent of the union's membership is involved. If the union should refuse to ask LO for permission or announce a strike against the will of the board, it loses the right to economic and moral support from all of the member unions in LO.

The Central Organization of Salaried Employees (TCO). TCO is comprised of 27 unions with 2,500 local branches. There are 529,000 members of which 300,000 are employed in private enterprises and 229,000 in state and municipal administration and services. About 75 percent of the employees not engaged in actual production—foremen, office employees of all types, sales personnel, and engineers—are affiliated with this organization.

The Swedish Employers' Confederation (SAF). SAF is by far the largest organization of employers in Sweden. Not only the greatest part of Swedish industry, but groups of enterprises engaged in handicrafts, transportation, and other services have associated themselves with this organization in order to present a common front in employer-employee relations. Forty-three employer associations belong to SAF. These associations involve some 25,000 enterprises with 1,200,000 employees.[25]

There are also a number of associations outside of SAF in banking and insurance, commerce, shipping, agriculture and forestry, and service trades. The cooperative movement and the fields of national and local government have employers' associations of their own. However, the policies laid down by the SAF usually set the pattern for the negotiations.

The SAF began as a defensive body to take care of the employers' interests in disputes with labor unions. This has meant that the top organization must maintain a united employer front, and that, in turn, has called for concentrated power. The employer associations must get SAF's approval of their constitutions or any amendments to them. Every labor contract must have the SAF's approval, and members are liable to penalties if they ignore this rule or break the employer front in an open conflict by making a separate agreement contrary to the SAF line. Finally, it gives financial assistance to its members during an open conflict, provided the conflict is legal and in conformity with the constitution of the SAF.[26]

Collective Bargaining. Industry-wide collective bargaining is the most usual form in Sweden. For example, there is one union for metalworkers. Both skilled and unskilled workers belong to it. However, this may differ from trade to trade. Nevertheless, there are certain points which are characteristic of the

[25] The largest association is the Swedish Metal Trades Employers Association with 1,689 members and 312,468 workers. The second largest is the Federation of Swedish Building Employers with 1,799 members and 97,014 employees. Other large employer associations are the Swedish Iron and Steel Works Association and the Swedish Textile Employers Association.

[26] T. L. Johnston, *Collective Bargaining in Sweden* (London: George Allen and Unwin, Ltd., 1962), pp. 68–81.

Swedish system. If neither the labor nor management federation in a given trade gives notice of termination of contract by a specified time—normally three months—before it expires, the contract is automatically renewed. Otherwise, the union usually makes the first move. It holds a contract conference to decide its requests. Delegates to such conferences, elected by the locals in proportion to their membership, vote on the new demands to be presented to management and elect negotiators. The corresponding organization on the employers' side discusses the specific demands of the union, determines the approach that should be followed, and marshals its bargaining forces.[27]

Collective bargaining is free from compulsory arbitration. Legislation enters only at three points: (1) it makes existing collective contracts enforceable and compels arbitration in cases of disputes over interpretation or application; (2) it makes the intervention of a government mediator obligatory if the parties cannot reach agreement in negotiations for new contracts; and (3) it requires one week's notice of strikes or lockouts if mediation fails.[28]

The collective bargaining contracts are concluded for a specific period of time—usually one or two years. When the contracts have been established, direct action, such as strikes, cannot be carried out during the period of the contract.[29] Disputes must be settled peacefully. If the terms of a contract have been violated, an employer can take the union into court and sue for damages, or vice versa. It is only after the contract has expired, that employers and unions are free to take any direct action to influence the terms of the collective agreement. During the period of the contract, peace prevails.[30] The individual employers can make their plans with a greater degree of assurance. This is especially important for competition which involves foreign markets where delivery can often be upset by labor disputes.

Government and Business

The Swedish government participates in the business sector of the economy through the ownership and operation of legal monopolies on alcohol and tobacco, transportation and communications media, certain public utilities, partial ownership in several iron ore mines and steel mills, and control of the Sveriges Kreditbank.

The Board of Telecommunications operates the telephone network and transmission facilities for radio and television. The production of radio and television equipment is entrusted to an independent company, Sveriges Radio, operating under a special charter which guarantees it complete autonomy. Radio and television activities are financed by special license fees—at present $6.30 and $21 a year—on families owning radios or television sets.

---

[27] *Ibid.*, pp. 89–97.

[28] Folke Schmidt, *The Law of Labor Relations in Sweden* (Stockholm: Almquist and Wicksell, 1963), pp. 263–278.

[29] Once entered into, a contract is binding all along the line, from the national federation to the individual employers and union members.

[30] Labor-management relations have been very good in Sweden. The number of days lost by strikes is negligible when compared to the number of days lost because of strikes in the United States.

The State Power Board is the largest purveyor of electric power in Sweden, controlling about 50 percent of total production. Government grants entirely finance the operations of the company. The Swedish government also owns, or has a controlling interest in, a limited number of business enterprises. Most of these companies have been created or acquired for reasons of public interest. Thus, the Norrbottens Jarnverk ironworks was built during World War II to increase domestic steel production and also to create employment in northern Sweden.[31] The Statens Skogsindustrier was created out of a number of private companies in the lumber, cellulose, and paper industries. These companies had difficulty in maintaining production in the 1930s and were taken over to keep up employment in a number of localities in northern and central Sweden.

The largest of the government owned enterprises is the iron ore mines, Luossavaara-Kurunavaara, with sales amounting to $189 million annually and with a labor force of 8,500. The total ore yield in 1969 amounted to 77 percent of Swedish iron ore production for that year.

However, private enterprise is dominant in the Swedish economy, and nationalization of industry has not been a part of the program of the Social Democratic party, which has been in office since 1934. The widely publicized cooperative movement is important only in retailing, the distribution of farm products, and housing.

No country in the world has used fiscal measures to the extent that Sweden has to influence the rate and volume of business investment. A system of freely chosen depreciation accounting techniques were permitted for a number of years, but was discontinued in the 1950s.[32] It was replaced by a stricter depreciation system which includes declining balance and straight-line methods. The new system is still regarded as very liberal by U.S. and European standards.

Although the Bank of Sweden has direct control over credit, the government prefers to use other devices to encourage business firms to follow policy goals. These goals are spelled out in the national budget. The national budget, as distinguished from the current budget, and the capital budget, pertains to national economic goals within which fiscal, monetary, wage, and price policies are to be worked out and coordinated in the national interest.[33] The national budget presents an appraisal of the outlook for the Swedish economy for the forthcoming calendar year: what may be expected to happen, for example, to gross national product, the rate of economic growth, wages, prices, and the like.

---

[31] Norrbottens Jarnverk accounts for 19 percent of all Swedish steel production. It represents an attempt by the Swedish government to industrialize the depressed area of northern Sweden.

[32] *Free depreciation* means that corporate taxpayers have the right to write off machinery and equipment for tax purposes in any way they see fit. Free depreciation provides an incentive to modernize for the reason that the entire cost of an asset could be written off during a tax year.

[33] Gosta Rehn, "The National Budget and Economic Policy," *Quarterly Review*, No. 2 (Skandinaviska Banken, 1962).

Economic policy coordination between the government, business, and labor is more extensive and thorough than in most European countries. This coordination is based on extensive consultations between the three groups, consultations which are based on the understanding that cooperation is necessary if Sweden is to compete successfully in the export markets.

Economic Planning

Economic planning of the French type, in which a set of goals or targets are provided as objectives to be achieved over a period of time and an actual planning mechanism provided to guide resources in the desired direction, does not exist in Sweden. However, planning is used in Sweden as a source of information for the government and private enterprise in the planning of public policy.[34]

Swedish planning takes the form of a long-term economic forecast which usually spans a five-year period.[35] The rationale of the survey is to provide information about the various sectors of the Swedish economy, so that relevant economic decisions can be made by government and private enterprise.

Previously, Swedish long-term planning was entrusted to independent committees appointed by the government. Later plans, however, were carried out within the Ministry of Finance, where a special Economic Planning Secretariat was established. Within the Secretariat, a Planning Council was created. This Council is composed of representatives of industry, labor, and public corporations, along with the economic experts of the government. It meets under the chairmanship of the Minister of Finance, and it is responsible for the development of alternative economic policies to be followed within the framework of the plan or forecast.

The current economic forecasts reflect a viewpoint that the individual's choice of consumption of goods and services produced by both the public and private sectors should be expressed by his preferences in the market place through prices that correspond to the cost of production to the economy. This arrangement ensures an optimum allocation of natural resources in relation to consumer preferences. The view is expressed that fees and taxes should be fixed at such a level that prices paid by consumers reflect social costs and that subsidies, which keep prices lower than actual costs, should be removed.[36]

A basic problem of resource allocation—the distribution of labor, which is in unusually short supply—confronts the Swedish economy. This problem of balancing the labor requirements of the public and private sectors of the economy is brought out in the long-term forecast. The supply of labor forecast is based on the following elements: forecasts of the population broken down

[34] In France, planning is an integral part of economic policy and has assumed the character of officially authorized plans. In Sweden, planning has no such official recognition. There are no Swedish plans.

[35] The forecast is called "The Swedish Economy, 1971–1975" and is published by the Ministry of Finance.

[36] Ingvar Svennilson, "Swedish Long-Term Planning—The Fifth Round," *Quarterly Review* (Skandinaviska Banken, Second Quarter, 1966), p. 38.

on the basis of sex, age, and marital status; forecasts of the labor participation rate in various groups of the population; and forecasts of the number of working hours per year.

The forecast indicated that the supply of labor would remain virtually unchanged, not only during the period 1971–1975, but during the decade of the 1970s as well. The Swedish government is now in a position to undertake policy measures which are aimed at increasing the quality and quantity of labor. These measures include a heavy emphasis on job training and retraining, the importation of workers from Finland, Italy, and other countries, and the movement of surplus labor from the farms and forests into areas of labor shortage.

The government is also able to plan in detail the development of those sectors of the economy in which production and distribution are directly its responsibility. It can also act for sectors in which it plays a more indirect, but nevertheless important, role in influencing production and distribution through the use of subsidies, construction permits, and other devices. Important sectors are agriculture and housing. For example, agricultural policy was based on the forecast of a decline in agricultural employment from 208,000 persons in 1970 to 180,000 in 1975.[37] This decline called for a policy which aimed at the consolidation of farm land into larger and viable economic units and at greater mechanization of agriculture to sustain an increase in production at a necessary rate of 5 percent a year to support the population.

Government planning, as applied to the private sector of the economy, involves the provision of information, through the use of the long-term forecast, for firms to follow in making policy decisions. No direct controls or coercion are used to see that firms make the right decisions, and in the application of general economic instruments, such as credit and finance policies, there is no discrimination between firms.

AN APPRAISAL OF THE SWEDISH ECONOMY

The Swedish economic system can be judged on the basis of how well it has accomplished the three basic objectives of full employment, economic growth, and price stability. A fourth objective, an equitable distribution of income, can also be included. In fact, as far as Sweden is concerned, this criterion may well be the most important, for a stated objective of Swedish economic and social policy is a movement toward greater equality in the distribution of income. The end result of this policy may well have results that extend far beyond Sweden. However, the Swedes have failed to define what constitutes a precise and exact end for their efforts to equalize incomes. So the question of how equal can you get is left hanging in the air.

Sweden has had a very high level of employment since World War II. In fact, the supply of labor has been so short that many workers have been brought in from other countries. Unemployment has averaged less than 2

---

[37] "The Swedish Economy, 1971–1975," *op. cit.*, p. 116.

percent a year since the end of the war. In 1972 the average unemployment rate was 2.2 percent. Full employment remains a paramount economic goal, and unemployment rates generally associated with full employment in the United States would topple any Swedish government.

However, if Sweden can be given high marks with respect to full employment, its marks with respect to price stability are at best average in comparison to other countries. During the period 1960–1964, household incomes increased 46 percent compared to a 22 percent increase in the consumer price level. During the period 1965–1968, household incomes increased by 29 percent while consumer prices increased by 11 percent. There was a significant change in the consumer price level for the period 1969–1972. The increase over the four-year period was 32 percent—an average increase of 8 percent a year.[38] Over the same period of time, real household income, which takes into consideration price increases, increased at a rate of 2.5 percent. In 1971 price controls were introduced and were limited primarily to goods and services considered important to consumers.

The rate of economic growth has been about average for Sweden when compared to other modern industrial countries. During the period 1950–1960, Swedish gross domestic product increased at a rate of 3.4 percent a year— a rate which was above that for the United States and the United Kingdom, but below the average rate of 4.0 percent which prevailed for 13 industrialized countries of Western Europe, and well below the 9.0 percent for Japan.[39] During the period 1960–1965, Swedish gross domestic product increased at an average rate of 5.4 percent—a rate above the average of 5.1 percent for the 13 industrial countries of Western Europe, and above the rate of 4.8 percent for the United States and below the rate of 10.1 percent for Japan. However, for the period 1965–1970, the Swedish average annual growth rate of 3.9 percent was below the average of 4.4 percent for Western Europe and was the lowest of the four Nordic countries.[40] The Swedish growth rate for 1970–1975, which reflects 1971 and 1972 data, is forecast at 3.7 percent—a below average rate for the Western European countries and the lowest for the Nordic countries. It is necessary to point out, however, that Sweden is a very highly developed industrial country in comparison to such countries as Austria and Spain.

Finally, and perhaps most important of all, Sweden should be examined from the standpoint of income distribution. The country has unquestionably one of the highest standards of living in the world, ranking second only to the United States in terms of per capita income. The trend in Sweden has been toward greater equality in the distribution of income. This has been achieved in part through progressive income taxation and transfer payments, both of which have a massive redistributive effect on personal income. The end result

---

[38] National Institute of Economic Research, *The Swedish Economy 1972* (Stockholm, 1973), p. 16 and p. 124.

[39] *The Swedish Economy 1971–1975, op. cit.,* pp. 12 and 116. The growth rates are in real rather than money terms.

[40] *Ibid.,* p. 116. The Nordic countries are Denmark, Finland, Norway, and Sweden.

is a redistribution of both money and real income which appears to be more equal in Sweden than in other Western countries. A negative factor is a tax burden which is the highest of any major country in the world.

It is apparent that inequality in the distribution of income is reduced through taxation. The impact can be measured by dividing Swedish taxpayers into quintiles on both a before- and after-tax basis. Table 13–6 reflects the impact of personal income taxes and social security contributions on taxpayers. There is a redistribution in the direction of greater equality because the proportionate share of the upper income groups in total income is reduced and the proportionate share of the lower income groups is raised. The progressiveness of the income tax structure brings this about because the effective rate of taxation—the ratio of total taxes paid to incomes received—increases with the size of income. This means, in other words, that the proportionate share of the total tax burden is greater for the upper income groups; hence, there will be a redistribution in the direction of greater equality.

TABLE 13–6

PERCENTAGE DISTRIBUTION OF SWEDISH INCOME EARNERS BY QUINTILES BEFORE AND AFTER TAXES, 1970

Quintiles	Percentage of Total Before Taxes	Percentage of Total After Taxes
Lowest	5.4	7.2
Second	9.9	13.2
Third	17.6	21.4
Fourth	24.6	24.2
Highest	42.5	34.0
	100.0	100.0

Source: Computations based on Table 13–5. It is to be emphasized that the data are based on the number of persons who were singly or jointly assessed for income taxes.

Transfer payments reduce income inequality even further because their distribution is heavily skewed in favor of households and individuals in the lower income brackets. However, the cost of income redistribution does not come cheap. Sweden leads all industrial countries with respect to the percentage of income increases that are swallowed up by income taxes. Moreover, Sweden ranks near the top of all industrial countries for the share of income increases that are eaten up by price rises. Some disenchantment with the cost of the welfare state was expressed by the Swedish voters in the 1973 elections when the best the ruling Social Democrats could do was to achieve a standoff with the opposition parties.[41] Disenchantment has also been expressed through an increased number of strikes in 1971 and 1972.

[41] Danish voters also expressed general discontent over high taxes and other costs of their welfare state in the December 1973 elections. Opposition candidates scored heavily on an anti-tax platform.

SUMMARY

Sweden, although a small country in terms of population, has an influence on contemporary Western society which is out of proportion to its size. Long known for its humanitarian activities during various catastrophies, Sweden has developed an economic system which is second to none in terms of providing a decent standard of living for everyone. An egalitarian society has been created in which extremes of wealth and poverty do not exist. To a certain extent this may be attributed to a fortuitous set of circumstances which have existed in the country, but probably more important has been the ability of the Swedes to develop measures which have placed an income floor under all types of persons. The major vicissitudes of life are covered through some form of social protection.

Sweden has gone as far as any country in creating a model society. Success has been achieved in maintaining a full employment, an adequate rate of economic growth, and an efficient allocation of resources between consumption and investment. However, this success has not been paralleled by success in preventing the development of continuously rising prices. Moreover, the costs of the welfare state come very high, for Swedish taxpayers carry a tax burden which is the highest of all countries. But, given the objectives of the welfare state which are a more equal distribution of income and the provision of social services to everyone, it is hardly surprising. The impact of high taxes on the Swedish economy is difficult to measure. Nevertheless, a generally low rate of savings has had an effect on investments, with the end result of a fairly low rate of economic growth. There also appears to be some disenchantment, reflected in the 1973 elections, on the part of many Swedish voters over the cost of the welfare state.

QUESTIONS

1. The Swedish economic system has been called the "middle way." What is meant by this term?
2. Income redistribution has been accomplished to a major degree in Sweden. Do you agree?
3. Discuss the roles of the current and capital budgets as instruments of budgetary policy.
4. Compare Swedish and French economic planning.
5. Discuss the various social welfare measures and how each is financed.
6. The basic institutions of capitalism—free enterprise, the profit motive, consumer sovereignty, and the private ownership of property—are left virtually intact in the Swedish economic system. Do you agree?
7. What specific role does the government play in the operation of the economic system?
8. Tax policy plays a fundamental role in resource allocation in Sweden. Discuss this statement.

RECOMMENDED READINGS

Adler-Karlsson, Gunnar. *Functional Socialism: A Swedish Theory for Democratic Socialization.* Stockholm: Prisma, 1969.

Lundberg, Erik. *Business Cycles and Economic Policy.* London: Allen & Univen, Ltd., 1957.

Samuelsson, Kurt. *From Great Power to Welfare State: 300 Years of Swedish Social Development.* London: Allen & Univen, Ltd., 1968.

Schnitzer, Martin. *The Economy of Sweden.* New York: Praeger Publishers, 1970.

————. *The Swedish Investment Reserve: A Device for Economic Stabilization?* Washington: American Enterprise Institute, 1967.

Secretariat for Economic Planning. *The Swedish Economy, 1971—1975.* Stockholm, 1971.

Sweden's Economy, 1950—1965. Stockholm: Svenska Handelsbanken, 1966.

Westerlind, Erik, and Rune Beckman. *Sweden's Economy: Structure and Trends.* Stockholm: Bokforlaget Prisma, 1964.

14

West Germany

INTRODUCTION

The Federal Republic of Germany, or West Germany, was created out of the western portion of the German *Reich*, which had been divided in 1945 into a British, an American, and a French zone of occupation. In 1949 free elections for a Parliament (*Bundestag*) were held, and the Federal Republic of Germany, with its capital at Bonn, was formally established as a federal republic made up of 11 states (*länder*) and West Berlin. A policy of decontrol of the economy was pursued under the direction of Ludwig Erhard, an economics professor who was to become Minister of Economics and then Chancellor of West Germany. He believed that the incentives of a free market economy would serve to liberate long dormant, productive capacities. His policies were enormously successful, and the West German "economic miracle" was created.

The reconstruction of the West German economy since the end of World War II has enabled the country to gain the position of one of the great industrial powers of the world and certainly the outstanding industrial country of the western European mainland. The task, however, was not easy, for when the Third Reich was defeated by the Allied Powers, Germany was divided into two parts. Eastern Germany, which consisted of the provinces of Prussia, Silesia, Pomerania, Brandenburg, and Upper Saxony, fell under the Russian sphere of influence, and from these provinces, the Republic of East Germany was formed. Western Germany, which consisted of the provinces of Westphalia, Bavaria, Lower Saxony, Württemburg, and the Rhineland-Palatinate, fell under British-French-American influence and eventually became the Federal Republic of Germany.

For practical purposes the history of current Germany begins with the end of World War II. Germany had lost the war, damage to industrial capacity was considerable, and the country was split in half. Yet, like the legendary phoenix, West Germany rose from the ashes to become one of the world's leading industrial powers. There were several factors that can explain this renaissance, which are as follows: [1]

[1] Henry C. Wallich, *Mainsprings of the German Revival* (New Haven, Conn.: Yale University Press, 1955). pp. 7–9.

1. The amount and extent of war damage was overrated. The amount of industrial capacity that was destroyed by allied bombing was counterbalanced by that which was constructed during the war. At the end of the war, Germany found herself with better than prewar industrial capacity. War damages and dismantling policies pursued by the allies led to replacement of old plants with newer, more modern ones.
2. Although split in two by the partition, the western part of Germany retained most of the prewar industrial base. This base was concentrated in the capital goods industries. These goods were needed, not only for German reconstruction, but for world markets in general. While other countries concentrated on the production of consumer goods for export, West Gemany concentrated on the production of capital goods.
3. A low level of imports and a favorable trade balance caused by the Korean War also contributed to the recovery of the West German economy.

Marshall Plan aid also played an important role in the revival of West Germany. Some 4.5 billion dollars were spent in helping Germany recover from its war losses. This aid supported the modernization of plants and equipment by supplying foreign exchange and investment funds.

Postwar Reliance on Market Forces. The German economy relied on market forces and incentives instead of controls to accomplish recovery from the devastation brought about by the war. Anti-inflationary and sound currency policies were pursued. To channel profits into investment and saving, income tax rates were modified in favor of savers and investors. A policy of free markets was adopted, but was by no means uniformly applied to all sectors of the German economy. This policy was carried out under the direction of the future Federal German Minister of Economics, Ludwig Erhard, who, with the support of the non-Socialist parties, gambled that the incentives of a free market economy would stimulate long dormant productive capacities. He felt that the function of the government was to provide the economy with principles and broad guidelines of economic policy. Government was to see that neither social privileges nor artificial monopolies impeded the natural process by which economic forces reached and maintained a state of equilibrium and that the operation of supply and demand was allowed full play.[2]

Erhard felt that the contradistinction was not between free and planned economic systems, nor between capitalist and socialist economic systems, but between a market economy with free price level adjustments and an authoritarian economy with state control extended over production and distribution.[3] In this market economy, any mistake in judgment in the management of production or distribution produced concomitant repercussions through price changes in the market place. In a state directed economy, the same mistakes would not be reflected in changes in the pricing mechanism, but would be covered up, eventually causing serious misallocation of resources. Market reaction to mistakes would be eliminated and the consumer deprived of all freedom of choice.

[2] Ludwig Erhard, *The Economics of Success* (Princeton: D. Van Nostrand Co., Inc., 1963).

[3] *Ibid.*, pp. 9 and 10.

Postwar German economic policy revolved around the combination of personal freedom and social welfare within the framework of a competitive economy. Social welfare programs became among the most comprehensive and extensive in Europe. The German government, in addition to its expenditures on social welfare measures, also relied heavily on tax incentives to stimulate savings and investment. In 1948 special depreciation allowances for various types of investment were introduced. High income tax rates, introduced subsequent to the end of the war to finance reparations and to combat inflation, were reduced to stimulate saving. Corporate tax exemptions permitted tax-free reinvestment of 10 or 15 percent of total profits.

Tax incentives were designed primarily to stimulate investment on the part of German enterprises. It was felt that the paramount postwar need was to rebuild productive capacity so as to increase production in all fields. In general, consumption was penalized through taxation, and private capital formation was promoted. This led to criticism that German fiscal policy favored the upper-income groups and discriminated against the working class. However, under conditions that were prevalent, this was probably the most direct way of stimulating economic growth in a free market system.

Postwar Monetary and Fiscal Policies. Postwar German monetary and fiscal policies were oriented toward production. Incentive elements favored the strong and discriminated against the weak. Considerable income inequality was permitted. Although the position of the economically weak and less viable segments of the economy was buttressed through the provision of a comprehensive social welfare program which consumed and distributed a sizable part of the national income, there is no question that the bulk of the economic gains went to business firms and individual entrepreneurs. Monetary and fiscal policies were tight and served to intensify competition among business firms to create markets for their products.[4] General policies aimed at stimulating aggregate demand and thereby insuring a sellers' market were avoided. To the contrary, aggregate demand was held relatively constant and aggregate supply was stimulated through various factors, such as tax incentives.

To a major degree, the free market policy adopted after World War II remains the policy of Germany today. Nevertheless, there are marked differences between the West German and United States economies. For one thing, a considerable segment of German industry is nationalized. Moreover, there is stronger government penetration and control over financial affairs in West Germany through state ownership of the central banking system and through the high proportion of transfer payments generated through the state budget.

THE ECONOMIC SYSTEM

A postwar reliance on a free market system represented somewhat of a break with traditional German reliance on state intervention in economic affairs, which predated Hitler by a considerable time period. The West

---

[4] Wallich, *op. cit.*, pp. 121–131.

German economic system, then, is a mixed economic system in which there is both public and private ownership of the agents of production. The bulk of German industry is in private hands, and pricing decisions are determined in the market place. It has been the government's stated policy to denationalize some of its holdings as it did in the case of the Volkswagen company in 1961. Distribution is also primarily a function of private enterprise with the government responsible for seeing that it is shared equitably by all income groups. To this extent, allocation of resources, as determined in a purely competitive market economy, is circumvented.

The West German economy can be divided into two sectors, private and public, each of which contributes to the total output of goods and services. The private sector is the most important in terms of consumption, production, and employment. The public or government sector is also important not only from the standpoint that it contributes to consumption and investment but also because it has come to play the paramount role in the maintenance of full employment and the redistribution of income. For a variety of reasons the government sector has entered into certain business activities that it shares to a greater or lesser extent with private enterprise. During the Bismarck era the railroad system was nationalized, and foundations were laid upon which the war economy of a later period could be built. Bismarck was also the chief architect of most of the social legislation which exists in Germany today.[5]

West Germany's gross national product for 1973 is shown in Table 14–1.

TABLE 14–1
THE WEST GERMAN GROSS NATIONAL PRODUCT FOR 1975

Expenditures at Current Prices		Billions of Dollars*
Private consumption		$231.08
Government consumption		88.56
Fixed capital formation		87.72
Machinery and equipment	$39.92	
Buildings	47.80	
Expenditure on stocks		− 1.12
Domestic expenditure		406.24
Net exports of goods and services		9.96
Exports	117.36	
Imports	107.40	
Gross national product (at current prices)		$416.20

Source: Deutsche Bundesbank, "Monatsberichte der Deutschen Bundesbank" (Frankfurt am Main, November, 1975), p. 43.

* The German currency unit is the Deutsche Mark. The rate of exchange between the DM and the U.S. dollar was 2.5 to 1 as of September 20, 1975.

[5] Bismarck was Chancellor of Germany from 1871 to 1890. He was a political pragmatist of the first order who realized that concessions to the working classes had to be made in order to check the rise of socialism. He sponsored social legislation in order to remove the causes upon which socialism was developing and to maintain military efficiency, which was dependent upon the health and happiness of the German people.

Public Finance

Almost any government activity influences the private as well as the public sector of an economic system, whether or not an effect is intended. Taxes divert resources from the private to the public sector of an economy, and the level of taxation relative to gross national product indicates the extent to which the influence of the state exists. In Germany the combined federal, state, and local budgets control about 35 percent of the gross national product. A considerable part of gross domestic investment is financed out of tax revenues, and income redistribution is facilitated by one of the most comprehensive social welfare programs in the world. However, the tax structure is heavily weighted against consumer expenditures, and the main thrust of fiscal policy has been toward capital accumulation, at first for reconstruction and subsequently for expansion of production capacity. Government savings as one source of capital formation have been high, averaging as much as 40 percent of total national savings. The government has also relied extensively upon preferential tax treatment to stimulate the rate of savings in the private sector of the economy, and the impact of tax policy on capital formation in the postwar period has been considerable.

In West Germany the budgets of the state and local governments constitute an important expenditure source in the economy. In comparison with the French public finance system, which is highly centralized, the German system allows the states (länder) to have large separate budgets, which, when combined with local budgets, provide a greater volume of expenditures than the central government. The social security system is similar to that of the French in that the tax-transfer arrangement is largely independent of the federal budget.

The German Tax System. The present tax structure of West Germany is primarily the inheritance of history and political processes. There is a similarity between the German and United States tax systems in that there is a *tripartite structure,* meaning that legislative authority over tax matters is divided between federal, state, and local governments, and certain taxes are regarded as the prerogative of each.

The German revenue system draws upon a large number of tax sources, the most important of which has been the turnover tax, which is now replaced by the value-added tax. The turnover tax has been the most important source of revenue for the federal budget, accounting for almost one third of total revenue. It was a *cascade tax* in that it was collected from nearly all types of transactions at all levels of production at a flat rate of 4 percent.[6]

The Value-Added Tax. The value-added tax was introduced in January 1968. It was devised in accordance with a Common Market tax harmonization

---

[6] The term *cascade* means that the turnover tax was cumulative. It was a multiple-stage tax levied on each transaction in the production process. At each stage, the gross turnover tax became an inseparable and unidentifiable part of the price, and at each succeeding stage the rate was applied to the total price, including all turnover taxes paid in previous stages.

directive which called for a value-added tax in all Common Market countries by January 1, 1970. The tax is levied at a general rate of 11 percent of value-added in each stage of the production process. There are numerous items, however, to which a lower rate applies. For example, many food and agricultural products are taxed at a rate of 5.5 percent, and exports and certain items and services are exempt from the tax. In the case of imports, the importer pays an import equalization tax equal to the value-added tax applicable to the same good produced domestically.

Excise Taxes. Federal excise taxes and customs duties are also an important source of revenue to the national government. Excise taxes are levied on a variety of commodities including tobacco, mineral oil, salt, tea, sugar, matches, and alcohol.[7] The manufacturer, producer, or importer of products subject to excise taxation is expected to shift the tax to the buyer by including it in the purchase price of the product. Revenue from the two major excise taxes on tobacco and gasoline account for approximately 15 percent of federal tax revenue, and the impact of the excise tax structure places a heavy burden on the individual taxpayer.

Income Taxes. Income taxes are levied by the states partly as a matter of historical right and partly under powers delegated by the federal government, and the proceeds are divided between the government and the states. Individuals pay a personal income tax at rates ranging from 19 to 53 percent, and corporations are taxed on distributed profits at flat rates and on undistributed profits at graduated rates. Income-splitting is permitted for personal income tax purposes in that the incomes of married persons are reckoned together, divided into equal parts, and each part subjected to the tax.

The federal portion of the proceeds from the personal and corporate income taxes amounts to 45 percent and the state portion, 55 percent. The state portion is allocated on the basis of the share of total income taxes collected by each state. Although this would tend to weigh the portions heavily in favor of the more densely populated and heavily industrialized states, there is a federal statute which provides for an equitable distribution of revenue among the various states. This is accomplished through equalization payments which are made by the affluent states to the needy states. All states are required to grant a part of their share of income taxes to the municipalities located within their territories.

Municipal Trade Tax. The municipal trade tax is the most important source of revenue for local governments. It is a tax on business profits, on business capital, and in some communities, on the payrolls of commercial enterprises. The basic purpose of the tax is to compensate local governments for the cost of maintaining schools, roads, police protection, and public welfare. Collection of the municipal trade tax is the responsibility of a community, and only business enterprises located within its boundaries are liable for the tax.

---

[7] A tax on beer is administered separately by the states and is an important source of revenue. In 1973 the beer tax accounted for about 10 percent of state revenues.

Tax Distribution. The tripartite structure of the German tax system is unique among European countries. The division of total tax resources results in a distribution of tax revenues among federal, state, and local governments in a ratio of roughly 5:3:1. In 1973, for example, total tax collections at the federal level of government amounted to $40 billion, total tax collections at the state level amounted to $22.9 billion, and total tax collections at the local level amounted to $10 billion.[8] This has meant a division of taxes, with the turnover tax the most important source of revenue to the federal government and the personal income tax the most important source of revenue to state governments.

Combined federal, state, and local taxes, including the very heavy social security levies, absorb approximately 38 percent of the German gross national product. Social security levies alone absorb 10 percent of the gross national product, and the total burden indicates the measure of the tax burden resting on the German economy. This burden, however, is mitigated by the high proportion of transfer payments and the existence of tax incentives to stimulate investment.

Table 14–2 presents revenue sources for the West German federal budget.

TABLE 14–2
WEST GERMAN FEDERAL BUDGET REVENUES FOR 1975

Sources of Revenue	Millions of Dollars *
Federal share of income and corporation taxes	$ 9,228
Value-added tax	10,588
Customs	1,002
Tobacco tax	2,426
Coffee tax	377
Minerals tax	4,410
Alcohol monopoly	890
Other taxes	567
Equalization fund and other minor items	598
Administrative receipts	504
Loans	1,527
Total receipts	$32,117

Source: Bundesministeriums der Finanzen, "Finanzpolitische Mitteilungen" (Bonn, February, 1976).
* 1 deutsche mark = $0.31.

Government Expenditures. Expenditure policy has emphasized a comprehensive social security system with constantly expanding individual benefits, public investment in the form of low-cost housing, transportation facilities and other civil construction, and economic assistance to private enterprise. In fact, a substantial part of public investment has been effected through the financing of private enterprise.

[8] Bundesministeriums der Finanzen, "Finanzpolitische Mitteilungen" (Bonn, February, 1970).

Germany became the first nation in the world to adopt comprehensive social security legislation. Current social security programs are extensive and costly. Social security levies, as mentioned above, amount to approximately 10 percent of the gross national product, and expenditures on social insurance and other welfare programs amount to approximately 12 percent of gross national product. Social insurance benefits supplement the wage of the average German worker by about 30 percent.[9]

Old Age and Survivors Benefits. Social security benefits are financed out of general revenues of the federal budget and out of taxes levied on the employer and employee. Old age and survivors insurance is financed by a tax of 8 percent of payrolls which is levied on the employer, a tax of 8 percent of earnings which is levied on the employee, and an annual subsidy provided by the federal government out of general revenues which amounts to approximately one third of the cost of the program. Cash benefits include: an old age pension, which amounts to 1.5 percent of the worker's assessed wage multiplied by the years the worker was insured; an invalidity pension computed in the same manner; a widow's pension which is 60 percent of the old age or invalidity pension; children's supplements, which, when added to the widow's pension, amount to 100 percent of the regular pension; and funeral grants of a lump sum of 20 to 40 days' earnings or three months' pension if a pensioner.

Sickness and Maternity Benefits. Sickness and maternity benefits are financed by a tax on the worker which ranges from 4 to 5.5 percent of earnings up to 10,800 marks ($3,857) a year, a tax on the employer of the same range on earnings up to the same amount, and contributions by the federal government out of general revenues which cover the cost of maternity grants.[10] Benefits include: sickness benefits, which amount to 75 percent of earnings up to 78 weeks; maternity benefits, which include a payment of 100 percent of earnings for six weeks prior to and eight weeks after confinement, and a maternity grant of 100 marks per birth; and medical benefits available to all with a small charge for prescriptions.

Unemployment Compensation. Unemployment compensation is financed jointly by a tax on the employer of 1.65 percent of payrolls and a tax on the employee of 0.65 percent of earnings. Benefits range from 40 to 90 percent of earnings. Benefits vary inversely with the wage class, with dependents' supplements of 9 marks ($3.30) a week for the wife and first child and three marks ($1.10) a week for other children. Benefits are payable for periods of 13 to 52 weeks according to the weeks of insured employment. The maximum earnings subject to unemployment taxation and benefits is 1,300 marks ($464.30) a month.

---

[9] *Ibid.*, p. 51.

[10] A characteristic of many European social security systems is their fragmentation into a number of funds or special systems. In Germany, for example, there are special systems for miners, public employees, self-employed artisans, self-employed farmers, and building and clock workers. Contributions and benefits vary according to the system. The contributions and benefits above pertain to the general social security system.

Work Injury. Work injury compensation is financed solely by a tax on the employer which varies according to risk, with the average contribution being about 1.5 percent of payroll. The federal government subsidizes the agricultural accident insurance fund. Benefits for temporary disability amount to 75 percent of earnings for a period of up to 78 weeks, and benefits for permanent disability amount to 66⅔ percent of earnings up to a maximum of 20,000 marks ($7,143) a month plus special supplements including a child's supplement of 10 percent of the pension for each child under 18.

Family Allowances. Family allowances are financed out of the general revenues of the federal government and are payable to families with two or more children. The allowance increases with the number of children, with 25 marks ($8.90) a month payable for the second child, 50 marks ($17.80) for the third, 60 marks ($21.40) for the fourth, and 75 marks ($26.80) for the fifth and subsequent children.[11] Education allowances of 30 marks ($10.70) a month are also paid to families with two or more children.

Public Investment Expenditures. Public investment from all government sources has accounted for approximately one fourth of total investment during the last ten years. The bulk of support has come from savings on the part of the federal government which have been derived from budgetary surpluses, funds secured from accumulations in the social security system, moderate amounts of government borrowing, both through bond issues and through direct credits from financial institutions, and surpluses in the budgets of the various German states.[12]

Housing is a major area of government support. An acute need after World War II was the repair and construction of residential housing. There was also the need to provide housing for the refugees from East Germany. To encourage the construction of housing, tax incentives and direct subsidies were offered by all levels of government. For example, newly built homes were exempted from the local real estate tax. Generous depreciation allowances were provided for the construction of houses and apartments, and rents for many dwellings were subsidized. Loans at subsidized interest rates as low as 1 percent per annum were also made to encourage housing construction.

All levels of government continue to be active in financing and subsidizing houses. Public support on the part of the federal government alone has averaged around $1.25 billion a year.[13] Housing construction continues to be supported out of subsidies financed by general taxes, interest subsidies, and accelerated depreciation allowances. Government subsidized housing has contributed to a higher level of demand than would otherwise exist in the

[11] The family allowance in Germany has been used as a device to increase the birth rate to compensate for the war losses sustained in the two world wars. As a percentage of total personal income, however, the family allowance is smaller in Germany than in France and Belgium, accounting for less than 5 percent of personal income.

[12] It is necessary to remember that Germany is a federal republic. The fiscal systems of state and local governments are much more important than in most European countries.

[13] Frederick Reuss, *Fiscal Policy for Growth Without Inflation: The German Experiment* (Baltimore: The Johns Hopkins Press, 1963), p. 189.

housing industry. Tax revenues have been channeled into housing investment, reflecting the postwar priorities of German fiscal policy. This means that the average German is subsidizing, to a certain extent, the cost of housing through the taxes paid to the various levels of government. In 1960 a person spent on the average 10.3 percent of income on housing, a low percentage for any industrial country. However, if taxes were calculated as a part of housing costs, the average German would pay more for housing. The housing market, then, is distorted by excessive stimulation of aggregate demand.[14]

A high proportion of savings, then, emanate from the government sector of the economy and are channeled into areas which are government approved. Agriculture has been another one of these areas. For example, agricultural enterprises are entitled to special depreciation provisions which are over and above the normal rate. Structural subsidies are paid to stimulate an increase in the size of the farming unit, and interest subsidies are paid to stimulate capital investment. Under the annual *Green Plan*, which is designed to improve the technical and economic organization of farms and to raise farm incomes, the federal government spent $1.36 billion in 1973, an amount which is considerably less than the total amount of subsidies to farmers.

It should be clear that combined federal, state, and local budgets absorb a very large percentage of the German gross national product, and many economic functions are influenced by government tax and expenditure policies. This means that a high degree of control over the economy can be exercised by governmental units through manipulation of taxes and expenditures. A wide variety of tax incentives have been used to stimulate economic growth, and many economic sectors have been favored by government use of tax revenues. Tax policy has sought to create incentives to work, save, and invest in business enterprises, but, in turn, heavy reliance has been placed on indirect taxation, such as the turnover tax and the value-added tax, which discriminates against consumption. Expenditure policy has sought to buttress the position of the average German by providing comprehensive social security measures.

Table 14–3 on page 322 presents a breakdown of the federal budget for 1973, showing the major expenditures.

Income Redistribution. The important thing to note concerning government outlays for transfer payments and goods and services is that they require the diversion of resources from the private to the public sector of an economy. To the extent that the government provides services, real resources are diverted to the public sector as a result of the purchase of goods and factor services by governmental units. The recipients of these services benefit through obtaining them at a price below their real cost as measured by the government expenditures necessary to provide the services. Transfer payments do not necessitate a direct diversion of real resources from private to public use, but they do require a diversion of financial resources, generally in the form of some portion of the consumer's current money income.

[14] *Ibid.*, p. 188.

TABLE 14–3
WEST GERMAN FEDERAL BUDGET EXPENDITURES FOR 1973

Expenditures	Millions of Dollars *
General services, including national defense	$11,917
Education and scientific research	1,282
Social welfare expenditures, including war pensions	12,489
Health and sports	76
Housing construction	598
Measures to promote economic growth	3,714
Public utilities and waterways	1,250
Transportation	2,448
General capital expenditures	1,700
General finance services, including interest on the national debt	4,890
Total expenditures	$40,364

Source: Bundesministeriums der Finanzen, "Finanzpolitische Mitteilungen" (Bonn, February, 1973).
* 1 deutsche mark = $0.40.

Table 14–4 presents the relationship between German gross national product and taxes, including social security contributions. Taxes, of course, provide the state with control over economic resources.

TABLE 14–4
A COMPARISON OF TAXES AND SOCIAL INSURANCE CONTRIBUTIONS TO GROSS NATIONAL PRODUCT IN WEST GERMANY FOR SELECTED YEARS (IN BILLIONS OF DOLLARS *)

Year	Gross National Product	Taxes and Social Insurance Contributions	Taxes and Social Insurance Contributions as a Percentage of GNP
1953	41.3	13.1	31.9
1958	60.9	19.0	31.2
1963	102.0	34.5	33.9
1967	130.7	46.1	35.3
1970	183.3	65.2	35.4
1972	235.5	85.1	36.2
1973	332.0	121.0	36.5

Source: Deutsche Bundesbank, "Monatsberichte der Deutschen Bundesbank" (Frankfurt am Main, October, 1973), p. 58.
* The deutsche mark was equal to $0.27 in 1953–1970, $0.31 in 1972, and $0.40 in 1973.

Transfer payments, that is, the payments from public sources to recipients of social insurance pensions, family allowances, and public assistance, amounted to 71 billion deutsche marks ($17.7 billion) in 1967. This amounted to 17.1 percent of German national income. However, as has already been mentioned, the development of the welfare state in Germany is not a recent phenomenon, and transfer payments, when expressed as a percentage of national income, have remained relatively stable during the 1960s. Moreover, German tax policy has relied on the provision of incentives to work, save, and invest in business enterprises, and has utilized as revenue sources turnover and other indirect taxes which impose relatively light burdens on upper incomes, the source of most personal saving, and on business investment. Furthermore, income tax rates have been subjected to successive reductions, especially the marginal rates on personal incomes in the upper brackets.

Fiscal Policy. West German budget policy has sought to avoid deficits, partly because of the difficulty of financing a deficit and partly as a result of legal restrictions confining public debts to those incurred for productive purposes.[15] Until recently, there has been no attempt to utilize the budget to offset short-term fluctuations in economic activity. Reliance instead has been placed on monetary policy for control of the business cycle.

The economic problems which brought down the Erhard government forced a reappraisal of this standard conservative budget policy. Over-expenditure in the public sector of the economy was a factor which was responsible for rising prices, and wage increases had outstripped gains in productivity. A recession occurred in 1966, and by the middle of February 1967 the number of unemployed workers in West Germany amounted to 3.1 percent of the labor force—a high rate for the economy. A provisional contingency budget was introduced, and countercyclical fiscal measures were used to stimulate demand. This contingency budget took the form of a Special Investment Budget, and in the spring of 1967, additional expenditures of 2.5 billion deutsche marks ($625 million) were provided for investments in the national railway system, postal services, and road building. Investment orders were also placed with the private sector of the economy. In spite of those additional investments, the countercyclical impact of the contingency budget was diluted and more than counterbalanced by contractions in budgetary spending on the part of state and local governments.

In June 1967, the Bundesrat (the upper house of Parliament) passed the Law for Promoting Stability and Growth in the Economy. In connection with the new law, Parliament gave approval to a required change in the Federal Republic's Basic Law. The provision for independent budgeting processes of the federal government and the states was altered to permit coordination of fiscal and economic policy actions at different levels of government. The separation of federal and state budgets had heretofore been an important obstacle to an effective countercyclical fiscal policy.

The law represents a delegation of fiscal powers by the German Parliament to the federal government. These fiscal powers are as follows:

[15] Under the *Basic Law* (the Constitution of the Federal Republic of Germany), the German government is not permitted to have an unbalanced budget. This has prevented use of the budget as an instrument of fiscal policy. The reason for this provision was to prevent legislative abuse of the budget.

1. To stimulate the economy in a recession, the Minister of Finance is authorized to finance supplementary public expenditures by borrowing up to 5 billion deutsche marks.
2. The federal government can suspend or restrict special depreciation allowances and the application of accelerated depreciation in a boom period.
3. The federal government, with prior approval of the Bundesrat, can restrict, for up to one year, new borrowing by federal, state, and local governments.
4. The federal government is authorized to increase or decrease income and corporation taxes by up to 10 percent, according to requirements of the business cycle.
5. As an antirecessionary move, the federal government is authorized, with prior approval of the Bundesrat, to introduce a tax credit of up to 7.5 percent of investments.
6. The federal government is required to submit to the Bundestag and Bundesrat an annual economic report which includes a declaration of its economic and fiscal policy objectives for the coming year.

The Banking System

The German banking system has a mixed public-private relationship. The central bank, the *Deutsche Bundesbank,* is publicly owned, but the commercial banks are privately owned. Two government financial institutions, the *Kreditanstalt fuer Wiederaufbrau* (Reconstruction Finance Corporation) and the *Industrie Kreditbank,* provide funds to business firms. There is direct government intervention in the flow of credit from the financial institutions to the various sectors of the economy through the provision of saving out of budgetary surpluses, which is made available for capital formation. Government lending to households and enterprises includes loans financed by its own funds, as well as loans made by public institutions which it controls. In addition, government authorities mobilize loan funds outside of the budget by subsidizing interest payments.

Central Banking. The historical and deep-rooted conflict between federalism and centralism is reflected in the development of central banking in Germany. The *Reichsbank,* Germany's first central bank, was formed in 1876; but, to placate the supporters of federalism, banks in the various German states were given the right to issue bank notes. In 1924 the Reichsbank was reorganized under the auspices of the Dawes Commission to make it more independent of the German government. In 1935 it was given the sole right to issue bank notes, but lost its autonomy during the Nazi period (1933–1945) when it became a monetary instrument which was subservient to the economic objectives of the government.

Following World War II, the Reichsbank was reorganized as the Bank Deutscher Laender, an interim central bank which existed pending the creation of a Federal Republic. However, it lost the function of note issuance to the central banks (*Landeszentralbanken*) of the German states. In 1957 it was reorganized into the Deutsche Bundesbank and given the exclusive right to issue bank notes. The capital stock of the Bundesbank was given to the federal government, and increased authority was also given to the government through the use of appointive powers which were granted to it. Members of the Directorate of the Bundesbank are appointed by the President of the Federal Republic.[16]

The current central banking system consists of the Deutsche Bundesbank and ten Landeszentralbanken (central banks of the states). The Bundesbank, unlike many central banks in other countries, operates with a considerable degree of autonomy with respect to open market operations and credit policy. It is, however, obliged to advise the government on all matters of importance in the area of monetary policy and to support general economic policies of the government, particularly in the area of currency stability.

The Bundesbank exercises control over monetary policy through various instruments which it can use to regulate the availability of credit and the liquidity of the banking system.

1. It has control over the rediscount rate and the rate it charges for advances on commercial paper. Moreover, the quantity of open-market paper which the Bundesbank stands ready to discount is subject to limits which are believed to be three times the liable capital plus the reserves of any given institution.

2. It has control over minimum legal reserve requirements for commercial banks and other credit institutions up to a maximum of 30 percent for sight deposits, 20 percent for time desposits, and 10 percent for savings accounts. Any credit institution that fails to meet reserve requirements is subject to a penalty surcharge which is usually 3 percent above the rate charged by the Bundesbank on advances.

3. It can engage in open-market operations by buying and selling Treasury bills and bonds, bills of exchange, and bonds that have been admitted to the official stock exchange.

4. It can encourage or discourage the placement of banking funds abroad by making it less or more expensive for commercial banks to make covered investments in the foreign exchange market, thereby increasing or decreasing the supply of funds available in the domestic money market.

Commercial Banks. German commercial banks are privately owned and are of three types: nationwide banks; state, regional, and local banks; and private banks. Commercial banks account for over 50 percent of total short-term deposits and short-term credits, but less than 10 percent of total long-term lending. German banks, remembering the banking crisis of 1931 when withdrawals of foreign short-term deposits brought down the superstructure of long-term credits, have pursued a highly liquid position with respect to loans.

There are three nationwide banks—the Deutsche Bank, the Dresdner Bank, and the Commerzbank. These banks have a nationwide network of branch banks. They have about one fourth of the short-term deposits and short-term credits of the entire banking system and conduct the bulk of Germany's international banking business.

---

[16] The Directorate of the Bundesbank is composed of the President, Vice-President, and no more than eight additional members—all of whom are appointed by the President of the Federal Republic.

There are 105 state, regional, and local banks which specialize in short- and medium-term lending. Some of these banks engage in general banking business; others are highly specialized. Underwriting is the main capital market function of these banks, and a large part of their holdings of bonds is related to the underwriting business. They also hold substantial amounts of fixed interest securities for their own accounts.

There are also private bankers who make short-term loans. Their strength stems from a close personal association maintained with their clients.

Savings Banks. Savings banks are municipally owned and are oriented toward local needs—housing, small business loans, and municipal projects. They provide the largest source of capital for the bond market and derive their funds from personal savings. Savings banks, as a rule, engage in both savings and short-term deposit transactions. Credits extended by the savings banks are mostly loans to medium-sized and small firms and to the handicraft industries.

There are also 12 central *giro institutions* (Girozentralen), which act as reserve depositories and clearinghouses and which carry out various banking functions, such as foreign exchange transactions and the issue of securities. Most of them are also provincial banks making long-term loans to communities and associations after raising funds by issuing bonds on the capital market.

Specific Purpose Banks. Government savings from budgetary surpluses and accumulations by the social security system have been most important in the development of the German economy. Some of these savings are loaned to private enterprises, partly through such specialized credit institutions as the Reconstruction Loan Corporation, the Equalization of Burdens Bank, and certain agricultural banks.

The Reconstruction Loan Corporation had as its original purpose the provision of loans for the reconstruction of German industry. It has now become the main instrument for the extension of long-term credits to developing countries in the framework of the German foreign aid program.

The Industry Credit Corporation provides short- and medium-term loans, primarily to the machinery construction industry and the chemical industry.

Monetary Policy. The Bundesbank has recourse to the standard instruments of monetary policy—control over the rediscount rate, control over minimum reserve requirements, and open-market operations—to accomplish stabilization objectives. Its influence on credit, however, has been obviated considerably during the postwar period through the existence of several factors which have been present in the German economy. For one thing, the interest elasticity of investment has been low, reflecting a strong investment demand, and interest rate changes via changes in the rediscount rate have had little effect. Furthermore, German banks have also possessed considerable excess liquidity during the postwar period and have not had to resort to rediscounting commercial paper to any significant degree. The existence of an export surplus has provided the foreign exchange to enhance the liquidity of the banking system. High interest rates have attracted foreign accounts which in turn has increased bank liquidity, thereby circumventing attempts at effective rediscount policy.

Monetary policy is invested with the primary responsibility for price level stability and for confining short-run fluctuations in levels of economic activity to moderate proportions. Credit restraint and easing has taken the form, primarily, of sharp increases and decreases in the rediscount rate. Excess reserves of commercial banks have been affected through changes in minimum reserve requirements. Open-market policy has been generally limited to Treasury bills.

Despite the factors mentioned above which reduce the impact of central banking policy on the German economy, monetary policy has contributed to the stability of the price level. During the period 1960 through 1973, the price level rose by 49 percent. A considerable part of the increase occurred during the 1971–1973 period when the economy was overheated. In 1971 the price level rose 5.4 percent, and in 1972 it rose 5.6 percent.

Government control over the supply of credit is more indirect than direct. As mentioned previously, a substantial part of savings during the postwar period has emanated from combined federal, state, and local governments' budgetary surpluses. Indirect influence on the capital market has been exerted through the allocation of government savings to government approved projects, such as housing construction.

Government incentives in the form of privileges and bonus payments have been used to increase the level of personal savings. Savers have received premium payments amounting to 20 to 30 percent for savings accounts and 25 to 35 percent for amounts held with building and loan associations provided that balances are immobilized for a specified period of time. Moreover, individuals in certain income brackets may receive greater premiums by deducting such deposits and premiums from taxable income.

Labor-Management Relations

The trade union movement in West Germany is dominated by one labor confederation, the *Deutsche Gewerkschaftsbund* (DGB), which was established in 1949 as a federation of 16 basic industrial unions comprising every segment of the German economy. For example, office and production employees in the textile industry are organized into a textile union. The DGB represents about one fourth of the workers in the West German labor force and is the successor to the separate, politically oriented trade union federations which existed before the Hitler era. It has approximately 7 million members. The three principal unions within the DGB are the metal workers, with approximately 2.2 million members, the public service and transport workers with 983 thousand members, and the chemical, paper, and ceramics workers with 526 thousand members. The multi-industrial form of organization is dominant in German trade unionism.

There are approximately 1.4 million workers who belong to other unions. White-collar workers and higher ranking civil servants, reflecting class division and higher occupational distinction, have their own unions. The white-collar workers belong to the *Deutsche Angestellten Gewerkschaft* (DAG), which has 500 thousand members. Civil servants belong to the *Deutscher Beamtenbund* (DB), which has 700 thousand members. These two unions, unlike the typical German union, are not multi-industrial in terms of organization.

On the employers' side, the principal organization is the German Confederation of Employers Association, comprising 37 national organizations that cover the major branches of industry and 14 industrial employers' confederations, which in turn are made up of local and regional associations. The basic employers' association, however, usually covers geographically a state and industrially a single product. These associations are responsible for collective bargaining with the union. Employers in Germany are better organized than workers and possess more of a united front in collective bargaining than their union counterparts.

Codetermination. A unique feature of labor-management relations in certain German industries is codetermination of business policies on the part of labor and management. Under the Works Constitution Act of 1952 and succeeding amendments, supervisory boards consisting of representatives from labor and stockholders were created in the iron, steel, and coal-mining industries. These boards must have equal representation from labor and stockholders, plus one representative who is supposed to be neutral. This neutral representative, who is selected by both groups, is supposed to function as a tie-breaker.

The Works Constitution Act also provided that each company in the iron, steel, and coal industries must have one labor representative on its board of directors. This person oversees all aspects of company personnel policies and practices.

The purpose of codetermination is to give workers a voice in determining public policy. There have been problems of employment, particularly in the coal-mining industry, and the unions felt that labor representation was necessary to protect the workers from arbitrary layoffs and reduction in salaries. The unions also felt that labor representation would ensure a more adequate distribution of company profits in terms of labor's share. Codetermination is in essence a social policy which emphasizes the role of the workers as potential capitalists. In practice, although union leaders were mesmerized with its potential, codetermination has not had too much influence upon the creation of worker capitalism.

Under traditional German collective bargaining procedures, the regional office of a union and the corresponding employers' association for the industry agree on wages and conditions of employment. The collective agreement is valid only in the geographic area for which it has been concluded. Agreements may be made to cover specific localities, states, or the Federal Republic as a whole. In any given case, the question of the applicability of a collective agreement depends on whether the place of employment—normally the employer's place of business—lies within the area covered by the agreement.

Demands of Labor. German unions exercised great restraint in their demands for wage increases during the first ten years of the postwar period, being content with a moderate share of gains in national productivity. The unions did not wish to retard the reconstruction of the German economy and were willing to permit large profits to encourage it. There was also a concern that immoderate demands would cause unemployment, for memories of the Great Depression were in the minds of many workers. The unions also did not want the responsibility for an inflationary spiral, the disastrous consequences of which were illustrated by the financial debacle which occurred after World War I.[17]

Since 1960, however, a labor shortage has been in evidence, and requests for wage increases and reductions in the workweek have become frequent. In 1971 new wage contracts resulted in an average wage increase of 12 percent, and in 1972 average wages increased by 10 percent. The year 1973 reflected continued union demands for higher wages, more fringe benefits, and shorter hours. Wage policies pursued in major neighboring countries to some extent produced a "demonstration effect" on the rank-and-file members of the German trade unions in that there has been pressure on the leaders to emulate gains made elsewhere. However, strike activity has been insignificant, particularly in comparison to the United States. A loss of 289,000 work days was recorded in 1972, mostly due to a series of wildcat strikes.

Third party participation in labor disputes in Germany, as compared to the United States, is more intensive in that in Germany there is more reliance on arbitration to settle wage disputes. This reflects the general German tendency to rely on the government to solve problems. During the Nazi period, all wages were set by decree, and during the Weimar Republic reliance was placed on compulsory government boards to conclude wage agreements. Third party participation is still lodged in government hands through the medium of Labor Courts.

Labor Courts adjudicate wage disputes between employers and unions with emphasis placed upon compromise between the parties rather than judicial determination. The courts are tripartite in that representatives of both employers and unions, as well as the government, are members. The government representatives are full-time employees making a career in the field of labor arbitration. In general, the system of Labor Courts has had the effect of reducing industrial conflict, but it also reduces the need for union membership and protection, for any worker can gain access to a court, whether he belongs to a union or not.

Government and Business

Government ownership of industry is partially concentrated in areas where state ownership is traditional. For example, telephone, postal communications,

[17] Employers were also more strongly organized than the unions and were in a stronger financial position, thus thwarting the use of strikes by the union. The federal government also made wage increases subject to stabilization controls.

and railway transportation are supplied by public enterprises. In addition, various public utilities, and to some extent bank services, are also owned and supplied by the public sector. Government ownership, however, also extends to areas that are the domain of private enterprise in the United States. Although the federal government has divested itself of a part of some industries, its ownership of others remains substantial. It is estimated that the federal government owns over two thirds of aluminum production, one third of iron-ore mining, one fourth of coal production, and one fifth of shipbuilding.[18] It is also estimated that the federal government owns commercial assets valued at around $2 billion, including stock in more than 3,000 enterprises.[19]

Participation on the part of the federal government in business is channeled primarily through several holding companies. One of them, Vereinigte Elektrizitaets und Bergwerke, A. G., controls subsidiaries which produce coal, lignite, and coke. Another holding company, Vereinigte Industrieunternehmen, A. G., holds interests in firms producing steel, aluminum, and chemicals. The third holding company, A. G. fuer Berg und Huettenbetriebe, has control over coal mining, transportation, and engineering firms. The federal government also controls titles to real estate properties through another holding company, Industrie Verwaltungs Gesellschaft.

Business Activity in the Third Reich. During the Third Reich, all of the economic activity in Germany, with the exception of agriculture and transportation, was centralized under a group—Industry, Commerce, Banking, Insurance, Power, and Handicrafts—and each functional group was subdivided into divisions. For example, the metal division was one subgroup in the Industry group. The metal division was further divided into subgroups—Mining, Iron Making, Nonferrous Metal, and Foundries. These subgroups were also organized along regional and geographic lines.

Mergers and cartels became a standard form of business development during the Third Reich. There was a strong, government sponsored concentration movement in industry and business. Thousands of small industrialists and business people were eliminated, and many new combinations and cartels were formed. Large firms were assigned the responsibility for founding and operating the new firms and industries made necessary by the national self-sufficiency programs. It was felt by the Nazis that cartels would result in greater industrial proficiency, and power over the cartel arrangement was transferred to the Minister of Economic Affairs, who could decide whether the arrangement was desirable. The Minister was given the power to make outside firms join cartels, and he could prohibit the establishment of new firms.

Postwar Business Development. Postwar Allied occupation policy was aimed at breaking the strength of monopolies and cartels. Deconcentration procedures were taken in the coal and steel industry, the chemical industry, and banking.[20] This action was designed to reduce the degree of monopoly which

---

[18] Based on personal estimates taken from Bundesministerium der Finanzen, *Beteiligungen des Bundes 1971* (Bonn-Bad Godesberg, 1971), pp 256–260.

[19] *Ibid.*, p. 257.

[20] This policy is similar to postwar occupation policy in Japan which sought to break up the zaibatsu combines.

existed under the Nazis. Decartelization policies were also followed. More extreme forms of cartels, such as sales syndicates and market quotas, were eliminated. However, firms, like Krupp, that had been ordered to divest themselves of parts of their industrial empires were able to avoid the implementation of these orders. In banking, the Allies broke up the three major banks which had dominated the prewar German banking system, but by 1957, the same three banks had been reestablished.[21]

Postwar German business development has been marked by a return to earlier patterns under which control over large sectors of the economy rests in the hands of a small number of business firms and bankers. Even though official government policy has sought to prevent continued mergers and business concentration, progress has been limited to some extent because of the opposition of the government's political backers in industry. The government's opposition to cartels was manifested in the Law of Cartels, which became effective in 1958 and was amended in 1965. Such business practices as price-fixing and market-sharing have also been curtailed to a degree. The concentration of German business has, to a certain extent, been inimical to the free market policy pursued by the postwar governments.

The federal government, then, exercises a degree of control over business in several ways, such as: through functions which in other countries are carried out by private enterprise, but which are publicly owned and operated in Germany; through the national budget, which absorbs and disburses a large part of the national income; through tax incentives which have been designed to stimulate savings and investment; and through a high degree of administrative authority which is wielded by government agencies. However, intervention in economic affairs is a tradition which predates the current government by a considerable time period. Bismarck used state intervention to make Germany a world power. During the Hitler period, intervention was carried to its ultimate extreme in order to prepare the economy for war. Actually, the postwar trend toward a more liberal free market economy represents a break with past traditions and a reaction to extreme state controls.[22]

Economic Planning

Unlike France, Germany has not utilized economic planning during the postwar period. In part, this may be attributed to the fact that German economic policy reflected the psychology of a people thoroughly disillusioned by the overt public controls imposed by the Nazis and, in part, to the Soziale Marktwirtschaft policy adopted by the Adenauer and Erhard governments, which involved the belief that maximization of welfare could be achieved by means of a system in which the role of the government is limited to enforcing competition in the private sector of the economy.

---

[21] The three banks are the Deutsche Bank, the Dresdner Bank, and the Commerzbank.

[22] It may be noted that articles 85 and 86 of *The Treaty Establishing the European Economic Community* are directed against arrangements which permit, restrict, or distort competition within the Common Market.

When the National Socialist party came into power in Germany in 1933, it adopted economic planning to cope with the depression. The First Four-Year Plan was introduced in May 1933, and was designed to deal with the problem of unemployment. Included in the plan were public works, subsidies for the employment of older workers, marriage loans, subsidies to stimulate building construction, restrictions on dismissals, and the reintroduction of compulsory military service. Expenditures on a national program of rearmament were also included in the plan.

In the fall of 1936, the Second Four-Year Plan was introduced. It, too, dealt with a specific problem, namely the need to make Germany self-sufficient so that it could wage war. The aims of the plan were to increase the production of raw materials, to increase agricultural production in general and especially in those lines which produced raw materials for industry, to distribute labor with special regard for the needs of military and armament industries, and to control and distribute foreign exchange. To facilitate these objectives, many phases of German economic life were brought under rigid government control. The government organized controls over prices and wages, international trade, and credit and investment operations.

Economic policy after World War II was away from economic planning and controls and toward a system of free enterprise which stressed competition and efficiency within a free market framework. The German economy again became the most productive in Europe, and the rapid growth rate in the gross national product averaged around 7 percent a year during the 1950s and early 1960s. Then the growth rate began to drop as the momentum which had propelled the economy forward began to decline and a recession occurred. The Erhard government was replaced by a coalition of the two major political parties. This coalition brought into office men such as Economics Minister Karl Schiller, who were disposed toward dropping the free market economic doctrine of former Chancellor Erhard and adopting more of a Keynesian policy of deficit spending and other fiscal measures. These men also felt that some sort of fiscal planning was necessary to bring more order into the sometimes chaotic federal and state fiscal relationships, so a medium-term fiscal plan was developed.

The Medium-Term Fiscal Plan. The Medium-Term Fiscal Plan was the off-shoot of a study prepared by the Economics Ministry in 1966 as a projection of economic prospects in Germany through 1970 for the European Economic Community. This study was transmitted to all federal ministries and to the states to be used as a common basis for medium-term budget plans.

The plan consisted of a series of projections or forecasts, as well as a plan of action, for the economy until 1971. Gross national product was projected to increase at the rate of 4 percent a year, and private consumption was projected to increase at the same rate. The individual components of investment were expected to increase at a differential rate. Public investment, because of anticipated further heavy demand for infrastructure and social investment, was to increase by 5.5 percent a year, while private investment in plant and equipment was to increase by 3.7 percent. For the labor force, an absolute decline was projected, attributable to a decrease in the rate of population growth. Labor productivity was expected to increase by 3.5 percent a year.[23]

The Medium-Term Fiscal Plan, however, is more than just a forecast of expected developments. It includes an investment program for special social and economic measures. The national budget forms the basis of the plan in that priorities are marked out for expenditures. Investment programs of public authorities have to be planned on the basis of budgetary projections covering the five-year period of the plan.

The plan gives equal priority to the following economic policy goals: price stability, full employment, stable economic growth, and a balance of payments equilibrium. Federal and state budgets are to be drawn up and managed in accordance with these objectives. Expenditures, particularly on investment, are to be adjusted year by year to conform to the economic situation. If aggregate demand is found to be excessive, provision is made in both budgets for allocation of funds to a special cyclical equalization reserve to be held by the Bundesbank. If economic activity shows a decline, additional expenditures will be undertaken from funds available in the cyclical equalization reserve.

AN APPRAISAL OF THE GERMAN ECONOMY

Principal responsibility in West German public policies for stimulating economic growth has rested on fiscal devices. Close to one fifth of federal government expenditures are devoted to physical investments in roads, schools, transportation, and particularly in housing. Savings derived from budget surpluses and the social insurance system have been diverted into investment in government approved areas, such as housing construction. The federal tax structure is heavily weighted against consumer outlays in that the turnover tax, now replaced by the value-added tax, and other taxes on consumption account for approximately three fifths of federal budget revenues. Numerous tax preferences are given for approved forms of savings and for various classes of business income, and the burden of the personal income tax weighs heaviest on the lower- and middle-income ranges.

Until recently the West German growth rate has been second only to Japan's in terms of annual increase. For the period 1950 to 1964, its gross national product increased at a rate of 6.7 percent a year compared to 3.1 percent for the United States and 9.6 percent for Japan. In terms of gross domestic fixed investment for the same period, the rate of growth was 10 percent for West Germany, 2.3 percent for the United States, and 16 percent for Japan.[24]

Using two time periods, 1950 to 1962 and 1950 to 1964, and using real national income valued at factor cost as a growth rate measure, the German economy exhibited the highest growth rate in Europe. In the period, 1950 to 1962, German real national income increased at a rate of 7.3 percent a year compared to 3.3 percent for the United States, 4.9 percent for France, and

[23] Unclassified material furnished by the American Embassy in Bonn, Germany.
[24] Angus Maddison, *Economic Growth in the West* (London: George Allen and Unwin, Ltd., 1964), p. 37.

2.3 percent for the United Kingdom. In the period, 1950 to 1964, the German growth rate in terms of real national income increased at a rate of 7.1 percent a year compared to 3.5 percent for the United States, 4.9 percent for France, and 2.6 percent for the United Kingdom. Italy ranked second to Germany among western European countries in terms of growth rates, accomplishing a 6 percent increase a year between 1950 and 1964.[25]

However, in more recent years the growth rate of the West German economy has become quite erratic. This fact can be observed in Table 14–5, which

TABLE 14–5

GROWTH IN REAL NET SOCIAL PRODUCT FOR WEST GERMANY, 1961–1973

Year	Growth Rate
1961	5.1%
1962	3.5
1963	2.9
1964	6.5
1965	5.3
1966	2.4
1967	1.1
1968	7.3
1969	8.1
1970	4.7
1971	2.9
1972	1.5
1973	3.7

Source: Statistisches Bundesamt, Statistisches Jahrbuch fur die Bundesrepublik Deutschland, 1973 (Wiesbaden: W. Kohlhammer Verlag, 1973), p. 490.

presents the rate of growth in real net social product from 1961 to 1973, with the rate expressed in terms of 1962 prices. *Real net social product* is defined as total goods produced and services performed less price increases that occurred during a given period.

Although the basic economic position of West Germany remains strong relative to other industrial nations, certain problems have developed. One such problem is inflation. In 1970 the general price level, as measured by the gross social product deflator, increased by 7.6 percent, or about twice the highest rate experienced since the upsurge connected with the Korean War boom. This inflation continued in 1971 and 1972, with a corresponding decline in real gross social product. One significant point in this connection was the deterioration in the growth rate of the West German economy relative to the French economy. In the first three years of the 1970s, the French real

[25] Edward F. Denison, *Why Growth Rates Differ* (Washington: The Brookings Institution, 1967), p. 17.

growth rate exceeded the West German growth rate. In 1972, for example, the real increase in French gross social product was 5.5 percent compared to 1.5 percent for West Germany.[26] Estimates for 1973 and projections for 1974 also show a West German lag relative to the French economy.

There are also other problems confronting the West German economy. For one thing, there is an acute shortage of housing in the major cities. There is also concern over pollution, which is a problem endemic to all industrial countries regardless of their political persuasion. In particular, the Rhine River has had its scenic beauty destroyed by the effluvia of the many industrial plants on its banks. There is some concern about the distribution of income which, if anything, may be more unequal than income and wealth distribution in the United States. Finally, there is general unrest among university students which may be attributed to a number of factors, not the least of which is an antiquated school system.

SUMMARY

The West German economy can be considered as a mix between private and public enterprise. The government has sought to establish a free market economy exempt from most controls. Policies have been pursued which can be considered as favorable to a free enterprise system. Certainly, from the standpoint of production and distribution, market forces determine each, just as in the United States. The pricing mechanism is the basic determinant, not some central authoritarian planner. Consumer sovereignty prevails in that the German people are free to purchase whatever products they desire.

Nevertheless, the government plays a much more important role in the economy than does its counterpart in the United States. A considerable segment of the economy is nationalized, and the government, through this segment, can influence the level of investment. Some nationalized industries are in direct competition with private industries for resources, but there is no striking economic consequence because public enterprise has coexisted with private enterprise since the days of Bismarck. There is also little danger that further encroachment on the private sector will occur on the part of the public sector. Since the end of the war, there has been no trend in this direction.

The government has made wide use of fiscal incentives to accomplish various socio-economic objectives. For example, fiscal encouragement has been directed toward housing construction. Private contractors have been accorded a variety of investment and tax allowances; they have been especially favored if they produce new homes to let at low rents. Tax credits and depreciation allowances have also been used to stimulate investment in ship construction to help rebuild the German merchant marine. On the other hand, special real estate taxes are levied to punish landowners who do not construct houses on their property. Savings are stimulated through the use of special premium allowances or tax exemptions.

An impressive portion of the West German national product is devoted to social welfare programs. These programs are extensive and are constantly expanding. Roughly half of government expenditures come under the purview of transfers, which is indicative of the welfare state character of Germany. Some

[26] Deutsches Institut fur Wirtschaftsforschung.

of the income redistribution effect of transfer payments has been counterbalanced by a shift from progressive income and corporation taxes to indirect taxes, such as the value-added tax, which are burdensome on the consumer.

Economic planning has not been a *fait accompli* in postwar German economic policy. However, recent events have prompted a rethinking concerning planning. First of all, the sharp recession in 1967 caused a shift in attitude away from the free market and conservative budgetary and monetary policies, with emphasis on price stability, toward a Keynesian-oriented economic policy which stresses economic growth, full employment, and balanced foreign trade, as well as price stability. Economic planning, however, is fiscal in nature and is designed to mesh government expenditures more closely with desired economic goals. Second, economic planning of the French type is favored by other Common Market countries.

The West German economy is among the healthiest and most viable of the world's economies. The 1973 victory of the Social Democrats provides a possibility that a move to the left in terms of planning, controls, and social welfare could occur.

QUESTIONS

1. Discuss the factors that were responsible for the rapid postwar recovery of the German economy.
2. Compare the West German and United States economic systems. Are there any major differences between the two systems?
3. Describe the West German tax system. Is there a similarity between it and the United States tax system?
4. Government tax and expenditure policies play a significant role in the operation of the West German economy. Do you agree?
5. Discuss the relationship of the Bundesbank to the West German banking system.
6. Fiscal policy in West Germany has shifted from a conservative, orthodox position stressing balanced budgets to a more Keynesian position. Do you agree?
7. Discuss the relationship of government and business in West Germany.
8. What are some of the objectives of the Economic Growth and Stability Law.
9. Economic planning has not been important in West Germany. Do you agree?

RECOMMENDED READINGS

Bailey, George. *Germans: The Biography of an Obsession.* New York: World Publishers, 1972.

Dahrendorf, Rolf. *Society and Democracy in Germany.* Garden City, N.Y.: Doubleday, 1969.

Jaspers, Karl. *The Future of Germany.* Chicago: University of Chicago Press, 1974.

Peck Reginald. *The West Germans: How They Live and Work.* New York: Praeger, 1970.

Schnitzer, Martin. *East and West Germany: A Comparative Economic Analysis.* New York: Praeger, 1972.

Sontheimer, Kurt. *The Government and Politics of West Germany.* New York: Praeger, 1973.

Wallich, Henry C. *Mainsprings of the German Revival.* New Haven: Yale University Press, 1955.

15

Modern Socialist Economies

INTRODUCTION

As mentioned previously, modern society offers two institutions through which resource allocation decisions are made. These are the market and government means of resource allocation. In reality, of course, no economic society allocates all of its resources through a single institution. Instead, each economy in the world is mixed, to one degree or another, between market-determined and government-determined resource allocation. Accordingly, a given national economy may typically be referred to as "capitalist" or "socialist" depending upon the degree to which it stresses the market or government means of allocation. A continuum can be used to show some of the major alternative techniques which can be used to affect resource allocation. These techniques range from those which are applied directly and completely by the government to those where the public sector's influence is very indirect. At one end of the continuum, government allocation influence is direct and complete, and at the other end market forces are dominant.

The socialist economies of today show considerable variation in terms of their positions on the continuum.[1] There are alternative allocative techniques which are used in different countries. There are some socialist countries that are mixed in that some functions are desocialized, while in others the state exercises all ownership functions which have not wholly or partly been transferred expressly by law to the private individual. But even under Stalinist command planning some form of market mechanism had to be tolerated. With the economic reforms of the 1960s, more elements of the market mechanism were incorporated or extended in socialist economies, such as a greater role

[1] The term "socialism" is used in preference to "communism" for the reason that the countries used in this section describe themselves as "socialist" and not "communist."

337

assigned to consumer preferences, considerable independence of enterprises, profit, the strengthening of material incentives to labor, and the use of various financial devices including interest and depreciation allowances. However, only Yugoslavia has adopted a form of market socialism.

No two socialist countries can be fitted into the same mold. In East Germany, for example, agriculture with very minor exceptions has been collectivized, while in Poland most of agriculture remains in private hands. There is private ownership of industry in East Germany and Hungary, but in the Soviet Union private ownership of industry is nil. However, there are various institutional arrangements which are common to the socialist countries. These arrangements are the subject of this chapter. However, before these arrangements are discussed it is first necessary to make reference to the economic reforms which were prevalent in the socialist countries in Eastern Europe, particularly those reforms which took place during the 1960s. These reforms are reflected in the most current character of the socialist economies.

ECONOMIC REFORMS

With the exception of Yugoslavia, the socialist countries of Eastern Europe were occupied by Soviet forces after the end of World War II. It was inevitable that sooner or later the Soviet Union would impose its type of economic system on these countries. Although this imposition did not occur at the same time for each country, by 1950 the basic rudiments of the Stalinist command type of economy had been established in Eastern Europe. This command economy was based on the ideological assumption that the only repository of human rationality is the Communist Party. Accordingly, the independent actions of individuals, groups, or institutions—which could only hinder the pursuit of rational goals—was replaced by the absolutist exercise of power by the party-state. This absolute rationality was embodied in the state plan, which prescribed practically all actions for each economic unit in the form of a state law to be carried out to the last detail. The same rigid relationship existed between the center and the unit, the state and the individual, in all walks of human life, particularly in politics, where it was seen as the only guarantee that the center could control the economy.

The advantage of a Stalinist command type of economy was that it ensured the structure of production and distribution according to the priorities postulated by the Communist Party. However, there was no scope for independence of decision making at the operational level. Producing units were bound by directive targets and a large number of other directive plan indicators. Economic accounting was done entirely in terms of physical units, and allocative decisions were not based on prices but on material balances. But the most important defect of the Stalinist command economy was its lack of flexibility and wastefulness. Resources were not allocated in the most efficient manner. There were shortages in the production of consumer goods, for top priority was assigned to the development of the capital goods industries. In each country under Soviet influence there was a common legacy of internal rigidity and resultant problems of economic performance. The attainment of Stalinist type objectives reinforced traditional autarky, nonspecialization, inappropriate specialization and small-scale economics—problems that were to plague Eastern Europe's development as a viable economic region.

To improve economic efficiency, a series of reforms were instituted by the socialist countries, particularly during the 1960s. The significant elements of these reforms involved a number of areas. Industrial and trading enterprises were given greater freedom to choose ways and means of plan fulfillment. Profit was accepted as the main indicator of enterprise performance, while the total number of success indicators were drastically reduced. Increased importance was attached to material as distinct from moral incentives. Planning was made less prescriptive and detailed; instead efforts were made to lay down broad targets expressed in value terms. Prices were brought more in line with production costs to reduce the need for state subsidies and to enable average enterprises to be profitable. Similarly, procurement prices paid to the farms were raised in relation to industrial prices, to encourage agricultural production and to improve living standards in rural areas. There was some overhaul of the retail and wholesale trade network, designed to improve services to consumers and to enable effective transmission of customers' preferences to producing enterprises. A greater role was assigned to finance and credit, with a flexible use of interest rates.

These reforms were by no means uniform in all of the countries. Yugoslavia, which was free from Russian hegemony, had more latitude in terms of reform actions. The other countries, within the limits of Soviet tolerance, were able to pursue different policy lines. The different policies which were implemented by the countries were related to their perception of economic performance and requirements. Rumania was less inclined than the other countries to vary from Stalinist economic institutions in that priority was given to the development of heavy industry. On the other hand, economic reform in Czechoslovakia, Hungary, and East Germany took the form of changes in price policy. Each adopted a multiple price system with some prices free, other prices varied within ranges, and some prices fixed. Production criteria of total quantity output at the enterprise level were replaced by monetary and qualitative criteria such as sales, costs, and profit.

Economic Reforms in Yugoslavia

In 1965 a series of economic reforms was introduced in Yugoslavia that hastened a trend toward decentralization which had started after the split with the Russians in 1948. These reforms were designed to achieve a socialist market economy through decentralized decision making and the use of market pricing. There were two basic objectives of the reforms: (1) improvement of the productivity of capital and labor and (2) a more balanced rate of economic growth. The reforms applied to nearly all parts of the economy and can be summarized as follows:

1. The fiscal system was decentralized. Several national taxes were eliminated, and all expenditures for the internal development of the national economy were also eliminated with the exception of the fund for the underdeveloped

republics. Major elements of public finance were transferred from the national government to the republics, districts, and communes.

2. The price system was reformed with the objective of eventually achieving the free determination of prices by market forces. Prices of goods and services were raised for the purpose of bringing them into line with those that prevailed in the international markets and also for the purpose of using them as instruments of development policy in combination with customs duties.

3. Reforms also took place in the banking system. Banks were organized into three broad areas of specialization—investment banking, commercial banking, and mixed banks. Banks were freed from direct government control, and their existence was made dependent upon funds provided by individual enterprises.

One unique characteristic of the Yugoslav economy, which has developed over time, is a reliance on decentralization of economic decision making and a dependence on the free market to accomplish the allocation of resources. Autonomy has been given to individual enterprises with regard to price and production policies and to the distribution of income between wages and investment. Within the limits set by national and international competition, enterprises are free to set prices, to decide what and how much to produce, and to distribute income from the sales of their products.

Economic Reforms in East Germany

Economic reforms in East Germany came under the heading of the New Economic System (Neues Oekonomisches System) which was first started in 1963. The focal points of the New Economic System were as follows:

1. To change the structure of the management system and economic administration and improve planning methods.

2. To direct enterprise interests into the direction desired for the whole economy through the use of material interests in the form of a self-enclosed system of economic levers.

3. To create necessary preconditions for more efficient monetary control.

A three-stage price reform was introduced in industry to encourage more rational assessment of costs and revenues and more economies in the use of scarce and imported raw materials which had been priced too low. These stages extended over a three-year period, 1964–1967. The reforms involved raising prices on most East German products. Efforts were made to relate prices more directly to real costs. However, the price reforms used cost-determined prices based on the value of labor as a variant of real value. This resulted in an average price which was too high for the labor intensive industries and too low for the capital intensive industries. This called for a look at the price system, and it was realized that labor alone is not the sole source of value. Capital also had to enter into the calculations, and labor and capital together would have to determine prices.

Another important aspect of the overall reforms was the acceptance of profit as the main criterion of enterprise performance. Prior to the reforms profit was used as an accounting device to ensure that enterprises covered costs out of their own resources and handed any surplus over to the state budget. To promote enterprise performance a system of incentives was tied to certain criteria. Incentives were based primarily on the volume of output, but efficiency of enterprise operations was affected adversely in that quantity was stressed at the expense of quality. When value of output was used as a measure of enterprise success, what usually happened was that only those articles containing the most expensive raw materials and components were produced. Incentives were based on the value of trade turnover; this criterion prompted trading enterprises to supply high-priced articles.

The New Economic System embraced the idea that the maximization of enterprise profit would ensure the quality and efficiency of production. Instead of tying incentive payments to the volume or value of output, payments are now based on profit. Given the tie between profit and performance, any increase in the profitability of an enterprise can be accomplished by producing what consumers and other enterprises want, on the one hand, and by reducing costs on the other. Profit is now generally calculated on the basis of the output actually sold, not merely produced. Moreover, improved systems of penalties are being adopted, whereby fines are deducted from profits, or receipts, for nonfulfillment of contracts, delays, poor quality, faulty specifications, and negligence.

Economic Reforms in Hungary

Hungarian administrative and economic reforms have also been designed to promote efficiency. Some effort was made during the 1950s to effect a liberalization of the bureaucratic and administrative framework. For example, in 1957 individual enterprises were relieved of the obligation to submit monthly and quarterly plans for the approval of higher authorities. In 1963 the guidance and control of enterprises, previously exercised by ministerial industrial boards, was turned over to newly organized trusts operated to maximize profits, with the component enterprises defraying the expenses. Another significant reform was made in 1964 with the introduction of capital charges in industry. Capital charges are annual payments made by enterprises to the state on fixed and circulating capital in their possession. It was recognized that interest is ideologically justified because capital is nothing else than materialized labor, and as such it should be rationally distributed, because it represents a means of economizing live labor.

However, the most important reforms took place in 1968. Enterprises were made independent economic units with the right to determine the structure of their production and sales. This policy conformed to one basic objective of the reform, namely, to relieve the planning authorities of the task of preparing intricate economic plans. Instead broad guidelines were provided for enterprises to follow. Enterprises were given latitude with respect to quality, styling and pricing. They were also given the right to determine their own production mix on the basis of their preferences. A modified market economy was permitted in which enterprises could react to consumer preferences. Neverthless, the central planning authorities were able to exercise some control over enterprise production through the use of economic levers designed to induce cooperation by making it more profitable to produce certain items. Thus, the government reserved for itself the final right to curb consumer preferences, particularly in the public area. Moreover, all major macroeconomic decisions concerning economic development, living standards, and investment and consumption remained in the hands of the state.

As is true of the economic reforms in the other East European countries, the state was ready to take away what it had given at the first sign of real independence. In Hungary enterprises and individuals discovered that indirect regulators and controls exercised by the state provided constraints which manipulated the market framework.[2] Moreover, there were no political reforms to accompany decentralization of economic decision making at the enterprise level. Although there was an effort to achieve decentralization of decision making, there was no corresponding effort to provide more autonomy in terms of political rights. In Hungary, as well as in East Germany and the other socialist countries, there has been no attempt on the part of the state authorities to relinquish their absolute political power. All economic decisions had to be made within the constraints of a highly circumscribed political framework. Inevitably the reforms came into conflict with ideological and political issues.

ECONOMIC PLANNING

The method of deciding key economic questions in socialist industry, e.g., what to produce, how much of each item, for whom, and the allocation of resources necessary to achieve the desired production and distribution, is through state economic planning. Although socialist economies make use of a system of money and prices, the prices of goods and services and those of agents of production are not determined by the competition of buyers and sellers in the market and hence are not reliable guides for the making of economic decisions. A socialist economic system has the ability to make economic plans and to see to it that these plans are carried out. This is because the productive wealth of the system, consisting of land and capital, is owned by society as a whole; and society, as reflected through the state, is the only business entrepreneur of any importance and controls most lines of economic activity.

So both production and distribution are implemented through the use of economic plans. Formally approved state plans, buttressed by rules of behavior and various types of incentives, govern production and distribution decisions. The plans represent an attempt to balance the supply of and demand

[2] For discussions of the reforms, see Barnabas Buky, "Hungary on a Treadmill," *Problems of Communism* (September–October, 1972), pp. 31–39; also Harry G. Shaffer, "Progress in Hungary," *Problems of Communism* (January–February, 1970), pp. 45–59. For Eastern Europe see Michael Gamarnikov, "Political Patterns and Economic Reforms," *Problems of Communism* (March–April, 1969), pp. 11–23.

for resources in order to achieve an equilibrium. In a market economy consumer choice influences resource allocation, but this is not true for a planned economy. Planning is not only concerned with every branch of economic activity, but embraces many aspects of socialist economic life. It is not content with merely making the system operate; it also has such objectives as increasing national wealth or the rapid industrialization of the economy. In other words, economic planning can have both short- and long-term goals. It relies on orders for its implementation; it is controlled by a central planning agency, by financial organizations, and, above all, by the political authorities.

Economic plans may be divided into several categories. First of all, there are general plans which may be laid down for a period of fifteen to twenty years. These plans are primarily concerned with long-term problems of structural changes on the national scale, technology, the training of labor, and the like. Secondly, there are medium-term plans, usually covering a period of five years and concerned mostly with changes in the capacity and rate of production of different industries and enterprises. This type of plan is subject to perpetual revision as it is carried out, and, as a matter of fact, there seems to be no real reason why the planning process should be broken down into five-year intervals. Thirdly, there are annual plans within each five-year plan. These plans provide a detailed description of production plans for the year and serve as a control mechanism to ensure compliance by the enterprises. Finally, there are quarterly plans within each annual plan, and even monthly plans for plants or groups of plants within specific branches of industries.

It is also necessary to distinguish between physical input-output planning and financial planning. Actually, economic planning consists of both types. The basic planning in the socialist countries is in real terms and involves physical output targets of the most important industrial and agricultural commodities, and the allocation of labor at the national level, the balancing and transfers of important types of raw materials and equipment, and total national capital investment. The financial plan is important as a control mechanism. It is used to control the execution of the national physical, or real, input-output plan. Although subordinate to the physical plan in the overall planning system, it is used to maintain a discipline in the physical planning process—a discipline which is imposed by the banking system. The financial plan is also used to maintain a balance between consumer disposable income and the volume of consumer goods and services available. It consists of three parts—the state budget, the credit plan, and the cash plan of the central bank. The importance of the state budget cannot be minimized for the reason that a considerable part of socialist gross national product flows through it. The credit and cash plans control the outlay of short-term credit and the currency and coin issued by the central bank. The latter plays an important role in financial planning because it exercises several control functions, such as seeing that credit loans to enterprises are used in conformance with physical planning objectives.

The state budget is an integral part of the financial plan. Its importance cannot be minimized for the reason that about half of the national income of the socialist countries flows through their budgets. It is through the state budget that the turnover tax, deductions from profits of enterprises, and the other fiscal resources of a socialist economy are collected and distributed. The state budget is a prime vehicle for the allocation of resources among various ends, whereas in a market economy the market is a device for the organization of economic activity, and it functions by transmitting preferences to producers who, in the process of adjusting output to correspond with these preferences, direct economic resources into alternative uses. The state budget is used as a control mechanism because it provides a considerable part of the investment funds for enterprises. These funds are provided for certain purposes within the framework of the financial plan.

There is in economic planning the need to balance plan targets with available economic resources. There are two ways in which this problem is resolved: (1) through the use of material balances or (2) through the use of input-output analysis. Material balances present an intended relationship between supplies and their allocation for specific commodities. The balances, which are normally expressed in physical units, provide a basis for the financial counterpart of the plan. Input-output analysis involves interbranch balancing which means that the economy is divided up into a number of branches, each of which has assigned inputs and outputs. These branches are presented on a statistical grid showing how much each economic sector buys and sells from every other major sector. For example, the grid shows how much of the output of the steel industry goes to the auto, construction, or chemical industries. At the same time it shows how much the steel industry itself receives from these other industries.

Mechanics of Planning

Economic planning is a complicated process in which production and consumption are controlled by the central planning authorities on the basis of predetermined economic and political objectives. Typically, priority has been given to the development of industries that will contribute the most to the attainment of national economic and political goals. Economic plans provide for a maximum rate of development of certain branches of an economy and lines of production through priorities in investment and materials and through human and financial resources. It is assumed that the accelerated expansion of certain key industries, such as the chemical, oil, gas, and power industries, makes it possible to increase the overall rate of growth of industrial and agricultural production.

The East German plan for 1973 can be used to illustrate the intricacies of economic planning. The plan was initiated in April 1972 by the State Planning Commission (Staatliche Plankommission). However, the plan is based on the policy directives of the Council of Ministers (Ministerrat der DDR), which is the highest administrative organ in East Germany. The Council is also responsible for the approval of the final draft of the plan. Guidelines for the working out of the plan are developed by the State Planning Commission to be sent to districts and municipalities and to all enterprises. The connecting links between the Planning Commission and the various economic and political units are the industrial, agricultural, and trade ministries. Each ministry is responsible for the application of control figures to its given area of jurisdiction. These control figures are also sent down to ministry subdepartments at district, county, and local levels.

The chart on page 346 presents the framework of the plan. The lowest link on the plan is at the enterprise level (kreisgeleitete Betriebe). The purpose of this dissemination is to provide information which can be used as a basis for plan formulation by all production and distribution units. After the control figures have been made available to the various economic units and the lower levels of government, there is a plan counterdesign which starts with the formulation of plans by industrial and trade enterprises, state farms, and other local economic units. These plans cover all phases of their operations. The plans, which can be considered as target plans, then travel upward for their integration into the national plan. At each administrative level the plans cumulate into a national whole. Also at each level the plans must be defended.

The numbers correspond to the various state administrative units and enterprises that are involved in planning. For example, number one represents the initiation of the planning process when the basic targets of the plan are sent to the ministries for transmission to the various industries under their jurisdiction. The black line represents the preparation and transfer of the plan. The ministries disaggregate the plan goals and transmit them to the respective executors. In East Germany the next step is number four when the plan directives go to the VVB's (Vereinigung Volkseigener Betriebe), which are associations of industrial and trade enterprises. Each VVB represents the most important link between the administration of the industrial system and the basic enterprise units.

The comprehensiveness of the plan is apparent. As has already been mentioned, the state budget is an integral part of the plan. There must be a reconciliation of individual enterprise needs to the availability of bank credit. Consumer needs must be balanced against the supply of producer's goods. Foreign trade also must enter into planning decisions. All of this is done during the period from April to September. By October the final process of reconciliation is done by the State Planning Commission. Once the plans have cleared the national ministries, they are merged into the draft plan in which the directives and policy objectives of the Council of Ministers is adjusted to planning aggregates. When the national economic plan is prepared, it is sent to the Council of Ministers for approval. Once approved the plan in essence becomes law, and it passes down the administrative ladder until it reaches the enterprises. It is to be emphasized that this annual plan is an operating plan which is to be followed within prescribed limits by all production and distribution units.

The basic method of East German economic planning involves the use of material balances which are usually carried on in physical terms and present an intended relationship between supplies and their allocation for specific

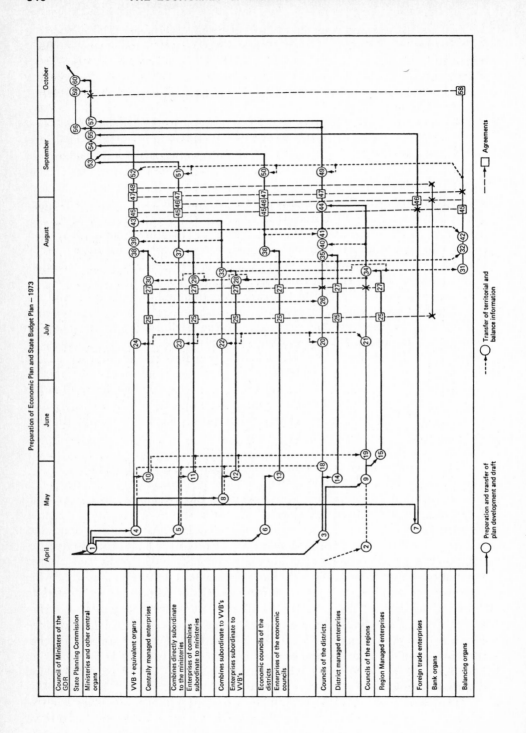

commodities. Material balances are drawn up for all of the important types of industrial and agricultural products. Targets are reconciled with the limiting constraints of available resources. The balances, which are normally expressed in physical units, provide a basis for the financial part of the plan. According to the existing practice in East Germany, the overall balance of the national economy comprises several flows which have to be harmonized, including production, consumption, and accumulation, and primary, secondary, and final distribution of national income. The material balance method is cumbersome to handle, and moreover it obscures the repercussions of economic changes.

Defects of Planning

In the case of a system of central plan directives, a powerful bureaucracy develops which generally identifies the movements and regularities of economic life with the internal norms of the state apparatus. This bureaucracy generally tries—regardless of its intentions—to perpetuate and consolidate its position. Every system of guidance has its internal logic; in the case of the central system of planning directives, this means that deficiencies are often due to the fact that enterprises are circumscribed in terms of planning directives. It is impossible to guide a complex and interdependent economy on a directive basis without running the risk of serious economic trouble. The hierarchical nature of planning and administration makes a socialist system unwieldy and not easily adaptable to the changes demanded by modern developments.

Under economic planning, not enough attention has been paid to problems arising at the microeconomic level. Socialist economies have tended to neglect the problems of management and utilization of resources at the operational level. Seen from a purely economic point of view, planning provides practically no incentive to be efficient. A dual system of decision making, which cannot be avoided in the absence of frequent enterprise, contains a danger of incongruity and divergence. Experience shows that it is not easy in practice to reconcile targets set at the central level, even though they may be optimal, with the interest of the enterprises so that they do not act contrary to social interest.

PUBLIC FINANCE

A major difference between the fiscal systems of the socialist countries and the leading nonsocialist industrial countries of the West lies in the role and size of the budget. In the United States there are three basic levels of government—federal, state, and local—and each level operates its budget in substantial independence from the other. However, in the Soviet Union and the People's Republic of China, as well as in the socialist satellite countries, the budget represents a financial control mechanism for carrying out the state economic plans. The budgets of both the Soviet Union and the People's Republic of China are centralized and represent a consolidation of all budgets—

national, republic, and local. The end result is the consolidated state budget which assumes the key role in the distribution of the national income in each country.

Significance of the State Budgets

The state budgets of the socialist countries are much larger in terms of the relationship of expenditures to national income than the budgets of the leading nonsocialist countries. About half of the national income of the Soviet Union and China flows through their budgets. The reason for the size of the state budget is obvious. Under the socialist system many things which would be financed in a capitalistic system by private enterprise or private individuals are financed by the government. So the budgets of the socialist countries are much broader in coverage than their counterparts in other countries. For example, investment expenditures, which in the United States would be financed by private enterprise, are financed to a considerable degree by the state budget in a socialist country. Many other expenditures, such as expenditures for health, education, and research, which would be financed at least in part by the private sector in a capitalistic economy, are financed out of the state budget.

In such socialist countries as the Soviet Union and China, the national economic plan sets forth the level and distribution of economic resources necessary for the fulfillment of national objectives. The state budget of these countries is an integral part of the financial plan, which reflects financially the national economic plan. The financial plan involves the cash, credit, and investment financing which is necessary to implement the attainment of the physical output goals spelled out in the national economic plan. It is through the state budget that the turnover tax, deductions from profits of enterprises, and the other fiscal resources of the government are collected and redistributed. The state budget is a prime vehicle for the allocation of resources among various ends, whereas in a market economy, the market is a device for the organization of economic activity, and it functions by transmitting preferences to producers, who, in the process of adjusting output to correspond with these preferences, direct economic resources into alternative uses. The state budget is used as a control mechanism because it provides a considerable proportion of the investment funds for enterprises. These funds are provided for certain purposes within the framework of the financial plan. This control restricts the opportunity of enterprises to indulge in investments outside of those which are specified in the plan.

Taxation

An outstanding feature of the fiscal systems of China, the Soviet Union, and Yugoslavia is the predominance of indirect taxation over direct taxation. This is surprising in view of the fact that Marxist doctrine would hold that the use of such taxes discriminates against the working classes because they are regressive and inequitable. However, there is a purpose for this reliance on indirect taxation. First of all, indirect taxes are easier to administer and harder to avoid than direct taxes. They are collected from thousands of enterprises rather than millions of individuals, and in the early stages of socialist development, this was important because the administrative machinery of government was not well developed. Second, the role of the government as reflected by the size of the national budget is more important in the socialist countries, so taxation by necessity must also be higher. Direct taxes would not provide the revenues which are necessary to support budgetary expenditures. The direct taxes would also have more of a negative impact on work incentives than indirect taxes.

Basic Types of Taxes. A very important tax in the Soviet Union is the turnover tax. It is applied primarily to consumer goods and is levied at early stages in the production process. It is a highly differentiated tax in that the rates vary from product to product and also from region to region. In addition to being a leading revenue source, the tax exercises an important control function in that it is used to regulate the level of aggregate demand. The tax is also often levied when, although goods are abundant, consumption is considered undesirable. For example, a high turnover tax is levied on such commodities as alcohol and tobacco and on such luxury items as furs and jewelry. The turnover tax is also used to regulate profits in that the rates can determine the amount of profits allowed to producers.

The most important source of tax revenue in China is the consolidated industrial and commercial tax which is levied on all enterprises and individuals engaged in industrial production, retail trade, importation of goods, transportation, and services. The rates are differentiated by products, and the tax is assessed as a percentage of total sales proceeds in the case of producers and retailers. For importers, the tax is levied on the total value of industrial imports, which includes cost, insurance, and freight (CIF) value and customs duties; however, for agricultural imports, the tax is levied on CIF value only.

The fiscal system of Yugoslavia was revised in 1965 in order to provide more autonomy to the republics and communes. The turnover tax, which was the most important source of revenue to the federal budget prior to 1965, was eliminated. This tax was of two types—a producer's turnover tax, which was levied on all products produced by Yugoslav enterprises, and a general turnover tax, which was levied on wholesale trade and imports. The turnover tax was replaced by a retail sales tax which is levied at the time of purchase on most items purchased at the retail level.

Deductions from profits represent another important source of revenue for the state budget, particularly in the Soviet Union. Profits, as defined in Soviet terms, can represent the difference between the total income received by an enterprise from the sale of its products and its production costs. They can also represent the difference between the government-determined price for a given commodity and the cost to an enterprise for producing it. When profits are made by an enterprise, they are utilized in two ways—one part is remitted to the budget and the other part is retained by the enterprise. The part which is returned to the budget can be viewed as a transfer of revenue rather than a direct tax. However, since it is a part of total profits over and above costs of production, it is incorporated in the final selling price. In this respect, deductions from profits can be considered to have the same effect as sales taxes since each can be shifted forward to consumers.

The personal income tax is not an important source of revenue in the socialist countries. For example, in 1970 the turnover tax accounted for 32 percent of total state budget revenues in the Soviet Union compared to 8.8 percent of total revenue for the personal income tax. In Sweden personal income taxes accounted for 60 percent of total government revenues—national and local—in the fiscal year 1973–74. The personal income tax is also the most important source of national government revenue in the United Kingdom and the United States. In China the personal income tax is a relatively minor source of revenue.

There are two reasons for the lack of reliance on the personal income tax in the socialist countries. First of all, virtually all wage and salary earners are employed by state enterprises or enterprises which are closely controlled by the state. Therefore, a personal income tax would only be an administrative device for doing what could be done with less trouble by adjustment of the wages and salaries originally paid. Second, the socialist countries rely on wage differentials to allocate labor. Material incentives play a very important role in stimulating worker productivity. It is felt that a direct tax, such as the personal income tax, would have a more negative impact on work incentives than indirect taxes. An indirect tax, such as a sales tax, is less visible than the income tax and would not have the effect of reducing the take-home pay of the worker. In the Soviet Union, the personal income tax on wage and salary earners was supposed to have been abolished after October 1, 1965. Although some staged reductions in the income tax have been carried out, the tax is still being used.

Fiscal Policy. There is little doubt that the three basic economic goals of full employment, price stability, and economic growth are highly desirable in both the nonsocialist countries of the West and the socialist countries. Both fiscal and monetary policy can be used to contribute to the attainment of these goals. Fiscal policy, as defined previously, deals with government receipts and expenditures. Receipts represent the flow of funds from the economy to the government and expenditures represent a reverse flow of funds from the government to the economy. The significance of fiscal policy lies in the fact that it deals directly with matters which immediately influence consumption and investment expenditures, and hence the income, of the economy. Monetary policy, as also defined previously, is concerned with the provision of money, defined to include currency and demand deposits at commercial banks. It seeks to maintain a balance between real aggregate demand and supply through control of the aggregate monetary demand for goods and services.

As has been mentioned in the chapters on the United States, Japan, and Western Europe, both fiscal and monetary policy carry responsibility for providing the conditions necessary for the attainment of the economic goals of full employment, price stability, and economic growth. Public investment in most of these countries is involved in the expansion of total productive capacity.

Tax policies have not only been concerned with stimulating private investment and thus promoting a higher rate of economic growth, but also with maintaining a balance between aggregate demand and supply. Reference has been made to the Swedish investment reserve, which is used to stabilize investment, and the surtax, which has been used in the United States and has for its objective a reduction in the level of aggregate demand as reflected in consumer and investment expenditures.

In the Soviet Union the turnover tax is the basic fiscal policy instrument which is used to achieve a balance between supply and demand. Consumer goods are in short supply relative to the demand for them. Soviet economic policy has usually stressed the development of the industrial goods sector of the economy and resources have been allocated for this purpose. Yet the Soviet workers receive income and have relatively few alternatives for spending it as far as consumer goods are concerned. The turnover tax is used to absorb the excess purchasing power of consumers. The production plans of the government provide that a given amount of goods be made available to consumers annually. On the other hand, in order to maintain incentives and partly because of errors in planning, consumers may receive more purchasing power than can be absorbed by the goods available to them. This excess purchasing power is siphoned off by the turnover tax which is applied at the various stages of production of the goods.

BANKING

Monetary systems vary considerably from country to country. This is particularly true when viewed from the standpoint of the relationship of central banks to governments. This relationship varies from the considerable constitutional independence which the Federal Reserve Banks possess in the United States to the integral role as an instrument of state economic policy which Gosbank plays in the Soviet Union. The United States is a country that always has been devoted to the doctrine of the separation of powers. Economic policy emerges from the interplay of various forces: the Federal Reserve Board certainly is free to hold, or openly advocate, rather different views in economic policy from those of the government. This is hardly the case in the Soviet Union or in China. On the contrary, Gosbank is an essential part of the Soviet economic control mechanism in that it contains the accounts of all state enterprises and can see that expenditures are made in conformance with basic economic objectives.

Central Banking

The central banks of the countries with mixed economic systems—France, Japan, Sweden, the United Kingdom, and West Germany—possess a considerable degree of independence from their governments in the determination of monetary policy. This is particularly true in West Germany, for the laws of 1948 and 1957, which provided for the creation of the Bank Deutscher Länder and the Deutsche Bundesbank respectively, provide the central bank (Deutsche Bundesbank) with considerable independence—an independence which it has in fact used. In France, on the other hand, the role of the central bank is more circumscribed in that monetary policy is decided by the National Credit Council. However, the Governor of the Bank of France has a key position on that body, and the regulatory power of the Council is exercised through the framework of the central bank.

In some respects there is a similarity among all central banks—socialist or otherwise. For example, Gosbank, the Bank of Japan, the Bank of France, and other central banks issue bank notes, serve as repositories for gold holdings, and make international payments. Gosbank serves as a fiscal agent for the Soviet government in that virtually all governmental receipts and expenditures flow through various deposit accounts. The same holds true of the People's Bank of China. In this respect, both are similar to the Bank of Japan, which has served since its inception in 1882 as the fiscal agent of the Japanese government. The Bank of Japan handles public receipts and payments, government debt, and Treasury accounts.

There is also a similarity from the standpoint of credit control between socialist and nonsocialist central banks. In France, for example, the central bank exercises tight control over the credit-creating banks. The central banks of the Soviet Union and China also control credit, but to a degree that is unheard of in the Western countries. In both socialist countries, the central banks are essentially *monobanks* in that they combine the functions of both central and commercial banking. These monobanks, with the exception of a few specialized banks, represent the banking system of each country and purvey most of the total credit. This fact means that they are provided with a control mechanism in that they can supervise the amount of credit granted and the purposes for which it is used.

Monetary Policy

The functions and instruments of monetary policy differ between the socialist and nonsocialist countries. Although the central bank is at the apex of the banking system in the two types of economies, there are different types of institutional arrangements. In Japan and the Western countries there is a well-defined commercial banking system and private capital ownership exists. Neither exists in the Soviet Union and China. In the nonsocialist countries imbalances between aggregate demand and aggregate supply are adjusted through the use of both monetary and fiscal policies; in the socialist countries reliance is placed upon fiscal policy.[3]

In the nonsocialist countries, monetary policy is a flexible instrument used by the central banks in response to changes in the market economy. The basic tools of monetary policy are control over the minimum liquidity requirements of commercial banks, changes in the rate of rediscounting short-term

---

[3] The Russian turnover tax, as mentioned previously, is an example of the use of fiscal policy to regulate consumer demand.

commercial notes, and open-market operations. The importance of each of these instruments varies from country to country. Monetary policy is implemented by the central banks through the commercial banks, with the ultimate objective of influencing changes in both the cost and the availability of credit. These changes are designed to affect the consumption and investment expenditures of both individuals and companies.

In the socialist countries, monetary policy is not used as an economic stabilization measure to effect a balance between aggregate demand and supply, and the basic policy instruments are irrelevant because the investment decisions are made by the state in the economic plan rather than by private enterprise operating within the framework of a market economy. Instead, monetary policy is a part of the financial plan and is concerned with controlling the amount of money in circulation and providing credit for enterprises. Its role is passive in that it is not used to correct disequilibria between supply and demand through changes in the cost and availability of credit. In other words, in Japan and the Western countries, monetary policy is a flexible instrument which is used continuously to respond to market changes, while in the socialist countries, monetary policy is inflexible and is used to expedite the implementation of the governments' financial plans.

Commercial Banks

A major difference between the banking systems of the socialist and non-socialist countries is the virtual absence of commercial banks in most socialist countries. In such countries as the United States and Sweden, commercial banks are a separate and integral part of the banking system. They are privately owned business firms operating for the purpose of making a profit. They provide facilities for time deposits on which depositors receive interest, extend credit to the great variety of borrowers by making loans and purchasing securities, and create and manage demand deposits. The essence of commercial banking in the nonsocialist countries is the extension of credit through the creation of money. Their ability to create spendable purchasing power in the form of checking accounts is the attribute which gives commercial banks a unique quality among financial institutions. Commercial banks in most nonsocialist countries are normally the largest single source of credit and the most diversified.

In the Soviet Union the functions of commercial banks have been assumed by Gosbank. In addition to serving as the central bank of the country, Gosbank has a monopoly over the provision of short-term credit. Each enterprise has an account in Gosbank, originally put there by the government, which is supposed to supply it with working capital, and when a sale is made between two industrial enterprises, the bank simply deducts the amount of the sale from the buyer's account and adds it to that of the seller. Under ordinary circumstances purchases and sales tend to offset each other, thus making no inordinate demand on an enterprise's working capital, but in the event that it is temporarily in need, it can obtain short-term credit from Gosbank. This credit is extended to enterprises for the purpose of procuring inventories and also for financing goods in transit.

Savings Banks

Savings banks exist for the purpose of making the accumulations of small savers available for use in financing the economic system, and savings are encouraged as a means of regulating consumer demand. Savings banks accept deposits from individuals and such personal organizations as trade unions, and pay interest on these deposits. They also perform other services, such as collecting rent and utility bills and selling government bonds. Most of their funds are invested in government bonds, and it is in this way that personal savings make their way back into the economy. Savings banks may exist as part of a nationwide system, as is the case in some of the satellite countries, or they may exist as a part of the central bank. The latter is the case in both the Soviet Union and China.

Special Purpose Banks

Special purpose banks are included in the structure of the socialist banking systems. For example, foreign trade banks operate to finance foreign trade transactions and to carry on a correspondent relationship with banks in other countries. Other banks exist as a channel for paying out to enterprises and institutions the funds provided by the state budget for investment. In the event that a particular enterprise is in need of funds for financing new construction, it may procure these funds from a special purpose bank in the form of a nonrepayable grant. If it is practical to finance the proposal out of future earnings, a short-term, interest-bearing loan can be arranged. An example of a special purpose bank is the Construction Bank of China, which is responsible for giving out nonrepayable investment grants and issuing short-term loans to construction enterprises. Agricultural banks also exist for the purpose of financing rural credit cooperatives. However, separate agricultural banks no longer exist in most socialist countries, and their functions have been assumed by the central banks.

There is diversity in the banking systems of the socialist countries. In the Soviet Union the central bank is a monobank because it combines the attributes of a central bank with those of commercial banks. A small number of special purpose banks also exist. In China the central bank is also a monobank, but there are more special purpose banks than in the Soviet Union. In both countries the central banks exercise important control functions. In Yugoslavia, however, the central bank, in terms of authority, more closely resembles the central banks of the nonsocialist countries than it does the socialist countries. Yugoslavia also has investment banks, commercial banks, and savings banks.

ORGANIZATION OF PRODUCTION AND DISTRIBUTION

In the socialist economic system, most productive and distributive enterprises are under the direct control of the state. There is some place for small private enterprises, particularly in Yugoslavia, but for the most part their operation is narrowly circumscribed. Some organizations are also left to local governments to operate on the grounds that their operation is largely of local importance. Such enterprises as public utilities, hospitals, theaters, and housing construction would fall into this category. Nevertheless, though the ownership and operation of these enterprises is entrusted to local governmental units, usually some agency of the central government has the ultimate responsibility for coordinating their operations within the general framework of the economic plans for the whole country.

The socialist state exercises a monopolistic control over the basic economic structure and resources of the country. It owns and operates large-scale industries, mines, power plants, railways, shipping, and various means of communications. It engages in farming on its own account through the institution of state farms, and it largely controls peasant agriculture through the institution of collective farming. It has an exclusive monopoly of banking and foreign trade, and it controls the domestic channels of distribution in its role as manufacturer, farmer, merchant, shipper, and banker. In the field of labor relations, it is the sole employer of note, and as such, dominates bargaining between itself and the employees. Although trade unions are allowed to exist, their function is purely subsidiary to the interest of the state, and strikes are illegal.

The Enterprise

The enterprise is the basic unit of industrial production. It has its own fixed and working capital, which is derived in part from the state budget and in part from bank loans and retained earnings. It is strictly subject to state planning and is managed by state appointees. Profits, if there are any, are turned over to the state treasury to be included as a part of revenue for the state budget, except for amounts which are assigned for retention by the enterprise earning them. Retained profit must, however, be used for specific purposes, such as bonus incentive funds. The enterprise is under an obligation to fulfill the production and financial plans set down by the state, which specifies targets or *success indicators* to be attained. These targets, for the most part, can be reduced to quantitative terms stated in physical or monetary units of measure. Quantity of output is often used as a success indicator, but often quantity may be achieved at the expense of quality or by providing a product mix that is not related to demand but which is easy to produce. Profit is also used as a success indicator.

When an enterprise is formed, it becomes an economic accounting unit with its own capital, both fixed and working, and its own account at the central bank. It then operates as a financial entity and is generally expected to conduct its affairs in such a way that income will cover expenses and leave some profits. However, the earning of profit is not a basic requisite for survival, as an enterprise can also operate with a planned loss. Prices of inputs and outputs are fixed, and the enterprise must operate within these constraints in fulfilling its plan, covering its costs, and making a profit.

The state prescribes the ultimate objectives to be sought by the enterprise in the annual national plan, and the enterprise prepares its own annual operating plan, which is an elaboration of the targets set forth in the annual national plan. This operating plan contains such targets as the volume of output and the introduction of new types of products. It also contains such information as the number of workers employed, cost of production, and the amount of wages payable to workers. The annual operating plan requires the approval of the central authorities before it can be implemented at the enterprise level. The operating plan is then formalized in terms of control figures and resource use.

In a country the size of the Soviet Union or China, one can well wonder how the operations of thousands of enterprises are coordinated. Although the managers of the enterprises have a certain degree of operational flexibility, major decisions regarding what to produce, how much to produce, and for whom to produce are made primarily by superior agencies. In both the Soviet Union and China there is a hierarchy of agencies that is responsible for developing and coordinating the economic plan. In the Soviet Union there are several agencies or organizations that can exercise some sort of managerial control. The state bank (Gosbank) can exercise monetary control since it holds the accounts of all enterprises. It can scrutinize an enterprise's receipts and payments to see if they conform to the objectives of the plan. The Ministry of Finance, in collecting tax receipts, can audit the accounts of an enterprise. Then, too, all industries in the Soviet Union are divided into functional groups under the control of industrial ministries which plan and control production and decide questions of technical policy, material supplies, financing, labor use, and wages.[4] As will be pointed out in the chapters which follow, there is also some decentralization of authority in the control of enterprises in the socialist countries.

Organization of Agriculture

The organization of agriculture has always presented a problem to the Communists because the peasants have always been hostile to efforts to collectivize and regiment them. For ideological reasons the Communists regard it as imperative that agriculture be collectivized, but early Soviet experiments with collectivization invariably ended in disaster. Eventually after most repressive measures were used on the peasants to enforce their compliance with Soviet collectivization policies, some sort of compromise was worked out whereby, in return for work on the collective farms, the peasants were given the privilege of farming their own private plots. This arrangement exists in other socialist countries as well. The degree of collectivization, however, differs considerably among socialist countries. In the Soviet Union there are a few

---

[4] The Communist Party also exercises control over the enterprises. Each industrial enterprise has a Communist Party committee elected from the personnel who are party members. This committee is responsible for stimulating the workers to carry out the plan. The committee can also report any irregularities at the enterprise.

individual peasants who own their land, but their numbers are exceedingly small relative to the total farm population. In Yugoslavia the opposite is true, for 80 percent of the agricultural land is privately owned and individuals are permitted to own up to ten *hectares* (about 24.7 acres) of land.

In comparing the relationship of the government to agriculture in the socialist and nonsocialist countries, the fundamental distinction lies in the pervasiveness of government control and administration of the whole socialist economic system, of which agriculture forms an integral part. The socialist state exercises a monopolistic control over the agricultural resources. It engages in farming on its own account through the institution of state farms, and it largely controls peasant agriculture through the organization of collective farming. Through control of the state budget and the banking system, it can control the allocation of monetary resources to agriculture. This branch of economic activity is also subject to the system of state economic planning.

Agriculture in the socialist countries is carried on by collective farms, state farms, and individual farmers. A *collective farm* is a production unit in which farm property is owned by the peasants and the produce is distributed according to their labor contribution. A certain amount of produce is also set aside for delivery to the state to be sold to consumers. A *state farm* is owned and operated by the government. Its annual budget and operating plans are prepared just like those of any state enterprise, and its equipment and machinery is owned by the state. It hires workers and pays them wages that are established by the states.

Marketing

In a socialist economic system the state is typically the sole producer and distributor of goods. It performs the principal marketing functions of buying and selling, transporting, storing, standardizing, and grading goods. The role of middlemen in the exchange process was decried by the Communists as a capitalistic invention designed to gain profits and was eliminated during the early stages of socialist development in the Soviet Union and other countries. This, however, failed to simplify the process of exchange, and in some respects there is a distinct similarity between distribution procedures in socialist and nonsocialist countries. In the Soviet Union, for example, the main channel of distribution for consumer goods is from producer to wholesaler to retailer to consumer, which also holds true for the United States. However, the Soviet government owns and controls each link in the production and distribution process.

Distribution at both the wholesale and retail level is usually the responsibility of two types of trading networks—the state trading network and the cooperative trading network. Although nominally collective, the cooperative network comes under close state control and is in fact little different from state trading. Both trading networks are governed by the annual economic plan. The plan determines the volume of goods to be distributed through the state and cooperative trading systems, and an effort is made to relate the volume of goods and services that will be made available to the income of consumers so that some sort of equilibrium is attained. Responsibility for the coordination of the distribution system is placed in the hands of a number of government agencies which perform such functions as drafting general plans for state and cooperative trade in accordance with the annual economic and financial plans and fixing wholesale and retail prices for state and cooperative outlets.

PRICING AND PROFIT IN A SOCIALIST ECONOMY

The problem of pricing in a socialist economy is of a different order of magnitude from that under capitalism. For one thing, prices do not determine the allocation of resources to the same extent as in a market economy. Moreover, pricing is not merely a question of economics, but also of ideology and politics. In terms of ideology they have a rationality of their own, for the law of value is the socialist rationality of prices. Value in the socialist frame of reference is the amount of labor embodied in particular goods and services. Labor is the only factor of production credited with the capability of creating value. So the price or value of anything is determined by the amount of labor which is required to produce it. The relative prices of two products will be in the same proportion as the amount of labor required to produce them. If two hours of labor is required to make a pair of shoes and five hours are required to build a cart, the price of the shoes on the market will be two fifths of that of the cart.

A hang-up over the labor theory of value has caused the socialists all kinds of pricing problems. For one thing, the theory virtually denies the role of demand in the determination of value. The idea of marginal utility is rejected because it is in conflict with the assumption that value is objectively determined by labor content, not by subjective valuation depending on the amount used. Moreover, the factor of scarcity has been ignored. The value of a thing in exchange for something else depends on the state of its supply and the state of demand for it. Behind supply and demand can be a great many interdependent determinants which cannot be ignored. When scarcity is considered, not only labor but capital and natural resources count as productive and value-creating.

However, pragmatism has transcended ideology in socialist pricing policies, so that the actual formation and structure of prices incorporate little of the labor theory of value. In fact, actual prices are arrived at through the use of different plan variants which recognize the scarcity of resources and the significance of demand. But the fact remains that no fully workable pricing system has been devised. Prices do not reflect factor costs, as rent and interest are not necessarily fully accounted for in them, and furthermore, different criteria for price setting are used for different categories of products. As a result, prices still do not perform a rational allocative function.

Producer and Consumer Prices

A dual price system operates in socialist planned economies—prices paid to producers and prices paid by consumers for retail goods. Producers' prices are those received by producing enterprises from other producing enterprises and from wholesale trading entities. The wholesale price is considered a producer price in the sense that it is a price charged by producers for the sale of a product when it leaves the factory. It consists of full production costs and the profit of the producers; it does not normally include distribution costs. Producer prices are normally based on an average cost for the entire branch of industry producing a given product. Included in average cost are not only wage payments and material costs, but capital charges and differential payments. In some cases, producer prices are actually set by the state at levels below average cost, so that enterprises operate with a planned loss, with the loss subsidized by state revenues.

Retail prices consist of all of the components which make up the prices charged by the producer to the retailer plus a retail price markup added as the last element of retail price formation. There is a virtual isolation between producer and retail prices in that what happens to the former has little impact on the latter. Retail prices are set to keep supply and demand in balance within the guidelines of the economic plan. However, the setting of prices is based on the macrosocial preferences of the planners rather than on the true interaction of supply and demand affected by consumer preferences. However, a certain amount of flexibility in retail prices is permitted. For example, "free prices," which are prices set by supply and demand, operate in the purchase and sale of certain agricultural products. Prices also may be allowed to fluctuate within ranges above and below the levels set by the state planning authorities.

The price structure of most products typically consists of production cost, profit of the producer, turnover tax, and wholesale and retail price markups. Profit, which is a matter for subsequent discussion, is designed to achieve a better use of resources at the enterprise level. The turnover tax occupies a distinct role in pricing in two ways. First, it is used to adjust demand to supply through the manipulation of rates on various goods. Typically goods in short supply or luxury goods carry a high rate. Secondly, the turnover tax is used to regulate profits. Since prices are fixed for the producer as well as the consumer, in effect the tax rates determine the amount of profits allowed to producers.

Price formation for a socialist enterprise may be described as follows: There is the enterprise price which consists of two components—enterprise costs and profits. Enterprise costs include material, wage, and social costs. The definition of these components differs from one country to another. One innovation in the field of enterprise pricing was the decision by such countries as East Germany and Hungary to permit enterprises to charge other producing enterprises, with the exception of the prices of most raw materials which remain set by the state. This, however, has led to distortions as monopolistic sellers have increased prices at will. These prices were passed on, where possible, by the purchasing firm.

A profit markup is the second component of enterprise price. This markup is set within ranges permitted by the state and represents what can be considered as an average for a given industry. Profit for individual enterprises can be above this average by either increasing production of articles which meet buyers' preferences or by reducing unit costs. From profit there is a deduction which goes into the state budget.

The turnover tax is added to the enterprise price to give an industry price. As mentioned above, the size of the turnover tax is determined by the required level of the retail price. The rate is differentiated to reflect different elasticities of consumer demand for different products. Typically the tax is arrived at residually, i.e., the retail price is fixed first to balance supply with demand, and the tax is the difference between this price and the price paid to the producer.

The wholesale price is really a margin which is added to the industry price. This margin is the price at which wholesale organizations sell to the retail network. In the absence of wholesaling organizations, an enterprise wholesale price may also be charged. The turnover tax is included in the enterprise wholesale price, and therefore is paid by the producer.

The retail price consists of all the above components which go into the making up of the price of a product. It can be viewed as a retail markup added as the last element of retail price formation. The markup may be fixed by the state or it may be flexible within prescribed limits. Free prices also are used along with ceiling prices in which the state prescribes a maximum retail markup.

A schematic presentation of price formation, which presents pricing policies followed by the East German clothing industry, is shown below.[5]

> Enterprise price (including cost and profit markup)
> + sales taxes = industry sales price
> + wholesale margin = wholesale price
> + retail margin = retail trade sale price

Profit

Profit is an interesting phenomenon in a socialist system. At first profit was decried as one of the most basic evils of a capitalist system. Although profit was used in socialist economies, it was created merely as an accounting device to ensure that enterprises tried to cover their costs out of their own resources where possible and then handed the surplus over to the state. But certainly profit was not the rationale for the existence of an enterprise. However, profit has come to have a new and important role under socialism. For one thing, it is used as a measure of enterprise efficiency. More important is the

[5] Staatsverlag der Deutschen Demokratischen Republik, "Gesetzblatt der Deutschen Demokratischen Republik," Teil 11, Nr. 24 (Berlin, May 10, 1972), p. 269.

attempt to link profit with incentives. It is now common to tie the reward system to enterprise profit, for profit may be distributed in the form of bonuses to both labor and management. The proportion of profit distributed in this manner comes under the heading of the material incentives fund.

In setting profit directives, state planning authorities use as the criterion, or base, average production costs in an industry producing a given commodity. Profit is expressed as a percentage of average cost and is set in combination with turnover tax rates and distribution markups. However, the use of a single average profit rate in the price set for a particular product does not result in a uniform rate of profit for all enterprises, because production costs vary widely among enterprises. Through the tying of profit to bonus funds, enterprise managers do have an incentive to reduce production costs. As an end result, however, some enterprises may make large profits while other enterprises may end up with a loss. Profit consists of the difference between receipts from total output and costs of production. Since profit is supposed to accrue to society in the first instance, a certain part of it has to be handed over to the state budget and the remainder is retained for use by the enterprise.

The profitability of an enterprise can be measured by comparing the profit to costs of production to obtain a profit rate. There are, however, weaknesses in this measure, and socialist planners are adopting other approaches. Profitability can now also be measured as the ratio of profit to the total annual average value of fixed assets and working capital. Fixed capital allocated to enterprises is no longer free, but is subject to capital charges now representing cost. The profit rate then becomes a composite of five factors which are as follows:

1. The average prime cost of an enterprise, which includes wages, materials used, interest, and depreciation of fixed capital.
2. The quantity of output actually sold by the enterprise.
3. The price at which the output is sold.
4. The average annual value of fixed assets.
5. The average annual value of variable assets.

Distribution of Profits

When an enterprise makes a profit, the first claimant is the state. A part of profit is allocated to the state budget, and the remainder is divided by the enterprise into a number of funds. Each fund is designed to accomplish a specific objective. There is a production development fund. Its purpose is to finance capital investment for the introduction of new technology, mechanization and automation, renovation of fixed assets, modernization of equipment, and for other purposes that are designed to develop and improve production. There is also a fund for social and cultural measures, which has as its purpose the improvement of worker morale and productivity. It provides revenue for the construction and maintenance of child-care centers, expansion of recreational facilities, support of athletic programs, and housing construction. There is also a reserve fund, which is used for the purpose of paying off long-term loans.

A simplified scheme of profit use for the individual state enterprise can be presented as follows:

Gross profits of the enterprise
Less payments to the state budget and interest on bank loans
Equal net profits of the enterprise, which are divided into

1. Production fund to finance fixed and working capital
2. Social and cultural funds to improve the social and intellectual life of the worker
3. Material incentive fund to stimulate worker productivity
4. Reserve or amortization fund
5. Profit residual that is not committed to any fund that goes to the state budget.

A specific example of profit distribution can be provided in the case of an East German state farm. The starting point in the distribution of profit is gross sales, which is obtained by multiplying the planned volume of sales per product by the set state price. From gross sales, production costs, including the cost of seed and fertilizer and depreciation, are deducted to get gross income. From gross income a deduction is made into the wage fund, and the remainder is called the socially clear income. This income may be considered as a residual that is divided between the state farm and the state. An example follows:[6]

Total sales		$450,450.45
Less seed, fertilizer, and other costs, including depreciation		225,225.22
Equal gross income		225,225.23
Less wage funds		90,090.09
Equals social clear income		$135,135.14
Less special costs	$22,522.52	
Less production levy	18,018.02	40,540.54
Equals gross profit		$ 94,594.60
Less land and production fund tax		18,018.02
Equals net profit		$ 76,576.58

INCOME DISTRIBUTION UNDER SOCIALISM

Income distribution under socialism can be examined in two ways. First of all, there is the Marxist theory of income distribution which is based upon an adaptation of Ricardian ideas, particularly with respect to a labor theory of value. Marx's theory of income distribution was a part of his overall theory of the development and decline of capitalism. In actual practice, however, there is a departure from his theory in the socialist countries today. Although this departure is explained away in part by the assertion that socialism is just a stage on the way to communism, the fact remains that income distribution in such countries as the Soviet Union and East Germany is tied to pragmatic economic objectives.

[6] H. Jorg Thieme, *Die Sozialistische Agrarverfassung* (Stuttgart: Gustav Fischer Verlag, 1969), p. 54.

The Marxist Theory of Income Distribution

At any given time—according to Marx—the way in which people earn a living is conditioned by the nature of the existing productive forces. These productive forces are three in number: natural resources, capital equipment, and human resources. Since people must make use of these productive forces in the process of making a living, some sort of relationship between people and the productive forces is necessary. Specifically, a property relationship is involved. People may own certain productive forces individually, as in a capitalist economy; or they may own them collectively, as in a socialist society. In addition to the relationship between people and the productive forces, there are interrelationships among people, since people find it desirable to cooperate and engage in social production, except under very primitive or isolated conditions. The relationships between people and productive forces and the relationships among people Marx calls the relations of production, and the sum total of these relations of production constitutes the economic structure of society.

The Marxist theory of income distribution is based on the labor theory of value which, in essence, asserts that the value of a commodity is determined by the labor time necessary for its production. Marx stated that the one thing common to all commodities is labor. Because labor power is the source of all economic or exchange value, exploitation exists whenever workers fail to receive the whole value of their output. Although all value is created by the workers, it is expropriated by employers in the form of surplus value which can be defined as the difference between the value created by the workers and the value of their labor power. The employers, or capitalists, are owners of the nonhuman agents of production—capital equipment and land. It is through their ownership of the physical means of production that the capitalists exploit the working class and extract surplus value from it.

Income in the Marxist schema is divided into two categories—surplus value, which is the source of all profit, and labor income. Capitalists try to wring as much surplus value out of their workers as possible to maintain or improve their relative share in the income total. The ratio of surplus value to labor income, or profit to wages, is really the foundation of the Marxist theory of income distribution. A rise in the ratio of surplus value to labor income represents an increase in the rate of exploitation. A decline in the ratio represents the reverse. Given the relationship between surplus value and labor income, the capitalists attempt to increase their share of the income total. They have the advantage over labor because a normal condition of a capitalist society is a continuous excess of labor supply over demand. This excess causes the market wage to fall toward a real wage equal to the minimum subsistence standard of living.

The traditional Marxist approach denies the role of demand in the determination of value. The idea of marginal utility is rejected because it is in conflict with the assumption that value is objectively determined by the labor content, not by subjective valuation of the amount used. So value in the Marxist rubric can be expressed in the formula $c + v + s$, where c represents raw materials and capital consumption, v represents variable outlays on wages, and s represents surplus value in the form of rent, interest, and profit. The c component, raw materials and capital, although clearly not labor, is explained away by Marx, who regarded it as stored-up labor from past periods. Thus, the remainder, v + s, represents net output which consists of the two basic income shares—wages and profit.

The distribution of income eventually precipitates the downfall of capitalism. This would occur after a series of business crises. Under capitalism there are certain inevitable forces at work to bring about its eventual collapse. There is a continuing struggle among the capitalists to increase their share of the total income. To do this, they try to wring as much surplus value out of their workers as possible. Hours become longer and women and children are employed. As long as there is a surplus of labor, the workers will receive no more than the value of their labor power. The intensity of competition among the capitalists also leads to capital accumulation, which leads to a decline in the relative share of wages in total income. But the end result is self-defeating for the reason that with falling wages, aggregate demand also falls, and the workers are not in a position to consume the products that the capitalists are turning out.

After the collapse of capitalism, two phases of communism are to occur. The first phase, which Marx called the "lower phase" or "socialism," is a transitional phase in which, among other things, income distribution is based upon ability rather than need. For the period of "social transition," the principle of distribution based on performance is necessary to create a society of abundance. So the term "socialists" is applied to the countries controlled by the Communist Party, including the nine Eastern European countries. These countries describe themselves as socialist—the Union of Soviet Socialist Republics. The higher phase, or communism, is to be marked by an age of plenty, distribution according to needs, and the absence of money. Individuals are supposed to derive satisfaction from being a part of such a social order— from contributing to it and sharing its ambience. All vestiges of capitalism are to disappear and the state is to wither away. However, when this higher phase is scheduled to begin is anybody's guess. In the Soviet Union some reference has been made about the second phase starting about 1980.

Income Determination

Income distribution is determined by the state within the framework of the economic plan. The total amount of wages to be paid, and the production counterpart to support the wage funds, depends on the division of the national income between accumulation and consumption and further of consumption between the social consumption fund and the wage fund. The total wage fund is partitioned into wage funds for all economic fields. In its economic planning, the government is able to determine the wages total for the economy by multiplying the planned number of workers by the rates of wages it has set. Wages are changed as seems necessary to effectuate government policy and achieve particular production ends. For example, in order to attract more workers to a given industry, wages paid by it may be raised while others remain static or are allowed to decline. Direct pressure on the part of workers would in general have little effect on wage determination.

The degree of state control over the wage fund at the microeconomic, or firm, level is smaller. Some latitude is allowed to enterprise managers in determining the size and the use of the fund. Typically the wage fund consists of several components, including basic wages. This component can be subdivided into two categories—time rates and piece rates. Both are based on work output indicators. In addition, bonuses may also be paid from the wage fund. The wage fund also provides for extra wages which are based on the difficulty of work, including payments for night, holiday, and Sunday work, and wages for state holidays, vacations, and participation in public duties. As it stands, typical workers receive payments according to their work grade from the wage fund plus a bonus based on a performance standard.

Another source of income is provided from the material incentives fund. This fund is tied to enterprise profit. The significance and success of the profit criterion lie mainly in the fact that a direct link has been established between profit and incentive payment so that it is in the interest of enterprise personnel—and at the same time of society—to strive to maximize enterprise profit. The proportion of enterprise profits channelled into this fund varies in different socialist countries. For example, in East Germany up to 20 percent of net profits can be placed in the fund. In East Germany, Poland, and Romania the size of the fund is based on complicated formulas in which a distinction is made between planned and above-plan profits, and further between profits made by exceeding production targets and those achieved by reductions in prime costs.

SUMMARY

Probably the most important difference between the capitalist and socialist countries is the role that economic planning plays in socialist resource allocation. Fundamental to the operation of planning is the public ownership of the agents of production, which joins industrial, agricultural, and trading companies into a single economic unit. Since there is no meaningful competition between rival firms, there is no price competition. In turn, the profit motive is rendered unimportant as an automatic regulator, which is its role in the market price system of a market economy. So in the absence of the market price system, economic planning is necessary to make the complex of state enterprises function. To organize the uninterrupted operations of these enterprises, full and exact account must be kept of the national requirements for their particular products and of the channels through which they must be distributed.

The state exercises a virtual monopolistic control over all economic resources. It owns and operates large-scale industries, mines, power plants, railways, shipping, and various means of communication. It engages in farming on its own account through the institution of state farms, and it largely controls agriculture through the institution of collective farming. It has an exclusive monopoly of banking and foreign trade, and it controls the domestic channels of distribution in its role as manufacturer, farmer, merchant, shipper, and banker. In the field of labor relations, it is the sole employer of note and as such dominates bargaining between itself and the employees. Although trade unions are allowed to exist, their function is purely subsidiary to the interest of the state, and strikes are illegal.

QUESTIONS

1. Why is it difficult to fit the socialist countries into a common economic pattern?
2. Discuss the purpose of the economic reforms of the 1960s.
3. What were the objectives of the Hungarian economic reforms?
4. Discuss the role of input-output analysis with respect to economic planning.
5. Discuss the process of economic planning as reflected in the East German plan for 1973.
6. Compare the role of the national budgets in the United States and the Soviet Union.
7. Discuss the new role of profit in a socialist economic system.
8. Compare the process of income determination in a market economy and a planned economy.
9. What is the link between profit and income distribution resulting from the economic reforms?

16

The Soviet Union I

INTRODUCTION

The Soviet economy depends on economic planning rather than on a market system to make the basic economic decisions of what and how much is to be produced and to whom it is to be allocated. Competition of buyers and sellers, which determines the prices of commodities, services, and the agents of production in a market economy such as the United States, is inoperative in the Soviet Union. Since land and capital are owned by the state in the name of society and since the state operates almost all lines of economic activity, it has the ability to make comprehensive economic plans and to see to it that they are carried out as thoroughly as possible.

It is also possible, as the Soviet Union has recognized in its recent economic reforms, to devise processes by means of which its economy could obtain some of the results of the market price system without actually having that system. In the early 1960s the rate of growth of the Soviet economy began to decline. This fact caused the Soviet leaders great concern, for the Utopia of abundance which they had envisioned in the immediate future was not close to being accomplished. There started an examination of many of the institutions of the command economy. In particular, there was concern over the need to reform the administrative mechanism for planning and managing the national economy.

In 1965 Premier Kosygin outlined a new system of planning, management, and incentives to be adopted for the Soviet economy. This system was to affect all areas of economic activity—agriculture, industry, transportation, and communications. To stimulate performances by enterprises, more of their profits were to be retained in specially created funds for bonuses, cultural expenditures, and investments. The payment of bonuses out of special bonus funds was designed to spur greater productivity on the part of the workers. Enterprise managers were allowed more freedom of action with respect to staffing patterns and wage rates. The enterprise also was being charged both interest on investment loans and rents on the use of land or other fixed assets. In agriculture, changes were made with respect to the operations of the state and collective farms—changes which were designed to increase output. Administrative changes in the operation of the Soviet economy also have been made.

Nevertheless, the planned economy is very much in operation. As stated above, the main objective of the Kosygin economic reforms was to make Soviet industry and agriculture more efficient. Although some of the institutions of a capitalistic system are being employed by the Russians, it can by no means be concluded that there is a convergence of the United States and Soviet economic systems. Central planning remains basic to the Soviet economic system, and the ownership of the means of production remains in state hands.

The Soviet Union is the largest country in the world in terms of land area and is larger than the United States and Canada combined. Its length from east to west is 7,000 miles, and from north to south it is about 3,000 miles. In metals and mineral resources, the Soviet Union can be considered one of the richest countries in the world. However, its resources have never been put fully to use because of great geographic impediments to transportation. Such rivers as the Dnieper and the Volga, which for a millennium were the chief mode of transportation, have retarded the development of rail and road transportation because of their length and width. Adverse climatic factors also impede the development of national resources.

From the standpoint of population, the Soviet Union is a little larger than the United States. Its population in 1974 was 249.1 million compared to 212.2 million for the United States. In one respect the populations of both countries are similar because each consists of a melange of different racial and ethnic groups. The people of the Soviet Union can be divided as Slavic or non-Slavic, or Russian and non-Russian. The Slavic group consists of Russians, Belorussians, and Ukrainians, and they were united by similar languages.[1] The non-Slavic group would consist of Estonians, Lithuanians, Tartars, Armenians, Georgians, and others. Slightly over half of the population of the Soviet Union can be classified as Russian. This group is limited primarily to the western, or European, part of the country.

The Soviet Union consists of 15 Socialist Republics. The largest is the Russian Soviet Federated Socialist Republic, which comprises 79 percent of the total area and 53 percent of the population of the country. The second largest republic in terms of land area and population is the Ukrainian Soviet Socialist Republic. Within the union republics, there are autonomous republics and regions which also reflect the ethnic diversity of the country.[2] For example, within the Russian Soviet Federated Socialist Republic there is the autonomous Soviet Socialist Republic of Yakutia, which has a land area of more than a million square miles, but is a very sparsely populated area far removed from Moscow. Its autonomy is largely a matter of administrative convenience. An example of an autonomous region is the Jewish Autonomous Region which is in the Asiatic part of the Russian Soviet Federated Socialist Republic.

[1] There are three subdivisions of Slavs—eastern Slavs (Russians, Belorussians, and Ukrainians), western Slavs (Poles, Czechs, and Slovaks), and Southern Slavs (Serbo-Croatians, Slovenes, and Buglarians).
[2] There are, in fact, over 170 different nationalities and more than 200 languages and dialects spoken in the Soviet Union.

THE POLITICAL SYSTEM

Perhaps the most important point that can be made with respect to the political system of the Soviet Union is the interlocking relationship between the Communist Party and the administrative units of the government. Political and governmental power in the Soviet Union is completely in the hands of the Communist Party. In other words, the Communist Party dominates the governmental administrative structure of the Soviet Union and has its members in practically all important offices and positions. Its policies are carried out by all governmental agencies and organizations.

Organization of the Government

The governmental administrative apparatus of the Soviet Union is divided into a multi-tiered arrangement with control extending from Moscow down to the rural soviets. The current arrangement is essentially as follows.

Territorial Administration. From a territorial administrative standpoint, the Soviet Union can be divided into several categories. First, there is the Soviet Union itself. As a federation of constituent republics, it has its own constitution. Then there are the 15 theoretically independent union republics which form the federation. Each republic has its own constitution, government, and party hierarchy. The republics are similar to American states, although they are generally larger in size.[3] A distinctive feature of Soviet public administration is the fact that most of these republics were formed primarily on the basis of nationality. The federalist structure of the Soviet Union can be regarded as a concession to the non-Russian peoples' nationalistic sentiments. However, administrative safeguards modify the formal federalism of the constitutional structure of the Soviet Union. The Communist Party itself is a single, unified organization which exerts a countervailing centralism to ethnic federalism. Moreover, the highest administrative organs of the country are centralized in Moscow.

National Policy Administration. The state apparatus through which national policy is administered can be divided into two pyramidal hierarchies—one is the Council of Ministers of the U.S.S.R. and the other is the Supreme Soviet of the U.S.S.R. The Council of Ministers is the executive branch of the Soviet government; the Supreme Soviet, the legislative branch.

The Council of Ministers. The Council of Ministers is responsible for the development of economic policy and the enforcement of laws passed by the Supreme Soviet. It is also responsible for exercising general guidance in the sphere of relations with other countries and for directing the general organization of the country's armed forces. It is elected by and is responsible to the Supreme Soviet. To assist the Council of Ministers in coordinating economic activity, there are a number of committees whose responsibilities are to provide the information needed for decision making. One important committee

[3] The Russian Soviet Federated Socialist Republic itself occupies a land area about twice the size of the continental United States.

is the State Planning Committee (*Gosplan*), which is responsible for the development of the national economic plans. There are five other committees—the All-Union Agricultural Committee, the State Committee for Science and Technology, the State Committee for Material and Technical Supply, the State Committee for Construction, and the CEMA Commission.[4] The Presidium of the Council of Ministers, which consists of a chair person and six deputies, one of whom represents each of the six committees, is the policy-making body. There is also a Council of Ministers in each of the 15 constituent republics.

The Supreme Soviet. The Supreme Soviet of the U.S.S.R. is the most important legislative branch in the Soviet Union. It is formally a bicameral legislature with coequal houses—the Soviet of the Union, whose deputies are elected on the basis of population, and the Soviet of Nationalities, whose deputies are elected on a territorial basis by nationality. The responsibilities of the Supreme Soviet are stronger in theory than in practice. In terms of real decision making it has little power and passes the bills that are submitted to it. A law is considered enacted if passed by both houses by simple majority vote in each. There are standing committees for each house comprising the following areas: credentials, plans and budgets, industry, transportation and communication, building and the building materials industry, agriculture, public health and social security, public education, science and culture, trade and public services, legislative proposals, and foreign affairs.

The Communist Party

Control of the government machinery in the Soviet Union is in the hands of the Communist Party, which is the only political party permitted in the country.[5] Although membership in the Communist Party is limited to a small minority of the total population of the country, it maintains firm control over every aspect of Soviet life through well organized and disciplined organization.[6] Communists are assigned to key positions in all institutions and enterprises in Soviet society. In factories, offices, schools, and villages, primary units called *cells* operate. Cells consist of at least three party members and are responsible for the recruitment of members and for the selection of delegates to the local party conferences which in turn select delegates to conferences covering a somewhat wider area, and this process continues until finally, in district and regional congresses, delegates are selected to the National Party Congress, which is supposed to be the highest body of party authority.

The Politburo. Power actually rests in the Politburo, the Central Committee, the Secretariat, and the various staff departments of the central apparatus in Moscow. The *Politburo* is, in effect, the supreme instrument of political power

[4] The Council for Mutual Economic Assistance (CEMA) is the consultative organ which coordinates the domestic and foreign economic policies of the U.S.S.R. and the European satellite countries.

[5] The Communists argue that political parties are class organs and that, if several parties were permitted, there would be a return to class antagonisms.

[6] In 1972 membership in the Communist Party amounted to approximately 14 million. This figure can be compared to the total population in the Soviet Union of 244 million.

in the Soviet Union. When the Central Committee is not in session, it is responsible for all phases of national life—foreign policy, domestic economic policy, and military policy.[7] There are 15 full voting members who exercise the prerogatives and responsibilities of national policy making, and seven candidate members who participate in varying degrees in the policy-making process. Most members of the Politburo have collateral duties, meaning that they serve in other capacities in addition to their positions as party administrators.

The Central Committee. The Central Committee is elected at the meeting of the National Party Congress. It is composed of the Politburo, Secretariat, Party Control Committee, and a number of individual sections including those called Cadres Abroad, Economic Relations with Socialist Countries, International Affairs, and Relations with Bloc Parties. The Central Committee has no effective role as a decision maker; that function is performed by the Politburo. It does, however, provide a forum or sounding board for the elaboration of the major policies of the Communist Party and its top leaders. It is also responsible for the dissemination of the aims and objectives of the leaders to officials in various departments in the central apparatus and also downward to the various party committees in the republics and at lower levels.

The Secretariat. The Secretariat of the Central Committee ranks second only to the Politburo from the standpoint of decision making. Unlike the Politburo, which has no administrative responsibility, the Secretariat is responsible for the administration of the Communist Party. It consists of 11 members who are elected by the Central Committee in plenary session—a formality, since the slate is drawn up in advance by top party leaders. There is an overlap between the Secretariat and the Politburo in the sense that several members serve on each organization. The Secretariat is responsible for providing the leadership for the professional party organization, which consists of a hierarchy of subordinate secretariats at the republic, oblast, and lesser administrative levels. This hierarchy is responsible for insuring the implementation of state economic policy by the various governmental organs. It is also responsible for the allocation and mobilization of manpower and other resources of the Communist Party.

Party and government structure parallel each other. For example, at the national or U.S.S.R. level, the basic party administrative units are the Central Committee, Politburo, and Secretariat; the basic governmental administrative units are the Supreme Soviet and the Council of Ministers with their respective Presidiums. The leaders of the party are members of both units. At the union republic level, the party administrative unit is the Central Committee and Secretariat, and the governmental administrative unit is the Republic Supreme Soviet and Council of Ministers. This interlocking relationship continues down to the rural soviet level. Although inefficiency may result at

[7] The Politburo of the Central Committee is not to be confused with the Presidium of the Council of Ministers of the U.S.S.R. and the Presidium of the Supreme Soviet. The last two are involved in the operations of the government as opposed to the Politburo, which is involved in the operation of the Communist Party.

lower administrative levels because of communication problems, there is no question but the interconnection of party and government and party domination of the government confer on Soviet public administration exceptional unity of control and uniformity of ideological perspective.[8]

THE ECONOMIC SYSTEM

It can be said that the leaders of the Soviet Union are committed to the view that the future of the country depends upon the Soviet economy's productivity and efficiency. Emphasis is placed on the organization of material production. This organization is based on two fundamental characteristics of the Soviet economy: (1) The economy is run by the allocation of resources by administrative decisions rather than by a market mechanism; and (2) its operations are governed by a priority system which over the years has given preference to capital goods and military and scientific development over consumer goods. Because of these characteristics, consumer sovereignty, which means that the production of goods is determined by the combined prices made in the marketplace by millions of consumers, cannot develop in the Soviet Union. Through its control over economic resources, the state can manipulate the share of gross national product which is to be allocated to consumption, and through its investment policies, the state can control the amount of inputs for those sectors of the economy that supply the consumer. Nevertheless, the Soviet leaders have heeded to some extent the expectations of the consumer for a higher living standard.

Economic Planning

The distinctive feature of the economic system of the Soviet Union is the fact that it operates on the basis of comprehensive economic planning. Fundamental to the operation of economic planning is the public ownership of the agents of production which has joined the multitude of industrial, agricultural, and trading enterprises together in a single economic unit. Since there is no competition among rival firms, there is no meaningful price competition. This, in turn, renders the profit motive impotent as an automatic economic regulator, which is its role in the market price system of a capitalistic economy. So in the absence of the market price system, economic planning is necessary to make the complex of Soviet enterprises function. To organize the uninterrupted operation of these enterprises, full and exact account must be taken of the national requirements for their particular products and of the channels through which they must be distributed. Conversely, every enterprise must be constantly supplied with raw materials, fuel, equipment, and

---

[8] This does not mean, however, that party and government organs function as two perfectly synchronized parts of a smoothly working administrative machine. To the contrary, there are cliques within the party and the governmental bureaucracies which often cause power rivalries or power disputes. These cliques have a vested interest in maintaining the status quo.

other means of production, the output of which must also be commensurate with national needs.

An important principle of economic planning in the Soviet Union is the priority given to the development of industries that will contribute the most to the attainment of national economic and political goals. Economic plans provide for a maximum possible rate of development of certain branches of the economy and lines of production through priorities in investments and materials and through manpower and financial resources. It is assumed that the accelerated expansion of certain key industries, such as the chemical, oil, gas, and power industries, makes it possible to increase the overall rate of growth of industrial and agricultural production. Economic planning also has political as well as economic overtones in that priorities in past and current plans have been given to industries which make the Soviet Union strong from a military standpoint.

It is necessary to stress the fact that there is a difference between formal and actual economic plans. In practice plans are changed often and some plans reflect aspirations. There constantly has to be a revision of targets to reflect changing economic conditions. As the socialist countries have been entering higher stages of economic development, the number of alternative uses for resources and the complexity of economic processes have greatly increased. Consequently, the possibilities of errors have been multiplying, threatening the economies with greater waste and dislocation than before. So the longer the planning period, the less precision can be introduced in terms of plan targets. What happens then is that planning, particularly for periods of five years or longer, is continuous and the plans are constantly supplemented and extended in the process of their implementation.

The economic plans differ in their functional character. There are physical output plans, which involve production, distribution, and investment goals, and financial plans, which are derivatives of these plans. Then, too, plans differ in terms of time limits. There are medium-term plans, which cover a period of five to seven years and which develop targets or goals to be accomplished during this time.[9] There are also annual plans which involve production plans to be followed by Soviet enterprises and other organizational units during the year. The annual plan can be considered an operational plan. Annual plans can be broken down further into quarterly or monthly periods. All of these plans are interconnected and interrelated, and it is important and necessary for planning agencies to ensure their unification in order to establish a proper relationship between production and consumption and between national requirements and resources. In terms of a frame of reference for the presentation of the methodology of Soviet planning, economic planning refers primarily to physical planning which involves product output and distribution, labor force utilization, and investment and which is developed on an annual basis.

[9] There are also long-range plans which extend for 15 to 20 years. These plans usually deal with a particular aspect of the economy, such as electrification.

The organization of economic planning can be divided into the following stages:

1. Drafting of the plan in conformity with the objectives of the Communist Party and the Soviet government.
2. Endorsement of the plan by relevant government administrative units.
3. Organization and control over the execution of the approved plan.

Planning in the Soviet Union is directed by the Supreme Soviet and the Council of Ministers. The actual plans are drawn up by planning bodies which may be divided into three groups—state planning bodies, ministries and departments, and the planning bodies of enterprises and organizations. The state planning bodies are the State Planning Committee (Gosplan), which is a part of the Council of Ministers of the U.S.S.R., the state planning committees of the union and autonomous republics, regional planning committees, and district and city planning committees. These committees draw upon the economic and cultural plans for the country as a whole and for individual republics, regions, and districts. In the ministries and departments, plans are compiled by planning boards and sections, and at the enterprise level they are the responsibility of planning departments.

Gosplan. The all-union Gosplan is the agency responsible for translating broad policy decisions made by the Council of Ministers and the Central Committee of the Communist Party into concrete programs. It has the responsibility for working out economic plans of all kinds and for their presentation for review by the Council of Ministers. It is also responsible for the supervision of the plans. Gosplan is organized into various economic planning sections for the branches of the national economy. One section is responsible for sector planning and is divided into the following sections: machine building, transportation and communications, consumer goods, agriculture, heavy industry, electrification and chemicalization of the national economy. Another section is responsible for the supply and distribution of materials, such as coal and metal products. This section provides a monitoring function over the supply of key materials. Gosplan is also responsible for setting wholesale prices for industrial and agricultural products and for setting retail prices. Through an institute which is attached to it, called the Scientific Research Institute of Economics, it also plays a leading role in theoretical economic research.[10] To check on Gosplan and its activities, there are various departments within the Secretariat of the Communist Party which serve as watchdogs.

Since the Soviet economic plan covers the entire economy, it is necessary to have planning units extending down to lower administrative units of government. Below the all-union Gosplan and subordinate to it in terms of planning are the union republic Gosplans. These Gosplans are responsible for the preparation of plans for all of the industries under union republic

---

[10] For the organizational structure of Gosplan, see Eugene Zaleski, *Planning Reforms in the Soviet Union, 1962–1966* (Chapel Hill: University of North Carolina Press, 1967), pp. 24–26; and U.S. Bureau of the Census, *The Soviet Financial System, Structure, Operations, and Statistics,* International Population Statistics Report, Series P–90, No. 23 (Washington: U.S. Government Printing Office, 1968), p. 13.

supervision. They are also responsible for developing recommendations pertaining to the draft production plans of all enterprises located within the territories of their respective republics. There are also the Gosplans of the autonomous republics and regional planning commissions at the oblast and kray level. They are responsible for drawing up plans for industry and transportation at the regional level, and for agriculture, social and cultural development, and housing and public construction. They also base their summary plans on plans developed at the rayon and rural soviet levels. The planning bodies at these levels draft the plans for enterprises under their direct control and check to see if they are implemented. There are also planning departments in industrial enterprises, state farms, and transport and trading enterprises. Their activities are guided by targets set forth in the national plan.

The Central Statistical Administration. A central agency of note which is concerned with the drafting and implementation of the economic plan is the Central Statistical Administration. It is responsible for providing Gosplan and the government ministries a flow of information on all facets of economic activity. There can be no effective planning without this flow of statistical data. The Central Statistical Administration, however, is independent of Gosplan and the ministries, for its purpose is to serve as a means of control over planning and over the powers of Gosplan. As is typical for any administrative apparatus in the Soviet Union, there are counterparts to the Central Statistical Administration in each of the 15 union republics, and there are statistical administrative units in the autonomous republics, krays, oblasts, and rayons. The statistical administrative units at the lower administrative levels are responsible for the collection of data from enterprises and from economic sectors for transmission to Gosplan, the Council of Ministers of the U.S.S.R., and other central government agencies. Thus, Gosplan is given a great mass of statistical data with which to work in developing specific ways and means of accomplishing the goals of the economic plan.

Drafting of the Plan. Control figures are drawn up by Gosplan before the five-year plan is drafted. These figures determine the prinicpal trends and general scale of economic development during the duration of the plan. These control figures cover the volume and distribution of national income, the overall volume of capital investment and industrial production in the more important branches of industry, the volume of output and state purchases of farm produce, the volume of retail trade, expected increases in labor productivity, and the monetary income of the population. These control figures are based on the economy's achievements in preceding time periods and on estimates of future manpower availability and progress in technology and labor productivity.

Stages of the Planning Cycle. When the plan is designed, it is a draft plan which outlines the basic economic development tasks for the plan period. This drafting phase transforms government and party objectives into numerical targets which determine the amount of resources to be allocated for specific purposes.

When the draft plan has been completed, it is sent for approval to the Central Committee of the Communist Party and to the Council of Ministers of the U.S.S.R. After the plan is approved, it is broken down by sections and sent to the appropriate national ministry or department for consideration. It is also sent to the Gosplans of the republics, which are also supposed to prepare plans for the economic programs of their particular republics and ministries. The draft plan is then sent to planning commissions at the regional and local levels and to enterprises. The purpose of this dissemination is to provide information which can be used as a basis for plan formulation at the enterprise level and also at the various local, regional, and national administrative levels. An enterprise, for example, would receive information as to the kinds, quantities, and qualities of goals whch it was expected to produce, quantities and kinds of labor, power, materials, capital goods, and other things which would be supplied to it, estimates of the productivity which the workers should achieve, and estimates of the workers' incomes and living standards.

After the control figures have been made available to the various economic units and the lower echelons of government, there is a plan counterdesign which starts with the formulation of plans by industrial and trade enterprises, state farms, and other local economic units. These plans cover all phases of their operations in great detail. For example, plans of enterprises set forth what they are to make, in what quantities, and by what combinations of labor and capital. These are target plans which are supposed to serve as a framework for annual operating plans. The plans then travel in an upward route to their eventual integration in the national plan by Gosplan. At each administrative stage the plans cumulate into a larger whole. From the primary producing units—industrial, agricultural, and trading enterprises, the plans move through local soviets, rayons, krays, oblasts, autonomous republics, and the various ministries and planning agencies at the union republic and national level.[11] Gosplan has the final responsibility for the preparation of the overall national plan. The problem is reconciling all draft plans into one national plan.

The process of reconciliation is the third stage of the planning cycle. Gosplan must adjust Politburo objectives from above with the aggregation of plans from below. It is also at this stage that various monetary plans are developed. These monetary plans, or financial plans as they can be called, represent a counterpart to the main economic plan which is expressed in physical terms. Two of the major financial plans are the state budget and the cash and credit plans of Gosbank. Each plan exercises important control functions which will be discussed later in the chapter.[12] The financial plans are

---

[11] For an outline of the preparation of the annual Soviet plan see U.S. Bureau of the Census, *The Soviet Financial System, Structure, Operations, and Statistics,* p. 51.

[12] There is also the consolidated financial plan, which includes the state budget and the cash and credit plans of Gosbank. In addition, it includes the profits of all state enterprises and allowances for depreciation, increases in savings bank deposits, and other financial resources.

approved and developed by the Ministry of Finance and Gosbank, and are reviewed by Gosplan in its preparation of the national economic plan. When the plan is prepared, it is sent to the Council of Ministers and the Central Committee of the Communist Party for ratification. Finally, the plan, with its tasks for each administrative and economic level, is passed down the line until it reaches the enterprise. The whole Soviet planning process is complex, for there has to be a flow of operational directives to the thousands of operating enterprises. Plans for various sectors must be coordinated with those of other sectors.

The Use of Material Balances. The basic method of Soviet economic planning has involved the use of material balances. These balances are usually carried on in physical terms and present an intended relationship between supplies and their allocation for specific commodities. Material balances are drawn up for all of the important types of industrial and agricultural products. An example of the use of material balances can be presented roughly as follows:

Product

Resources	Distribution
Stocks at the start of the planning period	Production and operating needs
	Capital construction
Production	Replenishment of state stocks
Imports	Exports
Mobilization of internal resources	Other needs
	Stocks at the end of the planning period
Total	Total

However, given the complexities of the production and distribution processes, the material balance method has become more cumbersome to handle. So it has been replaced to some extent with a system of interbranch balances which consists of working out a matrix of flows which look like a chessboard.[13] These flows represent an array of interrelationships between economic sectors. The economy is divided into so many branches and each of them is supposed to achieve an annual output of a given quantity. Each branch also uses a certain portion of its annual output. The remaining portion of each branch's annual output is to be delivered to other branches. That part of production over and above that used up in the branch and other branches during the year constitutes net material production. This total is devoted to consumption and investment.

[13] Interbranch balances, or input-output analysis, has not been fully adopted as a tool of Russian economic planning. On this subject see the following article: Vladimir G. Treml, Barry L. Kostinsky, and Dimitri M. Gallik, "Interindustry Structure of the Soviet Union: 1959 and 1966," *Soviet Economic Prospects for the Seventies* (Washington: Joint Economic Committee, 1973), pp. 246–251.

Economic planning has to reconcile a number of flows, including production, consumption, and saving; the utilization of labor resources; the distribution of national income; and personal money income and expenditure. The total amount of wages to be paid and the production counterpart to support wages, depends on the division of socialist national income between savings and the consumption, and further, of consumption between social consumption and wages. This leads to the problem of relating the total flow of wages to the total value of consumer goods and services. The maintenance of balance between incomes from work and the resources allocated to personal consumption is a part of distribution policy and especially of wage planning. As prices of consumer goods and services may change, this also involves the problem of maintenance of the purchasing power of wages and the relationship between nominal and real wages.

Conditions for Planning. The essential conditions for planning are present in the Soviet Union. The state is in full control of the land, factories, transportation, and the raw materials necessary for the production of all commodities. It controls the quality and quantity of the labor force, which enables it to supply the economy with the necessary labor to fill planned targets. Through control of money and credit, it finances construction and the operations of enterprises in accordance with the financial plan. To exercise compliance with the plan, the state, through Gosplan, Gosbank, and other organizations, can maintain control over the plan's execution. Gosplan in particular has the responsibility for checking on the progress made in implementing the plan. This is done through the hierarchy of planning offices that exist down to the lower administrative levels of government. The Communist Party also performs a control function in that its members hold positions of authority in all enterprises and they can supervise the implementation of the plan at the enterprise level.

Limitations of Planning. Nevertheless, the whole process of planning has its limitations. The plan may estimate that a certain number of workers, given certain supplies of machinery, land, equipment, materials, and power, will turn out a specific number of units of product of definite quality in a given period, but the results of the workers' activities may be anything but those which are expected. There is also a certain lack of coordination and inefficiency in planning which can be attributed to the existence of a comprehensive bureaucratic structure. Enterprises are separated from the decision-making agencies at the top by a number of intermediary agencies. This means that they are separated from other enterprises by agencies that must check purchase and sales requests and disburse funds. Another defect in planning is that the setting of general production norms or indexes fails to take into consideration differences in the characteristics of various enterprises. Also, over the years since planning was developed, the Soviet Union has grown into a complex and modern industrial nation with increasingly sophisticated production techniques and greater demands for quality specifications of materials. This, in itself, has complicated the central planning process and has caused a need for more detailed microplanning.

Public Finance

The operation of any modern state requires the collection of large sums of money for the financing of various public services and for the general administrative expenses of government. This is as true of the Soviet Union as it is of any capitalistic country. However, there is a great deal of difference in the ways in which the two forms of economic organization acquire and dispose of their revenues. In the Soviet Union government expenditures are very large in relation to national income, since the government has to make expenditures for operating industries as well as carrying on normal governmental functions.[14] Since the government has provided the expenditures necessary for the operation of industrial and agricultural enterprises, it would stand to reason that it would receive part of the proceeds derived from the sale of goods and services by these enterprises. Both the Soviet and Western capitalistic governments will necessarily devote substantial sums of their national incomes to general administrative expenses, to war and defense measures, and to various forms of social services, but in the case of the Soviet state, additional sums must also be made available to finance industry operation.

The Soviet State Budget. In the Soviet Union the national budget is of paramount importance since it provides for the accumulation and distribution of much of the national income. The national budget, or Soviet State Budget, as it is called, is a consolidated budget which provides for the expenditures and revenues of the national, republic, and local units of government. It is also closely related in terms of revenues and expenditures to the national economic plan. It performs an important allocative function in that it is the major instrument for financing many types of investment and for controlling the utilization of investment in accordance with planning objectives. The budget is also instrumental in decisions to divide the national product between consumption and investment.

The Soviet State Budget is made up annually for the calendar year. It is prepared by the Ministry of Finance and includes the all-union or central budget, the budgets of the autonomous republics, and the budgets of regional, urban, and rural administrative entities. Republic and local authorities prepare their own budgets in conformance with the objectives of the national economic plan.[15] When the tentative budgets are prepared, they are transmitted upward —local government budgets to their respective republic's ministry of finance, and republic budgets to the Union Ministry of Finance—and coordinated at each step with the national economic plan. When the total budget—all-union, republic, and local—is integrated, it is sent by the Ministry of Finance to the

---

[14] It is necessary to mention the fact that most state enterprises operate on the basis of what is called *khozraschet financing*. This means that they sell their products for money and use the resulting proceeds to finance normal operating expenses. However, the typical enterprise receives extensive support from the state budget. A major share of all capital investment of enterprises is financed from the budget.

[15] Only the principal headings or expenditures in the budgets require ultimate approval at the top of the budgetary hierarchy. Local and republic governments have some autonomy concerning expenditures for specific items such as fire protection and repairs of drains.

Council of Ministers of the Soviet Union for approval. After the Council of Ministers has made changes and recommendations, the Soviet State Budget is then presented by the Ministry of Finance to the Supreme Soviet for final approval by its members before it becomes the law of the land and is published. The budget often provides an indication of Soviet economic policies for the coming year, for it is a part of the country's overall economic and financial plan for each year and reflects priorities in terms of resource allocation.

The Soviet budget is presented in Tables 16–1 and 16–2. It represents the almost all-inclusive functioning of the state. Table 16–1 presents the principal sources of revenue for the state budget. Most of the revenue of the budget is derived from the operation of the national economy rather than from direct taxes on the incomes of individuals. The two most important sources of revenue are the turnover tax and deductions from the profits of state-owned enterprises. Both sources of revenue are obtained by setting the prices of goods at levels higher than the cost of production and appropriating the difference.

TABLE 16–1
ACTUAL REVENUES OF THE SOVIET STATE BUDGET FOR 1974 *

Revenues		Billions of Dollars †
Social sector		196.04
Turnover tax	72.28	
Deductions from profits	78.00	
Other receipts	45.76	
Private sector		31.33
State taxes on the population	19.24	
Receipts from Social Security	12.09	
Total revenues		227.63
Budget surplus		2.47

Source: *The USSR in Figures in 1973* (Moscow: Statistika, 1974), p. 38.

* Because of rounding, components may not add to the totals shown.

† The exchange rate is one ruble equals $1.30 as of March, 1974.

Expenditures of the state budget are presented in Table 16–2. There are four main categories of expenditures—expenditures to finance the national economy, social-cultural measures, national defense, and administration. Expenditures for financing the national economy and social-cultural expenditures account for four fifths of total outlays.

It can readily be seen that the main function of the state budget is the reallocation of funds within the economy. This reallocation process involves budget receipts of the turnover tax and deductions from profits, and budget expenditures on the national economy, social welfare programs, and national defense. The turnover tax and deductions from profits would represent an inflow of revenue into the state budget from the consumer and enterprise sectors of the economy. The turnover tax, for example, represents part of the

TABLE 16-2

ACTUAL EXPENDITURES OF THE SOVIET STATE BUDGET FOR 1972 *

Expenditures		Billions of Dollars *
Financing the national economy		103.5
Industry and construction	n.a.	
Agriculture and procurement	n.a.	
Trade	n.a.	
Transportation and communication	n.a.	
Municipal economy and housing and residual †	n.a.	
Social-cultural measures		77.4
Education, science, and culture	34.1	
Health and physical culture	12.2	
Social welfare measures	31.1	
Defense		21.8
Administration		2.2
Loan serice		n.a.
Budgetary expenditure residal ‡		6.2
Total expenditures		211.2

Source: *The USSR in Figures in 1973* (Moscow: Statistika, 1974), p. 39.

* Because of rounding, components may not add to the totals shown.

† Residual includes subsidies for state procurement of agricultural products, state gold purchases, allocations for geologic prospecting, and purchases of state reserves.

‡ This includes such items as budget allocations for increasing credit resources of long-term investment banks.

net income of society fully returned to the state budget to cover social-cultural measures, outlays for development of the national economy and other general state needs. These outlays represent an outflow of expenditures on enterprises, while other revenue in the form of salaries and transfer payments is directed from the budget to households. It can also be seen from looking at the state budget that the national government purchases large quantities of goods and services on its own account. An example would be national defense expenditures, which accounted for over 12 percent of total state budget expenditures in 1970.

The state budget usually shows an annual surplus of revenues over expenditures. This surplus has two important functions: (1) In terms of fiscal policy, it has an anti-inflationary effect on the economy and thus fits within the framework of the Soviet fiscal system; and (2) it is used to increase the resources of the State Bank (Gosbank). The two functions, to a certain extent, have offsetting effects.

Government Revenues. Government revenues are primarily obtained from two sources—a turnover tax and deductions from profits of enterprises. There is much less reliance on income taxation in the Soviet Union than in any of the countries with mixed economic systems.

The Turnover Tax. The turnover tax is one of the most important sources of revenue in the state budget. It was established as a revenue source in 1930 when Soviet industry, unable to support itself, needed additional revenue for further expansion. It represents a flexible and varied portion of the price and is delivered directly to the state budget in accordance with sales of goods on which the tax is levied. The tax is collected by wholesale distributing organizations, individual enterprises, and procurement organizations dealing with consumer goods and foodstuffs. As a rule, the following procedure is followed: If enterprises making goods subject to the tax sell them directly to buyers or to trade organizations, then the turnover tax is paid by the enterprises themselves according to the place of production of such goods; if, however, goods are sold through wholesale organizations, then the turnover tax is paid by the latter at the place of sale of the goods. The burden of the turnover tax ultimately falls on the Russian consumer, so that it can be considered to represent a part of the flow of funds between the state and households.

The Russian turnover tax performs several important economic functions. In addition to being a principal source of revenue for the budget, it also serves to absorb the excess purchasing power of consumers. The production plans of the national government provide that a given amount of goods be made available to consumers annually. On the other hand, in order to maintain incentives, and partly because of errors in planning, consumers may receive more purchasing power than can be absorbed by the goods made available to them at controlled prices. This excess of purchasing power is siphoned off by the turnover tax, which has the impact of an excise or sales tax, as it is applied primarily to consumer goods. It is not a fixed-rate tax, with the yield an independent variable, but, to the contrary, a tax where the desired yield determines the rate, which also varies in response to particular supply and demand conditions. Since the turnover tax is tied to output and is collected either directly at factories or at wholesale distribution outlets, it guarantees a steady inflow of funds to the budget and is easy to collect and inexpensive to administer. Moreover, it is a flexible device for establishing equilibrium prices on the bases of the level of output of consumer goods and disposable income.

In mid-1967 the Soviets effected a comprehensive and sweeping price reform, with significant changes in the wholesale prices for many goods—some up and some down. With all this, however, retail prices remained unchanged, and the effects were absorbed by the turnover tax. We have very little information on the new tax rates on specific goods. It is still true that such things as alcoholic beverages, tobacco products, cosmetics, and jewelry are taxed at high rates. The tax on vodka, for example, is about 90 percent of the retail price; that on cognac and fortified wines is around 50 percent. Tax rates on cotton and synthetic fabrics range from 45 to 65 percent of retail price.[16] Other products with substantial tax rates are motorcycles, passenger

[16] "The Budget of the Fourth Year of the Five-Year Plan," translation of an article by V. F. Garbukov in *FINANSY SSSR* (*Soviet Finances*), Joint Publications Research Service, *USSR Economy and Industry* (April, 1974), p. 13.

cars, television sets, refrigerators, watches, electricity, natural gas, and gasoline. Sugar is also taxed at a substantial rate.

There is, however, a trend toward freeing various commodities from the turnover tax. In 1967 the tax was eliminated on lumber, spare parts for agricultural machinery, and on second-hand commodities, and it was reduced on other commodities.[17] Exemptions from the turnover tax have also been used by the government to accomplish certain economic goals. For example, products produced for exports are exempted from the tax. Exemptions are also granted to encourage the development of new types of products or to support the development of local industry.

Deductions from Profits. The most important source of revenue in the Soviet budget is deductions from the profits of state-owned enterprises and organizations. For years, this revenue source ranked second to the turnover tax in importance. However, this relationship has changed. In 1960 the turnover tax accounted for 31.3 billion rubles and deductions from profits accounted for 18.6 billion rubles out of total budgetary revenues of 77.1 billion rubles. In 1972 the amounts of revenue collected from the turnover tax and deductions from profits amounted to 55.6 billion rubles ($67.8 billion) and 60 billion rubles ($73.2 billion), respectively. The 1974 financial plan, however, called for turnover tax revenues of 62 billion rubles ($80.6 billion) and revenues from deductions from profits of 62.6 billion rubles ($81.4 billion).[18]

Deductions from profits are payable on the actual rather than on the planned profits of enterprises, and such deductions vary from industry to industry. The rate for a particular enterprise is fixed on the basis of its financial plan for the year. The final selling price of commodities produced by the enterprise is designed to cover the cost of production and planned profits. The latter may or may not occur depending upon the efficiency of the enterprise. Each enterprise has the right to retain part of its profits for such purposes as expanding its fixed and working capital, and the government, in setting the rate of the profit deduction, takes this into consideration. Nevertheless, the amount of profits returned to the state budget is high and can account for as much as 80 percent of total profits.[19]

The distribution of enterprise profits falls into two categories—profits which are retained by enterprises and which are used to finance various incentive funds, and profits which are paid into the state budget. Retained profits can be used to finance an enterprise's material incentives fund, which is a part of the new economic reforms that have taken place in the Soviet Union. Its purpose is to provide an incentive system of bonuses to workers as a reward for increased productivity. Retained earnings are also used to finance an enterprise's social-cultural and production development funds. The former

---

[17] "Role of Tax Organs in Promoting Economic Efficiency," translation of an article by S. Miroschenko in *FINANSY SSSR* (*Soviet Finances*), Joint Publications Research Service, *USSR Economy and Industry* (July, 1968), p. 3.

[18] Garbukov, *op. cit.*, p. 3.

[19] *Ibid.*, p. 3.

is used to support various services which are provided to workers by an enterprise, and the latter provides a source of revenue for the expansion of fixed and working capital. Depreciation deductions also provide revenue for the same purpose. Profits which are paid into the state budget can be broken down into three categories—profits paid to the budget as a capital charge, profits paid to the budget for financing centralized investment, including credit repayment and expansion of working capital, and profits paid to the budget as a free or unused remainder. To an enterprise, this free remainder represents profits which are uncommitted to any particular fund or budget charge; to the state budget, it represents an important source of revenue.

Social Insurance Taxes. The remainder of the revenues obtained from the operation of the national economy comes from social insurance taxes paid by enterprises as a fixed percentage of their wage bill, taxes levied on organizations such as collective farms, and income taxes levied on individuals. The social insurance taxes are levied as a percentage of wages and salaries, and these taxes vary from industry to industry. The revenue is paid into a state social insurance budget which is administered by the trade unions. This budget is consolidated with the state budget, and revenue is transferred to republic and local budgets.

Personal Income Tax. Direct taxes on the population are unimportant in the Soviet revenue system. The personal income tax accounted for only 8.4 percent of total state budget revenues in 1972. It is progressive in nature, and in 1960 it ranged from a minimum of 0.15 percent to a maximum of 13 percent of monthly earnings withheld by the enterprises and paid to the Ministry of Finance.[20] The income tax is differentiated between economic groups, with certain groups, such as workers and salaried employees paying a lower tax than other groups, such as doctors, lawyers, and artisans, with incomes from private practice. The personal income tax was supposed to have been abolished in the Soviet Union by 1965. This has not come about, although some liberalization in the amount of income which is exempted from the tax has occurred. Since 1971, the amount of income exempted from the tax was 70 rubles ($91.00) a month.[21]

There is also a rural counterpart to the income tax, a so-called agricultural tax which is levied on farmers who earn an income from agricultural activities on their private plots of land. It has as its purpose to discourage farmers from spending too much time on their own land at the expense of their work on collective farms.[22] The tax rate is progressive and is based on the quantity of land in use rather than on the return on the land. As a source of revenue, the agricultural tax is of little importance, but it has a control function of regulating work.

[20] More current rates are not available.

[21] "Law on the USSR State Budget for 1974," translation of an article in *Ekono-micheskaya Gaseta,* Joint Publications Research Service, *USSR Economy and Industry* (February, 1974), p. 2.

[22] If farmers fail to work the stipulated minimum number of labor-days or work-days on the collective farms, the agricultual tax can be increased by as much as 50 percent.

Government Expenditures. Expenditures in the state budget are divided into four main categories—financing the national economy, social and cultural measures, defense, and administration.

Financing the National Economy. Expenditures to finance the national economy accounted for approximately 49 percent of total budgetary expenditures in 1971 and 1972. These expenditures include allocations to enterprises for capital investments and for working capital. Capital goods and construction industries are the major recipients of budget funds for investment purposes, for the government concentrates on growth-inducing investment in areas that constitute the base of economic power. Appropriations from the state budget are also used to finance the construction of transportation facilities, investment in state farms, and housing construction. State farms are government owned and operated and they are a major recipient of budgetary funds. Housing construction also enjoys a high priority in terms of allocation of budgetary funds because there is an acute housing shortage in the Soviet Union, particularly in the large cities. Funds allocated to housing construction are of two types: funds that are allocated to construction enterprises for building apartments and other dwellings, and funds which are made available to individual home builders in the form of credits.

As mentioned previously, the state budget redistributes income within the economy. Deductions from profits represent a withdrawal of income from the economy, but they reenter the economy through the budget as expenditures which are used to finance capital investment, increases in working capital, and housing. The turnover tax can also be considered as a device used to reallocate resources from consumption to investment.

Social and Cultural Measures. Expenditures for social and cultural measures, including education and training, public health, physical culture, and social insurance benefits, accounted for 36.6 percent of total expenditures in the 1972 state budget. A wide variety of social services are financed under the three subcategories of social and cultural measures—education, science, and culture; health and physical culture; and social welfare measures.

The first subcategory—education, science, and culture—amounted to 28 billion rubles ($34.1 billion) in 1972 and accounted for 16 percent of total budgetary expenditures.[23] Expenditures on education include construction and maintenance costs of schools, payment of teachers' salaries, and provision of financial support for students. Expenditures on science include the support of scientific research, and expenditures on culture include support for museums, expositions, and the fine arts. Other expenditures that are financed under education, science, and culture include the cost of disseminating political propaganda.

The second subcategory—health and physical culture—amounted to 10 billion rubles ($12.2 billion) in 1972 and accounted for 5.8 percent of total budgetary expenditures. Health expenditures cover outlays for medical and hospital facilities, training of medical personnel, and medical research. Physical

[23] See Table 16–2.

culture expenditures support the athletic programs, which are carried on throughout the Soviet Union. Unlike the United States, where sports receive no subsidy from the federal government, the Soviet Union subsidizes its sports and provides special dispensations to its better athletes.

The third subcategory—social welfare measures—represents expenditures for old age and disability pensions, sickness and maternity benefits, and family allowances. In 1972 expenditures on these social insurance measures amounted to 25.5 billion rubles ($31.1 billion) and accounted for 14 percent of total budgetary expenditures. Social insurance is financed by a payroll tax on enterprises which ranges from 4.4 percent to 9 percent, depending on the industry in which the enterprise operates. The government finances any excess of expenditures over and above total social insurance contributions, which in 1972 amounted to 9.4 billion rubles ($11.5 billion). Collection and disbursement of social insurance contributions is the responsibility of the Soviet trade unions, and administrative responsibility belongs to the Republic Ministries of Social Security, the Republic Minstries of Finance, and the Ministry of Health of the U.S.S.R.

Old age pensions in the Soviet Union range from a minimum of 45 rubles ($58.50) a month to a maximum of 120 rubles ($156.00). The retirement age is 60 years for male industrial workers with 25 years or more of work experience and 55 years for women workers with at least ten years of work experience. Workers in hardship areas of the country are entitled to a retirement pension at the age of 55 for men and 50 for women, with a minimum of 15 years' work experience. The retirement age of collective farm workers is 60 years for male workers with a minimum of 25 years of service and 55 years for women with at least 20 years of work experience. Reduced pensions, which are proportionate to the years of work experience, are paid to workers who have less than the requisite work experience for the basic pension. In addition to the old age pension, there is an invalidity pension which varies from 45 percent of earnings for partial disability to 65 percent of earnings for total disability. There is also a survivor's pension which varies according to the number of survivors. For three or more survivors, a pension of up to 85 percent of earnings, with a maximum set at 90 rubles ($117.00) is payable.[24]

Sickness and maternity benefits are also payable to all persons under the Soviet social insurance system. Russian workers are entitled to sickness benefits from the first day of incapacity until they return to their jobs or are declared invalids. These benefits range from 50 percent of monthly earnings for workers with less than three years of work experience to 90 percent of monthly earnings for workers with 12 or more years of work experience. Maximum benefits are limited to 10 rubles ($13) a day. Maternity benefits involve 112 days of paid maternity leave—56 days before and 56 days after the birth of the child. Payment ranges from 66.7 to 100 percent of average monthly earnings, depending on the length of employment. Medical benefits involve payment of general

[24] U.S. Department of Health, Education and Welfare, *Social Security Programs Throughout the World* (Washington: Social Security Administration, Office of Research and Statistics, 1972), p. 210.

and specialist care, hospitalization, laboratory services, and maternity care for workers and their dependents. Medicines are paid for by patients unless they are hospitalized, and patients also pay for the cost of special appliances.[25]

Work injury pensions are also paid to Russian workers, including those on collective farms. Temporary disability benefits are paid from the first day of injury until recovery. Minimum benefits are 30 rubles a month (1 ruble = $1.30). Permanent disability pensions amount to 90 percent of earnings up to 45 rubles a month, plus 10 percent of earnings above this amount. Maximum disability pensions amount to 90 rubles a month, with a supplement of 10 percent of the pension for one dependent and 15 percent for two or more. Pensions are lower in the rural areas and higher for persons engaged in difficult or dangerous work. In addition to work injury pensions, there are survivor's benefits, which vary according to the number of survivors. Maximum benefits range from 45 rubles a month for one survivor to 120 rubles a month for three or more survivors.[26]

The family allowance represents the fourth type of social insurance payment. It is paid to families with four or more children and ranges from 4 rubles a month for the fourth child to 15 rubles a month for the eleventh and each additional child. There is also a birth grant which is a lump-sum payment of 20 rubles for the third child and which rises progressively to 250 rubles for the eleventh and each additional child.[27]

National Defense. Outlays for national defense accounted for around 10 percent of total budget expenditures in 1972. However, the amount of 17.9 billion rubles ($21.8 billion) [28] understates the amount which was actually spent for defense-related activities because a substantial proportion of military-space research is carried out under expenditures for science. In 1972 total expenditures on science amounted to 14.4 billion rubles ($17.6 billion).[29] These expenditures include outlays for research and development for complex military equipment such as aircraft and missiles and for nuclear energy and space activities. The general defense category includes monetary and material allowances for armed forces personnel, payment for supplies and repair of combat equipment, maintenance of military institutions and schools, and military construction. When general defense expenditures are added to outlays for scientific research allocated under the category social-cultural measures but related directly or indirectly to national defense, total defense expenditures have ranged around 20 percent of the state budget and around 10 percent of Soviet gross national product.[30]

[25] *Ibid.*

[26] *Ibid.*

[27] The family allowance in most countries is paid to families with one or more children. The Russian family allowance suffers by comparison.

[28] The Soviet state budget has listed defense expenditures of 17.9 billion rubles for four consecutive years, 1970 to 1973.

[29] Garbukov, *op. cit.*, p. 5.

[30] Herbert Block, "Value and Burden of Soviet Defense," *Soviet Economic Prospects for the Seventies* (Washington: Joint Economic Committee, 1973), p. 178.

Soviet defense expenditures have placed a burden on the economy. For one thing, the best human and material resources are channeled into defense-related activities. Outside of these activities, the economy has generally been inefficient. In comparison to the United States, the Soviet Union provides a larger population with less than half of the goods and services available in the United States, and uses a labor force 45 percent larger and investing in real terms about the same amount. Policies and priorities favoring defense have worked to the detriment of agriculture in that it is possible to shift to this area material and human resources claimed by the military and space establishment. In addition, there is a trade-off between defense and nondefense resource use. The resources foregone for defense could have resulted in a higher standard of living for the Soviet consumer. The most apparent trade-off has been between defense weapons and producer durable goods, with decreases in the latter leading to a decrease in capital stock, one of the primary ingredients in the growth process. So it can be argued that Soviet defense expenditures have had an adverse effect on the growth rate.[31]

Administration. Budget expenditures for administration is another category of expenditures. This includes financing for local and central government agencies such as planning and financial bodies, ministries, government departments, and the courts and judicial organs. In this connection, it is necessary to remember that the Soviet state budget covers a scope of activities which is much broader than equivalent activities financed in the budgets of capitalistic governments. The state budget covers the planned expenditures for all of the national, regional, and local Soviet governments.

Money and Banking

Money plays a subordinate role in the Soviet economy. To some extent this reflects the traditional Marxist view on money, which largely represented a reaction against capitalism where money reaches its peak of development and influence. Moreover, primary reliance on planning is in real terms; a channeling of investment funds occurs through the state budget rather than through financial markets. As long as plan balancing is done in physical terms, there is little need for prices in planning. Since prices have generally been fixed according to administrative convenience, money values rarely indicate the value of goods in terms of real cost, and are, therefore, an uncertain guide to investment decisions. Money also does not provide automatic access to goods in the capital market. First, there must be authorization for the goods to be produced and, secondly, in addition to money, there must be plan authorization to acquire the goods.

This is not to say, however, that money is of no importance. Soviet money has many of the same functions as money in a capitalistic system. Within and outside the state sector, money serves as a unit of account; that is, all goods and services which are bought and sold are valued in monetary units. Money

---

[31] Stanley H. Cohn, "Economic Burden of Defense Expenditures," *Soviet Economic Prospects for the Seventies* (Washington: Joint Economic Committee, 1973), p. 154.

also functions as a medium of exchange in the Soviet Union in that wages and salaries are paid in terms of currency, and receivers of money can use it to purchase goods and services. However, the ownership of money does not give individuals command over the allocation of resources as it does under a capitalistic system, for resource allocation is determined by the national plan and not by the price system. It is also necessary to stress that money is an instrument through which the state maintains control over enterprises. The State Bank, acting as the agent of the planning authorities, allocates credit to enterprises in conformance with the plan. Finally, economic reforms, even to the limited extent they have been implemented, imply a more important role for money, particularly in the area of pricing.

Similar to the control over other sectors of the Soviet economy, there is a plan to control the monetary aspects—the financial plan—which parallels and is coordinated with the production and distribution plans for each period of time. The three essential components of the financial plan are the following: the state budget, which is responsible for resource allocation between consumption and investment; the credit plan, which regulates the granting of credits by the banking system to enterprises during a stipulated period of time; and the cash plan, which controls the supply of money in circulation. By use of the components of the financial plan, the planners seek to coordinate the operations of the monetary and financial aspects of the economy with the production of physical goods and services. The financial plan is calculated prior to the production plan because it determines the income and expenditure patterns of all important sectors of the Soviet economy.

The Soviet banking system possesses the following characteristics: [32]

1. Banking is centralized as a monopoly of the government. This means that through the direct operation of the banking system, the government can determine the volume of credit and hence the money supply.
2. The banking system is subordinate to the economic plan. It serves as an instrument of control through the verification of planned transactions.
3. Banks specialize according to functions. There are banks for savings and for investment. There is, however, a trend toward bank consolidation, and savings banks have become a part of the State Bank (Gosbank). For all practical purposes, Gosbank is the banking system of the Soviet Union because it provides for the cash and credit needs of the country.

The State Bank (Gosbank). The State Bank (Gosbank) is the keystone of the Soviet banking system. Within the framework of the centrally planned economy of the Soviet Union, it performs a number of functions:

1. It acts as the fiscal agent of the government in that it receives all tax revenues and pays out budgetary appropriations to enterprises and institutions.
2. It is responsible for granting short-term or commercial credit to all types of enterprises.

[32] Yves M. Laulan (ed.), *Banking Money, and Credit in Eastern Europe* (Brussels: NATO—Directorate of Economic Affairs, 1973), p. 9.

3. It carries the accounts of all business enterprises in the country. Each enterprise has an account in the State Bank which is supposed to supply it with working capital, and when a sale is made between two industrial enterprises, the bank simply deducts the amount of the sale from the buyer's account and adds it to that of the seller. This, as will be explained later, gives the central government control over the progress of each enterprise within the economic system.

4. It is responsible for the preparation of the credit and cash plans which are a part of the financial plan prepared by the Ministry of Finance. In this capacity, the bank is exercising a planning function which involves currency needs and credit expansion.

5. It is also responsible for the emission of currency and for holding all precious metals and foreign currencies owned by the Soviet government. As the bank of issue, it can issue money and withdraw it from circulation, thereby helping to regulate the supply of money available to enterprises and individuals in accordance with the cash plan.

Organization of the State Bank. At the apex of the State Bank is the policy-making head office, which is in Moscow. The administrative apparatus of this office is divided into several departments, which have a variety of responsibilities.[33] In addition to the main office in Moscow, there is a network of offices of the State Bank throughout the Soviet Union. These offices are of three types—republic, regional, and local. Each republic has a principal office which is responsible for the coordination of policy between the main office and regional and local offices. Regional offices are responsible for the supervision of local offices and the transmission of credit plans to the main office. They are also responsible for the conformance of local offices to the credit plans of the State Bank and for the dissemination of central bank policies into all areas of the Soviet Union. Local offices, of which there are some 3,500, serve enterprises, collective farms, and local government units.[34] They perform an important control function in that they possess the accounts of the various enterprises and collective farms and can enforce financial discipline in the sense that they can make sure that funds are used for only those purposes that are set forth in the financial plan. In addition to the republic, regional, and local offices, the State Bank also operates savings banks which are responsible for the accumulation of individual savings and the sale of government bonds.[35]

Financing the State Bank. The funds that are used to support the operations of the State Bank are obtained from several sources. One source is the

---

[33] George Garvy, *Money, Banking, and Credit in Eastern Europe* (New York: Federal Reserve Bank of New York, 1966), p. 38. Also see George Garvy, "Policies and Mechanics Related to Money," in Yves M. Laulan (ed)., *Banking, Money, and Credit in Eastern Europe* (Brussels: NATO—Directorate of Economic Affairs, 1973), p. 9.

[34] *Ibid.*, p. 124.

[35] Since 1959 developments have taken place within the Soviet banking system which have contributed to the greater centralization of the banking system and to the extension of the functions of the State Bank. In 1963 the savings bank system was merged with the State Bank, but the system continues to perform the function of serving as an outlet for the savings of the population. Savings are encouraged in the Soviet Union as a means of reducing the chronic excess of consumer demand over the supply of consumer goods.

state budget. Since the end of World War II, the state budget has annually shown an excess of revenues over expenditures. This excess is used to increase the credit resources of the State Bank. There are also other transfers of funds from the budget to the State Bank. For example, budgetary grants are made for capital purposes. Deposits of savings by the public in the savings banks operated by the State Bank are also a source of funds. These savings banks do not make loans to the general public. Part of the income derived by the State Bank is obtained from the difference between the interest paid on savings deposits and interest received from loans to enterprises. The reserves of the social insurance funds also provide a source of funds. Other sources are increases in note circulation and increases in the balances of enterprises and collective farms held on account with the State Bank.[36]

State bank resources consist of two major resource components which are presented in Table 16–3. These components are the monetary resources of private households and monetary resources of the socialized economy. Most payments between state enterprises are not settled by cash or check but by adjusting enterprises' bank accounts. These transfer payments are effected more or less automatically on the basis of delivery documents. Transfers of taxes and grants between the state budget on the one hand and enterprises and institutions on the other are made the same way.

TABLE 16–3
THE STRUCTURE OF MONETARY RESOURCES IN THE SOVIET STATE BANK (1970)

Items		Percentage
Monetary resources of socialist economy		71.4
Clearing accounts of enterprises	2.2	
Investment and other funds	26.4	
Bank funds	4.6	
State budget	24.7	
Monetary resources of private households		28.6
Savings deposits	19.7	
Cash	8.9	
		100.0

Source: Adam Zwass, Das Geld und Kreditwesen in Osteuropa (Vienna: Österreichisches Institut für Wirtschaftsforschung, 1973), p. 17.

Planning Function. One of the most important functions of the State Bank involves economic planning. The State Bank has the responsibility for the preparation of the credit and cash plans. These plans are approved by the Council of Ministers. The extension of loans made by the bank is carried out in connection with the credit plan and is granted for needs arising in the course of the fulfillment of the plans of production and distribution. Through

---

[36] Adam Zwass, *Das Geld und Kreditwesen in Osteuropa* (Vienna: Österreichisches Institut für Wirtschaftsforschung, 1973), pp. 11–17.

its drawing up of quarterly cash plans, the bank has a significant influence in determining the extent and composition of note issue. The purpose of the credit and cash plans is to adjust the supply of money to the real output goals of the national economic plan and to prevent expenditures outside of planning purposes. The credit and cash plans are used to implement the physical output plan and to preserve price stability. Both types of plans are used not only by the Soviet Union but by the other communist countries of eastern Europe and by China.[37]

The credit plan determines the amount of short- and long-term credit which is to be allocated to all enterprises and collective farms in the economy during the period of the national economic plan.[38] Both types of credit plans involve the preparation of a balance sheet statement which shows the sources and uses of funds.

The short-term credit plan is designed to provide loans to the various sectors of the economy for such purposes as financing the acquisition of inventories by enterprises. The sources of funds which are used to provide short-term credit are budgetary contributions, bank reserves and profits, balances of credit institutions such as savings banks, deposit balances of enterprises, and net changes in currency in circulation. The uses of funds include loans for the payment of wages, loans for temporary needs, loans against drafts in the process of collection, and loans for technological development.[39] It can be seen that the purpose of the plan is to collate the short-term needs of enterprises and collective farms with the supply of credit. This collation is carried down to the regional and local levels of the economy through the use of regional credit plans.

The long-term credit plan is prepared on an annual basis and is designed to provide loans for both productive and nonproductive investments which have completion dates of several years or longer. It, too, shows the sources and uses of funds during the year. The funds to finance fixed investment are obtained from three sources: loan repayments by collective farms, individuals, consumer cooperatives, and municipal enterprises; funds from the state budget, which include allocations for such purposes as construction, home building, and agriculture, and also temporary Treasury loans; and subsidies from the union republics, which are used to defray the cost of home building. The funds are used to provide loans to collective farms, individuals, consumer cooperatives, and municipal enterprises, and to repay temporary Treasury loans.[40]

The cash plan controls the amount of currency in circulation. It is prepared quarterly and consists of a balance statement which shows the inflows and outflows of money. The inflow of money represents deposits in the State Bank. These deposits represent currency receipts from a wide variety of sources—

[37] The banking system of the Soviet Union is a model which is followed by other communist countries with the exception of Yugoslavia.

[38] The national economic plan is in real terms. The financial plan, of which the credit plan is a part, translates real output into monetary terms.

[39] Zwass, *op. cit.*, pp. 9–10.

[40] *Ibid.*, p. 12.

tax payments, deposits to the accounts of collective farms, rents and municipal services, receipts from retail sales, receipts from amusement and personal services enterprises, post office and savings banks receipts, and receipts from railroad, water, and air transportation. Monetary outflows under the cash plan go for wage payments, pension allowances and insurance payments, payments for agricultural products and raw materials, consumer loans, expenditures for individual housing construction, and cash disbursements by various economic organizations.[41] The outflow side of the balance statement represents most of the money income payments of the Soviet Union. Withdrawals for wage payments constitute four fifths of total monetary outflows of the cash plan. Inflows into the State Bank represent the deposit of receipts of consumer expenditures which result from wage and other income payments on the outflow side. Thus, the cash plan is an instrument which is used to control the performance of the consumer sector of the Soviet economy in terms of the disbursement and use of money.

Control Function. The State Bank also exercises an important control over the operations of Soviet enterprises. Since all financial transactions of enterprises are legally required to be accomplished through the State Bank, this affords the bank an opportunity to view their economic performance with regard to real and financial plan fulfillment. Inasmuch as most transactions between enterprises are in terms of money through bank transfers, the flow of goods is necessarily accompanied by a counterflow of funds. By requiring that all purchases and sales of goods be matched against authorized payments and receipts, it is possible for the bank to exercise control over the budget of an enterprise as a regulator of production. The very status of an enterprise's account at the bank is an indicator of its efficiency. If it breaks even on its operation, its account should neither increase nor diminish. If it makes planned or unplanned profits, its balance at the bank will grow, but if it operates inefficiently and sustains losses, its balance will decrease.

It is clear that financial transactions that would normally take place directly between the parties to the transaction in capitalistic economies are obliged to be executed through accounts established in the State Bank where the transactions and the performance of the units carrying out the transactions must come under the close scrutiny of bank officials. This procedure is not in reality basically different from capitalistic bank settlement procedures since most transactions in capitalistic countries are also carried out through bank accounts, although these transactions are not as closely examined by capitalistic commercial banks. In the Soviet Union, every purchase or sale of goods and raw materials must be reflected in changes in the accounts of the enterprises involved. It is by way of this settlement process that the State Bank assumes its unique position to carry out many of its control functions.

Provision of Credit. Short-term credit accounts for an overwhelming percentage of the total credit granted by the State Bank. In 1964 it accounted

[41] *Ibid.,* p. 13.

for 91 percent of the total credit granted by the State Bank and the Investment Bank.[42] The most important purpose of short-term credit is to finance accumulations of inventories by enterprises. Another important use of short-term credit is to finance accounts receivable. This provides working capital to the seller of goods while payments are in the process of collection. Short-term loans must be made for purposes which are consistent with the credit plan. They must be secured by real assets, such as goods in process or finished goods, and must carry a fixed maturity date. Interest rates, which are practically uniform as to borrower and which vary from 1 to 2 percent per annum, are applied to all short-term loans, and penalty rates are charged on overdue loans. Interest proceeds are used as a source of revenue to cover the operating expenses of the State Bank. As an allocator of resources, interest does not play an important role in the Soviet Union.

The Investment Bank. The Investment Bank (Stroibank) assumed the function that was formerly the responsibility of the Industrial Bank, namely the long-term crediting of capital and consumer goods enterprises. It also assumed responsibility for the following functions: [43]

1. It has the responsibility for financing cooperative housing construction and the long-term crediting of individual housing construction and capital repair of houses in urban areas.
2. It finances the construction of schools, hospitals, and the like in urban areas.
3. It is responsible for investment financing in all state-owned sectors of the economy, excepting agriculture, transportation, communication, and state-owned housing construction.
4. It is responsible for the short-term crediting of contract organizations working on construction projects for which it handles budget grants.
5. It controls the accounts and expenditures of funds for capital repair and maintenance by contract organizations in the construction field.

The Investment Bank derives its funds from budget grants, which constitute the bulk of its investment assets, and from depreciation allowances and profits of enterprises. It is a result of the creation of a highly centralized banking system in which the State Bank plays the paramount role. The Investment Bank is an agent for the disbursement of budgetary funds in the form of grants to enterprises in accordance with their investment plans. Although most of its financing is long-term, it provides short-term working capital loans to the construction industry.

The Foreign Bank. Another Soviet financial institution is the Foreign Bank (Vneshtorgbank), which has been in operation since 1924. It is responsible for financing Soviet foreign trade and for carrying out a large part of Soviet international settlement operations. It is also designated as an agent for the State Bank in many dealings with regard to gold and foreign exchange. It provides the state budget with any surplus of export proceeds over the

---

[42] Garvy, *Money, Banking, and Credit in Eastern Europe, op. cit.,* p. 75.
[43] Zwass, *op. cit.,* p. 18.

amount which export producers would receive based on the domestic value of their products and pays subsidies to producers when export prices are below domestic costs. The Foreign Exchange Bank is organized as a shareholding bank with the State Bank owning two thirds of the shares. It has few offices of its own in the Soviet Union and, therefore, carries out its operations in the offices of the State Bank; abroad, it carries out its business through local correspondence banks.

SUMMARY

In their structural arrangement, both the Soviet government and the Communist Party resemble a pyramid with its apex representing control by a central government and party hierarchy. There is an interlocking relationship between government and party, with party officials controlling the administrative structure of each organization. This merging of authority at the top continues with parallel lines of party and government organizations extending downward through the whole Soviet system. In addition to its control and supervision over the government administrative apparatus, the party is organized in every Soviet institution.

In the Soviet Union economic planning is responsible for resource allocation. It is based on the public ownership of the agents of production. However, the size and complexity of the Soviet Union make it difficult for planning to operate efficiently. Economic planning consists of a system of plans. There is a single national plan for the economic development of the country and a subset of plans for different sectors of the economy (sectoral planning) and for different areas (territorial planning).

Economic planning can be divided into long-term and annual planning. The basic form of long-term planning is the five-year plan in which important targets are established. Annual plans are subdivisions of the long-term plan. These operational plans are particularly important at the enterprise level. Long-term economic planning is essentially investment planning, and annual planning is basically production planning. The long-term plan is the principal form of state economic planning.

Public finance in the Soviet Union occupies a much more prominent role in the economy than it does in the economies of the United States and western Europe. The state budget is very important, for through it flows a large part of national income. The budget is interrelated with the financial plan of the Soviet Union, which is used primarily as a check on the operation of the basic plan, which is expressed in physical value terms. The two main sources of state budget revenues are the turnover tax and deductions from the profits of state-owned enterprises. The turnover tax is used to regulate profits and to maintain a balance between aggregate demand and the available supply of consumer goods. Budgetary expenditures include allocations to finance capital investments and to provide working capital to enterprises. Expenditures on social welfare measures constitute a major expenditure item in the state budget.

The banking system in the Soviet Union is a monopoly of the government. Gosbank is the principal instrument of the system and can be called a monobank because it performs the functions of both central and commercial banks. It serves as a collection agent for the payment of taxes and other revenues by state enterprises and other organizations. It also serves as a control mechanism to assure that the flow of funds between enterprises is in accordance with the objectives of the national plan. Gosbank plays an important role in economic planning in that it prepares the credit and cash plans, which are a part of the financial plan.

QUESTIONS

1. Distinguish between the roles performed by the Council of Ministers and the Supreme Soviet of the U.S.S.R.
2. Discuss the interlocking relationship that is maintained between the Communist Party and the administrative units of the government. What does this relationship accomplish?
3. What is the difference between long-term and annual economic plans?
4. Discuss the procedures involved in the drafting and development of annual plans.
5. What is the role of the state budget in the Soviet economic system?
6. The turnover tax performs several important economic functions in the Soviet Union. What are these functions?
7. Why are direct taxes of little importance in the public finance of the Soviet Union?
8. In addition to performing central and commercial banking functions, Gosbank also performs control functions as well. What is the nature of these functions?
9. What is the role of the financial plan in the Soviet Union? What roles do the state budget and Gosbank perform in the formulation of the financial plan?
10. Gosbank is called a monobank. What is the meaning of this term?

RECOMMENDED READINGS

Bornstein, Morris, and Daniel R. Fusfeld. *The Soviet Economy: A Book of Readings,* 4th ed. Homewood, Ill.: Richard D. Irwin, 1974.

Campbell, Robert W. *The Soviet-Type Economies: Performance and Evolution,* 3d ed. Boston: Houghton Mifflin, 1974.

Garvy, George. *Money, Banking, and Credit in Eastern Europe.* Federal Reserve Bank of New York, 1966.

Gregory, Paul R., and Robert G. Stuart. *Soviet Economic Structure and Performance.* New York: Harper & Row, 1974.

Joint Economic Committee. *Soviet Economic Prospects for the Seventies.* Washington: 93d Congress, 1st Session, 1973.

Kaser, Michael. *Soviet Economics.* New York: McGraw-Hill, 1970.

Laulan, Yves M. (ed.). *Banking, Money, and Credit in Eastern Europe.* Brussels: NOTA—Directorate of Economic Affairs, 1973.

Nove, Alec. *The Soviet Economy: An Introduction,* 2d rev. ed. New York: Praeger, 1969.

U.S. Bureau of the Census. *The Soviet Financial System, Structure, Operations, and Statistics.* International Population Statistics Report, Series P–90, No. 23. Washington: U.S. Government Printing Office, 1968.

Zaleski, Eugene. *Planning Reforms in the Soviet Union, 1962–1966.* Chapel Hill: University of North Carolina Press, 1967.

17

The Soviet Union II

THE ECONOMIC SYSTEM

The organization of production and distribution is a fundamental problem which confronts all economic systems. Production involves decisions pertaining to the types and quantities of goods which are to be produced. Related to production is the matter of allocating scarce resources among competing alternatives to attain maximum output. Once the production of goods has taken place, the problem of their distribution arises. Distribution, or *marketing*, refers to the process by which physical goods are brought from producers to consumers. It involves the organization of channels of distribution, transportation, storage, finance, and inventory planning. These functions have to be performed regardless of the type of economic system involved. In the Soviet Union, they are performed by the government, which owns, administers, and controls all of the wholesale and retail distribution facilities.

Distribution can also refer to the division of national income in terms of money, real goods, and services among the suppliers of the agents of production. Most of the Soviet national income is distributed in the form of wages. The Soviets use monetary incentives, such as wage differentials and bonuses, as key devices for motivating workers. Profits are also a part of national income. Government enterprises in all fields of economic activity can make both planned and unplanned profits, but the significance of these profits is quite different from profits in the United States and Sweden. They belong to the government and are used for capital development and other purposes. As mentioned in the preceding chapter, deductions from profits constitute a major source of income for the state budget. Profits are also used as an index of the effectiveness of production of Soviet enterprises, and the extent of their retention by enterprises depends upon the promotion of greater productivity through better organization of production and through economies in the use of raw materials and energy. Interest also figures in the national income to some extent, particularly in the form of payment on the savings deposits of individuals.[1]

---

[1] Interest also takes the form of a rental charge for the use of capital. This charge is supposed to be levied only at the end of the period during which the capital has been utilized. Short-term credits provided by Gosbank to finance inventory accumulations of enterprises carry a rate of interest which is usually 2 percent.

In this chapter the organization of industry and agriculture in the Soviet Union will be discussed. In looking at this organization, it is necessary to examine the macroeconomic structures of industry and agriculture and their relationship to economic planning. To enforce planning in a country the size of the Soviet Union, there has to be a system of surveillance which is imposed by both government and party organizations. It is also necessary to examine the operation of individual industrial and agricultural enterprises, for they are the focal point of the primary, critical function of production. However, the production process in itself is incomplete until goods are distributed from producers to consumers. Also in this chapter, the role of unions in the Soviet Union and the process of income distribution among various types of workers will be discussed.

Organization of Industry

The organizational structure of Soviet industry is complex because an immense bureaucratic apparatus is necessary to plan and administer production and distribution policies in a country which is almost three times the size of the United States. There has, however, been a continual reorganization of the Soviet economic-administrative structure, the most recent occurring in 1965 when there was a change from the sovnarkhoz form of territorial organization to a ministerial form. The *sovnarkhoz* was a regional production council which had as its function the regulation of industrial enterprises in its area. It was established by Nikita Khrushchev in 1957 to effect improvement in the performance of the Soviet economy.[2] The Soviet Union was divided into 104 regions, each with a sovnarkhoz. The sovnarkhoz and its planning organs were made responsible for the development and implementation of plans for all industrial enterprises and other organizations under its jurisdiction. Individual enterprises received their production plans through their sovnarkhoz.

Administration of Industry. The administrative and policy-making framework of industrial organization resembles a pyramid, with the top being the Politburo of the Central Committee of the Communist Party and the bottom being the Soviet industrial enterprise. The Politburo is responsible for making major policy decisions, including those that affect industry. Then there is the Council of Ministers of the U.S.S.R., which is the most important governmental executive and administrative body in the Soviet Union, and Gosplan, which is directly subordinate to the Council of Ministers and which is responsible for the development of the long-term and annual economic plans. There is also the State Committee for Material and Technical Supply, which is also under the supervision of the Council of Ministers. This committee is responsible for implementing material and technical supply plans on a national basis and for ensuring that ministries, departments, and enterprises fulfill their delivery plans on time.

However, the direct links in the organization of industrial production are the all-union and union republic ministries, the ministries of the autonomous

---

[2] Prior to 1957 a ministerial form of industrial organization existed.

republics, regional and district departments and boards, and the enterprises. The all-union and union republic ministries are responsible for the allocation of material and technical resources to different industries. These resources are distributed according to plan through various central and regional supply organizations. Each ministry is divided into a number of administrative units called sectoral boards which are responsible for the administration of different industrial sectors within an industry. For example, the all-union Ministry of Machine-Tool and Instrument Industry has the following sectoral boards: heavy and custom-built machine tools; automatic lines and universal machine tools; precision machine tools; woodworking equipment; forging, pressing, and foundry equipment, cutting and measuring instruments; technological equipment; abrasive and diamond tools; hydraulic apparatus; general machine parts and items; and castings, forgings, punchings, and welded structures.

In 1973 changes were made in the administrative framework of Soviet industry. Ministries were given less control over Soviet enterprises, with their responsibilities limited to the formulation of overall policy in planning, investment, and technological improvement. More responsibility has been given to production associations, which can be considered as a form of trust that has control over the operations of enterprises in given economic fields. Each association is responsible for fulfilling that part of the economic plan over which it has jurisdiction and for facilitating the implementation of directives from the State Planning Commission and synthesizing recommendations of the individual enterprises under it. An association is also allowed to use part of its own earnings to form its special funds, to finance industrywide investment and research programs, to establish central incentive and bonus funds, and to cover the deficits of its unprofitable subordinates. One major unsolved problem, however, is the exact demarcation of competence between an association and an industrial enterprise.

The Soviet Enterprise. The enterprise is the basic link in the general system of Soviet production management and operates as a legal person engaged in production activity under the national economic plan.[3] It is under an obligation to fulfill its own production plan, which contains certain targets or success indicators that should be attained. It is required to operate under a profit and loss accounting system, and it has fixed and working capital which form the basis of its statutory fund, the size of which is shown on its balance sheet. It can decide how best to use the fixed and working capital assigned to it, providing that each is used for purposes which are stipulated in the production plan. An enterprise also has the right to make capital investments from funds that are set aside for amortization purposes and to fix the prices of its products within the limits set by the economic plan.

The Khosraschet System. Soviet enterprises operate under what is called a *khosraschet* system of organization. This means that they function as

---

[3] This means that an enterprise can own property, enter into binding contracts, sue, and be sued.

autonomous entities with their own profit and loss accounts. There are five basic characteristics of this system, which are as follows: [4]

1. Operational independence, within established limits, is assigned to khosraschet enterprises. Each enterprise has its own goals to meet and is given a fund consisting of fixed and working capital. There is freedom to utilize this fund within the constraints imposed by the plan. An enterprise is given an account in Gosbank into which proceeds from the sale of its products are deposited and from which payments are made to cover its own expenses. This, of course, means that Gosbank can exercise an important control function by monitoring the accounts of each enterprise.
2. Enterprises are generally supposed to conduct their operations in such a way that income will cover expenses and leave some profit. Fulfillment of its physical output goal, however, is the prime operational desideratum of an enterprise. Although financial self-sufficiency is desired, most khosraschet enterprises receive some sort of financial support from the state budget, particularly in the financing of capital investment.
3. Enterprises are supposed to meet their responsibilities in a prescribed manner, and they incur penalties if they do not. For example, fines are imposed by the government for late delivery of products.
4. Reliance on material incentives is another characteristic of the khosraschet enterprise. Funds are set aside to provide bonuses for superior performances on the part of workers.
5. Control by the ruble is exercised by Gosbank over all enterprises. This means that all enterprise transactions in value terms pass through Gosbank, and it can compare actual results with planned targets to see that there is no deviation from the plan.

The Tekhpromfinplan. Each Soviet enterprise has to prepare what is called a *tekhpromfinplan*,[5] which is its operating plan for the year. The tekhpromfinplan is a consolidated plan which includes the financial, output, and investment plans of the enterprise. It is prepared twice. The first is a preliminary draft and the second is a formally approved economic document. It is supposed to be developed within the framework of the long-term, or five-year plan, which is not only developed for the economy as a whole, but for each enterprise as well. However, operational targets and the allocation of resources for an enterprise are determined for the most part in the annual plan. The plan also functions on a quarterly and monthly basis.

The tekhpromfinplan contains a number of assigned indexes or success targets which are to be achieved by an enterprise. These indicators are as follows:

1. The volume of output to be produced and sold.[6]
2. The assortment and quality of output to be produced and sold.

---

[4] U.S. Bureau of the Census, *The Soviet Financial System, Structure, Operations, and Statistics,* International Population Statistics Report, Series P–90, No. 23 (Washington: U.S. Government Printing Office, 1968), pp. 35–37.

[5] *Tekhpromfinplan* may be translated as technical-industrial-financial plan.

[6] New ones added include labor productivity, gross value of output, assignments for reducing material and fuel expenditures per unit of output, and the size of basic incentive funds.

3. The aggragate amount of money to be expended for wages.
4. The amount of profits and level of profitability.
5. Payments to and allocations from the state budget.
6. The amount of funds to be spent on the expansion and improvement of production.
7. The introduction of new techniques and automation.
8. The volume of inputs in the form of material and technical supplies.

In terms of success, an enterprise is judged primarily by the volume of its sales and the amount of its profits, including savings made from economies in production. Constraints are placed on an enterprise in the form of fixed prices of both inputs and outputs and in limitations in the selection of inputs which are allocated to it. All prices, with the exception of those in the free agricultural market, are set by the government. In setting prices, an allowance is made for profits expressed as a percentage of average production cost for an entire industry. Individual enterprises will have differing rates of profits because of differences in production costs. *Profits,* then, can be defined in terms of the Soviet enterprise as the difference between its total income from sales and its cost of production.[7] In its annual operating plan, an enterprise lists its expected or planned profits as a percentage of total production costs. Its planned profits may be more or less than its actual profits. If they are less than actual profits, this is all to the good as far as the enterprise is concerned, for its material incentive fund is increased. On the other hand, an enterprise, or rather its manager, is embarrassed if its planned profits are above its actual profits, or worse, if it operates at a loss. Planned losses can also be made in certain industries, such as coal mining, where it is necessary to set prices below costs to stimulate consumption. These losses are covered by grants from the state budget or by income transfers from other sectors of the economy.

Organization of an Enterprise. In general a Soviet enterprise is organized along the following lines.[8] There is a director who is appointed by the state to run the enterprise. This director is governed from above by directives and rules of behavior which guide all decisions. However, the director is not rigidly circumscribed as to what can be done, but rather is somewhat free to operate in any manner so long as it is within the general framework of the national economic plan and the enterprise's operating plan. The director can influence the contents of the operating plan through familiarity with the resource needs and product specifications of the enterprise. The Soviet planning system, of necessity, has to permit a certain degree of managerial autonomy, for it is impossible to supervise in detail the operation of thousands of enterprises. Caution, rather than risk taking and innovation, appears to be an important characteristic of Soviet enterprise directors because it is easier and safer to work within established production procedures in the fulfillment of the operating plan.

[7] *The Soviet Financial System, Structure, Operations, and Statistics,* p. 104. Also see pp. 103–111 for the determination and treatment of Soviet enterprise profits.

[8] For an organizational chart of a Soviet enterprise see Barry M. Richman, *Soviet Management* (Englewood Cliffs, N.J.: Prentice-Hall, Inc., 1965), pp. 60 and 61.

Since the Soviet reward system has favored directors who fulfill or over-fulfill their plans, there have been frequent unfavorable results. Directors often have claimed overall plan fulfillment, when in fact the claimed production included subquality output, incomplete items, or an incorrect assortment of goods. To fulfill their plans, directors often have concentrated on goods of high value or items which are easy to produce.[9] This subterfuge is fairly difficult to detect, but the Soviet authorities are aware that it exists. The economic reforms have drastically reduced the number of targets or success indicators with which a director has to contend. Nevertheless, there is a community of interest, which tends to favor plan fulfillment regardless of the method involved, that binds the director and others who are directly associated with the enterprise.

In some respects the functions of a managing director in the Soviet Union are similar to those of an American managerial counterpart; in other respects, they are not. For example, there is a formal chain of command within both the Soviet and American enterprise, and both Soviet and American managing directors would operate through this chain. Also in terms of decisions involving the process of production, that is, quality control standards, budgeting, and production scheduling, there are similarities between Soviet and American managerial responsibilities. There would also be similarities with respect to personnel policies involving labor force utilization, promotions, and the development of wage norms.[10]

It is necessary to mention the role that the Communist Party plays in the operation of an enterprise. There is a local unit of the party in all enterprises which is supposed to act as the custodian of the nation's interest as opposed to the more narrowly circumscribed outlook of the industrial manager. Most managers, however, are members of the Communist Party, but, despite this fact, the party maintains its own independent hierarchy in each enterprise. At the head of this hierarchy is the party secretary, who shares responsibility with the director for plan fulfillment. The secretary is also supposed to keep the party informed of any adverse developments in the enterprise. Some ambivalence exists in defining the secretary's relationship with the director and with the party. The secretary can neither exercise excessive interference in the decisions of the director, nor be too lax from the standpoint of control.

However, as mentioned above, there is a mutuality of self-interest on the part of both the director and secretary which often works for collusion with respect to fulfilling the enterprise plan. Since each is judged and rewarded on the basis of the same success criteria, it is to their advantage to secure an easy plan or to produce the things that are easiest to produce to fulfill the plan. Since party and other officials are judged by the performance of enterprises under their jurisdiction, it is often to their advantage simply to stress plan

---

[9] See, for example, *The Many Crises of the Soviet Economy* (Washington: Committee of the Judiciary, U.S. Senate, 88th Congress, 2d Session, 1964).

[10] For a comparison of the roles of the Soviet and American manager, see David Granick, *The Red Executive* (Garden City, N.Y.: Doubleday and Company, 1960), and Richman, *op. cit.*

fulfillment, regardless of method. This places the burden of authority and control on agencies and officials at the national level, and pressures for change and innovation often have to emanate from this source.

The Soviet Reforms and Economic Incentives. Economic reforms were formally initiated in the Soviet Union in 1965 following a period of weakness in the economy. The period of weakness was reflected in a decline in the rate of economic growth from an average of 7 percent a year over the 1950–1958 period to 5 percent a year for the 1959–1964 period. Plant investments, which were already low in comparison to some Western countries, stagnated; production and installations of new capacities were delayed; and supply deficiencies in raw materials and intermediate products lowered the use of those facilities that did exist. The distribution system functioned poorly, quality of output was low, and there were long delays in the commissioning of new plants. It became apparent to the Soviet leaders that planning methods and economic organization clearly no longer met the needs of a modern industrial economy.

The development of a system of self-enclosed economic levers was of paramount importance within the framework of the economic reforms. These levers involved a change in the success criteria of enterprises. Profit was accepted as the main criterion of enterprise performance. To improve enterprise performance, a system of incentives was tied to certain criteria. Three incentive funds were created out of profits, from which bonuses were to be paid and limited kinds of investment could be financed.[11] The bonus system was designed to link the total wages of all workers with the overall results of the state enterprise. Reform of the price system constituted another economic lever. The price system was distorted, because state price formation offices had set very low prices in order to hold down production costs. Raw materials were also subsidized. Prices were revised in order to permit enterprises to cover capital charges and to earn a profit. Proper prices, coupled with the opportunity to make a profit, were supposed to stimulate enterprises to upgrade the quality of output and produce new products.

Although profit was accepted as the main indicator of enterprise performance, and although plan indicators regulating enterprise activities were reduced in number, the economic reforms developed a number of flaws.[12] For one thing, the economic reforms were introduced piecemeal, with some enterprises being converted to the new incentive system immediately, while others waited as long as five years to convert. Another flaw involved the fact that there was no accompanying program of political reform. In the realm of politics, there was no extension of individual autonomy—in short, no real change

---

[11] These funds are the materials incentives fund, the production development fund, and the fund for social and cultural measures and housing construction. The first and third funds are financed out of profits, and the production development fund is financed out of profits, amortization deductions, and money received from the sale of surplus equipment. The purpose of the production development fund is to finance capital investment.

[12] Gertrude E. Schroeder, "Soviet Economic Reforms an Impasse," *Problems of Communism* (July–August, 1971), pp. 36–39.

in the individual's subjugation to the state. The state through its vast bureaucratic framework refused to give up centralized management of the various sectors of the economy.[13] Control over the various economic levers—prices, profits, and incentive funds—was regulated by the state through the use of a series of complex formulas which determined how enterprises were to divide profits among various taxes and funds for profit-sharing, investment reserves, and social purposes. Prices failed to stimulate improvement in product quality as they bore little relation to cost.

In 1971 and 1972 changes were made in the incentive system for enterprises. As was mentioned previously, the purpose of these incentives was to promote efficiency. Monies for the funds were to come out of profits. To some degree, the incentive funds failed to promote their objective. For one thing, profitable enterprises paid bonuses to management and workers from the profits which remained after taxes, whereas unprofitable enterprises paid bonuses out of fictitious profits created by state subsidies. Since no distinction was drawn between the bonuses paid in the two types of firms, the bonus system failed to perform its designated function of rewarding economic efficiency. The incentive system tended to reward some groups, i.e., white-collar workers and managers, more than other groups, and failed to induce managers to economize on labor and capital costs and to innovate.

The newer changes made the incentive system more centralized. The sizes of incentive funds are set for each enterprise by its supervisory ministry.[14] Ceilings are placed on the size of bonus funds and the amounts individuals may receive. Ministries are also permitted to create centralized incentive funds for themselves. These funds can be paid to individual enterprises under given conditions. For example, they can be given to enterprises that increase the output of highest category products in their plans. They can also be used to supplement the incentive funds of enterprises that produce consumer goods that are in demand but that yield low profits. Uses of bonus funds have also been modified in that limits are placed on the increase of bonuses to management. Bonuses may be reduced or eliminated if an enterprise fails to raise product quality, overstates cost, or fails to fulfill plans for labor productivity.[15]

The economic reforms of 1965 and subsequent changes were designed to increase the efficiency of the Soviet economy. To promote enterprise performance, which is not necessarily the same thing as efficiency, the reforms linked profit to incentives, so that it was in the interest of the enterprise to maximize profits. Enterprise managers were given greater freedom to choose the ways and means of plan fulfillment. Nevertheless, there remained a dual system of decision making, with the state being unwilling to relinquish control over individual enterprises. Experience shows that it is not easy in practice

[13] See "On the Economic Theory of Socialism," in Oskar Lange and Fred M. Taylor, *On the Economic Theory of Socialism* (New York: McGraw-Hill, 1965). Lange regarded excess bureaucracy to be the greatest danger inherent in socialism.
[14] Gertrude E. Schroeder, "Recent Developments in Soviet Planning and Incentives," *Soviet Economic Prospects for the Seventies,* Joint Economic Committee, 93d Congress, 1st Session, 1972, pp. 33–37.
[15] *Ibid.,* p. 35.

to reconcile targets set at the central level with the interest of the enterprises. Moreover, Soviet bureaucracy is reluctant to relinquish any of its authority so that reforms, even though they may be successful, are regarded with suspicion. As a consequence, centralized planning and administration remain strongly entrenched.

Distribution of Profits. When an enterprise makes a profit, the first claimant is the state. A part of profit is allocated to the state budget, and the remainder is divided by the enterprise into a number of funds. Each fund is designed to accomplish a specific objective. There is a production development fund. Its purpose is to finance capital investment for the introduction of new technology, mechanization and automation, renovation of fixed assets, modernization of equipment, and for other purposes that are designed to develop and improve production. There is also a fund for social and cultural measures, which has as its purpose the improvement of worker morale and productivity. It provides revenue for the construction and maintenance of child-care centers, expansion of recreational facilities, support of athletic programs, and housing construction. There is also a reserve fund, which is used for the purpose of paying off long-term loans.

A simplified scheme of profit use for the individual state enterprise can be presented as follows:

Gross profits of the enterprise
Less payments to the state budget and bank loans
Equal net profits of the enterprise which are divided into:

1. Production fund to finance fixed and working capital
2. Social and cultural fund to improve the social and intellectual life of the workers.
3. Material incentive fund to stimulate worker productivity.
4. Reserve or amortization fund.
5. Profit residual that is not committed to any fund but that goes to the state budget.

Channels of Distribution. In the Soviet Union the government owns and controls every distribution outlet in the production process. There are two networks through which goods move—a material and technical supply network, which is responsible for moving supplies to and from industrial enterprises, and a state trading network through which consumer goods are sold. The key state agencies which are responsible for distribution are Gosplan, Gossnab, and the Ministry of Trade. As far as material and technical supplies are concerned, requirements are written into a plan for material supplies which is a part of the national economic plan. Gosplan is responsible for the development of this plan, and *Gossnab* (the State Committee of the U.S.S.R. Council of Ministers for the Supply of Materials to the National Economy) is responsible for carrying out plans for supplying materials and equipment drawn up by Gosplan. Gossnab is also responsible for the distribution of production which is not distributed by Gosplan. What all of this means is that materials and equipment are centrally allocated, and material transfers to enterprises must be authorized by the government and must be accompanied by payment of money on the part of the enterprise.

The actual distribution of supplies is carried out by various supply agencies attached to the ministries. These agencies function at both the national and republic levels. An enterprise estimates its output targets and input norms based on its proposed production plan and makes its requests, called *zaiavki,* for materials to a supply agency (*glavk*) which is part of the ministry that has ultimate jurisdiction over the enterprise. It is the responsibility of the glavk to ascertain whether or not the requests of the enterprise are legitimate, for in many cases enterprises pad their orders in order to enhance their chances of fulfilling their production plans. A fact of economic life for the director of a Soviet enterprise has been the inadequate provision of resources necessary to fulfill the production plan. An unsteady flow of supplies causes work stoppages and jeopardizes plan fulfillment; the disruptions spread through the economy in a chain reaction. In fact, a weakness in the Soviet economic system is the planning and distribution of supplies, and in spite of the many organizational reforms that have been introduced in the Soviet Union during the last 15 years, uncertainty in resource allocation still remains as a critical problem for enterprise managers.[16]

Consumer goods also go through various stages of distribution. At each stage, the characteristics of centralized allocation of resources are all present— estimation of needs, requests by enterprises, determination of delivery orders, and the transfer of funds. It is not until the final stage—retail trade—that goods are freely sold to the consumer. As is also true for the distribution of industrial supplies, planning of consumer goods involves a reconciliation of requests from wholesale or retail organs at the lower levels with the production and distribution plans at the higher levels. For example, a wholesale outlet may receive a request from retail stores for a certain commodity. These requests are transferred to the Ministry of Trade in the republic in which the wholesale and retail outlets are located. These requests eventually are transmitted upward to Gosplan. The allocation of consumer goods is determined in the overall national plan, and the amount of the particular commodity is allocated to the Ministry of Trade in the Republic and also to the republic Gosplan, which are responsible for delivery to the wholesale outlet. It, in turn, is responsible for the final delivery of the commodity to the retail stores.

The Ministry of Trade, which is a union-republic ministry, is at the apex of the consumer trade network.[17] It is responsible for the operation of a network of government stores that are located in urban areas. There is a Ministry of Trade in each republic, which has control over a number of wholesale outlets. Typically, government retail stores are under the control of a local city trade organization called a *torg.* The torg has within it trade departments which are responsible for supplying goods to the city and supervising the operation of the retail store system. Warehouses are also attached to the trade

[16] Thomas V. Greer, *Marketing in the Soviet Union* (New York: Praeger, 1973).
[17] *Ibid.*, pp. 14–45.

departments. Retail stores represent the ultimate link with the consumer. Retail prices are, for the most part, fixed by the government at levels which attempt to equate supply with demand. The retail price consists of several elements: production cost, profit of the producer, the turnover tax, and wholesale and retail markups. In other words, it consists of all of the components which make up the prices charged by the seller to the retailer plus a retail markup added as the last element of retail price formation.

In addition to the network of government stores, there is a consumer cooperative store network which also has its wholesale and supply system. Consumer cooperatives operate primarily in the rural areas. Like other organizations in the Soviet Union, they are formed in the structure of a pyramid, with local outlets at the base and the decision-making agencies at the republic and all-union levels at the apex. Prices are set by the Ministry of Trade usually at rates higher than those set on consumer goods in the urban areas. This is to compensate in part for higher transportation costs. Wholesaling is performed by government wholesale distributing units, the trade warehouses. Residents of a village or state farm are organized into consumer cooperatives and become shareholders. They are supposed to elect a governing board, a director, and an inspection committee, although actually there is little autonomy granted to local cooperatives.[18]

Labor Unions and the Soviet Worker

Labor unions exist in the Soviet Union, and workers are not only permitted but are encouraged to belong to them. Unlike their counterparts in the industrial countries of the West, unions do not enjoy a significant sphere of autonomous action. They do not have the right to strike, and decisions on wage rates, output norms, hours of labor, and similar matters are prerogatives of government rather than unions. These decisions are made on a national scale by the State Committee on Labor and Wages, which is a part of the Council of Ministers of the U.S.S.R. Such powers that unions do possess in the Soviet Union are in relationship to the operation of an enterprise. Although it was originally intended that important managerial decisions would be made by a troika of management, union, and party representatives, the role of the union declined in importance as the drive for industrial efficiency strengthened managerial authority. It can be said that in terms of a constellation of power, unions rank behind both management and party in an enterprise. They have certain functions which can be enumerated as follows:

1. They have the right to participate with management in the development of the economic plan for an enterprise.
2. They are responsible for the maintenance of worker discipline by discouraging tardiness, absenteeism, and worker turnover and by promoting measures to encourage productivity.

[18] *Ibid.*, pp. 55–63.

3. Management is required to obtain their permission in assigning workers to wage categories and in introducing regulations on piece-work and bonus systems.
4. Unions play an important role in the area of social insurance, and they carry out a variety of activities in connection with vacations, education, recreation, and culture.[19] They are responsible for the collection of social security contributions from enterprises and disbursement of cash benefits.
5. They have the right to express opinions on candidates nominated for management positions and to oppose discharges of workers that are initiated by management.

Nevertheless, the basic collective bargaining function, which unions perform in the Western democracies, has been emasculated in the Soviet Union. Unions are supposed to cooperate with management and function in the interest of the state and its national objectives. Although they have specific powers and responsibilities, they are subservient to the interests of the Communist Party.

Agriculture

Russia at the time of the czarist revolution of 1917 was predominantly an agricultural country. In the period immediately prior to World War I, agriculture underwent some dramatic changes. Under the Stolypin reforms of 1906, a large number of peasants were given legal title to the land they worked. The large landowner declined in importance and even disappeared from the economic scene. However, the deep-seated aspirations of the Russian peasantry, the desire to own and manage their own land, was to be thwarted when the Communists came into power. It was inevitable that an effort would be made to socialize agriculture, for many of the Communists believed that communism would never succeed in the Soviet Union as long as agriculture remained a small-scale, capitalistic enterprise.

During the early years of their regime, the Communists were faced with the problem of converting Russian farms into large-scale, efficient units capable of furnishing large surpluses of food for the urban and industrial population and providing large quantities of raw materials for industry. In 1929 the First Five-Year Plan went into effect. Huge state farms were established on old estates, and every effort was made to get individual peasants to pool their holdings and operate them as large, cooperative undertakings.

Initial efforts to collectivize agriculture were not too successful. In the first place, many of the more prosperous peasants refused to cooperate, and the government's relentless persecution of these *kulaks* deprived the collective farms of potential managerial ability. Second, many peasants killed and ate their animals before joining a collective farm, a practice that was encouraged by the fact that the government made heavy grain requisitions which left the peasants short of food and fodder. This heavy grain collection

---

[19] For the role of unions in social insurance see Gaston V. Rimlinger, "The Trade Union in Soviet Social Insurance: Historical Development and Present Functions," *Industrial and Labor Relations Review* (April, 1961), pp. 397–418.

brought a resumption of the old practice, which was prevalent under the czars, of hiding grain and decreasing the areas under cultivation.

By the end of the First Five-Year Plan, the basic structure of Soviet agriculture had been decided upon. This structure was based on two forms of collective enterprises—the state farm and the collective farm. The state farm was (and is) the full property of the Soviet government. It represents the main communist objective for agriculture—the peasants are truly proletarians with no property of their own.[20] The collective farm, as the name implies, was supposed to be a self-governing cooperative made up of peasants who voluntarily pooled their means of production and divided the proceeds. The first collective farms were basically of two types—collectives in which all livestock and implements were held in common by the peasants, who lived in communal buildings; and collectives in which the peasants were allowed to own livestock and a small plot of land as well as live independently of other members of the collective farm. The latter type of collective has become the prevalent form of agricultural unit in the Soviet Union.

Agriculture is controlled by the government through national economic planning. The supply and price of inputs, the share of output marketed, the prices paid for agricultural products, and farm income and expenditures are regulated by the plan. Overall procurement goals are established for agricultural products that are to be delivered to the government. These goals are disseminated downward by Gosplan to the Ministries of Production and Procurements in each republic and to lower administrative units in the provinces and districts. Given the procurement goals, which are supplemented by local requirements, each state farm and collective farm has to formulate a production plan. When this is done, each plan goes up the administrative line—district, province, and republic—to be examined and combined with other plans. Finally, the combined plans reach Gosplan for approval. Gosplan also is responsible for the determination of the production and use of such agricultural inputs as machinery and fertilizer. Material balances, which represent a balance sheet of the supply and demand for various inputs, are used in planning. Separate balance sheets are used for each input, with the left side showing the sources of inputs and the right side, its uses.

State Farms. State farms, as mentioned above, are owned by the government and operated as regular industrial establishments with managers and hired workers. Their annual budgets and operating plans are developed by the government, which is also responsible for the determination of wages paid to the workers and for the provision of livestock and equipment.

As originally set up, the state farms were extremely large. They were intended to increase agricultural production by enlarging the land area under cultivation, by utilizing modern, efficient farming techniques, and by serving as experimental stations and model agricultural centers. The state farm remains

[20] According to Marx, the ideal agricultural organization would be state farms where private ownership, no matter how insignificant it might be, could not exist and where all of the workers were to be paid by the government on the same basis as factory workers.

today as the highest form of a socialized agricultural unit and enjoys a favored position in Soviet agriculture. In recent years the number of state farms has increased considerably because some collective farms have been converted into state farms. Also, a number of specialized meat, dairy, and vegetable state farms have been created around major urban centers. In terms of physical output, they accounted for one fourth of total agricultural output—an amount which is adversely affected by the fact that many state farms are established in areas of low productivity.

State farms sell their produce to the government for processing and distribution through state stores, for stockpiling, and for export. The arrangement between state farms and the government takes the form of a contract which specifies the price to be paid for the commodity produced and the delivery date. There is usually a basic procurement price, subject to some regional variation, for each commodity. Prices can be used as incentives for changes in production. For example, if an increase in the production of dairy products or meat is desired, prices are raised. In this way, prices perform a function in allocating resources which is similar to their role in a market economy. Prices are also set at levels that reflect, at least in part, differences in average production costs on state farms operating in different areas of the country. Lower prices are paid in better land areas, reflecting the fact that no charge is made for land rent.

State farms are managed by directors who have the right to determine the total number of workers to be used on the farm, the planned production costs, the planned labor productivity, and other general factors of management control. Although this has meant greater independence of state farm management from central control, the basic policies to be followed are determined by the government, and directors must operate according to these policies.

Since state farms are entirely owned and operated by the state, workers are direct employees of the state and are paid a wage. This wage varies according to the type and the quantity of work done. Payments primarily take the form of piece rates that vary according to the classification of the worker. Specialists, such as agronomists, are paid on a monthly basis. Wages are paid from a general wage fund which must be provided for in the development of the state farm's overall operating plan. In addition, a bonus arrangement is provided for out of the material incentives fund which is separate from the wage fund.

The starting point in the distribution of profit is gross sales, which is obtained by multiplying the planned volume of sales per product by the set state price. From gross sales production costs, including the cost of seed and fertilizer and depreciation, are deducted to get gross income. From gross income a deduction is made into the wage fund, and the remainder is called the socially clear income. This income may be considered a residual that is divided between the state farm and the state. There is a deduction from profit, which also goes to the state. Remaining income is divided into various funds.

An example of the utilization of profit of a state farm is as follows:

Total sales		$1,300,000
Less seed, fertilizer, and other costs including depreciation		650,000
Gross income		$ 650,000
Less wage funds		260,000
Social clear income		$ 390,000
Less special costs	$65,000	
Less production levy	52,000	117,000
Net profit		$ 273,000
Less profits taxes		52,000
Net profit		$ 221,000
Less investment funds	$104,000	
Less enterprise funds	3,900	
Less social and cultural funds	48,100	156,000
Profit residual		$ 65,000

Collective Farms. The collective farm is the dominant type of agricultural organization in the Soviet Union when measured from the standpoint of number of farm units, share of land area sown, and number of workers employed. It may be defined as a form of agricultural organization in which varying numbers of individual peasants combine their resources and talents and operate on a collective basis. The land occupied by a collective farm is secured to it without payment and without time limit, and the livestock, implements, and public structures in its possession are considered to be its property. Each collective farm household, in addition to its basic interest in the collective property, is entitled to a small plot of land for private cultivation, housing, and such auxiliary items as productive livestock, poultry, and minor agricultural implements.

Differences from State Farms. Members of a collective farm are not paid wages, but share in the income of the individual collective farm. This income depends directly upon the crops which are produced. After certain deductions are made from the harvest, the remainder is distributed in kind among the collective farmers, or is sold for cash, which is then distributed, usually at the end of the year. However, with later agricultural reforms, there was a shift to a regular cash wage which is paid on a monthly basis. This reflects an attempt on the part of the government to use similar methods of wage payments for both collective and state farm workers.

Investment in collective farms is not financed out of the state budget, but from the income of the individual collective farm. From this income, the collective farm must pay an income tax and various current expenses, including those for administration and for educational and cultural purposes. An undivided surplus must also be set up to cover necessary capital expenditures.

Collective farms are also smaller than state farms in terms of size and number of workers employed per farm. In 1971 each collective farm had, on the average, approximately 380 households, 30,600 acres of land, 880 cattle, and 1,590 sheep and goats.[21] The number of collective farms in the Soviet Union is growing smaller. In 1940 there were 240,000 collective farms; in 1971 this number had been reduced to 32,400. This reduction can be explained by the fact that in recent years a large number of collective farms have been merged into larger collectives or have been converted into state farms for the purpose of increasing agricultural output.

Distribution of Income and Production. There are three claimants to the income and output of a collective farm—the state, the collective farm itself, and the members of the collective farm. The state has first claim on production. Prior to 1958, collective farms had to deliver to the government at low fixed prices certain specified quantities of crops and animal products. To acquire farm products cheaply had always been one of the main goals of Soviet economic policy. Also prior to 1958, payment in kind of a certain amount of produce had to be made to the Machine Tractor Stations. In 1958, however, the government introduced a single system of procurement prices, and agricultural products are now purchased from collective farms at a basic price for each product. Currently a wide variety of prices exists for most commodities depending on such factors as the type of market, quality, location, and the season when the commodity is marketed.[22]

There are two agricultural marketing systems in the Soviet Union—the state system and the private market system. Under the state system, the state assumes the responsibility for transporting and marketing all products it produces. For example, state-owned processing plants receive raw materials at a specified price, which is established by the government, and deliver the finished products to state stores and other outlets at specified prices, which are also set by the government. These products are then distributed to the consumer through state stores.[23] After the collective farms deliver procurement quotas of their product to the government, they are free to sell any surplus or remainder in the free market. This produce is usually sold in the immediate local areas because transportation is a problem. In some areas, the collective farm may provide its own facilities for retailing its products. Prices are set by ordinary supply and demand factors operating in the market.

The revenue derived by collective farms from the sale of their produce is used for several purposes. First of all, a number of general expenditures have to be met. These include contributions to a socio-cultural fund, production expenses for such items as fuel and fertilizers, insurance which is designed to protect the collective farm from the loss of its physical assets, and contributions to a capital fund for the purpose of acquiring capital goods. Prior to 1965, a

---

[21] U.S. Department of Agriculture, *Agriculture in the United States and the Soviet Union: A Statistical Comparison,* Foreign Agricultural Report No. 281 (August, 1972).

[22] The Russians have been reluctant to publish average prices received by all farms throughout the USSR for individual commodities.

[23] The state marketing system has proved to be inefficient, so the collective farms are now allowed to deliver their produce to stores and other retail outlets; for their produce they are allowed to receive the retail price less a discount.

standard 12.5 percent tax was levied against the gross income in cash and in kind of collective farms. However, in order to improve production incentives, changes were made in the tax in 1965. The tax is now calculated on the basis of net income, which is the difference between gross income and production costs plus deductions to the social insurance fund. A portion of net income which is equal to a profitability rate of 15 percent is exempt from the tax. The profitability rate is the ratio of net income to total costs. A tax of 12 percent is levied on the remaining net income.[24]

Wages paid to collective farm workers come out of a wage fund. The standard method of payment has involved the use of workdays. The *workday* is an abstract unit which is based on such factors as the quality and quantity of work performed and the type of work involved. Each worker must work a minimum number of workdays a year. The total number of workdays accumulated by a worker is divided into the amount of income available in cash or in kind for distribution at the end of the year. The result is a worker's income for the year. This system has been erratic over the years, and incomes of collective farm workers have lagged behind those of state farm workers. To remedy this defect, measures have been taken to raise incomes of collective farm workers up to a parity with incomes of state farm workers. The guaranteed minimum income, which in 1972 was 60 rubles ($73.17) a month, was made applicable to collective farm workers. A monthly wage system has been introduced. This places the worker's claim on a part of the income ahead of the claim of the collective farm instead of the other way around.

Private Plots. Private plots represent the third form of agricultural institution that exists in the Soviet Union. To a certain extent, they are almost an anachronism in that they represent the only substantial form of private enterprise that exists in the country. However, the fact that they do exist can be attributed to the fact that the Russian peasants have never been completely subverted to the idea that land should belong to the state and not to them. Although dwarfed in terms of physical size by the state and collective farms, the private plots account for an inordinately large share of agricultural output.[25] Although private plots and land holdings account for only 3 percent of all of the sown agricultural land, they contribute substantially to the production of livestock, dairy, and truck garden products. The bulk of the products produced on the private plots are high value products. In 1972 the private sector produced 35 percent of the total meat supply in the Soviet Union, 35 percent of the milk, 50 percent of the eggs, 65 percent of the potatoes, and 40 percent of the vegetables. Sales of products from private plots represent a substantial amount of the income of collective farms.[26]

[24] For example, assume a gross income of 2 million rubles and total costs of production plus social insurance contributions of 1.5 million rubles. Net income is 500,000 rubles. The profitability ratio is 33⅓ percent (500,000:1,500,000). Fifteen percent of the profitability ratio is exempt, or 225,000 rubles (225,000:1,500,000). Taxable net income is 500,000 minus 225,000, or 275,000 rubles. The tax is 12 percent of 275,000 rubles, or 33,000 rubles.

[25] The typical private plot is two thirds of an acre in size.

[26] Douglas B. Diamond and Constance B. Krueger, "Recent Developments in Output and Productivity in Soviet Agriculture," *Soviet Economic Prospects for the Seventies,* Joint Economic Committee, 93d Congress, 1st Session, 1973, p. 325.

The private sector of Russian agriculture can be classified into three categories—private plots which are held and operated by members of collective farms, private plots which are operated by state farm workers and by other state employees, and private land which is held by individual peasants. The last category is rare in the Soviet Union. Individual peasants who own and operate their own farms are located primarily in sparsely populated regions where the formation of collective farms is not economically justifiable. Ownership of private plots on collective farms represents a partial retreat from the complete collectivization attempts of the 1930s which had disastrous results. Although, in general, the attitude of the government toward private farming has ranged from encouragement to hostility, individual ownership and use of farmland is legal according to Articles 7 and 9 of the 1936 Constitution of the Soviet Union, providing it does not involve the use of private labor. Collective farm private plots are allowed as an entitlement under a 1935 statute.[27] It can be said, however, that the ultimate wish of the government is the elimination of all private holdings.

In addition to their private plot of land, collective farm workers are also allowed to own livestock and farm implements. The amount of livestock which farm workers are permitted to own varies according to the nature of the collective farm. The collective farmer is allowed to sell the produce which he grows on his plot of land. Prior to 1958, there was a compulsory delivery of a certain percentage of this output to the government at a price which was arbitrarily set far below its market price. This compulsory delivery could be regarded as a form of agricultural tax in that the same result is achieved by taking a part of farm produce at an arbitrarily low price as would be achieved by letting the farmers sell their crops for full market value and then taking a portion of their income by means of taxation.[28] In 1958 compulsory deliveries were abolished,

[27] The plot is given to the household for its personal use only. It cannot be sold or rented, and, if not used, it is taken away.

[28] This reasoning can be explained as follows: In the graph shown, P_2 represents the prices charged by the government to consumers, and P_1 represents the price paid to farms for their produce. The shaded area from P_2 to P_1 represents the tax.

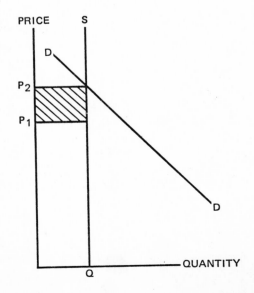

and the farmers are now free to sell their surplus produce in the open market. There are also the alternatives of selling the surplus through arrangements with the collective farm or of selling through consumer cooperatives.

State farm workers and other state employees are also allowed to farm private plots of land. The arrangements are similar to those on the collective farms. The private plots represent an entitlement which permits the worker to use the land for farming purposes. Surpluses from the plots can be sold in the free market. However, private farming, in general, has been a thorn in the side of the Soviet agricultural policy makers because many farmers, in pursuing their self-interests, have neglected their collective or state farm work to concentrate on production on their plots, which they can sell in the free market. Attempts to suppress the use of private plots have inevitably led to a decline in initiative on the part of the farm workers and a concomitant decline in productivity. So the private plots remain an anomaly under the Soviet system, an institution tolerated because of its importance in the production of high quality foodstuffs and because it makes the socialization of agriculture more palatable to the farmers.

An agricultural tax is paid by collective farm workers who derive income from private plots of land. This tax can be used as a control measure to insure that workers and their families work the prescribed minimum number of workdays. If workers or their families fail to work the minimum number of workdays, the agricultural tax is increased by 50 percent. State farm workers do not pay an agricultural tax on their income from private plots; instead, as regular employees of the state, they are subject to payment of the personal income tax.

Recent Agricultural Reforms. The performance of Soviet agriculture during the regimes of such leaders as Stalin and Khrushchev was, to say the least, rather poor. To a major extent, agriculture has been the Achilles' heel of the Soviet economy. Since the 1920s, agricultural output has barely kept up with population growth; and from 1958 to 1964, the food supply trailed the population increase. During the last years of Khrushchev's leadership, there were a series of failures on all agricultural fronts. Underinvestment in capital, excessive central planning and direction from self-appointed agricultural experts such as Khrushchev himself, and a general lack of economic incentives contributed to the stagnation of Russian agriculture. Many of the problems of Soviet agriculture can be attributed to the very low priority assigned to it by the Soviet leaders. Resources have been allocated to the development of the capital goods sector of the economy. Growth of heavy industry and development of military power have always enjoyed a higher priority than agriculture.

In recent years, beginning with 1965, a number of economic reforms were introduced and incorporated in the economic plans. These reforms had several basic objectives: to increase investments and other agricultural inputs, to increase labor productivity, and to improve the living conditions of the agricultural population.

One reform pertained to the operation of the state farms. From 1919, when they were first introduced, to 1963, state farms made an overall loss, with the exception of 1956. In 1963 nearly 70 percent of all state farms operated at a loss and required subsidies from the state budget. A model program of khozraschet financing was initiated on state farms. The state farms participating in this program have to finance their fixed and working capital from their gross incomes rather than from the state budget. They are also to receive the same price for their farm products as do the collective farms.

Another reform pertained to collective farms. In 1966 a new system of direct bank credits was introduced on an experimental basis. This credit is provided directly by Gosbank. Prior to 1966, credit was provided in the form of advances from state procurement organizations and no credits were given for labor payments. The payment system on collective farms has also been revised. Workers are paid on a monthly basis, and a wage system similar to that used on state farms has been adopted. Monetary incentives are being stressed as a stimulus to production, and wages are being raised to the levels that prevail on state farms.

The reforms on the state and collective farms now tend to make these two basic forms of Soviet agricultural organization resemble each other. Collective farms previously had been forced to provide resources for their own growth; state farms were subsidized by the budget. Collective farm workers were residual claimants on the farm's income; state farm workers received regular wages. Now farm workers receive a minimum income guarantee with part of their total income dependent upon the performance of the farm. Profitability is to be a major criterion of performance, and capital needs are to be financed from profits.

Soviet agricultural production has been quite erratic over time, as Table 17–1 on page 417 illustrates. It is necessary to emphasize the fact that not all of the agricultural problems can be attributed to Russian inefficiency. Some of the most recent difficulties can be attributed to a poor agricultural year in 1972, caused to a major degree by the weather, which resulted in the importation of more than 29 million metric tons of food and feed grains from the West.

Operating Results of Soviet Agriculture. An increase in the population and a rise in per capita income have combined to generate a constantly increasing demand for an improved product mix. However, there have been perennial problems of inefficiency, low labor productivity, and high production costs on both collective and state farms. Despite the fact that agriculture has received priority in the current five-year plan and in the economic reforms, labor productivity lags far behind productivity in the industrial area. To some extent the material incentive system, which is really more oriented toward motivating industrial workers, has failed to elicit a similar response among agricultural workers.[29] The end result of general inefficiency is that Soviet agriculture is one of the most expensive food producers in the world, a fact which redounds

---

[29] Michael E. Bradley and M. Gardner Clark, "Supervision and Efficiency in Socialized Agriculture," *Soviet Studies*, Vol. 23, No. 3, pp. 465–471.

TABLE 17–1

INDEX OF SOVIET AGRICULTURAL
PRODUCTION, 1965–1974

Year	1965=100
1965	100
1966	109
1967	109
1968	115
1969	110
1970	126
1971	126
1972	116
1973	119
1974	127

Source: Douglas B. Diamond and Constance B. Krueger, "Recent Developments in Output and Productivity in Soviet Agriculture," *Soviet Economic Prospects for the Seventies*, Joint Economic Committee, 93d Congress, 1st Session, 1973, p. 335; and estimates made by the U.S. Department of Agriculture.

to the disadvantage of the consumer because real income is reduced in comparison with that of consumers in other countries.

Comparisons can be made between agriculture in the United States and the Soviet Union. Agriculture contributes around 20 percent of the Soviet gross national product and employs one third of the labor force. In the United States agriculture contributes around 4 percent of the gross national product and employs 3 percent of the labor force.[30] Net farm output is increasing at a more rapid rate in the Soviet Union than in the United States. However, given the fact that agriculture has a greater impact on the Soviet economy, and the fact that the typical Soviet state or collective farm is many times larger than the typical American farm in terms of size and number of workers, performance clearly favors the American farm.[31] For example, farm efficiency, measured in terms of output per unit of input, is substantially higher in the United States than in the Soviet Union. The United States has made more capital inputs and has achieved greater yields.[32] The Soviet Union also lags far behind the United States in use of mineral fertilizers.

[30] F. Douglas Whitehouse and Joseph F. Havelka, "Comparison of Farm Output in the U.S. and U.S.S.R., 1950–1971," *Soviet Economic Prospects for the Seventies*, Joint Economic Committee, 93d Congress, 1st Session, 1973, p. 341.

[31] In 1970 the typical U.S. farm averaged 351 acres and employed 1.9 workers; the typical state farm averaged 99,578 acres and employed 635 workers and the typical collective farm averaged 26,508 acres and employed 26,508 workers.

[32] U.S. Department of Agriculture, "Agriculture in the United States and the Soviet Union," *Foreign Agricultural Report No. 92* (October, 1973), p. 2.

The United States produces more meat, eggs, fruit, corn, and soybeans than the Soviet Union. Average Soviet grain yields are less than half those in the United States. During the period 1967–1971, corn averaged 80.1 bushels per acre in the United States compared to 42.5 bushels per acre in the Soviet Union, and rice averaged 112.9 bushels per acres compared to 88.2 bushels per acre.[33] Soviet production of meat and eggs is only a little over half as much as output in the United States. Soviet beef and veal production per head of cattle as well as pork per hog are only about two thirds of U.S. output per head. Soviet milk and butter production is higher than U.S. output; however, U.S. milk yield per cow is more than twice as much as in the Soviet Union. In the production of fruit the United States is well ahead of the Soviet Union. However, the Soviet Union produces more potatoes, vegetables, and wheat. Per capita output of fruit, meat, and corn are higher in the United States.

Income Distribution

In a socialist country income is primarily limited to wages and salaries. It has been a socialist article of faith, which has been subject to question only recently, that labor is the only factor of production endowed with the capability of creating value. Therefore, labor should be remunerated to the exclusion of land and capital. The total amount of wages to be paid, and the production counterpart to support wages, depends on the division of socialist national income between accumulation and consumption, and further, of consumption between the social consumption fund and the wage fund.

National Income. National income in a socialist economy begins with the concept of the *net material product,* which can be defined either as the net contribution of the productive sectors of the economy (that is, gross production less the value of intermediate products and depreciation charges) or as the total income realized by the productive sectors. To put it more simply, the concept of socialist national income is that of national income produced and national income distributed. National income produced covers those activities that create material goods or help in the productive process; for example, gathering raw materials and processing them into finished products. National income distributed refers to the process of primary distribution of the income of the labor force, enterprises, and society by financial flows. This income can be divided into two categories. The first category of income is distributed to individuals and consists of gross money income before taxation of workers employed in the production process, money income and income in kind of farmers, and the value of net production from private activity of a productive character. The second category of national income distributed consists of gross profits before taxation of production enterprises, the turnover tax, and contributions of enterprises to social insurance.

[33] *Ibid.,* p. 6.

The distribution of national income may be shown as follows:

Primary Incomes of Individuals

1. Wages and salaries of the state sector of productive industries.
2. Wages and salaries of producer cooperatives.
3. Income of cooperative farmers from cooperative activities.
4. Income of cooperative farmers from private plots of land.
5. Incomes of individual farmers.
6. Incomes, private or otherwise, from other activities of a productive nature.

Primary Incomes of the Social Sector

1. Gross profits before taxes of productive enterprises.
2. Turnover taxes.
3. Contributions of enterprises to health insurance.

Socialist income accounting differentiates between productive and non-productive sectors. As these primary incomes of individuals and firms are generated only in the productive sectors, this flow of distribution gives no account of incomes of individuals working in the nonproductive spheres of activity, of unearned incomes of individuals with claims to transfer payments from public funds, and of enterprises operating in the nonproductive sectors. All of these incomes are included under the category of personal income, along with the primary incomes of individuals employed in the productive sectors.

Personal Income. The main difference between national income and personal income in a socialist system of national income accounts lies in the fact that only incomes of individuals and firms generated in the productive sectors—industry, agriculture, and others—are counted in national income, while personal income takes into account income earned in the nonproductive sectors as well. These sectors are education, health, justice, finance, and public administration. These sectors are considered nonproductive not because they are not useful, but because they don't contribute directly to the creation of material production. Thus, personal income in a country such as the Soviet Union would consist of wages and salaries of all workers employed in both productive and nonproductive industries, incomes of self-employed persons and independent entrepreneurs, and income from other sources including, for example, the income from the sale of agricultural products grown on private plots of land. Personal income would also include transfer payments of various types—family allowances, old age pensions, and other types of income transfers.

Personal income can be regarded as income generated in the process of redistributing the socialist national income. This process is effected by transfers between the state and society, between different sectors of society, and between different units of a public character. These transfers are realized mainly through the state budget, which is the most important instrument in modifying income flows in a socialist economy, and through a system of credits. Many transfers are payments by the state for which no service is provided in return, but which redistribute income to various groups. Examples are old age pensions and family allowances. Personal outlays include personal consumption of goods and services, taxes, and other payments. The end result is an economic balance that relates total money income of the population to their total outlays. An example of this balance is shown in Table 17–2.

TABLE 17–2
PERSONAL INCOME AND OUTLAYS IN A SOCIALIST ECONOMY

Income	Outlays
Wage fund (wages and salaries)	Consumption goods
Income of cooperatives and individual farmers	Services
Other income from enterprises (supplements)	Consumption of goods in kind
Imputed rent	Consumption of services in kind
Other labor and rental income	Total private consumption
Total income from work and property	Personal contributions
Government transfer payments	Personal tax payments to institutions
Total income	Total outlays

Table 17–3 presents a division of the major components of personal income in the Soviet Union for 1971. Also included in the table are direct taxes levied on the population. In the Soviet Union both taxes and transfer payments have a redistributive effect on income distribution. It is important to point out the fact that the price structure in the Soviet Union, particularly for food and basic services, is maintained at a low level to favor low-income consumers. The use of subsidies to maintain low prices for certain foodstuffs, transportation, and services is common. The prices charged by the state to consumers bear little relationship to the different production costs or the procurement prices paid to farms. Many consumer goods are priced below costs, but on the other hand prices for such luxury items as coffee and fruit are maintained at high levels. Price subsidies are a factor to consider when income distribution is examined.

As mentioned before, wages constitute the great bulk of personal income distributed in a socialist economic system. Although labor itself enjoys some freedom from central planning, there is a high degree of centralization and control over the determination of wages. The total amount of wages to be paid is set in the wage fund, which provides gross payments for all work done, including basic wage rates, payments based on piece-rate norms, basic salaries, premia and bonuses of all kinds, payments for overtime, and payments for night work and work on Sundays and holidays. The wage fund is linked to private consumption. Consumption, both collective and private, has to be planned in advance because it constitutes an integral part of the national economic plan, which cannot be constructed and balanced unless the size and structure of consumption are laid down. The planning of consumption necessitates the planning of the wage fund.

TABLE 17—3

PERSONAL INCOME IN THE SOVIET UNION FOR 1971

Components		Billions of Dollars *
Total personal income		$236.45
Wage and salary payments	$170.35	
Collective farm wage payments	17.11	
Household income from the sale of farm products	11.94	
Profits distributed to cooperative members	.18	
Military pay and allowances	4.23	
Transfer payments	32.64	
Less: Direct taxes (personal income and		
agricultural taxes)		16.65
Local taxes		.22
State loans		.36
Total disposable income		$219.22

Source: David W. Bronson and Barbara S. Severin, "Soviet Consumer Welfare: The Brezhnev Era," *Soviet Economic Prospects for the Seventies*, Joint Economic Committee, 93d Congress, 1st Session, 1973, p. 393.

* In 1971 one ruble = $1.21.

Wage Determination. Wages are determined by government fiat. In the Soviet Union, there are several state agencies that play a role in wage determination. Within the organizational framework of the Council of Ministers of the U.S.S.R., there is the State Committee on Labor and Wages. This committee is responsible for examining prevailing wage structures and practices within the Soviet Union. Within the committee there is the Institute of Labor, which does research on wage questions and policies. The committee takes this information and makes recommendations concerning changes in wages for various occupational groups. Gosplan and the Ministry of Finance also participate in the calculation of wages which are a part of the national economic plan. The total amount of wages for a given industry or enterprise would depend upon changes in the size and composition of the labor force, expected changes in the availability of consumer goods, and output and labor productivity plans. Once the total amount of wages has been determined for a particular industry, it is subdivided among each enterprise on the basis of the criteria mentioned above. Each enterprise, then, has its own wage fund from which it pays the wages of its workers.

Soviet economic reforms have provided a set of incentives to increase worker performance. Worker incomes come from two main sources—the regular wage fund from which wages are paid to all workers and the material incentives fund from which bonuses are paid. Money for the material incentives fund comes out of profits in accordance with standards prescribed by the state. Jurisdiction over bonuses was tightened by the state in 1972 and 1973. The amount of the bonus is set by Gosplan and implemented by ministries responsible for individual enterprises. The planned size of the material incentive fund is fixed for each year. Actual incentive funds may deviate from the planned funds, with the funds increased or decreased based on enterprise performance, which includes, among other things, the quality of the product produced and the production of new products.[34] The incentive funds are also tied to the government's efforts to produce more consumer goods.

Wage Differentials. Wage and salary differentials exist in the Soviet Union to a considerable degree. These differentials are based on several factors.

Within the factories, there are wage differentials which are based upon skills. In most industrial plants, there are six skill grades which are differentiated according to variations in skill from unskilled to highly skilled categories. The requirements for each grade are determined by the State Committee on Wages and the All-Union Central Council of Trade Unions. Differentials between the lowest and highest grade can vary according to the industry. These ratios, however, involve only the basic standard wage rate for each grade and do not take into consideration the fact that the use of piece rates and bonuses can cause considerable differentials in earnings among workers within the same grade.

Wage differentials are also based on conditions of work with hard or hazardous work commanding a higher premium than less arduous work. Within a given skill grade, there may be different gradings based on work conditions. Rates for work under hazardous conditions would carry a premium of as much as 30 percent above the basic wage rate.

The form of wage payment used also is responsible for wage differentials. Piece-rate workers are generally better paid than time-rate workers because under piece rates there is a direct correlation between output and payments.

Regional differentials also exist in terms of wage and salary payments. To attract workers to less desirable areas of the country where labor shortages are endemic, additional payments ranging from 10 to 100 percent of the base wage are added to all grades.[35]

Salary differentials also exist for engineers, economists, and white-collar employees. These differentials are based on the skill requirements of the job, the complexity of work, and the economic importance of the industry. There are various salary categories, which are similar to the wage grades used for the plant workers.

Wage Systems. There are several systems of wage and salary compensation used in the Soviet Union. These systems usually combine time rates or piece rates with bonus payments. In fact, time rates or piece rates plus bonuses cover most industrial wage earners.[36] The rationale of the bonus is to tie personal interests of workers more closely to the interests of production. Bonuses may be awarded on the basis of individual or collective performance. Individual bonuses are based on the performance of each worker as measured

---

[34] In the past, bonus funds encouraged enterprise managers to stress the volume of total output and quality was a neglected factor.

[35] Gertrude E. Schroeder, "Soviet Wage and Income Policies in Regional Perspective," *Association for Comparative Economics Bulletin*, Vol. XVI, No. 2 (Fall, 1974), pp. 3–20.

[36] A. S. Shkurko, "The Industrial Wage System in the USSR," *International Labor Review*, Vol. XC, No. 4 (October, 1964), p. 360.

against other workers, while collective bonuses reward a group of workers as a whole and are divided uniformly among the workers. Bonuses, however, are not always tied to the output performance of the enterprise, but may be awarded for other reasons. For example, workers can get bonuses for reducing waste or for coming up with suggestions that contribute to the efficient operations of an enterprise.

The economic reforms have intensified the incentive role of bonuses as a lever for achieving an increase in worker productivity and the rate of economic growth. As it now stands, Soviet workers receive fixed payments according to their grades from the wage fund of an enterprise plus a bonus which can come from the wage fund and from the material incentives fund. Workers could fall under one of three compensation categories: (1) Time rate plus a bonus. In this type of compensation system, wages are based on hourly rates which are set for each skill grade. In addition, bonuses are paid on either an individual or collective basis. These bonuses are often related to quantified standards such as output quotas, cost reduction, and material usage. In such cases, workers receive bonuses for the fulfillment and overfulfillment of individual or collective targets.

(2) Piece rate plus a bonus. The piece rate can be progressive, which means that earnings rise more than in proportion to output above the standard task. For example, at one time in the machine tool industry, progressive piece rates were as follows: An increase of from 1 to 10 percent in production over and above the standard task resulted in an increase in 30 percent in the piece rate; an increase of from 10 to 25 percent in production resulted in an increase of 50 percent in the piece rate; an increase of from 25 to 40 percent in production resulted in an increase of 75 percent in the piece rate; and an increase of from 40 percent and over resulted in a 100 percent increase in the piece rate. However, progressive piece rates have declined in importance and have been replaced primarily by straight piece rates, in which earnings vary in direct proportion to output. Bonuses are paid when an enterprise exceeds planned production targets. For example, in the engineering and building components industries, bonuses to workers amounted to 10 to 20 percent of normal piece-rate earnings if targets were met and 1 to 2 percent more for every percentage point in excess of the targets.[37]

(3) Straight time and piece rates. Straight time rates, usually monthly, would be paid to professional workers, such as doctors, teachers, and employees of various government agencies. Salaried workers for enterprises, such as engineers, managers, and technicians, are also paid time rates, but receive a bonus as well, provided that the enterprise achieves its targets. Under the reforms, bonuses to salaried workers come from the material incentives fund, the amount of which depends upon the profits an enterprise earns.

It can be said that the typical form of compensation for Russian industrial workers is either time rates or piece rates with bonuses. Before the economic reforms which were started in 1965, 67 percent of industrial workers received

[37] *Ibid.,* p. 361.

either time rates or piece rates with bonuses.[38] With more reliance placed on the use of material incentives to stimulate worker productivity, the percentage is probably higher today.

Reliance on material incentives is consistent with the philosophies of Russian leaders from Lenin to Kosygin. Both Lenin and Stalin emphasized the influence of material self-interest in the development of the Soviet economy and asserted that moral incentives were not enough. Khrushchev stated that it was completely wrong to oppose material incentives. There is a similarity in the use of monetary incentives in the Soviet Union and in the United States in that their objective is to tie the attainment of individual goals to the accomplishment of organizational objectives. In fact, through the use of the bonus system, the Soviet Union goes one step further than the United States, in that it ties incentives to such indexes as volume of output sold and profit made.

Nonmaterial Incentives. In the Russian economic system, material rewards are often combined with other types of noneconomic rewards in an attempt to achieve maximum effort on the part of the workers. For example, emphasis has been placed on programs which are designed to stimulate competition among individual workers, or among groups of workers, to see who can produce the most. Winners can earn individual or collective titles such as "Heroes of Socialist Toil" or "Communist Labor Brigade." These titles can carry with them considerable honor and prestige as well as such additional advantages as extra compensation and free travel passes. Medals are sometimes awarded, and plants are given a red flag to fly from the roof to show that their workers won in output competition.

There is also worker participation in the management of production. In all industrial enterprises, there are production conferences to which all types of workers—white-collar, blue-collar, engineers, and management—can be elected by various departments. These conferences meet to consider production goals, and they can make recommendations to the enterprise director who is supposed to consider them before making any final decision. If there is disagreement, members of the conference have the right to appeal to the trade union or Communist Party officials in the enterprise. However, although useful suggestions may emanate from the conference, there are reported drawbacks in that management may ignore proposals and that workers often strive to obtain easier work norms.

Moral stimuli are also used to motivate Russian workers. The Communist Party cadres and trade union officials are supposed to provide the moral motivation. A major task of the trade union is to promote what is called *socialist emulation,* which means the development of moral responsibility on the part of the workers to increase production for the interest of the state. Although glorious deeds of self-sacrifice on the part of workers may be resurrected from the past to spur workers on to greater activity, the union is supposed to provide the stimuli, through techniques such as motion pictures and lectures,

[38] *Ibid.,* p. 360.

to make them strive for improved performances and increased output. To stimulate socialist emulation, production contests are held between enterprises, and the winners receive red banners to fly from factory rooftops and cash prizes are given to those workers who have emulated the best.

Transfer Payments and Special Benefits. Money wages are only one source of a Russian worker's income. When various government expenditures for free subsidized consumer services, such as medical benefits and transfer payments, are taken into consideration, total money and real income can be increased considerably for the average Russian worker. Transfer payments account for around 15 percent of total personal income in the Soviet Union and have increased at a more rapid rate than wages and salaries.[39] In 1972 transfer payments amounted to 27 billion rubles ($32.9 billion) compared to personal income of 107 billion rubles ($130.5 billion). Consumer welfare has been stressed in recent years. Pensions and welfare grants have been liberalized and collective farms have been brought under social insurance coverage. In addition to transfer payments, Russians gain from subsidies on housing and basic foodstuffs. Russian workers also receive benefits from the socio-cultural funds of state enterprises.

The welfare of the consumer is receiving increasing attention in the Soviet Union. Among other things, priority is given in the economic plan to improvements in the quality and selection of consumer goods. Real disposable income of consumers has risen on the average 6.2 percent since 1965, as living standards have shown a marked improvement in recent years. Basic foodstuffs and services are maintained at a low price level to favor low-income consumers. Many consumer goods are priced below costs, but, on the other hand, prices for luxury goods and various consumer durables including automobiles, are maintained at very high levels. Moreover, disposable income has increased at a rate faster than the state's capacity to produce consumer goods and services, thus necessitating long delays in purchasing on the part of consumers.

Income Inequality. It is rather obvious that a truly egalitarian society does not exist in the Soviet Union, and it is a myth that the worker is first among equals. In 1972 the average monthly wage of Soviet workers was 130.3 rubles (about $158.90) and was less than two thirds of the amount necessary to maintain a family of four at minimum living standards.[40] This necessitates two income earners in a family. It is true, however, that income differentials in the Soviet Union have been reduced as the Soviets have raised the incomes of millions of low-income workers. Nevertheless, this point may be misleading, for there are certain privileges expressed in nonmonetary terms that redound to the advantage of the party elite, professional workers such as managers and engineers, and members of the intelligentsia. The difference between the income of the average worker and that of the privileged strata is striking and is

[39] David W. Bronson and Barbara S. Severin, "Soviet Consumer Welfare: The Brezhnev Era," *Soviet Economic Prospects for the Seventies,* Joint Economic Committee, 93d Congress, 1st Session, 1973.

[40] *Ibid.,* p. 379.

enlarged by special contributions from the state, including such benefits as private villas, personal limousines, and travel privileges.[41]

A general idea of income distribution in the Soviet Union can be gained by examining Table 17–4. This table presents a distribution of wages and salaries in the Soviet economy for 1966. Not taken into consideration are transfer payments, which would have a redistributive effect on income, or bonuses, which are not considered a part of regular wages and salaries. The table also fails to reflect special bonuses or privileges that typically redound to the advantage of special groups.

TABLE 17–4
DISTRIBUTION OF WAGES AND SALARIES IN THE SOVIET UNION FOR 1966

Wages and Salaries (Rubles per Month)	Percentage of Workers
30 and under 40	2
40 and under 50	9
50 and under 60	9
60 and under 70	12
70 and under 80	10
80 and under 100	18
100 and under 120	14
120 and under 140	10
140 and under 160	5
160 and under 200	10
200 and under 300	2

Source: P. J. D. Wiles and S. Markowski, "Income Distribution Under Communism and Capitalism," Soviet Studies (April, 1971), p. 503.

AN APPRAISAL OF THE SOVIET ECONOMY

There is no question that the economy of the Soviet Union made considerable progress during the periods before and after World War II. Today the Soviet Union ranks as one of the two major powers of the world and has proved capable of developing a military and industrial complex which rivals that of the United States. In the field of space technology, the Soviet Union has made a very important contribution, indicating the ability of the leadership to mobilize resources to accomplish certain objectives. In contrast to economies such as that of the United States, where the market dictates to a major extent how resources are to be used, the Soviet leadership can allocate resources into industries which build a base for further investment. Instead of diverting resources into the manufacture of automobiles or television sets, they are used to manufacture machine tools which can be used to produce more machine tools. This authority on the part of the leaders to influence production patterns through control over resource allocation has contributed to a rather high rate

[41] See, for example, John Dornberg, The New Tsars, Russia Under Stalin's Heirs (Garden City: Doubleday and Co., Inc., 1972), especially Chapter 3.

of economic growth in the Soviet Union during most of the period following World War II. Moreover, the Soviet economy has shown that it can maintain a high rate of investment independent of business fluctuations and the uncertain preferences of individuals. This means that the growth rate is not likely to be slowed by recessions, which sometimes impede the rate of economic growth in countries relying on the market system.

The performance of the Soviet economy has shown mixed results. Take, for example, the area of consumer goods production. Although there is no question but what the standard of living of consumers has increased dramatically, particularly since 1970, an imbalance in production has occurred. The speed with which new products and new production methods are introduced remains unsatisfactory. Market saturation and surplus production in some consumer goods areas have occurred. There are frequent bottlenecks and insufficient production in other areas. These developments reflect a general inefficiency of the whole planning and production system. Soviet planning has to adjust the production of consumer goods to conform more to the desires of consumers as reflected in an increased rate of total demand. Many problems, including servicing consumer goods, remain to be ironed out.[42]

The overall rate of economic growth as measured by changes in the real rate of gross social product has been good, but somewhat erratic. In 1971 the rate of real gross social product increased by 6 percent over the preceding year, a rate exceeded only by Japan among the major industrial countries.[43] In 1972 the real rate of growth of 3 percent lagged well behind the rates of the two preceding years. In comparison with other countries, the rate was lower than the growth rates for France, Japan, West Germany, and the United States. This was the lowest rate of growth recorded since World War II. However, the low rate was attributable in part to very bad weather conditions which caused a reduction in the output of agriculture. There were also delays during the completion of the new production facilities which contributed to the reduced rate of growth.

Comparisons can be made of the Soviet Union and the United States in terms of economic performance. The Soviet Union is larger in land area, population, and labor force participation. There has been a more rapid growth in the output of Soviet industry and agriculture since 1960. The main reason for this growth has been the leadership's willingness to devote increasing shares of national output to investment. Nevertheless, in absolute terms, the gap between the gross national products of the Soviet Union and the United States has increased in recent years. In 1973 the Soviet gross national product was $660 billion, slightly more than half that of the United States. Soviet economic

---

[42] For example, not only is there a shortage of automobiles relative to the demand, but there is a far greater shortage of filling stations and garages. There are 370 repair garages in the Soviet Union compared to 800,000 privately owned cars—one garage for each 2,200 cars.

[43] The gross social product of the Soviet Union excludes so-called "nonmaterial" services, banks, education, and the military from computation. This differs from the computation of gross social product of the Western countries, making comparisons somewhat difficult.

growth has generally exceeded that of the United States, particularly during the 1950s as the country recovered from wartime devastation. The pace gradually slowed, and since 1970 the rate of growth has been lower than that in the United States.

SUMMARY

The cornerstone of the Soviet economy is the industrial enterprise. It operates on the basis of an annual production plan which is integrated into the national economic plan. Its performance is based on a series of success indicators. Enterprises operate under a profit and loss accounting system, and their success is supposed to be judged primarily by the volume of their sales and profits. Each enterprise is run by a director or manager whose responsibilities are similar to those of managers of American enterprises. However, the government prescribes the policies of all enterprises are to follow in the national economic plan, and managers are confined by the targets and resource limits prescribed in it. There is a government and party heirarchy which plans and administers Soviety industry and, for that matter, the entire economy.

Agriculture has long been a problem in the Soviet Union. It has suffered because of underinvestment, excessive central direction, and lack of incentives. In terms of production and performance, it lags well behind agriculture in the United States. The United States uses more capital to achieve a greater output. Most equipment used on Soviet state and collective farms is not used at an optimum level because there is a chronic shortage of technical personnel. There has been a large-scale migration of younger workers, especially those who are trained, from the rural to urban areas. To arrest this urban migration and to promote greater efficiency in agriculture, economic reforms were introduced which have as their objectives the raising of rural incomes and living standards and the increasing of capital investment. Guaranteed minimum monthly payments to collective farmers have been introduced, and state farm workers have been put on the same wage system used for industrial workers. Although managers of state and collective farms have been given more autonomy, pricing of farm products remains in the government's domain.

Under the Soviet system, wages are regarded as remuneration for work in proportion to its quantity and quality. Incentives, both material and nonmaterial are used to motivate workers to produce with optimal efficiency. Reliance is placed on a bonus system which is tied to the level of enterprise profits, and wage payments to the majority of Soviet industrial workers can take the form of either piece or time rates plus a bonus. In addition to their regular monetary income, Soviet workers receive other benefits, such as free medical care and family allowances, which can raise total income by a considerable amount.

QUESTION

1. In some respects there are similarities in the operation of American and Soviet enterprises. Do you agree?
2. Discuss the role of profits in the Soviet economic system.
3. What is the purpose of an enterprise's tekhpromfinplan?

4. Labor unions in the United States and the Soviet Union have similar responsibilities. Do you agree? Explain your answer.
5. Distinguish the differences between state farms and collective farms.
6. How are state farms financed?
7. Income distribution in the Soviet Union is based on the Marxist concept of "from each according to his ability to each according to his need." Do you agree? Explain your answer.
8. To what extent does the Soviet Union employ nonmaterial incentives to stimulate worker productivity? Explain.
9. It has been stated that the Soviet Union relies on material incentives to stimulate worker productivity to an extent greater than any other industrial nation. Explain.
10. As you see it, what are the strong and weak points in the Soviet economic and political systems?

18

The People's Republic of China I

INTRODUCTION

China is the largest country in the world from the standpoint of population and third in terms of land size. The population is estimated to be around 865 million—a factor that presents both a blessing and a dilemma in terms of world geopolitics. The land area, however, presents a serious problem in that less than 15 percent of it is arable with the result that millions of Chinese depend upon small allotments of land for their subsistence.

From the year 1949, which marked the downfall of the Nationalist Chinese government, to the present, the Communists have worked to transform China into a communist economic system. Industrialization has been the primary economic goal. Economic policy has been directed toward the expansion of productive capacity in basic industrial commodities such as steel, coal, and petroleum. Agriculture has been put under state control and assigned the task of supplying raw materials to industry as well as feeding the population. During the earlier part of the development of the economic system, the Chinese looked to the Russians to provide the expertise and guidance necessary to transform China into a planned economy along Soviet lines. This approach, however, was discarded in favor of the use of idealistic extremism, as epitomized by the *Great Leap Forward,* to develop the economy.

The state prescribes the ultimate objectives to be followed by all Chinese. Society is regimented for the purpose of accomplishing specific economic and social goals. Unlike a capitalistic system where resource allocation is determined by price interaction in the market place, economic questions of what to produce, how much to produce, and for whom to produce are resolved by the state through comprehensive economic planning. Market forces have been replaced by state action developed by bureaucrats which involves plans, exhortation, rules of social behavior, and reliance on both material and non-material incentives.

On balance the performance of the Chinese economy has been reasonably good, particularly when the pre-1949 period is used as a frame of reference. Although the individual Chinese lives a Spartan and austere life by Western standards, basic material comforts, including an adequate food supply, are available to all. Moreover, there has been a gradual increase in the standard of living, with the quality of consumer goods and services showing improvement. In addition, China has made significant advances in the area of industrial development. An industrial labor force has been trained, and self-sufficiency has been attained in certain key areas, including the production of petroleum. New industrial complexes have been created throughout the country.

This is not to say, however, that the Chinese are free from problems. For example, capital accumulation is necessary to accomplish the development of an advanced industrial economy. There has to be a surplus for market exchange, and this is accomplished only by direct control over consumption. The agricultural base of the country can be easily disrupted by floods or other natural calamities, and these work short-term hardship on the mass of the population. An increasing population means that China must continue to increase its agricultural output on a small amount of arable land in order to sustain its living standard as well as provide the surplus which is the prime source of exchange for imports of industrial machinery. Finally, the ideological tergiversations of the Chinese ruling elite have contributed to a certain amount of economic and political instability.

DEVELOPMENT OF THE ECONOMIC SYSTEM

At the end of World War II, China was split into two factions, both of which had resisted Japanese incursions since the beginning of the Sino-Japanese War, which started in 1937. These factions were the Nationalists and Communists. Japan's defeat set up a struggle for control of occupied China extending from Manchuria in the north to Canton in the south. Although mediation was attempted by the United States, and a tripartite committee consisting of Nationalists, Communists, and the United States was set up to work out conditions for a coalition government, efforts proved short-lived and a civil war broke out which lasted from 1946 to 1949. The initial advantage possessed by the Nationalists in terms of territory and logistics was lost, and the Nationalist government was driven from the Chinese mainland by the Communists, who, by 1949, had become masters of the country.

The development of the Chinese economic system has gone through several stages during the period from 1949 to the present. The first stage, which lasted from the latter part of 1949 to 1952, was a period of consolidation during which the Communists laid the foundation for a national government. The second stage was the period of the First Five-Year Plan, which lasted from 1953 to 1957. This stage, which borrowed heavily from Soviet economic planning, marked the beginning of forced-draft industrialization along Soviet lines. The third stage was the Great Leap Forward, which lasted from 1958 to 1960. The rationale of the Great Leap Forward was the use of indigenous Chinese resources, particularly labor of which China had plenty, to drive the economy ahead at a faster pace. Russian style planning was abandoned in favor of this new approach toward industrial development. The fourth stage involved a return to economic planning after the collapse of the Great Leap Forward. This stage, which lasted from 1961 to 1965, involved the adoption of more rational economic policies toward industry and agriculture. The fifth stage, lasting from 1966 to 1969, was the Proletarian Cultural Revolution. In essence, the Revolution represented a regression to the political idea that only Mao Tse-Tung had the answer for everything. The sixth, and most current stage, began in 1970 and has marked a resumption of more orderly economic and political policies.

The Period of Consolidation, 1949–1952

When the Communists formally announced the creation of the Chinese People's Republic on October 1, 1949, they were able to formally begin the consolidation of power and the development of a new type of economic system. Certainly the task was not easy. Years of fighting and inflation had debilitated the economy. Widespread corruption had been rampant under the Nationalist government. The masses of the people were agrarian and illiterate and had to be trained and educated to fit into an industrial base which was to be the fountainhead for the development of the communist economic system.

Upon gaining control of the country, the communist regime stamped its imprimatur upon society through a series of nationwide reforms which attempted to refashion nearly every aspect of Chinese life. Of paramount importance was the redistribution of land to the peasants and the elimination of landlords as an economic class. This marked the first step toward *collectivization.* Then followed a series of organizational reforms beginning with the simplest form of social enterprise, the *mutual aid team,* and progressing through successive stages of so-called producer cooperatives to complete collectivization of the farms in 1957, during which time the peasant lost title to the land.

Economic Conditions. The Communists inherited inflation and a chaotic monetary system from their predecessors, the Nationalists. During the transitional period they relied upon the use of savings certificates which were tied to the wholesale price index as a device to ameliorate inflation. Interest payments, as well as the capital value of the certificates rose as the price index increased. Although the payment of interest for the use of capital is considered a device of capitalism, the Communists felt that the rationale for its use, namely, that savings would be diverted from hoarding into productive investment through the banking system, was justifiable. The purposes, then, of the savings certificates, were twofold—to attract and stimulate savings for capital formation and to stabilize prices.[1]

In the area of public finance, various reform measures were undertaken. One reform was the unification of a large variety of regional taxes

---

[1] The Communists also instituted a scheme of *real goods savings deposits* on which a *real goods unit,* composed of necessary commodities, that is, flour, rice, coal, and cotton cloth, was expressed in terms of a monetary value which was based on the wholesale prices of each commodity. The money value was determined every ten days, and the value of deposits was based on the current monetary value of the real units.

that had existed during previous regimes. Principal taxes were a tax on agriculture and a tax on industrial and commercial enterprises. There was also a general sales tax which was levied on all transactions, as well as an income tax on wages and salaries, but this affected only a small proportion of the population. Excise taxes and customs duties were also imposed. Centralized control and management over national revenues and expenditures was introduced in 1950, and tax collection was unified under central control by making the People's Banks agencies for collection throughout the country. In 1950 the budget was balanced—a contrast to most budgets in the preceding 30 years.

The banking and fiscal systems, then, were placed under tight communist control. Gold, silver, and foreign exchange were barred from circulation, authority to issue currency was turned over to the People's Bank of China, and private banks were systematically nationalized. Foreign trade was conducted by state trade companies which used only foreign exchange, thereby isolating the currency unit of China, the *jen min pi,* from foreign influence. As mentioned above, the tax system was consolidated under centralized control and the budget was balanced.

Elimination of Private Enterprise. The Communists also moved to break down the groups that were considered inimical to the best interests of the state. Landlords and rich peasants were either eliminated or neutralized, and their lands were distributed to the peasant farmers. Although at first left alone, private businesses were eventually harassed by profit taxes and made to sell to the state at low prices. Eventually, state trading companies were formed in all of the larger cities and towns. They provided the regime with an instrument for controlling inflation in that they provided important commodities to the government which could be placed in the market at strategic moments. The state trade companies also competed with private enterprises and ensured state control over output by private enterprises through orders and contracts. By degrees, private enterprises were eliminated from the economy and were replaced by state monopolies.

Results of the Period of Consolidation. On balance, the performance of the Communists during the period of consolidation was considered good. Stability was introduced into the monetary and fiscal systems of the country, and order was created out of chaos. The widespread corruption that existed under the bureaucracy of Nationalist China was eliminated. The transportation system was restored to operation, and a comprehensive program of public health and sanitation was introduced. The industrial base was restored, and the production and distribution of clothing and foodstuffs was increased. A campaign was also undertaken to increase the literacy of the Chinese people, and the Communists recognized that education had to be given top priority if internal growth and development were to be accomplished.

The First Five-Year Plan, 1953–1957

The First Five-Year Plan marked the second stage in the economic development of Communist China. To implement the Plan, the Chinese relied heavily on Russian expertise because planning had been used to develop the Russian economy and the Chinese wanted a model to follow. Soviet technicians were imported to develop the Plan and to run the factories. Agreements were reached providing for Russian aid in building or expanding electric power plants and in the supply of agricultural, mining, and chemical equipment. Russian financial aid took the form of low interest loans. The Russians also contracted for the construction of factories producing a wide variety of products including chemicals, synthetic fibers and plastics, liquid fuel, and machine tools. The Soviets also built modern iron and steel complexes, nonferrous metallurgical plants, refineries, and power stations, and they trained Chinese technicians to operate them. Sets of blueprints and related materials giving directions for plant layouts were also provided for the Chinese.

Objectives of the Plan. The First Five-Year Plan, then, represented Russian-style industrial development. It placed priority on the construction of heavy industry in order to create an industrial base for national power, and it aimed at doubling the value of industrial output over the period of its operation. Basically, there were five objectives of the Plan.

(1) Emphasis was placed on the development of basic industries such as steel, electric power, petroleum, and cement. This was to be accomplished with Russian assistance. According to the Plan, capital construction investment was to increase by approximately $18 billion over the five years and was to be allocated to the various sectors of the economy as follows: 58.2 percent to industry, with most of the amount going to heavy industry; 19.2 percent to transportation and communications; 7.6 percent to agriculture and forestry; and 15 percent to education, health, banking, trade, and other areas.[2]

(2) To facilitate the economic development of China, transportation was improved. New rail lines were built to connect the industrial centers with the remote provinces of the interior. The rail systems of north and south China were linked together by the construction of a major bridge at Wuhan. In addition to this construction, the rail lines which were already in existence were double tracked.

(3) The First Five-Year Plan also pursued a policy of industrial diffusion. The industrial base of the country had been concentrated in a few geographic areas, particularly in Manchuria. The desirability of developing regional industrial complexes as a military precaution was evident to the Chinese. The feasibility of this approach had already been demonstrated by the Russians,

[2] A. Doak Barnett, *Communist China and Asia* (New York: Random House, Inc., 1960), p. 42.

who had been able to survive the military onslaughts of the Germans, which had destroyed much, but not all, of Russia's industrial base in World War II. The Plan called for the construction of several major regional steel centers and ore-processing facilities at extraction points.

(4) To support industrialization, the educational system was revamped to give primary emphasis to technical education. Specialized schools and poly-technic institutes were created throughout China to provide workers with the technical expertise to man the factories. Everyone was guaranteed the op-portunity to receive an education, provided that the requisite ability was there.

(5) Agriculture was assigned a supportive role of feeding the masses, supplying raw materials to industry, and furnishing the exports necessary to provide for the imports of industrial machinery. The Plan aimed at increasing the gross value of agricultural production by 23 percent in five years. It also outlined plans for the eventual collectivization of agriculture. By the end of 1957, 33 percent of peasant households were to be in cooperatives, because the Communists were intent on achieving maximum state control over the peasants. Various goals were set for agricultural products. For example, grain production was to be raised 30 percent during the operation of the Plan.[3]

Implementation of the Plan. The First Five-Year Plan culminated in 1957. It was based upon massive Russian support which took several forms—the provision of technological expertise, financial assistance, supplies of machinery and equipment, and ancillary services involving the installation and operation of plants. Also, Chinese students were sent to Russia to receive technical train-ing. Savings to support capital formation were provided by taxes on consumers and on state-owned cooperatives, as well as by the relegation of agriculture to the supportive role of financing the importation of capital equipment.

Results of the Plan. The economic policies of the First Five-Year Plan resulted in a marked increase in the production of major industrial products. The output of crude steel increased from 1.35 million metric tons in 1952 to 5.35 metric tons in 1957. Electric power increased from 7.3 billion kilowatt hours in 1952 to 19.3 billion kilowatt hours in 1957. Coal production increased from 66.5 million metric tons to 130.7 million metric tons; cement production in-creased from 2.9 million metric tons to 6.9 million metric tons; petroleum production increased from .44 million metric tons to 1.46 million metric tons; and sulfuric acid production increased from 190 thousand metric tons to 632 thousand metric tons.[4] Moreover, Russian assistance had accomplished the training of thousands of Chinese technicians for work in industry. Additional plant capacity was created from the rehabilitation and reconstruction of plants existing prior to the start of the Plan as well as through the construction of

---

[3] Kenneth R. Walker, *Planning in Chinese Agriculture* (Chicago: Aldine Publish-ing Company, 1965), pp. 4–8.

[4] Arthur G. Ashbrook, "Economic Policy & Economic Results," *People's Republic of China: An Economic Assessment* (Washington: Joint Economic Committee, 92d Congress, 2d Session, 1972), p. 19.

large-scale, modern plants. Momentum had been accomplished in industrial production.

Agricultural gains were far less spectacular. Although production increased, it was barely enough to maintain the living standards of the rapidly increasing Chinese population, let alone to provide a surplus for export on the scale required to secure the necessary imports of machinery. However, it is necessary to remember that the main thrust of the Plan was the development of an industrial base. In agriculture, attention was given to increasing government control over the farms. Mechanization was to come later.

The Great Leap Forward, 1958–1960

In 1958 the Chinese decided to depart from the pattern of economic development set by the First Five-Year Plan and to use a new approach which relied on the idealistic fervor of the masses of workers and peasants to drive the economy ahead at a much faster rate. This approach was called the Great Leap Forward. It represented an example of idealistic extremism which substituted zeal for the material incentives developed under the First Five-Year Plan. China's enormous population was to be regarded as an economic asset and not a liability—the more people, the more hands to build socialism. Emphasis was placed on indigenous methods of production and the development of labor-intensive investment projects. National output in industry and agriculture was to be doubled and redoubled in a few short years, and hated imperialist powers, such as Great Britain, were to be surpassed in production. To put the basic objective of the Great Leap Forward simply, the population was to be harnessed to increase production and make China a great power.

The economic policy of the Great Leap Forward, as directed toward the various sectors of the economy, was as follows:

Agriculture. In agriculture, economic policy involved the formation of communes. Under communal organization, all vestiges of private property were eliminated. The communes marked the final stage in the transition of agriculture from private enterprise, which had existed during the first years of communist rule. The first stage in communist agricultural policy was land redistribution to the peasants. The second stage was the formation of material aid teams, which still left private property undisturbed. The third stage transformed the material aid teams into small cooperatives. Here the peasants divested their land and draft animals in the cooperatives with the right to withdraw them. The fourth stage was the formation of larger cooperatives out of a number of smaller cooperatives. The peasants received shares of produce according to their labor, and they were allowed to own plots of land.

With the coming of the communes, the peasants were not only deprived of the private plots, livestock, and implements which had been left to them by the previous collectivization, they also had to surrender their homes, and it was part of the idea of the commune that they should be rehoused in some kind of communal building. The purpose was to turn the peasants into mobile workers ready for any task in any area to which they might be assigned.

Under the commune system, peasants were required to perform non-agricultural tasks during the slack periods of the year, or they were drafted for mining, construction, or industrial work in their localities. Much of the rural population, so the Communists thought, was underemployed during at least part of the year. During this time, they reasoned, labor could be used for useful output such as dam construction and road development. Handicraft industries could also be created.

The commune was the highest form of collectivist agricultural development sponsored by the government. It was a multipurpose unit in that it carried out industrial as well as agricultural production. It was not only an economic unit but a military unit as well. It also was an administrative unit corresponding to a township and performing various administrative functions in the areas of agriculture, commerce, finance, and education. The membership of each commune was organized into various cadres which were responsible for work in agriculture and industry, as well as for the performance of other functions. The commune, the Communists hoped, would organize the entire work force behind a regimented, intensive campaign to develop both agriculture and rural industry.

An "Eight-Point Charter" for agriculture was developed by Mao Tse-tung. This included deep plowing (the furrows were to be increased in depth from less than one foot to as much as six feet), fertilizing, the repair and extension of irrigation systems, field management, close planting, pest control, the use of improved seeds, and the use of improved implements.

Industry. In industry, economic policy placed emphasis on the utilization of labor to create thousands of tiny industrial units throughout the country. This has been called facetiously "the steel mill in every back yard" policy. Again, the Communists planned to capitalize on the presence of a large labor surplus to accomplish rapid industrialization, particularly in the rural areas. During that part of the year when the rural population was underemployed, labor could be used for useful output. Small indigenous industrial plants were created to harness the energies of the labor force. These plants included handicraft workshops, iron and steel foundries, fertilizer plants, oil extraction, machine shops, cement manufacture, coal and iron ore mining, and food processing. The capital used to build the small plants came from the local communes and from taxes on state enterprises. Labor, however, was the key factor employed in the development of local industry.

Top priority was given by the Communists to the iron and steel industry. This was to be the key to industrial success that would enable China to overtake Great Britain in industrial production in 15 years. Lack of technology and equipment was to be replaced by mass fervor. After all, the Chinese leaders argued, who needs technicians? There is no reason why the smelting of iron and steel should belong to the few. Anybody can make steel. These sentiments were prompted by the fact that the Russian technicians and planners sent to help develop China were indeed a part of a technocratic elite, and they knew it. The Chinese observed this fact, hence the derogatory references mentioned above.

Some 80 million persons were involved in an attempt to create a do-it-yourself steel industry. Two million backyard furnaces developed throughout all of China. Many millions of Chinese worked day and night turning out steel, while millions of others labored with the extraction of iron ore and coal. The result was the development of a labor-intensive, small-scale, steel producing unit with a low capital-output ratio. Although the output of iron and steel was increased by the backyard furnace method, much of it was of poor quality, reflecting the absence of quality control standards and the necessary technical expertise. Production in other areas suffered as well because more than one tenth of the population was diverted from other pursuits, such as farm production, into the production of steel. The wear and tear on human resources was considerable, as might be expected when amateurs engage in steel making.

A dualistic approach was actually used in the promotion of industrial development. Simultaneous with the promotion of local industries was the pushing of the development of large-scale, modern industry. This was called the *walking on two legs policy.* The Chinese were anxious to accomplish industrialization and were impatient with the slowness of the Russian approach which based the rate of economic development on capital accumulation. Therefore, labor was substituted for capital, and a political approach which employed exhortation and shibboleths replaced economic logic.

Failure of the Great Leap Forward. The Great Leap Forward was not a success. Although industrial and agricultural output rose sharply in 1958, much of the gain was spurious. As mentioned above, the quality of the steel produced by the backyard furnaces left much to be desired. The products of many small plants were of such poor quality that most of them had to be scrapped. Production costs were high for many plants, reflecting an indiscriminate development of small plants in almost all industries. There was also a disregard for cost considerations at the local plant level because the most important success indicator was the degree to which the local cadre or leaders could fulfill or overfulfill quotas. This output was maximized at the expense of quality and cost, even though in many cases the quantity produced exceeded the quantity needed, and inputs of labor and raw materials could have been more effectively employed elsewhere. Also, a shortage of fuels and raw materials caused by the wastage involved in the backyard furnace method of production and by lack of adequate transportation facilities was responsible for the demise of many plants.

Agriculture. In agriculture, the pattern was the same. Output increased initially but slumped drastically in 1959. A severe food crisis occurred and shortages of raw materials were experienced, affecting exports adversely. Part of the problem can be attributed to a series of natural disasters, such as floods, which hit the mainland for several years in a row, but most of the problem can be attributed to the agricultural policies developed during the Great Leap Forward—policies that were similar to those pursued in the industrial sector in that technical expertise was replaced by the idea that zeal and fervor plus exhortations and slogans are adequate substitutes for science.

The basic cause of the agricultural collapse was the change in policy with respect to the relationship of the peasant to farming. Under the collective farm arrangement, he was left with a private plot to cultivate as his own, and his home was not touched. When communes replaced the collective farms, he was deprived of both home and land and forced to live and share communally. Political consciousness was supposed to replace all other types of incentives as the basic motivating factor behind his efforts. Output was based on ideology and was to be shared on an egalitarian basis. However, to the peasant, ideology was not sufficient to stimulate the effort necessary to increase output, reflecting the fact that a reward system must be based on some form of differential, monetary, or otherwise, if productivity is to increase.

Another cause of the agricultural problem involved the notion, also expressed in the industrial policy of the Great Leap Forward, that it does not take an expert to understand farming any more than it takes one to build a steel mill. Amateurs can lead experts and zeal can replace expertise. In the rush to increase output, technological constraints were ignored and untested farming techniques were often utilized over large areas. Irrigation systems, upon which most of the agriculture of China must depend, were often defective. There was much waste and inefficiency involved in the allocation of raw materials and capital.

Sino-Russian Relations. The Great Leap Forward also caused a rift in the relationship between the Chinese and the Russian advisers and technicians that had been sent to help them. In essence, the Russian blueprints for making China a self-sufficient world power had been ignored in favor of a development program that made little economic sense. The Russians believed that the communes would not work and that they had developed a program for agriculture that would work. The Chinese persisted in ignoring the advice of their Russian technicians despite the fact that Russia intimated that support would be withdrawn unless the Great Leap Forward was discontinued. In 1960 the Soviet technicians were withdrawn from China, and with them went the equipment, financial aid, and blueprints that had played the paramount role in the development of the Chinese economy during the First Five-Year Plan. This *en masse* departure of the technicians had a deleterious effect on the Chinese because they could not supply the expertise to replace them.

Alteration of Approach. Many of the aims and objectives of the Great Leap Forward were abandoned during the early 1960s. In agriculture, the private plots were restored, and the communes were replaced for the most part with more manageable units, such as production brigades that were responsible for output and farm management in several villages. Priority was placed on the increase of food production up to a subsistence level for the population. In industry, economic planning replaced exhortation and rhetoric as a model for economic guidance.

Some of the results of the Great Leap Forward are set forth in Table 18–1. It is necessary to point out that the gains in industrial and mineral production can be extremely misleading. Much of the output of steel was of low quality and had to be scrapped, and much of the coal which was mined was of inferior quality. The agricultural part of the Great Leap Forward was even more of a failure because there was a decline in the production of farm products which affected exports. This decline also caused shortages in food and consumer products. In 1959 millions of Chinese were mobilized to dig up wild plants and grasses which were to be used to produce synthetic foods, starch, chemicals, and medicines.

TABLE 18–1
CHANGES IN OUTPUT OF SELECTED PRODUCTS

	1957	1959
Agricultural Products (Million Piculs *)		
Rice	1,736	1,604
Wheat	473	486
Miscellaneous grain	1,053	832
Potatoes	438	432
Soybeans	201	204
Industrial Products (1,000 Tons)		
Steel ingots	5,350	8,630
Pig iron	5,900	9,450
Rolled steel	4,262	6,873
Cement	4,690	12,270
Mineral Products (1,000 Tons)		
Coal	130,700	347,800
Iron ore	19,370	66,860
Limestone	45,120	80,760

Source: K. C. Yeh, "Capital Formation in Communist China" (Rand Corporation, 1966), p. 26.
* 1 picul = 133.33 pounds

Economic and Social Readjustment Phase, 1961–1965

The period 1961–1965 marked a return to more orthodox economic and social policies. Economic planning, which was largely superseded by the Great Leap Forward, was resumed, and agricultural policy was modified to include smaller production units. For all practical purposes the commune was abandoned. Various forms of material incentives were restored, and farmers were again able to have private plots of land for their own use. Agriculture was given increased priority in terms of investment, while overall industrial investment suffered a retrenchment in favor of certain high priority industries, in particular those that contributed to the development of agriculture. Foreign trade, which had been previously tied to the Soviet Union, involved an exchange of basic raw materials for Western and Japanese machinery, technology, and grain in order to supplement domestic production.

The period of readjustment resulted in an improvement in output in many areas of economic activity, particularly in agriculture. Agricultural production, which had fallen to a low of 78 percent in 1961 compared to a base period of 100 percent in 1957, increased to 101 percent in 1965.[5] However, most of this increase was offset by an increase in population which necessitated purchases of wheat from Canada and Australia. Per capita gross national product, which declined from $128 in 1957 to $103 in 1961, increased to $129 in 1965.[6] Industrial production actually showed a decline in comparison to the Great Leap Forward period. However, this in itself is misleading, for useless industrial output was dropped as the small scale production units developed in 1958–1960 were closed down. Priority was given to the development of certain industries. For example, by 1965 the Chinese had become self-sufficient in the production of petroleum products.

Proletarian Cultural Revolution, 1966–1969

The Third Five-Year Plan was eclipsed by a political aberration of the first magnitude called the *Proletarian Cultural Revolution*. It was an attempt by Mao Tse-tung to mold Chinese society into his prescribed pattern. It placed primacy on ideological cant over scientific expertise and reverted back to the Great Leap Forward period in its attempt to replace material incentives with political ideology and also to denigrate any emphasis on technical excellence.[7] It aimed at annihilating, throughout China and particularly in the universities, any tendency toward a moderate or revisionist viewpoint concerning the role of communism in world affairs. Intransigence toward the Western countries in general and the United States in particular was to be maintained until Western influence was eliminated from Asia. The Russians also did not escape the general opprobrium that the Chinese engendered toward the West, because Mao was furious with them for drawing back from war and subversion in the interest of coexistence; and, with respect to the building of socialism, Mao deplored the use in Soviet economic practice of material incentives for the workers. He contemptuously referred to this practice as an example of *goulash communism*.

During the 1950s an education program was designed to service an expanding urban industrial economy based on the Soviet model. The education program was a success, but the program of urban industrialization was considerably less successful, particularly after the Great Leap Forward. This created severe social dislocations and political strains. The educated youth, indoctrinated to expect an urban life and an expanding industrial economy, had borne an undue share of the burdens resulting from a decade of stagnation,

---

[5] Ashbrook, p. 46.

[6] *Ibid.*, p. 47.

[7] A poster in a Peking park proclaimed, "We do not need brains! Our heads are armed with the ideas of Mao Tse-tung."

and they had faced large-scale unemployment, a lack of promotion prospects in industry and government, and an extensive recruitment for migration from urban areas to rural areas and frontier projects.

To accomplish ideological purity in the fabric of Chinese society, reliance was placed on a youth organization comprised of high school and college students, called the *Red Guards*. It was the function of the Red Guards to extirpate any bourgeoisie or revisionist tendencies that might still exist, particularly among some of the older element in society. They tried to accomplish a complete proletarianization of society through destroying the homes of the remnants of the former gentry and through ridiculing what was old and venerated. Universities were closed and educators examined to see whether or not their thoughts coincided with the purity of Mao-thought. Foreigners in general and Western diplomats in particular were excoriated by the Red Guard, and foreign influence as exemplified by long hairstyles for men was eradicated.

The rationale of the Proletarian Revolution was political as well as economic. It involved in part an attempt by Mao to develop a new socialist morality that would place the public interest above private individualism. There was the belief that Stalin had permitted the development of a new class structure in the form of a state bureaucracy which differed little from a capitalist class structure. What this had done is to separate claims of egalitarianism from the facts of special privileges of a small bureaucratic and technical elite. Moreover, Mao believed that Russia and other socialist countries had moved further away from the Utopian ideal of a perfectly egalitarian society by introducing material incentives and bonuses, which in themselves tend to differentiate among workers. An ethical revolution was needed, for people had to be changed in order to create a new order of society.

In some respects the Cultural Revolution had less of a disruptive impact on the Chinese economy than the Great Leap Forward. For one thing, there was less economic experimentation and the industrial infrastructure was left intact. Nevertheless, the Revolution was the source of widespread change that had an impact on the economy. Factories often had to suspend operations as ideological disruptions often resulted in shortages of raw materials. The index of industrial production fell below the 1966 level in both 1967 and 1968, and the average annual rate of economic growth declined by 2.5 percent for the period. Per capita gross national product declined from $137 in 1966 to $125 in 1968, but the index of agricultural production remained constant during the same period. Exports fell by 15 percent in 1967 and by 1.6 percent in 1968, while imports declined by 13 percent in 1967 and remained stationary in 1968.[8] There is a clear parallel between the dip in foreign trade and the impact of the Cultural Revolution. For 1967 the fall in exports corroborates a dip in industrial production, which is estimated at between 15 and 20 percent. However, in spite of the political and economic turmoil, Chinese living standards were maintained.

[8] Edwin F. Jones, "Cultural Revolution: In Search of a New Model," *People's Republic of China: An Economic Assessment* (Washington: Joint Economic Committee, 92d Congress, 2d Session, 1972), pp. 52–58.

The Post-Cultural Revolution Period, 1970–1974

The end of the Cultural Revolution ushered in another stage of Chinese economic development. For one thing, systematic economic planning in the form of the Fourth Five-Year Plan was reintroduced. Both the Second and Third Five-Year Plans were largely shunted aside by sudden shifts in Chinese political and economic policies—the former by the Great Leap Forward and the latter by the Proletarian Cultural Revolution. The Third Five-Year Plan (1966–1970) was designed to make China safe from external aggression and internal subversion. It proposed to secure minimum food needs by placing controls over farm development and population growth. Another objective was to secure a modern industrial base by stressing the development of technological growth industries.

The Fourth Five-Year Plan (1971–1975) has several objectives. In the area of industrial development, priority is to be given to the production of sophisticated electronic instruments including computers. Continued effort is to be given to increase the output of heavy industry, particularly iron and steel, hydrocarbons and chemical fertilizers. Agriculture, however, still remains the basis of the economy, and agricultural policy under the plan aims at making rural areas more self-sustaining. Investment is to be increased in various water conservation programs including the construction of dams, dikes, storage reservoirs, and irrigation canals.

The Impact of Policy Shifts on the Chinese Economy

In the period from 1949 to the present, the Chinese have oscillated between economic rationality and idealistic extremism in the development of their economy. This oscillation has had an uneven impact on the rate of economic growth, reducing it to a level lower than would have been the case with a more consistent economic policy. For example, the average annual rate of growth in real gross national product during the 1952–1958 period was 8.1 percent—a high average for a developing country.[9] During this period, the First Five-Year Plan was introduced. The Chinese relied heavily on Soviet economic aid and assistance and looked upon the Soviet economy as a model. Like the Russians, they used material work incentives extensively and emphasized the role of the technician and expert. The First Five-Year Plan witnessed very rapid economic growth. Major branches of industry were modernized and production more than doubled.

During the Great Leap Forward period, the annual average rate of economic growth declined to −6.6 percent. Dissatisfied with the degree of materialism and technocracy involved in the Russian approach to economic development, the Chinese decided to capitalize on revolutionary zeal as the appropriate method to accomplish economic goals. Radical institutional change was the key feature of the Great Leap Forward. In agriculture the collective farms were replaced by the communes, and private plots and free markets

[9] *Ibid.*, p. 52.

were eliminated. In industry, technological expertise was replaced with the notion that any peasant can build a steel mill. Industrial production was to be increased by using the large rural population to build small plants. Although quantitative gains were made in some areas of industrial output, quality declined. By 1960 the Great Leap Forward had disintegrated into general agricultural and industrial chaos.

The period 1961–1966 marked a recovery from the excesses of the Great Leap Forward. Ideological fervor was replaced by economic rationality. In agriculture the private plots were restored and peasants were allowed to engage in sideline activities which produced profits. Considerable emphasis was placed on increasing the supply of food to at least a subsistence level, and rural labor was redeployed to the growing of foodstuffs as opposed to the multiplicity of goals to which it was subjected during the Great Leap Forward. In industry emphasis was placed on the development of certain branches such as the chemical processing industry which produced chemical fertilizers for agriculture. As a result of the shifts in economic policy, the average annual increase in the rate of gross national produce was 7.8 percent for the 1961–1966 period.

The Proletarian Cultural Revolution represented a step backward in terms of economic growth. In the wake of its destabilizing conflicts, the regime faced the task of rebuilding a stable institutional structure and working out a new pattern of relationships between various groups. During the Cultural Revolution there was less physical damage to capital equipment than there was disruption of production and transportation which reduced current output, but averted long-term damage to the economy. The average annual rate of growth of gross national product during the period 1966–1968 was −2.5 percent, reflecting a general decline in industrial output of around 15 to 20 percent in 1967.[10] More important, the Cultural Revolution encouraged an ideological polarization within the regime and weakened consensus on the nation's fundamental values and priorities. For a considerable period of time confusion and latent ideological uncertainty will probably persist.

The post-Cultural Revolution period marked a return to relatively pragmatic, nonideological approaches to economic development. The success of these approaches was reflected in a much higher rate of economic growth for the 1969–1972 period. However, when all shifts in Chinese economic policy are taken into consideration, the average annual rate of economic growth over the years has been unspectacular. During the period 1952–1971, the average annual rate of increase in gross national product was 4.1 percent.[11] Using the period 1957–1970, the rate of economic growth was 3.1 percent. If China suffers no political or natural disasters, the economy may grow by about 4 percent annually during the next few years—enough growth to continue building the

---

[10] For a discussion of the impact of the Cultural Revolution on the Chinese economy, see Edwin Jones, *op. cit.*, and the statement of Ta-Chung Liu and Yuan-Li Wu in the Hearings on Economic Developments in Mainland China, Joint Economic Committee, 92d Congress, 2d Session, June, 1972, pp. 29–34, and pp. 65–69.

[11] Jones, *op. cit.*, p. 52.

foundations of national power and to maintain or slightly improve the standard of living.

THE COMMUNIST PARTY ORGANIZATION

The Chinese Communist Party consists of some 30 million members out of a population of 865 million. It has an all pervasive influence on the Chinese economic system in that it exists alongside every unit of organization in the country. All institutions—schools, plants, military units, and government agencies—have Communist party committees as counterpart organizations. Usually top-ranking management and supervisors are members of the Communist party. Requirements for membership in the Communist party are rigorous. Candidates must exhibit leadership ability and undergo a thorough and extensive process of political indoctrination. Party loyalty, in itself, is not a requisite for acceptance into the party; ability to lead and express one's thoughts are more important criteria.[12]

The hierarchy of power within the Communist party is discussed in the following paragraphs.[13]

The Politburo

The Politburo is the highest decision-making unit in the party. It is responsible for national policy formulation. All of the top members in the Communist party belong to it, and most members are responsible for an important area of specialization. Within the Politburo there is a five-member Standing Committee which formulates policies which are then evaluated by all members of the Politburo. The leader of the Standing Committee is Mao Tse-tung, who is Chairman of the Chinese Communist Party. The remainder of the Standing Committee of the Politburo consists of men who were associated with the revolution since its inception. In addition to the Standing Committee, there is a Secretariat which has the responsibility for maintaining a liaison between the central party organization and the party leaders in the provinces. Altogether, there are 21 members of the Politburo and four alternates.[14]

The Central Committee

The Central Committee consists of 319 members who are chosen by a National Party Congress.[15] The purpose of the Central Committee is to select members of the Politburo and clarify and discuss policies that have been decided upon by the Politburo. It also acts as a liaison between Peking and the provinces in that it furnishes the Chinese leaders with an insight into local conditions and how general policy can be adapted to them. Almost all

---

[12] Robert E. Ward and Roy C. Macridis, *Modern Political Systems: Asia* (Englewood Cliffs, N.J.: Prentice-Hall, Inc., 1963), pp. 157–163.

[13] A. Doak Barnett, *Uncertain Passage: China's Transition to the Post-Mao Era* (Washington: The Brookings Institution, 1974), pp. 185–245.

[14] *Ibid.*, p. 224.

[15] There are 195 full and 124 alternate members.

provinces and regions are represented on the Committee by the first party secretary for the region. The Committee transmits decisions to lower party levels, thus linking the top of the party hierarchy to its base. It also provides a means of achieving status for worthy party members.

The National Party Congress

The National Party Congress consists of 1,249 members elected for a period of five years by provincial party congresses.[16] It is supposed to meet annually, but, in fact, both elections and meetings have been held infrequently. The last Congress was held in August 1973. When the Congress meets, its actual function is to clarify policy which has been previously determined by the Politburo. Another function is to elect representatives to the Central Committee. However, the Central Committee has the right to convene a meeting of the Congress, but has failed to do so on a few occasions. This illustrates the fact that in Communist China the political system functions from the top down, not from the bottom up.

Other Levels of Organization

It can be said that the power organization of the Communist party resembles a pyramid with the Politburo representing the apex and local party cells the base. There are more than 1 million local level organizations that form the foundation of the pyramid. Membership requirements are strict. Applicants must be recommended by at least two party members and must undergo a probationary period of training during which they are examined for ideological purity. Applicants engage in the study of doctrine and self-criticism. The basic desideratum for acceptance into the party is leadership ability. Once the probationary period is finished and the applicants successfully survive their education, they are admitted to membership in the party. Then full participation in party life is mandatory. Membership provides upward mobility within the Communist hierarchy. Leaders in a factory are usually members of the Communist party. Membership also provides the opportunity to obtain additional benefits such as a higher education.[17]

ORGANIZATION OF THE GOVERNMENT

The administrative organization of the Chinese government is more decentralized than Communist party organization. The provincial governments have a certain degree of administrative autonomy. The national government, however, is dominant and can withdraw any powers it has granted to the provincial governments. Altogether there are 29 provinces, each with differing cultural characteristics and historical traditions. Some have been in existence since the 13th century.

---

[16] Barnett, *op. cit.*, p. 186.
[17] Herbert F. Schurmann, *Ideology and Organization in Communist China* (Berkeley: University of California Press, 1966), pp. 69–84.

The State Council

The State Council is the top decision-making unit of the national government. Its functions are to direct the conduct of internal affairs, develop and put into effect the national plans and provisions of the national budget, and guide the building up of the armed forces. It is divided into six departments: agriculture and forestry, culture and education, finance and trade, foreign affairs, industry and communications, and political and legal affairs. The State Council is selected by the Premier and ratified by the National People's Congress. The members are either full members of the Politburo or alternate members. The others, although Communist party members, are administrative personnel.

In addition, many of the government ministries have policy-making powers. The Ministry of Finance is responsible for the development of taxation and for budgetary appropriations. The Ministry of National Defense is responsible for policy pertaining to military programs. The Ministry of Commerce is responsible for the allocation of consumer goods, and the Ministry of Foreign Trade is responsible for the supply of imported equipment and raw materials to the various enterprises. The People's Bank of China is responsible for the allocation of funds to the state enterprises on the basis of their individual plans. It supervises the operations of state enterprises and their execution of the economic plans set for them.

The National People's Congress

While the State Council is the executive organ of the highest state authority, the National People's Congress is the supreme organ of state power.[18] Representatives are selected from provincial congresses, cities, national minorities, and the military. The National People's Congress is not a legislative body; its main functions are to endorse the policies of the state and to elect the Standing Committee as its acting body. Its function is to ratify the policies of the National People's Congress. The Congress represents the sovereign power of the people, as opposed to the State Council which represents the ruling power of the national government. This dichotomous, or parallel, system is based on the principle of democratic centralism, a system which to the Chinese means combined discussion and execution at the same time. The National People's Congress, then, exists for the purpose of discussion. It is a device through which various representatives of the diverse nationalities and regions are brought together in Peking to endorse the policies of the government. It also provides a useful liaison between Peking and the provinces and presumably establishes rapport between Mao and the leaders from the provinces.

Elections proceed upward through the local congresses to the National People's Congress. At the bottom of the pyramid are the local congresses. There are people's congresses at the county level, and at the provincial and regional levels. Movement is upward from one level to another, but direction emanates downward from the National People's Congress to the local units.

[18] The National People's Congress has met infrequently. The last time a full meeting was held was in the winter of 1964–1965. It is rumored that a meeting was called in 1973.

Other Units of Government

Below the national level of government, the Chinese Constitution provides for three additional government levels.

(1) The provinces, autonomous regions, and major municipalities represent the administrative units directly below the central level. Although a series of decentralization measures have given the provinces greater autonomy, particularly in the economic field, Peking possesses the ultimate power.[19] The provinces, regions, and municipalities possess local autonomy and representation on the unicameral National People's Congress, but do not receive the special attention accorded to the provinces in the bicameral legislative system used in Russia. Both China and Russia consist of a heterogeneous population which is reflected in the national character of each country. The Chinese provinces as well as the Russian provinces have acquired over time a distinct cultural character, and there is a provincial rather than a national identification on the part of the population.

(2) The counties, municipalities, districts, and prefectures comprise the next level of administration. The typical administrative unit is called the *hsien*, or county unit. It consists of various governmental departments which cover such areas as public finance, civil administration, commerce, industry, and social security.

(3) The villages, or rural governmental units, which are called *hsiang*, comprise the lower administrative unit. The hsiang was merged with the commune when the latter was formed, and for practical purposes, the two remain one and the same. Even at the hsiang level, people's congresses exist, and people's committees, having administrative directors, carry on the following functions: public finance, sanitation, civil administration, public order, commerce, and industry.

The Chairman of the Republic

Few people in the communist pantheon of heroes, including Karl Marx, attained an apotheosis during their lifetimes. Mao Tse-tung is one exception. His influence and thought permeate every aspect of Chinese life. His pictures adorn billboards and posters in every Chinese city, town, and hamlet, and his quotations and thoughts are presented over all communication systems. Passengers on airplanes and trains are also provided with his quotations over the public address system. To the Chinese, the eternal verities of life are to be found in the sayings of Comrade Mao. He is venerated and emulated in thought and in deed.[20]

The economic philosophy of Mao Tse-tung is simple. He wants to create an egalitarian society of which the workers and the peasants are the foundation. This egalitarian society would eliminate all material differences among people. Income differentials would be eliminated, and incentives based on

[19] It is necessary to remember that from an organizational standpoint, we are dealing with the China of the pre-Proletarian Cultural Revolution.

[20] Mao Tse-tung died in September, 1976, shortly before the printing of this text; thus, his death and its effect on China are not discussed here.

material rewards would be replaced by incentives based on a revolutionary desire to create a communist society of the Marxist-Leninist type. To achieve this society, Mao has played down the differences between the plant manager and the worker, the educator and the farmer, and the scientist and the manual laborer. In fact, the plant manager is required to work alongside of the workers at least part of the time so that he can achieve a proper perspective and not think that he has an elite position in society. The educator is required to work alongside the workers in the fields to learn the dignity of hard work and the proper set of values in communist society. The scientist also must put in his stint at hard labor. Class differences based on occupation and income, then, are to be broken down by this blending of work effort, but the end result on productivity and economic growth may well be disastrous.

SUMMARY

The Communist party itself has been unstable and changing. Initially it was small, predominantly young, and possessed high élan. However, it had to expand to maintain representation and control in the various sectors of society, and also to reward activists and leaders of sub-party organizations. The growing size and influx of disparate elements led to internal frictions and forced increasing resort to bureaucratic techniques of management and control. Although the Communist party had a rapid expansion, the rewards it could offer its members in the decade of stagnation declined, leading to demoralization at middle and lower echelons. The Proletarian Cultural Revolution, in its wrecking of the Communist party, did not destroy a strong and vigorous political institution, but rather one in an advanced state of decline.

Change and the impermanence of any particular form of economic and social organization have been the dominant features and realities of Chinese life since 1949. There has been a struggle between two lines of thought—between holders of Maoist and non-Maoist values—which has involved debate over whether to stress economics or politics, professional competence or egalitarian goals, material or ideological incentives, or orderly incremental change or sudden dramatic leaps. In the beginning, emphasis was placed on the orderly development of industry. Economic plans were prepared with the help of Soviet experts, who submitted to the Chinese a model inspired by their own plan. The Great Leap Forward shelved orderly planning goals for a more dramatic attempt to achieve instant self-sufficiency. The end result was a general collapse of industry. Then there was a period of readjustment, followed by the Proletarian Cultural Revolution, which was a manifestation of Mao's efforts to assert his personal power and vision, shake up China's bureaucratic structure, and revive revolutionary values. China's development over the immediate future will continue to center on a fundamental issue: Should the government stress rapid growth or egalitarian values and revolutionary social change?

QUESTIONS

1. Discuss the communist approach to economic problems during the period of consolidation, 1949–52.
2. Discuss the role of the Russians in the development of the First Five-Year Plan.

3. What were the objectives of the First Five-Year Plan?
4. The Great Leap Forward was an irrational departure from the methods and objectives of the First Five-Year Plan. Do you agree?
5. Discuss agricultural policy during the Great Leap Forward.
6. The Great Leap Forward can be considered a failure in its attempt to improve the development of industry and agriculture. Do you agree?
7. The Chinese felt that their large population was an economic asset which could be employed to increase production in industry and agriculture. Was this expectation borne out during the Great Leap Forward?
8. It has been said that Chinese economic policy between 1949 and 1973 has oscillated between economic rationality and idealistic extremism. Do you agree?
9. Discuss the organizational framework of the Chinese Communist Party.
10. What is the relationship between the Communist party and the organization of the Chinese government?

RECOMMENDED READINGS

Barnett, A. Doak. *Uncertain Passage: China's Transition to the Post-Mao Era.* Washington: The Brookings Institution, 1974.

Hsuing, James C. *Ideology and Practice: The Evolution of Chinese Communism.* New York: Praeger, 1970.

Joint Economic Committee. *People's Republic of China: An Economic Assessment.* Washington: 92d Congress, 2d Session, 1972.

Johnson, Chalmers (ed.). *Ideology and Politics in Contemporary China.* Seattle: University of Washington Press, 1973.

Richman, Barry M. *Industrial Society in Communist China.* New York: Random House, 1969.

Schram, Stuart R. *The Political Thoughts of Mao Tse-tung.* New York: Praeger, 1969.

Schwartz, Benjamin I. *Communism and China: Ideology in Flux.* Cambridge: Harvard University Press, 1968.

Wheelright, E. L., and Bruce McFarlane. *The Chinese Road to Socialism.* New York: Monthly Review Press, 1971.

The People's Republic of China II

THE ECONOMIC SYSTEM

The Chinese economy handles by means of economic planning most of the decisions which, under capitalism, are supposed to be made through the reactions of private individuals and firms to price relationships. The state prescribes the ultimate objectives toward which the Chinese industrial and agricultural enterprises should strive. Without market prices, reliance has to be placed on physical units of measure rather than on monetary units of measure in state planning and control. Output decisions are based on centrally determined targets and rationed allocation of resources among different sectors of production. Scales of priority are assigned to various sectors of the economy and maximum flows of resources are permitted to high priority sectors. During the First Five-Year Plan, about 85 percent of total capital investment in industry was allocated to heavy industry.

The Chinese have developed four formal five-year plans. The First Five-Year Plan (1953–1957) was patterned after the Russian plans and was developed with Russian assistance. State investment played a crucial role during the operation of the plan. From the standpoint of resource allocation, capital investment went to industry and transportation. The First Five-Year Plan set very high goals for industrial expansion. It called for the expansion of the gross value of output of producer goods by 128 percent over the 1952 level. It planned to produce 4 million tons of steel by 1957 and to raise cement production by 110 percent over the 1952 level. In agriculture, the plan set as a target an increase in the gross value of production of 23 percent in five years.[1] The Second and Third Five-Year Plans also established goals for industry and agriculture to attain—goals that were superseded by the Great Leap Forward and the Proletarian Cultural Revolution. The Fourth Five-Year Plan (1971–1975) places priority on the development of heavy industry.

Chinese economic plans are similar in their functional character to the plans developed in other socialist countries. There are the physical output plans, which involve production, distribution, and investment goals, and financial plans, which are derivatives of these plans. Then, too, plans differ in terms of time limits. There are long-range plans, which may extend to 30 years, and

---

[1] Choh-Ming Li, *Economic Development of Communist China* (Berkeley: University of California Press, 1959), pp. 29–61.

which usually deal with a particular aspect of the economy. Then there are the medium-term plans, which usually cover a period of five years and which develop targets or goals to be accomplished during this time. The normal frame of reference when one thinks of planning is the five-year plan. There are also annual or operating plans that involve production and distribution goals to be followed by Chinese enterprises and other organizational units during the year. Annual plans can be broken down into quarterly or monthly periods.

Formulation of Economic Plans

The national plan is a composite of a number of sectoral plans. There is a sectoral plan for industry which indicates what and how much individual enterprises should produce. This plan is subdivided into two parts—one for heavy industry and one for light industry. The plan also specifies the amount of producer goods and consumer goods that should be produced.[2]

Plans are also developed for agriculture and transportation. In agriculture, specific goals are set for consumption within the agricultural sector and for distribution to other sectors. The plan also covers all facets of agricultural production including crop rotation techniques and anticipated harvests. In transportation, the plan covers the construction of facilities, with particular emphasis placed on the development of the railways system. It also covers the anticipated volume of passenger and industrial traffic to be carried by the various transportation systems.

Another plan covers capital formation for individual economic sectors and is concerned with resource allocation as an end use. The plan includes a listing of the objectives of each capital project.

Other plans include a labor plan which involves the allocation of labor inputs in the various sectors of the economy. This includes providing an adequate supply of labor to meet anticipated demands. There are also plans which involve the allocation of materials consistent with the output plans of the industrial, agricultural, and transportation sectors, and the flow of products for consumption by the workers in agriculture and industry. The latter plan is subdivided into parts which involve the production of final products for wholesale and retail trade. These parts are further subdivided on the basis of geographic areas and trading companies.

There is also a cost plan which specifies relationships between wages and productivity as well as setting cost standards for enterprises to follow in each sector of the economy. It also provides for cost reduction goals. A plan for technology covers the provision of the latest developments in science and technology, including those from abroad, to the various sectors of the economy.

Plans for foreign trade, social and cultural development, and regional development also exist. The foreign trade plan covers export and import commodity targets and foreign exchange. The social and cultural plan covers

  [2] E. L. Wheelright and Bruce McFarlane, *The Chinese Road to Socialism* (New York: Monthly Review Press, 1970), pp. 129–142.

education, public health, and housing. It also includes the training of Communist party cadre. Regional development plans involve the development of areas of specialization and enterprise within various regions.[3]

Finally, a set of financial plans controls government income and expenditures with the objective of regulating resource allocation between consumption and investment and regulating the flow of credit from the banking system. There is also control over the financial plans of government ministries, enterprises, and communes.

The lack of market-determined prices makes it difficult for any planned economy to achieve a rational allocation of resources among the competing ends of production and consumption and to accomplish the production of goods as efficiently as possible. Apparently, the Chinese planners have not experienced great success with their plans for a variety of reasons: political bias which has favored the overfulfillment of plans at the expense of balanced economic growth; lack of adequate statistical data upon which to base planning; and lack of a desirable input-output balance between sectors, which can be attributed to a lack of flexibility in factor supply.

Mechanics of Economic Planning

The development of the national economic plan is the function of a number of government agencies which operate under the aegis of the State Council and which are responsible for the collection of statistical data, the allocation of resources, the formulation of plans, the supervision of production, the distribution of domestic and export goods, and the provision of finance for planned production expenditures.

Principal Agencies. There are several important agencies responsible for various aspects of planning.

The Bureau of State Statistics is responsible for data gathering. It occupies a staff position directly under the State Council.

The State Planning Commission and the State Economic Commission are responsible for planning. The State Planning Commission was established in 1952 and was patterned after the *Gosplan* of the Soviet Union. In 1956 the functions of the State Planning Commission were divided when the State Economic Commission was formed. The State Planning Commission was assigned the responsibility for the development of long-term planning, and the State Economic Commission was given the responsibility for short-term economic planning and coordinating current economic activity. The State Planning Commission has the responsibility for integrating all the individual sector and partial plans into the framework of the long-term plan. Targets are established which are based on data furnished by the Bureau of State Statistics. The State Planning Commission is responsible for the supervision of resource allocation to the various segments of the plan, and the State Economic Commission has the same responsibility for the short-term, or annual plan.

[3] *Ibid.*, pp. 134–135.

There is also a State Capital Construction Commission, which is responsible for long-term investment projects, and a State Commission for Science and Technology, which is responsible for basic research and development.

A number of state agencies allocate resources to various segments of the economy, control production and distribution, and administer financial plans. Labor allocation is the responsibility of the Ministries of Labor and Education, domestic raw materials are allocated by the Bureau of Material Supply, and imports of raw materials and supplies are the responsibility of the Ministry of Foreign Trade. Production is the responsibility of individual ministries and departments within ministries. There has, however, been a shifting and regrouping of production ministries as the Chinese strive for administrative efficiency. In conformance with the goals of the plan, the production ministries must transmit output targets to all enterprises under their jurisdiction. Using the data provided by the production ministry responsible for its operation, an enterprise develops a plan which is submitted to the appropriate agency within the ministry for its approval. Although some adjustments of control data are permitted at the enterprise level, overall conformance to the goals of the national plan is required.[4]

Distribution. Distribution is the responsibility of various ministries and state trading companies. Domestic distribution is the responsibility of the Ministries of Food and Commerce. The Ministry of Food is responsible for the distribution of food staples, and the Ministry of Domestic Commerce is responsible for the distribution of other consumer goods. The Ministry of Foreign Trade has the responsibility for the distribution of exports and imports. State trading enterprises handle the actual distribution of domestic and foreign goods. Distribution between producer-goods enterprises is handled by a purchasing and sales section within each enterprise.

The financial aspects of economic planning are handled by several financial institutions, such as the People's Bank of China and the Ministry of Finance. These institutions are responsible for the financial transactions related to the physical production involved in planning. The People's Bank determines the amount of credit to be made available to the various economic sectors in conformance with planning objectives. There is a financial plan, as well as a physical input-output plan, which includes sources and uses of funds for the economy. The financial plan is the monetary counterpart of the input-output plan, and provides a monetary definition of the physical output targets. It can be subdivided into banking and fiscal arrangements whereby the People's Bank of China and other financial institutions, such as the Agricultural Bank, provide financing for the plans of the individual enterprises and communes, and the Ministry of Finance is responsible for the development of budgetary expenditures and revenue collection under the financial plan.[5]

---

[4] The national plan is the annual plan rather than the long-term plan.

[5] Indirect control can be exercised over production since most transactions are in terms of money flows through bank transfers. Financial control over an enterprise can be exercised by matching purchases and sales of goods against authorized payments and receipts.

Planning and Industry

Implementation of the plan at the individual enterprise level is done through a chain of command which is downward from the ministry level to the enterprise level. However, in an attempt to accomplish some degree of decentralization, the Chinese have removed the control of many enterprises from the central industrial ministries in Peking to those of provincial and municipal administrations. The plan is broken down on the basis of administrative, territorial units—provinces and municipalities—and for these units, plan indicators are provided for industrial production in terms of branches of industry. Each enterprise is given a production plan to follow which involves the volume of output to be achieved. Control figures covering targets of volume or other targets, such as the trial production of new products, are set by the administrative unit directly above the enterprise, which is usually at the municipal level. Norms for utilizing equipment, for expenditures of raw materials and labor, and for the allocation of resources among enterprises can be set at this level. However, ultimate control over planning objectives is maintained at the ministerial level in Peking.

Individual enterprises must conform to the objectives of the plan, although autonomy is permitted to some degree in that managers can participate in the plan as it affects their operations and can make decisions pertaining to its implementation at the enterprise level. Obviously the planners at the top of the planning hierarchy are not in a position to best determine what resources are needed or what production processes should be employed at the local level. This the managers can do, and they can exercise a degree of autonomous decision making pertaining to resource allocation, factor inputs, and quantities of outputs. They can also exercise control over the use of funds and over wage incentives, subject to external constraints imposed by the plan—constraints which also may be ideological in nature. The attempt to replace material wage incentives with nonmaterial ideological incentives is an example of an ideological constraint.

Public Finance

Taxes in China reflect the relationship of the state to state-owned enterprises. The function of taxes is to ensure control through the state budget over a part of the incomes of state enterprises as well as over the financial and economic activities. The state budget itself is very important to the national economy, for virtually all economic sectors are owned by the state, and a very large part of all investment is undertaken with funds that are allocated by the budget. In addition, such normal government expenditures as national defense and social services are financed through it.

The Ministry of Finance is responsible for developing the national budget and for devising taxation and other sources of state revenue. It is also responsible for the financial supervision of other ministries. Administratively, it is under the Staff Office for Finance and Trade, one of six staff offices that are under the State Council. These staff offices comprise the administrative structure of the national government and perform supervisory functions in connection with the various ministries under their jurisdiction. The Ministry of Finance has under its jurisdiction several bureaus, including the Bureau of the Budget, which is responsible for the compilation of budgetary data, and the Main Tax Bureau and the Agricultural Tax Bureau, which are responsible for the collection of taxes. When the budget is prepared by the Ministry of Finance, it must be submitted to the National People's Congress for formal approval. Then it is returned to the Ministry of Finance for execution.

Government Revenues. Total budgetary revenue is obtained from both tax and nontax sources. In the tax revenue category, industrial and commercial and agricultural taxes comprise the bulk of tax receipts. Taxes are collected at various levels of government by a system of collection agencies and are paid into the People's Bank of China. In the nontax revenue category, profits from state enterprises, which are considered to be state property anyway, comprise the most important revenue source. Depreciation reserves and other income from state enterprises also constitute an important source of nontax revenue. Nontax revenue has increased in importance as a source of income for the national budget.

In the early stages of the development of the communist economic system, taxes were used for both political and fiscal purposes. Chinese fiscal policy during the period 1949–1952 had as its objective the attainment of price stability through control of the fiscal system. During this period a national tax system was established and efforts were made to balance the budget as an anti-inflationary measure through control over expenditures and through increases in revenue. Taxes were levied on wages and salaries and on the consumption of various commodities. Taxes were also used to reduce the influence of the private sector of the economy by diverting resources from private to public use. Income taxes were levied upon industrial and commercial enterprises and upon interest on bank deposits. A progressive tax was levied on agriculture to redistribute income from the landowners to the peasants. Tax policy, then, was used to discriminate against private enterprise.

Salt Taxes and Customs Receipts. Salt taxes and customs receipts are a carry-over from pre-Communist times. The salt tax is administered separately from other revenue sources by the General Salt Tax Administration.[6] The tax is levied on the state owned salt companies. Some attempt has been made to discriminate among users of salt, with salt for agricultural use being taxed and salt for industrial use not being taxed. Customs duties are collected by the Customs Administration, which is under the jurisdiction of the Ministry of Foreign Trade. An apparent function of customs duties is to serve as leverage for foreign trade negotiations with countries within or outside of the Chinese sphere of influence.[7]

---

[6] The salt tax has apparently become a part of the general revenue sources of the provinces. This change took place in 1959. It is an easy tax to administer at any level of government.

[7] George N. Ecklund, *Financing the Chinese Government Budget: Mainland China, 1950–1959* (Chicago: Aldine Publishing Company, 1967), pp. 25 & 27.

Agricultural Taxes. Agricultural taxes are usually levied in kind rather than in monetary amounts. One reason for this type of levy is that a problem which has faced the Chinese government is not a lack of adequate revenue, but rather a lack of an adequate supply of marketable agricultural products.[8] The tax is levied on the most important crop in each region—usually a grain crop, such as wheat or rice. Payment is made in grain, or if the predominant crop is not grain, it is converted into grain measurements to determine the amount of tax payable. When the grain or other agricultural produce is transferred by the collection agencies to the state trading companies for general sale, the amount is converted into cash and entered into the national budget as such.[9] In addition to the agricultural tax on grain and other commodities, a pastoral tax, which takes the form of a capital levy, is levied on livestock. There are also a number of minor taxes levied by local units of government on the sales of various types of agricultural produce.

Receipts from State Enterprises. The most important source of revenue for the national budget comes from a nontax source—receipts from state enterprises. A certain percentage of profits has to be remitted to the national government by each enterprise. Enterprises are also allowed to retain a certain percentage of profits as retained earnings to be used for working capital and capital investments. Profits, as defined previously, usually are the difference between the proceeds that each enterprise obtains by selling its products at state regulated prices and production costs and tax payments. Since the Chinese attach no significance to the capitalistic viewpoints on profits and their relationship to invested capital, the concept can be considered more in terms of a residual which belongs to the state after each enterprise has fulfilled the objectives set forth in national planning.

An example of how profits are remitted by state enterprises is the electric power industry. In practice, part of net operating revenues, which are all profits as far as the Chinese are concerned, is returned to the government, and part is retained in the electric power industry. That part which is remitted to the government is used to help finance expenses of investment in the electric power industry by the government, and that part which is retained is used to finance working capital, capital repair, construction of worker housing, and bonuses for managers. In 1956 total operating revenue in the electric power industry amounted to 930 million yuan ($378.05 million). Operating expenses—fuel, labor, and other costs—amounted to 320 million yuan ($130.08 million); depreciation amounted to 130 million yuan ($52.84 million); and taxes amounted to 50 million yuan ($20.32 million). Net operating revenue (profit) amounted to 430 million yuan ($174.80 million), of which 350 million yuan were returned to the government and 80 million were retained by the industry.[10]

---

[8] Jan Deleyne, *The Chinese Economy* (New York: Harper, 1973), p. 68.
[9] Ecklund, *op. cit.*, p. 57.
[10] John Ashton, "Development of Electric Energy Resources in Communist China," *An Economic Profile of Communist China*, Vol. 1 (Washington: Joint Economic Committee, 90th Congress of the United States, 1st Session, 1967), pp. 314 and 315.

Depreciation Reserves. A second important source of budgetary revenue is depreciation reserves for the amortization of fixed assets. Depreciation is charged only on the amount of fixed assets actually used in the production process. The Chinese feel that since capital is provided by the state to individual enterprises to be used, the depreciation reserve that is set aside to compensate for the wear of capital rightly belongs to the state. In the example of the electric power industry, the depreciation sum of 130 million yuan ($52.85 million) would also be remitted to the state.

The Turnover Tax. This form of revenue, which is common to all socialist countries, represents the difference between the producers' and the retail price, excluding the wholesale and retail margins for trading enterprises. These taxes apply mostly to consumer goods and some consumer services. The government imposes a turnover tax to separate retail prices from producer prices, and so is in fact redistributing nominal money incomes. Some consumer goods, such as foodstuffs directly sold by peasants to consumers, are free from turnover taxes. Whatever the basis of fixing this tax, the effective rates are highly differentiated. In a sense, the size of the turnover tax does not determine the level of retail prices—on the contrary, the magnitude of these taxes depends upon the predetermined price level.

Government Expenditures. The items of expenditure in the Chinese state budget are arranged according to their role in the creation of national income. More than one half of total expenditures is devoted to the financing of material production. Expenditures under this category would include allocations to state enterprises for capital investment and for working capital. Capital goods and construction industries are the major recipients of budget funds for investment purposes. Appropriations from the state budget are also used to finance the construction of transportation facilities, investment in state farms and housing construction. The provision of finance for stocks and reserves of materials and of subsidies to loss-incurring enterprises is also classified as productive expenditure. The financing of material production comes largely from two revenue items, deductions from profits of state enterprises and depreciation reserves. This means that although state enterprises remit most of their profits, they are returned in the form of capital investment expenditures.

Social Security benefits consist of old age and invalidity pensions, sickness and maternity benefits, and work injury compensation. The benefits are administered by the Ministry of Labor and are paid by employers. Coverage includes workers in factories, mines, and transportation, communication, construction, and public service. The old age pension amounts to 50 to 70 percent of average earnings for those who are 55 and older, and the invalidity grant amounts to 50 percent of average earnings. There is also a funeral grant, which amounts to one month's earnings, and a survivor's grant, which is a lump-sum payment that varies according to the years of employment.[11]

---

[11] U.S. Department of Health, Education, and Welfare, *Social Security Programs Throughout the World* (Washington: Social Security Administration, Office of Research and Statistics, 1972), pp. 52 and 53.

Sickness and maternity benefits also are provided by employers. Sickness benefits provide from 70 to 100 percent of earnings based on the length of employment. Maternity benefits provide 100 percent of earnings payable for up to 56 days before and after confinement. There is also a birth grant which is a lump sum equal to five feet of cloth. Medical benefits are also available for all workers and their dependents, but workers share certain costs, including 50 percent of ordinary medicines.

There has been a decentralization of the Chinese fiscal system, with more jurisdiction and control over revenue sources being given to provincial and municipal governments. The salt tax and various agricultural taxes were placed under control of local governments. Nevertheless, the national budget remains an all important control mechanism which transfers profits and taxes between state enterprises.

Banking

The banking system in Communist China represents a financial control mechanism for carrying out economic planning. All state enterprises and cooperatives have accounts with the banks, and control can be exercised since most transactions are in terms of money through bank transfers. Purchases and sales of goods by each enterprise can be matched against authorized payments and receipts. Government control over income and expenditures is also expedited through the credit and cash plans of the banking system as well as through the national budget.

The People's Bank of China. The People's Bank of China is the major banking institution and was formed in 1959 as the central bank of the country. It is under the administrational jurisdiction of the Staff Office for Finance and Trade and is responsible for the supervision of the financial transactions which correspond to the physical production plans. It is also an important control device which exercises a very important influence on the national economy. All state enterprises have accounts in branch banks under its direct jurisdiction. In this way, the People's Bank can exercise control because all expenditures and transfers made by the enterprises come under its scrutiny.

The People's Bank, as the central bank of China, has the following functions:

1. It is responsible for the issuance of Chinese currency.
2. It is responsible for the financing of credit to state enterprises. Funds to support credit expansion are obtained from the national budget, from retained profits, and from customer deposits.
3. It is responsible for the supervision of expenditures of state enterprises to see that they conform with national planning objectives.
4. It is responsible for the development of the Credit Plan and the Cash Plan, which are financial counterparts of the physical economic plans.

The Credit Plan. The Credit Plan involves the amount of short- and medium-term credit which is to be given to all state enterprises and agricultural communes by the People's Bank. The plan involves a balance sheet statement showing sources of funds and uses of funds. Sources of funds emanate primarily from one source—appropriations from the national budget which are obtained primarily from the earnings of state enterprises. Other sources of funds are from increases in savings deposits and currency in circulation and decreases in government deposits and deposit balances of communes. Uses of funds include increases in loans to industry, commercial organizations, and agricultural communes and cooperatives.[12] The statement should balance, and funds can be allocated only for purposes that conform to the national plan.

The Cash Plan. The Cash Plan is designed to maintain control over currency circulation, with the People's Bank responsible for the issuance of currency and the receipt of cash from state enterprises, communes, and government administrative units at all levels. This means that the People's Bank has control over the amount of money in circulation because it is both a starting point and a finishing point in the flow of currency throughout the system.

The Cash Plan consists of a set of cash inflows and cash outflows essentially in the form of a balance statement. Cash inflows include such items as retail sales receipts, savings deposit receipts, repayment of agricultural loans, deposits of communes, and public utility receipts. The total represents an injection of currency into circulation. Cash outflows represent a net withdrawal of currency and consist of wage payments by state enterprises and communes, government purchases of industrial and agricultural products, government administrative expenses, payments by the state to the individuals, management expenditures of state enterprises, new loans to agriculture, and withdrawals of savings deposits.[13]

The Credit and Cash Plans have to be coordinated with the physical production plans. A function of these financial plans is to provide financing for expenditures required by the production plans. This means that the People's Bank can supervise the operations of state enterprises to enforce conformance with production plans since purchases and sales of goods can be matched against authorized payments and receipts.

Other Financial Institutions. There are several specialized financial agencies, such as the Agricultural Bank, which also provide money to finance the transactions of enterprises in a specialized area of production. These specialized financial institutions, like the People's Bank, do not allocate funds independently of national planning objectives and thus have no influence on resource allocation as they would in a market economy.

The Agricultural Bank has as its functions the provision of agricultural loans and control over the mobilization of rural savings to provide a source of credit to the rural credit cooperatives which are responsible for the provision of credit to communes and to individual members of communes. Loans are

---

[12] S. C. Tsiang, "Money and Banking in Communist China," *An Economic Profile of Mainland China,* Vol. I (Washington: Joint Economic Committee, 90th Congress of the United States, 1st Session, 1967), pp. 332–334.

[13] *Ibid.,* pp. 335–337.

also made by the rural credit cooperatives to individuals for sideline undertakings involving private plots of land. The Agricultural Bank is under the jurisdiction of the State Council and is operated independently of the People's Bank. It has provincial branches and also branches which operate at the municipal, or *hsien,* level of administration.[14]

There are also several banks which are under the jurisdiction of the Ministry of Finance. One bank, the People's Construction Bank, is responsible for providing investment funds to enterprises. These funds are obtained from the national budget and do not have to be repaid. It is also responsible for providing short-term loans to enterprises for capital construction projects. Another bank, the Bank of Communications, is responsible for the distribution of nonrepayable funds from the national budget to state enterprises.

Interest has no significant role in resource allocation in the Chinese economic system. However, interest rates are charged on all loans by the banks to industrial enterprises, communes, and individuals, but the rates are far below the rates that would prevail under a system of free markets. Grants provided by the People's Bank to enterprises for capital investment are interest-free, but interest is charged on working capital loans to enterprises. However, interest charges are mostly paid by the state through a reduction in the profit tax liability.[15]

Organization of Industry

Although agriculture, providing the raw material for industry and food for a growing population, remains the foundation of the Chinese economy, any meaningful claim to a great power status must be based on the development of industry. The process of industrialization has been difficult, and the Chinese people have paid a price in terms of resources sacrificed to achieve this end. At the present the Chinese have a long way to go before they can match the industrial potential of the Soviet Union or any of the major Western industrial nations. Even within their own sphere of influence, the Chinese do not rival the industrial base of Japan, which today remains the only industrialized nation in Asia.

The Communist Take-Over of Industry. The Communists used similar policies for industry and agriculture when they assumed control in that a gradual approach was used to convert each from private enterprise to communism. Their first objective was to rehabilitate the economy which had been devastated by the civil war. By degrees private enterprise was eliminated. Some private industries were taken over by the Communists at the beginning, and the remainder were to be taken over in stages, with each stage proceeding toward the eventual state control over all enterprise. State trading companies were formed in all of the larger cities and towns. They were given a virtual

---

[14] Audrey Donnithorne, *China's Economic System* (New York: Praeger, 1967), pp. 412–414.

[15] Dwight Perkins, *Market Control and Planning in Communist China* (Cambridge: Harvard University Press, 1966), p. 136.

monopoly over wholesale trade and could set prices paid to private producers. Their orders and contracts were vital to the survival of private enterprise and thereby gave the Communists some control over output. Through their control of credit and taxation, the Communists were also able to discriminate against private enterprise industries.

By the beginning of the First Five-Year Plan in 1953, the Communists had assumed control over approximately 50 percent of industry, accounting for 60 percent of industrial output. This control had been secured in two ways, which are discussed below.

The "Five-Anti" Campaign. Through virulent attacks on private enterprise in the *five-anti* campaign of 1951–1952, which had as its objective the undermining of the position of private enterprise, the government was able to gain some control.[16] The "five-antis" were five evils—tax evasion, bribery, fraud against the government, theft of state properties, and leakage of state economic secrets—which presumably were being committed by private enterprise against the Chinese people. Fines and capital levies were imposed upon enterprises found guilty of perpetrating the evils, and employees were encouraged to denounce their employers to the state. It was made clear in this campaign that private enterprise eventually would be integrated into the socialist economy.[17]

Resource Allocation and Product Distribution. Through government control of resource allocation and distribution of final products, the government was able to exercise a strong influence over private enterprise. It controlled the railroads and most of the shipping facilities and could set prices in terms of distribution costs. It promulgated regulations which set forth the conditions under which private enterprises could operate. The government had control over the supply of bank credit, and private firms had no choice but to accede to terms. Through purchases and orders, the government made business firms dependent on it as their major customer. It also required the submission of production and sales plans for approval and exercised control over the distribution of earnings. Financial statements also had to be submitted to the government.

Achievement of Control. Harassment of private enterprise continued until 1955, and by degrees the private sector grew smaller. In that year the trend toward the socialization of all industry was accelerated when Mao Tse-tung called for the formation of joint state-private operation of industry. This coincided with the speed-up in the collectivization of agriculture. The Communists

---

[16] The "five-anti" campaign was also used to raise funds to support budgetary expenditures and to fight inflation. It had both economic and political objectives in that it provided new sources of funds as well as stirred up the populace against the capitalists.

[17] Government civil servants also came under attack in the "three-anti" campaign which was directed against corruption, waste, and bureaucratism. The "three-anti," like the "five-anti," was also designed to undermine or destroy any resistance to further change toward a socialist economy by certain classes in Chinese society. The civil servants were blamed for having yielded to middle class temptations.

felt the position of the private sector had been weakened to the extent that no resistance to the transformation to socialization would be encountered. They also felt that forced-draft industrialization was necessary to make China a world power and that private enterprise had to be eliminated to facilitate planning and control over the entire economy.

The elimination of private enterprise was rapid. By the end of 1955, most private firms were absorbed into state-private enterprises, and the owners were compensated in terms of interest based on their share of property taken over by the state. By the end of 1956, private enterprise, for all practical purposes, ceased to exist except on an individual basis. Small traders and peddlers were allowed to function, but even this group was eventually to come under state control.

With the transformation of private enterprise into state owned enterprise, the communist control over the economy was complete. The basic economic form industry was to take was patterned on the Soviet system, since the Chinese had no other system to emulate. Fortunately for the Chinese, the Russians were able to provide methods and technicians during the First Five-Year Plan to facilitate the organization of industry along Soviet lines. Specific goals were set for each industry in terms of its importance to the economy. To produce goods and services for the country's needs, some sort of organizational structure for the command of production had to exist. This led to the creation of administrative domains from the highest to the lowest levels of authority with power to make long-term decisions for the country as a whole and daily decisions by which an enterprise could be run effectively. A centralized control was developed and then later relaxed to provide for some decentralization in decision making.

Government Control of Industry. As has been mentioned, a number of ministries have been created as both departments of government and of economic activity. These ministries are in charge of industrial production for a whole group of related industries or a single industry. They do not produce anything but are merely control groups or administrative agencies. Within the ministries are a number of subdepartments or control groups that are responsible for the activities of a single industry, for data collection, for implementation of planning, for supervision of accounting methods, and for the development of new production facilities.

Industrial Chain of Command. The designation of authority is vertical. Between the ministries at the top and the enterprises at the bottom there is, as a matter of necessity, a chain of command which is responsible for the execution of national plans. Each ministry and subdepartment within it has a counterpart at the provincial and municipal levels. The span of control is direct in that the branch offices are responsible only to the ministry and, in turn, direct the units of production under their jurisdiction. This means that a large, intermediate, bureaucratic structure has been erected between the ministries and the local enterprises. Some degree of decentralization exists in that provincial and municipal administrative units have control over a number of industries, such as light industry and nonstrategic industrial enterprises, and they also have some control over resource allocation among enterprises. Managers of enterprises are permitted flexibility in terms of product mix planning.

There is another link in the chain of command between ministries and enterprises in the form of an industrial corporation which is either under the jurisdiction of municipal industrial branch offices or directly under the national ministries. The industrial corporation is responsible for the operation of a number of enterprises producing a homogeneous product.[18]

Some enterprises are directly under municipal authority, particularly if they produce a product that is used primarily in the local area. Other enterprises are directly under the national ministries. This occurs when an enterprise is producing a product which is of national importance or which is used for national defense purposes. Enterprises that use a new production process or that are established with foreign support and assistance are also under national ministerial control.

Ministerial relations with most enterprises, however, are indirect and are confined to the following functions:

1. Disseminating the details of the national plan as it would affect individual enterprises.
2. Allocating investment funds.
3. Planning and designing important capital investment projects.
4. Designing and developing important new products.
5. Training high level personnel for the enterprises.[19]

Industry-Party Relationship. A dual relationship exists in the organization of Chinese industry in that parallel Communist party committees exist at all levels of industry. Party committees exist at the provincial and municipal branch levels of the various industrial ministries and also at the local enterprise level. The main purpose for this dual role between professional managers and bureaucrats and the party committees is the coordination of national objectives. This is an attempt by the party to insure that enterprises and regional administrative offices do not stray from policy goals.

In setting prices, one element used by the state is productive costs, based on the average cost per product for enterprises in a particular industry. Another element is average profit for each product for these enterprises. Prices then should cover average costs plus an average profit for all enterprises within an industry. Taxes and the costs of distribution could also be added to give a final price which an enterprise can set for its product. Prices, then, should cover costs of production, which include labor, raw materials, and depreciation; profits, which can be expressed as a rate of return over cost; and taxes, such as the turnover tax.

There are different sets of prices which cover the production and consumption of commodities. There are procurement prices which cover the

---

[18] Barry M. Richman, *Industrial Society in Communist China* (Cambridge: Harvard University Press, 1969), pp. 62–68.
[19] *Ibid.*

acquisition of agricultural products, and ex-factory prices for industrial commodities, wholesale prices which involve the intermediate transfer of commodities from the production to the retail level, and retail prices which are charged to the ultimate consumer. There are also prices, called allocation prices, which determine the relationship of exchange between various enterprises producing different commodities.[20] These prices are determined in different ways. For example, ex-factory prices are determined by using average cost of production, taxes, and a margin for profits, and wholesale prices are comprised of ex-factory prices and the expenses and profits of wholesaling. Allocation prices of industrial commodities include ex-factory prices and various distribution expenses.[21]

In a country as large as China with a poor transportation system and a diverse industrial base, diffusion of responsibility for price determination is necessary. Decentralization has occurred in the setting of prices as well as in the control of industry. Local price variations exist and they are set by provincial and municipal governments. Apparently a dichotomy of responsibility exists between the national governments and local governments. For example, in 1965 it was reported that price changes were permitted for 76 kinds of fertilizers, agricultural insecticides, and agricultural machinery. Of this number, the prices of five items were controlled by the central government and the remainder were controlled by the provincial governments. The actual mechanics of price determination are the responsibility of the various ministries or bureaus, depending on the level of government, that maintain control over a particular industry.

Although the prices of most commodities are set by state agencies, managers of enterprises have some control over the setting of prices under certain conditions. For example, price changes can be proposed for products which are not standardized and for changes in design and product specification. Managers can also establish cost plus prices for minor subcontracting services—with the prices often providing for a profit margin of 15 to 20 percent to encourage product innovation.[22] In some cases, formal approval from a state agency is necessary for price setting; in other cases, approval is not needed.

Organization of Agriculture

Agriculture, since time immemorial, has been the foundation of the Chinese economy. It provides a living for at least 80 percent of the population and furnishes the raw material base necessary for the performance of the planned economy. Unfortunately for the Chinese, most of the land area is not conducive to the production of agricultural products. Much of China is mountainous and dry, and unfavorable soil and climatic conditions inhibit agricultural development in other areas of the country. In addition, there is a very large ratio of

[20] Wheelright and McFarlane, *The Chinese Road to Socialism* (New York: Monthly Review Press, 1970), pp. 81–86.

[21] *Ibid.*, p. 440.

[22] Richman, *op. cit.*, p. 70.

population to cultivable land, which reduces efficiency in production. This has meant that the country has had to operate at a margin which is very close to a minimum subsistence level. It has also meant that the Communists have had to face the problem of a growing population and a relatively small and technically backward agricultural base while at the same time trying to build up an adequate industrial base in order to become a major world power.

The Collectivization of Agriculture. As mentioned in the preceding chapter, agriculture went through several distinct phases of collectivization since the Communists came to power in 1949. At that time the peasant farms were privately owned either by landlords or by peasant owners. To win the support of the masses of the peasants, landless or otherwise, the Communists redistributed millions of acres of land and eliminated landlords as a class. Once the land was redistributed, peasants were allowed to operate the land as private owners. However, the peasants were not long left undisturbed. The Communists were merely marking time until economic control had been established over the other sectors of the economy.

Producers' Cooperatives. Agricultural producers' cooperatives were established in 1955. Farmers were organized into these cooperatives and had to pool their lands for cultivation. The land, however, was still held privately, and rent was paid by the cooperatives for its use. The cooperatives were run by central committees and were divided into production teams. The product was distributed by the cooperatives and the peasants compensated on the basis of labor contributed. Although land, animals, and implements, for the most part, were still privately owned, there was the continued trend toward the centralization of farm management.

Collective Farms. The next stage in the socialization of agriculture occurred in 1956. The agricultural producers' cooperatives, which had retained many of the elements of private property ownership, were consolidated into collective farms. On these collective farms the peasants were supposed to pool their land, animals, and livestock. Land now was no longer to be privately owned; it was to be collective property. However, the peasants were permitted to own small plots of land to be used for their own purposes.[23] They could produce and sell products from these plots. Similarly, domestic livestock and small farm implements were left in private hands. The peasants were formed into brigades, with brigade leaders given the responsibility for assigning workers their tasks. Income depended directly upon the crops that were produced, and workers were compensated on the basis of labor days contributed.[24]

---

[23] This plot of land was limited to an area which could not exceed 5 percent of the average per capita arable land on the collective farm. Its use was designed to make the collectivization process more palatable to the peasants.

[24] The *labor day* is a work unit which is based upon such factors as skill and physical exertion. Points are awarded for each day's work with premiums and deductions being given for overfulfillment and underfulfillment. Each member of the collective farm was rewarded on the basis of the number of points acquired relative to a norm or average that was established for each task.

The compensation was net of compulsory deliveries to the government of a certain percentage of the crop produced and deductions of taxes paid to the government. The collective farms were also required to set aside reserves for contingencies.

Communes. In 1958 the communes replaced the collective farms. A commune was designed as a multi-purpose unit which would perform administrative as well as economic functions. The *hsiang,* or local government administrative unit, was merged with the commune. The commune was responsible for both agriculture and industrial production.[25] It was considerably larger than the collective farm in terms of area and households. The typical commune contained around 24,000 people. The transition to the commune was rapid. The decision to form communes was announced in August 1958, and by the end of the year, some 750,000 collective farms representing virtually all of the peasant households had been formed into 26,578 communes.[26] All vestiges of private property ownership were removed. The peasants were organized into production brigades and teams.[27] The latter was the basic work unit and was given responsibility for the use of labor, land, animals, tools, and equipment. Living was communal. The peasants ate in mess halls, and the distribution of food was based in part on the needs of individuals and in part on work performed. Workers had to perform tasks that were by no means limited to agriculture, such as producing steel and mining coal.

The demise of the Great Leap Forward caused a shift in agricultural policies with respect to the communes. By 1962 several changes had been made. (1) The production team was given full rights of use of labor, land, and equipment, and it became the basic farm accounting unit.

(2) There was decentralization of the agricultural planning units in that the communes were divested of much of their authority, and the responsibility for production was shifted to production brigades and teams.

(3) Private plots of land were restored to the peasants, and the free market was permitted in which peasants were free to sell their produce for income. Pigs, which were in short supply as a result of Great Leap mismanagement, were returned to private ownership, and peasants were provided with incentives to raise pigs for sale to the government.

(4) Increased priority was given to the development of agriculture. During the First Five-Year Plan and the Great Leap Forward, priority had been given to the development of industry and the need to fulfill such grandiose objectives as overtaking the United Kingdom in steel production in ten years. When it became apparent that this was not likely to happen and

[25] The collective farm was only an agricultural unit.

[26] Marion R. Larsen, "China's Agriculture Under Communism," *An Economic Profile of Mainland China,* Vol. 1 (Washington: Joint Economic Committee, 90th Congress of the United States, 1st Session, 1967), p. 218.

[27] The basic agricultural units were the large production brigades which consisted of around 250 households and which were responsible for the coordination of work effort; the production brigade, which consisted of 30 to 40 households; and the production team of 6 to 20 households, which was the basic work unit.

chaos was occurring in the agricultural sector, it was necessary to change objectives. Agricultural policy focused on increasing inputs of fertilizer, equipment, and technology and outputs of grain, basic foodstuffs, and cotton.

Communes, Production Brigades, and Production Teams. Although divested of much of its administrative authority, the commune still exists to perform certain functions which are little related to agricultural production. It operates small industries and handicrafts within its jurisdiction and plays an important role in rural trading. It also directs disaster relief and emergency relief work involving flood control. The popular militia is also supported by the commune. However, it may well be that the eclipse and emasculation of the commune is temporary, particularly with the ideological ferment that has taken place in China. Certainly, the past 15 years of Chinese agricultural development have witnessed considerable experimentation and shifting of emphasis with respect to the appropriate organization of agriculture.

There has been a shifting of control over production downward from the communes to production brigades and teams, with the brigade consisting of usually several villages and the team consisting of one village or 20 or 30 households. The production brigade owns the land, but the important social unit is the production team. Although it has to contribute a certain percentage of its product to the brigade, it can devote a considerable part of its time to the raising of supplemental products which it is able to sell for income in the free market. The production brigade has the responsibility for the distribution of farm produce, the payment of wages, and the calculation of profits and losses. It is also responsible for banking and statistical data gathering.

Since 1961, then, the policy of the Chinese government has been to accord top priority to agriculture, with organization focused on the small, basic level of management—the production brigade and team. A private sector coexists with the public sector, although in time it may be eliminated.

State Farms. State farms are another type of agricultural organization that exists in China. All of the land, building, machinery, and productive equipment in general is owned by the government, and the farms are managed by government-appointed directors. The employees of the state farms are wage earners who have no more direct interest in the farms than industrial workers have in their factories, and they have no claim on the products of the state farms. The state farms typically specialize in the production of a single commodity, and they are mechanized to a much greater degree than the communes. In 1964, although state farms occupied less than 5 percent of the total cultivated area of China, they had 32 percent of the tractors, 50 percent of the mechanized farm tools, 82.6 percent of the combines, and 68 percent of the motor trucks.[28] Workers on the state farms are usually paid on a standard wage basis plus piece rates for exceeding a norm and are permitted to own small numbers of domestic animals, but no draft animals.

[28] Larsen, *op. cit.*, p. 223.

The state farm can be viewed as a large agricultural experimental station. Its purpose is to increase agricultural production by using modern, efficient methods and to serve as a modern agricultural center to give examples to other agricultural units throughout the country. Some state farms have been set up in remote areas to assist in land reclamation and development in an attempt to enlarge the land area under cultivation. It is estimated that in 1964 there were 6,400 state farms in operation in China.[29]

Heavy farm machinery, such as tractors, trucks, harvesters, and combines, are often owned by separate, government-controlled agencies—the machine tractor stations. This arrangement also existed in the Soviet Union at one time. The state farms utilize the machine tractor stations and make payment in kind or in cash.

Incentives and Income Distribution

It is apparent that the Chinese do not intend to rely entirely on wage differentials to motivate people, but, to the contrary, they intend to reduce the importance of nonmaterial incentives. Under the Proletarian Cultural Revolution there was an attempt to eliminate class distinctions based on wage differentials and occupational status. Educators were required to work side by side with peasants, and managers were required to spend at least part of their time working alongside the workers on the production line. The Chinese perhaps feel that an individual would not mind being poor or moderately poor if there were no prosperous persons with whom he could compare himself unfavorably. They obviously feel that small differences in income will prove adequate to provide incentives for all. However, only time and experience will prove whether they are right or wrong.

Incentives in China can be divided into material and nonmaterial incentives. The former relies on some form of income payment—wages, bonuses, and so forth—to motivate people to work; the latter relies on some form of external approval—prestige, power, public honors, and acclaim—to provide the motivation. Exceptionally diligent workers are given medals, and their names and accomplishments are mentioned over the radio and television and in the newspapers. The stimulus to support this form of motivation is the belief that a new ideology can be implemented in China—an ideology based on the creation of a proletarian society for the nation.

Material Incentives. Economic incentives involving differentials in income are used in China. However, there has been an oscillation in the use of material incentives over time. During the First Five-Year Plan the Russians introduced a wage system which tied rewards to performance. Income differentials existed between the engineers and technicians and the workers in the factories. During the Great Leap Forward, income incentives were criticized as being an example of right-wing communist revisionism, and income differentials were reduced.

[29] *Ibid.*, p. 221.

After the Great Leap Forward, there was a reversion to the type of incentives that existed during the First Five-Year Plan. Reliance was placed on piece rates to motivate increased productivity on the part of the workers. The enthusiasm engendered by the Great Leap Forward had palled by 1960, and performance on the part of workers and farmers declined, so material incentives linked to performance were utilized more and more. This continued until 1966 when the Proletarian Cultural Revolution occurred, and then material incentives were denounced as being capitalistic. Production, as a matter of economic policy, was to be achieved through reliance upon ideological motivation. It is apparent that the Chinese Communists have used economic incentives to accomplish specific economic policy goals in industry and agriculture; when these goals were accomplished, then ideology replaced material incentives in importance.

Types of Wage Payments. The Cultural Revolution had an impact on the form of wage payments to industrial workers. Piece rates, patterned after the Russian system, were abandoned during the Cultural Revolution, and remuneration was calculated monthly on the basis of the work norms per unit of time. Premium payments, which are awarded over and above wages, were also discontinued during the Cultural Revolution. Both piece-rates and premium payments contributed to the feeling expressed by Mao that the motivation of workers had shifted from devotion to the revolution to material considerations. The Maoist ideology calls for the suppression of material incentives at some point in time. It plans to rely solely on the workers social conscience to raise productivity. Material incentives, particularly those that encourage competition, and the profit motive were censured during the Revolution.

For both production and white collar workers, there are eight wage classifications. Classes 1 and 2 are for unskilled and part-time workers; classes 3 and 4 are for semiskilled workers; class 5 is for skilled workers who have passed a special examination, but who have no work experience; classes 6 and 7 are for skilled workers with work experience; and class 8 is for workers with extensive specialized knowledge.[30] Thus, Chinese workers are paid according to variations in skill from unskilled to highly skilled workers. There are also wage scales within classes. Wage scales by classes are also differentiated by industrial branch in line with the Chinese regime's priorities for differential industrial development. The highest paid workers are in the extractive industries, e.g., coal miners, and the lowest paid workers are usually in the consumer goods industries. For example, in 1970 the average monthly wage for coal miners was 80 yuan ($34.40) and the average monthly wage for textile workers was 55 yuan ($23.79).[31]

The wage differential between the highest and lowest wage categories is generally lower in China than in other socialist countries. As would be expected, this would be in conformance to Mao's desire to create an egalitarian

---

[30] Chien-jen Chen, *Die Lohnstrukture in der Volksrepublik China* (Berne: Swiss Eastern Institute, 1972), pp. 17–25.

[31] The yuan is worth approximately $0.43.

society. In the steel industry the average monthly rate for unskilled workers in 1970 was 34.5 yuan ($14.84) and the average monthly wage for skilled workers in the eighth, or highest, wage classification was 110.4 yuan ($47.47) —a ratio of 3.2 to 1.[32] There is a lower wage differential in the chemical industry, with the average monthly wage for unskilled workers amounting to 33.5 yuan ($14.41) and the average monthly wage of workers in the highest skill category amounting to 100.5 yuan ($43.22). These wage rates do not reflect the inclusion of bonuses or premiums for performance, which were supposed to have been done away with during the Cultural Revolution.

Managers and members of the scientific and technical intelligentsia are subject to different wage criteria. The standard wage payment depends on work experience, education, party loyalty, and other factors. The power and perquisites of being a manager have generally been emasculated over time by the belief on the part of Mao that no class difference should exist between managers and workers, or intellectuals and peasants. In some cases, managers earn less than highly skilled factory workers. Management responsibility is often limited in nature in that the general policy of an enterprise is laid down by the factory party committee. During the Cultural Revolution the party committee was frequently replaced by a revolutionary committee, which had as its objective replacing material incentives by ideological ones. However, there are indications that after the demise of the Cultural Revolution there has been a reversion back to greater reliance on material incentives and rewards for managerial performance.

Nonmaterial Incentives. Individual nonmaterial incentives also stress altruistic motivation. There is use of honors and symbols, such as titles, medals, and certificates of merit, to inspire greater effort on the part of the individual. With these honors go such perquisites as extra paid vacations, opportunities for advancement, and the chance to join the Communist party. There is also a technique called the *five good workers* where workers are selected for an award if they perform well on their job, improve their skills through study, help other workers with their jobs, engage in political study, and help other workers to accomplish ideological self-improvement. Medals and titles are given to those who merit the "five good workers" award. This is supposed to encourage other workers to emulate the accomplishments of the "good workers." In fact, the key motivating force is emulation—the desire to emulate some standard or individual and thus gain recognition and esteem by one's peer group. Special titles, such as *labor hero*, are given to workers who turn in performances in the Stakhanovite pattern—performances that are not easily duplicated and are to serve as an inspirational example to other workers.[33] Exceptional performances may win workers the opportunity to travel to Peking and perhaps meet Mao Tse-tung.

[32] Chen, *op. cit.*, p. 67 and p. 75.
[33] The Russian coal miner, Alexei Stakhanov, produced 102 tons of coal in six hours, well over the standard quota set for coal miners. As a result, he was lionized by the Soviet press, and countless honors were bestowed upon him. Other workers were urged to emulate his accomplishments, hence the Stakhanovite movement.

If little or no material distinction is to be made between either mental and physical labor or between managerial and worker responsibilities, can it be assumed that individuals will be motivated to go into those areas that require the most training or responsibility? In other words, why would a person train to be an engineer or doctor if the status and material benefits of either profession would be little or no greater than those attained by the worker in the factory or the peasant on the farm? Is not self-interest as expressed in terms of material gain and status a powerful motive? The Chinese, of course, would argue that material gain and status are symbols of decadent United States capitalism and Russian revisionism. Ideological motivation can make a person want to become a doctor, engineer, worker, or farmer. After all, in a society uncorrupted by Western influence, a person will want to choose an occupation on the basis of what personal contribution can be made to society and the state.

Income Distribution and Consumer Sovereignty. Land, labor, and capital are the three factors of production, and rent, wages, and interest are payments for their use. Of these payments, only wages have any real significance in China. The role of rent and interest in resource allocation is minor. As mentioned previously, interest is charged on certain types of loans by the banks. Interest is also paid by the state to former capitalists for properties which were expropriated. Rent is paid for housing, but like interest, is set at rates which are too low to perform any allocative function pertaining to housing and capital. Property income is nonexistent, for the land of the country is owned by the state and there is no separate class of people who, as landowners, receive rent as private income.

Wages, then, are left as the major factor payment, and these wages are determined by government action rather than by the free play of market forces. Wages are determined, in conformance with planning objectives, by the Ministry of Labor and by other ministries responsible for a particular area of production. That is, the economic plan specifies a certain total sum or fund which is to be used for wage payments in a given year and indicates how this fund is to be allocated among the different industries and enterprises in the country. Each industry and each enterprise thus knows in advance how much money it may pay out in wages during each year. This amount governs the number of workers an enterprise can hire and the wages it can pay.

Wages in the Chinese and Russian economic system have performed similar functions. They have constituted a device for evoking among the various occupations and industries of each country the distribution of labor which is appropriate for the carrying out of the economic plans. They have also provided a reward for accomplishment in production and an incentive to continued productive activity.

The Chinese have generally followed a low wage policy to make possible rapid capital accumulation. In general, wages have been set at a rate which has been considerably less than labor productivity. Another objective of the low wage policy has been to minimize inflationary pressures in the consumer goods market by keeping demand in urban areas in balance with the limited supply of consumer goods.[34] This has been done through control over the urban wage bill rather than through the use of general fiscal and monetary controls. The wage bill, which includes all wages, bonuses and subsidies which an enterprise can pay, is set by the national planning authorities.

In a capitalistic market economy, consumer preference, which is expressed through the price mechanism, determines what is to be produced, at what quality, and in what quantities. In Communist China, consumer preference or sovereignty does not exist in the sense that the consumer is able to influence, by his spending actions, the allocation of resources among various types of consumer goods. The production of consumer goods and services is determined by the state. However, consumers have freedom to choose among the various goods and services that are produced. In the absence of a market economy, it is difficult to relate consumer wants to what is being produced by the state. This problem is circumvented in part by having retail outlets and other commercial organs report to the planners the needs and requirements of the consumers. It is reported that the Chinese have considered the use of consumer surveys to find out what consumers really need.[35]

Freedom of choice does not necessarily redound to the advantage of all Chinese consumers. Even though a person may have the wherewithal to purchase a consumer good, such as an automobile, he may find that it is available only to the party elite. With disparities in income existing, although reduced during the Cultural Revolution, a rationing function is performed in that various desirable goods go to those who can afford to pay for them. With wages kept low as a matter of public policy, many consumers cannot afford most of the goods that are being produced.

AN APPRAISAL OF THE CHINESE ECONOMY

A considerable degree of ambivalence concerning political and economic goals currently exists in China. Ideological shifts have occurred since the Communists have been in power, which have caused a rather uneven pattern of industrial and agricultural development. The Cultural Revolution, with its emphasis on the supremacy of political idealism as opposed to economic materialism, represents the epitome of these shifts. After the Cultural Revolution, there was a revival of bureaucracy and party discipline and control under Chou En-Lai's leadership. To radicals within the Chinese leadership structure, such a restoration portends the arrival of elitism and revisionism and the undoing of everything the Cultural Revolution stood for. Until the conflict between idealism and political and economic pragmatism is resolved, policy goals will continue to remain in a state of flux.[36]

---

[34] Perkins, *op. cit.*, pp. 149–157.

[35] Donnithorne, *op. cit.*, p. 313.

[36] The Chinese press campaign in 1973 and 1974 to denounce the ancient sage Confucius is a case in point. The campaign branded Confucius as a class enemy who supported the slave-owning aristocrats against the forces of progress. This can be interpreted as a criticism of Chou En-Lai for restoring to office many party officials who were denounced as capitalists during the Cultural Revolution.

The density of population on a restricted cultivable area presents a problem in terms of economic and social development. There is the matter of a growing population which is increasing at a rate of between 2 and 2.5 percent annually. In the decade to 1959 the cities were growing by 8 percent annually, providing an upward social mobility that generated popular support for the regime and its institutions. In the decade to 1969 the cities declined in size. Internal migration continued, but was directed toward rural frontier areas and less densely populated areas. Social change continued, but without the hopes and optimism of the earlier period. Birth-control campaigns have been initiated, but their effects appear to be minimal.[37] But whatever the effect of birth-control programs, whether past or future, and whatever the rate of population increase, the country faces the problem of finding employment for persons coming on the labor market in increasing numbers. Given a projected population of 1.3 billion by 1990,[38] the pressures on employment, services, and food supplies will be exacerbated.

Agriculture is of paramount importance to the Chinese economy, not only because it must sustain the massive population, but it must also provide most of the raw materials for the consumer goods industries. Moreover, agriculture directly or indirectly supplies the bulk of the exports to finance imports. Declines in agriculture have had an adverse effect on the Chinese economy. Agricultural failures which followed the Great Leap movement were responsible for the starvation of an estimated 20 million persons. To solve the desperate food situation, the government was obliged to make important concessions to the peasants.[39] However, agriculture continues to remain a problem. In 1970 total grain output, estimated at 215 to 220 million tons, exceeded the 1957 figure of 185 million tons by a relatively narrow margin.[40]

The Communist party itself has been unstable and changing. Initially, it was small, predominantly young, and possessed high élan. However, it had to expand to maintain representation and control in the various sectors of society and also to reward activists and leaders of sub-party organizations. The growing size and influx of disparate elements led to internal frictions and forced increasing resort to bureaucratic techniques of management and control, reducing organizational enthusiasm and a sense of elite status. Although the party grew to 22 million members by 1966, the rewards it could offer its members declined, leading to demoralization at middle and lower echelons.

The future development of the Chinese economy is difficult to portend, particularly when considering the ideological convulsions through which it

---

[37] John S. Aird, "Population Policy and Demographic Prospects in the People's Republic of China," *People's Republic of China: An Economic Assessment* (Washington: Joint Economic Committee, 1972), p. 227.

[38] *Ibid.*, p. 328.

[39] These concessions were the freedom to cultivate private plots, the freedom to trade in rural markets, and the freedom to engage in subsidiary enterprises.

[40] Alva Lewis Erisman, "China: Agricultural Development, 1949–1971," *People's Republic of China: An Economic Assessment* (Washington: Joint Economic Committee, 1972), p. 121.

has gone. During certain periods of Communist control the rate of economic development was unquestionably high; during other periods the rate was very low. However, the launching in May 1970 of a space satellite and the development of nuclear capabilities indicate that the Chinese have achieved a great degree of technical expertise. But the pressure of population and an inadequate agricultural resourse base will continue to create internal domestic problems which it is doubtful that the shibboleths and slogans of Mao-thought can solve.

SUMMARY

China is similar to other Communist countries in that economic decisions concerning resource allocation are primarily the responsibility of the state. The market price system, which in a capitalistic system provides the means through which firms compete for the factors of production, does not exist in China. Without market prices to guide decisions concerning what and for whom to produce and the allocation of resources necessary to attain the desired amount of production, the Chinese must rely on economic planning. Physical production plans are developed which guide the decisions and operations of all industrial and agricultural enterprises. Financial plans, the monetary counterparts to physical plans, exist as a control mechanism to insure compliance with planning objectives.

To make agriculture more adaptable to planning, the Chinese have attempted to organize production in the form of comprehensive units, such as communes and state farms, where the activities of millions of peasants can be controlled. This enforced collectivization has also been designed to improve the efficiency of agricultural production through hoped-for gains in economies of scale. In recent years, there has been some decentralization of control, with the production brigade tending to supplant the commune as the basic agricultural unit. Private plots of land are owned by the peasants who are permitted to sell their produce in the free market.

The Chinese fiscal and monetary systems exercise a strong element of control over the economy. The national budget is important because much of the financial resources of the nation are collected and distributed through it. Tax and nontax revenues are disseminated through the budget to support capital investment in state enterprises. Monetary control is exercised through the People's Bank of China. All enterprises are required to have an account with the Bank, and purchases and sales of items can be matched against authorized payments and receipts. The Bank is responsible for the supervision of the expenditures of all state enterprises, and is also responsible for the allocation of financial resources under the Credit and Cash Plans.

QUESTIONS

1. Distinguish between financial and physical production planning.
2. Discuss the way in which resources are allocated under the Chinese economic system.

3. How are economic plans formulated and implemented in Communist China?
4. Discuss how industry is organized and controlled in China.
5. Profits exist in the Chinese Communist economic system, but do not have the same significance that they would have under a capitalistic system. Do you agree?
6. The state budget is an important control mechanism in the Chinese economic system. Do you agree?
7. Discuss the process by which agriculture was transformed from an essentially free enterprise arrangement to the communes.
8. What is the role of the People's Bank of China in the Chinese economic system?
9. The replacement of material incentives by political motivation should have no particular effect on individual initiative and productivity in the Chinese economy. Do you agree?
10. How are prices determined in the Chinese economic system?

20
Yugoslavia

INTRODUCTION

The Socialist Federal Republic of Yugoslavia represents a rather distinct brand of communism which is different from that prevailing in the rest of eastern Europe and the Soviet Union. The economy has been called a synthesis of state economic planning and a market economy.[1] It contains many features of a market economy, including the decentralization of management, the provision of credit for small-scale private enterprises, the formation of advertising associations to promote the distribution of products, and the use of personal incentives to accomplish desired economic objectives. There is also a constitutional guarantee of private peasant landholdings of up to 25 acres of arable land. There is a decentralization of economic decision making and a virtually complete autonomy of individual producing units, which indicates that the term *decentralized socialism* is applicable to Yugoslavia.

Economic planning is far less imperative than it is in other communist countries. The national five-year plan contains general sectoral targets which are not binding on enterprises. The plan is designed to guide each enterprise in the formulation of business decisions. Indirect policy instruments, such as taxation and bank credit, are used to implement the plan's objectives. The banking system, for example, can influence compliance with its targets by allocation of investment funds for capital formation.

Yugoslavia was formed in 1918, as an amalgam of Slavic groups, out of the countries of Serbia and Montenegro. With the dissolution of the Austro-Hungarian Empire, it included five Slavic groups—Serbians, Croats, Slovenes, Macedonians, and Bosnians—as well as Hungarians and Albanians. A centralized monarchy was created with the support of the dominant Serbian elements in the population and against the wishes of the Croats, who wanted a federal system of government that granted a certain amount of regional and ethnic autonomy. Antagonism between the Serbs and Croats characterized

[1] Janez Stanovik, "Planning Through the Market: The Yugoslav Experience," *Foreign Affairs*, XL (January, 1962), pp. 252–63.

477

the internal history of Yugoslavia between the two world wars. Although considerable autonomy was given to the Croats by the time of World War II, internecine rivalries existed between Serbs and Croats which even today the present government finds difficult to sublimate.

During World War II, Yugoslavia was occupied by the Germans. Resistance forces were split into two groups—the Chetniks, representing the exiled government of King Peter, and the Partisans, who were led by Tito and the Communist party.[2] The Partisans emerged as the stronger of the two groups and received the bulk of Allied military support. Those forces that had identified with Tito formed an independent base for the establishment of a communist regime at Belgrade at the end of the war. Since the liberation of Yugoslavia owed nothing to the Russian army but much to Tito and his supporters, there was no reason to be grateful or subservient to Moscow. It was for this reason that Tito could assert the independence of his regime from Russian domination. In 1948 Yugoslavia was expelled from the Russian-dominated *Cominform* for pursuing policies decided upon by its own leaders instead of Moscow.[3]

After the split with Moscow, Yugoslavia effected a rapprochement with the Western countries based on trade and aid and the desire to secure an alliance in the event of Russian aggression. However, in terms of foreign policy, it has pursued an independent line between East and West and has attempted to project itself as the leader of nonaligned nations, eschewing proximity to neither the Eastern nor Western military bloc. Although relations with the Russians have improved since the hard line Stalinist days, Yugoslavia's economic ties are essentially with the West, and there is participation in such Western economic organizations as the Organization for Economic Cooperation and Development and the European Economic Community.

Organizational Framework

The latest of several constitutions was drafted in late 1973. It is to retain the features of a federal system, with six republics and two autonomous regions. A problem confronting the drafters of the constitution is how to reconcile the national differences and desire for autonomy on the part of the Croatian and Serbian republics. Another problem confronting the whole

---

[2] The *Chetniks* were Serbian nationalists who desired an independent Serbia. The *Partisans* were primarily Croats and were led by Josip Broz (Tito), a Croat and also a Communist. Although Communists controlled at the top, considerable support was obtained from persons and groups of differing political opinions, who believed in Tito's call for national unity.

[3] The underlying cause of the break between Moscow and Yugoslavia was the fact that, in contrast to the neighboring satellite countries of Rumania, Bulgaria, and Czechoslovakia, the army and civil bureaucracy had not been created by emissaries of Moscow, but by the Yugoslavia Communists themselves during the resistance against the Germans and the civil war against the Chetniks. This meant that the Yugoslavs could proceed independently of Moscow's influence in both domestic and foreign affairs. Tito also visualized himself as the foremost Communist leader in eastern Europe and wished to establish his sphere of influence over Albania and Bulgaria.

rubric of the constitution is the replacement of Tito when he dies or retires. In 1971 a collective presidency was established as an amendment to the 1963 constitution. The collective presidency consisted of 23 members, including three from each republic, two from each autonomous region, and Tito as chairman. The number of members was later reduced to nine—one from each republic and autonomous region and Tito. In the event of Tito's death or retirement, it is intended that the representatives of the republics and autonomous regions would take turns in acting as chairman of the collective presidency. However, the collective presidency rests on fragile grounds as internal problems have made it weak, and its role is to be reduced. There has been a conflict between those persons who want more centralized control and those who want further decentralization.

Administratively Yugoslavia is organized as follows:

1. The republic has a president and legislative and judicial units. The Federal Assembly is the supreme organ of authority. It decides on changes in the Constitution, passes the federal laws, adopts the economic plans, and approves the federal budget. It also determines foreign policy and elects the president. There is also a Federal Executive Council which is responsible for the implementation of economic policy decided upon by the Federal Assembly.
2. There are the six republics and two autonomous regions. Each has a president, republic assemblies, and numerous specialized administrative agencies. Greater authority has been given to republics, as the federal government has sought to decentralize decision making and to encourage wider popular participation in economic affairs.
3. The commune, which has nothing in common with the Chinese institution of the same name, is a local government unit which forms the basic self-governing political entity in Yugoslavia. It would roughly correspond to a small city or county in the United States, and has three basic responsibilities: guiding economic affairs, including planning, investment, and supervision of enterprises; providing municipal services; and managing various social welfare activities.

The Communist Party

Yugoslavia is a communist country and the Communist party (League of Communists of Yugoslavia) is the only political party. In 1972 it had 1,200,000 members. The League is open to all citizens 18 years of age and over. Membership is apparently open to anyone who wishes to join, although the usual procedure is to have members or organizations serve as sponsors.

A Party Congress, which is held every four years, is at the apex of the policy-making hierarchy. It is responsible for the determination of the policy of the League, and it elects the Central Committee which heads the League in the interval between its meetings. The Central Committee implements the decisions of the Congress. It consists of approximately 130 members. Policy-making power, however, belongs to the 15-member Executive Committee, which is headed by the President of Yugoslavia and includes the secretaries of each republic's League of Communists and leading Communists from various areas of Yugoslav life. Within the Executive Committee, there is a five-member Secretariat for the areas of National Defense, Foreign Affairs, Finance, Trade, and International Affairs.

There is also a Republic Party Congress for each of the six republics. The main policy-making body is the Republic Central Committee, which consists of an Executive Committee, a Control Commission, a Political Secretary, and an Organizational Secretary. Representatives to the Republic Party Congress are elected at a district conference, which administratively consists of a district committee and a district secretariat. Finally, there are local conferences whose representatives are chosen from local party cells. Each local conference has a local committee and local secretariat.[4]

The economy of Yugoslavia has been undergoing a shift from agriculture to industrial development. There is a dependence on imports of basic raw materials and intermediate goods. Moreover, the pattern of growth and industrial development has been uneven, with the republics of Croatia and Slovenia accounting for 54 percent of the gross social product. In Table 20–1 the gross social product of Yugoslavia is presented on the basis of industrial origin, and also from the standpoint of expenditures. The Yugoslav national accounts are computed according to Marxist methods. The social product is equivalent to net material product plus capital consumption allowances. It differs from the concept of gross national product due to the omission from Yugoslav statistics of certain services. Normally, gross national product is calculated as about 114 percent of the Yugoslav gross social product.

TABLE 20–1

SOCIAL PRODUCT OF YUGOSLAVIA BY INDUSTRIAL ORIGIN AND TYPES OF EXPENDITURES, 1972 (Billions of Dollars *)

Industrial Origin		Expenditures	
Agriculture and forestry	8.3	Consumer expenditures	22.7
Industry	15.0	Public consumption	3.8
Construction	3.7	Gross investment	12.4
Transport	3.7	Increase in stocks	5.4
Trade and catering	8.4	Exports	6.5
Handicrafts	2.4	Less: Imports	9.3
	41.5		41.5

Source: *Statistical Yearbook of Yugoslavia* (Belgrade: Federal Institute of Statistics, 1973).

* The currency unit of Yugoslavia is the dinar. It is worth about $.17.

THE ECONOMIC SYSTEM

Yugoslavia possesses a unique, complex economic system, which combines elements of both a centrally planned and free market economy. One

---

[4] George W. Hoffman and Fred W. Neal, *Yugoslavia and the New Communism* (New York: The Twentieth Century Fund, 1962), p. 192.

unique feature of the Yugoslav economy is the workers' council, which is elected by all workers in each enterprise. The workers' council has extensive management powers concerning the operation of an enterprise. It approves the production plan, the hiring and firing of workers, the distribution of income to workers, and the annual financial statement. It also has control over the diversion of production and the use of investment funds from outside sources. The workers' council functions through a management board, which it elects from its members to perform the necessary decisions involving the day-to-day operations of an enterprise.

Another unique characteristic of the Yugoslav economic system is a reliance on decentralization of economic decision making and a dependence on the free market to accomplish the allocation of resources. Autonomy has been given to enterprises with regard to price and production policies and to the distribution of their incomes between wages and investment. Enterprises are legally independent in that their property is not owned by the government, but the property is held in trust by the enterprises for society as a whole. Within the limits dictated by national and international competition, they are free to set prices, to decide what and how much to produce, and to distribute income from sales of their products.

Economic Reforms

Economic reform in Yugoslavia has been developed beyond the direct influence of Soviet military power, and the country has been able to move farther and farther away from the Soviet model of economic and political development. The purpose of the Yugoslav economic reforms has been the development of a decentralized economic system, in part for political reasons, and in part to promote economic efficiency. The reforms have reflected a need on the part of the government to press for changes in resource allocation and administration in order to promote economic performance, while recognizing the interests of various nationalist groups within the country.

Minor economic reforms were initiated following Yugoslavia's expulsion from the Cominform in 1948. A major reform was carried out in 1952 when detailed annual plans were discontinued, substantial independence was granted to state enterprises, a greater role was assigned to the price mechanism, and a decollectivization of land was permitted. In 1953 the attempt to collectivize agriculture was abandoned. Further reforms were implemented in 1954 when centrally imposed output goals for enterprises were eliminated. However, steps to decentralize the economy and establish the socialist market system were intensified in the 1960s as economic problems, quantitatively expressed by an erratic growth rate and decreasing factor efficiency, developed. Moreover, given the fact that Yugoslavia had limited domestic markets and resources, foreign trade became an indispensable avenue for promoting technological progress. However, dependence on imports of raw materials and machinery created large deficits in the balance of payments. Given recurring crises in the economy, the government constantly had to intervene in the economy.

The economic reforms of 1965 speeded up the process of decentralization of economic management. Administrative elements of control were greatly reduced and transformed in terms of content and in terms of methods of intervention. It was felt that greater autonomy on the part of state enterprises would improve efficiency. The reforms were designed to achieve a socialist market economy through decentralized decision making and the use of market pricing. There were two basic objectives of the reforms—improvement of the productivity of capital and labor and a more balanced rate of economic growth. The reforms applied to nearly all sectors of the economy and can be summarized as follows:

1. The *dinar*, which is the Yugoslav currency unit, was devalued from 750 dinars to one dollar to 1,250 dinars to one dollar. A new dinar was then created in January, 1966, which was set at the equivalent of one new dinar to 100 old dinars and also at an exchange rate of 12.5 new dinars to one dollar. Export subsidies were eliminated and customs duties were reduced on most products by as much as 50 percent.

2. A major reform involved the decentralization of the fiscal system. Several national taxes were eliminated, and all expenditures for the internal development of the national economy were also eliminated with the exception of the fund for underdeveloped republics. Major elements of public finance were transferred from the national government to the republics, districts, and communes. The significance of the fiscal reforms is reflected in the fact that the budget revenues of the republics increased from 187 billion dinars ($31.8 billion) in 1964 to 359 billion dinars ($61 billion) in 1966, and the budget revenues of the districts and communes increased from 314 billion dinars in 1964 to 684 billion dinars ($116.3 billion) in 1966. The budget revenues of the national government, on the other hand, decreased from 776 billion dinars ($131.9 billion) to 748 billion dinars ($127.2 billion) during the same period.[5]

3. The price system was also reformed with the objective of eventually achieving the free determination of prices by market forces. Prices of goods and services were raised for the purpose of bringing them into harmony with those that prevailed in the international markets and also for the purpose of using them as instruments of development policy in combination with customs duties.

4. Reforms also took place in the banking system. Banks were organized into three broad areas of specialization—investment banking, commercial banking, and mixed banks. Banks were freed from direct government control, and their existence now depends upon funds provided by the enterprises. Each enterprise that contributes to the funds of a bank has some control over its operation through voting rights which are acquired in proportion to their contributions.[6]

Yugoslavia also passed investment legislation that allowed foreign firms to enter joint ventures with Yugoslav enterprises. This was the first such legislation

[5] "The Socialist Federal Republic of Yugoslavia," *Economic Surveys*, Table 9 (Paris: Organization for Economic Cooperation and Development, September, 1967), p. 24.

[6] No single enterprise is allowed to control more than 10 percent of the total number of votes in a bank.

passed in any communist country. Foreign firms are allowed to provide up to 49 percent of the capital in a joint venture with Yugoslav enterprises. A compulsory 20 percent of earnings has to be reinvested or deposited in a Yugoslav bank. Foreign investors are taxed on their income at the rate of 35 percent; however, taxes are reduced by as much as 50 percent on incomes over and above the compulsory 20 percent which are reinvested in the Yugoslav economy for five years or more.[7]

In 1967 a relaxation of state controls over exports and imports occurred. Restrictions on the imports of certain goods were lifted for the purpose of exposing Yugoslav enterprises to foreign competition. Most exports were also freed from state controls, and banks and enterprises were allowed to participate directly in foreign trade. No restrictions were placed on the imports of most raw materials, and importers were allowed to buy from the banks as much foreign currency as they needed to pay for imports of goods. The import of other goods was restricted, and enterprises could get only a set sum of foreign currency with which to pay for them.

Economic Planning

Yugoslavia has moved from a centralized planning procedure that copied that of the Russians, to a decentralized form of indicative planning that is more similar to French planning. This process of decentralization was developed at the time of the political split with Russia and has continued to the present. Whereas the early economic plans gave definite instructions to each Yugoslav enterprise pertaining to the methods and scope of production and distribution, the relationship between the current economic plan and the enterprises is entirely different. It contains a statement of economic and political objectives and a definition of the basic economic changes to be accomplished. The plan provides for certain measures designed to control the distribution of income of enterprises and cooperatives. Within the framework of the plan, efforts are made by the federal government to use methods which rely on the individual interests of the workers and the enterprises to produce in terms of the desired social product and national income. The federal government does not make detailed decisions concerning production, but leaves them to the enterprises to make. The economic plan serves as a guide for the production and distribution decisions of the enterprises.[8]

Current economic planning in Yugoslavia is the result of a process of decentralization which has been taking place over the last 20 years. During the First Five-Year Plan (1947–1951), the Yugoslav economic system was based on the complete centralization of management by the state and on government planning as the basic method for the allocation of goods and services. At that time the dominant conception of socialism meant the liquidation of the market system and its replacement by a system of economic

[7] In 1973 the U.S. firm, Gillette, agreed to participate in a joint venture with Yugoslavia Commerce of Belgrade to manufacture razor blades.

[8] There are annual and middle-term (five-year) plans. The fundamental elements in the policy of Yugoslav development are expressed in the five-year plans.

planning. This period of centralistic management of the economy lasted until 1951, and then a shift to a more flexible and less imperative type of planning occurred.

The First Five-Year Plan, 1947–1951. After World War II the transition to a socialist state occurred. A new Constitution was adopted that established a federation of six "people's republics" joined by a federal government to which major administrative powers were given. At that time, relations with Russia were excellent, and it was natural for the Yugoslavs to pattern their system after that of the Russians. Economic planning was adopted and all planning actions were initiated and directed by the government. Physical production quotas were assigned to each enterprise, and priority was placed upon the fulfillment of certain production targets. The federal budget was the instrument through which investment funds were provided for the enterprises. The budget had a dual responsibility of providing investment funds and restricting consumption through taxation in order to divert resources into the formation of capital.

The Economic Base. The First Five-Year Plan was concerned with the development of the economic infrastructure of the economy. Yugoslavia was a backward agrarian country. Although an industrial base existed, it was primarily confined to certain regions, and a considerable discrepancy in living standards existed between the various republics. The Plan aimed at the transformation of an agrarian economy into an industrial nation. Priorities in terms of resource allocation were placed on the sectors that could best accomplish this objective, such as the iron and steel industry. The Plan also aimed at the equalization of economic development between regions throughout the country. Allocation of investment resources was designed to favor the less developed republics over the more developed. Factories, transportation, and communication facilities were provided in the poorer republics.

In terms of total investment funds, the Plan provided for the expenditure of 278.3 billion dinars ($5.6 billion) over the five-year period. Priorities determined the allocation of these funds. Industry, mining, and electric power production received $2.3 billion, or approximately 41 percent of total investment funds. Transportation and communications received $1.5 billion, or approximately 26 percent of the funds, and housing, public services, and education, that is to say, social investment, received $1.1 billion, or 20 percent of investment funds. Agriculture, the least favored of all of the sectors, received only 8 percent of the funds.[9]

Operation of the Plan. The Plan provided an excellent example of how a command economy operates. Production plans were set which included specific quantities of a given commodity that was supposed to be produced during the course of the Plan. For example, in 1951, 4.4 million rubber shoes were supposed to be produced. In the Slovene Republic, 10,000 typewriters

[9] Albert Waterston, *Planning in Yugoslavia* (Baltimore: The Johns Hopkins Press, 1962), p. 92.

were to be produced during the same year. For 1951, 16,000 tons of tobacco and 304 million boxes of matches were to be produced in the nation as a whole.[10] Distribution of supply to various enterprises and industries and the rate of productivity increase per industry were also set by the central planning authorities.[11] The implementation of this planning, however, required the creation of a number of government agencies and a large bureaucracy. Each enterprise was required to complete detailed reports concerning the use of its resources, the number of workers employed, and its production goals.

Effects of the Plan. In general, the First Five-Year Plan was not successful. Quotas and goals were not fulfilled. Most of the targets were not reached, and between 1948 and 1952, national income increased at an annual rate of only 1.9 percent.[12] The existence of a large bureaucracy caused considerable administrative inefficiency. By 1950 the split with Russia had occurred, and the Yugoslavs felt that it was no longer necessary to adhere to a doctrinaire viewpoint of economic planning. A process of decentralization of the Yugoslav economic system began which gave rise to significant changes in the management of the economy. The basic characteristics of this process were the establishment of enterprise autonomy in economic decision making and the development of a market economy as a new form of integration among enterprises in the national economy. The process began with the elimination of administrative allocation of consumer goods. The centralized, ministerial system of economic management was replaced by a more localized form of management. Authority of the lower levels of government, particularly at the commune level, was increased, and enterprise ownership was transferred from the state to society. There developed the concept that property of an enterprise is not owned by the state, but by society, and a movement toward market socialism was started.

In the area of economic planning, the communes began to play an important role. They were given the authority to create and to liquidate enterprises, and the economic plans of the enterprises had to be based on those of the respective communes. The enterprises, or rather the workers of these enterprises, were represented in the Councils of the Producers, which constituted one of the two chambers of the assemblies of the communes. The role played by the communes, it should be repeated, goes far beyond the role of a political subdivision. They remain of enormous importance in the area of economic policy and planning.

Annual Plans, 1952–1957. During the period, 1952–1957, a series of annual plans provided the basis for projecting the economic and social development of the country. Economic planning shifted from a centralized command

---

[10] Svetozar Pejovich, *The Market Planned Economy of Yugoslavia* (Minneapolis: University of Minnesota Press, 1966), pp. 40–43.

[11] For each year that the Plan was in effect, annual plans were also established in which yearly targets were set. Each republic, district, and commune had to prepare annual plans which were extensions of the national annual plan.

[12] Waterston, *op. cit.*, p. 18.

procedural arrangement to a decentralized form of indicative planning, which has come to resemble French economic planning more than Russian economic planning. The system of fixed production quotas and prices was abandoned, and a devolution of planning controls occurred. Enterprises were permitted latitude in price setting and in the distribution of income. Although production goals were set in the plans, they were to serve as guideposts, and enterprises were left free to devise ways in which they would expand their output.

The Social Plan of Economic Development, 1957–1961. In 1957, a second five-year plan was developed. The basic goals of this plan were as follows:

1. A faster development of agriculture and industries producing consumer goods.
2. A reduction in the balance of payments deficit of the country.
3. A continued increase in personal consumption and general living standards.
4. The continued development through preferential treatment of the less developed areas of the country.

The highest priority was given to agriculture. Investment was to be increased by almost 200 percent for the purpose of increasing agricultural exports and reducing the dependence on imports. It was hoped that by increasing agricultural exports and reducing imports, the balance of payments deficit would be reduced. Branches of industry that supported agriculture, or which had a favorable export potential, were also accorded high priority.

The basic targets of the Plan included an increase in social investments of 71 percent and an increase of 39.8 percent in total investment in the national economy. It was projected that national income would increase at a rate of 9.1 percent annually during the term of the Plan.[13] Industry was expected to sustain an average annual increase of 11 percent, and agriculture, an average annual increase of 7.4 percent. Personal consumption was expected to increase by 41.9 percent, and housing and community service expenditures, by 72.5 percent during the five-year period. On the basis of anticipated gains in output by economic sectors, the Plan forecast an expansion in exports of 69 percent between 1956 and 1961.

The five-year plan for 1957–1961 was realized under unusually favorable circumstances, among which the most significant were: the normalization of political relations with the countries of the Soviet bloc, which brought about decreased investments in armaments; an increased share of international credits and financial aid, which contributed to an increase in the sources of revenue for capital accumulation; and two unusually good agricultural years in 1957 and 1959. The basic targets of the plan were achieved in four years, even though this was done with the help of factors which had little to do with the internal operation of the economy.

The Social Plan for 1961–1965. During 1959 and 1960 a new five-year plan for 1961–1965 was prepared. This plan proposed to coordinate the Yugoslav economy with the international market. Priority was given to the production of

[13] *Ibid.,* pp. 98 and 99.

basic raw materials, semimanufactures, power, and capital goods. The continued development of agriculture was also stressed. Investments were increased in industries, including tourism, that would contribute to a favorable export balance, and attention was also given to industries that produced import substitutes. Emphasis was placed on a more balanced rate of economic growth. An increase in personal and social consumption was another objective of the plan. As usual, development of the poorer regions of Yugoslavia remained a major objective.

The Social Plan for 1966–1970. The objectives of the Social Plan for 1966–1970 can be summarized as follows: [14]

1. There was to be an increase in the standard of living, particularly in the area of personal consumption. An increased proportion of national income was to be distributed to personal incomes, and the role of the federal government in terms of its effect on income distribution was to be reduced.
2. Continual emphasis was to be placed on the regional aspects of economic development. The plan not only specified the allocation among the republics of resources available for investment, but also the amounts to go to underdeveloped areas within each republic.
3. Monetary and fiscal measures were to be utilized to stabilize the domestic currency and the price level. Monetary policy was to be used to attain the necessary level of liquidity which is indispensable for production, distribution, and exchange. The growth in the volume of currency was to be at a lower rate than the real growth of production.
4. Greater emphasis was to be placed on education, scientific research, and the application of scientific and technical achievements. The main stress in the development of education during the plan was to be placed on increasing the enrollment of students attending secondary schools. The share of national income earmarked for investment in scientific research was to increase from 0.8 percent in 1965 to 1.1 percent in 1970.
5. Emphasis was also to be placed upon the modernization and reconstruction of productive facilities. Within the framework of industrial investment, the proportion of outlays in power production and metallurgy was to increase during the period of the plan. Modernization of transportation facilities to establish better links with production centers was also to be increased.

The Social Plan for 1971–1975. In January, 1972, after a delay of about six months, the Social Plan for 1971–1975 was announced. It has four basic objectives which reflect concern over internal problems. These objectives can be summarized as follows:

1. There is to be an effort to keep all forms of expenditures within reasonable bounds so as to ensure that between 1972 and 1975 prices increase by no more than 5 percent per annum.
2. Priority is to be given to the achievement of a more dynamic rate of industrial growth and a more consistent rate of increase in living standards.

[14] "Yugoslavia's 1966–1970 Social Development Plan," *Yugoslovenska Pregled* (Belgrade, 1966).

Up to 1975, the social product of industry is set to grow at a rate of 7.5 percent a year. Employment is to grow at a rate of 3 percent a year, with 900,000 new jobs to be created, and worker productivity is to increase at 5 percent a year. Gross industrial investment in fixed assets is expected to rise at an annual rate of 7.5 percent. The overall standard of living is targeted to increase at 7 percent a year. An external objective is to increase the rate of exports by 11 to 13 percent a year, while holding the increase in imports to 9 to 11 percent a year.

3. Another objective is to change the composition of output in favor of basic industries. A major problem in Yugoslavia has been bottlenecks attributable to lack of raw materials for industry. Emphasis is to be placed on the development of power, transportation, iron and steel, nonferrous, chemical, cement, and cellulose industries. Electricity output is planned to increase to 44 million kilowatt hours by 1975 compared to 26 million kilowatt hours in 1970. The steel production target is set at 4.5 million tons in 1975 compared to 2.2 million tons in 1970. Copper production is targeted to increase from 90,000 tons in 1970 to 150,000 tons in 1975, and aluminum production is to increase from 48,000 tons to 200,000 tons over the same period.

4. Priority is also to be given to an increase in the industrialization of the underdeveloped republics and regions in Yugoslavia. In particular, the republics of Bosnia—Hercegovina, Macedonia, Montenegro, and the province of Kosovo—are targeted to achieve an increase in industrial development at a rate 25 percent above that for the country as a whole.

Formulation and Implementation of Yugoslav Plans. There are actually three sets of plans in Yugoslavia—national, republic and commune plans. The Yugoslav national plan lays down the basic guidelines, targets, and aims of economic policy. Within the guidelines and objectives determined by the national plan and the plans of the republics and communes, Yugoslav enterprises and other economic organizations are free to formulate their own production plans. This is in keeping with the decentralization policies of the government and reflects the view in Yugoslavia that it is necessary to turn more and more authority in the sphere of economics from the government to the enterprises and communes. It also reflects the view that the workers, rather than the state, must decide on the allocation and use of the goods which they produce. This is done, as will be discussed later in the chapter, through the election of workers' councils who have vested control over the operations of all enterprises. Worker self-management fits in with the process of decentralized planning.

The national plan is prepared by the Federal Planning Institute and is approved by the Federal Assembly. The Federal Planning Institute consists of a number of technical divisions, each of which is responsible for the preparation of a certain part of the plan. These divisions include agriculture; forestry; transportation and communication; regional development; personal consumption and social welfare; investment; domestic trade and tourism; industry, power, and mining; and social product and national income.

The republic plans set for the republics the same objectives embodied in the national plan, allowing for special features of the republic economies.

Republic plans refer only to segments of the economy, and do not involve such subjects as foreign trade or balance of payments. The republics are free to set goals that go beyond the scope of the federal plan and are under no legal obligations to harmonize their plans with the federal plan. However, as the commune has emerged as the basic unit of government, republic plans have come to play a more limited role.

After the republic plans are completed, the communes prepare plans. The plans of the communes are more comprehensive and detailed than the republic plans and are prepared after consultations with various workers' organizations. They encompass such activities as planned tax policies and social welfare services. The communes, as well as the federal government, can influence compliance with planning objectives through control over policy instruments in the fields of credit, finance, and taxation. Neither the republic nor the commune plans must harmonize in detail with the national plan; nevertheless, these lower administrative units have to consider the overall frame of reference which is provided by the national plan.

The plans of the communes are worked out by the communal assemblies. Special committees within the assemblies are responsible for preparing the commune plans and these committees work in conjunction with local enterprises and other organizations in developing recommendations. Public discussions are also held, and a preliminary draft is developed.

Public Finance

During the first part of the postwar period the state was preeminent in all economic activities. All phases—production, distribution, exchange, and consumption—were included in government planning. Of all instruments of control available to the state during this period, the general state budget was the most important. It was composed of the federal budget, the budgets of the national republics, and local budgets. The general state budget was, for all practical purposes, one unitary fund, established by one authority, the national government. The general state budget served as the main distribution of investment funds. Its main sources of revenue were the sales tax, a form of profits tax from the socialist sector, and an income tax collected from the private sector.

The 1965 economic reforms had their effect on the public finance system of Yugoslavia. The first important change took place in 1964, when the investment funds were abolished and their resources were transferred to corresponding banks for investment, agriculture, and foreign trade, which at the same time took over the responsibility for the success of investment projects already begun. The basic goal of the 1965 tax reforms was to modify the scale and structure of taxation on Yugoslav enterprises in order to provide them with more financial resources. The process of decentralizing economic decision making and establishing a market mechanism system, which was the nexus of the 1965 reforms, carried over into taxation and expenditures of the national government. The producer's turnover tax, the business net profits tax, and the general turnover tax, all of which were major national taxes, were eliminated.

Tax revenues which were formerly returned to the republics in the form of grants and subsidies remained in the economy without formal government intervention. Yugoslavia also abolished all expenditures for intervention in the economy except the fund for underdeveloped republics.

Public finance in Yugoslavia, as a result of the reforms, is quite unlike that in any other socialist economy. For one thing, it is much more decentralized. As the federal government has withdrawn from its central role in the economy as a result of the market-oriented economic reforms, so the importance of public finance has declined. Unlike the centralized Soviet economy, with the all-important state budget, the Yugoslav public sector plays a less important role. It is only responsible for investment in a limited number of national schemes and the bulk of investment funds are provided by the commercial banks which are not state-owned.

The Yugoslav public sector consists of the federal budget, the budgets of the republics and communes, extra-budgetary funds, and the social security system. The extra-budgetary funds are largely used to finance infrastructure investment in less developed regions and are administered primarily by the republics. Table 20–2 presents the composition of revenues and expenditures for the budgets of the various political units in 1972. It is a requirement that these budgets must be balanced. The budget total of $7.96 billion represented

TABLE 20–2
BUDGETS OF YUGOSLAV POLITICAL UNITS FOR 1972

Items	Federal	Republics and Provinces	Communes	Total
Receipts (Billions of Dollars *)				
Personal		.27	.75	1.02
Taxes, of which		1.35	.70	2.05
sales taxes are		.46	.54	1.00
Stamp duties	.01	.03	.12	.16
Customs duties	1.67	—	—	1.67
Republic contributions	2.11	—	—	2.11
Other	.15	.53	.27	.95
Total	3.94	2.18	1.84	7.96
Expenditures (Billions of Dollars)				
Education, science	—	.19	.17	.36
Welfare	—	.29	.19	.48
Government	.22	.37	.92	1.51
Defense	1.71	—	—	1.71
Communities	.83	.92	.10	1.85
Economic development	.95	.29	.32	1.56
Reserves	.23	.12	.14	.49
Total	3.94	2.18	1.84	7.96

Source: *Statistical Yearbook of Yugoslavia* (Belgrade: Federal Institute of Statistics, 1973).
* The Yugoslav dinar equals $0.17.

about 50 percent of total public sector receipts and expenditures of $16.1 billion.[15] Excluded from the table are social security receipts and expenditures, and balances of the extra-budgetary funds. In 1972 total public sector outlays of $16.1 billion amounted to around 38 percent of gross social product— a low ratio in comparison to other socialist economies.

The Tax System. A major reorganization of the tax system was completed in 1965 with the result that certain taxes were eliminated, other taxes were revised, and new taxes were added. Taxes eliminated included the producer's turnover tax, which had accounted for 45 percent of total federal budget receipts; the net profits tax, which was paid by enterprises on their net profits, that is, the sum that remained after operating costs, debt financing, and regular salaries have been met; and the purchase tax, which was levied on the sale of specific items such as automobiles and furniture. The federal government was the sole collector and recipient of the above-mentioned taxes.

Sales Taxes. Currently, the sales tax is the main source of revenue for governmental operating budgets. A general tax rate of 12.5 percent is normally charged at the time of purchase on all items bought at the retail level. However, food, heating fuel, and electricty are exempt from the tax, and a higher rate is levied on other commodities. Items bearing higher rates are tobacco, with a rate of 60 percent; automobiles, with rates that vary from 12 percent on small cars to 100 percent on large, expensive cars; and alcoholic drinks. The federal government rebates 20 percent of the federal sales tax to each constituent republic based on the amount collected in each republic.

In addition to the federal sales tax, the communes and republics also levy sales taxes. Commune sales taxes average 6 percent of retail sales, and republics are authorized to levy a 2 percent sales tax. The sales tax imposed by both types of administrative units is confined to retail trade, is uniform within each territorial district, and has the maximum limits prescribed by federal legislation.

The Fixed Capital Tax. This is a tax which is levied on the fixed assets and buildings possessed by an enterprise. The amount of the tax was reduced from 6 percent to 4 percent under the provisions of the 1965 reforms. Agricultural enterprises, which paid no taxes on their equipment or buildings before the reforms, were made subject to the fixed capital tax. The federal government is the sole recipient of revenue from this tax source and uses the revenue to finance economic development in the less developed areas of the country and to finance infrastructure investments that benefit the nation as a whole.

Income Taxes. Significant changes have been made in the personal income tax in recent years. Before the 1965 reforms, the average Yugoslav worker paid a personal income tax of 17½ percent of gross income. From this amount, the federal government took 3 percent, and the republics and communes

[15] *Statistical Yearbook of Yugoslavia* (Belgrade: Federal Institute of Statistics, 1973), p. 25.

divided the remaining 14½ percent.[16] In addition, the average worker had to pay various contributions, which averaged approximately 26 percent of gross income, for retirement, health insurance, and other social benefits.

Following the reform, the average Yugoslav worker was to pay an income tax of 10½ percent of which 2½ percent went to the federal government and the remainder to the republic and commune governments. However, in 1966 the federal government levied an additional 2 percent tax on incomes to build up financial reserves to assist enterprises and other economic organizations, and the republic and communal governments also levied a similar amount for the same purpose. The additional 4 percent tax was temporary, and the revenue was used to provide credits to support the development of industries that had been adversely affected by the 1965 economic reforms. In 1968 personal income tax rates were made more progressive, particularly in the high income brackets.

Government Expenditures. A characteristic of the Yugoslav budgetary system is that it is decentralized. Jurisdiction has been transferred from higher to lower administrative units, and the growth of the budgets of the communes has increased. In 1972 the participation of the various administrative units in the total Yugoslav budget was as follows: federal government, 49.3 percent; republic governments and autonomous provinces, 27.6 percent; and districts and communes, 23.1 percent.[17] All sociopolitical units, with the exception of the autonomous provinces and districts, are independent in determining their revenue from taxes and contributions and in determining the rates.

Another characteristic of the budgetary system of Yugoslavia is that particular services are excluded from the budgetary accounts and are financed by means of special funds or by their own resources. Also outside of the budget system is a payment of interest by all Yugoslav enterprises on their business funds. This contribution goes to the federal government and is used for special federal intervention in the area of economic investment. For example, the federal government has a special fund for the improvement of areas of the country that are underdeveloped.

Social Welfare Expenditures. Social welfare expenditures are also excluded from budgetary accounts and are collected and administered by the communes and districts. The social security system is financed by contributions from workers' wages withheld by economic enterprises and public institutions. Private employers contribute for the persons they employ, and self-employed persons, such as artisans and shopkeepers, pay for themselves. The system includes old age and survivors pensions, sickness and maternity benefits, unemployment compensation, work injury and disability benefits, and family

---

[16] There was also an additional levy of 1 percent of incomes to provide funds for the rehabilitation of Skopje, a city that was severely damaged by floods. This levy is still in effect.

[17] *Statistical Pocketbook of Yugoslavia* (Belgrade: Federal Institute of Statistics, 1973), p. 96.

allowances. All wage and salary earners are eligible for full coverage under the social security system, while limited benefits—health protection and compensation for work-connected accidents in particular—are available to the remainder of the population. Although private farmers, craftsmen, and shopkeepers are eligible for health and old age benefits, they are not eligible for family allowances.

The family allowance is an important part of the Yugoslav social security system, and the monthly payments constitute a significant part of an average family's income. In 1972 the allowance was set at 40 new dinars ($6.80) a month for the first child, 36 new dinars a month for the second child, 32 new dinars for the third, 30 new dinars for the fourth, and 24 new dinars for the fifth and subsequent children.[18] The family allowance is paid for every child under 15, and it is continued for older children who pursue their education in secondary and higher schools. The allowance is reduced for families whose income is derived in part from agriculture.

An old age pension is payable to men who have reached the age of 60 and women who have reached the age of 55, provided that there has been 20 years of insurance coverage. Otherwise, the age is increased to 65 years for men and 60 years for women. The pension for men amounts to 35 percent of the highest 10 years of earnings, and for women, it amounts to 40 percent of the highest 10 years of earnings. There is also a survivors pension, which amounts to 70 percent of the pension paid or payable to the deceased, and there is a funeral grant, which covers burial expenses, plus one month's earnings or pension.

In addition to family allowances and old age and survivors pensions, sickness and maternity benefits are provided under the Yugoslav social security system. Sickness benefits are provided to all covered workers and amount to 60 percent of earnings for the first week of illness, 70 percent for the next 53 days, and 100 percent afterward. Maternity benefits amount to 80 percent of earnings and last for 105 days. General medical services are provided to everyone and include general and specialist care, hospitalization, laboratory services, and medicines and supplies. However, patients share in the cost of nonessential drugs.

Unemployment insurance is also provided under the Yugoslav social security system. Under Yugoslav law, unemployment compensation is paid until employment is found. However, if an employment office is unable to place an unemployed worker in a job that corresponds to his skills, it can refer him to a lesser job in terms of skill requirements. Unemployment benefits amount to 50 percent of earnings and are payable for a period of up to six months. This period can be extended up to a maximum of 18 months for workers who have 120 months of prior employment. Compensation is not paid to workers who have been discharged from employment or who refuse to accept jobs which have been provided by the employment offices.

[18] Data provided by the Embassy of Yugoslavia, Washington, D.C.

The Banking System

The 1965 banking reforms changed considerably the structure and operation of the banking system. Prior to the reforms, the banking system consisted of the National Bank of Yugoslavia (Narodna Banka Jugoslavije), which is the central bank; three specialized banks—one for agriculture, one for foreign trade, and one for investment—which were financed from the federal budget; six republic banks, which were responsible for the management of the republic investment funds; and approximately 375 local or commune banks, which were responsible for the needs of the communes. The local banks provided long-term and short-term capital for the communes and acted as the fiscal agents of the communes. Savings banks also existed and had as their function the collection of the surplus monetary media of the population and social organizations. They were allowed to grant credits for communal construction and consumer credit within the limits of the collected funds.

The purpose of the 1965 reforms was to continue the process of changing the Yugoslav banking system from the highly government controlled mechanism that it was during the early years of the development of the communist economic system into a decentralized system which would be more responsive to regional and local needs. The current arrangement is that of the National Bank, which is responsible for general central banking operations, and a system of specialized banks that are arranged according to the activity in which they engage. These banks fall into three categories—investment banks, commercial banks, and mixed banks.[19]

In 1965 all of the Yugoslav banks were divided into two basic groups. One group consists of the National Bank, which acts as a bank of issue and has other monetary functions as well, and the other group is comprised of commercial banks. This extension of credit is regulated by the Council of Banks, a common advisory organization in which all banks, including the National Bank, participate. It serves to coordinate the implementation of credit, monetary policy, and foreign exchange policies.

In addition to the issuance of bank notes as legal tender, the National Bank is also responsible for monetary policy. The post 1965 mechanisms of monetary policy which are available to the National Bank are: general or minimum requirements for bank liquidity, the maintenance of obligatory reserves of commercial banks with the National Bank, rediscount credit which is extended by the National Bank to commercial banks, control by the National Bank over the total volume of bank indebtedness, and qualitative control over the structure of bank credit. These instruments of monetary policy operate as follows:

1. As a minimum condition for commercial bank liquidity, the reimbursement period of at least 50 percent of total short-term credit must not exceed three months. In addition, the banks must always have sufficient amounts of liquid assets in their current accounts with the National Bank. These assets cannot exceed 6 to 8 percent of a bank's total sight deposits.

---

[19] George Macesich and Dimitrye Dimitryevic, *Money and Banking in Contemporary Yugoslavia* (New York: Praeger, 1973). This book presents a complete description of the Yugoslav banking system.

2. Commercial banks must keep obligatory reserves with the National Bank. Obligatory reserves are required for sight and time deposits. As an instrument of credit control, these reserves can be varied so that a bank's credit potential can be expanded or contracted by the National Bank. The reserves can be varied in an amount up to 35 percent of a bank's deposits.
3. The National Bank can set rediscount credit criteria for commercial banks which can affect their business policies, the structure of their assets, and the determination of the kinds and purposes of credits that can be discounted. There is also control over the length of the reimbursement period.
4. The National Bank exercises control over the volume of indebtedness of commercial banks. The commercial banks can obtain credit from the Bank only to the extent of their deposits. In order to increase their credit potential, the banks would either have to attract new deposits or build up their own credit capital.
5. The National Bank also utilizes instruments of qualitative credit control to exert a selective influence on the structure of short-term investments by commercial banks. This selectivity involves the stimulation of specific credits for exports, the sale of certain essential products, and the purchase of agricultural products.

Commercial Banks. Yugoslav banks are classified as investment banks, commercial banks, and mixed banks. Investment banks are responsible for the provision of credit for investment in fixed assets and working capital. They may also grant short-term credit. Commercial banks provide short-term credit to enterprises in order to assist them to carry on their business of manufacture and trade. Mixed banks combine the functions of the investment and commercial banks.

In addition to the regular commercial or *business banks,* which are organized and operated by enterprises and communes, there are other banks that are part of the banking system. There are three Yugoslav banks which provide special services. These are the former government-directed specialized banks—the Investment Bank, the Agricultural Bank, and the Foreign Exchange Bank—which, respectively, have the functions of channeling long-term domestic and foreign loans to industry, of extending long-term agricultural credits, and of granting long- and short-term foreign exchange credits. There are also six republic banks—one for each republic—which serve as investment banks, and district banks, which operate either as commercial or mixed banks.

A bank may be formed by enterprises or by socio-political communities, such as a commune, which provide the bank with the resources necessary to begin operations. Regulations require that not less than 25 enterprises or socio-political institutions invest their resources in the bank's capital fund. By doing so, they acquire the basic right to participate in the management of the bank. Apart from this participatory right, the investors also have the right to earn dividends on their share in the bank's credit fund. However, the investors also have to bear a proportional risk of bank losses.

Each bank has a special credit fund from which credit is provided and a special reserve fund which is designed to serve as surety for the bank's solvency. The credit fund comprises initial and subsequent investments made by the founders, that is, enterprises and communes, investments of other organizations which place their resources in the credit fund, and earned income. The bank's assembly is responsible for the determination of the distribution of total income into that which is allocated to the credit and special reserve funds, to that which belongs to the bank's workers, and to that which belongs to investors in the credit fund and to depositors as interest on their deposits.

The management of a bank is entrusted to a bank assembly, which consists of representatives elected from the organizations that provided the bank's capital. Representation on the assembly is proportional to the amount of investment that an organization has contributed to the bank. The assembly is responsible for the election of the bank's executive board, credit committee, and the managing director.

The Role of Interest. Under a capitalistic system, when quantities of capital funds are available for investment, the question of how they should be allocated is determined by the amounts of interest which firms in various fields of production are willing to pay for their use. The rate of interest will be determined in the market by the forces of supply and demand, and the rate plays the role of an allocator of resources. The underlying assumption is that if an economic entity is willing to pay more for the use of capital resources, the productivity of that entity is expected to be higher.

In Yugoslavia interest is also used as a device to allocate investment funds. Enterprises have to pay interest on borrowed funds and on their fixed and turnover capital. Since almost all of real capital is owned by society and since enterprises are entrusted with the use of this real capital, it is to the benefit of society to accomplish full and efficient utilization of these resources. This is ensured by charging interest for the use of fixed and working capital, the idea being that those who have no use for the capital will hesitate to hold it if they have to pay a certain price for its use. By granting loans to those who are willing to pay the highest rate for the privilege, the rate of interest plays the role of an allocator of financial resources. This rate of interest is not only applicable at the enterprise level, but also at the personal level, that is, the interest rate payable on consumer credit and on personal savings.

Maximum interest rates chargeable on credits are fixed by the Federal Assembly. Within the limits set by the Federal Assembly, interest rates can be fixed by the banks themselves in accordance with their business policies.[20] Under the conditions which have been created by the Economic Reforms of 1965 and 1966, Yugoslav enterprises and banks are supposed to show a much greater sensitivity to interest rates, so that interest charges will assume an increasing importance as an instrument of money and credit control and an item of operating expenses.

The Yugoslav Enterprise

The Yugoslav enterprise is the basic economic unit and may be started or expanded in several ways.

[20] In 1971 interest rate ceilings which caused earlier distortions in the economy were removed.

1. It may be formed by any governmental unit—commune, republic, or the national government.
2. It may be formed by individuals who have pooled their assets. However, at least five persons must be involved.
3. It may be formed by an existing enterprise or by the division or merger of two or more enterprises.

When the enterprise starts operation, it acquires an independent status even though its sponsors have committed considerable resources to its formation. Its assets become social property and the people which it employs have the right to self-government and to participate in the income of the enterprise on the basis of work done. It may merge with another enterprise provided that a majority of workers in both enterprises approve the merger. As a matter of economic policy, mergers have been encouraged in order to improve productivity and make Yugoslav firms more competitive in the international markets.

Yugoslav enterprises possess certain similarities to their American counterparts. Profit is the basic criterion of success for enterprises in each country, and each enterprise is independent in the pursuit of its business and development policies. Each can determine the volume and assortment of production according to its assessment of the market, and each can determine its pricing policies. Although economic planning exists in Yugoslavia, the government does not direct that specified quantities of products have to be provided by each enterprise, but instead relies on more indirect controls, including a reliance on pecuniary measures, to encourage compliance with national economic objectives.

Management of an Enterprise. In 1950 a law on economic organizations was promulgated which stated that the management of all enterprises would be given to their workers. That is, all factories, mines, and other enterprises which had been under state ownership since the coming to power of the Communist party in Yugoslavia were turned over to the workers of these enterprises to manage. The ownership passed from the state to society in general. Enterprises were defined, not as state property, but as social property, and workers were given the right to manage them, but not to own them. The key instrument through which this management would be accomplished was the workers' council, which in essence became the trustee of social wealth and the provider of self-management for an enterprise.

Since the adoption of the law on workers' councils in 1950, there has gradually developed a system of enterprise management under which managerial functions are shared by the workers' council and an enterprise director. The workers' council directs and guides an enterprise; the director manages it.

Workers' Councils. The workers' council is elected by the entire work force in any enterprise with at least 30 members, and the council may have anywhere from 15 to 120 members depending on the number of workers employed. Its authority is substantial. Within the limits set by the government, it has the right to decide what to produce and in what quantity and quality, and it is also responsible for the setting of prices, the determination of wages, and the distribution of profits. The last responsibility is one of its most important functions. It distributes enterprise profits in the form of wage bonuses to the various investment and social welfare funds of the enterprise. It also has the authority to divert the use of investment funds from outside sources.

Elections to the workers' council are held annually. As legally set forth, everyone in an enterprise who is over 18 years of age can vote. Although candidates are usually nominated by the labor union representing the workers, any group can submit its own list of candidates, provided it can obtain the support of one tenth of all of the eligible voters. Blue-collar, or manual, workers must be represented in proportion to their relationship with other groups of workers. Normally, around 75 percent of all representatives on the workers' council are blue-collar workers.[21] Members of the Communist party account for a high percentage of the members of the workers' council. Very large enterprises also have departmental workers' councils in addition to the regular council. For enterprises having fewer than 30 workers, all are members of the workers' council.

The workers' council chooses a management committee, which is its executive organ. This committee normally ranges from 3 to 11 members, and a certain percentage, usually 75 percent, must be manual workers. The management committee has the following responsibilities:

1. It is responsible for the development of the production plans of the enterprise.
2. It is responsible for the appointment of workers to important administrative positions.
3. It is responsible for the specification of wage and production norms and for ways in which to increase worker productivity.

Enterprise Directors. The director of a Yugoslav enterprise is accountable to the group that made the appointment, namely, the workers' council and the people's committee of the local commune. The director is appointed on the basis of a competitive examination and can be recalled at any time. Friction between the workers' council and the director often arises over the distribution of profits, with the workers' council tending to favor higher wage bonuses out of profits, while the director strives for increased investment. The procedure of recall is regulated by law. The workers' council has to petition the people's committee of the local commune in order to dismiss the director.[22] A joint commission consisting of representatives of the workers' council and the people's committee is created for the purpose of deciding whether or not the director should be recalled. If the commission decides to recall the director, the decision is final; however, if the commission decides to oppose the recall and the workers' council is opposed to the decision, the workers' council is dissolved and a new one is created. If the new council also favors recall of the director, then the people's committee must comply.

---

[21] Jiri Kolaja, *Workers' Councils: The Yugoslav Experience* (New York: Frederick A. Praeger, Inc., 1965), p. 7.

[22] Recall proceedings can also be initiated by the communes or other government bodies and by the Communist party.

Control of Enterprises. The Yugoslav enterprise operates within a different institutional framework than its American counterpart and is subject to more constraints. For example, the enterprise must coordinate its plan of production with the general development policies of the commune, republic, and federal government.

Economic Chamber. The enterprise is required to join a semigovernmental organization that enters into some phases of its business affairs. This institution is called the Economic Chamber and is set up at the federal, republic, and commune levels. The major administrative tasks with which the Chamber is charged are the allocation of foreign exchange quotas and the supervision of producer-consumer agreements for price increases. Another of its functions is to bring continuously to the attention of the managers of enterprises the current economic goals which have been established by the various levels of government.

Council of Producers. Another agency that exercises control over enterprises is the Council of Producers, which is established at the local, republic, and federal levels. Members are elected by only those persons who are gainfully employed. A function of the Council of Producers at the commune level is the inspection of the operations of an enterprise. It can also make recommendations concerning the operations. The enterprise also has to file periodic reports with the Council. At the national level the Producers' Council has authority over such matters as the annual plans, taxation, wages, and investment as they would pertain to an enterprise.

Relationship to the Commune. There is also an important relationship between the commune and the enterprise. The commune can provide financial support for an enterprise, and it can supervise the distribution of profits and audit the accounts of the enterprise. Through the people's committee, the communes can regulate various activities of an enterprise. As mentioned previously, the people's committee participates with the workers' council in the hiring and dismissal of the director. It can also participate in the setting of wages. The commune has some control over the provision of credit by the banking system to an enterprise in that it can underwrite or guarantee loans. The commune also has the responsibility for coordinating the production plans of all enterprises under its jurisdiction with its own plan. Although compliance on the part of an enterprise is not mandatory, continued failures to meet planning objectives can bring about the dissolution of the workers' council by the commune. Mismanagement of an enterprise can also bring about a dissolution of the workers' council by the commune.

Price Controls. Although prices in principle can be determined in a system of free markets, the federal government imposes a number of controls over the prices of certain commodities, and thus exercises some control over the pricing policies of enterprises. These price controls are designed to influence the distribution of income and also the development of certain sectors of the economy. There are various types of price controls including the following:

1. Ceiling prices are imposed on the production of certain commodities such as copper, zinc, lead, and aluminum. Such an upper price limit on these commodities takes into account the prevailing production costs and the average rate of profits.
2. Fixed prices are applied to tobacco and sugar. These prices represent both a maximum and a minimum.
3. Calculated prices are applied to a certain range of commodities, including such cereal and grain products as wheat, corn, barley, and oats, and such products as lard, salt, kerosene, and medicine and drugs. To calculate prices, fixed amounts are added to cover transportation and marketing expenses. To arrive at the cost of bread, for example, the Yugoslavs add to the basic price of wheat the cost of transportation, manufacturing, and also the profit margin.
4. A wide range of consumer goods are subject to a modified type of price control system called *evidence and control*. This system is used for goods that are considered important to the standard of living. When enterprises want to raise the price of important consumer products, they are required to show evidence to the federal government as to why prices should be raised. If the federal government has no objections, then an enterprise can raise the price of its product.

The government agency that is responsible for the administration of price controls is the Federal Institute for Prices. The Institute bases its price-setting decisions on two criteria:

1. The greater the priority the product possesses in terms of foreign exchange, the greater is the likelihood of its release from price controls.
2. When situations of short supply and strong demand or weak competition or monopoly exist for a product, the likelihood for price control is strong.

However, Yugoslavia has pursued a policy which aims at the elimination of most price controls. Indeed, if the economic reforms are to be capable of the desired performance, there has to be less rigidity in the price setting and adjustment process. Prices which are centrally fixed and remain unchanged over long periods produce contradictions in the context of changing costs on the one hand and consumer preference on the other. If buyers' markets are to be developed, production must be made to respond to demand, and flexible prices can achieve this more effectively than controlled prices can. Yugoslav enterprises are in a position to react to price changes expressed through consumer preferences.

The Operation of an Enterprise. The process of decentralizing economic decision making and establishing the market mechanism, which has taken place in Yugoslavia, has an effect on the operations of an enterprise. An enterprise can draw up its own plans for production independent of the national plan, but within limits prescribed by the plan of the commune. The production plan is approved by the workers' council after being put forward by the management committee of the enterprise. Once passed, the plan may be amended by the workers' council. Usually the enterprise is free to make its decisions pertaining to what to purchase and what to sell, and it can establish prices for its products unless they are subject to some form of price control. Distribution is not regulated, and an enterprise can bring out its goods in a comparatively free market which is guided by commercial principles.

The value of goods and services sold constitutes the gross or total income of an enterprise. The deduction of operating costs—excluding labor income, which is treated as a claim on income arising from current output and is not treated as a cost—leaves the net income of the enterprise. Operating costs cover outlays for the purchase of raw materials, depreciation, overhead costs, maintenance of fixed assets, research and development, insurance, interest on fixed and working capital, and payment of membership dues.

Maximum interest rates are prescribed by the Federal Assembly, but banks and other organizations are free to set interest rates within this limit in accordance with their business policy. Interest is paid on the total value of the fixed and working assets of an enterprise. Lower interest rates may be prescribed by federal law for certain enterprises or branches of industry that the federal government considers vital to the national interest or whose development the government wishes to promote as a matter of regional economic policy. Examples of industries that have received preferential treatment include mining, agriculture, metallurgy, transportation, publishing, and the manufacture of basic chemicals.

Investment Decision Making. A basic feature of the economic reforms has been the transfer of investment decision making from the national to the local level. To accomplish this, the flow of tax funds from business enterprises to the federal government has been reduced, the government dominated General Investment Fund has been abolished, and a larger share of enterprise earnings is being channeled into the reorganized banking system, which has become the main source of investment funds. The reorganization of the tax system, which occurred in 1965, was designed to increase the overall share of net income remaining in the hands of the enterprise. Table 20–3 on page 502 presents the distribution of net income for all Yugoslav enterprises for 1967 after the deductions of all operating costs except interest payments.

Distribution of Income. The income statement of a Yugoslav enterprise does not show wages as a cost of production; instead, after operating expenses are deducted, the net income is divided between an appropriation for personal income and for reinvestment.[23] The workers have the right to participate in the income of the enterprise on the basis of work done, and the workers' council decides on the amount to be paid out in terms of base pay and supplements.

[23] Rudolph Bicanic, *Economic Policy in Socialist Yugoslavia* (Cambridge: Cambridge University Press, 1973), pp. 106–109.

Income is set aside in a wage fund and is shared among the workers in accordance with a wage schedule adopted by the workers' council. To start with, a guaranteed minimum wage is assured all workers, and no worker can be paid less than this amount. Actual earnings, however, exceed the guaranteed minimum by a substantial amount, and the minimum assumes importance only when it cannot be covered out of the earnings of an enterprise. If this situation occurs, then the commune is required to make up the difference between the actual wage and the guaranteed minimum wage.

Base pay is determined by the workers' council and is based on hourly or piece rates which are worked out for each position in the enterprise. The actual amount that a worker can receive is related to the earnings of the enterprise and the amount of the wage fund. In the determination of base pay, priority is given to the more complex types of work that require greater vocational training and to the greater physical and mental efforts that are required in certain jobs. Base pay varies considerably between industries and between skills. For example, the ratio between the pay of an enterprise manager and an unskilled worker can be as great as 6 to 1.[24] There are also premiums for lowering of costs, quality of products, and increases in the productivity of labor in economic units, measured in actual performance above that planned. The top personnel can get premiums of up to 10 percent or more of income for successful management.

Personal taxes, such as income taxes and social security contributions, are collected by the communes from the enterprises and are portioned out to the

TABLE 20–3
DISTRIBUTION OF ENTERPRISE NET INCOME IN YUGOSLAVIA FOR 1967

Net income	Millions of Dollars *
Taxes on business funds	173
Interest on government and bank loans	246
Turnover tax	630
Contributions on personal income	1,030
Total tax and interest payments	2,079
Personal income in the form of wages, salaries, and bonuses	2,108
Enterprise funds and expenditures	1,805
Total income left to enterprises	3,913
Total	5,992

Source: U.S. Department of State, "Income Distribution of Yugoslav Enterprises" (from unclassified materials prepared by the American Embassy in Belgrade, June, 1968).

* The new dinar is worth $.08.

[24] *Ibid.*, p. 107.

federal government, the republic governments, and to the communes themselves. The base for tax computation is a worker's net pay, which consists of the base wage plus supplements which include a share of an enterprise's profits. However, deductions are made from gross pay, which consists of net pay plus taxes and social security contributions. For example, if a Yugoslav worker receives a net pay of 1,000 new dinars a month, the enterprise pays taxes and contributions on this amount, which would total 286.50 new dinars. Gross pay would total 1,286.50 new dinars. These levies have not affected the level of take-home pay, and from the worker's point of view, they are primarily a bookkeeping change since the amount withheld is included in gross pay.

An enterprise must divide its net income into funds which are used to pay the incomes of the workers and into funds which are used for various other purposes. There is a business fund which is used to increase the fixed and working assets of the enterprise, and a joint consumption fund which is used to finance the construction of houses for the workers, vocational training, and various social and cultural institutions that are used by the workers of the enterprise. In addition, there is also a reserve fund which is used for the purpose of meeting possible oscillations in business activities or to cover business losses. This fund is considered to be a permanent reserve which an enterprise is required by law to maintain to guard against emergencies. If the permanent reserve shrinks below a certain prescribed minimum, it must be replenished by the enterprise.

If an enterprise is unable to meet personal incomes that have been paid against the income it has earned or to meet the value of resources expended in its business, it operates at a loss. If it lacks sufficient resources in its permanent reserve fund to cover the loss, bankruptcy proceedings may be undertaken. However, most often the enterprise is restored to solvency by means of a recovery credit and other measures designed to eradicate the causes of insolvency. The recovery credit can be provided by other enterprises, banks, or the commune that has jurisdiction over the enterprise. In the event of liquidation, proceedings are commenced according to law before a court.

Agriculture

The organization of agriculture in Yugoslavia differs considerably from the organization of agriculture in Russia and China. The fundamental difference lies in the fact that about 80 percent of the agricultural land in Yugoslavia is privately owned. Yugoslav law permits the private ownership of up to 10 hectares (25 acres of land). Small land holdings are a dominant characteristic of agriculture in Yugoslavia. In general, a private holding must be farmed by the owner himself or his family without any outside wage-earning help.

Agrarian Reforms. The current agricultural arrangement began with the agrarian reforms of 1945 and 1953. Both reforms were based on the principle that land should belong to those who till it. In the agrarian reform of 1945, land was taken from large landowners, banks, churches, and other institutions that did not engage in agricultural production. Because the peasants had fought in the national liberation movement against the Germans, their land was not nationalized although a limitation of 20 hectares of land was placed on private holdings. Much of the land which was appropriated by the government was distributed to poor peasants. The remainder of the land went into the formation of state farms. However, the socialist sector of agriculture was not formed exclusively from land appropriated by the state, but was based in part on the state owned farms which had existed in Yugoslavia prior to the war.

Socialist Sector of Agriculture. The socialist sector of agriculture includes state farms, collective farms, and general cooperatives. State farms are owned by the federal government and are operated according to the system of workers' management in much the same way as the industrial enterprises. The state farms are designed to accomplish large-scale agricultural production and are of particular importance in the production of grain crops. The typical state farm controls around 1,000 hectares (2,500 acres) of land and receives from the government a high concentration of resources and personnel.

Land on the collective farms is state owned and is worked by the farmers in common. The produce is distributed according to the contribution of each member. In terms of its functions and operations it is similar to the Russian collective farm. The government encourages cooperation between the collective farms and private farmers; in some instances, private farms are worked by a collective farm on a sharecrop or cash basis. In this way farmers may retain possession of their land and benefit from the use of agricultural machinery, fertilizer, and farming techniques which are provided by the collective farm.

There are also general agricultural cooperatives which are jointly managed by the farmers and their own employees. The land is owned by the cooperatives and is farmed by private farmers who are paid in cash. The cooperatives provide the machines, implements, seed, and fertilizer. The cooperatives are also responsible for the marketing and sale of farm produce. The private farmers neither subscribe to business shares in a cooperative nor are they liable for its debts. Cooperatives and individual farmers may produce jointly, with profits shared in proportion to the contribution made by each partner, or the cooperatives may be responsible only for participation in the production process—furnishing services and equipment—and, in return, receive a fixed share of the profits of the farmers.[25] In most cases, the cooperatives and the private farmers conclude, in advance, contracts on production and the purchase of farm produce at fixed prices or at prices found on the market at the date of delivery.

Agricultural Bank. Agricultural credit is provided by the Agricultural Bank (Jugoslovenska Poljoprivredna). It grants short-term and long-term credit to agricultural enterprises and is responsible for supervising the use of the credit.

---

[25] For a discussion of the Yugoslav agricultural system, see Joel Dirlam and James L. Plummer, *An Introduction to the Yugoslav Economy* (Columbus: C. E. Merrill Publishing Co., 1973), p. 11.

It provides banking services in connection with the utilization of foreign exchange used in the agricultural sector and serves as a repository for the funds of the various agricultural enterprises.

AN APPRAISAL OF THE YUGOSLAV ECONOMY

Yugoslav communism is unquestionably more liberal and humane than the communism of the Soviet Union and its satellites. The reforms and the general attitude of the government indicate a flexibility and a willingness to experiment that is lacking in other communist countries. In order to honor promises to workers and to stimulate production, the government has decentralized management and has introduced workers' councils in economic enterprises. There are, however, certain problems which confront the Yugoslav economy.

From the beginning of its history, Yugoslavia has been confronted by a seemingly insoluble nationality problem. It is really a confederation of rather diverse ethnic groups which are difficult to weld into a homogeneous unit. Rivalries exist between regions and are exacerbated by the fact that economic development is extremely uneven between regions. The hope that surplus capital would flow more to the less developed regions of the country has not been realized. Neither Croatia nor Slovenia, which are among the most developed and richest republics of Yugoslavia, have shown much interest in investing in the underdeveloped areas of the south. Chauvinistic sentiment must be considered to be a key deterrent to the free flow of capital between regions.

Unemployment has been a problem which has confronted Yugoslavia. The transition from an agricultural to an industrial economy has not been smooth. Surplus labor from the farms has tended to migrate to the urban areas where employment has not always been available. In April, 1972 an estimated 310,000 workers were unemployed, or more than 4 percent of the labor force.[26] The unemployment rate during the 1960s was as high as 8 percent. Yugoslavia has eased its unemployment problem to some extent by exporting part of its labor force to other countries. In 1973, for example, more than one million Yugoslavs were working in the Western European countries. Yugoslavia's second largest source of foreign exchange is the remittances sent home by these workers.

There have been rather marked variations in Yugoslavia's rate of economic development. For example, economic growth has been lower than expected, with the result that many workers have migrated to jobs in more advanced industrial countries in Western Europe. The rate of economic growth, as measured by annual changes in the real social product, has varied over the 1967–1973 period from a low of 0.8 percent in 1967 to a high of 9.3 percent in 1969.[27] However, the average annual increase of 5.5 percent can be considered

[26] "Yugoslavia," *Economic Surveys* (Paris: Organization for Economic Cooperation and Development, 1973), p. 11
[27] *Statistical Yearbook of Yugoslavia* (Belgrade: Federal Institute of Statistics, 1973), p. 32.

as rather good in comparison to other countries. For example, using comparable data, the average rate of real growth for East Germany, the country with the highest standard of living of all the socialist economies, for the same period was 5.1 percent.[28] The real increase in Yugoslav per capita social product over the same period ranged from a low of 0.1 percent in 1967 to a high of 9.4 percent in 1969, with an average annual increase of 4.9 percent.[29]

Probably the most important economic problem confronting the Yugoslav economy is inflation. The period since the reforms of 1965 has been highly inflationary as a result of the gradual lessening of control over the economy and the move to a freer price structure. During the 1967–1973 period, consumer prices increased at an annual average rate of 10 percent in spite of the imposition of wage and price controls and attempts to limit the money supply.[30] Wages have increased at a faster rate than productivity. In 1972 money wages increased by 22 percent over 1971, while productivity increased by 4 percent. Inflation can be partly attributable to the fact that social considerations have prompted the government to allow inefficient firms to continue to operate. The effect, so to speak, is to remove the brake on wages and prices which the risk of a business failure might be expected to provide.

A concomitant problem has been a persistent deficit in the balance of payments, despite currency reforms. Like most developing countries, Yugoslavia imports more than it exports. But at the same time, it sells more services abroad than it buys. Therefore, Yugoslavia has a visible balance of payments deficit and an invisible balance of payments surplus. In the total balance of payments there is a deficit. This imbalance can be summarized as follows: [31]

	1967	1968	1969	1970	1971	1972
Exports (millions of dollars)	3,617	3,652	4,261	4,852	5,244	6,466
Imports (millions of dollars)	4,934	5,193	6,166	8,306	9,398	9,343
Deficit	−1,317	−1,541	−1,905	−3,454	−4,154	−2,877

It can be said that the Yugoslav economy is one of contrasts. It possesses the potential for rapid economic growth, but is vulnerable to inflation and balance of payments difficulties. With a mixture of a planned and market economy and a policy of accelerated industrialization, the government has transformed Yugoslavia from an agrarian to an industrial society. Industrial production for the period 1952–1960 grew at an average annual rate of 13.5 percent.[32] For the period 1960–1966 the rate was 9.5 percent, and for the

[28] Staatlichen Zentralverwaltung für Statistik, *Statistisches Taschenbuch der Deutschen Demokratischen Republik* (Berlin: Staatsverlag der DDR, 1973), p. 24.
[29] *Statistical Yearbook of Yugoslavia, loc. cit.*
[30] *Indek* (Belgrade: Federal Institute for Statistics, November, 1973), p. 7.
[31] *Ibid.*, p. 8.
[32] J. T. Crawford, "Yugoslavia's New Economic Strategy: A Progress Report," *Economic Developments in Western Europe* (Washington: Joint Economic Committee, May, 1970), p. 619; and *Statistical Yearbook of Yugoslavia, op. cit.*, p. 35.

period 1963–1972 the rate was 10 percent.[33] There were variations in the composition of industrial production, with manufacturing increasing at an average rate of 10.6 percent over the 1963–1972 period compared to an average increase of 4.6 percent for mining.[34] Industrialization has required some sacrifices on the part of consumers. Although productivity has increased rapidly, it has not kept pace with consumption demands, and this has caused some discontent and the migration of workers to Western Europe.

Comparisons of Yugoslavia and other socialist economies of Eastern Europe are difficult to make. For one thing, there are divergences in terms of differences in the level of economic development and resource availability. Moreover, some countries were more adversely affected by the war than others. A case in point is East Germany, which sustained not only massive destruction during the war, but also had to sustain reparations imposed by the Soviet Union.[35] However, East Germany had a prewar industrial base upon which to rebuild its economy. Czechoslovakia was also an advanced industrial country, particularly in comparison to Bulgaria and Rumania. There is also an exogenous factor, namely, Soviet influence on the economic process, that also affects comparisons of countries. Soviet control with respect to industrialization policies tended to fall more heavily on the developed economies of Czechoslovakia and East Germany than on the less developed economies.

Table 20–4 presents a comparison of the index of industrial production for

TABLE 20—4
A COMPARISON OF INDUSTRIAL PRODUCTION FOR YUGOSLAVIA AND OTHER SOCIALIST ECONOMIES, 1955–1970 (1960 = 100)

Country	1955	1965	1968	1969	1970	1971
Albania	46	139	209	237	251	268
Bulgaria	48	174	244	267	293	319
Czechoslovakia	61	129	156	164	179	191
East Germany	65	133	160	171	183	193
Hungary	70	144	175	180	193	203
Poland	63	150	190	207	225	240
Rumania	60	191	270	298	334	373
USSR	61	151	195	209	227	245
Yugoslavia	54	166	183	204	222	244

Source: Staatlichen Zentralverwaltung für Statistik, *Statistisches Jahrbuch der DDR, 1973* (Berlin: Staatsverlag der Deutschen Demokratischen Republik, 1973), p. 584.

[33] *Statistical Yearbook of Yugoslavia, op cit.,* p. 36.
[34] *UN Monthly Bulletin of Statistics* (New York: United Nations, April, 1973).
[35] Soviet occupation forces began with looting and dismantling of East German plants in 1945. They carried off timber, livestock, and industrial goods, and removed railroad rolling stock. Goods and services also had to be delivered as reparation for German damage done in the Soviet Union.

Yugoslavia, the Soviet Union, the Eastern satellite countries, and Albania, which ideologically is more aligned with China than the Soviet Union. Industrial production, as used in the table, refers to material production but excludes services and any form of nonmaterial production. Given the diverse economies and the lower industrial base from which the country had to start, it can be said that the performance of the Yugoslav economy has been good.

SUMMARY

The fundamental feature of the Yugoslav economic system is not state ownership of the means of production, but the self-management by workers and other direct producers of the operation of all economic organizations. The Yugoslav concept of communism is that society is a community of working people who create material wealth through their work. Thus, it is these working people who must decide on the allocation and use of the goods they produce. If working people are the leading social group, then the basic question concerns the construction of an economic system in which the active role of the producers and their associations will be strengthened and the economic and social role of the state will decrease and gradually disappear. According to the Yugoslav concept, the state, with its bureaucratic organization, represents an obstacle to progress, for it encroaches on the rights of workers to distribute income and to participate in the operation of the economy. The state is simply an institution which has replaced private capitalism in the socialist countries, but it imposes a new set of constraints upon the working people so that true socialism is never achieved.

In line with this viewpoint, a regionalization of macroeconomic management has replaced the centralized, ministerial system of state management. This has been achieved through the decentralization of management within the state apparatus and through the creation of local self-government in the commune, which is the basic form of social and economic integration in a region.

The policy of decentralization has extended over into the distribution of income. The 1965 reforms revised the Yugoslav fiscal system. The producer's turnover tax and the net profits tax were eliminated and were replaced by a sales tax levied on consumers. The largest part of funds for investment have been transferred to the enterprises. This change was accompanied by a reorganization of the banking system for the purpose of changing the distribution of investment resources.

A Yugoslav enterprise is managed by its workers through a managerial body called the workers' council. Workers' self-government and social management are supposed to encourage initiative and bring about a combination of centralized and decentralized decision making. The workers' council is responsible for the development of the plan and work schedule of an enterprise. It also makes decisions concerning basic matters of business policy and the use of the resources and funds of the enterprise. The workers' council selects a management board, which has the responsibility for enforcing decisions made by the council. Every enterprise also has a managing director who executes the decisions of the workers' council and the management board. The director is elected by the workers' council on the basis of public competition and is responsible to the council and to the management board for the performance of specific duties.

An enterprise acquires its resources either by investing part of its net profits in its business funds or by acquiring credit from banks and other creditors. Individuals or organizations may form an enterprise.[36] Production and price decisions are made by the enterprise, and there are relatively few restrictions placed by the state on its autonomy of operation. The enterprise operates within the framework of what can be called a socialist market economy in which it will either make a profit or a loss. In some cases, price decisions are affected by government decisions to channel consumption into a particular direction or to adjust the economic position of underdeveloped areas as a matter of national development policy.

As for economic planning, the Yugoslav type of plan differs considerably from the centralized command plans of the Soviet Union and other communist countries. Actually, it is closer to the French type of planning in that it does not contain rigid targets for industries to attain. To the contrary, it specifies only general goals for the economy. Republics and communes possess considerable flexibility in the development of their plans.

QUESTIONS

1. Compare the role of economic planning in Yugoslavia and in the Soviet Union.
2. What are some of the problems which have complicated the development of the Yugoslav economy?
3. What were the basic objectives of the reforms of 1965?
4. Compare the management of a Yugoslav and an American enterprise.
5. Discuss the operations of the National Bank of Yugoslavia in the monetary system.
6. In what ways do the Yugoslav and Chinese economic systems differ?
7. What is the philosophy that explains the reliance on worker self-management of Yugoslav enterprises?
8. Discuss how enterprises are operated and income is distributed in Yugoslavia.
9. In Yugoslavia, interest plays an important role in resource allocation. Do you agree?
10. What is the role of the commune in the Yugoslav economic and political system?

RECOMMENDED READINGS

Bicanic, Rudolph. *Economic Policy in Socialist Yugoslavia.* Cambridge: Cambridge University Press, 1973.

---

[36] The Yugoslav press in May, 1968 reported that a group of citizens collected 2 million new dinars ($250,000) and started the construction of a textile factory in Slavonska Orahovica. The new factory was to employ 60 persons, and its annual output was estimated to be 12 million new dinars.

Dirlam, Joel B. *Introduction to the Yugoslav Economy.* Columbus: C. E. Merrill Publishing Co., 1973.

Horvat, Branko. *Business Cycles in Yugoslavia.* New York: International Arts and Science Press, 1971.

Kolaja, Jiri. *Workers' Councils: The Yugoslav Experience.* New York: Praeger, Inc., 1966.

Macesich, George, and Dimitrije Dimitrijevic. *Money and Finance in Contemporary Yugoslavia.* New York: Praeger, 1973.

Milenkovitch, Deborah. *Plan and Market in Yugoslav Economic Thought.* New Haven: Yale University Press, 1971.

Popovic, Nenad O. *Yugoslavia: The New Class in Crisis.* Syracuse: Syracuse University Press, 1968.

Zaninovitch, George. *The Development of Socialist Yugoslavia.* Baltimore: Johns Hopkins Press, 1968.

21

The Economic Systems: Evaluation of Goal Fulfillment

INTRODUCTION

Full employment, price stability, and economic growth are basic goals of any economic system. To these goals, a fourth goal, the equitable distribution of income may also be added. It is the purpose of this chapter to evaluate the economic systems of the nine countries included in the book from the standpoint of attainment of these goals. To some degree comparisons of individual countries are difficult to make because the order of priority of goals differs among countries. Although a high rate of economic growth may be a prime economic desire for one country, a different goal may be of more importance to another. It is also necessary to mention the fact that noneconomic goals, such as the political freedoms of the individual in society are very important; however, their analysis is beyond the scope of this book.[1]

To provide a frame of reference, it is desirable to define each of the four goals.

Full Employment

The desirability of full employment is self-evident. It is the prime function of an economy to enable everybody willing and able to work to earn a living, and only a fully employed economy performs this function. However, it is hard to define what constitutes a fully employed labor force. At any given time some workers will be in the process of changing jobs or occupations; others will be experiencing temporary layoffs caused by the seasonal

---

[1] An area in which governments have shown flagrant neglect is in the care of natural resources. Land, air, and water have been spoiled freely. However, pollution cuts across ideologies. It is not a monopoly of capitalism as some would have us believe. The Soviet Union, too, has its pollution problems.

nature of their employment or by shifts in demand that reduce the need for some types of workers. In its 1962 Annual Report, the President's Council of Economic Advisers adopted an unemployment rate of 4 percent as a "reasonable and prudent goal for stabilization policy." [2] To the western European countries, this rate would be considered rather high.

Price Stability

Price stability is also a desirable goal. Inflation and deflation lead to the arbitrary redistribution of real incomes and real wealth, and if not contained can eventually cause an economy to collapse. However, price stability is difficult to define. Relative prices and changes in relative prices fulfill important regulating functions in a free enterprise economy. Price stability then would not refer to a completely stable and unchanging price. It means the absence of any marked trend or sharp, short-term movements in the general level of prices. Marked upward and downward trends and extreme short-term fluctuations in the price level are to be avoided. This does not mean that individual prices should not change; such changes are necessary if the price mechanism is to perform its allocating function.

Economic Growth

It is not difficult to reconcile the goal of full employment with the goal of economic growth. It is necessary to have growth in order to maintain stability of production and employment. Economic growth, however, can be defined not only to require an increase in gross national product large enough to absorb new entrants in the labor force but also to include increased per capita real income. The latter is a basic requisite for higher living standards. Economic growth in the sense of an expanding output of material goods and services is not an end in itself, but only a means to more basic ends. It provides the necessary resources to permit governments to discharge their ever increasing responsibilities without adversely affecting private consumption standards.[3]

Equitable Distribution of Income

A fourth goal, an equitable distribution of income, can be added to the three main goals of full employment, price stability, and economic growth. Although there must be an efficient production which provides balanced economic growth with full employment, the results of this production must be shared among members of society in such a way that it is felt to be

[2] *Economic Report of the President* (Washington: U.S. Government Printing Office, 1962), p. 46.

[3] To a certain extent there is a contradiction between economic growth and the quality of the environment. Economic growth results in part in smoke and fumes from more cars, litter from more cans produced, and pollution of streams from the increased output of factories. It is now also necessary to think about things which are tangential to the environment.

just and equitable. However, there is no absolute standard of income distribution that can satisfy everyone. Under a capitalistic system income inequality is justified on the basis that it is needed for the efficient allocation of resources. High prices are set on scarce agents of production and low prices on relatively plentiful agents. High prices tend to reserve the scarce agents of production for the uses which are most important and to keep them from being wasted in relatively unimportant uses. Low prices for more plentiful agents tend to lead to their use in large quantities. Differences in prices can also lead to a shifting of quantities of an agent from an area of plenty to an area of scarcity.

Role of Governments

Governments in the Western countries and Japan have come to play a very important role in the attainment of these goals. This role has taken two basic forms which have been mentioned repeatedly: (1) In order to absorb labor and other resources, they have entered their economies as important determinants of the level of aggregate demand. Keynesian economics has come to the fore, with the basic idea that full employment can be achieved through the use of adjustments in a country's fiscal and monetary machinery. Changes in taxation and government spending have influenced output, prices, and employment. Moreover, progressive income taxation and transfer payments have been used to create a more equitable redistribution of income. However, the extent of the redistributional effects of taxation and transfer payments varies from country to country.

(2) Governments also serve as a powerful force in the determination of productive capacity. There is public ownership of certain key industries, and there is also direct participation in the formation of capital. Government expenditures contribute to the health, education, and training of the labor force, and hence to productive capacity.

In the remainder of this chapter, the economic systems of the nine countries included in the book will be evaluated. Where value judgments have to be made, as in the case of national income, industrial output, and foreign trade, many problems arise, even if the countries concerned belong to the same economic system. However, where different social systems are involved, these problems are magnified because the bases, methods, and consistency of valuation differ fundamentally; and, moreover, socialist countries do not publish systematic returns. It is possible to make some general comparisons among the different economic systems with respect to such goals as full employment, price stability, economic growth, and income distribution. To some degree comparisons of individual countries are difficult to make because stated goals may differ.

THE AMERICAN MODIFIED MARKET ECONOMY

The United States is considered to be predominantly a capitalistic economy. Direct government ownership of industry is small, and there is a lesser degree of intervention in the economy than in the western European countries. Taxes, which provide a government with control over economic resources, are lower relative to gross national product in the United States than in the major western European countries.

It cannot be said, however, that the federal budget does not play an important role in the United States' political and economic life. It represents a proposed allocation of resources to serve national objectives between the public and private sector of the economy, and it also embodies the taxing and spending policies of the government for promoting full employment, price stability, and economic growth. In 1975 federal expenditures accounted for $356.9 billion.[4] This amount can be compared to a gross national product of $1.49 trillion. Purchases of goods and services accounted for $123.1 billion of total federal expenditures and transfer payments accounted for $131.7 billion.[5] Total expenditures of all levels of government in the United States amounted to $525.1 billion.

It is also necessary to look at the receipts side of the coin, for taxes as well as government expenditures redistribute income and perform economic stabilization functions. Taxes, as mentioned above, give governments control over economic resources. In 1975 federal tax receipts amounted to $283.5 billion compared to a gross national product of $1.49 trillion. A point which has been made throughout the book is that in countries with mixed economic systems, tax totals absorb a considerably higher percentage of the gross national product than in the United States, even after allowing for state and local taxes. For example, receipts from Swedish taxation and social security contributions amounted to 44 percent of the Swedish gross national product in 1967, while receipts from the same sources amounted to 29.8 percent of the United States gross national product. Thus, we can say that in Sweden the government is more deeply involved in the nation's economic affairs because of the larger percentage of the gross national product that flows through the public sector.

Governmental Role after 1929

However, the role of the federal government vis-à-vis the American economy has changed considerably since 1929. In that year, which was a pivotal point in the changing role of the federal government in the national economy, total federal expenditures accounted for 3 percent of the gross national product compared to 24 percent in 1975.[6] The federal government today has an impact on the economy in a number of ways, most of which were nonexistent in 1929.

Credit Aids. Federal credit aids—direct loans and insurance or guarantees of private loans—are provided for improvement of housing and encouragement

---

[4] *Economic Report of the President* (Washington: U.S. Government Printing Office, 1976), pp. 249, 250. The data is for the fiscal year.

[5] *Ibid.*

[6] *Economic Report of the President* (Washington: U.S. Government Printing Office, 1974), p. 327.

of home ownership, development of agriculture and other natural resources, redevelopment of communities and regions, promotion of business, and aid to education. In 1973 direct loans and insurance or guarantees amounted to an estimated $65.6 billion.[7]

Government Enterprises. Public enterprises, although small in number, contributed an estimated gross outlay of $31.1 billion in 1973.[8] They carry on operations primarily with the public, and are usually organized similar to private business firms. Some of them are incorporated enterprises; others are unincorporated. The outlays of some public corporations are considerable. In 1967 expenditures of the Commodity Credit Corporation and the Post Office Department amounted to $8.7 billion and $6.5 billion respectively.

Federal Grants. Federal grants to state and local governments have increased in importance in recent years. Broadly speaking, their function is to help solve particular public problems, such as education and housing. In the United States, political tradition is one of decentralized decision making, with wide discretion left to the states by constitutional reservation and political inclination. Barred from the kinds of intervention practiced by the western European countries, the federal government has utilized several means of accomplishing policy aims, among them the grant device. In 1975 total federal grants to state and local governments amounted to $48.3 billion.[9]

Federal Purchases. Purchases of goods and services measure the value of the gross national product consumed by the federal government. In 1975 purchases of goods and services amounted to $123.1 billion. State and local governments purchased $208 billion.[10] Federal purchases are classified into two major subcategories—defense and nondefense. The former accounted for $84.0 billion in 1975 and the latter, $39.2 billion.

Transfer Payments. The federal government also engages in a variety of transfer activities—unemployment benefits, retirement pay, veterans compensation, and other payments. Although transfer payments do not directly enter gross national product as a federal government expenditure, they are a part of personal income and are counted as part of gross national product when spent by the recipients. In 1975 transfer payments amounted to 13.9 percent of personal income compared to 3.1 percent in 1952.

Although federal government expenditures and taxation result in the diversion of resources from the private to the public sector of the economy, the extent is less than in the mixed systems of the western European countries. The relative importance of transfer payments as a source of personal income is a good measure of the degree of government intervention for welfare purposes. Their main effect is to redistribute income among individuals, social

---

[7] *Special Analysis, Budget of the United States* (Washington: U.S. Government Printing Office, Fiscal Year 1973), p. 66.

[8] *Ibid.*, p. 45.

[9] *Economic Report of the President, op. cit.*, p. 250.

[10] Federal government expenditures are for the fiscal year; state and local government expenditures are for the calendar year.

and economic groups, or geographic regions. When transfer payments are expressed as a percentage of personal income, the results for the United States for 1972 were 8.1 percent compared to 18.1 percent for France, 12.8 percent for Sweden, and 10.1 percent for the United Kingdom.[11]

Economic Goals

In the 1960s traditional concepts of public finance underwent a major change; government fiscal policies came to be viewed as instruments for influencing the magnitude and direction of income flows throughout the economy. As practiced by the Kennedy and Johnson Administrations, the "new economics" reflected the belief that economic stability—full employment without inflation—could be achieved through the use of fine tuning adjustments of the country's fiscal and monetary machinery. In 1962 the investment credit was introduced with the purpose of raising the level of investment. It permitted firms to deduct each year from their tax liability 7 percent of their investment outlays on machinery. Another example of the "new economics" at work was the income tax cut of 1964.[12] Its purpose was to assure an increase in total demand and hence an increase in the level of economic activity.

Full Employment. During the period from 1958 to 1963, the annual rate of unemployment ranged from a high of 6.8 percent in 1958 to a low of 5.5 percent in 1962. Regional unemployment was considerably higher in several areas of the United States. Certain coal mining counties in Kentucky and West Virginia had unemployment rates in excess of 20 percent for most of this period. By 1969 the unemployment rate had declined to 3.5 percent, the lowest rate since 1953. In part, this reduction was attributable to general economic policies designed to stimulate aggregate demand, and to manpower training measures which increased the skills, quality, and mobility of the labor force. Another reason for the reduction in the unemployment rate was the conflict in Vietnam. National defense expenditures increased from $50.1 billion in 1965 to $81.2 billion in 1969. To a considerable extent the increase in aggregate demand during the period 1965–1969 has been occasioned by war expenditures.

The unemployment rate turned sharply upward in the early 1970s, reflecting in part the cessation of the conflict in Vietnam. In 1970 the unemployment rate was 4.9 percent. In 1971 the rate had increased to 5.9 percent, but in 1972 the rate decreased to 5.6 percent, in 1973 the rate was 5.5 percent, and for 1975 was 8.5 percent. The President's Council of Economic Advisers suggested in 1962 that an unemployment rate of 4 percent should be taken as that rate compatible with economic stability. The choice of 4 percent was set as an interim target, given the existing structure of the labor market and prevailing

---

[11] *Economic Report of the President* (Washington: U.S. Government Printing Office, 1974), p. 253, and *OECD Economic Surveys for France, Sweden, and the United Kingdom* (Paris: Organization for Economic Cooperation and Development, 1973), pp. 49, 61, and 66.

[12] For the "new economics" at work, see Walter W. Heller, *New Dimensions of Political Economy* (Cambridge, Mass.: Harvard University Press, 1966), pp. 70–83.

opinion on the desirability of curbing wage rate increases and maintaining price stability. However, this target rate of unemployment, although generally accepted by a majority of economists as a desirable goal, has not been achieved very often. As a matter of fact, the unemployment rate over the last 25 years has been below 4 percent on only two occasions—during the Korean and Vietnam conflicts.

Price Stability. The maintenance of both full employment and price stability is a difficult policy goal. Although the annual unemployment rate was below 4 percent during the period 1966–1969, the consumer price index increased 14.6 percent during the same period. Inflation became a problem. During 1969 the consumer price index increased by 6.1 percent over the preceding year.[13] During 1970 the index increased at a rate of 5.5 percent, even though the Federal Reserve pursued a policy of restraint on money and credit in an effort to bring inflation under control. In 1971 and 1972 the performance of the American economy was better than other major industrial countries in that the consumer price index increased by 3.4 percent in each of the two years. However, in 1973 the consumer price index increased at a rate of 8.8 percent—the largest increase in over 50 years.[14]

The amount which any economy can produce in the short run with the existing resources, institutions, attitudes, and tastes cannot exceed certain limits, however great the demand. As unused resources become more fully utilized, there eventually has to be some sort of a trade-off or compromise between the goals of full employment and price stability in which part of one goal is traded for part of the other goal. For example, if full employment is the prime goal, inflation may be the direct consequence. If price stability takes precedence as the primary goal, then unemployment rates above the desired norm will probably be the logical concomitant. The desirability of full employment is self-evident. It is the prime function of an economy to enable everybody willing and able to work to earn a living. But price stability, too, is a desirable goal of economic policy. Inflation has a deleterious effect on an economy through changes in income distribution and through inefficient allocation of resources that eventually create a loss of output.

Economic Growth. Economic growth can be defined as an increase in real gross national product. It depends not only upon changes in an economy's potential for production, but also upon the extent to which that capacity is utilized. Without expansion of these productive capacities, it would be impossible for an economy to meet a variety of goals, all of which require resources. To maintain full employment continually, there must be a rate of economic growth sufficient to absorb new entrants into the labor force. Resources are also needed for services for which there is a continually increasing public demand, such as education and housing. An inadequate rate of economic growth reduces incentives to invest and innovate, and such a rate can aggravate social problems which are already in existence.

---

[13] *Economic Report of the President* (Washington: U.S. Government Printing Office, 1974), p. 3C4.

[14] The only comparable increase in the consumer price index was in 1918.

When President Kennedy came into office in 1961, there was concern over the low rate of growth in the economy of the United States relative to other countries, particularly the Soviet Union. During the period from 1951 to 1960, the average annual growth rates of the major industrial countries ranged from 8 percent in Japan to 3 percent in the United States. This relatively low rate of growth led to a related problem of unemployment, which by 1961 was as high as 6.7 percent. Fiscal policy measures were used to operate on the supply side of the economy to increase productive capacity. The Revenue Act of 1962 contained a provision for the allowance of an investment credit. Its use represented a desire on the part of the government to promote investment in specific assets and, through this promotion, to increase productive capacity and the rate of economic growth. Another approach was a reduction in personal and corporate income taxes in 1964. It was expected that the tax cuts would operate to stimulate both consumption and investment spending, thus bringing output closer to the full employment potential.

Partly as a result of these policies, the American economy sustained a continuous advance in terms of employment and output through most of the decade. Attributing this success to the "new economics," the *Economic Report of the President* cited the following gains made over the five-year period, 1964–1968: [15]

1. An increase in the gross national product of more than $190 billion, after adjusting for price changes. This amount was as large as the gain of the previous 11 years.
2. A decrease in the unemployment rate from 5.7 percent to 3.3 percent.
3. An addition of more than 8.5 million workers into the labor force.
4. A decrease by about 12.5 million in the number of people living below a defined poverty level of income.
5. An increase of $535 in the average income of Americans after taxes and after corrections for price rises.

However, from 1968 to 1974 the performance of the American economy has been marred somewhat by a resurgence of inflation, which continues to be a problem. The rate of economic growth has declined and the country drifted into an economic downturn in 1974 which was exacerbated by the energy crisis. In 1973 the spendable income of the average American, after allowing for price increases and taxes, actually showed a decline. The general conflict between economic growth and a cleaner environment has also not been resolved.

Income Distribution. Income distribution refers to claims on a country's national output that arise from the ownership of economic resources. The national income is allocated in the form of wages and salaries and in the form of various property incomes—rent, interest, and profit. It is necessary to go beyond this division into labor and nonlabor income, which is really an initial division of income, to examine the way in which a government can alter

---

[15] *Economic Report of the President* (Washington: U.S. Government Printing Office, 1969), p. 5.

income distribution. From the viewpoint of income redistribution, a more meaningful concept is that of *personal income*. This may be defined as money income actually received by persons or households, and it will differ from the national income because some income earned in the productive process does not find its way into the hands of individuals as money income earned. Examples are corporate retained earnings and social security contributions. Personal income can be redistributed through the use of a government's taxing and expenditure policies. Transfer payments can transfer income from one group or person to another group or person.

Recent decades have witnessed no real movement toward greater equality in the distribution of income in the United States. In 1972 families making more than $17,760, those who constitute the most affluent fifth of the nation's hierarchy, earned 41.4 percent of the nation's aggregate income.[16] Meanwhile, those in the bottom fifth, making less than $5,612 annually, took in 5.4 percent of the total income. In 1947 the bottom one fifth of all families received 5.0 percent of income, while the highest one fifth received 43.0 percent of income.[17] In 1947 the highest 40 percent of families received 66.1 percent of aggregate income compared to 33.9 percent for the lowest 60 percent; in 1972 the percentage relationship had shown virtually no change—65.2 percent to 34.8 percent. This stability is rather remarkable in view of the great changes that have taken place in the American economy. For one thing, it would be logical to expect mass education, particularly at the college level, to broaden employment opportunities and to break down class barriers. But it would appear that mass education has done little to reduce income inequality.[18]

Why is the spread between the upper and lower income groups so difficult to reduce? One reason is that the progressive income tax does not significantly redistribute income. That is partly because taxpayers in the highest brackets have a greater opportunity to take advantage of tax loopholes than those with low incomes. These loopholes serve to reduce the effective rate of the federal personal income tax to the point where the average rate of tax paid by the top 1 percent of taxpayers in 1967 was only 26 percent, even though the nominal, or marginal, tax rate on incomes ranged up to 70 percent. A second reason is that government programs aimed largely at helping low income groups—Social Security, welfare, Medicare, food stamps—have grown enormously. However, many of these benefits go directly to affluent persons too. In 1970, for example, 22 percent of all families with incomes of more than $25,000 received transfer payment benefits.

THE MIXED ECONOMIES OF THE MIDDLE WAY

Five highly industrialized and advanced democracies—France, West Germany, Japan, Sweden, and the United Kingdom—were covered in the section

---

[16] U.S. Bureau of the Census, "Current Population Reports, Consumer Income, 1971" (Washington: U.S. Government Printing Office, December, 1973), p. 32.

[17] *Ibid.*, p. 36.

[18] Christopher Jencks, *Inequality: A Reassessment of the Effect of Family and Schooling in America* (New York: Basic Books, Inc., 1972).

on the "middle way" economies. Although there are similarities between these countries, their institutional arrangements are very different. The size of the government sectors, the composition of expenditures, and degree of political centralization vary considerably. In Japan the public sector is relatively small, while in countries such as France and Sweden, it is quite large. For obvious reasons, a government which controls a relatively large part of the economy will have more opportunities to influence the economy than a government which controls a small part. The degree of government centralization is also important for fiscal policy purposes. Germany is organized on a federal basis, with state and local governments having autonomy on the expenditure side.

Role of the National Governments

However, the role of the national government in these countries is of paramount economic and social importance in several respects. First of all, the national budget is important because of its size relative to gross national product. It is the national budget that brings together most of the economic decisions a country makes. Expenditure decisions in the budget, as well as revenue decisions, affect the amount of income every family has to spend as well as the rapidity with which that income increases. Budget decisions affect purchasing power, employment, inflation potential, and the rate of economic growth. Decisions made in the budget affect the quality as well as the quantity of public services that are made available to a nation's citizens. Secondly, ownership of certain industries also gives the national government some leverage over the level of economic activity. Often these nationalized industries are very big capital users; although they may employ a small percentage of the total labor force, they have at times approached the point of being responsible for nearly half of all investment in productive industry as in France and the United Kingdom. Finally, although monetary systems vary from country to country, it can be said that there is much greater government control over money and credit policies in the mixed systems than in the United States. This control has generally been used to coordinate these policies with national goals.

Governmental Expenditures. Governmental expenditures are a part of an economy's total outlays on goods and services, and expenditures exert their influence by generating demand and, therefore, employment and income. For example, the Swedish national government's expenditures accounted for approximately 32 percent of the gross national product. In 1972 public investment on the part of the national government amounted to $2.06 billion compared to gross private investment of $4.6 billion. When public expenditures of local governments are added to those of the national government, combined public investment expenditures amounted to $4.6 billion.

However, it was pointed out that Sweden and France do not include most welfare expenditures in the regular national budget. In France, family allowances, old age pensions, unemployment insurance, and other transfers are carried in the social budget. In Sweden the basic old age pension scheme is the only part of the social security system that is incorporated in the national budget. The remaining components of the system are carried in autonomous budgets not presented as such to Parliament. In 1973 transfer payments to households from the autonomous budgets amounted to $3.9 billion. When local government expenditures were added to the expenditures of the national government, the total in relation to the gross national product of Sweden was more than 40 percent. Moreover, the National Pension Fund, which contains the contribution for old age pensions, is one of the largest institutions in the Swedish credit market.

Savings and Investment. The public sector's contribution to savings and investment is greater in the mixed economies than in the United States. Public investment is higher because of the importance of public enterprises. It includes not only social overhead capital, but a substantial share of what would ordinarily be considered private capital formation. In the United Kingdom public savings amounted to 6.7 percent of gross domestic product in 1972 compared to 15.6 percent for private savings, and public investment amounted to 7.1 percent of gross domestic product compared to 12.2 percent for private investment.[19] In Sweden public investment accounted for 11.1 percent of the gross domestic product in 1972 compared to 12.3 percent for the private sector.[20] In terms of fiscal leverage, the public sector can contribute significantly to aggregate expenditures and the growth of output.

Influence of the Public Sector. The public sector can exert its influence on an economic system in a number of ways. For example, in the United Kingdom, the public sector employs directly nearly 25 percent of the nation's labor force, and almost 60 percent of all workers with higher educations. It owns about 40 percent of total capital assets, and it is responsible for about 45 percent of the nation's annual fixed investments. About 60 percent of the nation's scientific and technical research and development is financed by government agencies. The size and structure of important private industries, such as agriculture and aircraft production, are affected directly by government decisions. Purchases by the public sector provide a large and, in some cases, dominant component of the demand for the products of other industries such as construction, pharmaceuticals, electronics, electrical engineering, and telecommunications.[21]

Economic Goals

As in other countries, the primary objectives in the mixed economies of France, Germany, Japan, Sweden, and the United Kingdom are full employment, a satisfactory rate of economic growth, and stable prices. To these, a

---

[19] Central Statistical Office, *National Income and Expenditures* (London: Her Majesty's Stationery Office, 1973), Table 6.

[20] Swedish Ministry of Finance, *The Swedish Budget, 1973–1974,* p. 32.

[21] Sir Richard Clarke, "The Management of the Public Sector of the National Economy," *Stamp Memorial Lectures* (London: University of London, The Athlone Press, 1964), pp. 6 and 7.

viable balance of payments position must be added, for these countries have economies which depend to a considerable degree on foreign trade. To complete the group of objectives, it is necessary to review the extent to which taxes and transfer devices, as well as public services, have been used to secure the desired adjustments in the distribution of income.

Full Employment. The performance of the countries with mixed economic systems with regard to maintaining a high level of employment has been excellent. Unemployment rates have rarely been above 3 percent during most of the postwar period, a record substantially superior to that of the United States, even allowing for differences in the measurement of unemployment.[22] During the period of 1959–1973, unemployment rates in the United Kingdom ranged from a high of 3.8 percent to a low of 1.4 percent. In Sweden, unemployment has averaged less than 2 percent since the end of World War II. In West Germany, the unemployment rate was the lowest for all western European countries during most of the 1960s. In 1973 the unemployment rate averaged 1 percent. Unemployment rates in France and Japan have also been extremely low in comparison to the United States.[23]

The economic and social significance of a given unemployment rate depends on the institutional features of a country and the weight that is attached to a low unemployment rate in the formulation of national economic policies. It has been pointed out that memories of high unemployment rates between World Wars I and II had a direct influence on economic policy in the United Kingdom, France, Sweden, and other countries in recent years.

It appears, however, that the governments of these countries have failed in their attempts to render compatible the apparently irreconcilable objectives of maintaining full employment and preventing inflation. The question remains of the economic costs of restraining rises in general price levels and improving international competitive positions through more restrictive monetary and fiscal policies—costs which are measured in terms of a short-run loss of employment and output.

Price Stability. Although the overall performance of the mixed economies has been good with respect to the maintenance of a high level of employment, the goal of price stability has not fared as well. In the United Kingdom, the average annual price increase since 1950 has been 4.1 percent, and in only five of those years prices have risen less than 2 percent.[24] Imports exceeded exports for each year during the period 1960–1969, and repeated crises occurred in the balance of payments. In Sweden, the consumer price index increased 37 percent during the period 1969–1973 and 62 percent during the decade of the

---

[22] Normally, it is necessary to add 0.5 to 0.8 percent to unemployment rates in the United Kingdom, Sweden, and other European countries to make the rates comparable to United States unemployment rates. An unemployment rate of 2.6 percent in the United Kingdom is comparable to an unemployment rate of about 3.4 percent in the United States.

[23] *Main Economic Indicators* (Paris: Organization for Economic Cooperation and Development, 1972), pp. 51, 55, and 67.

[24] *Lloyds Bank Review* (January, 1974), p. 59.

1960s.[25] Imports have exceeded exports for each year since 1960. In France the consumer price index increased by an annual average of 5.2 percent over a six-year period, 1967–1972.[26] In Germany the record in terms of price stability has been the best of the five countries. During the same six years, the German consumer price index increased at an average annual rate of 3.4 percent a year.[27] In Japan the consumer price index increased at an average annual rate of 5.9 percent for the same period.[28] However, inflation during 1973 accelerated, with Japan showing an estimated increase in the consumer price index of 18 percent.

By and large, the governments of these countries have concluded that the policies of restraint on their economies that preservation of the external value of the currency sometimes requires are no longer politically acceptable. Instead, the emphasis has been upon promoting full labor force employment and rapid economic growth, even though policies aimed at these objectives might have the ultimate effect of weakening the value of the country's currency. If the United States experience of the past three years may be accepted as a meaningful indicator, it would seem that the political fall-out from restrictive practices aimed at controlling inflation is not as great as has been assumed, and that tolerating inflation perhaps has greater adverse political impact.

Economic Growth. The rate of economic growth has ranged from the slow growth of output in the United Kingdom to an extraordinary performance by the extremely viable Japanese economy, which is the fastest growing in the world and now has the third largest gross national product among all countries. It has been said that the 21st century may well turn out to be the Japanese century.[29] However, the energy crisis and national concern over problems of pollution may well change that prediction. During the period 1950–1964 the average annual rate of growth of real gross national product in Japan was 9.6 percent. The increase in the average annual growth rate of the Japanese economy was even more spectacular for the period 1965–1973. At no time during this nine-year period was the real rate of growth less than 10 percent.

The performance of the German economy was almost as spectacular as the Japanese performance, particularly during the decade of the 1950s. However, in the 1960s the growth rate began to decline, reaching a low of 1.1 percent for 1967. The German economy rebounded in 1968 and 1969 and the real rate of growth increased to 7.3 and 8.1 percent for the respective years. From 1970 on, the German economy experienced a period of "stagflation," with the rate of growth averaging less than 4 percent. The growth rate of the French economy has been solid, with an average annual rate of increase in excess of 5 percent for the period 1960–1973. The Swedish growth rate has been unspectacular

[25] *Quarterly Review* (Skandinaviska Enskilda Banken, June, 1973).

[26] International Monetary Fund, *International Financial Statistics* (November, 1973), p. 2.

[27] *Ibid.*, p. 2.

[28] *Ibid.*, p. 2.

[29] Herman Kahn and Anthony J. Weiner, *The Year 2000* (New York: The Macmillan Company, 1967), p. 117.

in recent years, averaging 3.9 percent for the period 1965–1970. A similar rate
was maintained for the period 1970–1973. The growth rate for the United
Kingdom is the lowest among major industrial countries, regardless of the time
period used.

The growth performances of the countries with mixed economic systems
are summarized in Table 21–1. The growth rates during the 1970s show a

TABLE 21–1

GROWTH IN REAL GROSS NATIONAL PRODUCT FOR SELECTED COUNTRIES,
1950–1973

Countries	1950–1960	1960–1965	1965–1970	1971	1972	1973*
France	4.6%	5.8%	5.6%	5.0%	5.4%	6.5%
Germany	7.7	5.0	4.5	2.7	3.0	5.5
Japan	9.0	10.1	12.4	6.2	9.7	10.5
Sweden	3.4	5.4	3.9	0	2.2	4.0
United Kingdom	2.7	3.4	2.3	2.2	2.3	6.0
United States	3.3	4.8	3.4	3.2	6.1	6.0
Western Europe	4.0	5.1	4.5	3.1	3.7	5.5

Source: "Grundlinien der Wirtschaftsentwicklung 1974," Wochenbericht (Berlin:
Deutsches Institut fur Wirtschaftsforschung, December, 1973).
* Estimates.

marked decline over preceding time periods, reflecting in part inflation which
has become the major economic problem in Western Europe, Japan, and the
United States. This problem will be further exacerbated by the energy crisis
which has had a deleterious effect, particularly in Western Europe.

The mixed economies have maintained, for the most part, a respectable
rate of economic growth. However, problems have developed which may well
impinge upon the continuance of this record in the future. The effects of the
energy crisis upon the economies of Japan and Western Europe will be serious.
Until this problem is resolved, predictions of future growth are difficult.
Concern over environmental problems has caused some countries to reappraise
their economic policy goals. The Japanese government, for example, has called
for a policy of slower growth.

Income Distribution. It has been pointed out that taxes and transfer devices,
as well as public services, may be used to secure desired adjustments in the
distribution of income. Taxes, of course, provide governments with control
over economic resources, and expenditures are the chief means by which they
provide for social wants. The methods that governments have used most widely
to alter income distribution have been progressive income and inheritance
taxation. But for the most part the distributional effects of progressive taxation
have been minimal. The British income tax is progressive, and much has been
written in recent years concerning the strong influence of egalitarian considerations upon economic policy pursued by the British government since the end
of World War II. However, recent studies tend to dispute the idea that there

is a greater trend toward income equality in the United Kingdom. It appears that the trend was arrested in the period following 1957, reflecting several factors which have occurred since that time. First, the growth in employment income has slowed relative to self-employed income; second, rent, interest, and dividends have increased at an accelerating rate since the end of 1957.

The distribution of incomes after taxes has shown little change in the United Kingdom since 1957. In that year the top 1 percent of income recipients received 5 percent of total income after taxes. In 1965 the amount was 5.3 percent, and in 1967, the last year for which data are available, the amount was 5.0 percent. In 1957 the top 5 percent of British income units received 14.9 percent of after-tax total income, and in 1967 the amount was 15.5 percent.[30] There was an actual decline in the percentage of income taxes paid by the top 1 percent and 5 percent of income units. In 1957 the top 1 percent paid 35.3 percent of total income taxes and the top 5 percent paid 54.2 percent. In 1967 the respective amounts were 22.8 and 38.1 percent.[31]

It appears that Sweden and Japan may have more egalitarian societies than other countries from the standpoint of income distribution. One measurement of inequality is the distribution of personal income before taxes. When Sweden and Japan are compared to other Western countries, a smaller percentage of personal income is concentrated in the hands of upper income earners. Erik Lundberg, in computing before-tax distribution of personal income, found that Sweden and Japan had a less unequal distribution of income than Holland, West Germany, the United Kingdom, and the United States.[32] The highest 2.5 percent of income earners received 11 percent of income in Sweden and Japan compared to 28 percent in West Germany and 13 percent in the United States. However, income taxes average 30 percent of household income in Sweden compared to 10 percent of household income in Japan.

An international comparative analysis of almost any aspect of taxation is extremely complex. Attempts at simplification run the risk of inaccuracy and distortion. This is particularly true of tax burdens. Every major characteristic of personal income taxation varies widely among countries. Exemptions, allowances, and deductions are all treated differently. No accurate account can be taken of the tendency toward compliance on the part of taxpayers or of the efficiency of collection on the part of governments. Moreover, simple comparisons of tax payments make no allowance for the multitude of concessions and transfers which can radically alter the amount of net income.

Progressive income taxation, however, is not the only method used for the leveling of incomes: government expenditure is designed to the same end. In the mixed economies considerable revenues from taxation are paid out to the lower-income groups in the form of pensions and family allowances that add to their incomes. Tax revenues are also used to defray the cost of

---

[30] Central Statistical Office, *National Income and Expenditures, 1968* (London: Her Majesty's Stationery Office, 1969), p. 28.

[31] *Ibid.*, p. 28.

[32] Erik Lundberg, "Sweden's Economy in an International Perspective" *Skandinaviska Banken Quarterly Review* (First Quarter, 1971), p. 7.

living for many groups. Goods and services, such as food, housing, education, and transportation, are heavily subsidized by national and local authorities. Public expenditures which in some way contribute to the redistribution of income add up to no less than one quarter of assessed incomes in countries such as France, Sweden, and West Germany. In contrast to progressive taxation, government expenditures have had a much greater effect on the redistribution of income in these countries. Actually, the transfer of income by allowances and subsidies does not require progressive income taxation; it can be done by other tax forms.

Given the fact that taxes and transfer payments differ among countries, it is hard to make comparisons of income distribution. Moreover, some countries have favored a high rate of capital formation. Aside from the growth-inducing effect of capital accumulation, there is the multiplier effect on aggregate money income. There are also no criteria to indicate what is an equitable distribution of income, so value judgments become involved. Individuals and groups view an economic system from their own positions in society. Unanimity of opinion is therefore impossible, and it is highly doubtful if an agreed-upon concept of equitable distribution can be achieved. If such is the case, the actual effect of taxes and government transfer payments on the distribution of income will not be determined on the basis of any theory, but rather as a struggle among the dominant political forces at a particular period of time.

Table 21–2 presents a before-income tax distribution of income in Japan by quintiles for 1972. It can be said that the distribution of personal income in Japan, despite an emphasis on capital formation and economic growth, appears to be a little less unequal than similar distributions in the United States, France, the United Kingdom, and West Germany. However, social welfare benefits and services are lower in Japan than in these other countries. The tables exclude the effect of taxes and transfer payments.

TABLE 21–2
DISTRIBUTION OF JAPANESE PERSONAL INCOME BY QUINTILES, 1972

Quintiles	Percentage
Lowest quintile	8.4
Second quintile	13.4
Third quintile	17.8
Fourth quintile	22.2
Fifth quintile	38.2
Upper 5 percent	12.9

Source: Unpublished data provided by the Tax Administrative Agency of the Finance Ministry of Japan.

THE COMMAND ECONOMIES

In June, 1969 representatives of 75 communist countries from around the world gathered in Moscow for the third international summit meeting in the history of the communist movement. The Russians' purpose in calling the meeting was in part to divert attention from internal problems that existed in the Soviet Union and in part to attempt to salvage as much as possible their once uncontested primacy over the communist movement. Divisions within this movement were accentuated by the fact that two major communist powers, China and Yugoslavia, did not send representatives or even observers to the meeting. In fact, the Soviet Union was able to maintain its hegemony, enforced by the Russian army, only over the satellite countries of Eastern Europe. However, Rumania showed independence from the Soviet Union, particularly in the area of foreign policy, and was openly critical of Russian attempts at the summit meeting to read China out of the communist movement. Although Czechoslovakia was returned to the Soviet fold through the use of force, relevant problems—a stagnating economy and a sterile political system—remained unsolved or ignored.

Five years later, the Russians plan to call for another summit meeting. The divisions within the communist movement still have not been resolved. If anything, the schism between the Soviet Union and China has been widened, with some experts predicting an eventual war. Yugoslavia continues to maintain its political and economic independence from the Soviet Union and its satellites, and Rumania also continues to exercise its independence in the area of foreign policy. Even within the Soviet bloc countries, there have been variations from the Soviet economic model, which have been carried out in a series of economic reforms. However, these reforms have been very gradual, consisting of selective engrafting of certain elements of the market mechanism rather than in radical departures from central planning. The authorities have exercised caution, lest too much power is handed over to autonomous market forces.

It can be said that there are three principal variants of communism today. The first is Soviet communism, which involves a highly centralized command economy under which party officials and government bureaucrats in Moscow determine such details as how many tons of zippers will be produced. The second is Yugoslav communism, which offers a striking contrast to the Soviet variant. It is a new style of communism in which the Communist party guides but does not command the operation of the economy. The third variant is Chinese communism, or Maoism, which calls for a continuing class struggle under the dictatorship of the proletariat. The diversity of communism can be seen in a comparison of the main economic and political characteristics of the three countries.

The Soviet Union

The Soviet Union is the original fountainhead of the communist movement and the lodestar which guided the development of communism in other countries for the last 50 years. However, in recent years the lodestar has grown dim as nationalism rather than fealty to Moscow commands the attention of communist parties in other countries. Soviet communism can be called a bureaucratic dictatorship controlled by the Communist Party. Members of the party are to be found in all important positions in the political, economic, social, and even cultural life of the country. Thus, there is only one hierarchy of power which pervades every area of life, often with stultifying results.[33] The Soviet "establishment," which is the party bureaucracy, has as its overriding objective the maintenance of a power status quo.

Despite Lenin's predictions to the contrary, there is not a scintilla of evidence to indicate that any Utopian system has been created in the Soviet Union. Although the means of production have been socialized, and thus owned by the state as the representative for all of the population, it cannot be said that the state has acted as the compliant agent of the people in the production of goods and services. In fact, despite concessions from time to time, the reverse is true. In terms of production, not only has the Soviet Union failed to overtake the advanced capitalistic countries, particularly the United States, but grave deficiencies continue to exist in several sectors of the Soviet economy.[34] In the Soviet Union the slow growth of agriculture presents a serious problem. Perhaps the highest priority need is the expansion of agricultural output. Another major problem is an acute shortage of housing. There has been a sharp deterioration in urban housing and living conditions which has been exacerbated by migration from rural areas into the cities.[35]

The Soviet Union contends that its authoritarian form of social and economic organization is a particularly efficient instrument for dealing with the long-term problem of economic development. The claim of the Soviet Union that organization of society along Marxist lines is the most effective means of bringing about the rapid development of an economically backward nation rests upon Soviet success in the transformation of the country from a relatively backward peasant economy under the czars to the world's second most powerful industrial country in the space of less than a century. However, it has been conclusively demonstrated that the Soviet Union did not begin its Marxist experiment in a society nearly so backward economically as it would like the rest of the world to believe.[36] Although the Soviet growth rate has been impressive, it has been no more so than the growth rates of some of the Western countries.

Economic Growth. The Soviet Union has assigned the highest priority to an attainment of a high rate of economic growth, in part to demonstrate its

[33] However, this does not mean that Communist Party decision making is free from internal pressures. For example, even though they are at the bottom of the Soviet economic and social pyramid, peasants and workers can exert an influence on decision making. When collective or state farm workers respond to inadequate monetary incentives by poor work performance in the public sector, by transferring their energies to private plots, or by abandoning their jobs to seek better paying jobs in the industrial sector, they in effect bargain to improve their position. If more production is to be extracted from them, improved incentives have to be provided.

[34] The Soviet Union has also made no progress since the late 1950s in the pursuit of its long-standing goal to catch up with the United States in per capita consumption.

[35] In 1961 the Soviet urban population lived 2.72 persons to a room, compared to 2.60 persons to a room in 1923 and compared to the accepted maximum of 1.5 persons per room in the United States and western Europe.

[36] For example, see the OECD publication, *Science Policy in the USSR*, pp. 41–44.

superiority over those of the Western countries. By virtue of its control over the means of production and macroeconomic proportions, the socialist economy of the Soviet Union should have an effective system for sustained economic growth. However, the rate of economic growth of the Soviet Union has been somewhat erratic. For the period 1961–1965 the growth rate averaged 5 percent, with a high of 7.6 percent in 1964 and a low of 2.2 percent in 1963.[37] During the period 1966–1969 the average growth rate was 4.8 percent, with a high of 6.4 percent in 1966 and a low of 2.3 percent in 1969.[38] For 1970 the Soviet real growth rate was 6.2 percent, and for 1971 the rate was 6 percent.[39] However, in 1972 the real rate of growth dropped to 3 percent, the lowest rate since 1963. These rates were below comparable rates for Japan for the same time periods, but generally above the growth rates for the United States.

The real growth rate of the various components of gross social product illustrates a problem confronting the Soviet economy, namely, the unsuccessful results achieved in agriculture. In the Soviet economy, agriculture contributes approximately 20 percent of the gross domestic product and 50 percent of personal consumption. To some extent, agriculture problems in 1971 and 1972 can be attributed to adverse weather conditions and to some extent to general bureaucratic mismanagement. The poor agricultural performance had to be made up through sacrifices in other areas. Foreign deliveries were used repeatedly to relieve pressure on consumption. The disparity in the contribution of agriculture is reflected in shifts in gross production for various areas that have occurred over preceding years and can be presented as follows: [40]

	1970	1971	1972
Industry	7.0	6.3	5.2
Construction	6.3	5.0	5.4
Agriculture	11.0	2.0	−2.8
Rail transportation	4.2	4.5	3.8

Comparative studies of Soviet Union and United States output are difficult to make for the reason that the composition of economic aggregates vary. In the United States, for example, gross national product is measured as the final value of goods and services produced in a given time period. In the socialist economy of the Soviet Union, the closest concept to gross national product is net material product, which excludes those activities that do not contribute directly to material production. An example would be services. Given the difficulty of comparing different aggregates, some comparisons, although static at a given time, can be made. Using Stanford Research Institute estimates, Soviet gross national product was 46 percent of U.S. gross

[37] *Economic Performance and the Military Burden in the Soviet Union* (Washington: Joint Economic Committee, 91st Congress, 2d Session, 1970), p. 9.

[38] *Ibid.*, p. 9.

[39] Deutsches Institut für Wirtschaftsforschung, "Die Lage der sowjetischen Wirtschaft," *Wochenbericht* (May 17, 1973).

[40] *Ibid.*

national product in 1955 and 66 percent in 1970.[41] Department of Commerce estimates place Soviet gross national product at 54 percent of the U.S. total for 1970. Using net material product as a criterion of comparison, the Stanford Research Institute estimates Soviet net material product as 87 percent of that of the United States for 1970. On the other hand, the Central Statistical Agency of the Soviet Union provides an estimate of 66 percent for the same year.

Full Employment. A supposed advantage of communism over the market system is that unemployment can be eliminated through planned allocation of resources. The vagaries of the market place would have no influence over production. Work would be available for all. However, unemployment and underemployment exist in the Soviet Union.[42] Seasonal unemployment exists in many areas of the Soviet Union, and labor turnover rates are very high, causing frictional unemployment. Underemployment has long existed in the Soviet Union, particularly in agriculture. Also, many industrial enterprises have been forced to retain excessive staffs of workers because they cannot find jobs for them elsewhere. Others have maintained excessive labor forces in order to receive higher wage funds.

Unemployment, however, has ceased to be a major problem in the western European countries. The rates have been consistently low for a long period of time. Even when recessions occur, rates rarely get above 3 percent. So the Soviet Union can no longer claim superiority in the maintenance of a high rate of employment.

Price Stability. Presumably a planned economy should do a better job in maintaining price stability than a market economy. Costs can be kept in line and the supply of goods can be equated with the demand for goods through central planning. One method of balancing income to the population and consumer spending has been the manipulation of the turnover tax. However, over the years, there have been instances of inflation, sometimes open, sometimes concealed. During the period prior to World War II, a serious price and wage inflation occurred. It had as its origin the labor market, where an excess demand for workers caused wage rates to rise sharply. In general, however, inflation has been concealed, and reveals itself indirectly through rationing and through frequent breakdowns in material supplies.

Income Distribution. Taxes in the Soviet Union have a direct impact on the allocation of resources and the distribution of income as they also have in the market economies. However, the impact in the Soviet Union is greater, because the state budget occupies a more important role than do the national budgets of the United States and the western European countries. It is the chief vehicle through which the financial resources of the Soviet economy are distributed. It is instrumental in dividing the national product between

[41] Joint Economic Committee, *Soviet Economic Prospects for the Seventies* (Washington: U.S. Government Printing Office, 1972), pp. 122–125.
[42] *Labor Developments Abroad* (Washington: Bureau of Labor Statistics, U.S. Department of Labor, November, 1965), pp. 1–3.

investment and consumption and in allocating resources to investment in accordance with the national economic plan. Taxes not only provide revenue for the state budget, but also perform certain economic functions. The turnover tax not only is used to maintain a balance between the purchasing power of the consumer and the supply of goods, it is also manipulated to regulate the amount of profits allowed to producers. An agricultural income tax is utilized to discourage collective farmers from spending too much time on their private plots at the expense of their regular work on the collective farms.

By no stretch of the imagination can the Soviet Union be considered a "classless society." Income is distributed unequally, and income differentials based on wages and salaries may be as great, if not greater, than differentials in some of the market economies. In fact, at a symposium held at the Stockholm School of Economics, there was agreement among both Swedish and Russian economists that there was considerably more income inequality in the Soviet Union than in Sweden. There is a well-defined economic and social pyramid in the Soviet Union. At its apex are the important party functionaries in whom the ultimate power of decision reposes. Then there is a scientific and cultural elite who rank very high in the Soviet economic and social hierarchy. Closer to the pyramid base, there are the state bureaucracy and lesser party functionaries. Still lower, factory and enterprise managers comprise another group along with the professional workers—doctors, engineers, and teachers. A subgroup would be skilled workers and technicians. Finally, at the bottom of the social pyramid come the rank-and-file peasants and workers.

Transfer payments and the provision of various services by the state serve to redistribute income to some extent. It has been mentioned that transfer payments in one form or another can add as much as one third to a Russian worker's income. Medical care and other services are also provided the worker and his family. Education is available to the qualified regardless of status, but, in general, priority is given to the children of the elite groups. However, when transfer payments and public services are compared to similar arrangements in the Western countries, there is no particular differential which favors the Soviet Union. For example, the family allowance, one of the major transfers, is paid to families with four or more children in the Soviet Union, compared to families with one or more children in Sweden. There are no unemployment benefits in the Soviet Union, yet unemployment does exist. Old age pensions amount to 50 percent of average annual earnings; in Sweden the amount is 60 percent plus automatic adjustments for price changes. However, the Soviet Union can be rated ahead of the United States in terms of providing basic health and welfare measures for its people.

Yugoslavia

Yugoslavia presents a marked contrast to the Soviet Union. Its economy has been called market socialism, in which the free forces of the market are allowed to operate. Economic planning is more closely related to the indicative planning of the French than to the imperative planning of the Russians.

Yugoslavia, although still a long distance from the liberal democracies of the United States and western Europe, is the only communist country that has attempted to create a new type of Communist party which guides but does not command. This is consistent with attempts to achieve a decentralization of decision making in the evolving system of market socialism. In terms of foreign policy, the Yugoslavs have pursued a policy of nonalignment with either East or West.

Yugoslavia is a relatively underdeveloped country which has been willing to experiment and innovate in order to achieve its goal of industrialization. After a brief flirtation with agricultural collectivization, it began in 1950 a far-reaching program of experimentation with workers' self-management, decentralization of investment decisions, and freer markets, while retaining social ownership of capital goods. During the 1950s and early 1960s, Yugoslavia enjoyed a high rate of economic growth, and the industrialization of the country proceeded. Neither process, however, solved a severe balance of payments deficit at a rate of more than $200 million a year. A major reform of the economy became necessary.

The reform of 1965 had two objectives: the restructuring of prices and production to make Yugoslav goods competitive in the western European markets and the further decentralization of economic decision making. The dinar was devalued, tariffs lowered, and export subsidies abolished. Central control of investments was replaced by greater authority for local banks, and special taxes on enterprises by governments at all levels were eliminated or reduced. Increased reliance was placed upon the development of a quasi-market economy that would allow the free flow of resources to their optimum use. Federal expenditures were sharply reduced for the purpose of lessening the reliance of enterprises on state subsidies and increasing their reliance on the generation of internal funds for expansion.

In agriculture most of the land is privately owned in Yugoslavia. Private enterprise is permitted to the extent that a private employer can hire up to five workers. Restrictions have been dropped on the number of workers that can be employed in private enterprises serving tourists. The Yugoslav banking system is much more varied and decentralized than the monobanking system of the Soviet Union. Yugoslav banks now get most of their capital from business enterprises. The Yugoslav workers' councils represent a rather unique form of industrial self-management. They have the right to elect enterprise directors and participate in the development of annual production plans. Although there are some government-imposed limitations placed on the self-management of workers in Yugoslavia, it can be said that the workers' councils represent a unique experiment with industrial democracy.

Economic Growth. The economic growth of Yugoslavia has been erratic. In some years the growth rate has increased rather spectacularly; in other years the rate has been very low. Industrial output, which is a measure of economic growth, fluctuated from a high rate of growth of 16 percent in 1960 to below zero in 1967. The rate of output increased at an average rate of 9 percent for the period 1968–1972. The real rate of increase in gross national product has also fluctuated widely. In 1964 the real rate of growth was 9 percent; in 1967 the rate was 2 percent. In 1969 the rate of growth increased to 10 percent, and the average rate for 1970 through 1972 was 6 percent. However, on balance the performance of the Yugoslav economy in terms of maintaining a high rate of economic growth during the 1960s and early 1970s has been good.

Full Employment. Unemployment is a problem in Yugoslavia and is caused chiefly by the heavy influx into industrial areas of peasants from the countryside, where underemployment is so extensive that one fourth of those engaged in agriculture were released for other work. In 1972 unemployment in Yugoslavia was estimated at around 7.5 percent.[43] In fact, Yugoslavia's second largest source of foreign currency is the remittances sent home by Yugoslavs who have left to work in West Germany and other countries. It would appear that the ability of both Yugoslavia and the Soviet Union to achieve full employment is not superior to the abilities of the Western market countries. However, Yugoslavia has been traditionally an agricultural country which recently has experienced rapid industrial development. Some unemployment can be attributed to the transition to a mixed agrarian-industrial economy.

Price Stability. The Yugoslav performance in terms of the maintenance of price stability has been rather poor. Using 1963 as the base year of 100 percent, the price of consumer goods rose to 193 percent by 1972. Capital goods increased by 51 percent during the same period. The prices of agricultural products increased from 100 percent in the 1963 base period to 330 percent in 1972.[44] The year-to-year rate of increase in the cost of living index increased to 10 percent in 1970, and 17 percent in 1971. In 1972 the rate of increase reversed itself and stabilized at a rate of 6 percent. During the period 1970–1972 food prices increased at a rate of 33 percent, while capital goods prices increased at a rate of 25 percent.

Income Distribution. In terms of income distribution, the Yugoslav reward structure possesses some similarity to that of the Soviet Union. Certainly, there is no classless society. In 1959 average monthly earnings for a manager of an enterprise were five times as large as the average monthly earnings of unskilled workers in the enterprise. In 1961 average net monthly earnings for highly skilled workers was 2.4 times that for unskilled workers.[45]

China

The Chinese vision of a communist society, as expressed by Mao Tse-tung, is one of a classless society in which there is no distinction between manual and mental labor, in which state power will eventually disappear, and great

[43] "Yugoslavia," *Economic Surveys* (Paris: Organization for Economic Cooperation and Development, 1973), p. 10.

[44] *Ibid.*, p. 10.

[45] Bureau of Labor Statistics, "Labor Law and Practice in Yugoslavia," BLS Report No. 250 (Washington: U.S. Government Printing Office, 1963), p. 39.

abundance will be created for everyone. Experience indicates that this great abundance will be difficult to create in an overpopulated country with few natural resources.

Economic Growth. The performance of the Chinese economy has been mixed. During the period when Soviet planning methods were utilized, the growth rate was rapid. When the Chinese departed from the Soviet model to launch their own schemes, the growth rate was unimpressive. During the period 1952–57, the average annual increase in per capita gross national product was 6.5 percent—a rate exceeded only by those of West Germany and Japan.[46] This was achieved during the period of formal economic planning which was implemented by the Soviet Union. The accomplishment can be rated highly since the Chinese had little scientific, technical, and natural resources with which to start. There was, however, a very sharp decline in growth following the experimentation of the Great Leap Forward. Farm output declined sharply from 1958 to 1960.[47] The whole economy reverted backward from 1958 to 1961. Estimated per capita gross national product declined 14 percent and the domestic product for 1961 was 15 percent lower than in 1958. During the period 1962–65, the economy began to recover as the Chinese went back to a reliance on planning and economic incentives to stimulate industrial production. By 1965 estimated per capita income was back at the 1957 level.

By the end of 1969 the Cultural Revolution had run its course, and in 1970 the Fourth Five-Year Plan was initiated. There was a resumption of economic growth and gains in industrial capacity were made. Per capita income, which had at best remained constant during the period 1966–1969, showed an increase of 5 percent for both 1970 and 1971, and the gross national product index, with 1957 as a base set at 100 percent, increased from 122 percent in 1968 to 157 percent in 1972.[48] Industrial production in 1971 showed an average annual rate of growth of 6.5 percent compared to 1966. However, industrial growth has outstripped agricultural growth, with agriculture just sufficient to support the growing population at minimum standards.

Full Employment. Unemployment has been a problem in China, particularly in the urban centers. Unemployment and underemployment also exist in the rural areas. To a certain extent the rationale for the Great Leap Forward was based on the fact that China's population, especially in the countryside, was either unemployed or underemployed a large part of the year. Unused or underutilized labor was to be used in the development of small industry. Although this policy may have created employment, little else was accomplished, and as far as the urban economy is concerned, unemployment continues to remain one of the most intractable problems confronting the communist

[46] Ta-Chung Liu, "The Tempo of Economic Development of the Chinese Mainland, 1949–65," *An Economic Profile of Mainland China, Vol. I* (Washington: U.S. Government Printing Office, 1967), pp. 50 and 51.

[47] *Ibid.*, pp. 50 and 51.

[48] Joint Economic Committee, *People's Republic of China: An Economic Assessment* (Washington: U.S. Government Printing Office, 1972), p. 4.

regime. This urban unemployment has been dealt with in part by a policy of sending the unemployed to the countryside for temporary work in agriculture. The Chinese have utilized what is called a *hsiafang policy* to reverse the movement of people to the urban centers. The political and social dangers presented by urban unemployment have created greater political problems than rural unemployment.

Price Stability. The Chinese performance in terms of price stability is hard to measure. Prices are indirectly controlled through state control of commerce or through monetary and fiscal means.[49] The existence of excess demand relative to supply is reflected through the use of rationing on the part of the government. Excess demand for consumer goods has also been controlled through changes in wages. Taxes on consumer goods, such as the industrial and commercial tax, also absorb purchasing power. It can be said that inflation in China has been suppressed but not eliminated.

Income Distribution. Income distribution was based on Soviet wage methods. There was a heavy reliance on material incentives, such as piece rates and bonuses. There were wide variations in incomes among workers. For example, an income differential of 20 to 1 between top and bottom income earners was reported in 1958.[50] However, since that time, China's income policy, incentive system, and wage system, all of which were a part of the Russian plan for development, have been modified. Material incentives have been downgraded, and income differentials have been narrowed, particularly during the Proletarian Cultural Revolution. Nevertheless, the basic tenet of socialism, "to each according to contribution," remains applicable even in China, and it would be a mistake to assume that the Chinese society is a classless society.

SUMMARY

Any efficient economic system should achieve an efficient production with a high rate of economic growth, full utilization of resources, and a distribution of real income which is felt to be just. Comparisons have been made throughout the book of how production has been organized in different systems and how well basic economic goals have been accomplished. It has been pointed out that it is difficult to compartmentalize economic systems because variations exist in each which have to be considered. In some respects there are similarities between the mixed economies of the West and the centralized command economies of the Soviet Union and its Eastern satellites. For example, the redistribution of income is performed by the state in both the Western economies and the communist economies by means of taxes and transfers which alter the patterns of normal income distribution. Profits are, in spite of their planned character in the communist countries, a residual in both the market and command systems. In a modified market economy, such as the United States, the distribution of

---

[49] D. H. Perkins, "Price Stability and Development in Mainland China, 1951–63," *Journal of Political Economy*, Vol. 72, No. 4 (August, 1964), pp. 360–375.

[50] Victor C. Funnell, "Social Stratification in China," *Problems of Communism*, Vol. XVII (Washington: U.S. Government Printing Office, March–April, 1968), p. 18.

profits between dividends and reinvestment is the responsibility of management; in the Soviet Union planned profits are shared according to state regulations, with management and workers sharing in the subdivision of different profit funds.

This does not mean, however, that there will be a convergence of capitalism and communism, even though a series of economic reforms embracing some facets of capitalism have taken place in the communist countries. Although there may be some convergence in specific economic sectors, this in no way changes the fact that fundamental differences exist pertaining to the ownership of the means of production and the role of the individual in society—differences that are not likely to change in the future.

QUESTIONS

1. It can be said that both the United States and the Soviet Union are far removed from the true models of capitalism and communism. Evaluate this statement.
2. One of the important developments of the 20th century has been the attempt of governments to modify inequalities in the distribution of income. What procedures have been used?
3. In what ways does the government of the United States have an impact on the economy?
4. How would you evaluate the performance of the American economy in terms of achieving full employment and price stability?
5. How would you evaluate the Japanese economy in terms of goal fulfillments?
6. In general, the performance of the "middle way" economies has been superior to that of the United States in terms of fulfilling the goals of full employment, price stability, and economic growth. Do you agree?
7. The Soviet economy can be evaluated by comparing its economic accomplishments directly with those of the United States. Do you agree?
8. There are several variants of communism today. Explain each variant.
9. What are some of the strengths and weaknesses of the Yugoslav economy?
10. It is apparent that no Utopia exists in any type of economic system that exists today. Evaluate this statement.

RECOMMENDED READINGS

Dornberg, John. *The New Tsars: Russia Under Stalin's Heirs.* Garden City, N.Y.: Doubleday & Co., Inc., 1972.

Economic Report of the President. Washington: U.S. Government Printing Office, 1974.

Galbraith, John K. *Economics and the Public Purpose.* Boston: Houghton Mifflin Co., 1973.

Harrington, Michael. *Socialism.* New York: Saturday Review Press, 1971.

Heller, Walter. *New Dimensions of Political Economy.* Cambridge: Harvard University Press, 1966.

Joint Economic Committee. *Soviet Economic Prospects for the Seventies.* Washington: U.S. Government Printing Office, 1972.

Schnitzer, Martin. *East and West Germany: A Comparative Economic Analysis.* New York: Praeger, 1973.

Schultze, Charles L. and others. *Setting National Priorities: The 1974 Budget.* Washington: The Brookings Institution, 1974.

INDEX